The archaeology of classical Greece developed in the shadow of Greek historical scholarship, and it has restricted itself too modestly to the study of individual artefacts. A wide variety of modern developments in archaeology have been neglected. The contributors to this book review the history of the field and aim to demonstrate that modern archaeological approaches can contribute to a richer understanding of Greek society. They also insist that this complex, literate and highly unusual system of states poses important questions for archaeologists of other regions.

NEW DIRECTIONS IN ARCHAEOLOGY

Classical Greece

Editors

Wendy Ashmore
Department of Anthropology, University of Pennsylvania

Françoise Audouze
Centre de Recherches Archéologiques,
Meudon, France

Richard Bradley
Department of Archaeology, University of Reading

Joan Gero
Department of Anthropology, University of
South Carolina

Tim Murray
Department of Archaeology, La Trobe University,
Victoria, Australia

Colin Renfrew
Department of Archaeology, University of
Cambridge

Andrew Sherratt
Department of Antiquities, Ashmolean Museum,
Oxford

Timothy Taylor
Department of Archaeology, University of Bradford

Norman Yoffee
Department of Anthropology, University of Arizona

Classical Greece: ancient histories and modern archaeologies

Edited by
IAN MORRIS
University of Chicago

CAMBRIDGE
UNIVERSITY PRESS

Published by the Press Syndicate of the University of Cambridge
The Pitt Building, Trumpington Street, Cambridge CB2 1RP
40 West 20th Street, New York, NY 10011–4211, USA
10 Stamford Road, Oakleigh, Melbourne 3166, Australia

First published 1994

Printed in Great Britain at the University Press, Cambridge

A catalogue record for this book is available from the British Library

Library of Congress cataloguing in publication data

Classical Greece: ancient histories and modern archaeologies /
edited by Ian Morris.
     p.   cm.
Includes bibliographical references (p.) and index.
ISBN 0 521 39279 9
1. Greece – Antiquities. 2. Greece – Civilization – to 146 B.C.
3. Archaeology and history – Greece. I. Morris, Ian, 1960– .
DF77.C63 1994   938'.0072–dc20   93–6625 CIP

ISBN 0 521 39279 9 hardback
ISBN 0 521 45678 9 paperback

WD

For my parents

Contents

List of illustrations   *page* x
List of tables   xii
List of contributors   xiii
Acknowledgements   xiv

PART I HISTORY   1

1   Introduction
    Ian Morris   3

2   Archaeologies of Greece
    Ian Morris   8

PART II ARTEFACTS AND ART OBJECTS   49

3   Protoattic pottery: a contextual approach
    James Whitley   51

4   The riddle of the Sphinx: a case study in
    Athenian immortality symbolism
    Herbert Hoffmann   71

5   Looking on – Greek style. Does the sculpted
    girl speak to women too?
    Robin Osborne   81

PART III ARTEFACTS AS TRADED
OBJECTS   97

6   Positivism, pots and long-distance trade
    David W. J. Gill   99

7   Athens, Etruria and the Heueneburg: mutual
    misconceptions in the study of Greek–
    barbarian relations
    Karim Arafat and Catherine Morgan   108

PART IV ARTEFACTS IN THE
LANDSCAPE   135

8   Intensive survey, agricultural practice and
    the classical landscape of Greece
    *Susan E. Alcock, John F. Cherry and
    Jack L. Davis*   137

9   Breaking up the Hellenistic world: survey
    and society
    Susan E. Alcock   171

PART V RESPONSES   191

10 Response
    Michael Jameson   193

11 Response: the archaeological aspect
    Anthony Snodgrass   197

Bibliography   201
Index   239

Illustrations

4.6	Herse and Pandrosos.	74
4.7	Running satyr.	74
4.8	Athena.	75
4.9	Theban youths before the Sphinx on her pillar. Attic red-figured pelike (photograph courtesy of the Boston Museum of Fine arts).	75
4.10	Sphinx carrying a youth to an altar. Attic red-figured lekythos by Polion (photograph courtesy of National Museum of Athens).	76
4.11	Oedipus, Theban youth and heroes before the Sphinx. Attic-red figured pelike (photograph courtesy of Kunsthistorisches Museum, Vienna).	76
4.12	Shaman and thiasos. Astralagos by the Sotades Painter (photograph courtesy of the Trustees of the British Museum).	79
3.1	Jug with plastic attachments of snakes and mourning women (photograph KER 3438, courtesy of Deutsches archäologisches Institut, Athens).	*page* 58
5.1	Praxiteles, Aphrodite of Knidos. Copy of original of mid-fourth century BC. Vatican Museum (photograph and reproduction courtesy of Hirmer Verlag Munich).	83
3.2	Cauldron with griffin protomes (photograph KER 7103, courtesy of Deutsches archäologisches Institut, Athens).	58
5.2	Athena Nike temple balustrade relief panel, Athenian acropolis, late fifth century BC. Acropolis Museum, Athens (photograph and reproduction courtesy of Hirmer Verlag Munich).	85
3.3	Beaker or mug with fighting scene and plant-derived decoration (photograph KER 2975, courtesy of Deutsches archäologisches Institut, Athens).	59
5.3	Athena Parthenos. Miniature copy of second century AD of Pheidias' chryselephantine cult statue of the 430s BC. National Museum, Athens (photograph and reproduction courtesy of Hirmer Verlag Munich).	87
3.4	Lid from pyxis showing chariot scenes (photograph KER 3006, courtesy of Deutsches archäologisches Institut, Athens).	59
3.5	Krater used as grave marker, showing a sphinx (photograph KER 3432, courtesy of Deutsches archäologisches Institut, Athens).	64
5.4	'Amelung's Goddess', Roman copy of an original of the second quarter of the fifth century BC. National Archaeological Museum, Naples (photograph and reproduction courtesy of Hirmer Verlag Munich).	89
3.6	Rear view of krater in fig. 3.5, showing 'Orientalising' decoration (photograph KER 3430, courtesy of Deutsches archäologisches Institut, Athens).	64
5.5	*Kouros* from near Anavyssos, Attica, third quarter of the sixth century BC. Base gives the name 'Kroisos'. National Museum, Athens (photograph and reproduction courtesy of Hirmer Verlag Munich).	89
3.7	The Polyphemus amphora (photograph Eleusis 544, courtesy of Deutsches archäologisches Institut, Athens).	65
4.1–4.3	Sphinx vase by the Sotades Painter (photograph courtesy of the Trustees of the British Museum).	72–73
5.6	*Kore* from the Akropolis, Athens, 520s BC. Base names: dedicant as Nearkhos, sculptor as Antenor. Acropolis Museum, Athens (photograph and reproduction courtesy of Hirmer Verlag Munich).	91
4.4	Kekrops and Nike or Iris libating.	73
4.5	Aglauros and Erysichthon.	73

6.1   Attic black-figured hydria with SO graffito   100
      (photographs courtesy of the Fitzwilliam
      Museum, Cambridge).
6.2   Attic red-figured pelike and price   100
      inscription (photographs courtesy of the
      Ashmolean Museum, Oxford).
6.3   Attic black-figured Nikosthenic amphora   101
      and kyathos (photograph courtesy of the
      Fitzwilliam Museum, Cambridge).
6.4   Etruscan bucchero amphora and kyathos   101
      (photograph courtesy of the Fitzwilliam
      Museum, Cambridge).
7.1   Greece, Etruria and Hallstatt Europe: 110
      relative chronology.
7.2   The Etruscan states.   111
7.3   Neck detail of a Nikosthenic amphora   115
      (B64) signed by Nikosthenes as potter,
      from Cerveteri (photograph courtesy of
      The Johns Hopkins University,
      Baltimore).
7.4   The origins of Archaic and Early Classical   117
      imports in Etruria.
7.5   Cup by the Castelgiorgio Painter, from   119
      Vulci (photograph courtesy of the Trustees
      of the British Museum).
7.6   Principal sites in the Adriatic and   121
      west Mediterranean.
7.7   *Fürstensitze* with a hypothetical   121
      reconstruction of their territories.
7.8   Massalia and the *Fürstensitze*.   123
7.9   Imported Attic pottery from the   125
      Heuneburg (photograph courtesy of
      Professor Em. Dr Wolfgang Kimmig).
7.10 Proportions of Attic imports in Etruria and   127
      at Massilia.

8.1   Significant field survey projects undertaken   139
      in Greece since *c.* 1975.
8.2   Nemea Valley Archaeological Project,   140
      survey area.
8.3   Boeotia Survey, density of artefacts of all   141
      dates (© University of California Press).
8.4   North Jazira Project area, northern Iraq: 146
      archaeological sites, hollow ways, dry
      valleys and field scatters (© *Journal of
      Field Archaeology*).
8.5   Schematic zonation of land use with   155
      increasing distance from farm centres,
      using labour intensity values: (a) for
      Greece as a whole in 1955, and (b) for
      Melos in 1974.
8.6   The distribution of sites in the Nemea   158
      Valley Archaeological Project, 1984–9.
8.7   The Tretos Pass and the valley to the   159
      southwest.
8.8   Intensively surveyed block of land west of   161
      the Tretos Pass: (a) contours, toponyms
      and other modern features; (b) ancient sites
      and individual tracts, showing artefact
      densities.
8.9   Site PP 17 (late Hellenistic to early Roman)   162
      of the Boeotia Survey: comparison of the
      shape and extent of surface scatters of
      pottery and roof-tile with features detected
      by resistivity survey.
8.10 Map of site PP 17.   163
9.1   Sites mentioned in the text.   172
9.2   Locations of sites listed in table 9.1   178

Tables

3.1 Numbers of seventh-century sites in *page* 52
Attica, excluding Athens.

3.2 Seventh-century adult and child graves in the 54
Kerameikos.

3.3 Distribution of decoration on vases in the 55
Agora wells.

3.4 Child cemeteries in Attica. 56

3.5 Kerameikos cemetery: breakdown of 57
distribution of types of vases according to
context.

3.6 Scenes on Protoattic vases from the Agora 63
well groups and from the Kerameikos grave
markers and Opferrinnen.

6.1 Approximate values of various commodities 104
per cubic metre.

8.1 Estimates of manure production on Classical 154
farmsteads.

8.2 Archaic to Hellenistic sites in the study area. 159

8.3 Classes of pottery and other finds from sites 160
in the study area.

8.4 Pottery and tile counts from tracts in the study 165
area.

9.1 Major survey projects mentioned in the 176–7
chapter.

9.2 Changes in certain key areas in the study 187
regions.

Contributors

SUSAN E. ALCOCK
Department of Classics
University of Michigan
Ann Arbor

KARIM ARAFAT
Department of Classics
King's College
University of London

JOHN F. CHERRY
Department of Classics
University of Michigan
Ann Arbor

JACK L. DAVIS
Department of Classics
University of Cincinnati

DAVID W. J. GILL
Department of Classics
University of Swansea

HERBERT HOFFMANN
Podere Istine
Siena

MICHAEL JAMESON
Department of Classics
Stanford University

CATHERINE MORGAN
Department of Classics
Royal Holloway and Bedford New College
University of London

IAN MORRIS
Departments of History and Classics
University of Chicago

ROBIN OSBORNE
Corpus Christi College
University of Oxford

ANTHONY SNODGRASS
Museum of Classical Archaeology
University of Cambridge

JAMES WHITLEY
Department of Archaeology
University of Wales
Cardiff College

Acknowledgements

This book has been a long time in the making. Peter Richards and Colin Renfrew suggested the possibility of a *New directions* book on the social and economic dimensions of classical archaeology in 1988. Since then it has been through a lot of changes, and I want to thank the contributors for their patience with these. Most of the papers have been circulated between the contributors, and the process of mutual criticism has greatly strengthened the final results. These exchanges of ideas are acknowledged at the end of each paper. I also want to thank the contributors for enduring my editorial interventions and idiosyncrasies with good humour; to thank the University of Chicago for supporting the expenses of sending bulky typescripts and long faxes across the Atlantic; and above all to thank Frances Brown, Jessica Kuper, Jayne Matthews and Ruth Parr for struggling heroically with a messy and difficult typescript.

PART I

History

1

Introduction

IAN MORRIS

A *New directions* book on ancient Greece seems like an odd idea. Other volumes in this series take broad themes like *Symbolic and structural archaeology* (Hodder 1982d) or *Domestic architecture and the use of space* (Kent 1990); where they treat a single regional tradition, as in the volumes on the New World (Jones and Kautz 1981; Haas *et al.* 1989) or Europe (Renfrew and Shennan 1982; Rowlands *et al.* 1987), they still focus on topics like state formation or exchange. And of all the world's regional archaeological traditions, ancient Greece might be thought to be among the least likely to deserve a volume. It has its own massive literature and community of scholars. These archaeologists usually practise their craft in institutional settings different from those inhabited by most readers of the *New directions* series, and share few interests with them. Non-classical archaeologists tend to imagine specialists on ancient Greece working with statues, temples and inscriptions, attributing artworks to their creators and restoring masterpieces for the market.

All this is very different from the experience of most archaeologists. But it is also far removed from what many archaeologists of Greece do (see Snodgrass and Chippindale 1988). When the idea of this book was first floated in 1988, it seemed to me to have two main justifications: first as a way to convince non-classical archaeologists that Greek archaeology was not really as they imagined it, and second as a way to convince more classical archaeologists that a broader approach, influenced by recent developments in other archaeologies, would help the study of Greece. But in fact the number of die-hards who need to be convinced of either of these positions is quite small, and the process of assembling these papers forced me to think more carefully about why this project was worth undertaking. Of all the

things I could be doing, why edit a book on classical Greece in this series? And why should Cambridge University Press wish to publish such a book?

Time was when these questions would have seemed foolish: when it could simply be asserted that 'the Greeks aren't like the others'. Books from the earlier decades of this century have an easy self-assurance, a confidence that the simple fact that they dealt with objects from ancient Greece guaranteed them an audience. An attenuated form of this effortless superiority can still be found, and in a sense it is a self-fulfilling prophecy. The Greeks *aren't* like the others, because for generations now academics have chosen not to have them so. This alone, I think, justifies creating this book. In Ch. 2, I attempt to understand the archaeology of Greece by examining its history. Its origin can be traced, like that of most archaeologies, to the late nineteenth century. The most recent trend among historians of archaeology has been to see the formative disciplines of this period as providing a foundation myth for Euro-American civilisation (e.g. Trigger 1989: 73–147); but Greek archaeologists were themselves unlike the others in that they could claim to be researching the very cradle of Europeanness. They tied themselves more to classical philology than to world archaeology. Two forces were decisive in shaping the discipline. The first was the need to prevent archaeological data from challenging the Hellenist charter of 'Western Civilisation'; the second was the archaeologists' attempt to achieve high status by matching the highest standards of scientific archaeological method while remaining classicists. For much of the next century, archaeologists of Greece were remarkably successful in both these aims, although arguably as time went by the two goals became increasingly contra-dictory. I argue that the current sense of 'crisis' has been misrepresented as a conflict between theoretical and traditional archaeology, or even between young and old. In fact it is just one part of the general collapse of intellectuals' attempts to define what 'the West' is and should be. Archaeologists of Greece had neutralised their material to protect the set of beliefs which gave prestige to classical studies; now that these beliefs are crumbling, they are left defending nothing. The field's position is thus different from that of most other archaeologies, in which various crises of confidence since the 1960s have led to partial repositioning; but at the same time this history is crucial to understanding the functions of all archaeologies as forms of appropriation of the past. The roots of non-classical archaeologies can only be understood through their positions relative to the Hellenist core. Just as Herzfeld (1987) has shown that the very marginality of Greek ethnography to the 'main' area studies of modern anthropology gives it unique power to undermine our assumptions, the reasons for the isolation of Greek archaeology define the limits of contemporary 'theoretical' archaeology.

The title of my chapter, 'Archaeologies of Greece', betrays its starting point, Anthony Snodgrass' 1987 book *An archaeology of Greece*. But my analysis diverges from Snodgrass' in my belief that we can only understand contemporary practices through historical analysis. Surprising as it may seem, no full-length history of Greek archaeology has ever been written, and despite its length, Ch. 2 remains merely a preliminary examination. I have worked entirely from published sources, leaving untouched a vast wealth of archival materials. I have also bypassed important topics such as the relationships between Greek and Roman archaeology or the roles of museology and art markets in classical archaeology. My main aim is to frame the chapters which follow in a more sophisticated way than a conventional polarisation between 'new' and 'traditional' would allow. I argue that the authors, like the archaeological rebels of the 1960s New Archaeology and the 1980s postprocessualists, see a need to *refigure* the past. I use this word in two senses: first, that of finding a new starting point, changing the aspects of the record which are given importance and even the ways of writing about the past (cf. H. White 1973); and second, of reintroducing real people into the past.

There is a big difference, though, between a 1990s academic crisis and those of earlier decades. Here I develop a very important point made by Snodgrass when he chose to call his book *An archaeology of Greece*. He emphasised 'the studied use of the indefinite article . . . freely acknowledg[ing] that many other "archaeologies of Greece," of at least equal validity, could be devised' (1987: xiv). The papers in this volume present archaeolog*ies* of Greece. There is little agreement over how to refigure the past in either of these senses. Patterson (1989a) has pointed out that the post-processual archaeology is far more fragmented than either its proponents or its critics have generally realised, but the contributors to this volume have neither the rhetoric of a unified challenge nor even the assumption that they will replace, rather than exist alongside, earlier disciplinary practices. This book is no manifesto for a 'new classical archaeology', and, despite the series title, the contributors make no claim to monopolise 'new directions in Greek archaeology'. There are many other archaeologists working in similar ways. Instead, we have a recognition that in a changed world no amount of continuing success in pursuing research aims defined by nineteenth-century ideologies can give deep meaning or wide relevance to *the* archaeology of Greece. Any refiguring of the intellectual landscape of archaeology involves us in asking unsettling questions about what, and whom, the subject is for; and perhaps in accepting, and trying to make the best of, a plurality of answers (cf.

Stone and MacKenzie 1989; Layton 1989a; Gathercole and Lowenthal 1990).

The papers which make up the bulk of the book are structured around three topics, all of which are long established within Greek archaeology. The first is the artefact itself, the very essence of what we normally think of as Greek archaeology. The three contributors to this section take radically different attitudes towards objects. In Ch. 3, James Whitley looks at the contexts of use of seventh-century BC Athenian pottery, explicitly acknowledging Ian Hodder's influence; in Ch. 4, Herbert Hoffmann examines the iconography of one fifth-century Athenian vase in great detail, from a structuralist position; and in Ch. 5 Robin Osborne offers a poststructuralist treatment of a small group of Greek statues. The three papers share a rejection of the conventional producer-oriented approach to artefacts, instead exploring the perspective of the viewer or user. But beyond that they differ profoundly.

Whitley seeks to understand Athenian social structure from the ways in which pots were deposited in graves, sanctuaries and houses. His approach will be the most familiar to readers of *New directions* volumes, but much less so to the majority of classicists. He emphasises the total material assemblage, and tries to understand Athenian vases as a symbolic system through which conflicts were played out, rather than as individual objects. He concentrates on pottery because that is what dominates the archaeological record, but whenever possible he draws in metalwork, inscriptions and architecture. The key to this kind of archaeological structuralism is totality: *all* material must be shown to be explained. He thus explicitly rejects not only the long-established techniques of connoisseurship but also Osborne's attempts (1988a; 1989) to read individual seventh-century pots as texts, and finds no grounds for the assignation of meaningful content to particular painted decorations. He admits, as others have done (e.g. Tilley 1990: 65), that this approach makes it impossible to say what a specific pot 'meant' for its producer or any viewer. But for him that is less important than the potential the method has for unravelling the place of material culture within a system of exploitative power relations.

The other papers in this section diverge from Whitley's in that both concentrate on the response of viewers to individual artefacts as artworks. But at that point their similarity too ends. Hoffmann takes what was probably an object of fairly 'low' culture, a small red-figure pot in the shape of a sphinx, and tries to explain its form and decoration in the light of Athenian mythology. Working within a structuralist tradition owing more to Lévi-Strauss and Leach than to structural-functionalism, he seeks to unravel mythemes – the fundamental units of mythological thought – to understand how Athenians articulated the basic opposition of life and death. Where Whitley seeks a context for any specific pot in the total archaeological assemblage from the same period, Hoffmann finds it in a mass of literary evidence about sphinxes and death, which spans several centuries. Hoffmann certainly uses other archaeological evidence, such as the stone sphinxes placed over some Athenian graves in the sixth century; but his structuralism is a radical departure both from classical art history (with the exception of studies influenced by the so-called 'Paris School' (e.g. Bérard 1989b; Lissarrague 1990; Sourvinou-Inwood 1991)) and from the formalism emphasising the arbitrary nature of the sign which has been popular within processual and earlier phases of post-processual archaeology. It depends for its success on the existence of a rich iconography like that of fifth-century Athenian red-figure vase painting, in which mythical scenes can often be unambiguously identified; and on the existence of a strong (if chronologically disparate) body of mythological texts. As such, its direct relevance for non-classicists may be restricted, but its analogical value for the construction of an 'archaeology of mind' is unusually great.

Hoffmann assumes a fixed meaning for the symbols he discusses, and a community of knowledgeable observers; he defines his job as archaeologist as being to enter into this community. Osborne, on the other hand, takes it for granted that the audience for any Greek artwork was fragmented. Many lines of division are possible, but in this paper he focuses on gender. His subject matter is traditional enough, the 'high culture' products of Greek sculptors, but his methods are not. Starting from a group of problematic textual accounts of men's reactions to one particular statue, he traces a profound change in Athenian art around 500 BC. Before that date, he suggests, statues of women challenged their viewers by evoking something of women's power as objects of exchange; after 500, this vanished, and classical statues of women had little to say to living women. Osborne's methods differ from those of both Whitley and Hoffmann. He does not seek a context for his artefacts either in the total archaeological assemblage or in a web of texts (although again both classes of evidence play a part in his paper); his perspective is strongly empathetic, entering into the minds of viewers of the statue in a way which may be known to prehistorians through Hodder's treatment (1991: Ch. 6) of Ilchamus calabashes. Osborne's poststructuralist analysis poses a profound challenge to most approaches to Greek artefacts. His explanation for the transformation of statues of women at the end of the Archaic period, though, is framed in terms which will be familiar to Greek cultural historians: male citizens' attitudes to women were changed

by Cleisthenes' reforms of 508/7 BC, which restructured the Athenian citizen body. Both traditional archaeologists and contextualists might react to this in much the same way that Brook Thomas uses Jane Tompkins' book *Sensational designs* to typify what he sees as the limitations of the New Historicism as a critical method. While conceding Tompkins' success in deconstructing the canon of American literature, Thomas suggests that 'when she comes to write her own history, Tompkins abandons her up-to-date post-structuralist pose and returns to old-fashioned assumptions about literature and historical analysis' (1990: 185). Just as Whitley's approach to artefacts runs into problems when trying to treat the individual object, Osborne's reaches its limits in trying to re-situate the statues in historical context. The three papers in this section offer radically new and competing insights into Greek material culture.

Part III consists of two papers on Athenian painted pottery found outside Greece. Like the chapters in Part II, they try to shift the emphasis away from the Athenian producers towards the receivers' perceptions of the material (see Osborne 1991: 255–6). In a series of papers, David Gill and Michael Vickers (Vickers 1985b; 1987; 1990a; Gill 1987; 1988a–d; 1991; Gill and Vickers 1989; 1990) have argued that since the eighteenth century classical archaeologists have overvalued Greek painted pottery, out of a mixture of complicity in the art market and naïve positivism. This, they believe, has caused modern specialists to misunderstand pottery as an artistic medium; it should be treated merely as a pale reflection of the major media, silver and gold. These precious metal vases have mostly been melted down, but we can only write the history of Athenian pots if we constantly bear in mind the metal prototypes. In Ch. 6, David Gill summarises some of the most hotly debated points. He argues that Athenian vases were worth very little in the sixth and fifth centuries, and travelled overseas not as highly sought after works of art, but as saleable ballast to fill in the spaces between more valuable items of cargo. This has provoked fierce counter-arguments from some of the leading specialists (particularly Boardman 1987; 1988a; 1988b; Spivey 1991: 134–42), and the tone of Gill's paper reveals the seriousness with which the issues are taken. Gill asserts that classical archaeologists have assumed that finds of Athenian vases in Etruscan graves must mean both that Etruscans valued these pots highly and that there was an extensive pottery trade. Gill's attack on positivism is carried out independently from similar critiques within other archaeologies (e.g. Shanks and Tilley 1987; Kelley and Hanen 1988), and in a strikingly different style; instead of mounting a philosophical critique, he concentrates on specific empirical examples. The similarities and differences between the similar debates in different fields should be of wide interest to non-classical archaeologists.

In Ch. 7, Karim Arafat and Catherine Morgan take up much of the same evidence as Gill, but in very different ways. They too shift the perspective when looking at objects from that of the producer to that of the consumer. Combining the recent interest among ancient historians in Herodotus' literary representation of 'the other' (e.g. Hartog 1988; Cartledge 1990; cf. E. Hall 1990) with the prehistorians' emphasis on interpreting exchanged objects within the receivers' system of material culture, they compare the functions of Athenian pottery found in Etruria and in southwest Germany. Like Gill, they contest Athenocentric points of view, but they do so by detailed examination of the findspots of the pots within the settlement hierarchies of the two cultural systems. Their paper is addressed to Etruscan and Hallstatt archaeologies as much as to classicists. They argue that the recent vogue for core–periphery models which cast the Mediterranean world as a heartland compared to a central European fringe (e.g. Rowlands *et al.* 1987; Cunliffe 1988; T. Champion 1989) seriously distorts the evidence. Like Gill, they insist that anyone who wants to understand Greek objects in western contexts must take a position on Greek economic history. The works of Cartledge (1983), Finley (1985a) and Garnsey (1988) are cited with approval in both papers, but Arafat and Morgan see implications very different from Gill's.

The two papers in the fourth section reconceptualise the role of the artefact within Greek archaeology still more radically. Situating ancient remains within the modern landscape was critically important to the first main wave of Western visitors to Greece in the seventeenth century (Constantine 1989), and remained so when Greek archaeology was constituted at the end of the nineteenth century (see pp. 23–6 below). In this century some archaeologists became legendary for their knowledge of Greek topography; Eugene Vanderpool (1906–89) is said to have astounded generations of students at the American School (McCredie 1990). Alongside this tradition developed the conventional 'site survey', where archaeologists interested in excavating would scout out likely looking spots. These explorers discovered some remarkable sites, but they always subordinated the surface finds to subterranean remains. The notion of survey as an end in itself, well established in North American archaeology by the 1960s, was a late comer to the Aegean; but there is now a vigorous group of survey archaeologists in Greece, who have some claims to lead the field in methods of surveying artefact-rich landscapes.

The factors behind the explosion of intensive surveys in the 1980s are complex (see pp. 38–40 below). Economic,

political and intellectual changes all played a part, stimulating ecological and demographic interests among some Aegean prehistorians. Most of the earliest field projects which aimed to reconstruct regional environments, such as the Messenia survey in the 1960s (McDonald and Rapp 1972) and the Melos project in the 1970s (Renfrew and Wagstaff 1982), concentrated on the Bronze Age. But classical archaeologists were quick to see the potential of these techniques for the systematic understanding of settlement in later periods. Only fifteen years after Melos, it is taken for granted that any survey should employ consistent fieldwalking techniques and a battery of geomorphologists, and should collect and analyse finds of all periods. Increasingly, the site-oriented project is being abandoned in favour of plotting the continuous distribution of finds across the whole landscape. Aegean surveyors generally work at a level of intensity far higher than archaeologists in other parts of the world (see Cherry 1983; Bintliff and Snodgrass 1988a; 1988b). They consequently tend to cover much smaller regions, but produce incomparably more detailed pictures of rural settlement. In Ch. 8, Susan Alcock, John Cherry and Jack Davis show the kind of possibilities which this level of detail allows. Several surveys have noted that high-density artefact concentrations are often surrounded by medium-density 'haloes', both standing out from the general background scatter across the modern surface. Bintliff and Snodgrass (1988b; Snodgrass 1990; 1991) have argued from their finds in Boeotia that these haloes represent the dispersal of objects incorporated into farmyard manure piles in antiquity, and that their size and richness are good indices of the practice of manuring, and thus of agricultural intensity in different periods of the past. This is a revolutionary argument, but Alcock *et al.* challenge it, using the detailed data from their work in the Nemea valley. They examine similar medium-density artefact scatters, and claim to show that they are generally best explained as the workings of natural processes rather than human activity. They demonstrate the unusual potential of the Greek evidence by combining survey results with textual accounts of classical farming practices, arguing that the literary sources coincide with their interpretation of the surface remains. Their case against manuring is an implicit justification of a level of detail in recording surface data which goes far beyond what archaeologists in Greece committed to excavation or extensive survey would advocate (e.g. Popham 1990; Hope Simpson 1983; 1984). It also contrasts with the more *ex*tensive methods in use in many parts of the New World (e.g. Fish and Kowalewski 1990).

The 'new wave' of surveys in the past decade is transforming our knowledge of local settlement histories in Greece, modifying or overturning blanket descriptions of demographic changes based on throwaway comments in classical authors or extrapolated from the excavation of urban centres. But so far, relatively few surveys have been published in detail, and although there have been excellent general discussions of the historical implications of survey data (e.g. Osborne 1987a; van Andel and Runnels 1987), the question of how exactly these kinds of data are to be integrated with excavated or textual material has rarely been tackled. In Ch. 10, Susan Alcock attempts to overcome the difficulties to produce an historical account. Her subject is well chosen to exemplify the enormous potential of survey data.

The study of the Hellenistic world, conventionally defined as dating from the death of Alexander the Great in 323 BC to Octavian's victory at the battle of Actium in 31 BC, and spreading from modern Albania to Afghanistan, probably suffers from more vague generalisations than any other phase of Greek history. Alcock argues that it has been the victim of twin prejudices generated by the Hellenist research programme discussed in Ch. 2. First, many classicists assume a direct cultural progression from classical Greece to Rome and on to 'the West'; the death of Alexander the Great is treated as a watershed, after which Greek civilisation no longer had much to contribute to the European heritage. The second prejudice is even harder to deal with: geographically, most of the Hellenistic world falls within the sphere of 'the Orient', an undifferentiated mass not worth serious consideration. Classical scholarship has concentrated on the Greek cities founded by Alexander, which are often taken as an index of the Hellenisation of Oriental peoples. The division between 'Greek' and 'native', whether in Egypt, Mesopotamia or Bactria, makes it extremely difficult to understand the vast diversity of social processes at work. Alcock demonstrates that survey data allow us to overcome some of these problems, building a foundation for a non-Hellenist archaeology of the Hellenistic world. Text-based historians may be justified in hesitating to put great faith in surveys which can only date ceramics to five-hundred-year periods, and Alcock concedes that for many regions it is simply not possible to say whether demographic changes began before or after the Macedonian conquest. The main point, though, is that in a few regions, most notably within the modern national states of Greece and Jordan, she is able to show clear trends in settlement; and as more archaeologists come to see the technique's potential, the blank spots on the map will begin to disappear. Further, for all the uncertainties which surround the details of changes in particular areas, taken at an appropriately high level of generalisation – looking at trends spanning several centuries and across millions of square miles – she is undeniably able to document unsuspected variation in settlement history, showing decisively that the Greece-centred perspective has distorted our understanding.

Conclusion

The book ends with two responses, from Michael Jameson and Anthony Snodgrass. As I pointed out at the beginning of this introduction, no single argument unites the contributors, and there is no manifesto for a new classical archaeology. But I do see a certain similarity in these attempts to refigure Greek archaeology: by reshaping the century-old tradition of artefactual analysis to give greater prominence to people in the past, all the papers inevitably close the gap between archaeology and ancient history. By this I do not mean ancient history as non-professionals tend to imagine it, a military-political catalogue of kings and battles. Snodgrass (1985a; 1987: 36–66) has pointed out that classical archaeologists are themselves often outsiders to ancient history, and he has been particularly critical of their attempts to assimilate their work to such political narratives. Rather, the work of the contributors to this volume produces the kind of history which several postprocessual archaeologists have urged: a form of analysis which integrates material culture with larger social structures and with the intentions and perceptions of individual actors. The contributors renounce the unproblematised assumption of superiority which many classical archaeologists have made throughout this century, and admit that their work does not have a special claim to attention simply because the material they study is Greek. But this is not to say that Greek material has no special place at all. By writing a new kind of archaeological history, Greek archaeologists can stake a place within a wider set of debates, in which the unusual wealth of our evidence allows us to make a unique contribution.

2
Archaeologies of Greece

IAN MORRIS

A spectre is haunting archaeology – the spectre of history. Archaeologists study the whole of the human past, but grow uncomfortable when considering themselves as a part of that past. In this chapter I examine the past of the archaeology of classical Greece,[1] which is at once one of the most venerated and one of the most reviled archaeological traditions. I argue that this split personality is a product of archaeologists' lack of concern with the intellectual history of their own practices. The archaeology of Greece is intimately involved with a two-century-old project of under-standing 'Europeanness'. This quest ultimately underlies all Western archaeologies; yet Greece is commonly omitted from histories of world archaeology. We cannot expect to understand the structures of academic archaeology without putting them in the context of Hellenist thought and the archaeology of Greece.

There has been much discussion of the archaeology of Greece in the last decade, but its champions and its critics have both framed their analyses as ahistorical comparisons between classical and other, more theoretical styles of archaeology. For instance, John Boardman, describing the huge gathering of scholars at an international congress of classical archaeologists in Berlin in 1988, comments that 'Many of the papers treated subjects in a traditional way, trying to make sense of new discoveries, and making better sense of some of the long familiar, including some radical revisions . . . There were no signs of anxiety. Should there have been?' (1988c: 795). No, says Boardman, probably speaking for most classical archaeologists; but yes, say several other prominent figures (e.g. Wiseman 1980a; 1980b; 1989; Renfrew 1980; Dyson 1981; 1985; 1989a; 1989b; Gibbon 1985; Snodgrass 1985a; 1987; Bintliff 1986: 12–14). I suggest that this simple opposition between

'traditional' and 'new' prevents us from understanding Greek archaeology. I try to show its limitations by sketching the intellectual history of Greek archaeology. I seek neither easy remedies for perceived ills nor celebrations of past triumphs. Disciplinary history is not a miraculous form of auto-analysis which straightens out the hidden quirks of communities of scholars simply by airing them publicly; but it does force us to come face-to-face with the fact that our own academic practices are historically constituted, and, like all else, are bound to change.

The archaeology of Greek archaeology

I start with two examples of the dualism which dominates perceptions of the archaeology of Greece, remarkable only for the strength of their language. The first is from a self-proclaimed outsider, the former director of a major prehistoric excavation in North America:

> Classical archaeologists dig only selected parts of a site. They are interested primarily in the public precincts of a site, in the palaces, temples and tombs, and in the great religious and ceremonial centers . . . they dig only those sites which give evidence of having preserved architecture, or language texts, or objects of art . . . anthropological archaeologists dig in areas of a site belonging to the most menial aspects of life, such as the houses of the lowest-ranking people in the society, their work areas, their cooking fires, their garbage dumps . . . from now on, when I refer to archaeologists, I will generally be talking about *anthropological* archaeologists. (Struever 1985: 81–2)

The second comes from a former secretary of the French School of Archaeology at Athens:

> With all the swindling of a charlatan, the New Archaeology has waged a campaign of 'disinformation.' Simpleminded and Molièresque, like a terrorist, it has caricatured the parallel [classical] archaeology, seeing no difference between what was done a hundred, fifty, and twenty years ago. It was not Binford who had it right: it was Bayard, and Morgan, and Dumond. They were treated with contempt, but the future will show which check bounced. (Courbin 1988: 160–1)

This oppositional rhetoric is typical of the 'crisis litera-ture' which has appeared in the humanities in the last few years (see Megill 1985: 259–98), inviting us to take sides between 'new' histories, geographies, and so on, and 'traditional' methods. The split is often personified as a clash between generational groups, with the young and restless embracing new-fangled theories, while the old defend time-honoured facts. Different notions of academic activity are not examined *historically*. Some classical archaeologists seek a reasonable middle ground emphasising the strengths of both perspectives, but even this preserves the fundamental idea of a rivalry between old/traditional and new/anthropological archaeologies.[2] Preziosi suggests that in art history 'crisis writing over the past decade and a half seldom deals with issues and, arguably, a good deal of that has worked, certainly to a large extent unwittingly, to deflect or postpone engagement with the more profound problems facing the discipline' (Preziosi 1989: 2). I believe that the same is true in Greek archaeology.

I want to break down these unhelpful oppositions. I argue that in the late nineteenth century archaeological approaches to Greece were absorbed within an intellectual tradition of Hellenism which had its roots in eighteenth-century political struggles; and that since the 1950s, with the gradual disappearance of the social arrangements which had made Hellenism an important academic discourse, the classical disciplines as a whole and Greek archaeology in particular have been left without adequate intellectual justification. I identify the major problem in what Hayden White has called the 'prefiguring' of the object of study, 'the poetic act which precedes the formal analysis of the field, [in which] the historian both creates his object of analysis and predetermines the modality of the conceptual strategies he will use to explain it' (1973: 31). I suggest that an archaeology of Greece was created in and after the 1870s as a relatively innocuous sub-discipline within classics; that later generations of archaeologists were supremely successful in pursuing this vision of the field; that this vision was itself a product of a particular set of historical circumstances which are now passing away; and that it is time to *re*figure the discipline. 'Refiguring' has two dimensions: first, examining the history of Greek archaeology to understand how changing circumstances have undermined nineteenth-century assumptions about what is a worthwhile object of study, which I attempt to do in this chapter; and second, returning human beings to the centre of an intellectual landscape which has been systematically dehumanised, which the authors of the following chapters do. Simply seeing in 'anthropological' archaeologies (themselves enmeshed in similar historical problems) either the salvation of Greek archaeology or the corrosion of its standards obscures this crucial need to think about what an archaeology of Greece is *for*.

I aim to set individual archaeologists and institutions into their social and political contexts. Some readers may see this as an attempt to introduce politics into the discipline, and there certainly is a danger of sliding into self-serving polemics. Any historical account necessarily appears as biased to some readers simply through favouring one approach over other possible ways of writing. But the risk must be taken, especially in a field like classical archaeology, which has for too long avoided introspection. Bourdieu explains in his account of French academia that

> When research comes to study the very realm within which it operates, the results which it obtains can be immediately reinvested in scientific work as instruments of reflexive knowledge of the conditions and the social limits of this work, which is one of the principal weapons of epistemological vigilance. Indeed, perhaps we can only make our knowledge of the scientific field progress by using whatever knowledge we may have available in order to discover and overcome the obstacles to science which are entailed by the fact of holding a determined position in the field. And not, as is so often the case, to reduce the *reasons* of our adversaries to *causes*, to social interests. We have every reason to think that the researcher has less to gain, as regards the scientific quality of his work, from looking at the interests of others, than from looking into his own interests, from understanding what he is motivated to see and not to see. (Bourdieu 1988: 15–16)

The great difficulty, as Bourdieu emphasises, is how to explain patterns of thought and behaviour within academic groups without sinking into implausible conspiracy theories. He observes that 'What may appear as a sort of collective defence organized by the professorial body is nothing more than the aggregated result of thousands of independent but orchestrated strategies of reproduction, thousands of acts which contribute effectively to the preservation of that body because they are the product of [a] sort of social conservation instinct' (p. 150).

Historians of academic disciplines can be divided into two main types, internalists and externalists. The former concentrate on what goes on inside the discipline, the latter on the interaction between practitioners and outside forces. This neat distinction may be cross-cut by another, between cognitivists, who privilege the substance of research and the rational factors in its development, and noncognitivists, who emphasise political, ideological, psychological and other forces. The most successful intellectual histories combine all four methods, but this necessarily produces large books rather than introductory chapters (Novick 1988: 9). Most studies of archaeology have been written by extreme internalists and cognitivists, exemplifying more what Daniel (1981a: 10) called the 'back-looking curiosity' than a serious attempt to treat archaeology as an event in intellectual history (see Meltzer 1989). This is partly true even of landmark studies like Willey and Sabloff's *History of*

American archaeology (1980); while the brief 'historical' analyses of classical archaeology often verge on hagiography (see Dyson 1989a: 129–30). In the last few years there has been a reaction among prehistorians, and a new series of works has appeared, giving more weight to external factors (e.g. Trigger and Glover 1981/2; Sklenár 1983; Gero *et al.* 1983; Fahnestock 1984; Trigger 1984; 1985; 1989; 1990; Patterson 1986; 1989a; 1989b; 1990; Meltzer *et al.* 1986; Fowler 1987; Lamberg-Karlovsky 1989b; Silberman 1989; 1990; Stone and MacKenzie 1989; Christenson 1989; Pinsky and Wylie 1989; B. Arnold 1990; Malina and Vasicek 1990; Gathercole and Lowenthal 1990).

In this chapter I favour externalist and noncognitive forces. This has drawbacks, but in this context I believe it is the most useful approach. Unlike many recent writers, however, I emphasise the links between archaeology and other areas of the humanities and social sciences, drawing in particular on the critique of the history of ideas in Michel Foucault's earlier books. Foucault claimed that most intellectual historians trace what he called horizontal linkages, following ideas about a subject across the centuries. As Tilley recognises, there are major implications for archaeologists:

> the kind of framework which Foucault is criticizing has totally dominated all work in archaeology which has dealt with the history of the discipline. If we reject such a framework and take Foucault's criticisms seriously the implications are quite profound: we will have to rewrite archaeology's history. (Tilley 1990: 292)

Instead of the history of ideas, Foucault proposed the study of *épistèmes*, regimes of truth which subsumed all the intellectual activity of an age. He identified four such epistemes in Western Europe over the last five hundred years: the renaissance (*c.* 1400–1650), the classical (*c.* 1650–1800), the modern (*c.* 1800–1950) and the postmodern (*c.* 1950 onwards). Foucault's concepts are notoriously difficult to pin down, but in his clearest statement he explains that

> This episteme may be suspected of being something like a world-view, a slice of history common to all branches of knowledge, which imposes on each one the same norms and postulates, a general stage of reason, a certain structure of thought that the men of a particular period cannot escape. (Foucault 1972: 191)

Foucault replaced the history of ideas with the archaeology of knowledge, looking at vertical linkages, as he put it, between different forms of learning which co-existed in a single period. In *The order of things* (1970) he examined traditions of writing about living things, wealth and language since the fifteenth century, and argued that within each episteme these three areas of thought were all founded on very similar principles. He also claimed that scholars of grammar in the eighteenth century had more in common with contemporary natural historians or with the physiocrats than they did with the philologists of the nineteenth century, who took for granted – like nineteenth-century biologists and economists – an entirely different relationship between words and things. The history of ideas becomes an idle pursuit: we understand nothing unless we explain the episteme which gave coherence to the thought of each age.

But drawing on Foucault can be as disorienting as it is enlightening. Not only is *The order of things* seriously flawed (e.g. Gutting 1989: 217–26), but his goal of dissolving the repressive forces which restrict discourse made him as critical of externalist as of internalist accounts. He steadfastly refused to search for underlying social 'realities' which determined the forms of discourse. He described his method as producing 'a general history [which] . . . would employ the space of dispersion', as opposed to the social historian's normal approach, which 'draws all phenomena around a single centre – a principle, a meaning, a world-view, an overall shape' (Foucault 1972: 9–10; see Poster 1982; Megill 1987; H. White 1987: 104–41; O'Brien 1989). Foucault's refusal to discuss causation left his four epistemes as islands of thought separated by unbridgeable oceans.

I see two lessons in *The order of things*. First, archaeology has to be analysed in terms of other disciplines, as Malina and Vasicek (1990) have done. Any discussion of archaeology must consider its seminal thinkers, but it must also account for parallels between archaeology and very different disciplines. In this chapter I touch on the relationships between many fields, but I concentrate on two which are particularly important for my main arguments, classics and Orientalism.[3]

Second, we need to take account of Foucault's distinction between seeing epistemes as the 'negative unconscious' of thought, 'that which resists it, deflects it or disturbs it', and 'a positive unconscious of knowledge: a level that eludes the consciousness of the scientist and yet is part of the scientific discourse, instead of disputing its validity and seeking to diminish its scientific nature' (Foucault 1970: xi). That is, there is no point in reducing the history of archaeology to an account of 'Previous (Bad) Work in the Region', as Flannery (1976a: 373) puts it, followed by explanations for our forebears' obtuseness. Yet this is precisely the way most archaeologists have worked. Binford, for example, concedes that external factors influence the New Archaeology, but insists that the recognition that science can be affected by extrinsic factors or even fail to succeed at times is not justification for abandoning the goal of achieving an orderly pattern of accumulative growth in knowledge and understanding through scientific endeavours. (Binford 1982: 138; cf. Binford 1983: 233, n. 14; 1987: 402–3; Earle and Preucel 1987: 509; Schiffer 1988: 467–9; Watson 1991a; 1991b).

For Trigger, on the other hand, the same set of factors 'seriously calls into question the objectivity that the New Archaeology claimed on the basis of its positivist methodology' (1989: 324; cf. Lamberg-Karlovsky 1989a: 4–7). Oppositional rhetoric replaces analysis, trapping us within a for-or-against debate. By seeking out the 'positive unconscious', I try to show that the archaeology of Greece has functioned very well within the framework drawn up for it in the modern episteme, and that the crisis that some classical archaeologists feel is upon us is just a small part of a huge epistemic shift from modernism to postmodernism. I do not believe that archaeologists of Greece should merge themselves with any specific postmodern trend, but in an environment where such ideas dominate discussion, those who insist that classical archaeology remain aloof and those who cry out for unification within a single anthropological archaeology are equally guilty of narrowness of vision.

The argument

All archaeology is a form of what Ricoeur calls *appropriation*, 'the process by which the revelation of new modes of being . . . *gives* the subject new capacities for knowing himself' (1981: 192). One of the goals of the recent critical studies of archaeological history has been to understand how the discipline has helped academics to define Western society over the last century. In a series of studies, Rowlands (1984; 1986; 1987a; 1987b; 1989) has shown how archaeology has contributed to the notions of 'Europe' and 'Africa'; yet the most massive and ideologically influential of all archaeologies, that of classical antiquity, remains virtually unexplored (cf. Lowenthal 1990: 306–7). Greek archaeology has appropriated the past for political ends in a most extreme form, and its study ought to be central to any attempt to treat archaeology's place in Western thought. The very marginality of Greek archaeology to the concerns of most anthropological archaeologists merely adds to its importance. Herzfeld (1987) makes a similar argument that the ambiguous position of modern Greece as an object for ethnography – neither wholly 'us', those who practise academic research, nor entirely 'them', those who are practised upon – makes it an ideal looking glass to the ideological functions of anthropology.

At the centre of the late eighteenth-century shift from the classical to the modern episteme was a bundle of new ideas about Europeanness, which I will call *Hellenism*.[4] Its origins are complex, but it took its distinctive form – the idealisation of ancient Greece as the birthplace of a European spirit – in the context of nationalist disputes between France and the German states, and imperialist aggression by France and Britain against the Turkish empire. Hellenism requires a modification of Trigger's (1984) division of archaeologies into three types, each representing a different way to appropriate the past. His first type, what he calls nationalist archaeology, fosters unity in a modern state by concentrating on its times of ancient greatness; the second, colonialist archaeology, justifies the control of one region by another by demonstrating to the dominators' satisfaction that their victims were always inferior; and the third, imperialist archaeology, supports the world-wide ambitions of a few nations by downgrading the importance of local variations and regional histories. Hellenists created a continentalist rather than a nationalist view of the past, and did this by glorifying ancient Greece and insisting on its unique, or even superhuman, qualities. There was still room for disputes over which nation had the strongest claim on classical Greece, but it was generally agreed among Northwest Europeans and their colonists that they collectively held a monopoly on the Greek cultural heritage, and that this was crucial to the racial superiority which gave them a mandate to rule the world. This made any nationalist use of ancient Greece by modern Greeks problematic, which in turn made the practice of archaeology by the Greeks themselves a complex matter. Classical glories could bolster pride and promote unity, as in all nationalist archaeologies; but the periods and concepts appealed to had been appropriated and defined in advance by the West. The modern Greeks were cast in the role of living ancestors for European civilisation, and archaeology only reinforced this stereotype.

Hellenism had a minimal archaeological component throughout the nineteenth century, but archaeology in Greece underwent profound changes in the 1870s which were perceived as a potential threat to Hellenism. In the last quarter of the century all archaeologies of Greece were absorbed administratively and intellectually into classics, and their connections with the emerging broader discipline of archaeology were systematically severed. The archaeology of classical Greece was effectively neutralised, and slowly diverged in theory and method from other archaeologies, including Greek prehistory. This accelerated in the 1960s, when Greek archaeology was shielded from wider intellectual changes by its subservient relationship to classical philology, and consequently responded to these changes more slowly than did anthropological archaeologies. Since then, a general loss of faith in Hellenism has led some archaeologists working on classical Greece to question the direction the field has taken, but there has been no attempt to understand *why* archaeologists of different schools have such trouble communicating. I do not argue that 'traditional' archaeologists of Greece are stick-in-the-mud reactionaries, evil geniuses scheming to preserve white male supremacy, or victims of false consciousness; I simply assert the historical specificity of our archaeological practices and the need to face the changes taking place within the groups which pay for, produce and consume the results of our research. The kind of archaeology which has dominated classical Greece for a century has been extremely successful, but its audience is shrinking as part of a much wider set of changes. Fields of inquiry which are perceived, rightly or wrongly, to do little more than create a foundation myth for Western supremacy cease to be relevant within a new episteme which has no room in its regime of truth for such ideas of supremacy. Alternative accounts of the same phenomena are being sought, often in conscious opposition to Hellenist models (e.g. Amin 1989). Unlike some of the champions of multiculturalism, I am not suggesting that we should ignore the classical heritage; but changing circumstances demand that we rethink its significance.

I concentrate in this chapter on how the archaeology of Greece was brought within Hellenism, and what is happening now that that framework has been rejected by many academics. Foucault argued that a discipline under one episteme is so different from its successor in the next period that it makes little sense even to call it by the same name. Deprived of Hellenism, classics may disintegrate into its component parts, with Greek archaeology coming under the wing of anthropological archaeology; or it may be reorganised from within to continue to provide some distinctive model of the Graeco-Roman past. I identify three main responses within the discipline: first, ignoring the situation; second, reasserting the values of Hellenism; and third, attempting to problematise the role of Greek archaeology and to seek a new relevance. I suggest that the third of these is the most realistic course of action in the 1990s.

Categories of analysis

In addition to Foucault's epistemes, I use two other key concepts. The first is Thomas Kuhn's concept of the paradigm. Kuhn, a specialist in early modern science, found that looking at research as the cumulative growth of knowledge did not account for his evidence very well, and in *The structure of scientific revolutions* (1970 [1962]) he argued that scientific knowledge grows discontinuously.

Most of the time, he suggested, scientists act within a well-established paradigm, a set of assumptions and exemplary experiments or rules which define the problems to be approached and the methods to be used. The governing paradigm made progress easier by focusing research on a few topics and standardising language and presuppositions. Kuhn called such periods times of 'normal science'. The normal scientist is a puzzle solver within a secure framework, which he (less often, she) normally need not question. His results are shared with others in short papers, since lengthy explanations of aims are rarely necessary. But every so often there is a sudden change, a revolution in which one paradigm replaces another. All paradigms have anomalies which they do not explain well: this is what gives the normal scientist something to do. But, for reasons which vary from case to case, Kuhn argues, research will begin to focus on areas where the anomalies are particularly common or troublesome. The inability of science to explain its data then generates unease, which creates the space for a rebel – a Copernicus, Lavoisier or Newton – to propose an entirely different way of doing things. A new paradigm would explain some things less well than the old, but to succeed it had to provide a more coherent way to analyse what had come to be seen as the major problems in the discipline.

Kuhn's paradigms are not empirically comparable or refutable. There is no neutral language in which rival models can be tested against one another. Kuhn says that

> the proponents of different paradigms practice their trade in different worlds . . . both are looking at the world and what they look at has not changed. But in some areas they see different things, and they see them in different relations one to the other. That is why a law that cannot even be demonstrated to one group may occasionally seem intuitively obvious to another. (T. S. Kuhn 1970: 150)

After a brief struggle, normal science restarts, with the new governing paradigm now defining the legitimate problems. Anyone holding onto older conceptions is marginalised, and after a while sinks into obscurity. Kuhn insists that his model cannot simply be transposed to the social sciences or humanities (1970: 209; cf. Barnes 1977), and attempts to apply it to prehistory have serious problems (Kelley and Hanen 1988: 101–23; Trigger 1989: 4–12). Binford and Sabloff (1982) suggest that the complexity of archaeology creates groups of competing schools rather than a single paradigm. However, the paradigm is a good way to *describe* the intellectual positions I analyse below, with a Hellenist paradigm displacing Enlightenment models in the late eighteenth century, only to be challenged in turn after the

1960s. To some archaeologists in Greece, it is self-evident that we should read books by anthropologists and take soil samples; to others these are equally obviously uninteresting activities, and add nothing to the creation of better texts. No amount of name-calling between the two positions is likely to change this.

But Kuhn's model is less persuasive as an *explanation* of this history. His approach is noncognitivist, but it is strictly internalist (T. S. Kuhn 1977: 105–26). He assumes an autonomous community of scientists whose activities are guided solely by their paradigm; when he does mention external factors, it is usually to downplay them (e.g. 1970: 152–3). I argue that external factors have been crucial in shaping Greek archaeology.

My discussion of these processes draws in part on socio-logical analyses of professions. A series of studies in the 1970s (e.g. T. L. Haskell 1977; Larson 1977; Oleson and Voss 1979) examined how power accrued to self-defined specialists such as doctors, lawyers or academics who controlled particular bodies of knowledge, and how professional institutions – conventions, structures of employment, journals – reinforced the group as a whole and the hierarchy within it. More recent work (e.g. Abbott 1988; Perkin 1989; Derber *et al.* 1990) has emphasised the system of professions, and the need to study what goes on in one group in terms of its competition for prestige and power with other professions. I discuss the relationships between classics and Orientalism in some detail, but, as will become clear, a strictly institutional approach, while crucial as a way to compensate for the gaps in Kuhn's model, is not by itself adequate for understanding the archaeology of Greece.

Hegemony

This concept gained currency through Antonio Gramsci's *Prison notebooks* (1971 [1926–35]). Gramsci distinguished between political society, where an elite controlled the masses by force, and civil society, where an elite engineered consent to their rule through cultural hegemony. The reason why the proletariat did not overthrow capitalism, he argued, was that the capitalists ruled by consent; hence they had to be defeated not by old-fashioned tactics of a bloody revol-utionary 'war of movement', but by what he called a 'war of position', a cultural battle to raise proletarian self-awareness and expose elite hegemony as a weapon in the class struggle. He distinguished three different levels of hegemony, ranging from the 'integral', a virtually unqualified commitment, through 'decadent' to 'minimal', where there are strong challenges to authority, and the controlling group can only

hold on to power by *trasformismo*, incorporating the leaders of oppositional groups into an ever broader ruling class (Femia 1981: 46–7).

Gramsci's comments on hegemony can degenerate into the crudest use of a model of 'false consciousness' (Femia 1981: 43), but more recent studies combining them with Foucault's analyses of discourse (e.g. Laclau and Mouffe 1985) offer a more subtle tool for intellectual history. Smart suggests that:

> Hegemony contributes to or constitutes a form of social cohesion not through force or coercion, not necessarily through consent, but most effectively by way of practices, techniques and methods which infiltrate minds and bodies, cultural practices which cultivate behaviours and beliefs, tastes, desires and needs as seemingly naturally occurring qualities and properties embodied in the psychic reality (or 'truth') of the human subject. (Smart 1986: 160)

A hegemonic discourse is maintained not by propagating falsehoods, but by the dull hand of everyday experience and the constraints of language, which routinise the episteme into a 'natural' condition of life. For Foucault, academic disciplines were perfect examples of this, literally disci-plining their practitioners by driving out inappropriate statements (Foucault 1970: xiv; 1972: 17). Since the late nineteenth century, academic life has become increasingly professionalised (Heyck 1982: Engel 1983; Perkin 1989: 366–74) and the mechanisms for enforcing orthodoxy are powerful indeed. Aspiring archaeologists of Greece normally enter the field through B.A. and Ph.D. programmes involving years of exposure to the authoritarian processes of learning difficult languages and detailed, artefact-centred classes under the gaze of certified practitioners (see Redfield 1991: 6). These procedures vary from nation to nation, but even in such an unstructured context as the traditional British Ph.D., professional discipline is strong (Lewthwaite 1986: 79–80). As in all fields, to succeed in a dissertation students must internalise the skills which will allow them to have more success by publishing in quality journals and on university presses, and access to the funds which make research possible (Bourdieu 1988: 92–5). They must work within canons of language and presentation which limit the possibilities for what can be said (Nimis 1984; Dyson 1989a: 133–4; Peradotto 1989). The discipline guards itself through refereeing, and only those whose work conforms reasonably well will get through. I repeat that I am not rehearsing these points simply to debunk Greek archaeology; to most of us educated within such a hard school the products of others with the same background are likely to be more persuasive than those lacking such rigour. But at the same time, even the most original thinkers have to submit to these rules, and to collaborate in their reproduction (Bourdieu 1988: 112–18). Those who do not may be edged off the field by being denied access to its rewards (Herzog 1983; R. S. Turner 1983; Bernal 1987: 416–27; 1989a: 18).

But other factors unique to the archaeology of Greece make it especially easy to police potential scholars. In some of the Western academic systems a period of residence at the national school of archaeology in Athens is virtually mandatory for the serious graduate student. The schools provide a congenial base, a deep fund of experience and a wide range of services, without which research and field-work would be immeasurably harder. But they also act to expose novices to strong pressure from peers and professors to conform to 'proper' topics and procedures. This reinforces the mechanisms internal to the graduate student's home institution, and may provide a safety net for those whose advisors are academically eccentric – the 'extremist scholar-ship' identified by Muhly (1990: 84–6; cf. Bernal 1990: 125–31). All disciplines have their ideal career structure (e.g. Bourdieu 1988: 87), and the *cursus honorum* of fieldwork provides a third locus of control in archaeology; working their way up from wheelbarrow-pusher to trench supervisor and beyond, students are exposed to correct disciplinary practice and to the artefact-centred dogma, with as its final reward the grant of a body of material to work up into a thesis (cf. Foucault 1977a: 170–94).

Professionals who succeed are trusted to produce more professionals in their own image. Novick muses that

> If the maxim of the free market is *caveat emptor*, the slogan of the profession is *credat emptor*: 'the producer of these wares has been rigorously trained, and we vouch for both his competence and his ethics; the goods them-selves have been subjected to the most rigorous testing and criticism; you may therefore take them on faith'. (Novick 1988: 57)

It is a truism that academic policing works more through patronage and institutional loyalties than through public mutual criticism (Smelser and Content 1977: 7–26), but just the same it efficiently guarantees hegemony. The instruments of control – university departments, scholarly journals, learned societies, research centres, money, politics – run through this chapter, and provide continuity across a hundred-year survey. It is through these as much as through genius or the results of excavations that the archaeology of Greece has taken on and retains its characteristic forms; and it is through the dissolution of the entire modern episteme of which Hellenism was a part that alternative archaeologies have become important.

Great divides

The great tradition

One of the most influential analyses of the distance between the archaeology of Greece and other archaeologies is Renfrew's (1980) discussion of 'the great divide'. Renfrew takes an internalist position, arguing that the differences between North Americanist and classical archaeologies flow naturally from their subject matters:

> This new movement in America [the New Archaeology] stems, of course, from the bareness of the pre-Columbian record of archaeology: for centuries nothing happened of general interest to the student of world history – no Stonehenge, no Maltese temples. American archae-ologists, dismayed by their archaeological record, have sought refuge in theory and methodology, and spend their time talking about 'the elucidation of culture processes' and the production of 'laws of cultural dynamics'. (Renfrew 1980: 291)

Classical archaeology, he suggests, has a great tradition of detail about spectacular finds, which obviates the need for what he implies are the excesses of the Americanists. He traces the classicists' concern for detail to a philological tradition (1980: 288; see pp. 25–6 below), but otherwise adopts a timeless perspective. There is a classical great tradition; its absence in other fields has created a great divide; this must be bridged.

The 'great tradition' is Hellenism. Concern for detail is important for all archaeologists, but being concerned *exclusively* with detail is also part of a nineteenth-century hegemonic strategy which neutralised the threat that archaeology posed to Hellenism. As the Hellenist paradigm comes under pressure in the late twentieth century, the great tradition suffers with it. The great divide is not a conse-quence of the putative poverty of Americanist archaeology: it is one way in which classical archaeology is policed. Throughout this chapter I constantly return not just to this divide, but also to two others, which form part of the same discursive pattern. Through them the archaeology of Greece was made safe for Hellenism by being *de-peopled*. Power, conflict and social change – some of the major concerns of real people – are alienated from the realm of legitimate topics. Individuals reappear only as 'Great Men', whether the inspired artist like Pheidias or the wise statesman like Pericles, whose conscious decisions directly transform the passive material record.

A second divide: history and prehistory

The second divide is within Greek archaeology, and Renfrew himself exemplifies it. Much of his paper's impact came from his double legitimacy as both a leading anthropo-logical archaeologist and also as the director of important excavations in the Aegean. Since the 1890s, a line has been drawn through the Greek 'Dark Age' (*c.* 1200–700 BC). The time before the Dark Age is not properly classical. Very different theories and methods are tolerated in it, and are even encouraged in a kind of *trasformismo*, which allows those whose ideas cannot fit into classical archaeology (like Renfrew, now head of a Cambridge college) to enter the professional elite without friction so long as they remain in the time before 1200 BC. Most Bronze Age archaeologists remain 'traditionalists' (e.g. French and Wardle 1988), but since the 1960s a large minority has found more profit in contacts with other prehistorians than with classics. Renfrew (1972), for example, provided one of the best uses of systems theory in archaeology as an alternative to diffusionism to explain the rise of complex society in the Cyclades in the third millennium. This called for evidence which was simply not collected in standard classical fieldwork.[5] Some of the strongest challenges to Hellenist archaeology have seeped into discussion through initial applications in the Bronze Age. It is the soft underbelly of Hellenism, but the divide around 1200 is still strong enough to make it difficult for some Bronze Age specialists to understand the debates going on among classicists (e.g. Runnels 1989).

A third divide: history and archaeology

Classical archaeologists' training usually involved them in reading a good deal of the Greek historians, but Snodgrass (1985a; 1987: 36–66) shows that when they try to assimilate their work to history they usually look to the *wrong kind* of history, desperately seeking contacts with a political-military narrative. The Hellenist archaeology of Greece is saturated in historical texts, but it does not *produce* historical texts. The encounter between classically trained archaeologists and Greek material culture is reminiscent of Constantine's description of the response of similarly knowledgeable seventeenth-century travellers to the Greek landscape:

> the punning association of places and commonplaces, localities and loci . . . is a sort of appropriation of the place into the life and times of the modern traveller. What such a response or procedure most achieves is a feeling of continuity: continuity of the texts and of the landscape. No single factor in all the rediscovery of Greece is half so potent as this, the most obvious: the landscape survives and many of the fabulous places in it. (Constantine 1989: 11)

Archaeology becomes a source of illustrations to be pillaged in a bits-and-pieces fashion to lend colour to historical accounts based on other sources. The written word, even when excavated on inscriptions or coins, is separated from and made prior to other artefacts. Hayden White (1987: 1–57) argues that the emplotment of historical writing into narrative form presupposes a desire to moralise the events involved; by arranging their texts in self-consciously non-narrative forms, archaeologists deny themselves the possibility of telling a story of importance (see pp. 27–9 below). Archaeological data are not treated as needing explanation in terms of social action. Making archaeology part of ancient history, challenging as well as exemplifying assumptions about antiquity, depends on awareness of trends in other archaeologies and histories as well as on knowledge of the Greek language. Material culture is no passive mirror of social 'reality': the dynamic interplay between individuals and inherited institutions is partly carried out through manipulation of things, and it is this which gives archaeology its potential as a humanistic discipline (see Hodder 1982a; 1987a; 1987a; 1989c; 1991; Miller and Tilley 1984; Miller *et al.* 1989).

Hellenism

The Roman past

Frank Turner suggests that 'until the late eighteenth century most educated [West] Europeans regarded their culture as Roman and Christian in origin, with merely peripheral roots in Greece . . . In contrast to this visible, tangible and persuasive Roman influence, the Greeks simply had not directly touched the life of Western Europe' (1981: 1–2). Language was the most important part of this heritage. The claim that there was little interest in antiquities before the fourteenth century (e.g. Daniel 1950: 1–18) ignores good evidence for the collection of Roman art in the Middle Ages (Greenhalgh 1989), but there was definitely a change during the early Renaissance, when Italian artists began to draw inspiration from Roman sculpture and architecture (Gilbert 1977; Davos 1979). By the early sixteenth century French kings had begun to collect Roman statues as part of their claim to cultural hegemony as 'the new Rome' (Haskell and Penny 1981: 1–6), but Greek remains continued to be ignored, with the exception of the fifteenth-century Cyriac of Ancona (Weiss 1988: 131–44; Eisner 1991: 39–50). The ancient world was a powerful source of legitimacy and influenced all aspects of elite life, but it was almost entirely a textual creation, and a Latin one at that. This Latin pre-history is vital for understanding the development of Greek archaeology.

Classical Greek was used for official purposes in the Byzantine empire until the fifteenth century (Constantinides 1982: 151; Browning 1983), but in the west by AD 400 even an intellectual like St Augustine knew little Greek and cared for it still less (*Confessions* 1.13). Latin, however, was the ecclesiastical and diplomatic tongue, and its role in the Church gave it international currency. One of the main forces behind the expansion of higher education in the twelfth century was the need of increasingly centralised states for bureaucrats with a working knowledge of Latin, but not Greek (J. Bowen 1975: 79–87). The rediscovery of Aristotle, which did so much to transform Western intellectual life, was due almost entirely to Arabic versions, which now began to circulate in Latin translations (Dronke 1988; Luscombe and Evans 1988).

The political and literary functions of Latin declined in the fourteenth century as the use of vernacular tongues spread, but Latin-teaching professionals did not fade away. Instead, they shifted their emphasis from the Church Fathers to classical authors, especially Cicero, redefining Latin as a crucial part of the moral education of a gentleman (J. Bowen 1989: 164). Some acquaintance with Greek history was expected as background for Roman stories, but this came from Latin sources or from Latin translations of Greek authors. When around 1516 Machiavelli pirated the theory of the 'mixed constitution' – a perfect balance between democracy, oligarchy and monarchy – from the second century BC account of Roman politics written in Greek by Polybius, he probably did so via new Latin versions; there is no evidence that he knew Greek (Garin 1990). And when he used Polybius, it was in his detailed analysis of the political lessons for Florence of the first ten books of Livy's *History* of Rome.

Machiavelli used the mixed constitution to draw lessons for Florence from Roman history, which he knew would be familiar to any educated listener or reader. During the sixteenth and seventeenth centuries, Descartes, Bacon and other 'new thinkers' asserted that knowledge of classical texts was declining in importance compared to knowledge of science, and humanists as prominent as Casaubon accepted this; but as Grafton (1991) shows, this oversimplifies developments. Political theory continued to depend on Roman history. After Charles I introduced the concept of the mixed constitution into England in 1642, and particularly after the 'Glorious Revolution' of 1688, parallels were regularly drawn between England freed from the Stuarts and Republican Rome, freed from its kings in 508 BC (Weston 1960; 1984). Both were seen as examples of a balanced polity. Latin poetry, especially Virgil's polished masterpiece the *Aeneid*, exalting the ancestors of the first emperor Augustus, was acclaimed by Dryden and others as describing the ideal constitutional monarch. Latin models dominated English high culture to such an extent that the early eighteenth century is often referred to as the Augustan

Age (see J. M. Levine 1987). The ideals of the Enlightenment – power, sophistication, reason – found abundant echoes in contemporary perceptions of the Roman empire (F. M. Turner 1986; 1989b).

Johann Joachim Winckelmann

The great shift of interest from Rome to Greece – the rise of Hellenism – began in the mid-eighteenth century. For internalists, one man was decisive: Johann Joachim Winckelmann (e.g. Pfeiffer 1976: 183; Zinserling 1973; Borbein 1986). Born to a poor cobbler from Stendal near Berlin in 1717, Winckelmann gave himself a good Latin education and, after a patently specious conversion to Catholicism (he continued to sing old Lutheran hymns in his room (Constantine 1984: 136)), won the posts of librarian and president of antiquities at the Vatican. Prior to Winckelmann's arrival in Rome, papal administration of antiquities had been at best haphazard (Ridley 1992: 12–35), but he quickly took the situation in hand. Based on his knowledge of finds passing through Rome, he produced a major two-volume *Geschichte der Kunst des Alterthums* (1764 (English translation 1968)). Winckelmann adopted a four-stage scheme for Greek poetry proposed by J. J. Scaliger in 1608, and applied it to Greek sculpture. His first stage, set in the time before the Athenian sculptor Pheidias (mid-fifth century BC), was 'straight and hard'; the second, or Pheidian, was 'grand and square'. The third stage, in the fourth century BC, he named after Praxiteles, and called it 'beautiful and flowing'; finally, in the later centuries, art was imitative (Justi 1943; Pfeiffer 1976: 167–72; Constantine 1984: 92–127; Irmscher 1986; Käfer 1986. On his chronology, see A. Potts 1982).

Winckelmann was certainly influential. Herder, Goethe, Fichte and Schiller can all be said to have seen antiquity through his prism (Bruford 1962: 184–292), but the internalist and cognitivist perspective obscures more than it reveals about his place in the rise of Hellenism. Starting from the crudest externalist level, Winckelmann and his success could be seen simply as a product of the German cultural resistance to France, the self-proclaimed 'new Rome'. By the 1760s intellectuals opposing the French use of Rome could construct ideological alternatives drawing on knowledge of the far East and the New World, but Greece was still the obvious choice (but cf. B. Anderson 1991: 69–70).[6] Even in its subordinate position in early modern classical scholarship, Greece had richer associations for intellectuals than China, India or the Americas.

Protestantism was a mainstay of German resistance to France, and Luther's insistence on understanding Christianity *sola scriptura* – by the *Greek* text alone, unemcumbered by

Latin commentaries – encouraged identification with the Greek language. Sixteenth-century philologists saw links between German and Greek patterns of noun declensions, use of a definite article and large-scale reliance on particles and prepositions with verbs. And just as French kings could think of themselves as Roman emperors, squabbling German princes could identify with the warring Greek cities (Bernal 1987: 193, 203, 214). Winckelmann's popularity is best seen in this wider framework. As Bruford shows (1962: 27–39), in some ways Winckelmann merely reinforced tendencies long present in German elite culture.

By the late eighteenth century, interest in Greece was spreading. The French and American revolutions made all republicanism, even Roman, suspect to conservatives (Baeumer 1986). English scholars had occasionally drawn on Athens for political analogies in seventeenth-century debates about the division of powers (Roberts 1989), but they began to do so far more often after about 1770, at first to show the evil of democracy, and later to exemplify its 'constitutional morality' (Momigliano 1966: 56–74; Pappé 1979; F. M. Turner 1981: 187–234; 1989b; Wood 1988: 5–41; see pp. 29–31 below). Within France, the questions about the nature of liberty raised by the revolution were frequently debated in terms of a comparison with Athens. Sometimes this was done as a self-conscious historical comparison, as in Constant's 1814 *Spirit of conquest and usurpation* (Baker 1987: 453–61); more often, it was embedded within more complex cultural projects (Vidal-Naquet 1990: 161–243). The promotion of Greece was also useful in power struggles within the British elite. In the eighteenth century the universities reached the low point of their prestige – 'indifferent to examinations and standards, they functioned as finishing schools for the privileged classes' (J. Bowen 1989: 166) – and emphasis on Greek gave bourgeois teachers a weapon against the slothful aristocracy.

Winckelmann was part of a still wider movement, the intellectual revolt described by Berlin (1979: 1–24) as the 'counter-Enlightenment'. He was a key figure in the rise of Romanticism,[7] the search of the free soul for truth and beauty in spontaneous, natural creation. Narrowly construed, it was a consciously militant trend among young German, British and French artists, although some of the latter criticised it as an Anglo-German conspiracy (Fürst 1969); more broadly perceived, it was a major intellectual shift, Foucault's shift from the classical to the modern episteme.

Some see Romanticism as beating a middle course between reaction and revolution; others see it as a cult of the extreme, from ultra-conservatives like Chateaubriand to ultra-radicals like Shelley. Charles Nodier wrote that 'this last resort of the human mind, tired of ordinary feelings, is

what is called the romantic genre: strange poetry, quite appropriate for the moral condition of society, to the needs of surfeited generations who cry out for sensation at any cost' (quoted in Hugo 1957: 58). Hobsbawm (1962: 304–10) suggests that the economic and social revolutions of the late eighteenth century helped create groups of socially displaced young men and professional artists, who formed the 'shock troops' of the movement. Both groups felt cut off from a recognisable function, shouting the burdens of their souls into the dark and cursing the bourgeois philistine (R. Williams 1958: 48–64; Eagleton 1983: 18–22; Seidman 1983: 42–73). Romantic artists and intellectuals had little use for stable empires like Rome, Egypt and China. Small, intense communities, full of spontaneous emotion, originality, purity and childlike innocence were more interesting. The cultured Virgil was less exciting than divine 'folk poets' like Homer and the invented Ossian; Rome seemed decadent and corrupt next to the simplicity and hardness of the Greeks, especially the Spartans; and Roman art looked uninspired and derivative compared to Winckelmann's account of the liberty and spiritual simplicity of Greek sculpture. Youth and vitality were central themes in Romanticism, and Winckelmann's contribution was to see ancient Greece as the 'childhood of Europe'. His references to the Greeks as 'natural children' became, as Frank Turner says, 'an exceedingly useful and influential fiction' (1981: 42). The Greeks were the foundation from which all European culture sprang: and Winckelmann showed his readers paths back to it.

The German idealisation of Greece was to have important effects on classical archaeology. By the 1670s English and French travellers had begun to visit Greece (Eisner 1991: 50–62), and even if they rarely let their writings be influenced by what they saw, they insisted on the need to experience the landscape in person (Constantine 1989). German intellectuals did not feel this need. In spite of repeated invitations, Winckelmann never went to Greece, and his friend Johann von Riedesel is the *only* German known to have been there before 1800 (Constantine 1984: 128). German scholars rejected out of hand the physical experience of the ideal (cf. Said 1978: 52). As Papal Antiquary from 1763 until his murder five years later Winckelmann had access to nearly all sculptural finds from Italy and most of those exported from Greece. His letters kept North European scholars informed of discoveries, against which he constantly tested his theories of Greek art; but the only statues he handled (on which see Jenkyns 1980: 151–2) belonged to his fourth, 'imitative' period, or else were Roman copies (F. M. Turner 1981: 40). He worked largely from ancient literature about art, most of it Latin (Häsler 1973a). He was so critical of the digs which had begun at Herculaneum in 1738 and Pompeii ten years later that he feared 'a beating or worse' at the excavators' hands (Constantine 1984: 111). In spite of his talk of excavating Olympia with 100 workmen (p. 126) he never became involved in fieldwork. He preferred texts, and his fullest discussion of a specific statue was his bizarre interpretation of the Laocoön, a highly convoluted first-century AD Roman sculptural group, as an example of the 'noble simplicity and quiet grandeur' of Athens in the time of Socrates, around 400 BC (Butler 1935: 43–8; Brandt 1986; Andreae 1988: 46–52).

In the late eighteenth century, ancient Greece became a metahistorical concept, with the Hellenes themselves less and less subject to normal canons of analysis. Formulaic responses to an idealised Greece seemed called for. Jenkyns (1980: 13) suggests that 'to the German mind, Hellas became a sort of heavenly city, a shimmering fantasy on the far horizon'. Alexander von Humboldt, Prussian education minister in 1808–10 and a key figure in the rise of Hellenism, thought that Germans should see Greece 'at a distance, in the past, and removed from its everyday reality – only thus should the Ancient World appear to us' (quoted in Constantine 1984: 2).

Classics and German politics
By 1900 many wealthy Westerners visited Greece (Pemble 1987; Eisner 1991: 125–76), but the Hellenist attitude established before 1800 remained intact, largely because the unmatchable rigour of German academics carried the idealisation of Greece all over Europe and North America. Bernal (1987: 215–23) emphasises the role of the University at Göttingen in this. Göttingen was founded in 1734 as a professional centre for German scholars. Winckelmann himself stood outside this framework, but greatly influenced Heyne, the Professor at Göttingen from 1763 to 1812 (Constantine 1984: 92–8). The two were never friends, but Heyne dedicated his prize essay of 1778 to the master (Pfeiffer 1976: 171). Heyne began teaching archaeology in 1767, drawing on Winckelmann's letters and building up a cast collection. Among his students was von Humboldt (P. Connor 1989: 203). Heyne created a corps of classical scholars. The new professionals were initiated through the Seminar, where the Professor inculcated in them the skills of source criticism. This allowed a scholar to decide which ancient accounts to accept and which to reject, on the basis of identifying the authors' biases and the evidence which they could have had access to. The overarching paradigm controlling research was the concept of the *Zeitgeist*, or spirit of the age. Paradoxically, through the use of critical skills the Greeks were enshrined as being beyond historical criticism. History consisted of identifying the *Zeitgeist* which

belonged to each *Volk*. The spirit was rooted in the lands where the 'people' was 'born', and environmental determinism had a major role. Whatever happened to the *Volk*, it retained its immutable essence (Iggers 1983). In the case of the Greeks, all impurities were purged in the fires of source criticism to leave a race beyond comparison.

The new discipline, christened *Altertumswissenschaft* by Friedrich Wolf (another of Heyne's pupils), became a crucial concept in Prussian political ideology. Von Humboldt was appointed as education minister to repair national morale after Napoleon's annihilation of the Prussian armies in 1806. He made *Altertumswissenschaft* the basis of his new *Bildung*, an almost religious experience through education (Bruford 1975; Ringer 1979a), to rescue the fallen national spirit. He wrote that

> Our study of Greek history is therefore a matter quite different from our other historical studies. For us the Greeks step out of the circle of history. Even if their destinies belong to the general chain of events, yet in this respect they matter least to us. We fail entirely to recognise our relationship to them if we dare to apply the standards to them which we apply to the rest of world history. Knowledge of the Greeks is not merely pleasant, useful or necessary to us – no, in the Greeks alone we find the ideal of that which we should like to be and produce. If every part of history enriched us with this human wisdom and human experience, then from the Greeks we take something more than earthly – something godlike. (von Humboldt, quoted in Cowan 1963: 79).

Other nations did not leap to adopt the German system of Gymnasium and Seminar, but German scholarship was recognised as being more rigorous than anything available elsewhere. More importantly, *Altertumswissenschaft* was vindicated as a moral strategy by the Prussians' rapid recovery and their role in Napoleon's fall, and by the growth in German wealth and power thereafter. Von Humboldt's Hellenist *Bildung* was part of a package of liberalising reforms in 1807–12 (Hohendahl 1989: 255–61); but after a brief student revolt in 1817–19 a reactionary phase set in, and the *Bildung* was increasingly restricted to a meritocratic elite (O'Boyle 1969). Before the 1820s the Gymnasien typically admitted many students who would leave after a few years to enter non-graduate occupations. This had a 'democratising' effect, as some students from humble backgrounds were co-opted into the university elite. But as the century wore on two new factors emerged. First, another level of schools was set up for students aiming at non-graduate careers, turning the Gymnasien into elite institutions and stratifying education (Müller 1987). After 1834, the universities were effectively closed to anyone lacking a

Gymnasium education (Ringer 1979b: 34). Second, while the numbers of Gymnasien increased and the pool of applicants to the universities grew, the number of places in the universities expanded much more slowly, and the costs skyrocketed (Pilbeam 1990: 191–202). Classical education meant privilege, particularly after 1859, when Latin and Greek were dropped from the lower-order *Realschulen* in favour of modern languages and sciences (Ringer 1979b: 37). The *Humanismus–Realismus* debate which followed was essentially a conflict between the controllers of different types of institutions over shares of the student market and access to rewards (Hohendahl 1989: 261–70). Within the classical sector, a parallel debate grew up between a liberal historical wing (the *Sachphilologen*) and a narrowly philological and 'scientific' wing (*Sprachphilologen*), which was to have important consequences for archaeology (see p. 28 below). Classically educated graduates monopolised jobs in the state sector, education and law, but by the 1880s graduate unemployment was rocketing. One response was to increase science education in the universities; another was to tip the scales in favour of the bourgeoisie by reducing secondary school attendance among the children from the lower classes (Müller 1987: 37–8). In 1879 the German Association of Engineers insisted that Gymnasium Latin was required for a degree, thus asserting their professionalism and high caste (Pilbeam 1990: 177–80). But within twenty years the pro-science response had won. By 1900 classical education was being denounced as an archaism; the engineers now wanted to drop Latin qualifications, and the emperor had to intervene to allow this (Ringer 1979b: 39–40).

Despite the declining prestige of classics in Germany, it was at just this time that the system was being emulated overseas with the greatest eagerness. The radically different social and educational conditions in other nations meant that some aspects of German education were rejected, but the hierarchical and Romantic aspects of *Altertumswissenschaft* were embraced all over the West (cf. Ringer 1979b: 206–59).

Classics in Britain and the USA

In Britain, the German emphasis on the Greek language was useful in educational conflict. Degrees emphasising Greek were set up at Oxford in 1807 and Cambridge in 1824, but change was slower in the public (i.e. private and highly exclusive) secondary schools which could not match the Greek skills imparted in middle-class academies. In 1805 a court ruling even made it illegal for Leeds Grammar School (an elite medieval foundation) to abandon its traditional diet of Latin because this would be contrary to the founder's intentions (J. Bowen 1989: 168). The first of many

Commons committees was set up in 1816 to reform the system, just as von Humboldt had been empowered to do in Prussia, but without any way to enforce its recommendations. Britain in 1816 had just humbled Napoleon at Waterloo (with Prussian help), whereas Prussia in 1808 had been a defeated state in search of rejuvenation. Political will was lacking, and instead of forming part of a state-imposed *Bildung*, Greek was absorbed into upper-class education as an adaptive strategy to defuse bourgeois pressure. Headmasters of public schools played an important part in this, offering detailed instruction in Greek to give their pupils a better grounding for Oxbridge, and exerting pressure on the civil service to give those skilled in classical languages an advantage in the competitive entrance examinations (Bolgar 1979a). British education remained very different from German. The time which boys spent learning Greek could be small compared with that devoted to games, but these activities can be seen as part of a cult of the aristocratic amateur sportsman, which reunited perfectly with Romantic Hellenism in the new Olympic Games in 1896 (Hobsbawm 1987: 181–3; Robbin 1989: 162–82). This reshaping of German traditions to suit British needs took place at all levels; on the whole, the best British classicists remained 'brilliantly amateurish' when compared to the Germans (Shorey 1919: 48).

The situation in North America was different again. Nineteenth-century American intellectuals were acutely aware that in spite of their nation's growing stature, they remained culturally dependent on Europe. Americans wanting 'serious' education went to Germany, especially after 1850 (Diehl 1977). 'That Germany possessed the sole secret of scholarship was no more doubted by us young fellows in the eighteen-eighties than it had been doubted by George Ticknor and Edward Everett when they sailed from Boston, bound for Göttingen, in 1814', wrote Bliss Perry (quoted in Novick 1988: 21). Some were disillusioned by what they found, but many returned determined to pass the torch of scholarship to America. Knowledge of classical languages was less useful in defining an elite in America than in Europe, and education was rarely an avenue to wealth and power (Ringer 1979b: 249). The impetus for emulation of German practices came largely from the academics themselves, as a drive to establish professional standing. The call for an American Philological Association in 1868 spoke of an organisation of 'all professors of language of respectable standing in our colleges, universities, theological seminaries and other schools of higher education' (quoted in Shero 1964: 6). The Association was founded in the next year, uniting classicists in the Northeast and also formalising their hierarchy (Moore 1919; Calder 1984: 15–42; Benario 1989).

As in Britain, German goals were reformulated. The metaphysical *Zeitgeist* withered away, and the pragmatic American concept of 'science' replaced the idealist *Wissenschaft* (Nimis 1984; Novick 1988: 21–60; Halporn 1989). But the language of Shorey's anti-German polemic at the end of the First World War is revealing: 'despite a little fumbling and naïveté at the start, a sufficient number of the founders [of American classics] were entirely competent to play the game according to the German rules and possibly to devise American improvements' (1919: 41). He saw Americans as balancing British dilettantism and German pedantry, but *Altertumswissenschaft* remained the measure of man: national schools of thought were framed in terms of it. The German tyranny over Greece was all pervasive.

Other Western traditions led in the same direction. In France German universities were idealised (Weisz 1983: 61–3), and fifteen universities were opened in 1896–7 on the German model (Karady 1980; Singer 1982). As early as 1875 the Devonshire Report had criticised British schools for neglecting sciences (J. Bowen 1989), and educational progressives in the USA attacked high school classics in the 1880s (Hertzberg 1989: 71); but these assaults were mild compared to the Durkheimians' critique of French classics (Keylor 1975: 173–94). But despite these differences, the field developed along similar lines in all the Western nations. An idealised Greece was defined as the starting point of Europeanness; access to it was through long training in the Greek language; and, regardless of the ideologies of the early champions of Greek, a classical education came to be associated with political conservatism.

Hellenism, Orientalism, imperialism

The earliest surviving definition of *to Hellenikon*, 'Greek-ness', comes from Herodotus: 'we are one in blood and one in language; those shrines of the gods belong to us all in common, and there are our customs, bred of a common upbringing' (8.144.2). He framed this sentiment in opposition to 'the East' in his account of the Persian War of 480–479 BC, and the nineteenth-century definition of ancient Greece as the fountainhead of Europeanness was made in a similar context. We cannot understand Hellenism and its grip on Greek archaeology from a narrow disciplinary perspective. Hellenism was not an isolated growth. A full account would situate it in the kind of broad web of knowledge and power which Foucault examined, but I will concentrate on its inter-relations with Orientalism, which was invented at roughly the same time, and on how the two structures demarcated pure Europeans from tainted others. Both disciplines were tied to European military adventures in the East Mediterranean from 1798 to 1829, and they drew strength from their relationships with new ideas of race and early forms of imperialism.

Egypt

In the eighteenth century Egypt was regularly paired with Rome as an ancestor to whom European civilisation owed much. Napoleon's invasion of Egypt in 1798 was the zenith of this phase, but was also critical in transforming Egypt into a mirror to reflect the excellence of a purely European tradition deriving from Greece. Napoleon's army of scholars inscribed Egypt into twenty-three huge volumes of the *Description de l'Egypte* (1809–28). This massive project, like *Altertumswissenschaft*, surpassed all that had come before in its detail and scope, and developed a radically new language and attitude to its subject; but it worked very differently from Hellenism. Said argues that

> The *Description* thereby displaces Egyptian or Oriental history as a history possessing its own coherence, identity and sense. Instead, history as recorded in the *Description* supplants Egyptian or Oriental history by identifying itself directly and immediately with a world history, a euphemism for European history. To save an event from oblivion is in the Orientalist's mind the equivalent of turning the Orient into a theater for his representations of Orientalism. (Said 1978: 86)

Napoleon envisaged a two-pronged French regeneration of ancient Egypt, through scholarly knowledge and direct imperial administration. The revived Egypt would then become a source of renewal for Europe (Said 1978: 87; T. Mitchell 1991). His defeat and the British occupation of Egypt in 1801 changed all this, but the French academic project remained intact, even if, as Said (1978: 169) claims, it was 'imbued with a sense of loss'. The first 'modern' Orientalist, Silvestre de Sacy, typifies the French response. He won his influence precisely by reducing the Orient to something which could be analysed without leaving the libraries of Paris (pp. 127–8). Sacy's Orientalism achieved international success in much the same way as *Altertums-wissenschaft*. It allowed the European to know the East better than those who actually lived there could. The fact that Sacy, Renan and others could do this without setting eyes on the regions they studied only reinforced the message that the Europeans' power over the East was justified by their knowledge of it. Such a discipline had obvious appeal in Germany, where three factors – a relatively professionalised academic structure, the lack of a tradition of travelling scholars, and the absence of direct imperial involvement in the area – combined to produce a situation where few Orientalists visited the East before the 1870s (pp. 17–19, 52).

In Britain, with its military domination of the Near East, direct personal experience of the East retained considerable intellectual respectability (Kabbani 1986). Edward Lane's *Account of the manners and customs of the modern Egyptians* (1836) was explicitly offered as a response to the *Description*, as a triumph of British empiricism over French philosophy; but here too a library- and text-centred method had great appeal. Said argues that, despite all the national variations in style and politics,

> Ultimately, perhaps, the difference one always feels between modern British and modern French Orientalism is a stylistic one; the import of the generalizations about Orient and Orientals, the sense of distinction preserved between Orient and Occident, the desirability of Occidental dominance over the Orient – all these are the same in both traditions. (Said 1978: 225)

The assumption behind all the discourses was that the Orient was to be ruled by the West. Only in this way could anything be salvaged of its ancient contribution to the rise of the West, which was its only excuse for existing.

Beginning with Sacy himself in 1805, some Orientalists achieved status as political advisors; but Orientalism also required its scholars to take a subordinate place to classicists. The Hellenist worked on Greece, the point from which European success derived. The Orientalist worked on cultures which were either incompletely developed or degenerate, and which defined what Europe was not. Even those who emphasised the contribution of the East to the origins of Greek civilisation did so in language which represented 'the Orient' as fantastically ancient and unchanging, the possessor of a sterile wisdom which needed the youthful, original spirit of the Greeks to transform it into Europeanness. Only a few Orientalists refused to do this. The most notable was Champollion, the decipherer of hieroglyphics. For thirty years he was kept out of positions of authority by Hellenist and Christian rivals, and only preserved any credibility for Egyptology by playing the two factions against each other. His untimely death in 1831 was followed by (although it was not solely responsible for) a decline in the discipline. Even his decipherment was not taken seriously until the late 1850s (Leclant 1982; Marichal 1982). Egyptologists on the whole seem to have accepted their secondary role. Mogens Larsen uses the relief sculpture which Breasted designed to go over the door of his Oriental Institute, opened at the University of Chicago in 1931, to epitomise the scholarly niche which Orientalists accepted:

> The scene on the relief shows an ancient Egyptian scribe who hands over to a semi-naked Westerner a fragment of a relief with a hieroglyphic inscription . . . Behind the scribe are . . . the palace at Persepolis, the Sphinx and the pyramids at Gizeh. This, then, is the ancient Near East which, through the Egyptian scribe, hands over to the West the essential element in civilization, the gift of writing . . . Three buildings stand for this Western tradition: the Acropolis, a European cathedral and the US State Capitol at Lincoln, Nebraska, a modern skyscraper chosen here because it was built by the same engineering firm that was responsible for the Oriental Institute. (M. T. Larsen 1989: 230)

The Orient was important only in the distant past, and even then solely as a place from which the Greeks had taken certain ideas which they alone brought to fruition.

Other disciplines combined to urge Orientalists to accept this role. Even the most positive views of 'the East' subordinated it and its study to 'the West'. Montelius' synthesis of European prehistory in the 1880s, arguing for the diffusion of civilisation from the Near East, is a good example. German classical archaeologists such as Schuchhardt and Furtwängler opposed it vigorously, insisting that the inspiration for Mycenaean Greece came from northern 'Aryans', and that Semitic cultures were irrelevant. In Britain and France Montelius' theory was widely accepted, but the Orient was represented as having lost all power by the second millennium BC (Trigger 1989: 156–61). By the 1930s, Hellenists were so confident that they had practically written the East out of history – the history that mattered – altogether. Once again some German archaeologists went to extremes, and the notorious Gustaf Kossinna even claimed that the 'gift of writing' was a Stone Age Germanic invention (Trigger 1989: 166). Anglo-American archaeologists contented themselves with arguing that the transmission was late (*c.* 720 BC), was the result of Greek initiative, and was followed by a brilliant Greek reconceptualisation of literacy (Bernal 1987: 367–99). Said suggests that 'Most often an individual entered the profession [of Orientalism] as a way of reckoning with the Orient's claim on him; yet most often too his Orientalist training opened his eyes, so to speak, and what he was left with was a sort of debunking project' (Said 1978: 150–1). Many Orientalists were self-professed Hellenists, who showed their love for Greece by denigrating the East (p. 209; cf. Vidal-Naquet 1990: 245–65). In the same year that Breasted's Oriental Institute opened, the most famous of these scholars, Carl Becker, turned the nagging theme of Greek cultural borrowings from the East on its head by arguing that 'Islam' had stolen a 'Greek' humanistic heritage, but had lacked the creative imagination to understand it properly (Said 1978: 103–4).

The Greek War of Independence

The Greek War of Independence (1821–30) brought Hellenism and Orientalism together as opposites to create what Foucault (1972: 31–9; cf. Brown and Cousins 1986) called a discursive formation – a system of thought linking together statements on different themes within a single world view. Western philhellenes sought to regenerate Greece, which would then regenerate Europe, much in the way that Napoleon had looked at Egypt; but there were crucial differences. Napoleon had included Greece in his imperialist vision, saying in 1797 that his capture of the Ionian islands was more important than possession of the whole of Italy (Clogg 1986a: 46). But by the 1820s, the idea of directly controlling Greece had become unthinkable. Politics and Romantic notions of Greece were mutually reinforcing. On the whole, the Great Powers followed Metternich's policies after 1815, and opposed all revolutionary movements, for fear that like the French Revolution they would spread across national borders. The 'Holy Alliance' of Austria, Prussia and Russia actively backed the Turks in 1821; Britain remained aloof. French policy was ambivalent. The British seizure of the Ionian islands in 1814 still rankled, and there were hopes that an independent Greece would be a problem for London. The agents of renewal in Greece were to be the Greeks themselves, with the aid of individual philhellenes rather than imperial administrators.

The philhellenes had most contact with the *Philiki Etaireia* (Friendly Society), a secret society of expatriate Greeks founded in Russia in 1814, who aimed at Greek independence. By 1821 it had branches in all major Western cities, and perhaps 1,000 members (Geanakopoulos 1976). The *Etaireia* was initially divided between two policies. The first was nothing less than the restoration of Byzantium. Greek-speakers were scattered all over the Turkish empire, and many Greeks considered Constantinople as the obvious centre of Greek culture (Just 1989: 77–9). The *Etaireia*'s main effort was an invasion of the Danubian provinces, to create a rising of all Christians in the Turkish empire, led by the local Greek merchant and bureaucratic elites. This failed dismally. The *megáli ídea*, the 'great idea' of huge Greek state focused on Constantinople, remained important in Greece for a century (Tatsios 1984), but by 1823 most members of the *Etaireia* accepted a more limited goal, of setting up a small, 'revitalised' nation-state. It was for this that the philhellene volunteers of 1821–3 set sail, however mixed their motives may have been (St Clair 1972: 13–126; Dover 1988).

However, neither vision was shared by the only effective organisations within Greece, the Church and the bandits (Koliopoulos 1987: 39–66). Just observes that 'prior to the [war] there was never a single coherent political entity that went by the name of Greece (or rather, Hellas) or that construed its unity in terms of being Greek' (1989: 73). The uprising in 1821 was mainly a religious war. The Church would gain little from establishing a Western-style government in Greece, and the bandit captains would lose much. The philhellene military efforts were a complete fiasco, but in 1822 Kolokotronis destroyed a huge Turkish invasion force by bandit methods. This was a turning point. It was a complete defeat for the Western idea of regeneration, and by 1824 there was civil war within Greece between a 'military' or traditional party and a 'civilian', pro-Western group (Petropulos 1968: 19–33). But by guaranteeing at least the temporary survival of a free Greece, it encouraged the Great Powers to intervene directly. The Tsar claimed the right to protect all Orthodox Christians in the Turkish empire, and fear of Russian moves against Constantinople pushed Britain and France into more aggressive policies. The Turks' invitation to their nominal vassal Mohammed Ali of Egypt to invade Greece in 1825 should have reassured the Powers that the *status quo* would be preserved, but it had the opposite effect. His son Ibrahim brushed aside Greek resistance and captured Athens and Missolonghi in 1826, but the Egyptian presence in Greece merely completed the Romantic conception of the issues at stake. As Bernal puts it, 'Throughout Western Europe, the Greek War of Independence was seen as a struggle between European youthful vigor and Asiatic and African decadence, corruption and cruelty' (1987: 291). In the Treaty of London of July 1827 the Great Powers decided to mediate in the war, but the Turks refused; in October, the British, French and Russian fleets destroyed the Turkish navy at Navarino, and in April 1828 Russia invaded the Ottoman empire.

The Great Powers had no interest in the *megáli ídea*, and Navarino meant victory for the nation-state concept of Greece. There was no attempt to combine the Western and Orthodox models of 'Greece' (Dimaras 1980). The British government had rejected the Act of Submission in June 1825, a petition from one Greek party to place the new state under British protection; and the Greeks themselves were now to run the country, albeit under a king and a board of regents selected by Westerners. Hellenism was thus in a very different position from Orientalism after 1830. Greece, unlike Egypt, *was* renewed, but the attitudes of Westerners to the modern Greeks were complex. In 1821, Shelley, about to sail to fight in Greece, wrote in the preface to his *Hellas* that 'The Modern Greek is the descendant of those glorious beings whom the imagination refuses to figure to itself as belonging to our kind, and he inherits much of their sensibility, their rapidity of conception, their enthusiasm, and their courage.' Shelley drowned before he could depart; but against his account we might set that of a Prussian officer returning from Greece in 1822, who saw the Greeks massacre the defenders of Tripolitsa. 'Blind ignorance has succeeded Solon, Socrates and Demosthenes. Barbarism has replaced the wise laws of Athens' (quoted in St Clair 1972: 76). The philhellenes drove a wedge between ancient and modern as surely as the Orientalists had done, whether in Egypt or China. The Tyrolese Romantic Fallmereyer (1830: 143–213) argued that Slavic invaders had entirely replaced the 'Hellenic race' in the seventh and eighth centuries AD, and it became common in the West to suggest that the modern Greek population was one of 'Byzantinised Slavs', and in no way the heirs of the Hellenic *Zeitgeist* (Hussey 1978; Herzfeld 1982: 75–80). The Greeks were caught in an extraordinary cultural bind. Herzfeld suggests that

> the West supported the Greeks [in the war] on the implicit assumption that the Greeks would reciprocally accept the role of living ancestors of European civilization . . . Greece may be unique in the degree to which the country as a whole has been forced to play the contrasted roles of *Ur-Europa* and humiliated oriental vassal at one and the same time. (Herzfeld 1987: 19).

For the Greeks themselves the problems were considerable. Herzfeld identifies the crux of the matter: 'Unlike their European patrons, the Greeks were not seeking a return to a Classical *past*; they were instead seeking inclusion in the European *present*' (1987: 50). They were simultaneously Europe's oldest state and its youngest nation (Herzfeld 1982: 11–21). Under the first king, the Bavarian Otho I, the Great Powers repeatedly intervened in Greek policies (Psomiades 1976), even occupying Piraeus during the Crimean War. After 1863 a new king and his English-educated prime minister Trikoupis asserted more independence (Dontas 1966), but the problem of cultural identity remained.

The alliance of Romantic philhellenes, nationalist interests and academic Hellenists and Orientalists imposed on the people of the East Mediterranean its own version of their past, present and future. Some Westerners suggested that the Greeks were culturally inferior to all 'Europeans' except for the Lapps; and while many educated Greeks argued that they had made great strides in throwing off the influence of the Church and the Turks, they generally seem to have accepted their negative image (Angelomatis-Tsougarakis 1991: 118–45). The peculiar position of Greece, free yet dependent on its liberators, meant that its relations to the West were even more complex than those of the directly colonised portions of the Arab world (cf. Said 1978: 104–10). Some members of the new political elite wanted to unite the diverse groups within Greece into a Western-style nation-state (Tsaousis 1983). Western political ideologies did find audiences in Greece, and in 1843 a revolt opened the way to the adoption of a written constitution, but the Western social programmes of 1848 were simply reinterpreted within Greek bandit-politics (Brekis 1984). Against this background, many Greek intellectuals were as keen as those in the West to promote a Hellenist reading of antiquity, which gave Greece a special place in Europe (Kotsakis 1991: 65–70); but this also perpetuated the Greeks' reliance on Western approval of their use of their heritage. Romantic poetry and art rapidly caught on in Greece after 1830, becoming involved in a complex tug-of-war with nationalism (Dimaras 1982: 349–404; Beaton 1988). The creation of *katharevousa*, the 'purified' version of the Greek language, exemplifies this. By purging their tongue of 'degenerate' elements (usually explained as Turkish barbarisms) which distinguished it from classical Greek, academics like Koraes hoped to give their new nation a 'supra-cultural' vehicle for expression which would liberate them from their shameful Oriental past and their equally humiliating dependency on Europe (B. Anderson 1991: 72). The *diglossia* that this introduced gave the Greek elite a powerful cultural weapon in internal conflicts. In a moving speech on 'The present state of civilisation in Greece' delivered in Paris in 1803 (reprinted in Kedourie 1970: 157–82), Koraes argued that the classical heritage was indeed a problem for Greeks, but at the same time it was a challenge, and they would meet its high standards. But by continuing to make foredoomed attempts to return to the 'natural state' wished upon them by Western romantics, the Greeks were unable to challenge the role of 'aboriginal Europeans' which was foisted onto them. Political discourse continued to be defined in the West, and *katharevousa* played along with this (Sotiropoulos 1977; Herzfeld 1982: 17–18; 1987: 49–56; Lowenthal 1988; see also pp. 53–4 below).

The invention of archaeology

In spite of Winckelmann, archaeology had had little to do with the construction of Hellenism. Winckelmann and his heirs had worked mainly with texts. Not only were archaeological data unlike the evidence with which most classicists worked, but they also related to different aspects of antiquity. The insight they offered into everyday life and their potential for tracing change over time could pose threats to the ways of talking about Greece which Hellenism made legitimate. In the last decades of the nineteenth century some archaeologists tried to question norms, but these efforts were swiftly neutralised. Archaeology was reconstituted within Hellenism as an unthreatening subsidiary skill, just as Orientalism had been reduced to an illustrative discipline which threw the edges of Europeanness into sharp relief.

Four main factors need to be considered in the Hellenist take-over of Greek archaeology in the late nineteenth century. I present them in ascending order of the danger they posed to Hellenism.

Greek art

Throughout the nineteenth century, interest in Greek art was primarily Romantic. By returning to the source, modern artists could hold back the forces of corruption (especially those of industrialism and materialism) and through their own rejuvenated art could salvage Western society (Jenkyns 1980: 133–54; F. M. Turner 1981: 36–61; Lowenthal 1988). From Joshua Reynolds' *Discourses* at the Royal Academy of Art in 1769–1790 to Richard Westmacott's writings in the 1840s–50s, the debate was primarily textual, but there was also a parallel strain emphasising direct experience. Seventeenth-century visitors to Greece had shown considerable interest in its ancient art (Constantine 1984: 7–10; Käfer 1986: 15–32), but this intensified in the mid-eighteenth century. In 1751 the Society of Dilettanti in London sent Stuart and Revett to Athens to sketch its ruins (Eisner 1991: 71–2). Their book was long delayed, but in 1758 Le Roy published his *Ruines des plus beaux monuments de la Grèce*, and artists began to demand exposure to the physical remains of Greek art.

There was rapid escalation in what was considered adequate exposure. The first direct contact was provided by Greek pots from tombs in Southern Italy. Vickers (1987) argues that Sir William Hamilton, the British ambassador to Naples and a great collector, waged an advertising campaign to persuade Westerners that his vases were valuable, going so far as to hire Winckelmann – the ultimate authority – to contribute to their publication (Constantine 1984: 112). Instead of using the vases to question Hellenism, Vickers suggests, contemporary values were imposed onto the material by Hamilton's colourful agent d'Hancarville (see Haskell 1987) to inflate their market value. The campaign worked, and Hamilton sold his first collection of vases to the British Museum in 1772 for a staggering 8,000 guineas (Ramage 1990). The collection had great artistic influence. When Wedgwood threw the first six vases at his new factory in 1769, he decorated them with scenes from Hamilton's pots; and when Hamilton published his second collection in 1791, he made it a much cheaper set of volumes than the first to enable young artists to buy it to use for models.

Wedgwood gave the name Etruria to the Staffordshire

valley where he founded his factory, and many experts long continued to believe that Hamilton's pots were Etruscan. Even Hamilton thought that they were Campanian rather than Athenian. Sculpture and architecture from Athens itself were much more highly esteemed. In 1784, the Comte de Choiseul-Gouffier, French ambassador to Constantinople, sent Fauvel to Athens as his agent, armed with an official permit allowing him to draw and make casts of antiquities. But this was not enough for Choiseul-Gouffier, as his secret instructions to Fauvel make clear: 'Take everything you can. Do not neglect any opportunity for looting all that is lootable in Athens and the environs. Spare neither the living nor the dead' (quoted in St Clair 1983: 58; see also Eisner 1991: 80–1). Lord Elgin's embassy makes the escalation even clearer. The Napoleonic wars closed Italy to English travellers, and interest in Greece reached new heights among the adventurous (Angelomatis-Tsougarakis 1991: 1–24). When Elgin was leaving for Constantinople in 1798, his architect Thomas Harrison persuaded him that mere books no longer fired the imaginations of European designers; by sending men to Athens to make plaster casts of actual objects, Elgin could change the course of English art. He took up this idea with enthusiasm (St Clair 1983: 7–9). Fauvel had worked for years to be allowed to dig on the Acropolis, without success; but when the British drove the French out of Egypt and returned it to the Turks, Elgin won a permit to excavate and to take away whatever he found. Whether he had the right to tear statues off buildings is less clear (Hitchens 1987; Greenfield 1989: 61–71). He pulled down houses on the Acropolis and found statues beneath them, and had a huge statue at Eleusis dug out of a rubbish dump. He even planned to start large-scale digs at Mycenae and Olympia (Bracken 1975: 73–83, 94–5, 176; St Clair 1983: 89–110; Eisner 1991: 91–5).

For all their artistic influence, neither the 'marbles' nor 'Etruscan' vases contributed much to Hellenist discourse. Even the painters and later the photographers who visited Greece to depict its ruins represented them merely as extensions of a formalised, literary past (Tsigakou 1981: 26–9; Szegedy-Maszak 1987; 1988; Tomlinson 1991; Jenkyns 1992). The committee which discussed whether the nation should buy Elgin's statues in 1816 ended up debating Reynolds' theory of idealism, with the sculptures themselves becoming merely illustrative material. The idea that close study of antiquities could challenge modern understandings of the past was never raised. The basic rule, as Frank Turner explains, was that 'Writers appealed to Greece as an allegedly universal human experience, but the moral and social values of genteel upper-class English society set the parameters of that prescriptive experience' (1981: 51).

Nationalism

If philology gave western academics the tools to possess ancient Greece and to trace a line of power from it, archaeology took the matter one step further. By filling national museums with Greek statues and vases, governments could show their commitment to Hellenism and their civilised status, and also the strength of their power over ancient Greece. The unseemly squabble over the statues taken from the temple of Aphaia on Aegina in 1812 (Bracken 1975: 106–36) shows the lengths people would go to, with French, Bavarian and English agents chasing the shipment around the Mediterranean (St Clair 1983: 203–7). But like the artists, nationalist sentiment used archaeological finds to illustrate Hellenism, not to explore it. Once an acceptable stock of antiquities was built up, in Germany with the Aegina statues and in Britain with the Phigaleia and Elgin marbles, government and to some extent lay interest declined. The French acquired the Venus de Milo in 1820 (Bracken 1975: 159–71), but otherwise they got off to a slow start. They alone remained active in mid-century, sending state-sponsored teams to bypass the hazards of buying from private collectors. A 'scientific mission' descended on the temple of Zeus at Olympia for six weeks in 1829 with one hundred workmen. With the greatest difficulties, they carried off various sculptures (Weil 1897: 103–4; Bracken 1975: 176–9). France also set up a permanent school in Athens in 1846 at the encouragement of its small artistic community in Athens, as a spin-off from the international but mainly German-sponsored Instituto di Corrispondenza Archeologica in Rome, founded in 1829 (Radet 1901: 4–25). The French school dug on the Acropolis in 1852–3 and at other sites in the 1860s, but this work represented no change from art-collecting. The Greeks' own response to their past is a far more complex matter, however, which I will discuss below.

'Altertumswissenschaft'

The Greek War of Independence was a turning point in German relations with Greece. The German states provided over three hundred volunteers in the war, more than any other nation. The second wave of these, in 1822, was composed mainly of students, artists and intellectuals (St Clair 1972: 60–76). The chief impetus came from the Prussian government's decision in 1822 to stop volunteers from going, since revolution in Greece was being associated with the idea of 'regenerating' Germany through violent social change. The ban was effective in Eastern Germany, but several Southern and Western German states encouraged philhellenism as a way to resist Prussia. The philhellenes suffered appallingly, and many of those who came home were embittered against the modern Greeks (St Clair 1972:

111–26), but nonetheless the new generation of academics felt no need to keep ancient Greece at arm's length.

Germans interested in antiquities found themselves pulled by two contradictory forces. On the one hand there were the methods pioneered by Winckelmann, which, as Otto Jahn's career shows, remained powerful (Bazant 1991); on the other, there were the philological methods of *Altertumswissenschaft*. If rigorous, comprehensive and detailed analysis were applied to antiquities, it might stimulate new ways of looking at the past. Some of the leading English classicists in the 1870s certainly feared that this might happen (F. M Turner 1981: 180–1). A large-scale detailed excavation which treated the minutiae of its finds as seriously as the textual critics treated theirs would produce evidence for daily life and change through time which could not be handled adequately within the existing frameworks.

Internal crises in disciplines are often brought to a head by outsiders who do not share conventional wisdoms, and this is what happened in Greece. The catalyst was Heinrich Schliemann, who began to dig at Troy in 1870. For all his Romantic adoration of Homer, Schliemann was an outsider to *Altertumswissenschaft*. His personal fortune cut him free from institutional controls, and, although the early seasons at Troy were more destructive than instructive, his demonstration that excavation could go beyond the recovery of sculpture brought him international fame (D. Turner 1990).

German Orientalism had long been distinguished from the French and British varieties by its lack of connection to direct colonial rule, but German nationalism changed rapidly with Bismarck's rise to the Prussian chancellorship in 1862 and the unification of Germany in 1871 (Wehrli 1970; Hobsbawm 1990: 101–30). Schliemann demonstrated German intellectual pre-eminence in yet another field (cf. W. D. Smith 1991: 84–7), and the new nationalism was decisive in the decision to excavate at Olympia. The French school at Athens had been considered a source of national pride and a focus for patriotism since its foundation in 1846 (Radet 1901: 150), and in the 'age of empire' the Great Powers all scrambled to assert their status in Greece through academic imperialism. Greece thus differed again from the Near East by remaining an independent state with room for all to establish their physical presence on her sacred soil through scholarly institutes. A German Institute was set up in 1874, the year that Schliemann moved to Mycenae (Jantzen 1986: 1–16).

Schliemann's shortcomings can be exaggerated (e.g. Calder and Traill 1986; cf. J. Herrmann 1992). He showed the possibility for a rigorous archaeology of Greece. But it was Ernst Curtius (1814–96), not Schliemann, who achieved a synthesis of excavation and *Altertumswissenschaft*. Curtius was more conventional than Schliemann, but was by no means a traditional classicist. He received a solid philological education, and went to Athens in 1837–40 as tutor to the sons of his friend Brandis, who was to be literary advisor to Otho I. While there Curtius lived briefly on the acropolis, and met with leading archaeologists. He became interested in topography. He visited Olympia in 1837, and recorded his plans for future work in a long letter (Weil 1897: 106, n.). His three-year absence from Germany had left him on the margins of academic life, so he returned to Halle and gained his doctorate in 1841. After a public lecture about the acropolis in 1844 he was appointed as tutor to Prince Friedrich Wilhelm. He took up a regular academic post in 1850, and two years later began trying to raise money to dig at Olympia. In spite of having Alexander von Humboldt and the Kaiser as supporters, he was unsuccessful. There was some interest in finding statues of athletic victors by the most famous sculptors (Gerstenberg 1949), but, with the Aegina sculptures already in Munich, there was not enough enthusiasm to launch new excavations. The crown prince of Bavaria had bought the theatre on Melos in 1816, but let it wait for twenty years before he got round to having it excavated (Bracken 1975: 159). Giuseppe Fiorelli had shown that stratigraphic recording at Pompeii helped him to recover artwork (Daniel 1950: 165), but this had little effect in Greece; it took Schliemann's finds to make the obstacles disappear. In 1875 Curtius began to dig (Hodgkin 1905/6).

Sculpture was not his main interest. He agreed that all finds should belong to Greece, and retained only the right to make casts and moulds of objects within five years of their excavation (Weil 1897: 110–15). He wanted to clear the entire precinct, to understand the relationships of the buildings (H.-V. Herrmann 1972: 203–6; Bittel 1980). The Austrian Alexander Conze had dug with similar aims in the sanctuary on Samothrace in 1873 and 1875 (Conze *et al.* 1875; 1880), but Curtius' operation was on a vastly larger scale. Although recording and collection strategies were minimal by modern standards, Curtius still generated artefacts and information in unprecedented quantities (Weil 1897: 115–52; Fellmann 1972: 37–44). He did find works of art (though not the statues of victors) and buildings named by ancient authors, but it was the more mundane aspects of the excavation which threatened to create problems. As Bowen observes, 'archaeology undermined the highly romantic, idealized image of ancient Hellas which provided ruling class ideology, and on which dons and public school masters could wax lyrical' (1989: 177). Olympia even more than Troy or Mycenae needed a new technical language and a new style of emplotment into a text, both of which drew more on the practice of archaeology in other parts of the world than on Hellenist procedures.

World archaeology

Archaeology of a recognisably modern kind can be said to have begun in Denmark around 1800 in Thomsen's chronological researches (Gräslund 1987). Kristiansen (1981) and Trigger (1989: 73–86) link the precocity of Danish archaeology to the rise of a middle class wishing to set itself off from French and German cultural domination, and turning to prehistory as a uniquely Danish possession. Barthold Niebuhr, Denmark's most important classicist of this period, provides a valuable contrast. Described by Bernal as 'reactionary even by the standards of the counter-revolutionary age' (1987: 300; *contra*, F. M. Turner 1989a: 103–4), Niebuhr turned his back on Danish nationalism: he wanted to study at Göttingen (his father prevented him and sent him to Kiel, then a Danish city) and when he was able to do so abandoned the Danish civil service to join the Prussian government.

The early transmission of Thomsen's system to Scotland and Switzerland may be seen in similar social terms, along with its rejection in Prussia (Böhner 1981). British and French archaeologists concentrated on palaeolithic problems, for which the Scandinavian approach was little help; but by the 1880s comparable versions of archaeology were adopted all over Europe (Trigger 1989: 110–63; Bowler 1989). Prehistorians often worked with assumptions similar to the Hellenists', seeking to find the origins of Western uniqueness, but the existence of an alternative disciplinary location for the archaeology being practised in Greece compounded the dangers of systematic excavation. The idea that archaeology – *all* archaeology – was an independent science with its own methods and observation language was as potentially subversive for Hellenism as it was attractive to some archaeologists. The study of Greek material culture need not be tied to Hellenism; it could be influenced by anthropologists or historians, and might even be carried out by non-classicists. On the one hand, it was in the interests of archaeologists to make their subject as distinct as possible, and to emphasise skills such as knowing how to control stratigraphy, to classify pottery sequences and to date artefacts; on the other, it was in their interests not to cut themselves off completely from classics, which held vastly higher professional prestige than archaeology. Archaeologists who were devoted Hellenists, as most of those active in Greece were, used the new methods and skills to carve out a niche for themselves within classics. If classicists ignored the new developments in archaeology, their archaeology would not live up to the highest standards of 'science', which in the last quarter of the nineteenth century would be a fatal flaw; but left unchecked, these forces could make Greek archaeology largely independent of classics.

The battle for Greek archaeology

Writing archaeology

The eighteenth-century tradition of connoisseurship merely illustrated Hellenism; nationalism was coherent with Hellenism, but by 1870 competition enhanced the possibilities for change; the application of *Altertumswissenschaft* to antiquities posed problems; and the possibility that archaeology might become a separate discipline at the end of the century threatened to allow free rein to such research. Much was at stake.

But by 1900 Greek archaeology had been neutralised, turned into a blank page on which to inscribe Romantic Hellenism. The solution to the problems which philological-style archaeology might raise was to banish people from its discourse, only to re-introduce them at the end of the story as free Romantic beings who by spontaneous decisions could alter the direction of a passive material culture. The standard text for Greek archaeology was set up as the artefact-centred monograph, describing in great detail the architecture, sculpture, small finds or pottery from a specific site. The goal of the archaeologist was to fit this descriptive pattern as comprehensively as possible. The ideal research strategy was to spend several seasons with a huge team excavating a major sanctuary or city, which would then be published as an imposing series of books. Olympia again provided the model, with its five volumes of *Ergebnisse* (1896–7). The level of detail in these works and those that followed them is astonishing.

Shanks and Tilley claim to see a similar attitude in British prehistory in the 1980s:

> The objects remain detached from a historically located materiality, from the question of their meaning other than that of objectivity (a meaning which belongs to the historical present): the objects are simply manipulated by neutral reason. So the past is, in effect, presented with identity papers and locked up. There is a place for everything and, apparently, everything is in its place. The tendency, ideal or *telos* is a total administration of the past. (Shanks and Tilley 1987: 18; cf. Tilley 1989a; Hodder 1989a)

But there is a difference between the site reports which they criticise and the practices enshrined in Hellenist archaeology at the end of the nineteenth century. As Shanks and Tilley themselves show (pp. 18–24), the excavation report is but one part of a larger discursive system, including synthetic and synoptic works. The goal of a total, objective record of an excavation is of course impossible, but texts like the site report are the centre around which any empirical archaeology must revolve. Deetz (1988; 1989) suggests that we

should think of detailed site reports and similar texts as archaeography, standing in the same relationship to archaeology that ethnography does to ethnology.

Foucault (1970: xv) opened *The order of things* by quoting an entry in a Chinese encyclopaedia from a story by Borges, listing the categories animals may be classified under. These headings – ranging from animals 'having just broken the water pitcher' to those which 'from a long way off look like flies' – seem bizarre, and perhaps the categories pioneered in the Olympia reports will one day seem equally strange. However, as Snodgrass shows (1987: 14–24), in the meantime the zeal with which classical archaeologists pursued the illusory goal of recording 'everything' has made it possible to adopt a wider range of approaches to material from Greece than is the case in supposedly more rigorous regional traditions like colonial North America. In spite of Shanks and Tilley's concerns (1987: 16–17), there is no reason to suppose that many archaeologists are likely to want *less* detailed site reports in the foreseeable future; and with the advent of interactive electronic texts, we will probably be able to expect vastly fuller accounts of fieldwork.

The problem with Hellenist archaeology is not its commendable level of detail, but the idea that in archaeology mastery of a vast body of artefacts is *all* that there is. This produces an exaggerated version of what Preziosi (1989: 31–6, 54–79, following Foucault 1972: 195–228) calls 'the panoptic gaze' of the art historian: the notion that the creator of an academic text has viewed his or her facts objectively from 'a point where all contradictions are resolved, where the incompatible elements can be shown to relate to one another or to cohere around a fundamental and originating contradiction' (Foucault 1977: 128). The panoptic gaze allows the archaeologist to order all the data: anything *not* visible from the vantage point, itself chosen on the basis of assumptions which are rarely made explicit, is *a priori* not worth discussing. It is this choice of vantage point which constitutes the *prefiguring* of an historical field, an essentially poetic act which determines what can be talked about (H. White 1973: 30–1). In the late nineteenth century, archaeologists of Greece decided that the compiler and classifier of excavated data in a multi-volume site report was the ideal creative persona.

Since Winckelmann's time, the major literary form for the student of antiquities had been the narrative. Even authors who published private collections of objects concentrated as much on narratives about the development of art or its mythical themes as on 'publication' in the modern sense (von Bothmer 1987a: 185–97). In the 1880s, this style of writing began to take a second place to non-narrative texts, above all the excavation report. Preziosi (1989: 47) distinguishes between two ways in which art historians have interpreted what he calls the 'absent content' of artworks: first, 'in the direction of a *Zeitgeist* or *Kunstwollen* or of ethnicity in general; or of social, economic or historical forces of which the maker [of the object] is but the instrument of transmission'; and second, 'in the direction of creative or libidinal impulses and energies and for which, again, [the artist] may serve as an instrument'. Both interests can be found in any text in Greek archaeology; but in the late nineteenth century there was a significant shift towards the first perspective as the ideal point from which to view Greek antiquities. Winckelmann in the 1760s had merged chronology into a Romantic obsession with the timeless creative powers of the Greek genius; by the 1880s, interest had turned decisively towards dating and race.

The publication of collections of pottery provides a good example of the change in styles. Furtwängler's (1885) catalogue of the vases in Berlin was a landmark: eschewing old-fashioned narratives, Furtwängler listed 4221 vases and classified them by fabric, period and shape. Even more unusually, he attributed the vases to specific styles. The period 1880–1914 saw the start of several long-term projects to publish complete corpora of sculpture, sarcophagi, coins and vases, but according to von Bothmer (1987a: 200–1) it was not until Beazley's 1927 catalogue of the red-figure vases in the Ashmolean Museum that the most famous of these, the *Corpus vasorum antiquorum*, 'could put its best foot forward and become respectable'.

The analytical text had one major advantage over the narratives of the earlier nineteenth century: it was written in the language of science. As Hayden White puts it, 'To many of those who would transform historical studies into science . . . [a] discipline that produces narrative accounts of its subject matter as an end in itself seems theoretically unsound; one that investigates its data in the interest of telling a story about them appears methodologically deficient' (1987: 26). Archaeologists writing non-narrative texts aligned themselves with the *Sprachphilologen* and were able to claim to be more scientific than *Sachphilologen* for whom re-presentation in narrative was the highest form of explanation. Like philologists, archaeologists 'did not read (*lesen*) ancient literature [or the material record], they read it to pieces (*zerlesen*) in their frenzied search for raw materials from which to make new lexica and handbooks – but never a new vision of the past' (Grafton 1991: 215). The new-style archaeologist prefigured his or occasionally her domain as one where categories of artefacts formed the objects of analysis, and ordering them stylistically/ chronologically was the main form of explanation. It was possible to dispute others' orderings, to subdivide or blur categories, to fight over the chronological structure which justified the ordering, or to promote new groups of artefacts

(coarse wares, bones, etc.) to the rank of those worth discussing; but going beyond this would risk the charge of antiquarianism or eccentricity.

The rise of the scientific site report and catalogue made narrative inappropriate for legitimate archaeologists. This meant that archaeology could not tell a story. It could not challenge narratives based on literary texts (themselves often narratives in the first place) and could not, therefore, challenge the central sub-disciplines of classics; and it could not make the kind of moral/political judgements of the past which are implicit in the narrative form (cf. H. White 1987: 14). Some historians see calls for a return to narrative as a mask for conservative agendas (e.g. Kousser 1984; Bogue 1986), but precisely the opposite was the case in Greek archaeology. By emplotting their texts as 'analyses' rather than narratives, Greek archaeologists won scientific status but (like Egyptologists earlier in the century) surrendered the disciplinary high ground – the right to shape the story of the relationship between the Greeks and the West – in return for a secure, if rather small, niche within Hellenism.

Some archaeologists resisted these pressures, but the problem was that once they abandoned the security of their place within classics they lost influence. Three British figures illustrate this. The earliest is the maverick Charles Newton, keeper of antiquities at the British Museum in the mid-nineteenth century. Newton was a pioneer in fieldwork, excavating classical sites in Turkey in the 1850s. He was unusual in not being particularly interested in using Greek art to combat the moral corruption of modernity. He rejected the 'childhood of Europe' approach to Greece, and tried to use a wide range of evidence for everyday life and religion. He was more in tune with anthropology than most classicists of his time. Like the anthropologists, he took an evolutionary view, concentrating on how art changed through time (F. M. Turner 1981: 63–5; cf. Stocking 1987). He was as Eurocentric as any Hellenist, but his emphasis on change began an archaeological critique of Hellenism. Newton was an important supporter of the British School at Athens (Waterhouse 1986: 11). His interest in change may have helped the early British concentration on the Bronze Age, although he took no action when informed about Knossos in 1879–84 (Hood 1987), and Arthur Evans saw him as hostile to Aegean prehistory (McDonald and Thomas 1990: 67). Within Britain he seems to have been perceived more as a pioneering fieldworker than as a theorist (e.g. Gardner 1894/5). As early as the 1860s he challenged Hellenist approaches by using the huge number of vases he had given the British Museum to teach students a new way to explore Athenian society (F. M. Turner 1981: 117), but only a few followed his lead.

One of these was Jane Harrison, who was among the first women undergraduates at Cambridge. She later recalled:

> We Hellenists were, in truth, at that time [in the 1860s] a 'people who sat in darkness', but we were soon to see a great light, two great lights – archaeology, anthropology. Classics were turning in their long sleep. Old men began to see visions, young men to dream dreams. I had just left Cambridge when Schliemann began to dig at Troy. (Harrison 1965 [1921]: 342–3)

The possibility that Greek archaeology could be at home among anthropologists was felt all over Europe. German classicists defeated it completely (Whitman 1984), but in Britain a few anthropological archaeologists achieved professional success. Harrison started her publishing career with a very traditional, idealising treatment of sculpture, but by 1903 she was using evolutionary anthropology, French sociology and excavated evidence to argue that the Olympian gods rested on an older stratum of demons and spirits (Peacock 1988: 55–90). She identified an evolution from matrilineal to patrilineal descent and saw all Greek religion as deriving from ritual (Harrison 1903; 1912; F. M Turner 1981: 115–34; Peacock 1988: 179–222; Schlesier 1990). But archaeologists showed little interest in her work; her followers in the so-called 'Cambridge School', including such luminaries as Francis Cornford and Gilbert Murray, were exclusively philological. A. B. Cook, who was more of an archaeologist, was always rather marginal to the school (Ackerman 1991: 1, n. 2). Ackerman (1972: 218) describes her as 'always basically an archaeologist rather than a philologist', and she was invited in 1890 to join the German Institute at Athens; but she herself wrote that 'By nature, I am sure, I am not an archaeologist' (1965: 343). She survived the First World War by ten years, but her combination of disillusionment at the state of classics, an obsessive interest in Russian mysticism and her intense personal rivalries with several leading classicists alienated her still further from mainstream academics (J. Stewart 1959: 171–200; Ackerman 1971; 1991: 4; Peacock 1988: 223–44; Africa 1991: 29–32). Her research became merely a by-word for the dangers of reading too much outside the field of classics. Few modern archaeologists share her enthusiasm for Frazer, and she was often sloppy or worse in her use of the Greek evidence, but the complete disappearance after 1914 of her attempt to produce a dynamic, people-centred approach to Greek archaeology is a testimony to the hegemonic power of Hellenism.

The most successful anthropological archaeologist of Greece was William Ridgeway, who combined archaeology, anthropology and German comparative philology, but brought with it the kind of unreliability which Muhly (1990) identifies as the hallmark of the academic 'eccentric'. According to one obituary, 'To him the conviction of separate Northern and Southern strains in the Greek race was almost a psychological necessity, for there was much in classical Greece that repelled him, and he was implacable against "the old Southern vices" . . . In strict logic he was weak, especially from his way of using all kinds of evidence, strong and weak alike, in support of a theory of whose truth he was convinced' (Conway 1926: 331). Conway thought that Ridgeway had been kept out of a fellowship at Caius College in 1881 by 'partisan feeling', and his influential paper 'The authors of Mycenaean culture' was blocked by the editors of the new *Journal of Hellenic Studies*. The editors ultimately resigned over this (Conway 1926: 327–8), but he received the same treatment from the journal in 1887 and 1895 (Ridgeway 1908: 11, 16). His work was fiercely resisted in the 1880s, and when he returned to Cambridge from Cork in 1892 it was not as a classicist but as Disney professor of archaeology. In spite of thirty-four years in the chair, a period as president of the Royal Anthropological Institute and a knighthood, he had no more impact on the shape of classical archaeology than Newton or Harrison.

Greek historiography

But the failure to establish an anthropological Greek archaeology did not mean that a depersonalised, non-narrative approach to artefacts was the only possible outcome. Once secured within classics, archaeology was commonly perceived as the handmaid of history, and the state of this field therefore had great importance for the direction taken by Greek archaeology. Through much of the nineteenth century the history of Athens was important in liberal critiques of society, but by the 1880s historians were generally denying that ancient Greece was relevant to modern politics. The historians' retreat from commitment meant that instead of becoming accomplices in radical social criticism, archaeologists of Greece were allotted the innocuous role of shielding the textual world from disruption by material culture.

Thanks to Frank Turner's work (1981: 187–263) the trend is clearest in Britain, although it was by no means restricted to that country.[8] From its emergence in the late eighteenth century until the middle of the nineteenth, Greek history had been intensely political. As we have seen (p. 17 above), the Greek states appealed to Romantics, but they also provided conservatives with a case study of the disastrous effects of democracy. William Mitford, author of the first large-scale *History of Greece* (10 vols., 1784–1810), is a fine example. Edward Freeman, later Regius Professor of History at Oxford, characterised him as 'a bad scholar, a bad historian, a bad writer of English', but also as 'the first writer of any note who found out that Grecian history was a living thing with practical bearing' (Freeman 1880: 127, n.). Mitford had no use for German scholarship, and even among conservatives his treatment of Greece was odd. Instead of praising Sparta as an alternative to democratic Athens, Mitford complained that the Greeks had no idea of what a balanced constitution was. He saw a decline from moderate Homeric monarchs to the republican nightmares of Athens and Sparta, before the Macedonians set up a political system of the eighteenth-century British type. His original attitudes to slavery, tyranny and Macedon were all strongly tied to his Tory political beliefs (F. M. Turner 1981: 196–204; E. M. Wood 1988: 10–16). As a reviewer in *Blackwood's Magazine* put it in 1819, Mitford looked at 'everything in the bright PAST of antiquity with an eye cooled and calmed by the reflection and experience of the troubled PRESENT in which himself [sic] had lived' (quoted in F. M. Turner 1981: 203). Implicit – and sometimes explicit – in all ten volumes were his horrified reactions to the American and later the French experiments in republicanism and democracy.

Mitford was massively influential, if only because no alternative text existed; but by 1820 liberal thinkers were turning to Greece. To George Grote, a successful banker and leading Whig, Mitford's *History* was a major prop for elite anti-democratic ideology. Grote took advantage of a request to review an innocent book on Greek chronology to attack Mitford in a leading liberal journal, with a political explicitness which stands in sharp contrast to the detached stance expected from twentieth-century scholars. Grote the empiricist has been remembered by Greek historians; Grote the politically engaged critic of knowledge has generally not. He argued that

> There is no historical subject whatever which more imperiously demands, or more amply repays, both [liberal] philosophy and research; and when we recollect the extraordinary interest which the classical turn of English education bestows upon almost all Grecian transactions, and the certainty that a Grecian history will be more universally read than almost any other history, we regard it as highly important that the most current work in this country on the subject should be fairly and correctly appreciated. (Grote 1826: 280)

The problem was partly methodological; Grote observed that 'we are made painfully sensible of the difference between the real knowledge of the ancient world possessed or inquired for by a German public, and the appearance of knowledge which suffices here' (p. 281). Grote was rightly proud of his mastery of continental skills (see F. M. Turner 1981: 87–92), but it was (liberal) understanding of Greece *by the public* which he sought. He made the political

implications clear in his peroration, suggesting that Mitford's high reputation

> is a striking proof how much more apparent than real is the attention paid to Greek literature in this country; and how much that attention, where it is sincere and real, is confined to the technicalities of the language, or the intricacies of its metres, instead of being employed to unfold the mechanism of society, and to bring to view the numerous illustrations which Grecian phenomena afford, of the principles of human nature. It is not surprising, indeed, that the general views of Mr. Mitford should be eminently agreeable to the reigning interests in England; nor that instructors devoted to those interests should carefully discourage all those mental qualities which might enable their pupils to look into evidence for themselves . . . few works would more effectually conduce to this than a good history of Greece. (Grote 1826: 331)

Grote himself was too busy to write such a history, being closely involved with the First Reform Bill of 1832, which widened the electorate by about half; and from 1833 he was active in Grey's Whig government (he was also instrumental in changing the names of the political parties to Conservative and Liberal). He was a leading figure in the extreme Liberal group known as the Philosophic Radicals, urging further electoral reform, but this collapsed after the 1841 election (see Newbould 1990). Disillusioned by his failure to radicalise the Liberals, Grote turned to writing a fully political *History of Greece* (12 vols., 1846–56; see M. L. Clarke 1962; Momigliano 1966: 56–64; Pappé 1979; F. M. Turner 1981: 213–34).

Grote argued that Athenian democracy exemplified the 'constitutional morality' which Britain could have attained if it had followed his agenda. Turner (1981: 218–21) notes the links between Grote's discussion (1847: 57–67) of Cleisthenes' reforms of 508/7 BC and his comments on parliamentary reform in an 1831 pamphlet. For Grote, the success of fifth-century Athens was due to the unity fostered by Cleisthenes' total overhaul, while the failure of Liberal ideas in the 1830s grew out of the incomplete nature of the First Reform Bill.

Such political engagement was widely welcomed; it was taken for granted that Greek politics provided lessons on modern politics. It was only the nature of the lessons that was disputed. Even the conservative Freeman was to recall his feeling that 'to read the political part of Mr. Grote's history . . . is an epoch in a man's life' (1880: 169). But by the 1880s ancient historians were turning away from the belief of Grote's generation that politics – either British or Athenian – could regenerate society. Two factors were at work. The first was the replacement of 'men of letters' like Grote by specialised academics who claimed greater legitimacy by being more 'scientific', but thereby surrendered the right to be general social critics (Heyck 1982). The second was the abandonment of liberalism by the educated classes. The Third Reform Bill of 1884 extended the franchise to agricultural workers with fixed abodes (as had in a sense been normal in classical Athens), swelling the electorate to over four million. This and Gladstone's Irish Home Rule Bill (1886) scared many of the bourgeois off liberal policies (Harvie 1976). Greek historians did not respond to the experience of mass politics by returning to Mitfordian views – Grote's attacks had made this impossible; instead, as Turner concludes, 'Students of and participants in the democratic politics of England in the last third of the century repeatedly denied that modern democracy resembled the democracy of Athens' (1981: 251). By 1900 any historian taking a Grotean position that Athens held lessons for modernity would have been regarded as an academic eccentric. This remained true until the 1950s (Finley 1985c: ix–xii); and the only attempt to reassert a similarity between Athenian and modern democratic politics is still more recent (M. H. Hansen 1989).

Grote's Liberalism was just as Hellenist as Mitford's Toryism (Bernal 1987: 326–30); for instance, in spite of his prominence in the 1820s, Grote was marginal to Whig involvement in the Greek War of Independence (Rosen 1992: 278). A Greek archaeology aligned with Grote would still have been part of the larger intellectual project of legitimising the descent of Western power from the Greek fountainhead. But using archaeology within a critique of politics would nevertheless have led to a very different discipline, requiring an approach something like those championed by Newton, Harrison and Ridgeway.

A case study: Americans and Greeks

Rather than try to trace the growth of Hellenist archaeology through a broad but superficial survey, I have chosen to examine in more detail a single national tradition. The obvious candidate is American archaeology. The USA had kept out of Greece's problems for much of the nineteenth century, in spite of the strong philhellenist feelings of some educated Americans (Pappas 1985). But by 1939 American archaeology had become the most powerful of all the foreign presences in Greece.

Charles Norton

The American sense of cultural inferiority to Europe in the nineteenth century created an exaggerated version of the rivalries between the various European powers, and was central to the development of American archaeology in

Greece. The founding figure of American archaeology was Charles Eliot Norton, in whom all four of the major factors discussed on pp. 23–6 above came together. Norton's father had been prominent among the New England Unitarians, and was linked with European Romantic intellectuals. Charles sat on Wordsworth's knee as a baby, and was fast friends with Carlyle and Ruskin – both major contributors to the British study of Greek art (Sheftel 1979: 3–4). Like these thinkers, Norton saw the humanities as

> the strongest forces in the never-ending contest against the degrading influences of the spirit of materialism . . . The need is great, I say, for those who hold the humanities in this esteem, and above all for those who recognise in classical studies, largely interpreted and rightly understood, the quintessence of the humanities, to unite in the assertion and maintenance of these studies. (Norton 1900: 8)

Norton became Harvard's first Lecturer in the History of the Fine Arts as Connected with Literature in 1874. The German Institute at Athens was founded in the same year, and Norton's decision in 1879 to create an Archaeological Institute of America (AIA) was precipitated by hearing that the Cambridge classicist Jebb was trying to set up a British School. Norton admired European scholarship but felt that Americans could equal it (H. A. Thompson 1980). Dort suggests that 'two objectives, to secure for America its due share in the fieldwork in the lands of antiquity and to bring great works of Classical art to this country, were clearly the primary motives in Professor Norton's mind' (1954: 195). As Norton himself said in 1880, 'what we might obtain from the old world is what will tend to increase the standard of our civilization and culture . . . [if] we are ever to have a collection of European Classical Antiquities in this country we must make it now' (quoted in Hinsley 1985: 55).

He was also in touch with the rise of archaeology as a discipline, and made genuine efforts to reconcile this with Hellenism. His first circular in 1879 advertised the AIA as a society 'embracing the sites of ancient civilization in the New World as well as the Old'. The second series of the AIA's organ, the *American Journal of Archaeology* (*AJA*), was announced in 1885 to be 'devoted to the study of the whole field of Archaeology, – Oriental, Classical, early Christian, Mediaeval and American' (quotations from Donahue 1985: 3, 5).

But right from the start there were struggles between archaeology and Hellenism. At the first annual meeting, in 1879, Francis Parkman suggested 'that the main purpose of the Society would be to promote the study of American Archaeology', but William Everett favoured concentrating on 'things outside our own country lest the young Americans should lose all interest in what is beyond America'. There was a replay a year later, with Parkman insisting that the acquisition of knowledge and not the 'acquisition of objects' was the aim. A Mr Parker replied that 'the Institute should not begin its work at a point where the civilization was inferior to our own instead of superior', and Norton had to intervene to keep order (Dort 1954: 196–7). Norton's position was difficult, trying to control forces that pulled in several directions. He never questioned Hellenist control over Greek archaeology, and wrote to Carlyle in 1880 that 'My interest in this new Archaeological Institute of ours springs from the confidence that it may do something to promote Greek studies among us' (cited in Sheftel 1979: 5). But his idea of archaeology belonged to the Romantic, pre-professional era, and in spite of his admiration for Curtius' work (Sheftel 1979: 3) he was uneasy with the neutralised would-be scientific archaeology. In an address to the AIA in 1899 he observed that 'a pitfall has opened up before the feet of the archaeologist . . . there is risk in the temptation, which attends the study of every science, to exalt the discovery of trifling particulars into an end in itself' (1900: 11).

By then, the polymathy of the AIA had collapsed. The editor of the *AJA* insisted that he was 'desirous that American Archaeology in particular should once more become an important feature of the work of this Institute, and that it should find more frequent representation in the pages of this JOURNAL' (J. H. Wright 1897: 3–4), but after the 1880s the AIA sponsored little work outside the Mediterranean. Donahue suggests that

> Although interest in the New World was mandated in the founding documents of both the AIA and the *AJA*, American subjects, despite the best attempts of its students, did not receive the same emphasis as classical topics. By the early years of the twentieth century the divergence between Old and New World studies became serious enough to necessitate extensive discussion and some practical readjustments. In hindsight, it is clear that centralization in a field expanding so rapidly in so many directions could never have been sustained for long; *it was natural* that organizations and publications should grow in response to the needs of the various areas of concentration. (1985: 8; emphasis added)

There was nothing natural about this split. Larger organisations like the American Historical or Anthropological Associations, or the Modern Languages Association, did not break up. American archaeology split into classical and non-classical components in the 1880s because of a near-total acceptance of Hellenism among those working in Greece, and their lack of interest in anything outside the classical

tradition. This was not simply an academic preference. A sense of cultural decline into aestheticism dominated the 'Gilded Age', and a *Bildung*-type improvement of society through classical antiquity was an important political idea. Hinsley suggests that 'To men of Norton's background and education the burden of public enlightenment was tangible and serious, a noblesse oblige that served at the same time, they believed, as the surest route to peaceful, gradual social improvement in community and nation' (1985: 56).

Not only was Americanist archaeology unimportant in this political agenda, but its colonialist attitudes and lack of chronological detail (Trigger 1989: 119–29) also made it unappealing within Hellenism. Unlike the identification most classicists had with Greece, Trigger (p. 206) suggests that Americanists felt 'alienation' towards the peoples they studied. Most archaeologists of Greece wanted to belong to the respectable great tradition of classics, rather than to the new and weak field of 'archaeology'. A group of amateurs tried to set up a Society for American Archaeology in 1879, the same year that the AIA was founded, but this collapsed through lack of support. Americanist archaeology remained a largely amateur field for another generation, with the Bureau of Ethnology (another 1879 foundation) providing what little structure it had (Meltzer 1983; 1985: 249–50). The contrast between the AIA's struggle over establishing a School of American Research in Santa Fe in 1906–12 (Hinsley 1986) and the relative ease with which the American School in Athens went forward in the 1880s is revealing.

For all Norton's fears of scientism, classicists could not ignore what had been done at Olympia, even though systematic excavations produced evidence that Greece was not the simple world that Hellenism implied. As Herzfeld shows, the simplicity/childlike innocence of the past is a crucial theme in Hellenism (1987: 53–61). But what could be done was to produce a Hellenist archaeology which created a past with no substantial human content and no room to discuss social change, by making the object of archaeology not the people who created the material record but the material record itself, here in the present. Far from questioning Hellenism, the archaeology of Greece contributed powerfully to it, possessing antiquity in the most direct way imaginable.

The founding of the American School of Classical Studies at Athens in 1881 was a major part of Norton's plans. The School contested European dominance and helped to organise a group of professional archaeologists under the aegis of classics. It would 'afford to young American scholars similar advantages to those offered to their pupils by the French and German schools already existing there' (Norton 1900: 5). The AIA, replaying the intentions of the

American Philological Association, aimed at 'uniting the teachers of classical studies of the leading colleges and universities throughout the country' (p. 8). The School contributed to this, and also helped to create hierarchy within the new profession. The School was put under the charge of professors from Harvard and Brown. It was, its first official historian tells us, 'not only an American institution on Greek soil . . . [but also] an intercollegiate project, the oldest in America except the Harvard-Yale boat race' (Lord 1947: vii). As early as 1881 there were doubts about who should be allowed to join when Dartmouth and Wesleyan Colleges offered to contribute money. It was officially decreed that 'any decent college that wishes to forward the interests of the School may do so' (quoted in Lord 1947: 7), with the chairmen deciding who was 'decent'. The first large extension of the School's base in America only came in 1919, when Edwin Capps, the chairman who did most to professionalise American archaeology in Greece, raised the number of contributing institutions to thirty.

Fieldwork was essential to Hellenist archaeology, and the School was digging by 1886. The first large project was Waldstein's at the Argive temple of Hera in 1892–5, a direct imitation of the German 'big dig' approach at Olympia. The massive excavation at an urban or religious site employing hundreds of workmen was already the ideal. Not only did it yield art treasures, but it also generated the wealth of smaller finds on which archaeologists had started to depend to define themselves as a distinct group, leading to the inevitable series of monographs. It allowed excavators to appropriate for themselves the past of famous cities and sanctuaries; and it made the most prestigious fieldwork so expensive that only the foreign schools of the Great Powers could carry it out (see Dyson 1989b: 215–16).

Hellenist archaeology and modern Greece

The American School soon got involved in a competition to dig at Delphi which illustrates a fundamental theme in the relationships between Greeks and the foreign schools. Every archaeological event in a sense increased the prestige of Greece, but this prestige was translated into another symbol of Greece as a passive representation of the birth of the West. In 1885, Norton learned that the Metropolitan Museum in New York was expanding, and that it would have room for many new finds. He set about raising money and looking for a good Greek site. Delphi was widely held to be the most promising spot, and in a letter written in 1889 Norton even suggested that American interest in the site 'was one of the motives that led to the foundation of the Archaeological Institute in 1879' (quoted in Sheftel 1979: 8). However, the French had dug there in 1861, and had first claim among the foreigners. The main problem was that the village of Kastri

overlay the site, and would have to be moved, at great cost. Some Americans felt that it would be unethical to seize Delphi from the French, but others thought it would be more of an honour than an embarrassment. In 1889, W. G. Hale wrote to Norton, saying (according to the AIA secretary's summary):

> Tricoupi [i.e. Trikoupis] stated unequivocally that we could have the concession if we came with the money. He said the French 'were not patient persistent excavators.'
>
> 'The advantage to the country would be greater if another nation [than Greece] should undertake the task. Greece needed to be more widely known. The work of the Germans at Olympia has benefited the country more than if the same excavations had been accomplished by Greeks.'
>
> 'The Greek Archaeological Society would prefer to have the Americans undertake the work.' (Quoted in Lord 1947: 59)

The heritage of Olympia was unquestioned: the French and the Greeks themselves were undesirable because they did not live up to these standards, and in any case, it was assumed that only the Americans could come up with the kind of funding required.[9] The French ended up making trade concessions to secure their rights, and feeling that the Greeks had deliberately tempted the Americans in order to raise the price of the site from about $25,000 to $80,000 (Lord 1947: 58–62; Sheftel 1979: 7–8).

The Greek government and the people of Kastri did rather well out of their quiet resistance, but only at the cost of reinforcing the West's hegemony. However, there were also more active forms of resistance. Greek intellectuals were developing their own Romantic model of their past, positing a Greek *Zeitgeist* which was equally present in classical, Byzantine and modern times. Relatively few Westerners were impressed, but this 'native model' did have some successes. In 1913 Richard Burrows, a philhellene of the old style, began trying to establish a Koraes Chair of Modern Greek and Byzantine History at King's College, London, where he had just been appointed Principal. Prime minister Eleftherios Venizelos committed the Greek government to paying for it, but when this proved impossible, Burrows enlisted the support of the Greek community in London. After some difficulties Arnold Toynbee, then best known for his official account of Turkish atrocities in Armenia (Toynbee 1916), was appointed. Toynbee was no orthodox Hellenist, and many readers of his *A study of history* (1934) were to find his rejection of European superiority shocking (McNeill 1989: 159–66); but even he was not prepared to countenance non-Western interpretations of ancient Greece. His inaugural lecture shows the difficulties Greek intellectuals had in making their voices heard. John Gennadius, a former Greek minister to Britain, opened for Toynbee with a speech nearly as long as the new professor's, defending the unchanging Greek spirit and urging Toynbee to condemn the use of demotic Greek. Toynbee, however, had his mind on higher things, and spoke in Herodotean style about Greece as the meeting place of East and West, concluding that Greek history and world history were really much the same thing (Toynbee 1919). As in Hellenist archaeology, this glorification of ancient Greece could work both for and against the modern Greeks. The following year Toynbee clarified his position in another public lecture, laying out his vision of fifth-century Athens as the founding point of Europe: 'When Ancient Greek civilisation may be said finally to have dissolved, our own civilisation was ready to "shoot up and thrive", and repeat the tragedy of mankind' (Toynbee 1920: 51). Toynbee saw a Greek genius which was peculiar to antiquity, and which had subsequently been taken over by the West, leaving the modern Greeks with little. His refusal to see a timeless Greek essence led to tensions with the chair's sponsors, which were exacerbated by his sympathy for the Turks in the war of 1920–2. When his five-year term ended in 1924 he was forced out of his chair in spite of a public outcry, to be replaced by F. H. Marshall, a Byzantine and Ottoman historian more acceptable to the sponsors (Clogg 1986b; McNeill 1989: 92–120).

Greek control over the finances of the Koraes chair gave their point of view a certain leverage; in archaeology, Greek resistance was less successful. The main exception was Mycenae, where Tsountas rightly rejected the view of Jebb and others that the site was 'non-European'. Tsountas, like Gennadius, argued that Schliemann's discoveries showed that the Hellenic spirit was not restricted to the fifth and fourth centuries BC, but could appear in many times in many forms – including that of the late nineteenth century (Bernal 1987: 368). However, a divide between 'classical' and 'prehistoric' Greece – or 'Hellenic' and 'Helladic', as some called it – was already appearing. Tsountas' resistance could be defined away by claiming that the Helladic *Volk* was not truly 'Greek'; as Bernal notes (1987: 391), some of the most intense efforts in Greek archaeology in the first quarter of the twentieth century went into studies of Bronze Age ethnicity. Western scholars kept control of the rules of archaeology, and Greek involvement with their own past continued to be deeply ambiguous. The Greek government encouraged Western nations to set up foreign schools in Athens, and Trikoupis went to some trouble to donate land to the British in 1884 and Americans in 1887 (Lord 1947: 26–7; Waterhouse 1986: 6–7). The presence of the schools repeated the prestige/domination relationship.

Archaeology had been part of the Greek cultural dilemma since liberation. The sense of a connection with antiquity was strong among wealthy Greeks who had travelled in the West (see Petrakos 1987: 248–60), and archaeological organisations appeared all over the country after 1829 (pp. 17–18). The first law to prevent random excavation and export of antiquities was passed in May 1834. A state Archaeological Service was founded in 1835, and an Archaeological Society of Athens in 1837. Standing on the Acropolis in 1838, Rizos-Neroulos, the first director of the Service, proclaimed that 'It is to these stones that we owe our political renaissance' (quoted in Tisgakou 1981: 11; cf. Petrakos 1987: 22–3). The new street plans drawn up for Athens in 1831 and 1834 built in the idea of the city as a living museum of European origins as well as the capital of a modern nation. The whole settlement was to be shifted north to expose the area where the Agora, the ancient political and commercial centre, was known to have been. However, the lack of provision for those whose houses were demolished to make room for the city's wide new thoroughfares combined with the influx of immigrants, soldiers and bureaucrats from Nafplion in 1836 meant that this open space soon filled up with houses (Travlos 1981: 393–4).

The earliest Greek activities examined monuments mentioned in ancient sources (Rankavis 1837; Travlos 1981: 395–8; Petrakos 1987: 23–46). There was a movement away from Athens in the Society's fieldwork after 1870, just as the foreign schools began to seek rights to excavate (Petrakos 1987: 46–71). Whether this should be seen as an attempt to compete with the Westerners is unclear.

The concentration on periods of the greatest past glory is typical of Trigger's category of nationalist archaeology (1984: 360), but once again there is a difference: every excavation and expropriation of land added to the image of Athens as a frozen point of departure for 'Western civilisation' as much as it did to creating a sense of the Greek nation.

The Athenian Agora

Successive governments limited building in the area of the Agora, but by 1924 it was decided that if a large excavation was ever to take place there, it would have to begin soon. The context is important. The Greeks had just suffered a shattering defeat at the hands of the Turks, and in July 1923 had surrendered extensive territories. Over a million people were relocated from these areas over the next few years, and the population of Athens nearly doubled between 1920 and 1928. These immigrants regarded themselves as culturally distinct from the mainland population, and even today a sense of difference persists (Hirschon 1989). There had been a military coup in October 1923, and in April 1924 a plebiscite abolished the monarchy. A major display of Greek prestige might help Venizelos hold onto power and mollify the increasingly influential reactionary elements in Greek politics (Close 1990). However, Greece was in another financial crisis; by 1933 some 65% of state expenditure went on servicing the national debt, and exports fell from an annual average of $125 million between 1922 and 1930 to just $49 million in 1933 (Clogg 1986a: 116–25; Mazower 1991). The Archaeological Society was practically bankrupt, and in the whole period 1924–44 it limited its fieldwork in Athens to just two small digs (Petrakos 1987: 129–33). The state did not have the money on hand to buy out the 7,000 (Shear 1932: 98) to 10,000 (Capps, in Lord 1947: 201) residents of the Agora, and a bill of expropriation was rejected by parliament (Capps 1932). Hints were made that the Americans – the only archaeologists who might raise the sums needed – would be allowed to carry out the project instead of the Archaeological Service. Armed with an anonymous gift of $250,000 from John D. Rockefeller in 1927, Capps won the concession and the expropriation went ahead, in spite of strong opposition from the displaced locals.

The Agora excavation raised Hellenist archaeology and the professionalisation of the American School to new heights. In 1931–9 alone, Rockefeller contributed one million dollars to the dig: 365 buildings were demolished, and 250,000 tons of earth removed from an area of 16 acres. In 1891, the American School had conceded that its students were less competent excavators than the French and Germans (Lord 1947: 81); by 1936, Leslie Shear Sr. had trained a sufficiently large group that he could carry out work in eight different parts of the site, and the recording of vast quantities of data was organised in increasingly effective ways (Shear 1938: 314–18). In 1928 the AIA officially recognised that the School was the main institution involved in Greek archaeology, and should be entirely responsible for the Agora (Lord 1947: 205), and in the same year the Greek government ruled that any foreigner wishing to do fieldwork first had to win approval from his or her school in Athens (Zaimis and Petridis 1928: article 2). In December the School completed its monopoly by forbidding Americans to undertake collaborative projects with Greek archaeologists without the School's permission. In 1929 Capps announced that the School would finally have its own journal, which began to appear in 1932 as *Hesperia*.

The Agora was the culmination of the big-dig approach. Even the other foreign schools could not compete with the resources needed for this kind of work. It generated a wealth of material that has kept researchers busy ever since, cataloguing and publishing in the approved manner, and masking the need for any more explicitly theoretical approaches to the historical significance of the evidence.

When there is so much to be done just controlling the material, other concerns must be secondary. The professional programme is self-reinforcing. If a group within the discipline had been systematically excluded from access to the data, it might have produced a situation where the dominant practices were criticised; but exclusion from unpublished artefacts meant exclusion from the discipline, and the artefactual discourse remained intact. The 1930s, a decade of uncertainty and relativism in so many of the human sciences (Novick 1988: 168–278), was the golden age of Hellenist archaeology.

Beyond Hellenism

Dyson (1989b: 215) suggests that 'While young Turks in anthropological archaeology have been slaying their ancestors, the dutiful in classical archaeology have been worshipping theirs', but two generations after the start of the Agora project, the innocence of Hellenist archaeology has gone. In this section I examine some of the factors at work in Greek archaeology since 1939, ranging from the intellectual and individualist to the epistemic. I argue that the main force is a process of political and intellectual change operating at the very highest level, affecting all aspects of the Western human sciences – what Foucault called the shift to the postmodern episteme, or in Fredric Jameson's words 'the cultural logic of late capitalism' (1991: 1–58). The intellectual terrain laid out in the late eighteenth century, which gave the fledgling Greek archaeology its institutional purpose when it emerged one hundred years later, has shifted beneath our feet.

Greece at war, 1941–9

The first set of factors to consider is political changes within Greece and in the relationships between Greece and the Western powers. The German occupation of Greece in 1941 halted most fieldwork, although the occupying forces did some excavation (Jantzen 1986: 53–6), and work continued on artefacts generated by the big digs. The most striking feature about archaeology in the forties and fifties, though, is its continuity with pre-war research. The Greek government banned foreign excavations in 1945 until such time as the Archaeological Service had returned to strength, but an exception was made for the Agora, which was back in action by May 1946 (H. A. Thompson 1947: 193–5). In spite of the horrors of the occupation (Hondros 1983), the German Institute resumed digging at Olympia in 1952. Post-war digs were generally on a smaller scale than those of the 1940s, but the strategy remained the same.

However, this was not a foregone conclusion. The brunt of the resistance against the Germans had been borne by the

Communist-dominated EAM/ELAS forces, who by mid-1944 controlled most of the country. They had between half a million and 2 million members, and their leaders confidently expected to take control after the German withdrawal (Sarafis 1980). But Great Power interest in Greece had not subsided, and in October 1944 Churchill and Stalin cemented an agreement giving the Soviets a free hand in Rumania, Bulgaria and Hungary in return for leaving Greece to Britain (Stavrakis 1990: 11–47). Six thousand British troops were sent to Athens to back up a new 'government of national unity', but in December they were forced onto the defensive by ELAS. A settlement was reached in February 1945, but civil war seemed inevitable (Iatrides 1972: 251–5; Vlavianos 1992: 55–78). The Communists set up a Democratic Party to protect their interests against the state army. Early in 1947 the British decided that in spite of a tradition of dominance over Greece going back to 1825, maintaining a force there was simply too expensive (see Alexander 1982). The Americans stepped in to fill the breach, guaranteeing economic support to pro-Western governments in the Truman Doctrine of March 1947. Greece was the cornerstone of anti-Communist strategy (H. Jones 1991). At first ELAS had the upper hand in the civil war, but the struggle ended in October 1949 with the complete defeat of the Communists (Woodhouse 1976).

This was crucial in preserving Hellenist archaeology. A Communist victory would almost certainly have aligned the Greeks' own archaeology closely with Soviet practices. In the Stalin era this was a very restrictive doctrine, and would have meant a profound reorientation towards ethnicity, the material bases of society and class conflict (Trigger 1989: 229–33). Western archaeologists might have retreated into still more conservative approaches, but it would have been difficult to fund fieldwork in a Communist country. Ideological conflicts between Greek and foreign archaeologies could have called Western fieldwork into question, making it more difficult to sustain a Hellenist archaeology. The civil war and the Marshall Plan averted this, and Greek intellectual life entered a Western-dominated period of what Tsoucalas (1981) calls 'cultural regression'.

Sir John Beazley

During these years, when it was difficult or even impossible to carry out fieldwork, the scientific publication of artefacts already in museum collections began to attain an importance at least equal to that of excavation reports. A series of major analytical monographs appeared, which are still fundamental texts fifty years later. Furumark's *The Mycenaean pottery: analysis and classification* should probably be regarded as the first of these, although its relationship to the general

trend is complex. Mycenaean pottery had, ever since Schliemann first broke the soil, been regarded as more in need of rigorous classification. Furtwängler, one of the pioneers of the modern collection catalogue, also published syntheses of Mycenaean pottery (Furtwängler and Löschke 1879; Furtwängler 1886). Furumark was clearly not simply responding to the difficulties of excavation. He conceived the idea of his book as an assistant on the Swedish dig at Asine in 1928, and had carried out the bulk of his work by 1937 (Furumark 1941: xvii–xviii). The book provided the foundation for a flourishing sub-field of Mycenaean ceramic studies producing ever-finer divisions of chronology, and the number of non-digging pottery specialists grew. A new feeling emerged among some archaeologists (which the hazards of new fieldwork no doubt encouraged) that enough data had now been accumulated to make synthesis worthwhile.[10]

The major achievement of this period was without doubt Beazley's staggeringly comprehensive series of catalogues attributing tens of thousands of Athenian painted vases to artists, schools, manners, circles, etc. (Beazley 1956; 1963; 1971). Beazley's work was no more of a direct response to the perils of the 1940s than Furumark's; he had never been a field archaeologist, and had begun his programme as early as 1910. However, his methods were extremely appealing in the new political and military context. In a wartime lecture at London University on 'The future of archaeology' he observed that

> It is sometimes thought that the museums have been worked through, and that for fresh light on ancient art and archaeological problems the world is dependent on new excavations. Our [ideal] student will not be of this opinion, but will realise that from the enormous stores of objects already above ground, secrets incalculable in number and importance can be won by keen and patient scrutiny. (Beazley 1989 [1943]: 100)

As von Bothmer puts it, 'His example served as an inspiration and challenge to his friends, colleagues, pupils, and followers – museum curators, university professors, excavators, students, collectors, and lovers of antiquity alike.' His achievement was to transform 'What had been in the nineteenth century the prey of diverse and divergent scholarly stabs at a complex and confusing mass of minor monuments . . . into a proper discipline, well ordered and sorted out, in which no aspect had been neglected' (1987a: 201). During the wars it was perfectly possible to be a major figure in Greek archaeology without ever breaking the soil.

The most remarkable feature of this methodological

revolution is that it was carried through without creating any problems for Hellenism as a system of thought. Vickers (1985b: 122–6; 1987: 100; 1990a; 1990b; Gill and Vickers 1989: 300–1) portrays Beazley as a Romantic, suggesting that he was particularly influenced by Ruskin and William Morris. Vickers' argument has weaknesses (Boardman 1987), but Beazley's position squarely within the Hellenist tradition can hardly be questioned (Robertson 1985: 20), and the underlying assumptions of the Arts and Crafts movement do seem consistent with his writings (see Wendy and Kaplan 1991: 9–28). He followed the same path as Charles Norton, promoting the study of ancient art as an antidote to the corruption of materialism and industrial society. This is hardly surprising; by the late Victorian era the emergent academic professions had come to define themselves largely by such anti-industrial rhetoric (Perkin 1989: 119–21), and, as Danny Miller (1987) shows, alienation from material mass production united thinkers regardless of other political or social attitudes.

Paradoxically, Beazley's 'unqualified success, essentially unchallenged authority, and general reluctance to explain in print how he looked at vases' (Kurtz 1983: 69) have created their own problems. Von Bothmer says, 'I do not believe that Beazley himself would ever have considered his word to be the last, for he never stopped acquiring new knowledge or refining and perfecting his method' (1987a: 201); Robertson argues that 'The main work [of attribution] *has* been done . . . other approaches are and should be in the forefront of study now' (1991: 9). Even some of Beazley's greatest admirers express fears that he left little to do in the field of vase painting studies as traditionally defined. The question 'where do we go after Beazley?' is frequently raised (e.g. Hoffmann 1979; Iser-Kerenyi 1979). One response has been for research to spread downwards and outwards, concentrating on lesser-known artists or classes of material, and spreading into regions and periods formerly considered peripheral.

Another solution is to return to narrative, drawing on the mass of detail provided by new analyses since the 1940s. Pseudo-biographical monographs on individual artists and studies of the evolution of specific motifs have multiplied in the wake of Beazley. A few grander works on entire vase painting traditions have also appeared. Furumark (1941: xviii) promised such a history of Mycenaean vase painting, but never delivered, while Beazley did give us an important series of lectures on the development of Athenian black-figure vase painting (1951). But narrative has made more headway in the Bronze Age than in classical periods (e.g. Betancourt 1985; Walberg 1986). Archaeologists' energies continue to be directed primarily towards analysis of objects

rather than discussion of the past. These texts fail as narratives, but they have been successful in avoiding disrupting the way in which the intellectual landscape had been prefigured. The subject matter of classical art history and the panoptic gaze of art historians remained unaltered; accounts of the chronological development and mutual influences of vase painters, sculptors and architects can be rewritten every generation. The major exceptions are scholars influenced by structuralism and its successors or by feminism (e.g. Keuls 1985; Bérard 1989; Beard 1991; Sourvinou-Inwood 1991; Hoffmann, this volume; Osborne, this volume); but their attempts to produce genuine cultural history remain 'eccentric' within the Anglo-American tradition. Osborne (1991) points out that both Vickers' approach and structuralism shift the focus from the individual producer of art to the consumer. He looks for ways of 'allowing the artist back in' (1991: 271) while preserving the insights of Bérard's school, but such flexibility is unusual.

The problem is exacerbated by Beazley's notorious unwillingness to discuss methods. He did not explicate his technique of 'keen and patient scrutiny' beyond saying that it 'consists of drawing a conclusion from observation of a great many details' (1918: v). Kurtz (1983: 69) argues that it was based on the methods pioneered by Morelli in his studies of Italian Renaissance painting. Robertson (1985: 26) endorses this, and suggests that 'Beazley in his early articles is clearly working under the direct influence of Morelli and Berenson in their studies of Italian vase painting; and he treats Attic red-figure too unquestioningly, I feel, as an entirely comparable field.' Beazley seems to have used Renaissance analogy as an alternative to a sociology of Attic vase painting. Robertson's summary of Beazley's achievement is revealing:

> by distinguishing the development of Attic vase-painting (black-figure, red-figure and white-ground) in terms of individual artists – master and pupil, colleagues and rivals, who learned from and influenced one another – he saved us from a schematic structure like that by which we distinguish the phases of Minoan or Helladic pottery; and instead we are able to watch the way in which the art was shaped by real men over three hundred years, much as we can watch the way the painters of Florence or Siena or Venice shaped the programme of their schools over later centuries. (Robertson 1985: 19–20)

But, as Robertson points out, this is not really the case. Beazley transferred a vague notion of an artistic 'school' from Botticelli to works in the style of the Berlin Painter, and Robertson accuses him of oversimplifying other complex relationships, such as that between Group E and Exekias (pp. 26–7). It is not at all clear what a 'school' is, or even a 'painter'. In the latest edition of the *Beazley addenda*, Robertson (1989) felt compelled to add a preface trying to define just what Beazley meant by these terms. We end up not being able to see how Athenian pottery production – let alone Athenian art – was shaped by active agents. Beazley's categories are no less schematic than taxa like Late Helladic IIIC1c; they just have friendlier names. When Beazley did talk about the painters' social context or the conditions of artistic production he relied primarily on literary sources, with archaeology used in the classic Hellenist manner, to provide illustrative material (see Beazley 1989 [1943]: 99). Far from exhausting the Hellenist approach to vase painting, Beazley's remarkable achievement has reinforced it. He left us with an incomparably tight chronology for sixth- to fourth-century Athens, but the net result was to alienate human agency still further from Greek archaeology, by providing the appearance of a humanistic discipline without requiring archaeologists to think about the functions of painted vases in Athenian social action.

Economy and society in modern Greece, 1949–89

Dyson (1989b) suggests that economic changes have made the greatest problems for Hellenist archaeology. In the thirties and forties big digs were cheap for foreign schools because exchange rates and Greek financial underdevelopment made Western money go a long way, but in the fifties Karamanlis' more orthodox fiscal policies changed this (Woodhouse 1982: 95–116). Patterson (1986) identifies roughly contemporary problems in the funding of Americanist archaeology. In both cases the main response to the spiralling costs of large projects was not to change fieldwork methods but to shift from private funding to grant applications to foundations and government agencies. However, it became difficult for archaeologists to transport large groups of experts and students out to Greece each summer or to hire huge gangs of workmen. As before the war, a few archaeologists with private incomes could maintain themselves year-round in Athens, but it was getting harder for excavations to generate enough material to employ teams of scholars in its description. Costs rose still more sharply after the energy crisis of 1973. Some excavators adopted more intensive recovery techniques which sustained the flow of artefacts to describe and classify, but this posed new dangers by generating types of evidence which required non-classical expertise. The important American excavation at Nichoria typifies this. Although primarily a Bronze Age site, it also produced Dark Age and Byzantine remains, which were studied in unusual detail. But, according to Muhly (1980: 101), 'In the words of one of its critics, it is the archaeology you do when you do not find

anything.' Survey has been an alternative response. One major advantage is its cheapness, but, like the seeds and bones from intensive excavations, the artefacts it finds require new skills. The first systematic surveys in Greece were carried out by Bronze Age archaeologists (see Cherry 1983); and significantly the first post-Bronze Age specialist to organise such a project was Michael Jameson (1976), as much a text-based historian as an archaeologist (Jameson, this volume).

Struggles against colonialism in all its forms made the 1960s and 1970s a difficult time for Eurocentric archaeologies in Africa, Asia and the Americas (Robertshaw 1988; Layton 1989a; Trigger 1990). In Greece, the replacement of Karamanlis by George Papandreou's Centre Union in 1964 marked the beginning of more independent policies. Papandreou ended the teaching of ancient Greek in schools, but support for Western archaeological involvement in Greece and the larger commitment to NATO continued. After the Colonels seized power in 1967 there was a distinct cooling in diplomatic language between Greece and the West, but this was not followed up by either side in any significant way (Xydis 1972; Trehold 1972). The Colonels restored ancient Greek in schools and indeed made *katharevousa* the sole language of education in 1967 (N.N. 1972; 'Athenian' 1972: 92), although this was reversed again in 1976 (Dimaras 1983: 237). After the fall of the Colonels in 1974, a steady diplomatic drift began away from American control, largely in response to the US support of the junta (Couloumbis 1991). In 1980 even Karamanlis was hinting that the future of Greece lay more with Europe than with the US (Iatrides 1983: 150), and the country entered the European Community on 1 January 1981. More radical changes were in the air, as Papandreou's son Andreas led the socialist PASOK party to electoral victory that year on a platform which, for the first time since 1947, questioned American hegemony. Attitudes towards the West began to harden (Clogg 1986a: 218–28; Coufoudakis 1987; Verney 1987; Konstans 1991). In 1983 Melina Merkouri began a vigorous campaign for the return of the Elgin marbles to Greece (Hitchens 1987), only to discover that the Council of Europe shared Fallmerayer's 150-year-old view that modern Greeks have no racial affinities with ancient Greeks and that this justified Britain's turning down the request (Greenfield 1989: 91–2). Since 1928 Greek law had limited each foreign school to three permits to excavate each year (Zaimis and Petridis 1928: article 2; 1932: article 37), but various loopholes were now closed and the law began to be enforced more vigorously (Merkouri 1982: articles 2–3; Kardulias, forthcoming). In 1988 the law was extended to cover surveys too. The tougher Greek attitudes in this period formed part of a world-wide pattern of nationalist resistance to Western archaeologies (see Kelley and Hanen 1988: 137–43).

Anthony Snodgrass

Academics like to see the early days of their own disciplines in terms of the impact of giant intellects, but they are usually unwilling to accord such status to anyone still living. But if anyone can be cast in a Winckelmann-like role in post-war Greek archaeology, it must be Anthony Snodgrass. Other archaeologists, such as Sir John Boardman, the Lincoln Professor at Oxford, may have had a greater influence than Snodgrass; but his research represents an unparalleled departure from traditional practices. Snodgrass came into British classical archaeology in the 1950s by a conventional route. He studied at Oxford, and was Boardman's first doctoral student, writing his dissertation on the by then well-established topic of the archaeological evidence for armour and weapons in the Dark Age. This material had been studied by historians interested in Homeric warfare and the 'hoplite reform', a supposed change in tactics around 650 BC, which was seen as having a crucial effect on the rise of the Greek city-states. Snodgrass made a thorough collection of the evidence (1964). The Dark Age was rapidly being 'colonised' by British classicists applying to its pottery techniques similar to those used by Beazley for later periods, and producing analytical works of the same type (e.g. Desborough 1952; Coldstream 1968; Benson 1970; see Whitley 1991: 45–53, 70–3). However, it also had a certain chronological marginality, and its problems and methods overlapped with those of Bronze Age archaeology. Further, the questions Snodgrass was addressing had been formed largely by text-based historians. Historians have been in the forefront of disruptive demands for quantification in Greek archaeology (e.g. Finley 1975: 93–100; Humphreys 1978: 109–29), and in appeals for a 'new classical archaeology' (e.g. Cartledge 1986). Snodgrass' first major contribution was to put the archaeological evidence on a sound footing by rigorous cataloguing, quantifying his data to demolish earlier impressionistic accounts of the change from bronze to iron; but this led him directly to using his material to comment on theories of social change in Archaic Greece (Snodgrass 1965a). Finally, the fact that the weapons he based a large proportion of his research on were made from iron distanced his work from much contemporary archaeology. The objects had little aesthetic appeal, and perhaps for this reason had never been subjected to systematic analysis. The researchers with whom Snodgrass had most in common were not art historians, but archaeologists of the Iron Ages of other parts of Europe and the Near East, and from an early stage Snodgrass addressed much of his writing to the questions they were asking (e.g. Snodgrass 1965b; 1980a; 1989a).

Snodgrass extended his research to a more comprehensive study of the Dark Ages, which included a rare theoretical statement:

> The method of this work is empirical . . . it is to examine the whole period in chronological sequence scrutinizing the evidence as it comes, assembling the facts and endeavouring to face them. This sounds banal enough, but in this instance it involves abandoning the normal priorities of the historian, the literary scholar or the Classical archaeologist. (Snodgrass 1971: vii)

Snodgrass' innovation was to extend the traditional rigour of classical archaeology to all artefacts, and even more importantly, to concentrate as much on contexts of deposition such as burials, houses and votives as on the objects themselves. The closest parallel for his work was not Desborough's roughly contemporary and more conventional *The Greek Dark Ages* (1972), but the earlier work *The origins of Greek civilization* by the ancient historian Chester Starr (1961). Snodgrass' questions were those more of the historian than of the classical archaeologist, and his methods those more of the prehistorian than of the classicist.

Snodgrass, like many archaeologists of the Greek Bronze Age, saw demography as a prime mover in social change (1977). From this concern he became, after Michael Jameson, the first major scholar of post-Bronze Age archaeology to champion intensive surface survey (Bintliff and Snodgrass 1985; 1988a; 1988b; Snodgrass 1989b; 1990; 1991). Some of his earlier claims (1982) for the inherent superiority of the information collected in surveys over that generated by excavations have since been moderated (1987: 99–131), but even so his position is perceived as being over-stated or even misguided by some classical archaeologists (e.g. Boardman 1988c: 796; Popham 1990).

Snodgrass' blend of traditional strengths and innovative ideas has been recognised in Britain by his appointment to the Laurence chair of classical archaeology at Cambridge in 1976 and in the USA by his selection in 1984 as only the third archaeologist to give the prestigious Sather classical lectures at Berkeley (Snodgrass 1987). Boardman (1988c: 796–7) asks the question 'Is there a "British School" [of classical archaeology]?', and answers 'Probably not: there are too few of us spread over the whole range of studies', but Snodgrass could plausibly be said to stand at the head of such a group. As he and Chippindale say in introducing a collection of papers on classical archaeology in *Antiquity*, 'If, together, they are taken as some kind of manifesto for a "new Classical archaeology", then so be it' (1988: 725).

The first feature of Snodgrass' new classical archaeology is its eclecticism. Quantification, wide-ranging comparisons and varied interdisciplinary borrowings are all grist to the mill so long as they lead to new ideas about ancient society. Its second characteristic is overlap with ancient history. It is common to see archaeology as a zero-sum game, diminishing in value as the amount of written evidence increases, with a cut-off point between 1200 and 700 BC, after which archaeology provides mainly art-historical information. Snodgrass has ignored this, pursuing social archaeology into the fifth century BC (Snodgrass 1980b), and some of his students have gone on to Hellenistic and Roman times (e.g. Osborne 1987a; Gallant 1991; I. Morris 1992; Alcock 1993).

Snodgrass insists that unless classical archaeologists move closer to anthropological archaeology, they will become irrelevant to the general discipline of archaeology, with which Greek archaeology should have more in common than it does with classics (1987: 1–13). The favourable responses to his book and the similar arguments of other prominent classical archaeologists (e.g. Wiseman 1980a; 1980b; 1989; Dyson 1981; 1985a; 1985b; 1989a; 1989b) suggest that this view is widely shared.

Epistemic change

A plausible explanation for current challenges to Hellenist archaeology could be built up from these factors. Greater problems in producing the sort of evidence with which earlier generations had worked led to a search for new ways to use the material already available or to create new kinds of evidence from smaller projects. One way was to classify and date objects with ever greater precision; another, pioneered by Snodgrass, in an area where classical archaeology intersected with ancient history and prehistoric archaeology, was to concentrate on the social meanings of finds and their contexts of deposition. This stimulated awareness that similar problems were being tackled in more effective ways by archaeologists working in other parts of the world, and provoked a sense of crisis in some archaeologists. This level of analysis has much to recommend it, but it is only part of the story.

The appearance of critics within Greek archaeology has coincided with a fragmentation of the very anthropological archaeologies in which the critics seek salvation. Both phenomena must be seen as part of a wider set of changes, as *all* areas of the Western human sciences have been transformed, in what Foucault described as the disintegration of the modern episteme. The expression 'postmodernism' began to be used commonly in the mid-1970s, first among architects and then all across the humanities. If anything, the word is even harder to define than Romanticism or Hellenism. Novick suggests that the term 'is symbolic of a circumstance of chaos, confusion, and crisis, in which everyone has a strong suspicion that conventional norms are no longer viable, but no one has a clear sense of what is in the making' (1988: 524). Definitions abound. Jencks, who popularised the word among architects, sees the crucial element as 'double coding', an ironic awareness of the impossibility of individual freedom from the constraints of what has already been done and said. The architect draws eclectically on a wide range of earlier styles in a spirit of pluralism: 'the architect must design for different "taste cultures" . . . and for differing views of the good life' (Jencks 1991: 8). In postmodern architecture, literature, art or scholarship the modernists' imposition of a single inter-national style is abandoned in favour of participation with active users of cultural products, in a piecemeal approach allowing constant room for choice and individuality. The pose is ambivalent, at once critical of the links between space, speech or action and the perpetuation of relationships of domination, and yet accepting such links and mocking the innocence of any attempt to escape complicity in them (Hutcheon 1989: 1–10).

Some on the political Left see this decentring of the individual subject into a pastiche of overlapping discourses as a retreat from political engagement. Fredric Jameson argues that this has caused the waning of affect, as the anxiety of self-conscious solitude disappeared; the dis-appearance of depth models of the world, such as the dialectical distinction between the essential and the apparent, the Freudian between latent and manifest, the existential between authentic and inauthentic, and the semiotic between signifier and signified; and the loss of a genuine sense of the past as a place where alternative realities can be found. He characterises postmodern culture as shallow and schizo-phrenic (1989; 1991; Kellner 1989b). Habermas goes further. Defending what he calls 'the project of modernity', a philosophical current running from Kant and aimed at grounding human reason in a universal logic, he sees post-modernism as the culmination of twentieth-century despair in the possibility of objective rationality, and thus as an extreme form of neoconservatism (Habermas 1984; 1985; Jay 1985; 1991; Rorty 1985; Bernstein 1985; D. Rasmussen 1990). But in a direct response to Habermas, Lyotard agrees that postmodernists reject 'making an explicit appeal to some grand narrative, such as the dialectics of the Spirit, the hermeneutics of meaning, the emancipation of the rational or working subject, or the creation of wealth' (1984: xxiii), while denying that this is a rejection of the emancipation of the human spirit. Rather, he claims, 'Postmodern knowledge is not simply a tool of the authorities; it refines our sensitivity to differences and reinforces our ability to tolerate the incommensurable' (p. xxv). Knowledge becomes 'many different language games – a heterogeneity of elements. They only give rise to institutions in patches – a local determinism' (p. xxiv).

Others disagree on some or all of these points (e.g. Hutcheon 1988: 97–106; Greenblatt 1990). This is worth emphasising because lack of consensus is one of the few features of postmodernism on which all can agree. In a more cynical vein, Callinicos suggests that:

> The discourse of postmodernism is therefore best seen as the product of a socially mobile intelligentsia in a climate dominated by the retreat of the Western labour movement and the 'overconsumptionist' dynamic of the Reagan-Thatcher era. From this perspective, the term 'post-modern' would seem to be a floating signifier by means of which this intelligentsia has sought to articulate its political disillusionment and its aspiration to a consumption-oriented lifestyle. (Callinicos 1990: 115)

The baffled observer could be forgiven for seeing in all this merely a fog of waffle and academic posturing, but there are some shared themes. Key among them are the decentring of the subject, an approach that rejects the primacy of the panoptic gaze (see p. 27 above): the piecemeal use of the past without regard for context; and the refusal to accept any totalising 'metanarrative' which would provide a coherent meaning in history. One result has been a rejection of traditional ways of identifying truth and objectivity – in anthropology (Marcus and Fischer 1986; Geertz 1988; Manganaro 1990; Sanjek 1990), philosophy (Bernstein 1983; Lang 1986), sociology (Giddens and Turner 1986; Giddens 1990), legal studies (Kelman 1987), psychoanalysis (Gellner 1985; E. R. Wallace 1985), geography (Lowenthal and Bowden 1976), history (Novick 1988: 415–629; 1991; Berkhofer 1988; Ankersmit 1989; Kloppenberg 1989; Zinn 1990; Hollinger 1991; Megill 1991), archaeology itself (Hodder 1989a; Bapty and Yates 1990), and above all in literary criticism (Eagleton 1983; Felperin 1985; Veeser 1990), which has increasingly displaced anthropology as the paradigmatic form of inquiry into the human condition (Hunt 1989a). In many cases this 'collapse of the centre' has led to fragmentation. Some scholars hold to Eurocentric views going back to the nineteenth or eighteenth century; others replace their lost faith with a new certainty based on positivism and quantification; others adopt various forms of relativism. The dividing lines are not always political. Some Marxists resist postmodernism, fearing its tendency to fragment scientific knowledge into incompatible discourses, and postmodern philosophers like Baudrillard have become the darlings of the Right (P. Anderson 1983; Novick 1988: 563–72; Kellner 1989a; Gallagher 1990). In extreme cases, established disciplines seem about to disintegrate into sub-specialities which cannot communicate with each other.

These attitudes are antithetically opposed to the aims of classical scholarship since the late eighteenth century. The central concept of tracing the evolution of the West as the descendants of Greek culture has little relevance to the concerns which are coming to dominate academia. Robert Connor (1989) provides a sketch of the effects of this shift, which he characterises as a move from the Old Humanities, focusing on public behaviour, to the New Humanities, concerned with more private issues. He suggests that the dominant view before 1960 was that:

> since our universities advanced the public good by educating citizens, and (it was to be hoped) leaders, these future power-holders should study power and its impli-cations within the intensely political cultures of the Greeks and Romans. In doing so, they would gain perspective on their own society, discover the values that should govern the use of power and at the same time be introduced to the literary tradition that shaped their culture. Thus the universities would contribute to a better world. This was a powerful rationale until driven topsy-turvy in the struggles of the late 1960s. Suddenly the noble rhetoric came home to roost. Student radicals and once-trusted colleagues told us if we wanted a better world, then the universities had better become vehicles for social and political change, here and now. Everything except immediate political reform became suspect. We all know the arguments and battles of that era and the reaction that set in in the 1970s. The results are evident today: a concentration on private concerns and some-times even private worlds. Fantasy literature cohabits happily with guides to success and affluence. (W. R. Connor 1989: 29)

The net result is that classicists

> have lost something, for one of [the] effects is that it is much more difficult for the classical humanities to claim a central role in liberal education. And if the claim is made, it is much more difficult to deliver the goods . . . What do we have to put in the place of the old educational rationale that selected, presented and interpreted a canon of classical writers because of their critical concern with power and the holders of power? We have lost that rationale and not yet found a substitute. (W. R. Connor 1989: 34)

Foucault (1970: 232–6) suggested that students of language took longer to adopt the modern episteme around 1800 than did students of wealth and living things because of their privileged position in the eighteenth-century episteme. The same is true of classicists since the 1960s. In the nineteenth century, classical philology held the academic high ground;

adjusting to a more fragmented postmodern world forces it to concede this position. If classicists persevere with their long-established goals and methods, they will sink into the same kind of obscurity that has enveloped Egyptology since 1880; if they move into the mainstream of the New Humanities, they have to surrender their claims to a superiority that needs no demonstration, and prove their value to the academic community. It is a double bind. Bourdieu notes the same problem in his comments on the classics in France in 1968: 'the previously dominant, who find themselves, unwittingly and in spite of themselves, gradually led into a subordinate position, contribute as it were to their own decline by obeying a sense of statutory grandeur which prohibits them from changing gear and operating the necessary reconversions in time' (1988: 127)

The situation is still more difficult for classical archaeology. Created in the late nineteenth century as a technique which insulated an idealised ancient Greece from potentially dangerous evidence for difference, conflict and change, it is left without any function if the set of ideas it was invented to defend are abandoned.

Alternative archaeologies

So it is not simply a matter of classical archaeologists being marginalised because they have not kept up with the gurus in Albuquerque or Cambridge. Other archaeological practices are just as implicated in the intellectual movements of the last thirty years as is the study of Greece. Trigger argues that the New Archaeology of the 1960s was merely the 'intensification of the functionalist and processualist trends that had already been developing in American and West European archaeology since the 1930s' (1989: 295; cf. Sabloff 1989), but both it and the subsequent postpositivist reaction are typical of the conflicts which have divided all areas of research in the humanities and social sciences. New Archaeologies emerged at the same time in Britain and the USA (D. L. Clarke 1962; 1968; Binford 1962; Binford and Binford 1968), and although there were national differences (Shennan 1989a; Trigger 1989: 284–317), both disciplines and to some extent the 'logicist' archaeology of France (Gallay 1986; 1989; Gardin 1987) can be recognised as belonging to a single genre which offered the security of positivism in a world where old verities were disintegrating.

The New Archaeologists have written their own history in internalist and celebratory modes, sometimes casting themselves in the role of Kuhnian revolutionaries (e.g. Kushner 1973; Sterud 1973; Watson 1991a; 1991b; *contra* Meltzer 1979; Wobst 1989). Clarke suggested that archaeology was moving through a three-stage process from consciousness to self-consciousness to critical self-consciousness, when 'attempts are made to control the direction and destiny of the

system [i.e. archaeology] by a closer understanding of its internal structure and the potential of the external environment' (1973: 7). Archaeology is seen as being powered by introspection, its 'loss of innocence'. Binford presented the rise of the New Archaeology as a personal odyssey away from innocence, a struggle against naïve, unphilosophical empiricists who believed that the archaeological record spoke to them without conscious theorising. The crucial stage in his creation of a scientific archaeology came when the ethnologist Leslie White drew his attention to the logical system of Carl Hempel. The value of this borrowing has been questioned even from within the New Archaeology tradition (e.g. Kelley and Hanen 1988: 29–60; Gibbon 1989), but Binford went on to describe how his scientific vision won over the younger and more open-minded archaeologists by its self-evident superiority over the old, as he moved from dismissal from the University of Chicago to a triumphant standing ovation at the American Anthropological Association (Binford 1972: 6–13). Hill (1972: 61) argued that the New Archaeology had overthrown the traditional methodology because the latter had been unable to solve its own major questions; while Leone (1972: 21) suggested that the traditional archaeology had been so successful on its own terms that it had left archaeologists with nothing to do, and they had therefore invented New Archaeology. The New Archaeology represented itself as a complete break with the discipline's past, declaring history redundant (Pinsky 1989: 52).

These pseudo-histories are as crudely dualist as anything we find in Greek archaeology. More recently, though, Earle and Preucel (1987) have defended the principles of the New Archaeology by comparing its history with that of geography. They identify a shift in both disciplines in the 1960s from normative to positivist approaches, with the appearance of a New Geography as well as a New Archaeology; followed by the rise of 'radical' variants of both in the late 1970s. However, no explanation is given for why the two disciplines developed in parallel. Patterson (1986) and Trigger (1989: 289–324), on the other hand, have developed critiques of the New Archaeology which concentrate on its economic base. Patterson describes the traditional 'Eastern Establishment' coming under attack in the 1960s from a more professionalised 'Core Culture' based in the Midwest and South, championing the New Archaeology (cf. Binford 1972: 340). This should be linked to changes in the social origins of American archaeologists after 1945, when the GI Bill made higher education available to a wider (though still predominantly white and male) section of the population (Kelley and Hanen 1988: 122–8; Deetz 1989). Patterson goes on to see in the attack on processualism led by Ian Hodder in the early 1980s a situation where 'many academics, especially younger ones, simultaneously express feelings of privilege, marginality, insecurity and power-lessness in the face of the university reforms and social transformations that are currently taking place' (1989a: 556).

In the most extended analysis, Trigger explains the American New Archaeology as part of the transition from a colonialist to an imperialist mentality. He attributes its initial success to the economic boom of the 1960s, and a confident, dominant middle class writing materialist naturalisations of their own position as the inevitable outcome of an evolutionary process. The New Archaeology accommodated itself to American pragmatism by justifying its findings as socially useful while castigating other archaeologies as irrelevant (cf. Tilley 1989d: 105–6); and, he argues, its emphasis on generalisation fitted well with US economic and military interventionism. The implication of cross-cultural 'laws' was that local traditions were unimportant; all could be subsumed within a single American discourse. Trigger claims that 'While New Archaeologists may not have been conscious agents in the promotion of United States political and economic hegemony, their programme appears to have accorded with that policy' (1989: 315). He links the subsequent emphasis on demography, ecology and catastrophe theory in the 1970s to failures in American foreign policy, especially in Vietnam, and growing uncertainty in the middle classes (pp. 289–324).

Trigger argues that world-wide economic upheavals in the 1970s increased the relevance of its second phase (see Gibbon 1989: 81–7) for 'the insecure middle classes of other Western nations' (p. 323). But while American New Archaeology progressed from colonialist themes (justifying the destruction of native American culture) to imperialist (justifying American interventionism), British New Archae-ology can be seen as retreating from colonialism towards nationalism, or at least Eurocentrism. The 'second radio-carbon revolution' of the 1960s demanded a rethinking of diffusionist prehistory, and Renfrew's work (1972; 1973; 1978) on multiple invention and local systemic change has been treated as part of a similar rethinking of Orientalism, creating a distinctly 'European' developmental trajectory as early as Neolithic times (D. D. Fowler 1987: 236–7; Bernal 1991: 65–74). Similarly, Rowlands (1986; 1987a) has argued that Gosden's (1985) alternative to centre–periphery models is part of a modernist fantasy, projecting the concept of 'Europe' back into prehistory; and Tim Champion (1986) accuses Wells (1984) of legitimising current ideologies by inventing a 'Thatcherite enterprise culture' in Iron Age Europe.

So far, though, few archaeologists have rushed to find a place within postmodernism. Danny Miller (1984) drew attention to the importance of architectural theory for archaeologists, and has argued that archaeology provides a middle path between the modernist alienation from mass culture and the postmodern tendency to rejoice in the shallow and shoddy (1987). Tilley (1989b) provides a self-consciously Foucauldian analysis of the language of the Cambridge inaugural lecture, and several studies of the textual emplotment of archaeology (e.g. 1989c; 1990). Shanks and Tilley (1987: 29–45, 243–6) embed their critique of the New Archaeology within an appeal for critical archaeology informed by recent literary theory and philosophy; and Hodder (1989b) directly addresses the impact of postmodernism on archaeology. Hodder's *The domestication of Europe* (1990) and Tilley's *Material culture and text* (1991) are the first book-length studies of prehistoric archaeology to draw heavily on poststructuralist ideas, and Hodder's students Bapty and Yates have published a series of seminars as *Archaeology after struc-turalism* (1990). These works have provoked strong reactions. Binford criticises them as 'irrationalist' (1983: 233), 'silly chauvinistic' and 'nihilist' (1986: 465); Lamberg-Karlovsky explodes that 'The proliferation of such twaddle is perhaps only comprehensible in the narcissistic appreciation of self – a strong component of all that passes as "post-modern." One can only hope that such inane, post-modernist, reflexive, critical, post-structuralist abscesses do not afflict archaeology' (1989a: 13).

Conclusions

I am not arguing that archaeologists of Greece must become postmodernists. Only one or two papers in this volume could be given such a label; the other authors ask social or economic questions about the archaeological record, and are often concerned with 'old-fashioned' issues of public power. What I am saying, though, is that over the past thirty years the Hellenist idealisation of Greece as the unique origin of the West has been widely rejected. Since Greek archaeology acted largely to defend that idealisation, its potential contribution to scholarship is open to serious question. I have suggested that most recent critics of Greek archaeology have argued that we should orient our work towards a wider archaeological audience. The problem is that there is no united 'interpretive community' (cf. Fish 1980: 338–55) to which we can appeal. Anthropological archaeologists are if anything even more divided than classicists. The New Archaeologists' faith in themselves as disinterested scien-tific observers passing objective judgement on relevance (e.g. Binford 1982; 1989) now seems naïve, but no persuasive case has yet been made for alternative sources of legitimacy (see Hodder 1991; Tilley 1989d; Stone 1989).

I see three possible broad responses for archaeologists of

Greece. The first, and most favoured, is to deny the existence of the problem. If enough scholars do this, then the discipline may continue in its well-trodden paths, following the example of nineteenth-century Egyptology. Egyptologists purchased the right to continue in their narrowly textual and philological paradigm by surrendering to classics the right to redefine Egypt as an unimportant culture. The professional cost was high, and classicists in Britain are now paying the same price after the Conservative government claimed the right to define irrelevance and to punish it through the Education Reform Bill of 1988 (Janko 1989). However, unwillingness to think about the social context of academia can have different results. This became clear when the editorial board of the *American Journal of Philology* published a narrow definition of what constituted the proper study of classicists in 1987. A furious debate arose which crystallised as the book *Classics: a profession and discipline in crisis?* (Culham *et al.* 1989). The policy statement issued by the new editor of the equally respectable *Transactions of the American Philological Association* three years later (Goldberg 1990) provides a much broader view of classics and illustrates the strength of the resistance to the conservative position. Generally, both cases seem to support Connor's view of the movement towards the New Humanities. Feminist alternatives to the androcentric political canon are proving to be particularly effective (see Keuls 1985; Hallett 1989; Richlin 1989; Skinner 1989; Pomeroy 1991), but involve recognising that ancient Greece is one interesting historical case among many, with no claims to a special position of importance beyond the mere fact of its antiquity; and even in that it must yield pride of place to Egypt and the Asian civilisations.

The second response reasserts the wide relevance of ancient Greece in the 1990s. The most serious work of this kind comes from neo-conservatives in America. Allan Bloom's *The closing of the American mind* (1987) is the clearest example, building up an image of an undefined 'relativism' which is posing a terrible threat to an equally vaguely defined 'Western civilisation'. Bloom singles out feminism as 'The latest enemy of the vitality of classic texts' (1987: 65), and the only response to such enemies, he claims, is the detailed study of a small and fixed group of works which are said to enshrine – for those educated to read them – the eternal moral values of an intellectual elite. His project has been championed by former Education Secretary William Bennett. In an idea going back to T. S. Eliot and Gadamer (Eagleton 1983: 39–40, 72–3) there is said to be a Western tradition within which all valid thought operates. The American new right is able to exploit a growing popular feeling that the university system is too left wing and too research oriented (i.e. too intellectual; see Sykes 1988;

Wilshire 1990; Kimball 1990) to argue that a return to what they identify as the basics will, like von Humboldt's *Bildung* in Prussia, revive the nation. This is an old idea in America (Hofstadter 1961), but the emphasis on classics gives it a new twist. Although Bloom's methods have been severely criticised by classicists (e.g. Nussbaum 1987), in a cynically professional sense this reactionary trend offers more hope for ancient Greece than most other approaches: Bloom would make Greek a central part of elite education. Enrolments for classes in Greek language and civilisation are rising: everyone wants access to the fountain of knowledge and morality. But Bloom's panacea offers little to even the most conservative archaeologist. His only comment on the subject is that 'a few humanities departments . . . have been able to escape respectably into the sciences, such as archaeology' (1987: 375). His classics has no place for archaeology at all. The canon does not need to be defended against the potentially disruptive implications of the material record, because it does not share the totalising ideal of nineteenth-century scholarship. It is only concerned with a very small group of authors. Most of the literary evidence which survives from antiquity is irrelevant; archaeology is even more so.

The third response is to recognise that the archaeology of Greece as it has been structured for the last hundred years is the product of a particular set of historical circumstances, and that these circumstances are now passing away. For a century the simple fact that the objects which archaeologists were studying came from ancient Greece was adequate justification for the discipline's existence and high level of funding. That is no longer the case; but there are no easy alternative sources of legitimation at hand. Historians have found it easier to criticise elitist, racist and sexist discourses like Orientalism than to replace them (e.g. Prakash 1990; B. Lewis 1990; Inden 1990: 213–70; cf. M. Levine 1992), and archaeologists of Greece are in a similar position.

'Problematising' is one of the most overused words in the vocabulary of the New Humanities, but it is the only one which describes the task facing Greek archaeologists. Ignoring the narrowness of the nineteenth-century definition of the subject, rejoicing in it or condemning it are all equally pointless. For the first time since the beginning of this century, we need to think hard about why we should study the material culture of ancient Greece, and what benefits a fuller understanding of it will bring to anyone. I am not rejecting the notion of an ideal of disinterested scholarship in favour of a political agenda; I simply argue that our century-old concentration on chronology and attribution is itself ideological, and, moreover, belongs to an ideology which is hard to justify in the 1990s. Redfield (1991) argues that there is a 'natural opposition between philology and democracy', philology being at root a form of traditional authority (Weber 1947: 341–5) which is at odds with modern society. Certainly we might cast ourselves, as Redfield puts it, as defenders 'of a certain standard' of rigour in resistance to a general decline. Many intellectuals have taken on the role of social critic, but using this to justify continuing current practices in Greek archaeology would require a sophisticated level of argument which has so far been lacking, and would itself constitute a radical political agenda.

I have no simple answer to such a large and complex question. Each of the papers in this volume represents a different response, and the authors frequently contradict each other. If there is anything postmodern about the collection, it is in this open-endedness. But as Fish recently observed, trying not to rule out any particular approach does not constitute an answer to anything; 'you cannot not forget; you cannot not exclude; you cannot refuse boundaries and distinctions' (1990: 311). In the end, the direction the field moves in has to be the cumulative result of thousands of decisions about research and teaching taken by individual archaeologists around the globe. I think that drawing attention to the factors which have influenced such decisions in the past, as I have tried to do in this chapter, is likely to have more impact than a string of dogmatic assertions about what we should do next. But all the same, I will conclude with some tentative suggestions about the areas where I see Greek archaeology having the greatest potential to make meaningful contributions to a broad range of scholarly fields – if that is what archaeologists of Greece want to do.

Bradley (1987: 119) attacks prehistorians of Britain for acting 'as if the true task of the archaeologists is not to say anything *yet* – if the subject is to come of age, it must amass more and more primary observations'. Snodgrass has made the important point (1987: 14–17) that the wealth of evidence already accumulated in Greece gives the discipline unique potential. I believe that we can only begin to fulfil this potential by reversing some of the decisions of the 1870s and bridging the three 'great divides' which I identified on pp. 14–15 above; and that by doing this, we can give Greek archaeology a central place within the human sciences.

The first of these divides was between classical and anthropological archaeologies. This is where Snodgrass and others have concentrated their criticisms. My disagreement is not with the notion that archaeologists of Greece must be familiar with the theories, methods, data and conclusions of both anthropologists and archaeologists of other areas, but rather with the assumption that such awareness is a panacea that will cure our ills. The second divide was between classical and prehistoric archaeologists in the Aegean. Many of the latter group have already forged strong links with anthropological archaeologists in other regions, with

obvious benefits for their research. Attempts to cross the Dark Age and to bring prehistorians' methods into classical Greece have already had some success, most notably through the rise of intensive surface survey.

While both these processes are important and beneficial, I think that it is the bridging of the third divide, separating archaeologists from historians, which holds the greatest promise. The textual evidence for Greek social and economic history is limited, particularly once we leave Athens; archaeological evidence, properly treated, can partly remedy this problem. Further, the use of archaeological data in ancient history is not a zero-sum game. As Finley (1975: 101) observed, 'it is often the case that the usefulness of archaeology to history increases with an increase in [textual] documentation'. The social archaeologist of a text-producing society can work in far more subtle ways than the prehistorian.

An integrated Greek historical archaeology has still greater potential at a time when archaeologists are especially receptive to the idea of archaeology as long-term history. Unfortunately, many of the archaeologists seeking links seem not to have had much experience of the *practice* of history, basing their appeals for a humanistic archaeology on examples drawn from Weber, Collingwood and Sahlins rather than from more concrete work (e.g. Shanks and Tilley 1987; Hodder 1991). In ancient Greece we have an opportunity to develop a genuinely historical archaeology in which social structure, individual agency, ritualised behaviour or economic factors can all be directly incorporated into our analyses rather than introduced as explanatory *dei ex machina* to put 'meaning' into abstract, formal patterns detected in the archaeological record (cf. Tilley 1990: 65–6). Interestingly, some of the strongest moves towards historical analogy in archaeology are being made by specialists in ancient Greece (e.g. Bintliff 1991; Snodgrass 1991b). The social archaeology of more modern societies which are better provided with textual evidence could be even more valuable to the development of archaeology as a whole; such historical archaeologies are developing (e.g. McGuire and Paynter 1991), but ancient Greece nevertheless has remarkable potential in this regard.

Such a social-historical archaeology requires us to re-figure our approaches to the past in two senses. First, there is the sense intended by Hayden White (1973) in his discussion of the *pre*figuring of the historian's intellectual landscape: we have to shift our perspective radically. Classical archaeologists have tended to make understanding the material record as it exists in the present the ultimate goal of their inquiries. Adopting the historian's role means treating the evidence as the means rather than the end; we have to concentrate on the social roles of material culture in antiquity, even if this means that we spend more time talking about objects which have not survived than those which have. The second sense follows directly from this. In abandoning what Preziosi (1989) calls the 'panoptic gaze' of the art historian, we fragment our perspective into the countless points of view of actors *in the past* – that is, we re-figure classical archaeology in the sense of treating material culture as something used by real people in pursuit of their social goals. The contributors to this volume go about re-figuring Greek archaeology in different ways. Osborne, for instance, favours detailed discussion of ancient responses to individual objects, while Whitley examines statistically an entire corpus of pottery from one region, and Alcock compares settlement patterns over vast areas. Some of the authors concentrate on bringing into Greek archaeology methods which are well known in other archaeologies; others aim to combine artefactual and textual data in a single framework. The methods deployed are eclectic, but the papers do share two themes: the need to problematise the practice of Greek archaeology, and the need to make the ancient Greeks themselves rather than the archaeological residues they left behind them the main subject of analysis.

Wiseman (1989) suggests that many of the problems of classical archaeology would disappear if its practitioners were educated, as they often are in Britain, in archaeology departments in universities, rather than in classics departments. The implication of my argument is that this may not be true; archaeologists of Greece need as much contact with historians and literary critics as with anthropologists and other archaeologists. In the late nineteenth century, it was essential for the well-being of classics that Greek archaeology should be insulated from disruptive outside influences; in the late twentieth century, precisely the reverse holds. But the breakdown of barriers has costs. Most obviously, if we expect archaeologists of classical Greece to be comfortable dealing with concepts derived from the study of ancient Mesoamerica, the French Revolution or reception theory we cannot expect them to be as familiar with classical philosophy, literature or languages as has been the case in the past. There are formidable obstacles to be overcome if archaeologists of Greece are going to transcend their appointed role as an inferior kind of classicist. How quickly and how widely the great divides will be bridged is anyone's guess.

I have consciously tried to avoid concluding with a call to arms or even an apology for reform in any very specific direction. In reflecting on archaeologies of Greece, three points have struck me most forcefully: the success of a single archaeology of Greece over the last century; its intimate links with an historically specific and increasingly threatened set of ideas; and the potentially vast range of archaeologies of Greece which might challenge it over the next few years. The most that the historian of an academic discipline should hope to do is to draw others' attention to the particular forces which at one point or another influenced the development of the field; and archaeologists of Greece often seem unaware that *any* historical forces are involved in what they do. My aim is to stimulate greater self-consciousness in thinking about what Greek archaeology is for. I advance this interpretation of our history to provoke others to prove it wrong.

Acknowledgements

I did most of the reading for this paper and some of the writing in the Spring of 1990, as a Junior Fellow at the Center for Hellenic Studies in Washington DC. I thank the Director and Senior Fellows of the Center for their support, and the University of Chicago for giving me this time on leave. I wrote most of the text in June and July 1990, while I was teaching a Summer class at the University of Chicago on '*Black Athena* and the ideology of classics'. I thank the members of the class for making me think harder about my ideas. The final version was completed while I was a Scholar at the Chicago Humanities Institute in January to March 1992; I thank Norma Field and the Scholars of the Institute for their interest and help. This chapter has benefited greatly from comments and criticisms made by David Aftandilian, Martin Bernal, Margot Browning, Paul Cartledge, Jack Davis, Steve Dyson, Mihalis Fotiadis, Charles Hedrick, Michael Herzfeld, Herbert Hoffmann, Nick Kardulias, Kathy St John, Anthony Snodgrass, George Stocking, Bruce Trigger, Peter White and James Whitley, although of course none of them agrees with all of it.

Notes

1 'Classical' is often used by historians in a technical sense to describe Greece between the Persian invasion of 480 BC and the death of Alexander the Great in 323 BC, but I take it here in its wider sense, meaning the canonically defined core periods of Greek and Roman civilisation, from roughly 700 BC to AD 500.

2 It is not easy to find a single satisfactory term to embrace the whole range of theoretically inclined archaeologies which have appeared in the English-speaking world and beyond in the last thirty years. Embree (1989a; 1989b), after polling a number of archaeologists, suggests that 'theoretical archaeology' might be the best phrase, but since this perpetuates the theory/practice dualism at the

heart of much of the crisis literature, I prefer to use Struever's expression 'anthropological archaeology'. The main danger of confusion with this term is that Struever was advocating and Courbin attacking the 1960s North American New Archaeology, not its post-processual critics; but similar attitudes probably prevail between classical archaeologists and postprocessualists (although, as Snodgrass (1987: 6–11) shows, anthropological archaeologists rarely feel the need to address classical archaeology at all).

3 My discussion of Orientalism draws heavily on Said (1978). Said's account has been criticised for displaying many of the same hegemonic tendencies that he attacks in others (e.g. Clifford 1988: 255–76; R. Young 1991: 119–40), but that does not lessen its overall usefulness. Greek and Near Eastern archaeologies are often grouped together as sub-specialities of a larger discipline of 'classical archaeology' (which is certainly how Struever used the term on p. 8 above), which could itself be seen in Said's terms as a species of Orientalism. It might seem strange to speak of classics and Orientalism as two separate fields, but I will argue that they are two inseparable disciplines – Said's Orientalism could not function with Hellenism, nor the idealised 'Greece' without its cardboard 'East'.

4 'Hellenism' is used here as a shorthand expression to cover a broad range of literary and political ideas. I distinguish it from philhellenism, but it does not seem necessary to draw repeated distinctions between the various shades of English, French and American Hellenism or the more virulent German neo-Hellenism of the nineteenth century. Like Droysen's original coinage of the word *Hellenismus* to describe the world conquered by Alexander the Great (see Alcock, this volume), Hellenism derives from the ancient Greek *Hellenismos*, the *imitation* of things Hellenic.

5 The Minnesota Messenia Expedition had already begun to provide this with a large-scale survey, significantly aimed at 'Reconstructing a Bronze Age environment' – the subtitle of its publication (Macdonald and Rapp 1972) – rather than an ancient Greek environment; but Renfrew's systemic approach inspired much new work in this vein.

6 Herder always provides an exception to generalisations about German intellectuals' appeal to Greece as a counter-balance to the French use of Rome. He was highly critical of the German tendency to admire a mythologised Spartan culture more than their own, and also drew on Kant's account of the Iroquois and Delaware Indians as well as on literary sources about ancient Greece in his cultural critiques.

7 'Romanticism' is notoriously difficult to define; in 1948, one literary critic counted 11,396 significantly different definitions (Cuddon 1979: 586). The topic is perhaps best approached through the works of individual artists and thinkers, rather than broad generalisations: see, for example, McGann 1983; Christiansen 1988; Roe 1988; Mellor 1988.

8 There was a similar development in Germany, from Droysen's attempts between the 1830s and 1880s to link Greek and Prussian history (see also McGlew 1984; H. White 1973: 83–103) to the general rejection of presentist approaches to Greece in the last quarter of the century shared by both Burckhardt and the 'mere philologists' whom he saw as opposing him (Weintraub 1988).

9 There seems to be no good reason to doubt Hale's account; Trikoupis was staunchly pro-Western, and Greece was in the middle of a severe financial crisis (Clogg 1986a: 90–3).

10 New finds have of course been important, particularly for the final phases of Mycenaean pottery, which had been poorly represented in the 1930s. See Mountjoy 1986.

PART II

Artefacts and art objects

3

Protoattic pottery: a contextual approach

JAMES WHITLEY

The Protoattic style of pottery, which prevailed in Attica between 700 and 600 BC, has always occupied an unusual position in the history of Greek vase painting. Attic Geometric and Attic black-figure were two of the most influential styles in their respective periods: Attic Geometric, though not widely traded, was widely copied; and black-figure is found in large quantities all over the Mediterranean world. In comparison to both previous and subsequent periods in Attic vase painting, Protoattic appears both eccentric and provincial, especially in relation to the dominant seventh-century school of Greek vase painting, Protocorinthian. Most of those who study Protoattic avoid claiming to perceive any enduring aesthetic value in the works they study, and attempts to place Protoattic in the mainstream of the development of Greek vase painting have always had a slight air of desperation about them.

Protoattic is then usually studied not for its critical, but for its historical interest. Protoattic vases are not great works of art (which is not to say that they are not art). They are merely our principal source of evidence for seventh-century Attica. Two kinds of historical interest direct the study of Protoattic: an art-historical interest in the development of Attic art; and a social historical interest in seventh-century Attic society. Hitherto, art historians have dominated the study of Protoattic. They have sought to improve our understanding of the techniques and iconography of Attic vase painting in the seventh century, so that we can begin to explain the commercial and artistic success of later black-figure (for example Beazley 1951: 1–16). Social history has by contrast received less attention from archaeologists, since social history is usually seen as the province of the textual historian (see Osborne 1989). Yet seventh-century Attica is still essentially a prehistoric (albeit partially literate) society

known to us largely through its material culture. Its social history is therefore a proper object of study for the archaeologist.

This characterisation of the seventh century may strike some historians as surprising. After all, later fifth- and fourth-century authors refer to a number of events in the seventh century. Aristotle (*Constitution of Athens*, 2–3) describes the pre-Solonian constitution; both Herodotus (V, 71) and Thucydides (I, 126–7) relate the story of the conspiracy of Cylon; and Herodotus (V, 81–9) tells the story of Athens' war with Aegina (see also Dunbabin 1937). Some of Solon's poems also date from the very end of the seventh century, and Plutarch's *Life of Solon*, though written down in the second century CE, has usually been regarded as a key document in the reconstruction of early Attica. Our only really solid piece of evidence however is the fragments from the re-publication of Draco's law on homicide, apparently copied from a seventh-century original.[1] Collectively, these stories do not enable us to construct a narrative, still less a social, history of seventh-century Attica. Even if the incidents recorded actually took place, the reason for their preservation as stories bears little relation to their probable historical importance. The 'Conspiracy of Cylon' was remembered by other political families because of the embarrassment it caused the Alcmaeonidae (see Rhodes 1981: 79–84). The war with Aegina served as an excuse for fifth-century Athenian hostility towards that island, and in any case it cannot be dated precisely.[2] Doubts have even been cast on Draco's 'law code' (see note 1). The few other historical facts from seventh-century Attica really tell us very little (S. P. Morris 1984: 104–7). Neither a constitutional nor a social history of Attica can be created from these sources alone, which is perhaps why many scholars (S. P. Morris 1984; I. Morris 1987; Osborne 1988a; 1989) have started to re-examine the archaeological evidence.

Paradoxically, an additional reason for studying Protoattic (and other seventh-century pottery from Attica) is the paucity of the material evidence. Unlike Peloponnesian *poleis* such as Corinth or Argos, Athenians did not invest in public, monumental religious architecture. Experiments in temple building and roof construction took place elsewhere. Sanctuary deposits in Attica are much poorer in metals and other valuables than those of Peloponnesian states (see table 3.1 and S. P. Morris 1984: 9–12, 99–100, 104–7). There are far fewer graves, particularly adult graves, in seventh-century Attica than in previous or subsequent periods (see table 3.1; I. Morris 1987: 72–109; Camp 1979). There is, in almost every respect, a trough in the material record of Attica in the seventh century. Thus, though there is very little Protoattic or even Subgeometric pottery (see again S. P. Morris 1984: 9–11) compared to either

Table 3.1. *Numbers of seventh-century sites in Attica, excluding Athens (for information see index)*

No. of sites with seventh-century material	33
No. of sites with Subgeometric material	16
No. of sites with Protoattic material	20
No. of sites with other seventh-century material (Protocorinthian, relief pithoi, etc.)	9
No. of ritual sites	13
No. of domestic sites (certain)	4
Total number of cemetery sites (certain)	11
Adult cemeteries	2
Child cemeteries and grave plots	3
Mixed (adult/child) cemeteries	6
Probable cemetery sites	7
Probable domestic (settlement) sites	1
Total number of probable adult graves (Athens included)	63
Total number of probable child graves (Athens included)	131

Geometric or black-figure, pottery and the contexts in which it is found is our chief source of evidence for seventh-century Attica.

The traditional approach to Protoattic vase painting is one of connoisseurship: the attribution of vases to hands and workshops, and the definition of personal 'styles' arrived at by the isolation of idiosyncrasies of draughtsmanship. Connoisseurship, narrowly conceived, has been taken as the *sine qua non* of archaeological analysis. For art-historical purposes this approach has been quite adequate. Stylistic phases have been defined, and a workable chronology constructed. J. M. Cook's (1935) technical classification of Protoattic into early (where orientalising motifs are introduced), middle (where colour is added) and late (when Corinthian innovations such as incision are finally adopted) has, with minor modifications, stood the test of time well. But the traditional approach also has its dangers. It can create a false sense of intimacy with historically remote 'artistic personalities', personalities which are often largely the creation of the individual scholar. This approach also tends to treat artistic development as autonomous, as somehow separate from the conditions which made such art possible. For the writing of a social history through material culture it is, to say the least, inappropriate.

Protoattic scholarship has not always been quite so narrowly circumscribed. It is true that pioneers in the field, such as Böhlau (1887), were primarily concerned with defining the distinctive features of the early Archaic pottery of Attica. But, before the immense prestige of Beazley and his method had come to overshadow the study of Attic pottery, other questions were not neglected. There is, for example, an interesting discussion by Kenner (1935: 130–4) of the role of Protoattic 'louteria' in cult practices. So contextual studies are not entirely new in this field; merely unusual.

What then is meant by the term 'contextual approach', and why might it be preferable to other approaches? A contextual approach places social and archaeological context in the forefront of any analysis. Sceptics may point out that any attempt to relate Greek vase painting to Greek culture and society is contextual, and in a sense they are right. Many iconographic studies, notably those by French scholars, are contextual in this sense. My use of the term, however, derives from Ian Hodder (1982a; 1982b; 1987b; 1991: 118–46) who is interested in material culture both in its broader, social context, and in its narrower, archaeological context. Contextual archaeology sees the production, use and deposition of artefacts as being connected in a necessary and intimate way. Contextual archaeology stresses that artefacts are always used and produced *for* some purpose, a purpose which we can sometimes infer from an analysis of their ultimate context of deposition. Artefacts cannot be understood in isolation from the contexts in which they occur. The material culture of any particular society embraces context and use, as well as form and decoration. In a broader sense, the shape and decoration of material culture, and the nature of that society's 'depositional practices', are seen as being related, as being the product of a particular social structure or social order. Contextual archaeology tries to bridge the gap between the broad generalisations of processual archaeology on the one hand, and the study of particular classes of material on the other. This approach might be seen by some as inherently 'structuralist'. But such an approach is, I would argue, the *sine qua non* of any attempt to write a cultural history from archaeological evidence.

As I see it, the term contextual approach has precise methodological implications. A contextual approach tries to relate archaeological context to social context, not directly, but by viewing archaeological deposits as records of particular types of social behaviour. Interpreting deposits in such social terms demands two things: a quantitative analysis of and statistical comparison between types of deposits; and ethnographically or historically derived social models to explain types of 'depositional behaviour'. By comparing which types of material appear in which it is thought that we can arrive at an understanding of both the value and the social use of material culture. A contextual approach is both statistical and sociological. It asks: what kind of behaviour does this deposit represent, and then, what kind of society would produce such deposits?

An interest in social context rather than vase painting *per se* also helps to direct the focus of this analysis. I am interested in Protoattic, the Orientalising figured pottery produced and used in Attica, and how these vases relate to the tastes and practices of seventh-century Athenians. I am not primarily interested in vases whose shape and decoration may relate to Aeginetan tastes and circumstances. The Aegina deposits (fully discussed by S. P. Morris 1984: 19–36) will only be brought in by way of contrast.[3] However, painted Protoattic vases cannot be considered independently of the other kinds of pottery produced and used in Attica at the time, such as Attic coarse and handmade wares, Subgeometric, and Protocorinthian and Corinthian imports.

Pottery in seventh-century Attica

Before discussing these other styles, it is perhaps worth underlining the way in which Protoattic marks a decisive break with the Late Geometric style of vase painting. Protoattic is primarily a *stylistic* innovation. The technical advances – the addition of colour in Middle Protoattic, the use of incision in the Late period – are few, and represent the gradual, not to say grudging, acceptance of developments which had taken place earlier elsewhere. Early Protoattic in particular was not a period of great change as regards iconography. As Theodora Rombos has shown (1988: 35–7, table 1) the greatest increase in the iconographic repertoire of Attic vases took place in Late Geometric II. Both Late Geometric II and Protoattic vases were dominated by figured decoration, but the range of iconographic themes decreases markedly from Late Geometric II to Early Protoattic. The stylistic changes that took place were of two kinds. First, Orientalising motifs, in particular plant-derived and other curvilinear motifs, begin to replace the Geometric ornament on large vases. The subsidiary ornament ceases to be rectilinear and becomes curvilinear. The shape and scale of vases took longer to change. It is only in Middle Protoattic that pots again assume the proportions of the Late Geometric I 'Dipylon' vases. By Middle Protoattic too, new shapes had developed which owed less and less to the Geometric tradition. Vase shapes had by this time lost their Geometric rigidity, their outlines now in harmony with the predominantly curvilinear decoration.

Protoattic is then a truly Orientalising style, one among many in seventh-century Greece. But the advent of Proto-attic also marks a split, a bifurcation in the Attic pottery tradition. For a brief period, Orientalising and Geometric styles had co-existed (J. M. Cook 1947; Brokaw 1963), and

it is only after 700 BC that the Protoattic style became fully established. Some Attic potters, however, continued to produce shapes in the Geometric tradition, decorated in a rather careless fashion with 'Geometric' motifs. This is the pottery we can Subgeometric, which is by far the most common ware in Attica in the seventh century. Such an aesthetic 'split personality', where Geometric and Orientalising have become alternative styles between which a potter, painter or consumer could choose, can also be paralleled in other, earlier periods in Greek vase painting. In ninth-century Knossos, for example, vase painters could and did alternate between a 'Geometric' and an 'Orientalising' style, the so-called Protogeometric B. Sometimes these alternative styles are to be found on either side of the same vase (Coldstream 1984). In Attica such eclecticism was not tolerated. Yet the very existence of alternative styles has important consequences for our understanding of seventh-century Attic taste. For when alternatives exist, 'natural' conservatism becomes an impossibility. The conservative cannot help but distinguish himself by his conservatism; the conformist loses an absolute standard to which he can conform.

Despite this split, the distinction between Protoattic and Subgeometric is not always that clear cut. Many Protoattic vases continue to be decorated with motifs which are also found in Late Geometric II. Moreover, the extent to which a Protoattic vase can be called Orientalising is often a matter of degree rather than kind. Some vases are 'Protoattic' only in shape. Some are described as having Orientalising motifs, motifs which are distinguished from Geometric solely because they are curvilinear rather than rectilinear. Others are decorated with the kind of plant-derived motif whose antecedents can be traced back to the Near East; and yet others are painted with the kind of composite creatures (such as the Sphinx; see fig. 3.5) which have a long and distinguished ancestry in Egyptian and Levantine art. There are clearly degrees of Orientalising, and I have tried to reflect these gradations in my tabulations. But there is rarely any problem when classifying any vessel as Subgeometric or Protoattic. The shapes of each class of pottery are quite distinct. No figured scenes are to be found on Subgeometric vases, whose decoration, eschewing the Oriental, is generally of the simplest kind.

It has been clear for some time that these types of pottery – Protoattic, Subgeometric, coarse wares and imported vessels – occur in different quantities in various contexts in seventh-century Attica, but no-one has as yet tried to give statistical expression to these differences. Before a preliminary analysis of this kind is attempted, it will be useful to describe the contexts in which various types of seventh-century Attic pottery occur. As will become apparent, the common-sense distinction between burial, 'ritual' and domestic deposits requires some refinement before any useful statistical comparison can be made.

The contexts: burials

As Ian Morris (1987: 61–9) has pointed out, the burial practices of seventh-century Attica emphasise the distinction between adult and child (see tables 3.1, 3.2, 3.4 and 3.6). For the most part, children and adults are buried in separate cemetery areas – if not separate cemeteries, then separate grave plots. These spatial divisions are emphasised by the differences in burial practices for adults and children. Children's graves are usually inhumations, often contained within a pithos or amphora. Adult inhumations are rare, but adult cremations common (see table 3.2). These particular distinctions between dead adults and dead children were evident in the late eighth century BC, but in other respects seventh-century Attic mortuary practices represent signifi-cant departures from what had gone before. It is now very rare for adult cremations to receive individual grave goods within the grave. The rich female graves, which had been such a persistent feature of Attic burial customs in the Dark Ages (Whitley 1991), 'disappear'. This may be due to a change in burial customs – seventh-century cremations are much more effective in reducing human bones (Kübler 1959: 83–5). Grave offerings are now no longer placed in the grave itself, but in a separate offering channel or offering place (Opferrinne, Opferplatz or Opfergrube; see Kübler 1959), usually placed outside the edge of the funerary mounds or tumuli which begin to be constructed in this period. Such mounds seem to be built only over adult cremations. Mounds of this type, with their offering channels, occur in the Attic countryside at least from the late seventh century onwards – the sites of Vourva and Vari are typical of this pattern. But it is only in the Kerameikos that we can trace their architectural development in any detail.

Funerary mounds begin modestly in the early seventh century when they are simply low mounds over a grave. But fairly soon these mounds acquire stone or ceramic grave markers (see figs. 3.5 and 3.6), and gradually become larger.[4] During the course of the seventh century other forms of funerary architecture appear (Kübler 1959: 80–94). The rectangular earth marker, the 'Erdmal', seems to have been current from the mid-seventh century onwards. By the end of the century, 'Grabbauten', mudbrick rectangular tombs, become the predominant form of grave architecture (see I. Morris 1987: 129–31). This gradual trend towards monumentality is the inverse of late eighth-century practice, when many graves were unmarked above ground but richly furnished with grave goods.[5] It seems to hark back to an

Table 3.2. *Seventh-century adult and child graves in the Kerameikos (after Kübler 1959; 1970; Schlörb-Vierneisel 1966: 11–16; Freytag 1975)*

Adult/child	Adult	Child	Total
Graves without grave goods (excluding Opferrinnen)	20	3	23
Graves with grave goods	9	13	22
Inhumations	5	13	18
Cremations	24	3	27
Graves with grave marker (ceramic or stone)	10	0	10
Graves with grave building or monument (not mound)	7	0	7
Graves with grave mound	18	0	18
Graves with offering trenches (Opferrinnen) or similar	13	0	13
Total graves	29	16	45

earlier eighth-century pattern, the period of the Dipylon graves with their elaborate ceramic grave markers.

The relevant mortuary contexts for comparison therefore are: (a) adult graves; (b) children's graves; (c) offering trenches; and (d) grave markers.

Other contexts

Similar distinctions can be made between types of 'ritual' deposit. With the exception of Sounion (Staïs 1917), the major state sanctuaries of seventh-century Attica, such as the Acropolis, Eleusis and Brauron, do not possess impressive remains, nor are they rich in votive deposits. Architecturally Attica lags behind the Peloponnesian states, and the quantity and quality of seventh-century votives from Attic sanctu-aries does not bear comparison with Perachora, the Argive Heraeum, or Olympia (S. P. Morris 1984: 9–11, 99–100, 104–7; de Polignac 1984). The 'peak sanctuaries', altars probably dedicated to Zeus found on many hills in Attica, such as the sanctuary on Mt Hymettus described by Langdon (1976), or the 'Kultplatz' on Turkovouni whose finds have been published by Lauter (1985b), have by contrast produced much pottery, though little Protoattic. Then there are the tomb cults at the Mycenaean tholos tombs of Menidhi (Wolters 1899; Callipolitis-Feytmans 1965: 44–8; Hägg 1987; Whitley 1988) and Thorikos (Bingen *et al.* 1965b: 30–9; 1969: 30–4, 37–9), and the apparent votive deposits over an Early Geometric child's grave in the Agora (Burr 1933; H. A. Thompson 1968: 60). These again form a

Table 3.3. *Distribution of decoration on vases in the Agora wells (after Brann 1961; 1962; R. S. Young 1938: 139–94)*

Agora wells	C	D	E	F	G	H	S	Total
Protoattic, total	30	4	1	18	8	14	8	83
Protoattic, shape only	16	2	0	4	1	4	4	31
Protoattic, Orientalising	9	1	1	13	7	9	4	44
Protoattic, animals and composite creatures	6	0	0	4	2	2	2	16
Protoattic, human figures	0	1	0	3	0	2	1	7
Protocorinthian and Corinthian total	18	2	0	6	2	2	1	31
Protocorinthian and Corinthian linear decoration	18	2	0	6	1	0	0	27
Protocorinthian and Corinthian Orientalising	0	0	0	0	1	2	1	4
Imports (fine)	0	0	0	0	3	0	0	3
Imports (coarse)	0	0	0	7	0	0	1	8
Subgeometric	60	11	4	23	29	45	10	182
Coarse wares (local)	12	5	0	11	6	7	4	45
Terracottas:								
domestic	9	4	0	5	3	13	6	40
votive	6	5	0	1	3	4	0	19
Stone objects	0	0	0	5	0	1	0	6
Other	0	15	0	0	0	1	0	16

coherent group, the character of whose finds is quite different from those from peak sanctuaries.

There are a number of excavated seventh-century settlements in Attica whose deposits we might expect to be useful. However the material available for comparison is disappointing. Although much was recovered from the excavation of Lathouresa (Walter 1940: 177–8; Lauter 1985a: 4, 5–7) nothing is as yet available for study. The quantity of material from Thorikos, Velatouri (Bingen *et al.* 1967b: 9–19) is meagre, and the Protoattic pottery recovered from elsewhere in Thorikos does not come from good contexts (Blondé 1978; van Gelder 1978). Only a few sherds are noted as coming from the seventh-century house in the Athenian Agora (Brann 1962: 110; H. A. Thompson 1940: 3–8). Here again the Agora well deposits (Brann 1961; R. S. Young 1938; 1939: 139–94) provide the best comparanda.

Preliminary analysis

Protoattic has often been considered a special, 'ceremonial' class of pottery. Brann, for example (1961: 306), states that 'In the seventh century, as in the preceding period, there was still a wide rift between ceremonial and use pottery', Protoattic being the ceremonial style. If a distinction between 'ceremonial' and 'use' pottery were being rigidly maintained, then we could expect to find Protoattic largely in 'ceremonial' (that is ritual) and not domestic contexts. But a statistical comparison between ritual and domestic deposits

does not bear this out. In some sanctuary deposits, particularly in the 'peak sanctuaries' (Langdon 1976; Lauter 1985b) the vast majority of pots found are Subgeometric, with only one or two Orientalising sherds. Although exact quantification is not possible, it seems that at the tholos tomb at Menidhi and at Thorikos more pottery that is truly Orientalising is to be found (Whitley 1988; see site index). The same is true to a lesser extent for the votive deposit over an Early Geometric child's grave in the Agora (Burr 1933).

More importantly perhaps, the Agora well deposits appear to indicate that Protoattic pottery was as common in the domestic sphere as it was in ritual contexts (see table 3.3). Although Subgeometric vases are much more abundant overall, Protoattic vases are at least as common in these well deposits as Attic household wares. It may be objected that these deposits are dumped fill (that is secondary deposits), not use fill, and that therefore their domestic character can be questioned. Certainty is not possible, but there are several reasons for thinking these deposits to be largely domestic. For one thing, the shapes of Subgeometric and household wares seem to relate directly to such domestic activities as preparing food and drawing water. Large numbers of stone tools, loom weights and spindle whorls have also been found in these deposits. Furthermore, if Protoattic was purely a ceremonial and Subgeometric simply a use ware, then these kinds of pottery should be found in spatially distinct parts of the Agora. The proportions of Protoattic and Subgeometric should therefore vary considerably between individual well

Table 3.4. *Child cemeteries in Attica (for references see grave index)*

	Phaleron	Eleusis	Thorikos	Kerameikos	Total
Protoattic, total	12	2	3	13	30
Protoattic, shape only	5	0	2	2	9
Protoattic, Orientalising	7	2	1	10	20
Protoattic, animal and composite figures	0	2	0	3	5
Protoattic, human figures	0	1	0	0	1
Protocorinthian and Corinthian total	45	2	7	9	63
Protocorinthian and Corinthian linear decoration	40	2	?	6	?
Protocorinthian and Corinthian Orientalising	5	0	?	3	?
Subgeometric	75	11	42	8	136
Coarse wares	9	10	12	9	40
Hand-made vessels	5	7	1	0	13
Other imports	?	?	?	?	?
Other	10	0	7	0	17

deposits which are widely separated within the area of the Agora excavations, always assuming that they were filled from dumps close by. But such variation is not to be found (see table 3.3). In fact, the proportion of Protoattic to Subgeometric varies hardly at all from well to well.

It is therefore, I think, a mistake to see Protoattic as a ceremonial ware, used only in ceremonial contexts or on ceremonial occasions (*contra* I. Morris 1987: 156–67). It is true that most of the more elaborate Protoattic vases from known contexts come from graves, or grave contexts broadly speaking. If the Agora well deposits demonstrate that Protoattic was not exclusively a funerary style, then an examination of Attic children's graves shows that Subgeometric was not exclusively domestic. The proportion of Subgeometric, Protocorinthian and Protoattic vases in the child cemeteries of Phaleron, Thorikos and Eleusis is not that different from the proportion found in domestic contexts. Indeed the proportion of Protoattic in these graves is actually lower than in the Agora well deposits (see table 3.4). The only adult or mixed cemetery where we can compare grave contexts in detail is the Kerameikos (see site index). Here of the twenty-nine adult and sixteen child graves of the seventh century that have been found, only nine adult graves were furnished with grave goods, whereas thirteen children's graves received some kind of offering (see tables 3.2 and 3.5). This is not to say that adult graves were poorly regarded. Eighteen adult graves are marked by mounds, ten by stone or ceramic grave markers (see figs. 3.5 and 3.6).[6] Whereas the memory of the dead children was effaced after the completion of the funeral ceremony, the memory of the deceased adults was maintained by these visible, tangible *semata* (but see D'Onofrio 1988). Nor were adult graves

entirely devoid of offerings. Thirteen of the adult graves were associated with Opferrinnen, offering channels in which numerous and often highly decorated vases (e.g. figs. 3.1, 3.2, 3.3 and 3.4) were placed alongside remains of a ritual meal. Offerings were, however, rarely if ever placed within the grave proper. An adult grave, in seventh-century Attica, was not a fine and private place, but a public monument, with an open space for post-funerary ritual.

As will be clear from table 3.5, most of the Protoattic pottery recovered from the Kerameikos comes from these offering channels (fifty-two out of a total of eighty-one vases). Subgeometric vases are hardly to be found in these contexts, although there is a fair quantity of Protocorinthian. Moreover many of the Protoattic vases from these offering trenches seem to have been specifically produced for the post-funeral 'Opferrinne' ceremony. Many vases are furnished with elaborate plastic attachments, such as snakes and mourning women (fig. 3.1) or griffin protomes (fig. 3.2). Such vases cannot have been useful in any utilitarian sense, and indeed they are not to be found in any domestic deposits in seventh-century Attica. Both the consumption and, to a lesser extent, the production of Protoattic was therefore restricted. It was rationed, its use confined to certain contexts and occasions. But, as I have tried to show above, this rationing was not by context and occasion alone. The majority of Protoattic vases are found associated not simply with graves, but with adult graves. If Ian Morris (1987) is right in thinking that only a minority of adults in seventh-century Attica received burial beneath these grave mounds, a minority we think of as an elite, then the use of Protoattic was not rationed so much by occasion, as by status. The finds of Protoattic pottery therefore relate directly to the status of

Table 3.5. *Kerameikos cemetery: breakdown of distribution of types of vases according to context (after Kübler 1959; 1970; Schlörb-Vierneisel 1966: 11–16; Freytag 1975)*

	Opferrinnen, Opferplatzen, etc.	Adult graves	Grave markers	Child graves	Total
Protoattic, total	52	9	7	13	81
Protoattic, shape only	2	2	0	2	6
Protoattic, Orientalising	41	6	5	10	62
Protoattic, animal and composite figures	30	4	4	3	41
Protoattic, human figures	17	1	2	0	20
Protocorinthian and Corinthian total	24	4	0	9	37
Protocorinthian and Corinthian linear decoration	7	2	0	3	12
Protocorinthian and Corinthian Orientalising	17	2	0	6	25
Subgeometric	0	2	0	8	10
Coarse wares	1	3	0	9	13
Hand-made vessels	0	0	0	0	0
Imports	0	0	0	0	0
Other	3	2	0	0	5

the deceased person whose memory was the focus of the 'Opferrinne' ritual. Certainly the quality of the Protoattic pottery from these offering trenches is outstanding when compared with other seventh-century Attic material. In particular, the Kerameikos mugs (fig. 3.3; see also S. P. Morris 1984: 84–6) and the lids from some of the pyxides (fig. 3.4) found in the Kerameikos Opferrinnen are amongst the finest examples of the Protoattic style.

Similar grave mounds, or rather tomb complexes with mounds, adult cremations without grave goods, and Opferrinnen, can be paralleled elsewhere in Attica, for example at Vourva (Staïs 1890a; 1890b), Vari (Papaspyridi-Karouzou 1963) and Tavros (Schilardi 1975). Although the reports from Vari are unclear, it seems that all the late seventh-century pottery from these sites came from the offering trenches, and not the cremation pits themselves. Ian Morris (1987: 152) has argued that all these Opferrinne/ tumulus complexes are the burial areas of an elite. This interpretation depends on our accepting a number of still controversial propositions. Morris argues that the 'trough' in the material record of seventh-century Attica, in particular the drop in the number of recoverable graves and the relative increase in children's graves (see table 3.1) is due not so much to a natural disaster such as a drought (Camp 1979),[7] or to a presumed war with Aegina (S. P. Morris 1984: 107–15; Dunbabin 1937), as to what he calls a rationing of the privilege of visible recognition at death. He believes that most seventh-century Athenian adults were disposed of in a manner that makes them archaeologically 'invisible'. I will not rehearse all Ian Morris' arguments here, but simply state

my preference for sociological explanations, and social models, which take some cognisance of the *longue durée* and which can be re-examined in the light of future research, over *ad hoc* contingent explanations.

Ian Morris' sociological explanation for the drop in the number of 'visible' graves, and thus for the rationing of 'visible' burial by status, can help us begin to explain the small quantities and restricted distribution of Protoattic pottery. Decorated, Orientalising pottery, like visible, high-status burial, was rationed. Its consumption and use was confined to an elite. It remains to consider what kind of an elite may have existed in seventh-century Attica, and to underline what a contextual analysis of Protoattic has told us about this elite's 'depositional behaviour'.

Attic society in the seventh century and in the Dark Ages

'Elite' here is a relative term. I would argue that, despite indications of the existence of some kind of formal, pre-Solonian constitution, political power in seventh-century Attica was still based on personal loyalties and kinship ties (I. Morris 1991). To assume otherwise, to believe that the *archon* and the *basileus* held a 'monopoly of force', or that there were other office holders with real and extensive responsibilities (Lambert 1986), is to render incomprehensible the faction-fighting that was endemic in Athens from the time of the Cylonian conspiracy to Cleisthenes. It is a mistake to believe that *formal* reconstructions of a constitution, a *politeia*, can lead to any real understanding of the power structure of an early *polis* like Athens. It is simply to transfer the prejudices of an Aristotle, and of the Whig theory of history, to the seventh century. The elite of seventh-century Attica might be no more than the heads or chiefs of family groups, the *Eupatridae* who constantly needed to bolster their authority by claims of a privileged relation to distinguished ancestors or heroes. Clearly the elite of seventh-century Attica did not indulge in expensive dedications to the gods. The relative poverty of offerings in Attic sanctuaries in this period, and the scant signs of Attic participation in pan-hellenic cults and festivals is an indication that sanctuaries were not at this time arenas for the competitive display of wealth and piety. This is particularly

surprising when we consider the numbers of eighth-century Attic tripod dedications on the Athenian Acropolis and at Delphi and Olympia (Touloupa 1972; Morgan 1990: 43–7, 140–1) and the large numbers of marble dedications on the acropolis of sixth-century date (Raubitschek 1949; Stoddart and Whitley 1988).[8] These material indications cannot easily be reconciled with the picture of seventh-century Attica painted by some historians, with the majority of the population groaning under the yoke of an exploitative, Eupatrid aristocracy (Aristotle *Constitution of Athens*, 2.2 and 5; Forrest 1966: 145–60). Nor is poverty a sufficient

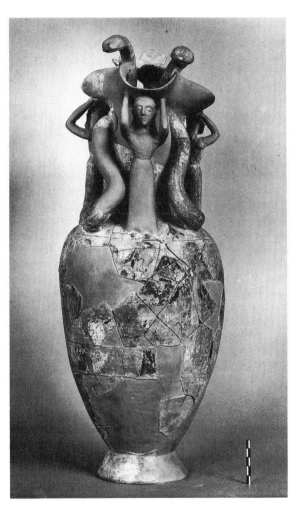

3.1 Jug with plastic attachments of snakes and mourning women. Kerameikos no. 149 (Kat. Nr. 49) from Opferrinne γ, Anlage XI in the Kerameikos.

3.2 Cauldron, with griffin protomes. Kerameikos no. 148 (Kat. Nr. 52) from Opferrinne γ, Anlage XI in the Kerameikos.

explanation for this apparent reluctance on the part of Athenians to participate in the agonal spirit of seventh-century Greece. The explanation lies in the persistence (or recurrence) of distinctively Attic patterns of behaviour which have their antecedents in the Dark Ages.

The pattern of behaviour I am talking about is called social rationing. It is a means of maintaining the coherence and identity of an elite through exclusive access to certain items of material culture. As Appadurai (1986a), amongst others, has pointed out, in pre-market economies, the significance of goods is often primarily political. Goods, and many aspects of material culture, can be seen as 'coupons or licences', which have a direct relevance to the social system. As Appadurai (1986a: 25) puts it: 'The social systems in which coupons and licences function is geared to eliminating or reducing competition in the interests of a fixed pattern of status.' In some societies where social rationing is found, the production and consumption of items is governed by strict rules. Only persons of known and recognised rank are entitled to certain items and certain emblems or motifs. This is a pattern which can be observed today in such areas as the Waigal valley communities of Nuristan (N. Jones 1974). Such a pattern is also very characteristic of ninth- and early eighth-century Attic society, as I have argued more fully elsewhere (Whitley 1986: 166–93, 362–6; 1991: 116–62). However they are still sufficiently unfamiliar to merit repetition.

Athenian Geometric pottery has usually been regarded as the paradigm of the Geometric style (Coldstream 1968: 8). It is a style which, before the eighth century, generally eschewed images, and relied on purely aniconic motifs. Early and Middle Geometric I pottery represents this style at its most accomplished and austere. This is a dark ground style, which achieves its effect through the careful arrangement of rectilinear ornament. Athenian Early and Middle Geometric I pottery is distinguished from Protogeometric

3.3 Beaker or mug (one of the 'Kerameikos mugs') with fighting scene and plant-derived decoration. Kerameikos no. 73 (Kat. Nr. 20) from Opferrinne β, Anlage IX in the Kerameikos.

3.4 Lid from pyxis, showing chariot scenes. Kerameikos no. 75 (Kat. Nr. 28) from Opferrinne β, Anlage IX in the Kerameikos.

not only in the range of its motifs but in the stricter grammar of their arrangement.

This stylistic change is paralleled, in the tenth and ninth centuries, by changes in the mortuary sphere. In Proto-geometric times (1025–900 BC), rules had been established which defined certain burial types. Men were usually interred in neck-handled amphorae (often accompanied by swords), women in belly-handled amphorae (almost invariably accompanied by dress pins, and sometimes with a fibula). Children were not cremated, as were adults, but buried in cist graves. These distinctions were not emphasised by the choice of motifs used on the main burial urn. No close correlations can be observed between artefact types, the age and sex of the deceased, and the decoration on the burial urns (Whitley 1991: 97–116).

In the ninth century (900–800 BC), such correlations do become evident. Particular motifs found on grave markers and burial urns are found in regular, recurrent association with particular pot and metal artefact types. In particular, circular motifs are to be found on the burial urns (belly-handled amphorae) of a small class of rich female graves[9] in association with gold, bronze fibulae, dress pins, gold rings and ivory. Such motifs are also found on the kraters which mark a group of less well-preserved male graves in the Kerameikos.[10] These graves are not extravagantly rich, but they are exclusive. Particular design elements and particular artefacts are confined to these two classes of grave (Whitley 1991: 117–37). Ninth-century symbolic forms are charac-terised by exclusivity and selectivity, by 'conspicuous parsimony' (Appadurai 1986a: 30). Access to formal burial (I. Morris 1987: 79–81) and to the use of certain artefacts and motifs had become the preserve of a particular stratum of society. An aristocracy had emerged that defined itself on the principle of exclusivity, rather than the extravagance of its display. This is not true everywhere in ninth-century Greece. In Knossos, variety and eclecticism in both pot styles and burial forms are the predominant theme (Whitley 1986: 307–24). In ninth-century Lefkandi, there is a great increase in the quantity of gold items deposited in graves (Popham *et al.* 1980: 216–25, 417–20), which, if anything, must indicate an increase in ostentation in the funeral ceremony at this time.

This Athenian aristocracy, I have argued, went to great lengths to prevent other groups from usurping these symbolic privileges. This I term social rationing, and it is something that can be observed in present-day societies studied by anthropologists. In Nuristan, for example (N. Jones 1974), a society which Oswyn Murray (1980: 68; 1983) has suggested offers close parallels to 'Homeric' society, there is a strict regulation of symbols according to birth and achieved rank (N. Jones 1974: 184–5). The

meaning of decoration is direct and obvious. It refers to social status.

Such societies dislike exotic artefacts, since their style and iconography cannot easily be fitted into the existing symbolic order, an order which relates directly to social needs. Appadurai (1986a: 31–48) has drawn attention to the role that exotic material culture may play in pre-market economies and societies. As he puts it (Appadurai 1986a: 33):

> The politics of demand frequently lies at the root of the tension between merchants and political elites: whereas merchants tend to be the social representatives of unfettered equivalence, new commodities and strange tastes, political elites tend to be the custodians of restricted exchange, fixed commodity systems and established tastes and sumptuary customs. This antagonism between 'foreign' goods and local sumptuary (and therefore political) structures is probably the fundamental reason for the . . . tendency of primitive societies to restrict trade to a limited set of commodities and to dealings with strangers rather than kinsmen or friends.

Exotic material culture can therefore be extremely disruptive to an established social and symbolic order based on rationing and sumptuary laws. This is a major reason why many societies try to keep the 'foreign' at arm's length. One notable feature of the Attic Dark Age ceramic sequence, as contrasted to those of Euboea or Knossos, is its continual resistance to exotic material culture (Whitley 1991). Exotic elements are confined to metalworking, or, when they do intrude into pot painting, as in the animal friezes on Late Geometric I belly-handled amphorae, are subordinated to native, Geometric principles of design (Coldstream 1968: 37–41; Whitley 1986: 194–225; 1991: 137–44). In this respect Attica is unusual. Euboea, Crete and many other parts of Greece (apart from the Argolid) had a much more eclectic attitude towards exotic material culture (Whitley 1991: 45–53, 184–94). This resistance to the exotic accounts for much of the aesthetic success of Attic Middle and Late Geometric pottery. But it also makes for a certain inflexi-bility, especially when the symbolic and social systems are so closely connected. The disruption of the symbolic order affects the social order, and vice versa.

There are many indications that the late eighth century was a period of rapid change and innovation, and so of both social and symbolic disruption (Whitley 1986: 226–50; 1991: 162–80). Whether or not we take the innovations of the late eighth century as indicating the rise of the *polis*, we cannot begin to explain the appearance of such a wide-ranging complex of innovations without positing some kind of major, indeed revolutionary, social change (de Polignac 1984; Snodgrass 1980b). In Attica a symptom or a by-product of this change is the gradual breakdown in the canons of the Geometric style (Coldstream 1968: 87–90), which I would claim indicates a disruption in the symbolic order which had been used in the reproduction of Attic society. At the very least, the acknowledged variety and unevenness of the Late Geometric II style in Athens must register a deep certainty about taste.

At a time when the conventions of Attic Geometric were slowly breaking down, many other communities in Greece were beginning to adopt Oriental and Orientalising imagery, motifs and other conventions in their pot painting. Communities such as Corinth, whose Geometric tradition was less well established, and the cities of Euboea, whose pottery tradition had always been much more eclectic than Athens, were in the forefront of these developments (R. M. Cook 1972a: 46–65, 104–5). This adoption of the elements of an alien material culture has usually been seen as a natural and welcome development. But this view is misplaced. Societies vary greatly in their attitude towards the exotic, and in many societies there is a certain ambivalence about foreign artefacts and styles (see again Appadurai 1986a). In the modern world, the feelings of many non-Western peoples towards the material culture of the West are mixed, often displaying a bewildering combination of cupidity and hostility. Moreover the extent to which a particular culture will adopt elements from another society, and the manner in which such adoption takes place, are often mediated by the role which certain artefacts and styles play within that society. A good modern example of how cultural attitudes to material culture determine the pace and nature of 'acculturation' can be found in modern India (broadly 1700 to 1930 CE), as discussed by Bayly (1986). Bayly discusses at some length the changing use of cloth in India during the period, and what this might tell us about social history. For Indians, cloth was much more than a simple commodity. The production and distribution of cloth was mediated by a whole host of cultural attitudes and institutions. It was partly through the distribution of cloth that rulers demonstrated their concern for the governed, and won their consent. Cloth was a medium of reciprocity between ruler and ruled. The use of colour in cloth reflected complex cultural attitudes to caste, religion and purity. When foreign, chiefly British, cloth began to appear in the eighteenth century, the degree to which it was accepted depended on how it fitted in with the native Indian system of values. Red British cloth was fairly quickly and willingly adopted by Indian sepoys because the colour red already possessed distinctly martial overtones within Indian society. But in most respects these attitudes hindered the acceptance of British cloth within India. Indians

never really accepted the British view that cloth was simply a commodity like any other, and cloth eventually became an effective symbol of resistance to British rule. Many of Gandhi's political campaigns, for example, set out to discourage Indians from using foreign cloth. These campaigns depended for their success as much upon these latent cultural attitudes as upon simple dislike of the British.

There is a common assumption amongst many archaeologists that the products of a 'superior' culture will, almost automatically, be found attractive by simpler societies living on their periphery. But the Indian example should demonstrate that the acceptance of foreign styles and foreign artefacts, even from a 'superior' culture, is strongly affected by social and cultural values. It is clear at least that the societies of Early Archaic Greece varied greatly in their attitude both towards the Orient and towards Orientalising art. In ninth- and early eighth-century Attica, native material culture had had a direct and obvious relationship to the reproduction of the social order, and the distribution of Oriental goods had been severely restricted. For Attica, the sudden increase in the availability of exotica in the seventh century must have posed peculiar problems. It set up a conflict between two 'regimes of value' (Appadurai 1986a): one willing, or even eager to follow the path laid down by Corinth and endeavour to 'Orientalise'; and the other wishing to restrict the use of exotica as far as was possible. So, in Attica, an ambivalent attitude towards the Near East would have arisen. Exotica and Orientalia, with their connotations of a rich world beyond the provincial horizons of seventh-century Attica, would have been felt to be as desirable as they were disruptive. One possible solution to this ambivalence would have been the rationing of both the production and consumption of artefacts with 'Oriental' connotations; a restriction of their use to contexts which were both prestigious and liminal. There were two aspects to this solution. Orientalising pottery was only produced for certain high-status people and occasions; and Orientalising pottery was, in general, disposed of in contexts far removed from daily life. Confining the use of Orientalising pottery to ritual meals held to honour the dead was a way in which the 'high status' of the exotic was acknowledged and its disruptive effect minimalised by its removal from day-to-day living.

So far I have talked solely about pottery. Can this 'rationing' model be applied to other aspects of material culture in Athens, poor though they are? Of the metalwork, most seventh-century Attic bronzes do appear to be Orientalising, rather than Geometric, in style, and this marks a break with the eighth century. Like the pottery, all the bronzes have been found in liminal, ritual contexts, far removed from the domestic sphere. There are ten bronze vessels from two seventh-century graves in the Kerameikos (Kübler 1970: 556–8), all decorated in an Orientalising, or rather a daedalic, style. There are also eleven griffin protomes from the Athenian Acropolis (see note 8), a respectable number, though far fewer than in other parts of Greece. There is too little gold or ivory (Kübler 1970: 559) for any useful comparison with the eighth century to be made. It is at least unusual however that the most 'Orientalising' aspects of eighth-century Attic material culture had indeed been ivory and gold work (Coldstream 1977: 123–6, 130–2). Perhaps this is another indication that the Athenians were, in some respects, even less receptive to foreign influences in the seventh century than they were in the eighth.

There is one area, however, where Athenians appear to have been very receptive to new ideas ultimately derived from the Near East: that is, in their use of that new 'technology of the intellect', the alphabetic script. Here there is a continuity with the eighth century. The Dipylon oinochoe is one of the earliest Greek inscriptions, and several others found in Attica appear to date to the eighth century (Immerwahr 1990: 7–8; Powell 1991: 158–67). This tradition is carried on into the seventh century with the large number of graffiti found on Mt Hymettus (Langdon 1976). The quantity of graffiti and dipinti found elsewhere in Attica between 700 and 620 BC is not great however (Immerwahr 1990: 9–14). It is easy to exaggerate the importance of literacy in seventh-century Attica. The number and type of inscriptions indicate that, in this area at least, Attica was 'in step, with other regions of Greece, but no more than that. The widespread use of alphabetic writing for public purposes, for dedications and for funerary monuments, is largely a sixth-century phenomenon (Stoddart and Whitley 1988). It is only from the late seventh century (620 BC) onwards that inscriptions (dipinti) come into general use on Attic vases, where they are employed to clarify a mythological or narrative scene (Immerwahr 1990: 20–3). Again, as with the dedicatory inscriptions and the funerary monuments, the real change takes place towards the end of the seventh century.

So my interpretation of Protoattic is at least consistent with what little we can infer from Athenian metalworking, which, like Orientalising pottery, tends to appear in liminal contexts. The hesitant use of alphabetic scripts in the seventh century, when compared with the situation in either the eighth century or the sixth, is also broadly in keeping with the 'rationing' hypothesis. But the 'rationing' system which had been re-created in the seventh century was significantly different from that which had prevailed in the ninth. In both systems the production and consumption of high-status items was restricted. In the ninth century, however, rationing was primarily by *status*; material symbolism had a direct

relationship to social rank. In the seventh century no such relationship can be discerned. Instead of rationing by status, we have rationing both by status and by occasion. The liminality of funerary ritual, its removal from day-to-day living and its proximity to the world of the dead is as important a feature of the system as the connection between high status and Orientalising decoration. There is no longer any direct relationship here between particular design elements and the social hierarchy as such. Instead, we have an ambivalent, rationing solution to the 'problem' of what to do with exotic material culture that is both highly sought after and highly dangerous. This solution, I would argue, was appropriate for an insular, reactionary society which was slow to adopt most of the characteristic innovations of early Archaic Greece.

Image, context and society

This interpretation of Protoattic helps to explain why there was so little of it – many people were simply prevented from acquiring it through a restrictive system of production and distribution. In any case, many might have preferred the homely Subgeometric, which did not have disruptive foreign overtones. But does this interpretation stand up to any kind of contextual analysis? It cannot be the whole story, for if it is, we cannot explain the quantities of Protoattic pottery which turn up in the Agora well deposits. Some Protoattic was used in or near the domestic sphere, and in some respects Protoattic was no more than an elite style, or a style with 'elite' overtones. But it does at least fit in with a picture of an insular and conservative Attica, one slow to adopt such innovations as temple building or hoplite warfare.

There are further indications of Attica's isolationism, ones that may be found in the iconography of Protoattic vases. One of the peculiarities of the Protoattic found in Attica, rather than the 'Protoattic' found in Aegina, is the paucity of mythological representations. Here I am using the term mythological representations in the strict sense, meaning those representations which either narrate or allude to a known myth. I exclude composite mythological creatures, such as sphinxes, which are of Oriental origin and may not yet have been assimilated into Greek myth by this time. On these strict criteria, there are only eight mythological representations on seventh-century vases found in Attica, whereas there are an equal number of 'Protoattic' and Protocorinthian vases found on the much smaller island of Aegina (Fittschen 1969).[11] Most of the Attic representations are late – they are associated with the Nessos painter and his school – whereas the Aeginetan examples date from the middle of the century. Again, a pattern of restricted, controlled consumption might help to explain hesitancy of

Table 3.6. *Scenes on Protoattic vases from the Agora well groups (after Brann 1961; 1962; R. S. Young 1938; 1939: 139–41) and from the Kerameikos grave markers and Opferrinnen (after Kübler 1959; 1970; Schlörb-Vierneisel 1966: 11–16; Freytag 1975)*

	Agora, well groups	Kerameikos, grave markers	Kerameikos, Opferrinnen
Geometric motifs	4	5	10
Orientalising motifs	36	5	25
Plant-derived motifs	11	2	17
Humans (simple)	4	1	3
Animals (simple)	17	2	24
Chariot scenes or horse and rider	2	2	7
Fighting scenes/warriors	1	0	2
Composite creatures	0	3	10
Mourning women	0	0	8
Snakes	?	0	2
Total vases	42	7	47

those painters working in an Attic environment to experiment with mythological or narrative representations.

Contextual analysis also reveals certain iconographic preferences which the rationing hypothesis might help to explain. These preferences become apparent when the Protoattic vases from the 'domestic' well deposits in the Agora on the one hand and those from the offering trenches in the Kerameikos on the other are compared. Stock generic scenes, scenes which have identifiable antecedents in the Geometric repertory of representations, such as chariot scenes (fig. 3.4), fighting scenes (fig. 3.3), or single human or animal figures, are common in both contexts (see table 3.6). But mourning women, and composite, 'mythological' creatures such as sphinxes are hardly to be found in the well deposits. Whilst the absence of mourning women from well deposits is hardly surprising, the relative frequency of composite creatures on vases either deposited in the Opferrinnen or used as grave markers is unusual. Sphinxes are particularly common in funerary contexts. They are found represented on ceramic grave markers (fig. 3.5; Kübler 1970: plate 78), on vases found in the Opferrinnen (Kübler 1970: plates 25, 58, 77) and even in the form of plastic thymiateria (Kübler 1970: plates 32–5).[12] As Hoffmann argues (this volume), by Classical times, sphinxes are considered to be 'liminal' creatures, whose composite character makes them particularly appropriate for occasions when the dead meet the living. But in the seventh century, sphinxes – and composite creatures in general – are the most clearly Orientalising and exotic element in the Protoattic repertory. Their occurrence in primarily funerary contexts is, at this time, as much a product of their 'foreignness' as it is

of their liminal or composite nature. Sphinxes were images whose Oriental connotations were highly charged, and thus images whose ambivalent quality would be more deeply felt. Their exotic qualities make them appropriate images for the honouring and commemoration of the dead, but also images which it would be desirable to keep away from day-to-day living. So their use was rationed, restricted to the ceremony and liminality of death. Images on Protoattic vases used in the domestic sphere generally have a respectable Late Geometric ancestry. They were images that had already been assimilated into the visual culture of seventh-century Attica, images which had already been domesticated.[13]

A contextual study of Protoattic may then have shed some light onto social history. But has it improved our understanding of individual pieces? In what sense would contextual analysis modify our understanding of the best known Protoattic vases, those vases which, in scholars' eyes at least, have a place of honour in the tradition of Attic vase painting? One such piece is the Polyphemus vase (fig. 3.7; after Mylonas 1957; 1976: 91–2), a Middle Protoattic neck-handled amphora, whose iconography has recently been re-interpreted by Osborne (1988a). The iconography of the vase is certainly unusual: on the neck we have the scene where Polyphemus is blinded by Odysseus and his companions; on the neck, a scene of one animal attacking another; and on the lower body Perseus and the Gorgons (the Gorgons having cauldron heads). Osborne sees these images as being related and having a common theme: death as the deprivation of the senses. The viewer, moving from the top, observes the blinding of Polyphemus, and then the two animals, and then his/her gaze is returned, and frozen, by the

Gorgons – who ought, if they were real, to be depriving the viewer of his/her senses. In this way the viewer becomes caught up in the image. Osborne does not simply look at the iconography, but also pays some regard to the context of this vase, that is to the circumstances of its deposition. The vase was used to contain the remains of an infant. It was placed on its side in a trench, neither face up nor face down, and the infant was accompanied by a number of smaller vessels placed inside the vase. These circumstances justify, according to Osborne, our seeing the images on the vase as concerned with death. The imagery then is a meditation on death, where the use of the vase for burial and the thematic unity of its imagery reinforce one another. This meditation ultimately reflects a cultural attitude, one current in the seventh century, and distinct from later Classical and earlier Dark Age attitudes to death. In this way, Osborne uses iconography to write a kind of social history, or rather an *histoire des mentalités*.

But if the imagery on this vase were truly representative of seventh-century attitudes to death, then we should be able to read such attitudes out of the iconography of other Protoattic vases. Osborne's interpretation should make sense within a wider context. But here we run into a difficulty: most children's graves in seventh-century Attica were furnished with Subgeometric rather than Protoattic vases (see table 3.4). Interments of children or infants within highly decorated vases of this type are something of a rarity. Nonetheless, there are other examples of a child being interred within an elaborately decorated Protoattic neck-amphora (as opposed to a mere pithos). These occur fairly regularly in the main child cemeteries: one, perhaps two, in the Phaleron cemetery (gr. 18, R. S. Young 1942: 35–6, fig. 18; perhaps another, Couve 1893); two others in the Eleusis cemetery (gr. zeta 10, Mylonas 1975: 251–3; gr. VI, Skias 1912: 32–3, plate 14). There is also the unusual child's grave from the slopes of Mt Hymettus (Böhlau 1887: 43–4 n. 109, plate 5). On none of these vases do we find the same kind of imagery as on the Polyphemus amphora. Even on the most highly decorated of these vessels, such as the Hymettus amphora, none of the themes of the Polyphemus vase is repeated. It would strain even Osborne's ingenuity to interpret the conventional fighting scenes on the Hymettus amphora as being primarily concerned with death as the deprivation of the senses. Of a possible total of 131 children's graves in Attica, a maximum of six are interments of this kind. It is not so much the content of the imagery on the burial amphorae as the fact that these vases were highly decorated in an 'Orientalising' manner that marks these graves out as important.

Large vases of this type (neck or neck-handled amphorae) are not confined to the graves of children. The Athens Nessos amphora for example seems to have come from an

3.5 *Krater used as grave marker, showing a sphinx. Kerameikos no. 801 (Kat. Nr. 115) from Grabbau x, Anlage LVI in the Kerameikos.*

3.6 *Rear view of krater Kerameikos 801, showing 'Orientalising' decoration.*

offering trench (Opferrinne) in Piraeus street (see site index). Osborne's death-as-sensory deprivation interpretation could, by stretching the meaning of the terms a little, also be applied to the imagery on this vase, with its scenes of Gorgons and of Heracles slaying the centaur Nessos. But it is significant that this vase comes from the Piraeus street grave plot, close to if not part of the cemetery from which the Dipylon vases came. If the 'Dipylon' is indeed an aristocratic grave plot, and if I am correct in thinking that highly decorated Orientalising vases, like visible burial, were more strictly rationed in the seventh century than in either the late eighth or the sixth, then the vase can properly be seen as an exceptional post-funerary offering to an exceptional individual. When it comes to the particular features of the imagery, however, I can say almost nothing that is new. The iconography itself has little in common with that found on other Late Protoattic vases from offering trenches, such as

3.7 The Polyphemus amphora, from gr. Γ6 in the West Cemetery of Eleusis.

those from the Kerameikos (see figs. 3.1–3.4) or the Kynosarges amphora (see index).

In the Nessos amphora we have reached the limits of contextual analysis. Contextual analysis is very good at outlining the general patterns of stylistic and iconographic preferences. It has helped us to understand why certain images (composite creatures, snakes) are common in burial contexts, and why other images are more prevalent in well deposits. Moreover by placing certain 'iconological' interpretations in their broader context, it has helped to assess their wider interpretive claims. Osborne (1988a) may be right in his interpretation of the Polyphemus amphora, but any attempt to extend such interpretations, to read mentalities out of images alone, must bring the broader context of the deposition and use of such artefacts into account. Osborne's (1988a; 1989) approach is still largely that of the art historian, who, for the most part, is reluctant to consider the mucky details of context and deposition.

When it comes to the details of iconography, however, contextual method is not enough. We have to adopt different approaches. More can no doubt be achieved by traditional methods, and it is too early to say what the long-term value of 'poststructuralist' interpretations such as Osborne's (1988a) will be. In any case, I am not so much concerned with the details of iconography, as with the very different social uses of 'Protoattic' and other kinds of seventh-century pottery. I have tried to show that the use of an Orientalising style was rationed, both to high-status contexts and to liminal occasions (such as the burial ceremony). The use of Protoattic reflected a peculiarly Attic ambivalence towards the newly internationalised and Orientalised world of the seventh century.[14]

Protoattic (that is the Protoattic of Attica, not the 'Proto-attic' of Aegina) was a style that sensitively registered the tensions of seventh-century Attica – a conservative society proud of its autochthony and suspicious of the exotic, but nonetheless attracted by and caught up in the wider 'Orientalising' world. While Orientalising imagery was still viewed suspiciously as foreign, Oriental imagery could not be assimilated into the visual culture of seventh-century Attica, a fact which perhaps explains its hesitant use. Oriental imagery and artistic conventions were only finally and successfully assimilated when they were used to convey native, Greek myths, but this is an achievement that is as much Corinthian as Athenian.

Acknowledgements

This article is an expanded version of papers given at the Archaeological Institute of America conference in Boston in

December 1989, and at small seminars in Columbia University in New York (March 1990) and at Cardiff, Wales (February 1991). I would like to thank all those who offered their comments on those occasions. I would also like to thank Ian Morris, Sarah Morris, Robin Osborne, Anthony Snodgrass and my wife, Rachel, for comments on earlier drafts of this paper. This is not meant to imply that any of them agrees with anything that I have to say, or that they are in any way responsible for any remaining omissions or mistakes.

Notes

1 Although Draco is credited with a complete 'law code' by Aristotle (*Constitution of Athens*, 4–5; *Politics* 1274b, 15–18) the only epigraphic evidence we possess is the late republication of his law on homicide (Stroud 1968; see also Stroud 1979). Whether or not there was anything more to Draco's *nomoi* or *politeia* than this remains uncertain. See the remarks of Hignett (1952: 5): 'It is now generally agreed that the constitution ascribed to Draco in the *Athenaion Politeia* must be rejected on internal grounds as the invention of some oligarchical pamphleteer who wrote in the last quarter of the fifth century.' Nor is there any necessary connection between the law on homicide and the conspiracy of Cylon, other than the historian's optimistic belief that, in protohistoric times, fragmentary pieces of evidence must somehow relate to one another.

   The best discussion of the whole question of the pre-Solonian constitution is that of P. J. Rhodes (1981: 65–97). R. W. Wallace (1989: 3–47) manages to find some other, very late, 'sources' for seventh-century Attica, whose relevance is as obscure as their value is questionable.

2 See Dunbabin (1937: 8): 'The archaeological evidence thus fails to provide, or even confidently suggest, a date for the war.'

3 Some discussion of the Aegina deposits is, however, clearly in order. These are the largest deposits of 'Protoattic' pottery. They have been fully published by Eilmann and Gebauer (1938) and recently re-examined by Sarah Morris (1981; 1984). I am reluctant to include this material in my discussion of Protoattic, since I agree with Sarah Morris that, whatever the origin of the potters and painters who made these vases, they were made *for* Aeginetans. That is, the shape and decoration of these vases reflect the taste of seventh-century Aeginetans, not seventh-century Athenians. It is true that, in many respects, this Protoaeginetan material is very similar to Protoattic, but perhaps no more so than it is to Euboean or other Island Orientalising styles. Even if it is conceded that these vases derive from an Attic tradition of potting and painting, I find it difficult to believe that these vases could be exports. They are too large and too ungainly to be readily transportable. I must conclude that they were made to suit their Aeginetan consumers. This hypothesis would at least help to explain the large number of shapes found in this deposit which are, to put it mildly, rare in Attica: shapes like the ovoid pedestalled krater. There are no such vases from good contexts in Attica that I know of. The shapes of the vases seek to reflect very un-Attic tastes and preferences. To sum up:

A Most of the vases in the *Aegina Funde* are ovoid kraters, a vase form almost unknown in the Kerameikos grave deposits.
B None of the characteristic shapes of Attic Protoattic, such as the neck-amphora found at Eleusis (Mylonas 1957), is to be found in the Aegina deposits.
C Equally, bell kraters, 'mugs' and plastic attachments, common in the Kerameikos, are not to be found in the Aegina deposits.

   All this suggests a difference in local tastes which we can only explain if we concede that the Aeginetan vases were made for Aeginetans, and the Athenian for Athenians.

4 It could be, however, that all grave mounds were originally covered with stone or ceramic grave markers. The manner in which mounds A to H were superimposed on one another means that there is no possibility of earlier grave markers being left in place (see Kübler 1959).

5 Although some late eighth-century graves did continue to have grave markers of one kind or another, many of the best-furnished Late Geometric graves have none, for example the rich grave at Erechtheiou street (Brouskari 1979), grave VDAk1 in the Kerameikos (Freytag 1974) and graves XVII (G21:17) and XVIII (G12:9) in the Agora (R. S. Young 1939).

6 These figures are based on the fully published graves from the Kerameikos, not on the incompletely published graves (see site index).

7 The inadequacy of the drought hypothesis is particularly evident when it is used to explain the simultaneous strength of Aegina and the weakness of Attica in the seventh century. Attica is a part of the mainland, and an area of relatively high relief; Aegina is an almost flat island. Simple geography then makes it likely that Attica will receive more rain than Aegina. As John Cherry

(1981) has pointed out, islands are always much more vulnerable to climatic fluctuations than is the mainland. It is therefore almost impossible to imagine that a drought which affected Attica would not, simultaneously, devastate Aegina. To mix metaphors a little, if Attica sneezed, Aegina would have caught pneumonia.

8 There are surprisingly few seventh-century bronzes from the Acropolis, at least few which can be assigned to the seventh century on the basis of de Ridder's (1896) catalogue. By my estimate there are only sixteen (numbers after de Ridder 1896): 250, 261, 431–40 (griffin protomes), 442, 445, 756 (Egyptian import?) and 774; see also S. P. Morris 1984: 99–100.

9 These being Kerameikos G41 (Kübler 1954: 235–6), Agora gr. H16:6 (Smithson 1968) and Kriezi street gr. XII (Alexandri 1968).

10 In particular, Kerameikos G2 and G43 (Kübler 1954: 210–12, 238–9).

11 Using Fittschen's (1969) numbering system, the Aeginetan examples are: GV6, SB34, SB51, SB105, SB80, SB115, SB117 and [SB51]; the certain Attic examples are GS3, GS4, SB35, SB50, SB61, SB62, SB85 and SB111; the doubtful Attic examples GV10, SB52, SB62 and AF5. It could be objected that the criteria I employ are too strict, and there are always numerous problems in identifying 'myths'. It is not clear, for example, that the term 'myth' should be restricted to myths known from literary sources, as Snodgrass (1987: 132–69) has often emphasised.

12 Sphinxes continue to play an important role in funerary art in the sixth century in Attica, and even into the fifth (see Hoffmann, this volume). They are particularly common on sixth-century marble grave stelai (Richter 1961).

13 It is true that 'Orientalising' decoration is as common in the Agora well deposits as in the Kerameikos offering channels. But this fact is less significant than it seems. All that is meant by 'Orientalising' motifs here is those motifs which are curvilinear but which are neither figured nor plant-derived. These motifs generally occupy a subordinate position in the decorative scheme ('wave crest motifs' are an example of this type, see fig. 3.6). Plant-derived motifs, which are also of Oriental origin, and which usually occupy a much more prominent position on the vase, are much more common in Kerameikos grave contexts than in the Agora well groups.

14 I may here be accused of exaggerating the unusual position of Attica *vis-à-vis* other regions of Greece. In the Argolid too there is a decline in the number of visible graves in the seventh century when compared with the eighth (A. Foley 1988: 34–5). There is also remarkably little seventh-century Argive pottery (Foley 1988: 56–79). The amount of Protoargive, Orientalising pottery is particularly scanty (Courbin 1955; Bommelaer 1972). Since the Argolid was another region of Greece which had a rich Geometric tradition, and which, like Attica, was notably unreceptive to Near Eastern 'influences', it might seem that the argument I have put forward for seventh-century Attica might also be applied to the Argolid in the seventh century. But this would be to ignore the rich votive deposits found in the Argolid in the seventh century, particularly those from the Argive Heraeum (Waldstein 1905). In this respect, and unlike Attica, the Argolid was in step with other, advanced regions of Greece, such as Corinth. I doubt whether the situation in the Argolid in the seventh century was essentially the same as the situation in Attica.

INDEX

Abbreviations used in the index

Bibliographic abbreviations

AA	Archäologischer Anzeiger
AAA	Athens Annals of Archaeology (Arkhaiologika Analekta ex Athenon)
AD	Arkhaiologikon Deltion
AD A	Arkhaiologikon Deltion, meros A, Meletai
AD B	Arkhaiologikon Deltion, meros B, Khronika
AE	Arkhaiologiki Ephemeris
AJA	American Journal of Archaeology
AM	Mitteilungen des Deutschen Archäologischen Instituts, Athenische Abteilung
AR	Archaeological Reports (supplement to JHS)
BCH	Bulletin de Correspondance Hellénique
BCH Chr	Bulletin de Correspondance Hellénique, Chronique des Fouilles en Grèce
BSA	Annual of the British School at Athens
CVA	Corpus Vasorum Antiquorum
Ergon	To Ergon tis en tais Athenais Arkhaiologikis Etaireias
JHS	Journal of Hellenic Studies
PAE	Praktika tis en tais Athenais Arkhaiologikis Etaireias

Non-bibliographic abbreviations

C	Corinthian (pottery)
DAI Athens	Deutsches archäologisches Institut in Athen
EPA	Early Protoattic
G	Geometric

KER   Kerameikos photo number (DAI Photoarchiv)
LG   Late Geometric (after Coldstream 1968)
LPA   Late Protoattic
MPA   Middle Protoattic (black and white style)
PA   Protoattic
PC   Protocorinthian
SubG   Subgeometric

Note

I have based my study largely on published material, and not on a prolonged and detailed scrutiny of the objects themselves. The index, and many of my statistics, will probably have to be revised in the light of Ludger Hunnekens' 'Frof. archaische Vasenmalerei Attikas' (PhD dissertation, Freiburg 1987) which I have not yet been able to see.

Index I: Athens: seventh-century material from Athens

ACROPOLIS: (i) vases, see Graef and Langlotz 1925: xxxi, 34–40; from later excavations *JHS* 72 (1952), 93, pl. VI.4b; *AE* 1952: 160–1, pl. 9: 3; 66, no. 8; (ii) possible seventh-century column bases, see Nylander 1962; (iii) bronzes, see de Ridder 1896.

AGHÍOU DIMITRIOU grave? PA sherds, *AD* 19: 2 (1964), 55.

AGORA graves
Grave 2, *Hesperia* 20 (1951), 85–6; Graves II–VII, VIII?, IX?, X (R. S. Young 1939: 21–44).

AGORA wells
Well C (R. S. Young 1939: 139–94); Well D (R. S. Young 1938); Wells E, F, G, H, S (Brann 1961; 1962) and *Hesperia* 8 (1939), 212; 16 (1947), 210; 22 (1953), 39.

AGORA houses and other settlement deposits
House under tholos (H. A. Thompson 1940: 3–8; Brann 1962: 110); other settlement, *Hesperia* 25 (1956), 48; R. S. Young 1939: 105–38.

AGORA ritual deposits
Seventh-century votive deposit (Burr 1933; *Hesperia* 37 (1968), 36–76).

AIOLOU/SOPHOKLEOUS streets (junction of): perhaps some seventh-century material, *BCH* 86 (1962), 644.

ACHILLEOS street: probable child's grave, *AD* 29: 2 (1973/74), 123–4.

AKTAIOU/NILIOS streets (junction of): perhaps some seventh-century material, *AD* 23: 2 (1968), 36–8.

AREOPAGUS: graves, seventh-century in date? W. Judeich, *Topographie von Athen* (Munich: C. H. Beck 1931), 400.

DIAKOU/MAKRIYANNIS streets (junction of): a few G and SubG sherds, *AD* 25: 2 (1970), 59.

DIMITRAKOPOULOU street: possibly some seventh-century sherds, *AD* 27: 2 (1972), 53.

ERMOU street: Archaic (seventh-century?) sherds, *AD* 30: 2 (1975), 20–1.

KAVALOTTI street: Archaic well, possibly some seventh-century sherds, *AD* 29: 2 (1973/4), 90.

KERAMEIKOS: north and south of Eridanos, graves included in the statistics; 37 adult and children's graves with mounds, grave markers, Opferrinnen, etc. (Kübler 1959; 1970); 7 graves, *AM* 81 (1966), 11–16; child's grave and Opferrinne, *AM* 90 (1975), 49–81.

KERAMEIKOS: incompletely published graves, not included in the statistics, apart from the total number of graves: 2 adult cremations and 2 children's graves (and perhaps one other), *AA* 1964: 434–5, Abb. 28–30; Bau Z graves, one child's grave and several damaged adult graves, *AA* 1983: 221; *AA* 1984: 32–3.

KRIEZI street: Grave IV, seventh-century with inscription, *AAA* 1 (1968), 26; Archaic grave, XXXII, seventh-century? *AD* 22: 2 (1967), 95; see also *AD* 23: 2 (1968), 67.

KYNOSARGES: seventh-century SubG, Protoattic and 'Orientalising' vases from graves, including the Kynosarges amphora, *BSA* 2 (1895–6), 22–5; *BSA* 12 (1905/6), 80–92; *JHS* 22 (1902), 29–45.

MEIDANIS street: 3 graves, late eighth- or early seventh-century, *AD* 19: 2 (1964), 58–60.

NYMPHAEUM Archaic sanctuary, with possibly some late seventh-century material, *Ergon* 1957: 5–12.

OLYMPIEION PA material, from destroyed graves? *PAE* 1886: 14, pl. 1; *Hesperia* 28 (1959), 251–2; *BCH* 84 (1960), 634.

PARTHENONOS/ROVERTOU GALLI streets (junction of): seventh-century terracottas; shrine? *AD* 21: 2 (1966), 71.

PIRAEUS street 'Dipylon': seventh-century vase? *AM* 17 (1892), 205–8; Grave VIII and seventh-century pithos, *AM* 18 (1893), 115–17, pl. VIII; 134, fig. 30; PA vases, *AD* 17: 2 (1961/2), 22–3; Archaic (seventh-century?) graves, *AD* 21: 2 (1966), 63; grave XVIII with PA amphora and possibly 5 more seventh-century graves, *AD* 23: 2 (1968), 82, pl. 45; Nessos (Athens NM 1002) amphora, from pyre or Opferrinne, *AD* 1890: 4–5; V. Staïs and P. Wolters, *Antike Denkmaler* I.5 (1891), 46–8, pl. 57; Beazley 1956: 4–5.

SAPPHOUS street: child's grave XIV with PA amphora, graves X and XVIII also possibly seventh-century, *AD* 23: 2 (1968), 89–92; seventh-century sherds? *AD* 32: 2 (1977), 27–8.

SYNGROU Avenue: Archaic wall, G (SubG?) sherds, *AD* 20: 2 (1965), 90.

THEOPHILOPOULOU street no. 16: SubG cremation grave, VII, *AD* 23: 2 (1968), 61.

VEIKOU Avenue: G and A sherds, seventh-century? *AD* 25: 2 (1970), 47.

VOULIS/PANEPISTIMIOU streets (junction of): G, A and 'Orientalising' (i.e. seventh-century?) sherds, *AA* 1927: 346–7; *AD* 9 *Parartema* (1924/5), 68–72.

Index II. Attica: seventh-century material from Attica, outside of Athens

ACADEMY: hero shrine of Academos: (i) graves: 8 early seventh-century children's graves, *PAE* 1956: 47–54; other graves (grave 4, etc.), *PAE* 1959: 9–10 and *PAE* 1960: 318–23; grave T.12, cremation? *AD* 17: 2 (1961/2), 20–1. (ii) Ritual deposit? or seventh-century house, *PAE* 1962: 5–11.

AGRILEIKI: seventh-century peak sanctuary with SubG sherds, *PAE* 1935: 154–5; Langdon 1976: 104–5.

ANALATOS: EPA hydria (Athens NM 313) from grave? Böhlau 1887: 34–9; J. M. Cook 1935: pls. 38b, 39.

ANAVYSSOS: (i) SubG vases from tombs, *PAE* 1911: 110–31, esp. 120 and pls. 15–17; (ii) EPA vase, from tomb? J. M. Cook 1935: 188–9, pl. 51c.

ANO VOULA: possible settlement, seventh-century? SubG sherds, *AD* 29: 2 (1973/4), 60.

DRAPHI: seventh-century tombs with EPA and MPA pottery, *BCH* 80 (1956), 246–7; 81 (1957), 517–19; 82 (1958), 681, fig. 23.

ELEUSIS: (i) early excavations, with seventh-century cemetery evidence, *AE* 1885: 169–84, pls. 8–9; *AE* 1898: 29–122, esp. pl. 4; *AE* 1912: 1–39, esp. 5, 32–3, pl. 14 (grave VI); (ii) west cemetery, general: graves gamma 10, 13, 17, 21, 25, 27, 28 and 39; graves delta 7 and 14; graves zeta 9, 10 and 12, lambda 1 and 2, theta 22 and iota 29 (Mylonas 1975); (iii) Polyphemus amphora from grave gamma 6 (Mylonas 1975: 91–2; (iv) sanctuary (Mylonas 1961: 63–76).

HYMETTUS: main peak sanctuary (sanctuary of Zeus Ombrios and Altar of Herakles), with much SubG pottery and a very little PA (Langdon 1976).

HYMETTUS: Hymettus, Prophitis Ilias hill, near Koropi, seventh-century? peak sanctuary, *PAE* 1949: 5–74; *PAE* 1950: 144–72; Langdon (1976: 5–7) does not think that any material is or could be seventh-century.

HYMETTUS: Elimbo, child's skeleton in MPA amphora (Böhlau 1887: 43–4).

KALYVIA KOUVARA: EPA vase from tomb? (J. M. Cook 1935: 177, pls. 44, 45, 46a).

KERATOVOUNI: peak sanctuary with SubG cups (Langdon 1976: 103).

LATHOURESA (near VARI): settlement with SubG and perhaps some PA pottery (Lauter 1985a); *AA* 1940: 177–8.

MARATHON: (i) cemetery, perhaps with SubG vases, *PAE*

1934: 29–38; *PAE* 1939: 27–39 esp. 33, pl. 6; (ii) settlement, perhaps with 'Orientalising' pottery, *AAA* 3 (1970), 14–21 esp. 17, pl. 3; 18, pl. 4.

MEGALO MAVROVOUNI: peak sanctuary, black-glazed and SubG sherds (Langdon 1976: 102).

MENIDHI: 'hero cult' in Mycenaean tholos tomb, with numerous PA vases; for publication of material see Wolters 1899; Callipolitis-Feytmans 1965: 43–65; for further discussion see Whitley 1988: 176 n. 21; Hägg 1987: 94–6; Kenner 1935: 130–4.

MT MERENDA: peak sanctuary, PA and SubG sherds (Langdon 1976: 103).

MERENDA: cemetery (i) LGIIb or early PA vase from grave, *Ergon* 1960: 30–7; (ii) child's? burial in seventh-century relief pithos, *AE* 1969: 217, n. 9.

OLYMBOS: late seventh-century painted funerary plaque from grave? *BSA* 50 (1955), 58.

PHALERON: mixed cemetery (46 children, at least ten seventh-century adult graves, and many undatable adult inhumations without grave goods) with both PA and SubG vases; *BCH* 17 (1893), 25–30, pl. 2, 3; *AE* 1911: 246–56, esp. 246–51; *AD* 2 (1916), 13–64; R. S. Young 1942; Beazley 1956: 7.

PROPHITIS ILIAS: peak sanctuary, with PC aryballoi and 'Phaleron' cups (Langdon 1976: 104).

SOUNION: sanctuaries of Athena and Poseidon: (i) hero cult to Phrontis? (Abramson 1979); (ii) sanctuary deposits, with large numbers of seventh-century 'Oriental' imports including scarabs, etc., *AE* 1917: 168–213.

SPATA: grave groups: (i) 'Orientalising' vases from grave, *AD* 6 (1920–1) *Parartema*, 131–8; (ii) SubG kotyle (J. M. Cook 1947: 147, fig. 6b); (ii) EPA hydria in Vlastos collection, from grave? (J. M. Cook 1935: 177, pls. 46b, 46c).

TAVROS: graves; 3 PA graves and pyres, *AE* 1975: 107–14, 122–49.

THORIKOS: (i) west cemetery, graves T.13, T.50, T.83, T.104, T.87, T.127, T.126, T.128?, T.113, T.111, T.109, T.124, T.137, T.146, T.132, T.151, 16 children's graves (Bingen *et al.* 1965b: 19–29; 1969: 59–86; 1967a: 34–6; 1967b: 42–8, 31–56; 1969: 72–108; 1984: 72–150); (ii) south cemetery, graves T.6, T.10, T.17, T.8, T.7, T.2, T.12 and T.4, 7 children's graves and one adult grave (Bingen *et al.* 1965b: 16–17; 1969: 47–58); (iii) settlement on Velatouri with some PA pottery from 'fill' contexts (Bingen *et al.* 1967b: 9–19; Blondé 1978; van Gelder 1978); (iv) 'hero cult' with offerings in Mycenaean tholos tomb I, with PA but mainly PC and C vases (Bingen *et al.* 1969: 30–4, 37–9).

TRACHONES: graves, at least 15 seventh-century graves, with a minimum of 2 adult cremations and several children's graves, *AM* 88 (1973), 1–54.

TURKOVOUNI: altar of Zeus, seventh-century peak sanctuary with much SubG and very little PA pottery (Lauter 1985b).

VARI north cemetery: seventh-century grave complex with several tumuli, adult? cremations, offering trenches and much PA pottery. The reports from this are very confused, but there seem to be three main deposits: (i) from 'tymvos I', large PA kraters with stands and large PA lekaneis (from graves or offering trenches?); Papaspyridi-Karouzou 1963: 5–14, 15–36; *AA* 1935: 172–5; *AA* 1939: 224–30; *AA* 1940: 126–34; *AJA* 41 (1937), pl. 8; (ii) related deposit from offering trench (Brandopfer), *AA* 1937: 121–4, Abb. 8–12; *AA* 1940: 176; Papaspyridi-Karouzou 1963: 46–9; (iii) vases from graves around (grave groups not reconstructable, although it does include one child's pithos burial), *AA* 1936: 123–5; *AA* 1937: 122–3; *BCH* 61 (1937), 451.

VARI east cemetery: tombs 1–4, 9, 10, 15, 16, 18, 19, 21; probably mainly adult graves with PA and SubG pottery, some (2, 3) with pyres, *AD* 18: 1 (1963), 115–32; *BCH* 109 (1985), 32–47.

VOTANIKOS: (i) Metrodoros and Geminou streets, Archaic graves, seventh-century?; (ii) Prophetou Daniel street, seventh-century settlement evidence? *AD* 33: 2 (1978), 21, 24–5.

VOURVA: late seventh-century grave complex with 7 graves, several tumuli and 2 offering trenches, and much late PA pottery, *AD* 1890: 105–12; *AM* 15 (1890), 318–29.

VRAVRONA (sanctuary of Artemis at Brauron); seventh-century lekythoi and aryballoi; *Ergon* 1959: 13–20; *BCH* 86 (1962), 664–83.

4

The riddle of the Sphinx: a case study in Athenian immortality symbolism

HERBERT HOFFMANN

Ritual and religion are taboo subjects in archaeological circles. Only a perverse few continue their studies in this dangerous field.

(Orme 1981)

In this chapter I examine the British Museum's Sphinx vase from Capua (figs. 4.1–4.8), a remarkable plastic rhyton (drinking vessel) attributed to the Athenian potter Sotades and dated to the middle of the fifth century BC.[1] Much of what I say about this object will make better sense against the background of a fundamental premise: that the thousands of Greek painted vases found in the temples, tombs, houses, wells and rubbish pits of the ancient world represent relatively inexpensive offerings in imitation of objects made of precious metals, the gold and silver plate off which ancient Greeks and Etruscans dined (see Vickers 1985a; 1985b; 1986; 1990a; 1990b; 1990c; Gill, this volume, Hoffmann 1988; forthcoming). I believe that the reason why so much pottery and so little costly metal has been found in excavations of classical Greek and Italian sites lies in a phenomenon first identified and discussed by that remarkable prehistorian Gordon Childe (Childe 1945; cf. Sherratt 1989). Childe argued that as societies evolve and become more sophisticated, grave goods not only fail to keep pace with growing wealth but actually become poorer. As societies evolve they become thrifty; gold and silver tableware are used, melted down, reworked and passed down the generations for heirs to inherit (cf. Parker Pearson 1982, and the alternative approach of Cannon 1989). Among the classical Greeks wealth was no longer conspicuously wasted (buried with the dead) as in barbarian fringe societies such as the Thracians and Scythians. Clay vases and figurines – mere symbols – came to be substituted for *realia*. In the late eighth

century the men of the still poor city-states were occasionally buried with their bronze armour, and women (more often) with their jewellery. In later cemeteries graves become poor as cities become rich (Snodgrass 1980b: 54, 99–100; cf. de Polignac 1984). By the sixth century, Athenian grave furnishings consist almost entirely of pottery and clay figurines – often very beautiful but bearing little or no relation to a dead person's real wealth in life. Burial and votive offerings – both in the temple and the household – were, I am convinced, the primary contexts for the deposition of black- and red-figured Greek pottery and are the *sine qua non* for the understanding of its imagery (see Gill 1988b; Gill and Vickers 1990; Vickers 1990a).

In Athens in this period special legislation was probably passed around 500 BC forbidding not only the destruction of wealth in funerals but also the erection of costly tombstones (Humphreys 1980: 101–2; 1983: 85–7; Vickers 1990a: 111; I. Morris 1992: ch. 5). During the later sixth and much of the fifth century BC vases assumed the functions held earlier (and again in the fourth century) by grave reliefs and funerary epigrams. The shapes of these objects, and often their decoration, evoke the banquet, which throughout antiquity remained the focal nexus connecting mortal man with the gods, the heroes and the dead (Nock 1944; Hoffmann, forthcoming). This, it seems to me, is why the most important function of painted pottery can, like Pindar's poetry, be described as 'the creation of immortality'.

Whereas ethnological and archaeological interpretations of ancient material culture are generally concerned with reconstructing ancient ritual, my interest here is different. My concern in this paper is with investigating passage symbolism on a Greek votive or mortuary offering as a form of symbolic mediation. My theoretical line of departure is Hegel's premise that the purpose of art is to 'reveal truth and represent the reconciliation of contradictions'.

The Sphinx vase I

As Lippold (1952: 89–95) first saw, the London sphinx vase is a ceramic facsimile of a gold and silver rhyton. The metal original, like its 'sister', the Amazon vase in Boston (Hoffmann and Metzler 1990), consisted of two pieces: a sphinx statuette (the stand) and a removable *keras* (the drinking horn). It is unlikely that the pottery version ever actually contained wine, since it is unpainted on the inside. The projecting spout between the sphinx's paws (absent from a second, simplified, version found in the same tomb (Beazley 1963: 870 no. 89) probably represents the tip of the *keras* as a symbolic, vestigial reference to the function of the original as a rhyton (from *ruein*, to flow). I discuss the ritual significance of rhyta and the spouted/spoutless distinction elsewhere (Hoffmann 1989), where I use the expression 'heroic passage' to designate the symbolic importance of the shape.

Description of the plastic form

The sphinx is seated on her haunches on a rectangular plinth. She has the head of a beautiful woman, the taut and sinewy body of a dog or a young lioness and the avian sickle-wings with which vase painters characterised certain supernatural females such as sirens and gorgons. The inscrutable expression on her face is achieved by the dot-in-circle pupils of her eyes, an iconographic convention designating demonic beings. The eyes themselves are framed by lashes in dilute glaze, creating an appearance of wide-eyed, harmless innocence. Her hair is covered by a patterned cloth (*sakkos*) except for a gilt hair roll worn like a diadem over the forehead. Her lips are slightly parted as though she were singing her oracular song (Euripides, *Phoenician Women* 48, 1507). On her breast she wears three gilded gorgon medallions strung on a cord.

The Sphinx as tomb monument

The Sotadean Sphinx is the 'Theban Sphinx' of tragedy (Robert 1915; Simon 1981; 1982). I shall give the story as it is told by Sophocles in *Oedipus Tyrannus* and *Oedipus at Colonus*. King Laios and Queen Jocasta rule over Thebes. Their son Oedipus is exposed to die because an oracle tells Laios that Oedipus will one day kill him. Oedipus survives and is brought up by a shepherd at Corinth. On reaching manhood, Oedipus goes to Delphi to find out who his parents are. He is told by the oracle that he will kill his father and marry his mother. To avoid this fate, he leaves Corinth and on his way to Thebes kills Laios in a supposedly chance encounter (significantly at a crossroads). Arriving in Thebes, he finds the city plagued by the Sphinx, a female monster

who destroys all those who cannot solve her riddle. The hand of the newly widowed queen is promised to anyone who will deliver the city. Oedipus solves the riddle and the Sphinx commits suicide or is killed by him. He marries Jocasta and has four children by her, but upon discovering the true nature of their relationship Jocasta commits suicide and Oedipus blinds himself, thereby attaining supramundane insight (on the relationship between blindness, seeing and understanding in Greek myth, see Sourvinou-Inwood 1989: 164 and n. 113).

But back to the pottery sphinx. The object is a tomb monument in miniature, a token for the marble sphinxes that until their interdiction half a century earlier were mounted on grave stelai in cemeteries throughout Attica (Richter 1961). Where lies the connection between tomb monuments and the myth of the Sphinx? Obviously in the Sphinx's riddle, as we shall presently see. Archaeologists have generally explained the role of these tomb sphinxes as being like that of watchdogs: to 'guard against and punish those who would disturb

the dead' (Vermeule 1979: 171). Their *raison d'être* seems to me to be more complex. Beginning with Freud, the focus of scholarly attention to the Sphinx has been its connection with Oedipus and his myth. With the exception of Bammer (1989), a sense-connection between the myth and the Greek funerary practice of setting sphinxes on tombs has not been drawn (see Moret 1984 for bibliography). To understand why some Greeks placed sphinxes on or in tombs, or painted sphinxes on pots destined for the dead, I feel that the anthropological concept of *boundary* needs to be explained. I shall digress briefly on this subject, drawing on Leach's (1976) theory of taboo.

Leach's underlying premise is that our perceptions of time and space are socially constructed, and that spatial and

4.4 Kekrops and Nike or Iris libating (detail).

4.1–4.3 Sphinx vase by the Sotades Painter. London, British Museum, E 788.

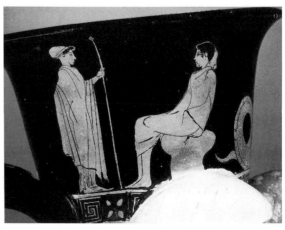

4.5 Aglauros and Erysichthon (detail).

temporal boundaries interrupt the natural space-time continuum with strips of 'no-man's land' and 'no-man's-time'. Being of a paradoxical nature – neither this nor that yet both – boundaries are inevitably sources of conflict. In anthropological terms, the crossing of boundaries from one category, state or status to another, such as from child to adult or from living citizen to ancestor, requires special techniques (rituals) to insure that the transition proceeds smoothly. These are called rites of passage, or transition rituals, the most important being births, initiations or marriages and funerals.

Contact between categories such as 'this world' and 'the other' take place in a middle ground of ambiguous time and space, which functions as a bridge. This is the realm of myth and mythologising imagery with its fantasmal products which commonly straddle and join the categories of animal, human and divine. The myths open a line of communication to the invisible (metaphysical) world which they simultaneously serve to create. By this 'mytho-logic', imaginary creatures (= images) such as sphinxes by virtue of their paradoxical middle-ground characteristics are eminently suited to be mediators between 'worlds'.

The mortuary sphinx, that enigmatic creature with animal, human and super-human features, by mixing up three ontological terms in a single image focuses attention on the interstices between categories. This gives rise to excitement (taboo) because it suggests a confusion of taxonomy – of categories which must normally be kept apart. By referring to, and creating, the betwixt-and-between world of the metaphysical imagination, the Sphinx is communicating in a single enigmatic image that which can only inadequately be expressed in words: that contact with divinity, the ultimate source of power, is exciting but at the same time dangerous,

since it links life with death. The territory the Sphinx occupies is the middle ground, or space of passage, and this is why the mortuary aspect of her nature is stressed in Athenian tragedy (e.g. Sophocles, *Oedipus Tyrannus* 1200–1; Euripides, *Phoenician Women* 1019–66), where her myth is part of the funerary lament.

The Sphinx, however, has another highly disconcerting aspect, which is underscored by the three gorgon masks fastened to her breast. The myth of the gorgon Medusa, it will be recalled, is that she paralyses men with her stare, turning them into stone. Like Medusa, the Sphinx represents death with the face of a woman.

The riddle of the Sphinx

To label the Sotadean Sphinx as a 'symbol of passage' and leave it at that would be too simple. She was, after all, sent by Hera to confront and devastate the Thebans with her riddle (Apollodorus 3.57–8). The riddle is a piece of folklore: 'What is it that has one name that is four-footed, three-footed and two-footed?'. 'Man', replies Oedipus, 'for as an infant he crawls on all four, in his prime he walks upon two,

4.6 Herse and Pandrosos (detail).

4.7 Running satyr (detail).

and in old age he takes a stick as a third foot' (Apollodorus 3.53–4). Athenian vase painters dwell on the enigmatic aspect betokened by the riddle. Take the Oedipus Painter's kylix in the Vatican as an example (Beazley 1963: 451 no. 1). Here the Sphinx is shown perched on her lofty column, a landmark on the road of heroes. Oedipus is seated before her pensively. As Hartwig noticed a century ago, the Sphinx's eyes are half closed: she is in trance. The words *kai tria* – and three' – issue from her mouth (Hartwig 1893: 664). It is well known that in riddles and folktales things often come in threes or happen thrice, three being a magic or sacred number all around the world. In Greece moreover, as still in many cultures, the dead were buried on the third day, called *ta trita*, when offerings of wine were made (Harrison 1903: 288). The celebration which marked the end of mourning seems also to have been called the *trita* (Kurtz and Boardman 1971: 144–6). The Sphinx's speech bubble *kai tria*, while alluding to the third part of her riddle ('three-footed'), appears to have had further content. The number three stands for transition, the overcoming of the duality represented by the number two (cf. Usener 1903; Jeanmaire 1939: 448–9). This may explain not only the deeper meaning

of the Sphinx's riddle but also its connection with Greek initiation and mortuary practice.

The Sphinx as an initiation paradigm

As a reference to the third foot, the infirmity of old age, the Sphinx's terse *kai tria* is obviously a *memento mori*, but it is also more than that. On numerous Athenian vases depicting the Sphinx theme – especially pelikai and column kraters, two shapes commonly used to hold the ashes of the cremated dead – Oedipus is joined or replaced by one or more 'anonymous' youths either standing or seated on rocks or campstools (fig. 4.9). They generally have their mantles drawn over the backs of their heads in a ritual gesture of mourning, expressing readiness to 'die' (Hoffmann 1989; forthcoming). The Theban youths waiting for their doom between the Sphinx's claws are in reality Athenian ephebes, the city's future hoplite warriors, awaiting initiation: 'dying'

4.8 Athena (detail).

4.9 Theban youths before the Sphinx on her pillar. Attic red-figured pelike. Boston Museum of Fine Arts 28.49.

(experiencing the terror of death) in order to be 'reborn' (Moret 1984; La Fontaine 1985: 117–40).

Moret gives many examples of the Sphinx as a paradigm for hoplite initiation in Athenian vase painting, but two are particularly instructive about fifth-century city-state ideology. On a red-figured lekythos in Athens (fig. 4.10; Beazley 1963: 1172 no. 18; Moret 1984: no. 26) and a head-vase in the Metropolitan Museum (Beazley 1963: 1550 no. 6; Moret 1984: no. 27), the Sphinx has snatched a youth from his family and carries him towards an altar. The youth, whose eyes are wide open, is shown abandoning himself unhesitatingly to his fate like a novice during his initiation (cf. La Fontaine 1985). By placing initiatory 'death' in the same semantic category as blood sacrifice, the imagery here imbues initiation with the index of a consecration.

What, then, does initiatory 'death', the temporary dissolution of the ego, have to do with physical death, the permanent dissolution of the body? What logic links

initiation with a funeral and makes the Sphinx into an Athenian mortuary offering? The answers are complex (see Hoffmann 1989). In order to answer both questions fully we must first distinguish between two substantially different categories of initiation prevalent in ancient society. The initiation I have been discussing so far has been the hoplite initiation, the common Athenian rite of passage accomplishing the transition from youth to adult male. Jeanmaire (1939) argued that hoplite initiation was a survival from a tribal ritual, providing the novice with a death experience which transformed him from a fledgling into a fearless warrior who, having experienced the terror of death in life, would not flinch from it in the extremely frightening experience of hoplite battle (see Hanson 1989: 55–104). The military aspect of hoplite initiation was paramount: it was a communal affair of the *polis*. But Athenians also knew of a more esoteric initiation, often undergone during the second half of life. This was more

4.10 Sphinx carrying a youth to an altar. Attic red-figured lekythos by Polion. Athens, National Museum 1607.

4.11 Oedipus, Theban youth and heroes before the Sphinx. Attic red-figured pelike. Vienna, Kunsthistorisches Museum 3728.

private, although it too increasingly became a concern of the state. Mystery initiation (see Burkert 1987) involved what I have called an 'indirect rebirth' experience (Hoffmann 1989), this being the *tekhne* (art or method) of most mystery rites throughout antiquity. Indirect rebirth means passing through the experience of death vicariously, via the death and rebirth of a divinity, which usually involved the ritual re-enactment of a death-rebirth myth.

In the famous ceremony celebrated annually at Eleusis, one's own personal death was assimilated symbolically to the *kathodos* (descent into the underworld) and *anodos* (rising, resurrection) of Persephone, which were in turn patterned on the death and rebirth of vegetable life. For the male citizen, initiation into one or more of the various mystery cults which flourished in Periclean Athens was not without connection to his earlier hoplite initiation, with which it shared a tripartite structure; but a vertical dimension was now added. For the majority of Athenians, mystery initiation may simply have offered pious reassurance, 'the promise of a blessed life beyond the grave', as Nilsson (1948: 155) put it. This may be seen as a denial of death (cf. Becker 1973; *contra*, Garland 1985); but for some it also provided *gnosis*, the mystic or contemplative 'awakening' which Heraclitus (*c.* 500 BC; frag. 62, Diels) called 'living one's death and dying one's life'. What I am suggesting is that a Sphinx as a tomb or a temple offering will, true to her polyvalent nature, have invited at least two basic interpretations.

The picture on a pelike by Hermonax in Vienna (fig. 4.11; Moret 1984: no. 71) neatly illustrates this. Oedipus leaning on his stick listens to the Sphinx sing her oracle, while around the vase seated heroes and standing youths – representatives of the past and present generations – 'witness' the proceedings. The polyvalency of Athenian initiatory imagery is here epitomised in a single eloquent image, bringing us back to the riddle and *kai tria*. The final *telos* of life ('end' or 'outcome', from *teleo*, 'I fulfil') is the *telos thanatoio*, or *telos* of death (as in Homer, *Iliad* 9.416). Initiatory 'dying' provided the core experience for the realisation of this goal, which for fifth-century Athenians was coequal with immortality. The Sotadean Sphinx thus proclaims the time-*less* dimension of reality. Her *ainigma*, or concealment, can also be seen to be the correlate of *aletheia*, 'unconcealment', or revelatory knowledge (Hoffmann 1989).

The Sphinx vase II

Description of the red-figured painted decoration

The two flat, irregularly shaped panels between the sphinx's fore legs and her hind legs each contain a single figure. In the left panel (with the sphinx facing us) a satyr runs along swinging a club. He turns his head to look back and gestures excitedly with his open hand. The right panel shows a girl or a young woman holding a spear. She wears a chiton and a himation and her hair is held in place by a sash. On the bowl above there are three pairs of figures. In front is Kekrops, the legendary first king of Athens, who is shown on no less than five other Athenian rhyta (Webster 1972: 178). Kekrops is identified by his sceptre, by the regal diadem in his carefully groomed hair and by the fact that the lower part of his body has the form of a snake. A winged goddess holding an oinochoe ministers to him. The serpent-king, who supports himself on his lotus-tipped sceptre, holds a *phiale* (libation bowl) for the sacrifice he is about to perform. He has removed his chlamys, folded it and placed it over his shoulder for the occasion. To Kekrops' left, back-to-back with him, a youth, fourteen at most, sits attentively on a rock facing a *parthenos* (unmarried girl) wearing a chiton, a himation and a *sakkos*, proper Athenian dress. She holds a sceptre tipped with a lotus bud, like Kekrops'. The youth is wrapped in a himation and has drawn a corner of it over the back of his head – again, a ritual gesture of mourning. To the right of Kekrops, a running girl with flying hair gestures to a second with the palm of her hand turned up as if urging her to follow. The one wears a sleeveless peplos, the other a chiton and himation. The first has a diadem in her open hair, the second has her hair in a *sakkos*. The hands of the latter are muffled by her garment like those of the seated youth in the scene to the left. These fine distinctions are important.

Kekrops and his children: the myth of autochthony

Although the iconography is unparalleled, the general sense seems clear enough. Kekrops, who was said to have been born from the earth rather than from a woman (Apollodorus 3.14.1), is characterised here, as so often on Athenian vases, as a man above the waist and as a snake – a dangerous animal – below, to emphasise his chthonic nature and to establish him as a being that slips easily between realms. Like the Sphinx, he too is a nature–culture hybrid, his 'serpent form' (Euripides, *Ion* 1163–4) suiting him perfectly for his role as the royal ancestor credited with inventing rites of passage, the city's earliest rituals. The Athenians, sometimes called *Kekropidai* (children of Kekrops) liked to think of Kekrops as their oldest ancestor, and his name is closely linked with the mythological notion of a Golden Age in which men neither worked nor grew old and died (Kron 1976; R. Parker 1986). Kekrops and his race were timeless and therefore deathless, and since no one died there was no need for women's wombs for procreation. Men were autochthonous, 'born of the earth'. Only when Pandora, the common ancestress of all women, opened her jar full of evils (Hesiod, *Theogony* 561–616; *Works and Days* 94–105) did mortality appear. The notion of immortality, then, is linked in Greek thought with the triumph over the female, held to be responsible for death – as in the myth of the Sphinx. It is linked also with denial of the need for sexual reproduction (Phillips 1984: 16–24; W. Shapiro 1988) and in the final analysis with Greek homosexuality. This is the fuller meaning of the myth of Kekrops and of autochthony.

This venerable founder has returned to offer sacrifice – become necessary since the passing of the Golden Age – and preside over the sacred proceedings being acted out in his name. The nature of these proceedings is spelled out by the various figures to the right and the left in the scene. Both the youth and the second running *parthenos* are characterised as initiands by their muffled hands, and he also by his cowled head (Moret 1984: 36; Hoffmann 1989: 81). Kron (1976: 68–70) suggests that the youth might be Erysichthon, Kekrops' only son, the Athenian cult founder who died 'heroically' young. The standing maiden with the sceptre would then be Aglauros, Kekrops' oldest daughter, who, as *kourotrophos* ('in charge of raising young boys') was the patroness of ephebic initiation (Burkert 1985: 244; Vidal-Naquet 1986: 97).

I would tentatively identify the running *parthenoi* with Kekrops' other daughters, Pandrosos (literally 'all-moistening') and Herse ('dew'), nymph-like nocturnal dancers (Euripides, *Ion* 496) who seem like their sister to have been associated with initiation rites (Burkert 1966). In their familiar myth, the daughters of Kekrops were pursued by a serpent (cf. Kaempf-Dimitriadou 1979: no. 266) and driven mad/possessed for their curiosity (Euripides, *Ion* 271–4; Hyginus, *Stories* 166; Pausanias 1.18.2). The wildly excited one with the flying hair seems to be running towards Erysichthon and Aglauros and exhorting her more timid sister to come and have a look.

The neat differentiation of the two running maidens is striking: they form an opposed pair. Whereas the demure one with muffled hands and *sakkos* appears to be a novice, the other is characterised by her open hair as an 'ecstatic female', an initiate who knows and can show the way. Adopting an open, polysemic and beholder-based mode of interpretation, I would suggest that the initiation hinted at in this scene – pendant to the initiation of Erysichthon on the other side of Kekrops – should be read as being of an ecstatic, orgiastic kind (Martino 1976: 204–8; Bremmer 1984; Bérard and Bron 1986; 1989).

If *thanatos kalos*, the 'good death' in war, was the ideal destination of every youth as a future hoplite, the corresponding *telos* of every *parthenos* was to marry and produce male offspring in order that the ranks might be closed again

(e.g. Thucydides 2.46). Daughters must leave their families, sons replace their fathers (Vernant 1980: 45–70). Here the paradox of Kekrops, the incarnation of autochthony, being simultaneously the inventor of marriage (Vidal-Naquet 1986: 216), moves into the foreground. Whereas hoplite initiation was the obligatory passage ritual for boys marking their entry into the community, nothing quite comparable existed for girls, since marriage was for the Athenian female what war was for the male (Vidal-Naquet 1986: 129–56, esp. 146; Dowden 1988; *contra*, Sourvinou-Inwood 1986; cf. also Brulé 1987). Marriage is not, however, referred to directly in this scene. Instead, it is characterised by the spirited female ebullience which in Athenian red-figured vase painting in this period usually betokens maenadic activity. Ought we perhaps to think of the wild-haired Kekropid as the leader of a maenadic thiasos? The iconography is vague, perhaps deliberately so, but as Bremmer (1984) points out, maenadism with its temporary experience of ecstasy fits well with several other female rites of vaguely initiatory character which all share the function of reconciling women to their dull and isolated marital lives. Her closest parallels in the Sotades Painter's work are the ecstatic women on his London astragalos (fig. 4.12; Beazley 1963: 765, no. 20; Hoffmann 1986: 180).[2]

The winged goddess can be called either Nike or Iris (Beazley (1963) often uses the names interchangeably). These are the winged females most commonly represented in the company of gods and heroes on Greek vases, sometimes with their names inscribed. Both act as mediators or messengers of the gods; Iris perhaps because the rainbow to which her name refers creates a bridge between the earth and the sky, Nike ('victory') heralding the fame of Kekrops (thus Webster 1972: 178) but referring also to initiation as a *telos*, a victory over death. Whether Iris or Nike, the presence of the winged goddess creates divine reality and underscores the importance of the events depicted. The libation poured by Kekrops will seal, or confirm, the sacred rites referred to by the imagery. Representing the theological principle of generation (Harrison 1912: 261–75), Kekrops appears here in his full splendour as an Athenian Abraham, the spirit of *palingenesia*, or 'life back again'. The ceremony he and the winged goddess are performing now comes into focus as the point of convergence of a cluster of signs and symbols. Like every sacrifice, whether of flesh or of a substitute such as wine, libation separates the pure from the impure and involves a death and a rebirth in a new form (Burkert 1985: 70–3). The focal act of libation here links the visible and the invisible worlds and brings the past and the future together in the nexus of present ritual action spelling immortality.

These tentative suggestions seem to be supported by the figures on the sphinx's base: the female spear-bearer and the running satyr. The former can only be Athena, who may be seen here in the role of Parthenos (virgin), or (depending on the beholder's ideological orientation) Phratria, who was worshipped during the feast of Apatouria at the conclusion of the hoplite initiation rite (Plato, *Euthydemos* 302D). Apatouria was also the Athenian confirmation festival at which the year's newly initiated young men and the newly married young women were entered into the phratry lists, thereby confirming the young in their new status in life: the males ready for military service, the *parthenoi* for marriage and childbirth. Whether as Parthenos or as Phratria, Athena would be representing the citizen's obligation to the city.

The running and gesticulating satyr informs us that Dionysos is nearby (reminding us that the myth of Kekrops and his children is part of a larger cycle including Theseus, Ariadne and Dionysos, as well as Oedipus (Lévi-Strauss 1963: 213–18)). The Dionysian satyr-reference would seem to be the chthonic and mystic (Eleusinian) aspect of the god, amply attested by Aristophanes in his comedy *The Frogs* (Jeanmaire 1978: 387–8; Segal 1961). The club-swinging satyr may thus be parodying Heracles, the prototypical mystery initiate. In this context, we should also remember Kekrops' Eleusinian connection (Moret 1984: 164). His daughter Herse mothered Keryx, one of the two founders of Eleusis. Athena could then be read alternatively as representing the close connection of Eleusis with the Athenian *polis* (Athena = Athens). But here we are on less safe ground.

Recapitulating: we have described the Sotadean Sphinx (the object's plastic form) as an anomalous third term, a mediating bridge connecting this world with the Other. In Greek mythology such bridges are also created by the hero-ancestors, who manage, by an elision of metaphor and metonymy, to be human and divine at the same time. Kekrops (the object's red-figure decoration) is an example of such elision. As a god-man, he takes on liminal attributes analogous to those of the Sphinx. Kekrops and the Sphinx together open the way to movement across borders. Immortalising imagery is seen as being complementary to ritual action. In this wider anthropological perspective there is no hiatus between the shape and the painting of the Sotadean rhyton. Quite the contrary: they move together!

Appendix

As mentioned above, the myth of Kekrops and his children is part of a larger cycle that includes Oedipus and the Sphinx. The juxtaposition of the Sphinx and Kekrops, in other words, has a further ideological dimension, and Lévi-Strauss in his brief exposition of the Oedipus myth (1963: 206–31) penetrated to the bottom of their deeper connection. The official religious doctrine of the Athenians says that man is autochthonous, and that Kekrops, the first king, grew out of the soil like a plant. This created a problem:

> The myth has to do with the inability of a culture which holds the belief that mankind is autochthonous to find a satisfactory transition between this theory and the knowledge that human beings are actually born from the union of a man and woman. Although the problem obviously cannot be solved, the Oedipus myth provides a kind of logical tool which relates the original problem – born from one or born from two? – to the derivative problem – born from different or born from the same? (Lévi-Strauss 1963: 216)

In this perspective, the contradiction addressed by the imagery of the Sphinx and of Kekrops and his children can be considered as the affirmation of official ideology (Kekrops, autochthony) and simultaneously its denial. Whereas Lévi-Strauss' analysis of the Oedipus myth unfortunately remains a fragment, it is a tribute to this great scholar that his general argument is clearly so consistent with the evidence of the Sotades Painter's Sphinx vase as it has been presented in this paper.

On Lévi-Strauss' analysis of Oedipus and the Sphinx see especially Edmunds 1983 and Spencer 1990. As Edmunds points out in his Proppian folkloristic analysis: 'For Lévi-Strauss overcoming the sphinx is reduced to a denial of autochthony, and the riddle solving has practically no significance.' Peradotto (1983) offers an insightful re-analysis of Oedipus à la Lévi-Strauss.

Vernant 1989, containing astute observations on sphinxes and other female killers, was not available to me at the time of writing; cf. also D. Williams 1992.

4.12 Shaman and thiasos. Astralagos by the Sotades Painter. London, British Museum E 804.

Postscript

My thinking about 'the function of Athenian vases in Athenian social action' (Morris, this volume) proceeds along two paths. The one is pragmatic; it is connected with the concrete function(s) of Athenian black- and red-figured pottery referred to at the beginning of this paper. The other, founded on the empirical basis of function, is concerned with content ('meaning'). I am interested in exploring the symbolism of Attic vase imagery as mediating the structural contradictions inherent in Athenian society. This of course implies studying Attic vases in the context of Greek religion. I am interested, finally, in seeing what sense can be made of the painters' *jeux d'images*. Geertz's 'thick description' (1973: 3–30) comes close to approximating my own method: observing the intricate interweaving of plot and counterplot with the aim of drawing large conclusions from small, but very densely textured facts. The three cardinal questions posed by the Sphinx vase – 'Where do I come from?', 'Who am I', 'Where am I going?' – therefore form part of a discourse of contemporary relevance.

Further to my method: I work outward from the iconographic analysis of details and simultaneously inward from the matrix of religious, social and historical context. As my inquiry progresses, I increasingly focus and limit, and at some point my interpretation gels into a logical synthesis of foreground and background. This is essentially a *Gestalt* approach to iconology, corresponding to the outlook propagated in academic psychology by Wertheimer, Koehler, Arnheim and others, and in art history by Panofsky (1955). *Gestalt*, for which there is no adequate term in English, is approximated by 'meaningful organised whole'. As Arnheim (1969) puts it: 'We don't see three isolated points, we make a triangle out of them.' I might add that I am less interested in 'getting it right all along the line' than in opening up Greek vase imagery to further and deeper exploration. If this paper goes some way to counteract the current devaluation of ritual and religion in the field of archaeology due to 'Western culture's schizophrenia concerning its own ritual life' (Orme 1981: 219), my purpose will have been served. It is not that initiations and funerals go entirely unnoticed in modern life; it is simply that the specialist and secular bias characteristic of mainstream contemporary academics has banished the study of passage rites as a respectable field for archaeological inquiry. Ritual and religion, it is felt by many, are best left to theologians.

In dealing with the complex passage symbolism of a single Attic vase, understood as being part of the 'total burial assemblage' that includes the funeral rite of passage (I. Morris 1992), I hope to have drawn attention to an important aspect of Attic vases hitherto ignored: their vital function as part of the Athenian immortalising system. Owing to the frequent structural mutuality of their imagery with sacrificial and mortuary ritual, the vases of the age of Pericles – regardless of whether they were employed as votive offerings or as grave goods – contribute substantially to the creation of symbolic immortality (Hoffmann 1988; 1989; forthcoming).

Acknowledgements

This paper draws on research for my forthcoming book on Sotadean imagery which was supported by a generous grant from the Deutsche Forschungsgemeinschaft (DFG). My thanks are due to Brian Cook, Lucilla Burn and Dyfri Williams for their kind assistance and for supplying the necessary photographs, and to Ian Morris for his comments on an earlier draft.

Notes

1 Lippold 1952: 89–90, fig. 11; Beazley 1963: 764, no. 8 (Sotades Painter, Kekrops and Nike, with two women (daughters of Kekrops?)); Kron 1976: 93–4, pl. 11 (Kekrops with Nike or Iris; Erysichthon with his mother or sister; the Kekropids); D. Williams 1988: 44–6, fig. 50e; Lexicon Iconographicum Mythologiae Classicae I: pl. 213, 29 (Aglauros).

2 I will return to maenadism and what Vidal-Naquet (1986: 217) characterises as the 'exclusion of women from the body politic' in my forthcoming book on Sotadean imagery.

5
Looking on – Greek style. Does the sculpted girl speak to women too?

ROBIN OSBORNE

The visitor to a Greek sanctuary or cemetery in the sixth century BC will have come face to face with sculpted images of women, both mortal women and goddesses. The visitor to a Greek sanctuary two centuries later will also have confronted statues of females. But the sculpted women of the fourth century looked very different from those of the sixth. The changes in the style of sculptures during these two centuries have been much discussed, but they have been discussed very largely from the formal point of view, with the stylistic features of one period represented as the natural result of the development of the stylistic features and trends of the preceding period. But the communication which a work of art makes with the viewer is a communication in which the style plays as large a part in the message as the 'content', for it is the style as much as the content which determines the viewer's response.[1] In this paper I want to bring back the viewer and examine the changing images of women in sculpture from the point of view of women. What image of women do these sculptures present to the male and to the female viewer? How do the stylistic differences between the sculptures affect the image projected?

The sculpted goddess

I want to start with the most famous of all statues in antiquity: Praxiteles' Aphrodite of Knidos, carved in the middle of the fourth century BC (fig. 5.1). There are two reasons for starting with this piece: first, 'In the Aphrodite of Knidos, whether or not there were other naked Aphrodites before her in classical art, there can be no doubt that Praxiteles created something profoundly new: a figure designed from start to finish, in proportion, structure, pose, expression to illustrate an ideal of the feminine principle'

(Robertson 1975: 391). This is a statue seen by classical art historians as a radically new image. The second reason for choosing this piece is that we possess abundant testimony on the reaction of viewers in antiquity to it. Several of these viewers are separated by four hundred years or more from the sculpting of this statue, and they cannot be taken as guides to contemporary reaction, but they do give us reactions from viewers who, unlike ourselves, had not been trained in the artistic values of the Renaissance, and whose reactions to female sexuality were unaffected by the Christian tradition. These two advantages outweigh, for my purposes, the disadvantages caused by the loss of the original statue, so that our own reactions have to be based on Roman copies of the work.

From the various ancient comments on the Aphrodite I will quote three: an epigram ascribed to the philosopher Plato (if genuine then fourth-century BC); an account by the ancient encyclopaedist Pliny the Elder (first-century AD) and a fictional piece included with the *belles-lettres* of Lucian (second-century AD).

First, the epigram:

> Paphian Kythereia came through the waves to Knidos
> Wanting to see her own image.
> She gazed all round in an open space and
> Said: Where did Praxiteles see me naked?
> Praxiteles did not see what he should not, but
> The iron carved such a Paphian goddess as Ares desired!
> (Page 1976: Plato xxv.
> Cf. *Palatine Anthology* 16.159–63, 165–70)

Second, Pliny:

> There are works of Praxiteles in the Ceramicus at Athens, but before all the works not only of Praxiteles but all in the whole world is the Venus which many men have sailed to Knidos in order to see. Praxiteles made two statutes of Venus and sold them at the same time, the other of clothed appearance, which the Coans, who had the choice, preferred against it, when he had offered them at the same price, because they judged it serious and modest: the Knidians bought the one the Coans rejected and it has had a very different fame. Later King Nicomedes wanted to buy her from the Knidians, promising that he would pay off the whole of the city's debt, which was huge, but they preferred to endure everything, and not without reason, for Praxiteles ennobled Knidos by that image. The whole of its small temple is open, so that the likeness, which, it is believed, was made with the goddess's favour, can be seen from every side. The same wonder is provoked by every view. They say that one man, seized with love, when he had

hidden himself in the night, grasped the statue and that a spot marks his desire. (*Natural History* 36.20–1)

Third [Lucian]:

When we had enjoyed the plants to our fill we entered into the temple. The goddess is sited in the middle, a most beautiful artistic work of Parian marble, smiling a little sublimely with her lips parted in a laugh. Her whole beauty is uncovered, she has no clothing cloaking her and is naked except in as far as with one hand she non-chalantly conceals her crotch. The craftsman's art has been so great as to suit the opposite and unyielding nature of the stone to each of the limbs. Kharikles, indeed, shouted out in a mad and deranged way, 'Happiest of all gods was Ares who was bound for this goddess', and with that he ran up and stretching his neck as far as he could kissed it on its shining lips. But Kallikratidas stood silently, his mind numbed with amazement.

The temple has doors at both ends too, for those who want to see the goddess in detail from the back, in order that no part of her may not be wondered at. So it is easy for men entering at the other door to examine the beautiful form behind. So we decided to see the whole of the goddess and went around to the back of the shrine. Then, when the door was opened by the keeper of the keys, sudden wonder gripped us at the beauty of the woman entrusted to us. Well, the Athenian, when he had looked on quietly for a little, caught sight of the love parts of the goddess, and immediately cried out much more madly than Kharikles, 'Herakles! What a fine rhythm to her back! Great flanks! What a handful to embrace! Look at the way the beautifully delineated flesh of the buttocks is arched, neither too wanting and drawn in too close to the bones themselves, nor allowed to spread out excessively fat. No one could express the sweetness of the smile of the shape impressed upon the hips. How precise the rhythms of thigh and shin extending right straight to the foot! Such a Ganymede pours nectar sweetly for Zeus in heaven! For I wouldn't have received a drink if Hebe had been serving.' As Kallikratidas made this inspired cry, Kharikles was virtually transfixed with amazement, his eyes growing damp with a watering complaint . . . (*Amores* 13–14)

[Lucian] continues with the story of the young man who made love to the statue.

I want to draw attention to three features of these accounts. First, that the statue is said to induce an overtly sexual thrill in the viewer. This is seen not only in the anecdote of the young man leaving his mark on history, told by Pliny and [Lucian], but also in the reaction of the imaginary party visiting the temple in [Lucian]'s essay. Second, the high priority on seeing the statue from all round. Pliny states that the statue was so placed as to be seen from every side, in strong contrast to what was usually the case with a cult statue, and [Lucian]'s story, although implying that in fact it could not be seen from *every* side, stresses the special lengths to which the Knidians had gone to make the back as well as the front visible (compare *Palatine Anthology* 16.169.1). Third, the conviction that Praxiteles must have used a model; as well as the epigram cited, other writers claim that the statue was modelled on a mistress of Praxiteles', although they disagree about the identity of the mistress (Phryne in Athenaios 590, Kratine in Poseidippos [Jacoby 1925–58: 447 F1]).

What is it about the statue that calls forth these reactions? Neither the fact of nakedness (there were other naked female statues by the time of Pliny and [Lucian]) nor the skill in carving (about which we can only speculate with the original lost) are likely to be sufficient. Account needs also to be taken of the pose. Modern scholars have felt that Aphrodite's pose, and in particular what she is doing with her right hand, needs to be explained. 'The lifting of the drapery from the vessel and the movement of the other hand imply that the goddess has been washing and did not mean to be seen naked. It is noteworthy that at all periods of Greek art, when women are shown without clothes their nakedness is motivated: it is a situation where nudity is natural . . . The convention, one of the most characteristic and influential of Greek art by which a man can be shown naked in any action or context without regard to practice or probability, is never extended to the representation of women' (Robertson 1975: 392). 'Even in the fourth century, when prejudice had become relaxed, Praxiteles felt obliged to justify the nudity of the Knidia by the suggestion that she was preparing to bathe' (Carpenter 1960: 216). Or, for the right hand: 'The missing right hand covered the crotch, an action that was accepted as the automatic result of modesty: it is exaggerated into a self-conscious coyness in later Aphrodites' (Lawrence and Tomlinson 1983: 189–90); 'The right hand is brought across in front of the pudenda – a gesture that from repetition now seems prudish or banal, though here there is no hint of self-consciousness' (R. M. Cook 1972b: 137).

The scholars' story is that the representation of the female body was generally taboo, and was acceptable only if realistically 'motivated' (but the claimed explanation of the taboo in K. Clark 1956: 65 is fantasy). At the same time, however, that the publication of the naked female body is deemed to have been acceptable if it reproduces the scenes in which the private female would have been naked, it is felt necessary to have this statue acknowledge that it is public, not private, by the gesture of the right hand.

If we examine further the mismatch between the representation of men and the representation of women, which Robertson points to, it becomes clear that the simple story of taboo and modesty will not do (cf. Pollock 1987a: 50–90). Not only is it common to have the male represented naked without regard to plausible context, but it is actually not at all normal, whether in sculpture or on pots, to have the male represented naked in those situations in which he would privately have appeared naked, or indeed to have the male represented in private, domestic, space at all. Try to find a *man* washing or bathing (as opposed to oiling himself in the gymnasium). The only interior spaces in which men are regularly represented are the workshop (a public space) and the symposion, but symposion scenes are closely related to scenes of outdoor revelling. Men do appear in indoor scenes when they are shown with women (Webster 1972: ch. 16). Broadly speaking, two things can be said of the *classical* sculpted man: that he is a public actor, and that he does not acknowledge the presence of the viewer. As far as sculpted men are concerned, we are anonymous spectators who happen to have glanced their way but who can make no demands on their attention. The sculpted girl, by contrast, inhabits a different world, a world which includes private space as well as public, and indeed the public contexts in which women are shown tend to be very restricted (Webster 1972: ch. 17; Bérard 1989a). The contrasting presentation of mortal men and mortal women comes out very starkly from the Athenian grave reliefs of the fourth century BC: men are shown in public roles (as soldiers, athletes and so on) and in an explicitly public or indeterminate space, or occasionally on the threshold of the domestic space; women are shown in explicitly private space and engaged in domestic roles (Friis Johansen 1951). With goddesses the situation is different. Seeing any god was a potentially dangerous experience for a mortal, and to see a god when that god did not want to be seen was something which, if possible at all, brought a heavy punishment. Sculptures of gods and goddesses thus re-present a highly charged moment, the epiphany of the deity, and they represent the deity as that deity chooses to present itself.

But where does Praxiteles' Knidian Aphrodite stand with respect to these conventions? Both ancient and modern commentators agree that Aphrodite is engaged in the private activity of bathing, but that the gesture of the right hand acknowledges that a viewer has intruded into that public space. Thus, in as far as this is a private scene, Aphrodite is represented as a woman, but in as far as she acknowledges the spectator she is represented as a goddess. The merging of the artistic conventions thus presents a goddess, but one seen as a woman might be seen; this is the sculptural equivalent of the narrative of the goddess surprised bathing which is

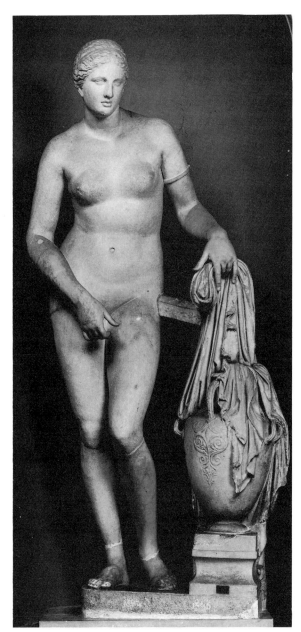

5.1 Praxiteles, Aphrodite of Knidos. Copy of original of mid-fourth century BC. Vatican Museum.

manifested in a number of myths, invariably with drastic consequences for the viewer (e.g. Antoninus Liberalis, *Metamorphoses* 17.5; Kallimakhos, *Hymn* 5; Photius 1466–7a). The viewer of the sculpture is put in the fantasy position of being able to see Aphrodite naked with impunity: Praxiteles represents the unpresentable.

But Praxiteles' Aphrodite does far more than simply exploit the productivity of the clash between the conventional representation of women and the conventional representation of a goddess. For at the same time that it invites the construction of a narrative it gives no particular purchase to any particular narrative. Is Aphrodite about to bathe or has she bathed? Modern scholars disagree without appearing to notice the fact (Robertson 1975: 392; Carpenter 1960: 216; Charbonneaux *et al.* 1972: 211). Have we surprised the goddess, or was she in fact preparing to receive us? Is the metonymic urn to be filled, full or empty?

That the viewer cannot resist completing, or trying to complete, a narrative for this Aphrodite can be seen not only from the amatory response of the characters in the ancient stories but also from modern scholarly observations. 'From the full front the hand conceals the junction of belly and thighs, but again the least movement reveals it' (Robertson 1975: 392). Or Kenneth Clark in a long comparison of the relation between viewer and sculpted goddess in the Knidian and Capitoline Aphrodites:

> Approach the Knidian from the direction to which her gaze is directed, her body is open and defenceless; approach the Capitoline and it is formidably enclosed. This is the pose known to history as the Venus Pudica, the Venus of Modesty, and although the Capitoline is more carnally realistic than the Knidian and the action of her right hand does nothing to conceal her magnificent breasts, a formal analysis shows that the title has some justification. We can see why in later replicas this attitude was adopted when the more candid nudity of Praxiteles would have given offence (K. Clark 1956: 79)

As the modern critic feels obliged to move round the statue, to occupy the position of the object seen by the goddess as well as to look on as a third-party spectator of the goddess' surprise, so also the imaginary characters of [Lucian]'s story feel themselves obliged to see the statue from all round. The result of this becomes very clear from [Lucian]: the goddess of whom a glance is stolen, before whom the stupor of fright and love is the only possible response, to whom love must be made, successively as the viewer adopts changing positions before her, is fragmented and reduced to 'love parts' as she is encircled. This is the incomprehensibility of beauty enacted, destroying the possibility of any present narrative. As Roland Barthes saw:

'Beauty (unlike ugliness) cannot really be explained: in each part of the body it stands out, repeats itself, but it does not describe itself. Like a god (and as empty), it can only say: *I am what I am*. The discourse, then, can do no more than assert the perfection of each detail and refer "the remainder" to the code underlying all beauty: Art. In other words, beauty cannot assert itself save in the form of a citation' (Barthes 1975: 33). But Kallikratidas' response in [Lucian] is not just the reaction of a particular mortal to an encounter with, as it were, the Platonic 'Idea' of the beautiful: it is also an essentially sexual response. For the Athenian's fragmentation of Aphrodite's body is part of his attempt to comprehend the female body in terms of the male: his cry arises only when he can pretend that this is a young boy lover that he has before him, that this is a Ganymede. In Freudian terminology this is a classic case of the fetishism of the female form: 'Parts of her body are taken out of context and made to function both as erotic thrills and threatening dangers for the male viewer' (Pollock 1987b: 242; cf. Pollock 1987a: 120–54; Mulvey 1987).

Clark wrote of the Knidian Aphrodite that 'beyond the geometrical harmony, there is, in her whole bearing, a harmonious calm, a gentleness even, much at variance with the amatory epigrams which she inspired' (K. Clark 1956: 76). I have tried to show, by contrast, that it is precisely the delicacy with which she is posed that created the amatory epigrams. But if that is true, then it must also be clear that the viewer whom I have in the above account struggled to keep sexless, is assumed to be male. Aphrodite may be the first female nude in Greek sculpture, but she is already centrally placed in the tradition of the Western nude: 'Her body is arranged in the way it is, to display it to the man looking at the picture. This picture is made to appeal to *his* sexuality' (Berger 1972: 55, of Bronzino's *Allegory of time and love*).

But we should resist Berger's further move in implying that because the female nude of art and the girlie pin-up both offer up their femininity to be surveyed they belong to the same category. Praxiteles' goddess does not feed the male appetite in at all a straightforward way. This is in part a matter of Aphrodite being in a very strong sense a sculpture in the round: placed as a cult statue in a temple the official view of the statue is certainly the full-frontal one, but placed in such a way as to be seen all round it is in fact up to the viewer which position he adopts, and as he adopts a particular position so he opens up or forecloses the possible narratives. 'Pin-up and softcore pornography's interest in the female body is confined to a small repertoire of parts – those which mark the woman as feminine, not-male, different' (A. Kuhn 1985: 38), but Knidian Aphrodite allows the viewer, like Kallikratidas in [Lucian], to make his own selection. According as he adopts a position the viewer is, or is not, the viewed person who has called forth the 'gesture of modesty', he is viewer or voyeur; Aphrodite smiles for him or at him or both; and so on. Both actor and observer, not simply in turn but at the same time, the viewer finds himself and his male appetite, his male sexuality, framed. Before this goddess (who is not as unselfconscious as Cook imagines, from some points of view not unselfconscious at all) the viewer becomes himself self-conscious; for as he occupies the position of the viewed, the object of Aphrodite's gaze, so he becomes the actor observed by the viewer who watches the drama from the full-frontal position. The invitation to drama is clearly seen in the way in which [Lucian] has the Aphrodite seen by a *group*. This is not a statue at which you can gaze in private.

Rich though the message of this statue is about male sexuality, it has very little to say about female sexuality. What separates Aphrodite from the Page 3 girl also stops her saying anything to women. The Page 3 girl may invite female 'sexual enjoyment, sexual freedom and active participation in heterosexual activity' (Holland 1987: 111), but this statue does not. That Robertson could call this statue an illustration of 'the ideal of the feminine principle' is indicative of the way in which the 'feminine principle' is constructed by male desire.[2]

Praxiteles' Aphrodite is an uncommonly powerful work, but is it breaking new ground as Robertson claimed? In an attempt to answer this question I want to look at two more sculptural representations of goddesses, one an architectural relief and the other a cult statue. The architectural relief is part of the balustrade put up around the temple of Athena Nike on the acropolis at Athens in the 410s, and it shows Nike, the divine personification of Victory, adjusting her sandal (fig. 5.2). No ancient reactions to this work survive, but here is the account of Jerome Pollitt (1972: 115–18):

> The most conspicuous example of the new style is found in the reliefs of the parapet which surrounded the graceful little Ionic temple of Athena Nike on the Acropolis. These reliefs, which ran around three sides (north, west, and south) of the bastion on which the temple stood, depicted Nikai (Victories) erecting trophies and bringing forward sacrificial bulls in the presence of Athena, whose seated figure appears three times on the frieze (one on each side). The expressive effect of the Nikai was created almost wholly by the carving of their drapery. Smooth surfaces where the drapery is pressed against the body, revealing the anatomy beneath it, are contrasted with deep swirling furrows created by the use of a running drill. The relief medium enabled the sculptors to carry these furrows beyond the surface of the body itself, creating patterns of line and of light and

shade which were totally independent of anatomical structure and could be elaborated for their own sake. The impression the Nikai give of being calligraphic designs quite as much as sculptural figures is further reinforced by their often arbitrary and only vaguely functional actions. The pose of the 'Nike adjusting her sandal', for example, strikes one as a formal device designed to provide a semi-circular pattern in which the sculptor could give a virtuoso's display of his ability to vary the texture of the drapery in a series of parallel ridges; and the animated Nike from the north side of the parapet who is enwrapped in a beautiful flourish of waving furrows seems to lay her hand on the head of the adjacent bull only as a token of duty. In these sculptures ornamental beauty has become an end in itself and to a great degree has usurped the role of meaning or 'content' in the

5.2 Athena Nike temple balustrade relief panel, Athenian acropolis, late fifth century BC. Acropolis Museum, Athens.

specific narrative sense. It is true that they do have a general overall theme – victory, and that the Nikai may be thought of as engaged in a very casual processional movement towards Athena, but compared to the Parthenon frieze where each group of figures was planned so as to contribute through both its form and meaning to a single great design and subject, the parapet seems almost aimless. The very fact that Athena appears thrice, like an ornamental motif, seems to say that the subject is just for show and that it is the ornamental function which counts. The Nikai perform a beautiful ballet, but the choreography seems designed to divert one from giving too much thought to the question of just what the dance is about.

Leaving aside, here, the claim that form and content are separated in these reliefs, I want to concentrate on Pollitt's contention that the sculptor was only interested in the calligraphic design, the Nikai simply constituting a frame on which this is hung. The Nike adjusting her sandal provides the most appropriate framework for this consideration since she is the only figure whose action can truly be said to be gratuitous. But what is her action? She is traditionally known as the Nike Sandalbinder, but others refer to her as Nike *un*tying her sandal (Woodford 1986: caption to fig. 209). Nor will the neutral 'adjusting her sandal' do: the truth is that the sculpture does not make explicit the action. Still less does it make explicit the motive. As soon as we ask *why* Nike is taking off/putting on/adjusting her sandal we raise the further question of what this Nike was doing before, and what she is about to do. And to answer, or try to answer, this question is to attempt to construe the sculpture.

Any such attempt immediately involves the viewer not in admiring the calligraphic design of the drapery, but in trying to read the actions of the body beneath the drapery. But for all that the clinging drapery has been called 'a transparent veil over what is in effect a female nude' (Robertson 1975: 391), the body here will not construe and the drapery cannot be removed. The lower part of the body is effectively in profile or close to it, while the upper part of the torso is close to being frontal. Not only does the drapery mask the very awkward transition involved here by masking the position of the left hip, but it also renders initially credible the combination of an almost upright back with breasts aligned at an angle of 45° (with the result that the right breast is improbably close to the right thigh) and the fact that if you put the right leg down on the ground it proves longer than the left.

Is the impossibility of construing this relief a product of incompetence? Is it proof that the pattern was all that the sculptor was interested in? Perhaps, but another explanation is worth canvassing. What the semicircular patterns of the drapery folds, and what the unreally small distance between breasts and right thigh, do is create a focus to the composition, and this focus is not upon the binding or unbinding of the sandal, nor is it upon the now missing head: it is precisely upon the 'junction of belly and thighs' which is also the area most deeply concealed in dark pools of shadow and multiple folds of cloth. Like it or not, viewers find their attention focused upon a female body which cannot be construed. Here is a Victory which eludes the male viewer; desire is tended and cultivated and representation is (a)voided. This is 'a radically dehiscent image whose construction further disintegrates the longer one examines it' (Bryson 1984: 175 of Ingres' Grande Odalisque, to which I owe a considerable debt here). As with Praxiteles' Aphrodite, so with this relief the viewer is framed, and here that framing takes the form of constructing a promise that this winged victory can be real, can be sited in the life in which sandals are removed and put on again, and then of having that promise necessarily unfulfilled. The convention that in a man's world of war Victory should be represented as a woman is here put under close scrutiny as both what representation is and what Victory is are questioned.

But if Praxiteles' nude cult statue of Aphrodite and the relief of Nike fiddling with her sandal can both be seen to play upon male desire, male sexuality, and male expectations and values, and to say nothing to women, what of the most important new cult image in classical Athens, the cult statue of Athena Parthenos by Pheidias in the Parthenon (fig. 5.3)? Although again we know this statue only from later copies, these make it very apparent that we are dealing with a statue of a very different kind from either of those we have looked at so far. It differs in scale (it was colossal), in material (it was made of gold and ivory), and in the complexity of the iconography: not only did Athena have griffins and a sphinx on her helmet, a gorgon on her breast, a victory on her outstretched hand, and a snake by her feet, but her shield had scenes of Amazons fighting on the outside, of gods and giants fighting on the inside, her sandals had scenes of lapiths and centaurs fighting, and the base of the statue showed the birth of Pandora. Moreover, the viewer was prepared for his encounter with the goddess by the sculptures of the temple as a whole (Osborne 1987b).

This is not the place to attempt to unravel the complex of ideas explored by this monument, but a few general points can be brought out. Although known as the statue of Athena Parthenos, it is not Athena's maidenly qualities but her involvement in the warlike activity of men that is stressed by the accumulation of scenes and symbols of war. From top to bottom it is Athena's participation in the male world of martial combat that is brought out, with two motifs excepted:

the Gorgon on Athena's breast and the scene of Pandora on the base. Since Freud's classic analysis of the gorgon Medusa, the sexual connotations of the gorgon do not need to be emphasised (Freud 1977: 351; cf. Napier 1986: 83–134). The story of Perseus' decapitation of Medusa enacts male fears of being unmanned in the encounters of war and in encounters with women, and the not uncommon

5.3 Athena Parthenos. Miniature copy of second century AD of Pheidias' chryselephantine cult statue of the 430s BC. National Museum, Athens.

practice of having a gorgon's head blazon on one's hoplite shield turns this threat onto the enemy. But worn on her breast by Athena, the gorgon's head acquires a new charge. Athena may offer Victory, but she does not thereby remove the dangers of war or change the stakes involved.

This challenge not to forget Athena's own sexuality is reinforced by the presentation of the birth of Pandora on the statue base. Pausanias, in his description of the statue, notes this in the following way: 'The birth of Pandora is worked on the base of the statue. Hesiod and others have written in their poems that Pandora was the first woman to be born' (Pausanias 1.24.7). Pliny seems to have said that the birth was shown with twenty gods present (Pliny, *Natural History* 36.18 reads 'There are twenty gods being born', but this is manifest nonsense and straightforward emendation gives the sense 'Twenty gods are present at the birth'), and from models of the Athena Parthenos and a neo-Attic relief in Rome it seems that the base presented a central frontal figure of Pandora flanked by standing and sitting deities with the rearing chariot team of Helios at one end and the departing horsemen of Selene at the other. If this is correct then this composition echoed the scene of the birth of Athena herself from the east pediment of the Parthenon and the array of gods observing the arrival of the Athenian procession with the peplos on the east frieze. Thus the worshipper coming from the east and entering the temple was presented with three parallel scenes in turn: the gods are seen to observe first the birth of Athena from Zeus; then the arrival of the autochthonous Athenian worshippers; finally the birth of Pandora fashioned from clay. But, as Pausanias' invocation of Hesiod makes clear, the birth of Pandora cannot be separated from her indiscretion which brought misery to man (Hesiod, *Theogony* 570–612; *Works and Days* 70–105; cf. Vernant 1980: 168–85). The viewer had to face up to the question of how he or she related to these very similar but also very different creation stories, the creation of the immortal goddess and the creation of the mortal woman. Both men and women are challenged to find a place in the service of the city, but it is the man, whose martial duties the cult statue brings to the fore in all its other scenes, who is left uncomfortably reminded of his inability either to cope with, or to survive without, the female sex.

The sculpted mortal woman

Classical statues of goddesses, I have argued, address themselves most powerfully and most richly to men and have little directly to say to women.[3] I now want briefly to show that the same is true of Classical statues of mortal women, and then to look back into the late Archaic period and claim that this had not always been the case.

I take as my example of a Classical statue of a woman a piece from the early fifth century which is, on the face of it, rather short on explicit sensual charm, by comparison with the Nike balustrade figure or Praxiteles' Aphrodite: 'Amelung's goddess' (fig. 5.4). This is perhaps the most heavily draped of all ancient statues, the heavy himation covering all but face, left hand, bottom inches of tunic, and feet. Chronologically not far separate from the last of the *korai*, a series of small changes mark this out as very different: the expression is much more severe, the dress plain and sober, the right hand invisible, and the head slightly turned. This turn of the head ensures that, unlike the *korai*, this is not a 'statue to be met' (Martin Robertson's phrase). The turn of the head ensures that we are not ourselves the sole object in the gentle drama in which this figure has a part; it turns us into spectators at a drama.

But what is the drama? The clues are few: the extended left hand was restored by Amelung to hold a flower, but we cannot know if that is right. Whatever is extended, to whom is it offered or from whom received? Even if the hand held nothing some exchange is taking place, an exchange to which we are witness but to which we are not party. To get any further in the analysis of this narrative of which we are given a glimpse, we must turn to the information that will have been given on the statue base. One late copy of this statue is inscribed 'Europe' on its base, and Martin Robertson has ingeniously argued that a figure on a late fifth-century krater by the Kekrops painter, which is certainly a representation of this statue seen from the side and with minor adjustments, should be identified as Europe (Robertson 1957). Once we have the name Europe then our puzzle as to what this modest woman is engaged in is given an answer: the name Europe gives us a narrative, and for all the ancient variations in detail, that narrative is basically a narrative of *rape*. What then is the exchange to which we are witness? Given the subtitle 'This woman was/will be a victim of rape by Zeus', the inarticulate signs constituted by her difference from the tradition of *korai*, her right arm clasped to and drawing attention to her breast, her gaze which resolutely refuses to engage with the viewer's, all become redolent with meaning. The viewer, who approached the statue and looked to read the inscription thinking that he was observing a fragment of someone else's drama to which he was merely a spectator, finds himself the one whose gaze is shunned, himself being warded off, himself framed as an outsider. But Europe's story is again one of male desire, this narrative too is a narrative that speaks to men. To caption this statue 'Europe' is the ancient equivalent, in some ways at least, of the modern advertising slogan 'Underneath they are all lovable', and it has cognate overtones for women (Coward 1987).

Like Praxiteles' Knidian Aphrodite and the Nike fiddling with her sandal, Amelung's 'goddess' challenges the viewer to construct a narrative in order to comprehend the image, and like them this statue makes the construction of a definitive narrative impossible and ensures that the act of building a story frames the viewer and exploits and exposes his male desire. Faced with any of these statues, as faced with the Athena Parthenos, men are reduced to a common denominator, and the factors which separate one man from another are shown up as superficial. But it is by exploiting the male image of what it is to be a woman that all these sculptures achieve their effect, not by questioning that image; and no independent voice is allowed to women, no purchase given to the woman viewer. For all the marked changes in style between these sculptures there is no basic change in the way in which women are construed.

But if the classical construction of women stays unchanged through all the changes of sculptural style in the 150 years after the Persian Wars, was it itself an inheritance from the Archaic period? Was the major stylistic change that occurred early in the fifth century also of no importance with regard to the question of what sculptures had to say to women, or did *this* stylistic change at least make a difference?

Archaic free-standing sculpture is dominated by two types, the *kouros* and the *kore*. The *kouros* is a naked beardless male, standing with arms by sides, left leg advanced, and gaze straight ahead. The *kore* is a draped female figure, either with feet together or with one slightly advanced, one arm by the side and the other either folded across the breast or held out with some object, a bird or a piece of fruit, for instance, in it. In Attica, at least, both *korai* and *kouroi* were used both as dedications to the gods in sanctuaries and as markers on tombs (D'Onofrio 1982). On tombs *kouroi* always mark dead men, *korai* dead women, but men dedicate *korai* as well as *kouroi* in sanctuaries, and female deities receive *kouroi* as well as *korai*. Thus *kouroi* and *korai* stand neither universally for the deity nor universally for the dedicator: they have a life of their own.

Despite their similar configuration and use, the differences between *korai* and *kouroi* are important. Hands by his sides and feet flat on the ground, the *kouros* refuses any engagement in a narrative, gives no purchase to any identification as athlete, warrior, or god (fig. 5.5). His resolutely forward gaze makes contact with nothing but the viewer whose own gaze is mirrored. The *kouros* re-presents man to himself and to god and god to man (Osborne 1988a). *Korai* too gaze straight ahead and have their feet firmly on the ground, but more is at stake here than an exchange of looks: for these are dressed up statues whose offered or received gifts hint at a narrative (fig. 5.6). Before the *kore* the viewer is called to take part in her story, not merely to subsume her identity.

As dedications on graves, *kouroi* and *korai* were accompanied by inscriptions, and the difference between *kouroi* and *korai* as sculptures is paralleled by the difference between the inscriptions. The simple dedicatory formula 'X dedicated me to Y' is frequently found on both *kouroi* and *korai*, as is the fuller 'X dedicated me to Y as a tithe'. Few *kouros* dedications follow any other form.[4] *Korai*, by contrast, not infrequently bear dedications expanded in

5.4 *'Amelung's goddess', Roman copy of an original of the second quarter of the fifth century BC. National Archaeological Museum, Naples.*

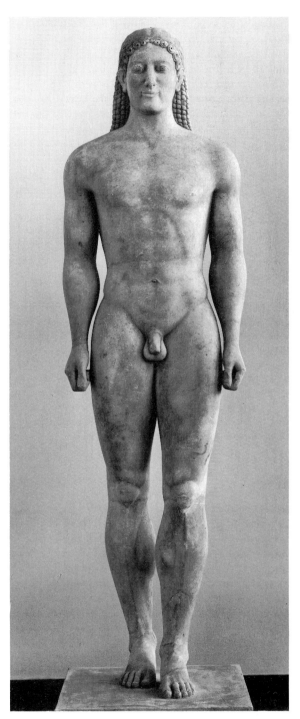

5.5 Kouros *from near Anavyssos, Attica, third quarter of the sixth century BC. Base gives the name 'Kroisos'. National Museum, Athens.*

various ways. One of the earliest *korai*, Nikandre from Delos, is inscribed 'Nikandre dedicated me to the far-shooter of arrows, the excellent daughter of Deinodikos of Naxos, sister of Deinomenes, wife of Phraxos' (P. A. Hansen 1983: 403 = Lazzarini 1976: no. 157 = Richter 1968: no. 1), situating her very surely in a man's world. The tithe idea gets expanded in the inscription on 'Antenor's *kore*' from the Athenian acropolis (fig. 5.6), traditionally restored to read 'Nearkhos the potter dedicated me as a tithe of his works to Athena. Antenor the son of Eumares made the *agalma*' (P. A. Hansen 1983: 193 = Lazzarini 1976: no. 636 = Richter 1968: no. 110 = Raubitschek 1949: 197); and again on a base from the Athenian acropolis which is the only Athenian dedicatory inscription to use *kore* of the object dedicated (as opposed to referring to Athena as the '*kore* of Zeus'): 'Naulokhos dedicated this *kore* as a tithe of the catch which the sea-ruling one with the golden trident gave to him' (P. A. Hansen 1983: 266 = Lazzarini 1976: no. 639 = Raubitschek 1949: 229).

The term most frequently used in the inscriptions to refer to the statue is not *kore* but, as in Antenor's *kore*, *agalma*. A simple example of this is another Athenian acropolis base: 'Aiskhines dedicated this *agalma* to Athena having vowed a tithe to the child of great Zeus' (P. A. Hansen 1983: 202 = Lazzarini 1976: no. 680 = Raubitschek 1949: 48). More complex are the ideas conveyed in a slightly earlier dedication: 'Alkimakhos dedicated me to the daughter of Zeus, this *agalma* as a votive offering and he boasts that he is the son of a good father, Khairion' (P. A. Hansen 1983: 195 = Lazzarini 1976: no. 732 = Raubitschek 1949: 6). A further Athenian example associated the sculptor in this act of relating to the goddess: 'Lyson dedicated to Pallas Athena a tithe of his own possession, and Thebades the son of Kyrnos made this gracious *agalma* for the goddess' (P. A. Hansen 1983: 205 = Lazzarini 1976: no. 638 = Raubitschek 1949: 290). Outside Athens the only certain uses of *agalma* on *korai* come from Samos where Kheramues dedicated two *korai* to Hera, one inscribed 'Kheramues dedicated me to Hera, an *agalma*', and the other 'Kheramues dedicated me to the goddess, a very beautiful *agalma*' (P. A. Hansen 1983: 422 with note = Lazzarini 1976: nos. 727–8 = Richter 1968: nos. 55–6).

Agalma is not only used of *korai* in the Archaic period in epigraphic dedications: on the Athenian acropolis it is firmly attested for sculptures of horses, or horses and riders, for a four-horse chariot group, and for seated figures and figure groups (Raubitschek 1949: 374, 234, 248, 155, 273, 64, 336, 40, 295 (= P. A. Hansen 1983: 183, 190, 194, 212, 224–7, 234), 195, 206; P. A. Hansen 1983: 281, 285, 289–92). With a single exception, however, *agalma* is never used of *kouroi*. Not only were *kouroi* dedicated on the Athenian acropolis,

but there was a sanctuary full of *kouroi* dedicated to Apollo Ptoios in Boiotia, none of which is referred to as an *agalma*, although *agalma* was used of three non-*kouros* dedications there (P. A. Hansen 1983: 302, 334, 423 = Ducat 1971: nos. 141, 262, 238 = Lazzarini 1976: nos. 856, 796). The one exceptional use of *agalma* on a *kouros* comes from Samos, where the leg of a *kouros* is inscribed 'Kharmues dedicated me to the goddess, a very beautiful *agalma*' (P. A. Hansen 1983: 423 = Lazzarini 1976: no. 727), that is, it is dedicated by the same man who dedicated the two *korai* with identical or near-identical dedicatory epigrams.

In the face of the strength of the epigraphic testimony for *korai* as *agalmata*, and the very weak testimony for *kouroi* as *agalmata*, claims that 'le formule, homérique et traditionelle, *perikalles agalma*, convient à n'importe quel type d'offrande, mais particulièrement à un *kouros*' (Ducat 1971: 386), or that '*Agalma*, come si è visto, può essere un oggetto di qualunque genere, anche se fra gli *agalmata* hanno netta prevalenze la statue, generalmente di *kouroi* o *kourai*, cioè di offerenti ideali che con hanno alcun rapporto specifico col dedicante' (Lazzarini 1976: 96), seem insufficiently well founded. It is worth exploring the possibility that the two sorts of statue related humankind to the gods in different ways. In tragedy, for example, a heroine *in extremis* is on several occasions likened to an *agalma*. In Euripides, we read, 'Taking hold of her gown she tore it from her shoulders to her waist beside the navel, and showed her breasts and her body, most beautiful, like those of an *agalma*' (*Hecuba* 558–61); and 'Well, what hill is this I see, with sea-foam flowing around it? And there is some image of a maiden, chiselled from the very foam of the rock itself, an *agalma* made by a skilled hand' (*Andromeda* fr. 125 Nauck; cf. *Helen* 262–3. I am indebted to Edith Hall for these references). In inscriptions of the Classical period and later '*agalma* customarily designates the statue of a god' (Lewis and Stroud 1979: 193), but in the Archaic period its use is much wider: 'Founded on the same symbolism of wealth, the *agalma* puts into action sacred powers, social prestige, and bonds of dependence among men; its circulation through gifts and exchanges, engages individuals and mobilises religious forces at the same time as it passes on possession of goods' (Vernant 1980: 360; cf. Gernet 1981: 73–111). In identifying *korai* as *agalmata* the inscriptions situate them in this world of exchange of precious objects whose value cannot be exhausted by putting a price on them, but is bound up with social prestige and sacred powers.

The *kore* which insists that she is part of a narrative, comes offering and receiving gifts, and demands a response, embodies just this idea of exchange. In a society where women are the prime source of symbolic capital, where it is women who are given in and move with marriage, where it is women who confer prestige by their movement and by the gifts they bring, and where the women have special access to religious power because they alone can hold certain priesthoods, including some of those most central to the community such as the priesthood of Athena Polias at Athens, and they alone can celebrate certain central rituals (there were no festivals limited to men in classical Greece, it appears, but there were several restricted to women, including the most widely dispersed of all Greek festivals, the Thesmophoria), it is not just appropriate but inevitable that *korai* be used to mark the relationship between *men* and the gods, and that by coming face-to-face with a *kore* the viewer should be obliged to enter into an exchange. *Kouroi* reflect a man's gaze back on a man, and demand and provoke introspection; *korai* draw men's attention to the necessary exchange outside themselves, and to the world where dressing up in finery, offering gifts and offering them in a particular manner, where women, matter.[5]

Korai were appropriate gifts to the gods, returns to the gods for their goodness in bestowing economic capital, only because of their value as symbolic capital in the exchanges between men. In the act of the man who repays the god for a successful fishing season by dedicating a *kore* we see part of the 'endless reconversion of economic capital into symbolic capital'; Naulokhos' *kore* signals his success, wealth and power and legitimates his claim to authority. But the use of the *kore* in this context reinforces the position of women which made it possible in the first place. Naulokhos' dedication creates symbolic capital not only for himself but for women. *Korai* as dedications speak to women too, and they speak of power: the role of women as objects of exchange opens up for them a role as agents able to extract a price for the offering they bring; theirs is a hand outstretched ready to receive as well as to give.

But if *korai* as dedications carry a burden of ideas quite other than that borne by *kouroi*, so also as funerary monuments they encourage a rather different sort of mediation on death and the dead. Scarcity of evidence renders all hypotheses in this area fragile, but the accompanying inscriptions on funerary *korai* seem to support the claim that they had a distinct role. Three inscriptions survive from *korai* grave-markers. One is simple: 'Alas for the dead Myrrhine, whose marker I am' (P. A. Hansen 1983: 49 = Jeffery 1962: no. 54). The other two are longer and more complex: '[Philton](?) set down this memorial of his dear child, a memorial fine to behold and Phaidimos made it' (P. A. Hansen 1983: 18 = Jeffery 1962: no. 44); 'Marker of Phrasikleia. I will always be called *kore* having been allotted this name by the gods instead of marriage. Aristion of Paros made it' (P. A. Hansen 1983: 24 = Jeffery 1962: no. 46).

5.6 Kore *from the acropolis, Athens, 520s BC. Base names: dedicant as Nearkhos, sculptor as Antenor. Acropolis Museum, Athens.*

The formula 'I am a marker of X' is plentifully paralleled for the male dead, including dead marked by *kouroi*. The epitaph of [Philton]'s daughter belongs to a small group which draws attention to the beauty of the monument. A stele from Kalyvia Kouvara in Attica reads 'This is the monument of Arkhias and his dear sister; Eukosmides had this fine monument made and skilled Phaidimos placed the stele on it' (P. A. Hansen 1983: 26 = Jeffery 1962: no. 48); a *kouros* base from the Piraeus gate of Athens reads: 'This is the marker of the boy Nelon son of Nelonides, and it was he who had this delightful memorial made to a good son. Endoios made him' (P. A. Hansen 1983: 42 = Jeffery 1962: no. 19). Phrasikleia's epitaph, by contrast, is unique in its identification of statue and dead girl and the direct role ascribed to the god in bringing that situation about. The peculiarity of this epitaph comes out particularly clearly when it is compared with that on the base of the funerary *kouros* of Xenophantos: 'His father Klebolos placed this marker to the dead Xenophantos to stand in place of his *arete* and *sophrosune*' (P. A. Hansen 1983: 41 = Jeffery 1962: no. 9. For the sense of virtues lost, cf. Jeffery 1962: nos. 2, 23, 49, 51, 56 (all for men), and more general expressions of grief in nos. 16, 24, 25, 31, 50). Both inscriptions draw attention to what was lost in death, but while Klebolos looks to his son's good qualities in life as he lived, Phrasikleia laments the future life of which she was deprived, and sees death as an exchange substituted for the exchange of marriage.

In a sample of three, arguments from silence can scarcely be broached with confidence, but it is to be noted that no funerary *kore*, and no archaic stele on the grave of a woman, makes the direct address to the passer-by and viewer which is far from infrequent in archaic grave epitaphs for men, both on *kouroi* as in 'Stand and shed a tear at the tomb of the dead Kroisos, whom Ares came and slew as he stood in the first rank' (P. A. Hansen 1983: 27 = Jeffery 1962: no. 57), and probably on stelai, as in 'Looking upon the memorial of Kleitos the deceased son of Menesaikhmos shed a tear; he died a *kalos*' (P. A. Hansen 1983: 68 = Jeffery 1962: no. 67). Nor is a woman involved in either of the two Archaic grave stelai which invoke a 'nameless first person mourner', to which David Lewis has drawn attention (1987): 'Looking at this tomb of the young Autokleides I feel pain . . . ', and 'I shed a tear looking at this tomb of the dead boy Smikythos who has destroyed the good hope of those who loved him.'[6]

All this might be held to encourage the view that *korai* and *kouroi* function in discrete ways as funerary markers, ways that connect closely with differing attitudes to male and female dead. *Kouroi* with their mirroring gaze and refusal to constitute another's story turn the fact of death back upon

the viewer, promoting contemplation of death as loss, and sympathy that comes from putting oneself, or having oneself put, in the position of the deceased. The male life is presented as constituted of virtues and martial achievements, both of which death puts an end to. *Korai*, by contrast, have a narrative of their own. The object-bearing hand involves them in a transaction in which they are both clearly separated from the viewer and into which, by their forward gaze, they draw the viewer. Death is construed not in terms of loss, but in terms of an exchange: the monument itself is a positive return for the loss of life; setting up a *kore* fine to behold leaves a beautiful mark in the world where the woman once was; the value of the marriageable girl is translated into the statue which stands in her stead for the future as a thing of delight. But this is not a thing of delight to behold and pass by, it is a thing of delight which gains its value from the exchange which it transacts: as the woman's value was intimately connected to her being 'given' in marriage, so the *kore* acquires, creates, value by the exchange with the viewer which the frontal gaze insists upon.

That *korai*, like classical statues of women, are playing parts in a drama scripted by men is undeniable; but the particular drama in which they act, and the part which they play, is strikingly different. For the *kore* plays an active starring role, vital to the plot of the 'institutionally organized and guaranteed misrecognition which is the basis of gift exchange and, perhaps, of all the symbolic labour intended to transmute, by the sincere fiction of a disinterested exchange, the inevitable, and inevitably interested relations imposed by kinship, neighbourhood, or work, into the elective relations of reciprocity' (Bourdieu 1977: 171). And in this role she speaks to women too, encouraging the realisation of the power which belongs to those who create, as well as to those who possess, symbolic capital. Essential in giving the *kore* a speaking part is her forward gaze: 'Her look of allure is always directed at us, her eyes always engage with ours' (Holland 1987: 110); written of the Page 3 girl, this observation is no less true of the smiling *kore*. Just as the imaginary 'narrative' which surrounds the Page 3 girl and situates her in real life is the key to her speaking to women too, so with the *kore* the gaze unpacked by the object-bearing hand and the fine costume ensures that she has a message. The Classical sculpted girl, by contrast, parades before but will not engage with the viewer, and her part in her drama is a non-speaking one. The narratives she suggests frame the male viewer and make him scrutinise his own desire, but however much they prove good for men to think with, they say not a word to women.

I set out in this paper to explore the question of whether and in what ways the images of women communicated by Greek sculpture changed over time. In the course of it I have examined sculptures of widely divergent styles and of several different types, from the formal cult statue to the private dedication, from low relief to three colossal gold and ivory dimensions. It requires relatively little training in Classical sculpture to be able to distinguish the drapery treatment in the Nike parapet reliefs from the drapery treatment in Amelung's 'goddess', or the treatment of flesh in either of those from its treatment by Praxiteles. Within the broad ambit of Classical sculpture both style of execution and content (that is, what precisely the sculptor chooses to portray) vary very palpably. But I have argued that none of these changes make any basic difference to the way in which these sculptures present women. From Europe to Aphrodite of Knidos the sculpted woman is presented for observation, the viewer is given the option of being a fly-on-the-wall at the, often overtly trivial, drama in which this female character is engaged. The woman is presented to the viewer's gaze as an object to behold, an object to sense. From the severe drapery of Europe through the transparent drapery of the Nike to the undraped flesh of Knidian Aphrodite, the sculptor's skill is devoted to evoking a sensory response as he offers a tactile experience to the viewer whilst allowing the viewer the fiction of maintaining an aloofness from the action in which the sculpted woman is engaged. By contrast, the viewer of the Archaic *kore* is unable to stand aloof, he is directly implicated in the woman's gaze and made to enter into an exchange, not offered a free gift on the side. Here is none of the particularity of the classical narrative of Pandora or Nike or Europe or Aphrodite, here is woman establishing her centrality in the male world of exchange, exploiting her symbolic role in order to make clear that woman, that sexual difference, lies at the root of symbolic possibility in general.

What is it that makes the *kore* function in a way so different from Classical statues? What is it that lets the male viewer off the hook after the Archaic period? On the face of it, the most important change is the change of pose: what the *kore* has that later sculptures of women lack is the frontal gaze and the hand extended towards the object of the gaze who is also the viewer of the sculpture. The engagement of the *kore* with the viewer is essentially established by these two features. But these two features themselves are closely related to and indeed dependent upon a further development: the new interest in the sculptural representation of particular forms rather than of types. Where the *kouros* and the *kore* stand for man and maiden but not for particular men or maidens, classical sculpture models human forms in a less generalising way, and achieves its effects at least in part by evoking the possibility that this is a *particular* human being. This increasing suggestion that a *particular* narrative is

being referred to by the gestures and poses of the sculpted figures makes it possible for the viewer to be a spectator at a tableau. It enables all sorts of additional subtleties to be introduced into the spectator's reactions to the sculpture because of the allusiveness of the associations of the particular narrative, but it also insulates the viewer from the direct impact of the sculpted action.

But if the changing style of sculptures of women does, in this one instance, have profound implications for what those sculptures have to say, not just to men but to women too, what is it that determines the change of style? Are we dealing here merely with a chance product of a 'naturally evolving' sculptural style, or is the change in artistic expression linked to wider social change? There is no doubt that in the Greek world in general, and in Athens in particular, the period from 550 to 450 saw very marked changes not only in the mechanics of political life but in various aspects of social expression.

Elite public expression changed in two ways closely related to the theme of this paper. These are marriage and burial. Of marriage Vernant has written:

> One can speak in terms of a break between archaic marriage and marriage as it became established within the framework of a democratic city, in Athens, at the end of the sixth century. In the Athens of the period after Cleisthenes, matrimonial unions no longer have as their object the establishment of relationships of power or of mutual service between great autonomous families; rather, their purpose is to perpetuate the households, that is to say the domestic hearths that constitute the city, in other words to ensure, through strict rules governing marriage, the permanence of the city itself through constant reproduction. (Vernant 1980: 60)

Although it is necessary to be careful not to overstate the case for a change in the use of marriage, for there can be no doubt that marriages continued to be made at Athens for broadly political reasons (witness the intertwining of the major families shown by Davies 1971: Table I), that there *was* a change is undoubted. The marriages between the elites of different cities for which there is much evidence from the seventh and sixth centuries (a Kypselos appearing as archon at Athens in the early sixth century, Peisistratos' marriage to Timonassa of Argos, Megacles' marriage to the daughter of Cleisthenes of Sicyon) are no longer a prominent feature in Athenian fifth-century history, and after 451 BC were effectively ruled out by Pericles' citizenship law which limited Athenian citizenship to those with both an Athenian father and an Athenian mother. Vernant noted that in Archaic marriage two contrasting aspects of the union are stressed:

As a daughter offered in marriage to a foreign *genos*, she fulfils the role of wealth put into circulation, weaving a network of alliances between different groups, just as do the *agalmata* exchanged at the wedding, or the herds that, in order to win his wife, the husband must present to her father. But as a mother who bears a man children that are truly his own and that directly continue his line, she is identified with the cultivated land owned by her husband, and the marriage has the significance of an exercise of ploughing, with the woman as the furrow. (Vernant 1980: 73; cf. Gernet 1981: 289–302, especially 299)

Pericles' citizenship law put all the emphasis on the latter aspect of marriage, ruling out the former aspect except within the boundaries of the *polis*. Thus in the fifth century women are effectively removed from the realm of *agalmata* – a suggestion to which the epigraphic record lends some support as we have already seen. Ties between elite families in different cities certainly continued, but they were carried on by different means, not involving the exchange of women (see Herman 1987 on the developing institution of ritualised friendship).

Marriage was one of the two ceremonies at which the doings of the elite impinged on the wider mass of citizens. The other was burial. Tradition in Classical Athens had it that at the beginning of the sixth century Solon, as part of his measures to improve Athenian social relations, restricted funerary display (Plutarch, *Solon* 12.5, 21.4–5). The restrictions Solon is supposed to have imposed are such as to leave no material trace, and it is clear that in other ways at least funerary display continued, with impressive built tombs and elaborate sculpted grave monuments (including *kouroi* and *korai*). Cicero (*De legibus* 2.25.64–5) claims that some time after Solon a law was passed limiting the size of grave monuments (or more precisely the labour that went into them) and certainly at around the end of the sixth century sculpted grave monuments disappear from Attic cemeteries, not to reappear until three quarters of a century later. This disappearance approximately coincides with an enormous increase in the proportion of Athenians who got buried with some pottery grave goods in their tombs (I. Morris 1987: 72–3 and fig. 22). Exactly what is happening is unclear, but we seem to be witnessing mass emulation of those features of elite burial which could feasibly be emulated by the poorer members of the citizenry and forcible suppression of those features which could not be emulated. In the middle of the fifth century almost the only Athenians whose deaths were celebrated by the erection of monuments were those who died in war, whose names were displayed, according to the artificial tribal affiliations created by Cleisthenes, on pillars erected in the Kerameikos cemetery, and even these

men were listed by personal name alone with no patronymic or demotic, so that it was in fact impossible to attach securely a name from the list with a particular person. All these names were necessarily those of *men*.

Less secure, but also suggestive, are the changing practices with regard to making dedications to the gods. The Athenian acropolis, which in 500 was packed with sculptures dedicated to individuals (some of whose dedicatory epigrams have been studied above), looked completely different fifty years later, and by the end of the fifth century it was packed with buildings erected at the expense of the city and celebrating the communal festivals of the city. Part of what made the difference here was the sack of the acropolis by the Persians, which destroyed the archaic dedications for the Athenians and preserved them for us in the pits where they were buried when the Athenians tidied up. But was the Persian sack the only factor involved? Unless the archaeological record, not only from the acropolis but from other Attic, and indeed Greek, sanctuaries is very deceptive, elite dedications never dominated sanctuary space after 480 in the same way as they had before. It seems that sculptures of men and women cease to be central to the mediation between human and divine: the *agalma* has been hijacked to be solely a statue of a deity.

It is difficult to believe that all these changes are independent. None, certainly, can plausibly be seen as cause of the other, but the general similarities between them point to their all being correlated with broader social change. Do they also correlate with political change? For the political historian the major event at the end of the sixth century in Athens is the democratic reform of Cleisthenes, giving an increased formal role to the people, ensuring the participation in the day-to-day running of the city of men from all over Attica, and promoting the idea of equal rights to have one's views heard. Herodotus, an outside observer writing perhaps around 420 BC, had no doubt that it was this promotion of citizen equality which transformed Athens, turning her into the crucial political and military power in Greece (5.78). The meagre records of Cleisthenes' reforms in our ancient sources (Herodotus 5.69; [Aristotle] *Constitution of the Athenians* 21) do not allow us to see in detail what he actually did in the social realm, but by the time we can observe Athenian politics in detail in the fifth century there is no doubt that it is no longer in the hands of rival factions centred on a particular family or charismatic leader, as Athenian politics had been in the sixth century. Directly or indirectly, therefore, Cleisthenes' 'cobbling together' (Farrar 1988: 1) of democracy had involved an attack upon established relations and on all that sustained them – 'feasts, ceremonies, exchanges of gifts, visits or courtesies, and, above all, marriages' (Bourdieu 1977: 171). Assisted in part by events outside its immediate control, Athenian democracy was able to offer a substitute for the 'symbolic' violence of the archaic *polis*: overt violence – against the Chalcidians and Boeotians immediately the Spartan threat to establish Cleisthenes' rival Isagoras as tyrant had disappeared, against the Aeginetans in the 490s, against the Persians in 490 and 480/79, in the establishment of her empire, against Sparta and Sparta's allies. This overt domination by the city over outside powers transcended the demand for symbolic domination within the citizen body; indeed one of the things that the lists of war dead was doing was asserting that the Athenians were a single body, not divisible into parts. Whether forcibly excluded or simply rendered unattractive by the success of the new image of what it was to be Athenian, symbolic capital was no longer avidly accumulated.

The changing demands made of and by Athenians can be seen to correlate with artistic change in two ways. At the most obvious level, two of the most important areas of artistic expression, individual funerary monuments and individual dedications, were, explicitly or otherwise, ruled out. It was not just the monuments themselves that had ceased to be acceptable, but also, for this was intimately bound up in them, what they expressed. More overtly in some cases perhaps than in others, these monuments had constituted a claim by those who had them made and erected to stand in a privileged way for mankind at large both in the face of natural forces (especially death) and in the face of the gods. They erected their life as the model life for all to think with and through. For the classical Athenian the horizons had narrowed, it was important for the political and social relations of the city that it was now the *citizen* who was privileged, and that it was the *citizen's* life that should be the model for all. While the *individual* citizen continued to be effaced, the status and values of the citizen were required to be invoked. This created a demand for, and sympathy with, works of art that could suggest the particular status of the human beings represented as well as simply their humanity. It is against this background that the change from the *kore* as the outstanding sculptural monument of the late sixth-century Athenian acropolis to the Parthenon sculptures as the outstanding sculptural monument of the late fifth-century Athenian acropolis needs to be seen.

Finally, let me return to the images of women. Is the sea-change in the sculpted image of woman merely a by-product of a change of artistic style which came about in connection with events essentially independent of any question of women's roles? Hardly so. 'Athenian politics shaped man's self-understanding along civic lines' (Farrar 1988: 276). The premium put upon *man's* self-understanding, and the focus of reflective questioning on 'the connection between *politics* and the human good' (Farrar 1988: 276, my emphasis) eclipsed and silenced women as much in life as in art. If the argument of this paper has anything to recommend it, it is the artistic expression of this Classical Athenian obsession with *man* as a political animal which laid the foundation for the treatment of women in the whole tradition of Western art.

Acknowledgements

This paper was originally written for a seminar in Cambridge organised by Jas Elsner; I am grateful to him for the invitation and to that audience and subsequent audiences in Oxford for comments. I am particularly in debt to Simon Goldhill, Edith Hall, Richard Hawley, John Henderson, David Lewis and Ian Morris for their criticisms and contributions of ideas and material which have much improved this paper. They should not, however, be held responsible for the result.

Notes

1 I talk here of 'the viewer's response'. Not all viewers react in the same ways to works of art in our own society and there is no reason to believe that all viewers will have reacted identically in past societies. Likewise the same viewer may react differently at different moments. Nevertheless for the work of art to be a work of communication at least some degree of shared reaction must be experienced by different individual viewers, and artistic 'style' is one of the factors which affect the sorts of ways in which the viewer responds.

2 But does this statue speak to women if what Aphrodite is seen to be doing is pointing to and conspicuously drawing attention to her genitals? Against this I note two points: first that the direction of Aphrodite's gaze ensures that there are always three people present – Aphrodite, the object of her gaze, and a 'voyeur'; and second, that the recuperation of the female genitals as the imagery of a celebratory affirmative exposure of female sexuality is highly problematic. On this second point see Pollock 1987b and Tickner 1987.

3 That women did look at sculpture (e.g. Euripides, *Ion* 184ff; Theokritos 15.76ff) and that there were some women artists (Kampen 1975; Pomeroy 1977) does not alter this point.

4 A *kouros* of colossal size from Delos has its base inscribed 'I am of the same stone, both statue and base' (P. A. Hansen 1983: 401), and the twin *kouroi* from Delphi traditionally known as Kleobis and Biton seem to

have had a long inscription on their base, which survives only partially. It is to be noted that the number of inscriptions which can be securely attached to their dedications or markers, or even to a particular type of dedication or marker, is very small, and that this renders all generalisation hazardous.

5 I borrow heavily here from Bourdieu 1977. Note especially p. 179: 'Thus we see that symbolic capital, which in the form of the prestige and renown attached to a family and a name is readily convertible back into economic capital, is perhaps the most valuable form of accumulation in a society in which the severity of the climate (the major work – ploughing and harvesting – having to be done in a very short space of time) and the limited technical resources (harvesting is done with the sickle) demand collective labour.' An introduction to these ideas can be found in Appadurai 1986a.

6 Autokleides' stele from Nikaia was first published in *Horos* 4 (1986), 31–4. Smikythos' stele base, from Athens, appeared in *Mitteilungen des Deutschen Archäologischen Instituts, Athenische Abteilung* 78 (1963), 118–22, no. 4 (= *SEG* XXII.78 = P. A. Hansen 1983: 51, although there it is wrongly restored).

PART III

Artefacts as traded objects

6

Positivism, pots and long-distance trade

DAVID W. J. GILL

The 'positivist fallacy' in classical archaeology has been receiving much attention in recent years. Are we only to discuss what has survived in the archaeological record? Are we permitted to create models to try and understand the artefacts which have come down to us? Do we privilege certain categories of material?

The recent debates about the nature of trade and the ancient economy have largely passed classical archaeology by, or at least the Greek element in it. M. I. Finley's *The ancient economy* (1985a [1973]) is relatively silent on the archaeological evidence, and Garnsey *et al.*'s *Trade in the ancient economy* (1983) allows an archaeological contribution, for instance Snodgrass on 'Heavy freight in Archaic Greece', but there is little on the role of Greek pottery in trade.

The same cannot be said for Roman pottery where there has been much helpful work on the 'rigorously anonymous' wares (Finley 1985b: 23). For example, Morel (1983) has drawn our attention to the ways that pottery can be used to measure trade in other commodities, and Fulford (1978) has used archaeological analogy, in part through medieval port records, to come to terms with the import of pottery to Roman Britain. Likewise Chinese porcelain has been seen as saleable 'ballast' alongside other items of trade such as tea and silk (Hobhouse 1985: 107). However when we come to Greek pottery there are some who hold a very different position. It is a world in which we are told 'Corinthian vases were being carried for their own sakes, as objets d'art, or at least best plate' (Boardman 1980: 17) or that 'much pottery was traded as a commodity in its own right, and not for its contents' (Arafat and Morgan 1989: 336). It is this approach which Snodgrass (1980b: 126) has challenged. He sees that 'economic reconstruction' in the Greek world has been

hindered by this 'positivist fallacy' characterised by an assumption 'that the importance of a class of evidence for antiquity stands in some relation to the quantity in which it survives to be studied today'. He draws particular attention to 'painted pottery' – not 'vases' – whose production he views as 'a very minor component of the economy' (pp. 127–8). In particular he suggests that we should be 'wary' of 'economic conclusions' which are based 'on the evidence of painted pottery alone' (p. 128).

The privileging of Greek painted pottery since at least Sir William Hamilton has certainly distorted our picture of the way that pots were transported (Vickers 1987). For example, Michell in his *The economics of ancient Greece* could write about pots – or perhaps they should be vases (cf. Gill 1990: 229) – finding in antiquity their 'last resting place in the collection of some connoisseur' (1957: 295). His model for Black Sea trade also deserves to be noted if only as one of the stepping-stones in the debate: 'we can well imagine how, when in search of a cargo of grain, the shipmaster would pack a few choice specimens [of pots] in order to tempt the wheat merchants of South Russia' (p. 297). Are these attitudes obsolete or do people continue to hold these views?

Sostratos

One way to approach this problem is by turning to a stone anchor found at Gravisca, the port of Tarquinia, in Etruria. This was inscribed, 'I belong to Aeginetan Apollo, Sostratos son of [. . .] dedicated me (*epoiese*)' (e.g. Cristofani 1985: 185, no. 7.1.9). Now in Herodotus (4.152) a merchant of this name appears: 'wherefore the Samians brought back from it [sc. Tartessos] so great a profit on their wares as no Greeks ever did of whom we have any exact knowledge, save only Sostratos of Aegina, son of Laodamas; with him none could vie.' There is an Aegina link, the same name, but unfortunately the patronymic is missing on the anchor. A range of commercial graffiti scratched underneath the feet of the Athenian figure-decorated pots have been added to the discussion. A common graffito is that of *SO*. An example of this is provided by a black-figured hydria in Cambridge (GR.2.1952: Johnston 1979: 82, Type 21A, no. 65), showing Athena mounting a chariot (fig. 6.1). These *SO* marks are quite common, especially on pots from Etruria; for example, thirty-two from Vulci and eleven from Tarquinia. A black-figured column-krater in the Museum of Classical Archaeology, Cambridge (Johnston 1979: 82, Type 21A, no. 62; Spivey and Stoddart 1990: 94, fig. 45) has two inscriptions on the base: *laso* and *so*. The form of the lambda and the alpha, and an interpretation of the first part of the inscription as *la[kythos]* led Johnston to believe that the writer of this inscription was an Aeginetan. The other graffiti do not help to identify an Aeginetan, and indeed some may even be Attic (Johnston 1972: 421). Johnston then goes on to suggest that 'From here it was an obvious though by no means necessary step to equate SO with the Herodotean Sostratos' (p. 419). Although other personal names starting with So come to mind (e.g. Sosias, Socrates, Sophocles), Johnston is certain enough of his identification to write that 'we may confidently assume that Sostratos,

6.1 Attic black-figured hydria with SO graffito.
Cambridge, Fitzwilliam Museum GR.2. 1952.

6.2 Attic red-figured pelike and price inscription. Oxford,
Ashmolean Museum, loan.

whose mark in any case is the most frequent, exported many more Attic vases, both large and small. What else he took to Etruria we cannot say' (p. 422). Or that 'the turning over of stones and vases has surely now brought more worldly substance to yet another of the engaging walk-on characters of Herodotos' work, and that in a scene set in an Etruscan port' (p. 423).

One is thus asked to believe that Sostratos at Gravisca was indeed the same Sostratos as the one in Herodotus, and moreover that it was he who inscribed, or had inscribed, an abbreviated form of his name on pots which he carried to Etruria by ship. Although these strands may be 'persuasive' for some (e.g. Johnston 1990: 440), this seems to take the available evidence too far and the whole question should perhaps be left open. One area raised by Johnston is that these pots imported in antiquity 'were apparently as popular in Italian markets as they are in European [ones] today, and we may surmise that Sostratos was not slow to appreciate this' (Johnston 1972: 422). This view of pots as *objets d'art* to be appreciated and highly valued is one that appears in Boardman's *The Greeks overseas* (1980: 17) and even in work by historians who today talk of 'the fine-art market in Etruria', and Corinthian pots as the 'Wedgwood of the seventh century' which were purchased as 'luxury goods

bought for their artistic quality' (Salmon 1984: 106, 110, 113).

Specialisation

One strand of evidence taken by some to support the case that Greek pots, and especially Attic ones, were 'highly prized' in antiquity is the predominance of certain shapes in the tombs of Etruria. Some Attic shapes are clearly related to bucchero ones: in particular the so-called Nikosthenic amphora and the kyathos (figs. 6.3, 6.4). The majority of the Attic shapes are found in Etruria, the Nikosthenic amphora almost exclusively at Cerveteri. This has been interpreted as follows: 'In the case of both the amphora and the kyathos we can note a specialization of interest in the Italian market . . . We may note that both shapes give evidence of "product research"' (Eisman 1974: 52), or that 'this sort of ingenuity ensured a brisk market' (Boardman 1980: 202). This 'specialisation' allowed Eisman to reject the traditional model of Greek pottery trade which he describes as follows: 'a merchant strolling through the Kerameikos past Nikosthenes' shop is supposed to take a fancy to the Nikosthenic amphorai displayed (*pace* Beazley), buy them and then sail off to try to sell them' (pp. 52–3). Owing to the predominance of these pots in Cerveteri, Eisman felt unable to accept this model. Rather

these products, it would seem, were made 'to order'. It would have been a risky business venture to make products which had no market in Athens on the *chance*

6.3 Attic black-figured Nikosthenic amphora and kyathos. Cambridge, Fitzwilliam Museum GR.3. 1962 and GR.10. 1937.

6.4 Etruscan bucchero amphora and kyathos. Cambridge, Fitzwilliam Museum GR.1. 1934 and GR.19 1952.

that a merchant might buy the small quantity and sell it in the proper market. A much more reasonable hypothesis is that at the time Nikosthenes brought the strange shaped 'foreign' vase into his shop he already had a sale. Indeed, if one is allowed to speculate a bit further, he probably demanded payment in full, if not a substantial advance. After the first year there was probably a set agreement for a certain amount of the special vases to be picked up at specific times. (p. 53)

Thus there is a specialised market-orientated production with contracts, long-term orders and advance payments. Indeed elsewhere he sees the appearance of a kyathos in Russia as a 'shipping error' rather than a reflection of less specialised marketing (Eisman 1975: 77). A further type of specialised shape is the Tyrrhenian amphora which is seen by some as an example of Athenian potters catering for Etruscan delight in 'colourful story-telling' and that their nonsensical inscriptions merely reflect Etruscan ignorance (Boardman 1980: 202), rather than forming part of their general decoration.

However, Eisman's interpretation is ceramo-centric. Do we really believe that Etruscans sent pots to Athens as models for potters? Were there really advance orders? Perhaps we should approach the problem from a different angle. Critias (quoted in Athenaeus 1.28b–c), writing in the late fifth century BC, draws our attention to trade in Etruscan gold cups and bronzework. More important for Etruria was the trade in metals, especially iron. If we take the case of Populonia, opposite the island of Elba, it is possible to make an estimate of the level of this trade. The slag-heaps from iron-working are estimated as weighing 2 million tons, with an estimated annual extraction of ore at 10–12,000 tons over four centuries. If 8 kg of iron can be produced from 50 kg of ore then this represents an annual production of 1600–2000 tons of iron (Gill 1987: 85). This in itself would require around twenty ships, of 100 tons, to export such quantities of iron annually. It is against this level of activity that we should understand the import of Attic pottery. If we take the 5,000 known imported Attic pots from Etruria (Martelli 1979; Meyer 1980), the rate of import is not as significant as one might at first imagine. If we take the level of imports over two centuries, then this represents only twenty-five pots a year, which does not compare well with the hypothetical twenty ships leaving Populonia annually. If we take a positivistic stance, it might well appear that even in the busiest period of 525–500, Attic pots were only arriving in Etruria at a rate of less than sixty a year (Gill 1991a).

If we accept that the movement of pottery can reflect trade in the opposite direction, then it might be worth considering the case of Athens and the grain supply. Few would now accept Adcock's (1927: 174) view that 'the corn-barons of the Crimea soon became amateurs of Attic pottery and terracottas' but some would continue to argue that painted pottery was a major trade commodity. If we take Garnsey's suggestion 'that Athens never in a normal year had to find grain from outside Attica, narrowly defined, for more than one-half of its resident population' or that 'Attica was capable of feeding in the region of 120,000–150,000 people . . . under normal conditions', then with a population of 200,000–250,000 to feed it is possible to make an attempt to outline the scale of imports (Garnsey 1988: 104–5). If each person consumed 230 kg of grain per year, and there was a need to import grain for between 50,000 and 100,000 people, then the level of imports would be between 11,500 and 23,000 tonnes (287,500–575,000 medimnoi). (This does not of course take account of wastage.) In terms of shiploads, each carrying 3,000 medimnoi, this would be the equivalent of 100 to 200 ships per year under normal conditions (Gill 1991a).

If so many wheat-bearing ships were sailing to Athens in a 'normal' year (and we leave aside other seaborne imports such as slaves, timber and metals) then where does this leave the export of Athenian pottery? The 20,000 Athenian black-figured pots known in 1974 (Boardman 1974: 7) (and in 1987 there were some 16,500 figure-decorated items not in Beazley's work: Boardman and Kurtz in Carpenter 1989: ix) – and many of these have been found at Athens and in Attica – could have been exported by 100 sailings a year over five decades at a rate of four pots per voyage (Gill 1991a).

The value of pots

The high status normally assigned to Greek pottery in the ancient world has been challenged in recent years by Vickers (1984; 1985b). Leaving aside the 'grey areas' (cf. Spawforth 1989) of whether or not Greek silver was kept in a patinated state, he has drawn attention to the somewhat flimsy evidence which has been used in the past. Boegehold (1987) in the recent exhibition catalogue of *The Amasis Painter and his world* wrote of Attic potters as follows:

> We do know one thing. Some of them had extra, disposable income. Potters made dedications on the Acropolis frequently enough so that as an identifiable class of dedicators, they outnumber all others. Some dedicated modest terracotta plaques, but others dedicated works in stone or bronze by famous sculptors, such as Endoios and Antenor. (Boegehold 1987: 19, fig. 4a–b, 28)

Yet such conclusions rest on far from convincing evidence. Boegehold chooses to take Nearchos' dedication of a *kore* by

Antenor as his example. Yet even a quick glance at the inscription shows that the crucial words *ho kerameus* are not present, and alternatives, such as the toponym Eleuthere]us, are equally possible. Some of the problems relating to these dedications have been discussed elsewhere (Gill and Vickers 1990: 6–8), but we should notice that even Johnston in his discussion of 'Amasis and the vase trade' (presented in the conference linked to the exhibition) now accepts that some of these inscriptions 'cannot be said with any conviction to be that of a potter' (Johnston 1987: 135).

There is a view that because pottery is frequently found in tombs – and the majority of complete or semi-intact pots now in our museums found their last resting-place in such funerary contexts – it was considered to have been valuable in antiquity (Gill 1988b: 737–8). For example it has been suggested that 'the ancient Etruscans collected Greek pottery (although not systematically) which they prized highly, imitated, and buried with their dead' (Moon 1979: xvii), or that 'Corinthian vessels clearly had value to receptor communities . . . since they appear in burials' (Morgan 1988: 337). One of the best examples is Beazley's discussion of Attic pots from a tomb at Capua where they are described as 'peak of possessions' (Beazley 1945: 158), a term used by Pindar to describe a gold *phiale* at a symposium (*Olympian Ode* 7).

Pots, of course, had some value – even if low – in antiquity, but we should be careful about equating their presence in a tomb with high value. Indeed inheritance customs might dictate that those things which were valued were kept above ground for the benefit of the living and rather substitutes for the wealth were placed in the grave (Hoffmann 1988: 152; Gill 1988b: 738). Could the use of imported pottery in the tomb be rather a reflection of the Etruscan choice to dispose of surrogates rather than valuable items? Could the visual images have held meaning for the funeral? This is a field for further investigation.

One area of disagreement in the discussion of pottery distribution is whether or not this counts as part of a 'luxury trade'. We might wish to use the term as it is employed by Hasebroek (1933: 51) where it is taken to mean 'something desirable but not indispensable'. Such a view is followed by Cartledge (1983: 4, 14) and Snodgrass (1980b: 127), where it is applied to painted pottery. Vickers (1986: 162), however, questions the use of luxury in this context. If we equate luxury in the ancient world with *truphe* or *luxus*, then perhaps we need to use the word with caution. Luxury objects for a luxurious standard of living might include painted ivory (e.g. the Kul Oba plaques) or gold-figured silver plate (e.g. the finds from Duvanli in Thrace) (Gill and Vickers 1990: 4–5).

Commercial graffiti

The value of pots in trade can be seen through the marking of pots with prices. These price inscriptions frequently consist of the name of the pot shape, the price (frequently prefixed by *TI* for *time*), and the number of pots in a consignment. Underneath an Attic red-figured pot on loan to the Ashmolean Museum is a graffito; following a ligatured *al* or *ma* (which may be a personal name or the name of the pot), there is a *ti* followed by the numerals for 3.5 obols, and then four strokes representing four units (fig. 6.2). In other words this pelike, attributed to the 'Achilles painter', was part of a consignment of four pots each one costing 0.88 obol. (Even if the price is thought to be in drachmae, the pelike would only be worth 5.25 obols). Although such a low price might disturb some, we should recall that the highest recorded price for a pot in antiquity was 3 drachmas (found on two red-figured hydriae), and even a belly-amphora attributed to the 'Berlin painter' only cost 7 obols (Gill 1991a).

Another example is a red-figured oinochoe attributed to the 'Bull painter' in Newcastle upon Tyne (Shefton 1970: 60–1, no. 14). Underneath is a complex inscription, which seems to have been cut before firing, that is to say at Athens, as it is covered by a red miltos wash. There are three sets of inscriptions. The first is a price: 1 drachma and 4 obols. The second is a batch mark: 20. The third states *poi* which probably should be expanded to *poikilai*, 'with painted decoration'. The inscription thus gives a price of 0.5 obol per oinochoe.

These price inscriptions may give information on a series of different shapes and probably reflect the export of batches. A red-figured pelike from Naples lists a range of vessels: *stamnoi, oxides, lekythia mik, lekythoi dik, oxybapha* (Johnston 1978a). There are then noted the size of the batches, 3, 11, 50, 6, 13, and finally the prices, which range from 7 obols for each pelike to 3/50 obol for *lekythia mik*. Similar lists may be found marked on red-figured bell-kraters, which regularly sold for 4 obols each (Gill 1991a).

The price inscription on the Newcastle oinochoe seems to have been added at Athens, so is it fair to talk in terms of these prices as export values? Many, but not all, of these price inscriptions refer to pots found outside Athens. However one piece of evidence which needs to be considered is a price marked on a red-figured bell-krater in New York. On the underside in Cypriot script is marked a unit cost of three. Although some have tried to see this as representing 3 sigloi (as the Persic standard was in use on Cyprus), it seems to have been forgotten that there were Persic obols in circulation on Cyprus. Indeed three of these obols were the equivalent of 4 Attic obols, a price which regularly occurs in commercial graffiti (Gill 1991a).

When faced with so many marks on pottery some have rightly observed that there must have been some organisation, however loose, behind the trade in painted pottery. However it is rarely noticed that commercial graffiti also occur in other types of consignments. On the underside of a silver mug from Dalboki in Thrace (and now in the Ashmolean Museum, Oxford) there is marked an inscription, *sky* (Johnston 1978b). Such marks occur frequently on pottery and relate to the name given to that shape of vessel. In this case *sky* may be expanded to *skyphos*. Unfortunately the melting-pot seems to have removed other examples of this type of inscription; indeed Attic plate rarely survives (Gill and Vickers 1990). However it seems possible that the arrangement for the export of Attic and other silver plate was at least as organised as that for pottery.

Trademarks have also thrown light on what some have seen as a second-hand market in Greek pots. Many have been puzzled by the phenomenon that Attic pots found in Etruscan tombs carry *kalos* inscriptions, which praise Athenian youths from the social elites. This has been explained as the pots ordered for particular feasts at Athens, hence the topical names, and then sold off afterwards where they were purchased by Etruscans who are seen by some as 'a rich but artistically immature and impoverished people' (Boardman 1980: 199). Others have sought an alternative by suggesting that 'possibly the vases were long on public display in the potters' quarter before sale or choice for shipment' (Boardman 1975: 88). Johnston (1979: 40–1) has, however, demonstrated that different types of mark appear on groups of pots 'related by workshop' which would lend support to those who believe that pots went straight from place of production to the external markets.

The value of pots in antiquity has attracted much recent comment. John Boardman has attempted to show that 'Athenian decorated pottery was not cheap and that it was as valuable and profitable a trade commodity as most that any classical ship took on board' (Boardman 1988a: 33; 1988b; and endorsed by Arafat and Morgan 1989: 336). He attempted to calculate the value of pots and then compare this with other commodities; I would, however, disagree with the validity of some of his data, and it is clear that his calculations do not correspond with his published tables (Gill 1988a; 1991a). There perhaps needs to be a note of caution, as there are few known prices for pots and other commodities. It is clear from what evidence is available that his assertion does not hold. If we take a selection of items which includes metals, foodstuffs, and pots then their value in drachmas per cubic metre ranges from 28 for painted pots, and 37 for ceramic tiles, to 98 for oil and 95 for wheat, and

Table 6.1. *Approximate values of various commodities per cubic metre*

Painted pottery	28–67 dr
Ceramic tile	37–89 dr
Wine	41–438 dr
Barley	57–114 dr
Wheat	95–305 dr
Oil	98–547 dr
Lead	514–1285 dr
Silver phialai	79,300–113,300 dr
Gold phialai	952,200–1,620,000 dr

beyond that 514 for lead and 952,200 for gold (table 6.1). From these figures, ceramic tiles could be more valuable than figure-decorated pots, and metals considerably so (Gill 1991a).

Pots as containers

One of the great red herrings in the study of pots and trade has been the suggestion that figure-decorated vessels were themselves containers of wine and oil; some seem to have served as containers for perfumed oil. Although few would continue to use this argument, it has been used to dismiss pots from discussions of trade and export. Thus Garnsey (1988: 110) can write: 'It is unsafe to infer the existence of a substantial export trade in wine and oil from the wide diffusion of decorated vases.' However it is clear, as Finley (1985b: 23) for example recognised, that pots can mirror trade in other commodities.

The fact that fine pottery might accompany amphora-based commodities need not restrict us to think only in terms of wine, oil and fish-sauce. For example, an Etruscan amphora from the Giglio Island shipwreck was found to contain olive stones (Bound 1985: 68, fig. 6). A painted inscription on a fragmentary Palestinian bag-shaped amphora of AD 450–530, a shape normally associated with the wine trade (Peacock and Williams, 1981: 191 class 46), showed that it had, at one time, contained pistachio nuts (Shelton 1991: 276, no. 12, pl. xxi; Gill 1991b).

Quantification

Finley (1985a: 33) has called for more quantification of excavated finds of pottery so that trade can be measured. The tabulation of ceramic finds from Etruria has plotted the decrease in Corinthian and East Greek pottery and the increase in Attic imports (e.g. Martelli 1979). Such a swing was seen by Beazley as follows:

By the middle of the sixth century [Attic vases] have penetrated everywhere, and above all, the great Etruscan market is in the hands of the Athenians. Their monopoly of fine pottery remained almost unchallenged for over a hundred years. (Beazley 1926: 600)

This art-historical approach to trade is taken one step further as he continues:

The earliest Attic artist whose name we know is the vase-painter Sophilus. Sophilus was by no meant a dolt; but it was not such men as he who beat the Corinthians for ever from the field. It was men like Ergotimus and Clitias, the maker and the painter of the François vase . . . a marvel of minute yet masculine work. (pp. 600–1)

Do we really believe that Greek pottery was exported purely through its artistic merits or could there be other reasons?

Certainly quantitative studies have allowed comparisons between different areas and cities. Attic black-glossed pots seem to have arrived at Camirus on Rhodes and Marion on Cyprus at very similar rates until towards the end of the fifth century when numbers rose on Cyprus, perhaps owing to increased demand for copper during the Peloponnesian War; the break-off at Camirus at the end of the fifth century is due to the synoecism of Rhodes (Gill 1988c: 179, fig. 2, 180). A glance at a comparison of Attic pottery from Etruscan cities shows that Caere, Tarquinia and Vulci, with relatively easy access to the coast, have higher black-figured imports than the inland cities of Orvieto and Chiusi where access was by river. Interestingly Bologna's peak corresponds with the levels of imports at Orvieto and Chiusi rather than what is happening at Spina on the coast (Martelli 1979; Meyer 1980).

Spina itself is unusual as the levels of imports seem high at a time when they were falling elsewhere. Indeed the levels are such that the cemeteries have been described as 'probably the greatest single source of fine Athenian vases in the Greek world, or outside it' (Boardman 1980: 228). It is probably not adequate to think of Spina's prosperity purely in terms of agricultural products from the Po valley. Rather, as Nash (1985) has proposed, changes in central Europe away from the Rhône and Marseilles, gave greater emphasis to the Alpine passes, northern Italy and the Po valley. Thus Spina found itself as a port linking the societies of central Europe with the Greek world. Indeed one possibility of trade is that the warrior societies were supplying slaves to the urban communities of the Greek world. Is it not worth considering that the large quantities of pottery at Spina represent the southward movement of bulky cargoes of slaves down the Adriatic?

The chronological horizon for the emergence of Spina is one that coincides with other ports around the Mediterranean. During the excavation of one of the houses at Spina, built on a dune of virgin sand, several sherds of Attic black-figured pottery were found. Pots of this style appear to make the refoundation of the port at Al Mina, Woolley's level 4, after a gap of some fifty years (Gill 1988c: 180). This horizon should now be placed sometime after 480 if we accept the reinterpretation of the so-called Rectangular Rock-Cut Shaft at Athens (Francis and Vickers 1988). Does this adjustment mean that we should now see renewed Mediterranean-wide trading activity – mirrored by the pottery – in the years immediately after the Persian Wars?

Shipwrecks

The controlled excavation of shipwrecks has shown us several things (A. Parker 1990). First, that fine pottery seems to have been exported alongside other commodities. There has yet to be found a shipwreck which has conclusively been shown to have contained pots alone. Early reports of the Dattilo shipwreck said to have been carrying a cargo 'almost exclusively of BG [black-glossed] tableware' (Wilson 1988: 125) seems to have been premature. Second, wrecks such as that off Giglio Island were found to have been carrying pottery of several different fabrics, which reminds us that pots produced in one area could be carried by ships from another area (Bound 1985). It is to this area of the geographical origins of the traders that we can now turn.

One of the few ancient references to the trade in pottery appears in pseudo-Scylax where Phoenicians are recorded as exchanging Athenian pots, perfume and 'Egyptian stone' for various animal skins and ivory in west Africa (Gill 1988d: 6–7).

Shefton (1982) has reminded us that Phoenicians are likely to have been responsible for the westward transport of Early Protocorinthian kotylai and SOS amphorae which have been found in some quantity in Spain. Indeed the appearance of eastern silver plate in Etruscan and Campanian tombs with these kotylai and amphorae may also hint at Phoenician activity in Etruria at an early stage. The appearance of Attic black-glossed Castulo cups in north Africa and Spain during the second half of the fifth century BC may indicate the continuing activity of this trade. Moreover the levels of Attic black-glossed pottery at the western Phoenician city of Sabratha match those in Spain during the fourth century BC (Gill 1986).

It is noteworthy that the Phoenicians are re-emerging in modern scholarship as the carriers of Greek pottery. For in the 1930s A. Blakeway (1933) in his discussion of the appearance of Greek pottery in the West before colonisation, the so-called 'trade before the flag' debate, refused to give the Phoenicians 'the credit of having carried the Greek Geometric pottery of the eighth century to the West'. Rather for him the appearance of Greek pottery was evidence for Greek commerce.

Although few would wish to argue along the same lines as Blakeway, his thesis was one that sought to attack the Hasebroek (1933) position. Blakeway's aim was to restate the importance of trade in a pre-colonial era, and to do that he had to dismiss any who would suggest that non-Greeks were involved. It is in this connection that I turn to Al Mina. To the question of who founded this 'trading station', Boardman (1980: 40) responded with 'the finds'. The appearance of Euboean wares was for him firm evidence that Euboeans founded the port, even though there is an equally strong possibility that non-Euboeans (or even non-Greeks) carried it there.

This tradition of seeing Al Mina as a Greek port goes back to Woolley (1938: 15) who in 1938 had described the merchants as Greeks. His interpretation was based in part on a twentieth-century view of twentieth-century trade in the eastern Mediterranean. He commented that in Alexandretta (Iskenderum) in the 1930s 'heads of business firms are seldom Syrians, and it is likely to have been so in the past' (p. 16). This comment is linked to his interpretation of the site at Al Mina: 'at al Mina, where the foreign trade was exclusively with Greece, the handling of the trade can scarcely have been done by others than Greeks or Levantines of Greek origin' (p. 16). Yet of the Greek inscriptions which he cites, two are from jar handles, and a third is from a stamped amphora handle (p. 145, fig. 20). These were clearly imported items and need not reflect on the ethnic background of the merchants. There is a Greek graffito on the wall of a Late Geometric skyphos from the site (Johnston 1990: 476 D) but its presence is surely no more significant than a Greek graffito on a piece of Attic black-glossed pottery from the Phoenician site of Sabratha (Gill 1986: 276–7, 287, pl. 64a, no. 91).

Even pottery can be misleading. Some of the pottery found in the early levels used a multiple brush and this was seen as an indication of 'Greek hands' at work (Boardman 1959). The ground gained in the argument, by asserting that Greeks and especially Euboeans were actively involved in the east, must be shaken by recent scientific analysis of the pots in question which can now be shown to have a Cypriot origin (R. E. Jones 1986: 694–6). The presence of Greeks in the east is a central one to present theories about the adoption of Semitic script by the Greek world, as well as the influence of the East on Greek art and thought (cf. Boardman 1990: 170). It is clear that such theories need to be reassessed on the grounds of the recent evidence.

A similar approach in identifying traders or settlers by

their pottery is taken when trying to explain the different proportions of imported wares at Tocra in Cyrenaica (Boardman and Hayes 1966: 14). Such a thesis, if followed to its logical conclusion, would suggest that the population of eighteenth-century England (or at least the social elites) was predominantly Chinese.

Politics and trade

This misunderstanding of the role of pottery and trade has started to influence the ways that we view states interfering with commerce during times of war. In particular, surprising views have been expressed about the appearance at Corinth of Attic pottery; we are supposed to imagine the consternation at Corinth because, as one recent commentator has described it, the citizens 'could not communicate with an Attic potter to order anything specific or depend upon receiving anything at a specific time' (Herbert 1977: 4). B. R. MacDonald (1982) has attempted to identify the amounts of imported Attic pottery at Corinth and in Corinthian settlements during the Peloponnesian War. Imports continued to arrive at Corinth despite the war, and MacDonald (p. 118) explains this in terms of warring states not interfering 'with the trade of a non-essential item such as pottery'. Yet such a view is not adequate as it does not explain the movement of pottery between producer and consumer. Are we to believe that pots alone travelled between the centres and therefore there was no interference? Or if they accompanied other commodities which have not survived in the archaeological record, why was this trade allowed to continue? Perhaps the problem is that trade in commodities tends to be viewed in terms of the producer state, rather than seeing merchants as free from any ties.

The positivist fallacy and chronology

The positivist fallacy has also been applied to chronology, where it requires 'the evidence of excavations to express itself in the language of historical narrative' (Snodgrass 1987: 62). Although one might choose to disagree with the new historical framework which M. Vickers and the late E. D. Francis have proposed (see most recently Francis 1990), it is no longer possible to pretend that the present Studniczka-Langlotz chronology is without flaw. Archaeological deposits which have fragments of 106 pots in more than one layer, sometimes separated by up to 3 m, are not likely to be carefully stratified deposits (Francis and Vickers 1988). Stratified pottery from underneath the temple of Aphaia on Aegina cannot be later than the construction (Gill 1988e; 1993). Three unstratified Late Geometric sherds alone should not be presented as belonging to a pre-destruction layer at Hama because this would help to retain a high chronology (Francis and Vickers 1985). The old chronology might be correct, but if it is to be retained then it should be re-argued and not be allowed to stand on flimsy evidence (cf. Biers 1992).

We have already had cause to note problems with the chronology at Al Mina, and certainly it is probably better to try to define the general chronological horizon into which the pottery falls than to choose a date which automatically tries to relate to the historical record. The Corinthian aryballoi from the Giglio Island shipwreck (Bound 1985: 68, fig. 9, 69, figs. 13–14) belong to the horizon defined by Early Corinthian pottery (cf. Payne 1931: pl. 21, 6 [no. 496B] and 7 [no. 488]). This is a period when the settlement at Naucratis in Egypt was established (although there is one scrap of Transitional Corinthian pottery which is said to be from the site: Boardman 1980: 121, fig. 138). However, this poses a problem. Herodotus (2.178) tells us that the foundation dates to the reign of Amasis (568–526 BC), but the pottery, on the orthodox chronology, to '630–620 BC' (Bowden 1991). If the movement of pottery is more usually due to the currents of trade in other commodities, then perhaps we would expect the earliest pottery to belong to a phase after the foundation of the *emporion*, rather than an earlier settlement, unattested in the literary sources. In any case the role of the settlement viewed through the ceramic finds is bound to be challenged by the Naucratis stele of

Nektanebos II which records the movement of gold, silver, timber and worked wood through the port (Gunn 1943). There are clearly some problems which have yet to be resolved.

Conclusion

It has been usual to see the distribution of Greek pottery as a reflection of demand for *objets d'art* by societies which could afford them. The low value of pottery in antiquity, demonstrated by commercial graffiti, has forced us to review the privileged position which it has held in modern scholarship. Shipwrecks have reminded us that pottery could accompany trade in other commodities and that the nationality of traders need not be the same as that of the potters. The appearance of non-Greeks in the literary sources as the carriers of pottery should encourage us to rethink the view that the spread of Greek artefacts indeed represents the spread of the Greeks overseas.

Acknowledgements

I am particularly grateful to Michael Fulford, Ian Morris, Robin Osborne and Michael Vickers for their comments on earlier drafts of this paper, as well as the participants of seminars in Oxford and Reading who have helped to clarify some of the areas of discussion.

7

Athens, Etruria and the Heuneburg: mutual misconceptions in the study of Greek–barbarian relations

KARIM ARAFAT and
CATHERINE MORGAN

Artefacts made and decorated within self-conscious local traditions, especially those in regular use, reflect and reinforce the identities and priorities of the societies which produce them. When they move beyond the boundaries of the producer society and are integrated within the material cultures of other social groups, they acquire new roles and meanings. Hence it is possible to think of such artefacts as commodities with ascribed, but redefinable, social identities and value (Appadurai 1986a; Kopytoff 1986). Fine decorated pottery is such a case in the Archaic and Classical Greek world, and in this paper we shall explore the ways in which the products of one particularly well-documented regional school, Attic, were integrated into the material systems of non-Athenian communities. Not only does this problem bear directly upon issues of social values, it also has implications for the study of trade and contact between societies. Extensive discussion of the archaeological evidence for Mediterranean trade has made much of the potential role of pottery (e.g. Boardman 1988a; 1988b; Gill 1988a; Johnston 1979: 33–5; Morel 1983; Snodgrass 1980a: 126–9; Vallet and Villard 1963), which is still tacitly regarded as a consistent and comparable component in the material cultures of most regions of the Greek world, and thus as a reliable basis for generalisation about the direction and strength of inter-regional contacts within and beyond the Mediterranean (as illustrated by the arguments of Gill 1988c). Such generalisations have gained particular significance as a result of the popularity of core/periphery models (derived principally from the work of Wallerstein 1974; cf. Braudel 1972; Woolf 1990), via which inter-regional relations within and beyond the Mediterranean have come to be described primarily in the economic terms of supply and demand (T. Champion 1989: 1–21; Rowlands 1987c).

Attempts to chart the relationship during the sixth and fifth centuries between a core of Greek or Mediterranean consumer states and the dependent barbarian periphery which supplied them have proved popular amongst European prehistorians (e.g. Brun 1987; Collis 1984: ch. 4; Cunliffe 1988: ch. 2; Frankenstein and Rowlands 1978), especially those who face the difficulty of interpreting Mediterranean goods on their sites. This approach has superficial attractions, not least for the way in which it forces high level integration of data across a wide area. Yet, as we shall show, it glosses over variations in production, modes of exchange and the role of different categories of material culture in a fashion that is less than satisfactory.

Attic pottery and Athenian trade

Athenian black- and red-figured pottery has long been the subject of chronological and iconographical study (R. M. Cook 1972: 287–327, cf. Beazley 1951; 1956; 1963; Boardman 1974; 1975; 1989), and we now have detailed knowledge of stylistic developments and the careers of individual potters and painters. Equally, resource distribution, the social circumstances governing the organisation of production and marketing, and the local role of iconography and particular vessel types all form background conditions for the production of fine pottery which circulated widely beyond producer communities, and these conditions help to explain the diversity of local ceramic styles in Greece from the early Iron Age onwards (D. Arnold 1985; Rice 1981; 1984: ch. 4; 1987: ch. 6; van der Leeuw and Pritchard 1984: introduction). In the case of Attica, there is a comparatively large body of evidence for all of these aspects of local ceramic ecology (Arafat and Morgan 1989).

Throughout Greece, Attica included, decorated finewares belong within that category of artefacts which reinforce regional boundaries, whilst others, such as architecture, sculpture or metalwork, cross them (Hodder 1982a: chs. 3, 4; Morgan 1990: 85–9; Morgan and Whitelaw 1991). Unlike state inspired architecture or sculpture, pots were first and foremost personal possessions and their iconography reflects changes in individual interests and self-perception (Arafat 1990a: 175–7). In Attica, for example, there is a trend away from episodes which can be read directly by individuals as representations of aristocratic ideals (funerals, battles or chariot scenes), and which mainly appear on vases used as markers on wealthy burials during the eighth century (Ahlberg 1971a; 1971b; Snodgrass 1987: 148–50), towards the incorporation of similar themes into allusive, mythical episodes (Osborne 1988a). This accords well with the slow process of political integration visible in other aspects of material behaviour (e.g. I. Morris 1987), diverting the attention of individuals from factional interests and towards purely personal, or communal concerns coincident with the interests of the emerging state (Arafat and Morgan 1989: 329–36; Morgan 1990: chs. 1, 6; Starr 1986: chs. 3–6). Although never a tool of factional propaganda or a prominent medium for the display of elite wealth, Attic vases reflected in their iconography interests generally appropriate to individuals as citizens of the state (Boardman 1984: 240; R. M. Cook 1987; H. A. Shapiro 1989: 1–17). Thus we find allusions to Athenian achievements, such as the capture of Aegina in 458, reflected in scenes of Zeus' pursuit of Aegina (Arafat 1990a: ch. 3), or developing political interests, shown in changing depictions of the Amazonomachy or of Theseus, founding father of the Athenian state (Gauer 1988; Boardman 1982).

It is unusual to find Attic finewares produced specifically for a foreign market, and here we emphasise that we are considering only finewares and not container vessels (including amphorae) or coarse and cooking wares whose spread was largely governed by functional criteria, and which present separate problems beyond the scope of this chapter. A rare and exceptional case of fineware production for the Achaemenid empire involved just a few workshops (notably that of Sotades *c.* 460–50, and slightly later, the Kleophon painter: de Vries 1977), and most production was geared to home needs. The basic unit of production was probably the extended family, the oikos, whose wealth lay primarily in land, and who supplemented its income by craft production (Arafat and Morgan 1989: 314–29). A degree of flexibility was possible in scheduling production to suit the demands of the agricultural cycle, especially when sailing seasons and the visits of negotiatores were limited to short periods in any year, but Athenian producers could not greatly expand or contract their activities to suit foreign demand (even if it existed). There is no evidence to suggest that any Greek state encouraged the industrial production of goods to exchange for foodstuffs (Finley 1965; cf. Garnsey 1988: 110). Equally, no region of Greece (or indeed the Mediterranean) lacked the resources or technology to produce its own finewares; there is no evidence for the regular movement of clay in the Greek world and many factors militate against it.[1] Acquisition of the right clay is a prerequisite for the production of good fineware, but mixing of clays was rarely a viable proposition in the manufacture of glazed wares, and it is unlikely that any society would choose the vulnerable course of basing its local fineware style on imported clay. Equally, it seems unlikely that a community would regularly sell its best clay, and second rate clays would offer few advantages. So in view of the existence of locally significant variations in ceramic style, the wide distribution of basic resources for pottery production, and locally based patterns of work, it may seem hard to understand why fine pottery circulated comparatively widely across state boundaries.

Unlike marble or essential commodities (such as metal), pottery cannot be classified as heavy freight (Cartledge 1983: 12–14; Snodgrass 1980a: 126–9; 1983) and was rarely a primary component of any cargo (although the notion that low value goods were used as ballast is hard to support in shipping terms: A. Parker 1990: 342). Yet even if fine pottery was just a space filler, it is important to consider how and why Athenian vessels moved on the scale that they did (especially as they were rarely traded for their contents: Johnston 1979: ch. 8). Recent studies have focused upon the value of pottery of all kinds (often without discrimination) as a commodity of trade (Boardman 1988a; 1988b; Gill 1988a; Johnston 1979: 33–5); John Boardman, for example, has attempted to consider the relative cost of carriage, and the profit to be made from pottery in relation to the overall content of an 'ideal' Athenian cargo (1988a). Since the lower the value of the raw material converted into an exchangeable item, the higher the relative degree of profit which *could* be made from that exchange, the commercial value of pottery lies in its relative cheapness and ability to earn a quick profit *if* there was a market and a suitable gap in the hold. As a move beyond analogy and an attempt to consider the place of pottery in Athenian cargoes, this is a step in the right direction, but it does not encompass variation in the presence, proportion and origin of each commodity according to route. We know very little about the structure and role of individual trade routes, and although wreck evidence is valuable where preserved, there is so little of it that general trends are hard to identify with confidence (Gibbins 1990; A. Parker 1990). In fact, wrecks highlight the variety of roles which pottery could play in a cargo: the Archaic Giglio wreck is notable for the range of Corinthian pottery (aryballoi and oinochoai) carried with Etruscan and Phoenician amphorae (Bound 1985), whereas the Porticello wreck of *c.* 400 carried bronze statuary as its main cargo (plus amphorae and bullion) and such pottery as has been found consisted of utilitarian wares for the use of the crew (Eiseman and Ridgway 1989: ch. 3).

Trademarks were applied to vessels at the place of production, and the range of local scripts on Attic vases (e.g. Etruscan, Ionian and Aeginetan) suggests that traders from other areas of Greece and Etruria visited Athens to obtain vases for shipment (Johnston 1979: ch. 11; 1985; 1987). The great majority of some 2,500 underfoot marks known from the late seventh until the fourth century occur on Athenian vases, in contrast to Corinth, where vessels of Corinthian manufacture bearing dipinti have them almost exclusively in Corinthian script (Johnston 1979: 234–5). Furthermore, in

Archaic and early Classical times it is impossible to trace any significant correlation between Athenian interests and regions where Attic pottery is found (B. R. MacDonald 1979). One might therefore argue that Athenians played a very small part in shipping Attic pottery, and that Athens either could not or would not handle directly the bulk of trade in her own products. However, evidence is very limited, and as a cautionary tale it is worth noting that even in the fourth century, when sources are more plentiful, it is possible to construct opposing arguments, that most traders were Athenians or that most were not, using more or less the same evidence (cf. E. Cohen 1990; M. H. Hansen 1984; P. Millett 1983). Nevertheless, available evidence does suggest that there was less overlap between the groups involved in production and trading in Athens than, for example, in Corinth, and the general picture is one of *ad hoc* negotiation between Athenian producers and shippers or purchasers.

There is therefore nothing self-evident in the import of pottery decorated in the traditions of other social groups. The decision to acquire wares originally produced by Athenians for their own purposes was an important one, and in this article we shall focus upon the nature of the relationship between producer, carrier and purchaser in examining underlying reasons for the decision to use finewares made and decorated to suit other people's social requirements. The value placed on fine pottery today, both for its qualities of preservation and for its art-historical interest, is unlikely to be the same as its ancient material value (Gill 1988b; Vickers 1986; 1987; 1990b). Yet this only heightens the need to consider its specific role in each individual producer and importer society, and to understand how and why it was exchanged; whatever one's views on the value of pottery (and however one chooses to approach the concept of value), one cannot avoid the issue of why pottery was circulated and the contexts in which it was used. It is therefore unfortunate that studies of trade and exchange have concentrated upon the actions of traders and the effects of the market upon Athenian potters, yet have failed to relate them to the structure of markets and to consider links between patterns of contact and the role of imported pottery within the material cultures of receptor communities. Ethnographical and historical analogies have forced us to re-examine certain assumptions about the role of fine pottery (e.g. Gill 1988d; Vickers 1984: 90–1), but generalisations, cautionary tales and non-structural analogies are no substitutes for testing models on specific Greek data. We shall therefore pursue these issues by investigating the role of Archaic and Classical Attic finewares in two contrasting Mediterranean contexts, Etruria and Hallstatt Europe, two societies which differ greatly in their organisational affinity to the *polis*

world, and thence their comprehension of 'Greek' culture (fig. 7.1).

Etruria

Etruscan society

On a general level, the pattern of Etruscan state development and the factors underlying it show certain general similarities with the Greek world, especially in trends such as an eighth-century population rise, agricultural intensification and settlement nucleation (cf. d'Agostino 1990a). Contacts and material exchange (on a small scale) were resumed in the eighth century after a post-Bronze Age hiatus, and from this time onwards, Greek pottery regularly occurs on Etruscan sites and 'Italian' metalwork appears at several Greek sanctuaries (d'Agostino 1990b; Kilian 1977; Kilian-Dirlmeier 1985). Yet the Etruscan states are also significantly different in their settlement organisation, structures of government and the role of local elites. These factors helped to create a distinctive indigenous pattern of development which owes nothing to the Greek state, and a cultural boundary between

	GREECE (Athens)	ETRURIA	W EUROPE
1200			
	LH IIIC		HALLSTATT A1
1100	SM	PROTO	HALLSTATT A2
		VILLANOVAN	
1000	PG		HALLSTATT B1
900	EG		HALLSTATT B2
800	MG	VILLANOVAN	HALLSTATT B3
	LG		EIA
700			HALLSTATT C
600	ARCHAIC	ORIENTALISING	
			HALLSTATT D
500		ARCHAIC	
400	CLASSICAL	CLASSICAL	LA TENE 1a/A

7.1 Greece, Etruria and Hallstatt Europe: relative chronology.

Etruria and the Greek world which is quite different from divisions between Greek states (Stoddart 1989), and which must have affected the movement of a category of artefact as culturally specific as fine decorated pottery.

By the Archaic period, southern Etruria was divided into a series of small polities, each consisting of a defined territory containing a primary centre linked to an entrepôt, and sometimes a secondary centre also (fig. 7.2). Although archaeological interest in anything other than art and tombs is a recent development (Stoddart 1987: ch. 2), field survey in a number of regions enables us to trace the settlement changes which accompanied state formation (Guidi 1985;

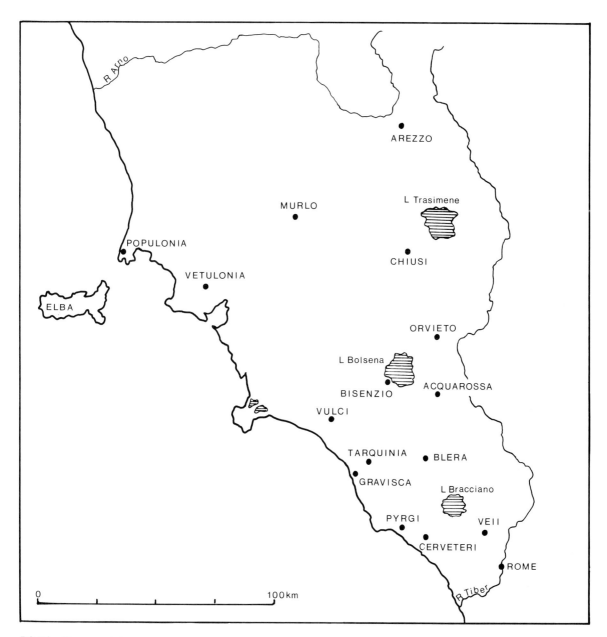

7.2 The Etruscan states.

Potter 1979; Stoddart 1987: chs. 6, 7). Nucleated centres which formed the basis of city states began to develop from the end of the tenth century, mainly on the sites of Late Bronze Age settlements (d'Agostino 1985; di Gennaro 1982; Mansuelli 1985); the pace of change quickened during the eighth century, and a constant filling out of the landscape produced, by *c.* 500, an unbalanced settlement structure with a heavy concentration on primary centres, pressure on land near nucleated settlements and greater use of marginal land (Potter 1979: 69–87, ch. 4). During this period, a steady increase in population was accompanied by the development of increasingly complex social ranking and administrative institutions, and also an intensification and diversification of agriculture (with associated technological changes such as terracing, hydraulic engineering and drainage) and engineering projects, including the creation of a road system, all of which required the organisation of labour (Ward-Perkins 1962).

Although the lack of detailed area excavation makes it difficult to generalise about urban functions and development, reflections of the urban focus of political and economic power include restrictions on trading activity, the distribution of inscriptions (Stoddart and Whitley 1988) and especially the high degree of ritualisation (Edlund 1987: ch. 3). Monumental religious buildings, such as the ritual complex of Piazza d'Armi or the extra-mural Portonaccio temple and sanctuary complex (both at Veii), are an essentially urban phenomenon, and by the sixth century one also finds burials concentrated in formal funerary areas on roads leading from cities (Colonna 1985a: chs. 4 and 6; Spivey and Stoddart 1990: 110–26). As the authority of urban elites was consolidated through the sixth and early fifth centuries, so the boundaries of state territories were occasionally marked with shrines such as those at Punta della Vipera, or Foce della Marangane on the boundary between Cerveteri and Tarquinia (Stoddart 1987: ch. 7.3.1).

The development of the Etruscan countryside is closely related to the needs of the elite concentrated in urban centres. Large country farmsteads within state territories (Barker 1988) provided wool, textiles and wine to satisfy the tastes of developing elites (vine trenches and pressing equipment have been found at the villa at Blera, for example: Ricciardi *et al.* 1985), and whether or not olives and vines were indigenous to Etruria, the beginnings of systematic polyculture during the sixth century coincide with state formation. The importance of the products of the countryside to urban life is reflected in the choice of ritualised feasting as a means of expressing elite status, and in the relatively frequent appearance in wall painting of subjects involving the hunting, preparation and consumption of food (*Alimentazione*). Furthermore, the emergence of large urban

centres in the southern coastal area itself produced a form of economic zoning within Etruria, as more conservative northern regions (especially those inland) developed agricultural specialities (notably viticulture) to suit southern markets. Northern society was considerably slower to adopt the changes in material behaviour and settlement ordering evident in the south (and certain areas and aspects of life remained very different: Cristofani and Zevi 1985; Stoddart 1987: ch. 3). With the exception of the northern city of Chiusi, imported Attic pottery was confined to southern urban centres and their entrepôts.

Imported Attic finewares consist almost exclusively of vessels (cups, kraters, hydriae and amphorae) which could be used for the symposia of urban elites. From *c.* 650, greater social stratification and centralisation of power was accompanied by the development of an increasingly elaborate and varied elite material culture (Camporeale 1985). From the seventh, and especially the sixth centuries onwards, wall paintings show elite pastimes including feasting (Cristofani 1987) and agonistic activity; boxing at Tarquinia (Jannot 1985), for example, or the armed dance which appears in a number of media (Camporeale 1987; Spivey 1988). Horse-riding and hunting also appear in tomb depictions, and in view of the fact that horses played a minimal subsistence role (rarely appearing in faunal deposits), horse-owning seems to have been largely an elite preserve. Ritualised feasting and drinking also have a long history; drinking vessels first appeared in quantity especially in graves during the eighth century (along with (largely Athenian) SOS amphorae in the graves of chieftains: Jones and Johnston 1978: 103–4, 119–20), and increased in popularity with the spread of indigenous viticulture through the sixth. Bruno d'Agostino (1989) makes the point that the symposium was the 'emblem of seigneurial ideology' and that it was used as such by the new classes which emerged during the sixth century with the development of trade and commercial agriculture. Since the wealth of the countryside rested on production for urban elites (Barker 1988) and for limited export (cf. Bound 1985), elite activities depended upon, and perpetuated the structure of, agricultural exploitation of state territory. Thus the activity for which Attic imports were used had a well-defined and long-established place in the structure of elite behaviour.

The material culture of the urban elite in each major centre appears increasingly uniform over time, and reflects shared economic values and ruler ideology (Stoddart 1987: ch. 8.2.3). Yet it is possible to identify local styles and production places for certain classes of artefact which were then widely exchanged (Bouloumié 1982: 776–7; Camporeale 1985: 84), e.g. bucchero at Cerveteri (T. Rasmussen 1979: 148–50), or to a lesser extent, bronzework at Vulci (d'Agostino 1985: 46), and the development of exchange networks within Etruria runs parallel to that of external trade. From the time of the resumption of strong links with the Eastern Mediterranean during the Orientalising period, foreign access to Etruscan markets was increasingly controlled and focused upon city centres via the development of entrepôts as formal centres of contact (Baglione 1988; Martelli 1979: 38–9; 1985). This system maintained a restriction of access to those communities which contributed to the expression and maintenance of elite status (cf. Whitley, this volume); the wide range of foreign amphorae at Gravisca, for example, contrasts markedly with the primarily local distribution in the hinterland (Boitani 1985; Colonna 1985d; Slaska 1985). Entrepôts were highly ritualised, and cosmopolitan in a way that urban centres were not; Gravisca and Pyrgi had Greek-style temples with inscriptions in Greek, Phoenician and Etruscan (Colonna 1985a: chs. 3, 5–7; Edlund 1987: 75–7; F. Ridgway 1990), and Greek cults and Greek-inspired religious architecture were generally confined to entrepôts and did not extend into urban centres via any form of 'Hellenisation' (Torelli 1983: 482–5). Specific links between individual entrepôts and urban centres ensured an urban concentration of imports, but also limited the access of foreigners to Etruscan communities, since access to one port did not guarantee access to all. Clearly, such a system of proliferation of foreign connections operated for the benefit of Etruscans rather than for the ease of traders.

Attic imports

The import of Athenian finewares represents foreign contacts which, although not the earliest or even the most direct, differ significantly from previous connections. Earlier links with Corinth, via her western colonies, had an artistic impact resulting in the production of Etrusco-Corinthian pottery, but were comparatively weak and short lived (effectively over by *c.* 550; Szilágyi 1975). Corinthian activity in the West was focused on her colonies in southern Italy and Sicily, and there is little evidence for direct trade between Corinth and Etruria. Equally, very little Etruscan material has been found in Corinthia (Macintosh 1974; Shefton in T. J. Dunbabin 1962: 385–6). Although Juliette de la Genière (1988) has sought to identify specific Corinthian forms (notably kraters) which may have been produced for the Etruscan market, as yet we know too little about the full range of Corinthian production to draw such conclusions. Corinthian pottery in the colonies seems to have fulfilled a very specific and important social role: it is mainly found in wealthy graves and sanctuaries (insofar as excavation biases permit such conclusions) and was probably one of the many means used to express the identity and status of colonial

citizens and the community as a whole in relation to the mother city (Arafat and Morgan 1989: 335). The strength of the demand for Corinthian finewares in the western colonies may be reflected in the extremely faithful copies produced by Corcyra (Farnsworth *et al.* 1977), and it continued into the fifth century, when local imitative schools in west and central Sicily began to fill gaps in supply (Zimmermann-Munn 1983: 149–69). Corinth's main interests therefore lay in southern Italy and Sicily, and she may even have avoided direct contact with Etruria (perhaps because of the potential for conflict over land or political interests). There is no evidence (in the form of trademarks) of Etruscans buying Corinthian pottery direct from Corinth, and such vessels as they had probably came via the colonies (e.g. Livadie 1985).

In addition to their appearance in Etruria, Attic black- and red-figured wares occur under very different circumstances in southern Italy and Sicily (increasing in numbers at a time when they were becoming scarcer on the Greek mainland: Boardman 1979: 36–7). In turn, they acted as models when local schools of red-figure were established in Lucania, Apulia, Campania, Paestum and Sicily from the second half of the fifth century (Mayo 1982; Trendall 1989). Attic imports complemented the long-standing Corinthian connections noted above, and it is possible that part of the attraction of Attic fineware lay in its very different appearance; it also lacked the sociopolitical connotations attached to Corinthian, and since its technique offered greater scope for the creation of a rich, varied, but purely local iconography, it could serve as a springboard for the creation of distinctive local styles. The fifth-century Atticising South Italian schools offered the first viable and readily available alternatives to Corinthian imports and copies, and may therefore also have played a role in the long process of changing material behaviour in relation to the evolution of community identity. South Italian red-figure originated *c.* 440 and continued to be produced into the late fourth century. It is technically derived from Attic proto-types and certainly depended on the long-established skills of Greek colonists (Shefton 1967; Trendall 1989: 14–15). It is likely that Attic potters migrated to start workshops, but suggestions relating a migration to a supposed temporary decline in Athenian production are extremely tenuous (B. R. MacDonald 1979: 210–14; 1981). Whatever its origins, South Italian red-figure was a distinctively local style, which used and developed Attic shapes (often beyond their period of fashion in Athens) in addition to certain local ones, and employed a range of iconographical themes concentrating on everyday life (Trendall 1989: 9–13; 1990), and largely subsuming mythical episodes into tragic and comic theatrical scenes. Attic wares served merely as a basis for the creation of a colonial iconography which reflects a very different perception of 'Greekness'.

The role of Attic pottery in Etruria is quite different from that of Corinthian, or of Attic in South Italy and Sicily. First, the limited number of shapes found in Etruria contrasts with the wider and more balanced range found in Italy (which includes amphorae, pelikai, kraters and lekythoi). Even if there were no other evidence for independent patterns of supply, it would be hard to see how the Etruscan cities could have acquired sufficient supplies of the shapes they needed from areas to the south. Second, even allowing for biases in excavation, the great majority of imports in Etruria ended up in tombs, as symbols in mortuary display, and since they served their function by virtue of being imports they were not widely copied (a point to which we shall return). Indeed, many of the material trappings surrounding elite activities were used in this way: container vessels like amphorae, with commodities inviting to the elite, are not commonly found outside cemeteries and entrepôts (Boitani 1985; Slaska 1985). The chronology of Attic imports is closely linked to the expansion of elite funerary display (at most centres, elaborate chamber tombs began to appear during the sixth century, and wall painting and rich goods reached their height during the fifth).

Trademarks form our main source of evidence for the origins of those involved in the carrying trade. As Alan Johnston notes, a high proportion of all marks on Attic vases were found in Etruria, but the scripts represented (and the presence of dual numbering systems) suggest that although Etruscans were involved in shipping Attic pottery, most vessels travelled in non-Athenian Greek and other ships working their way through to Etruria (Johnston 1979: 5, 49, 238, ch. 4; 1985). Even if they were not directly involved at every stage, Etruscans provided the impetus for trade on the basis of their detailed knowledge of the structure of local markets, and Etruscan dipinti reveal the active role of Etruscan agents in re-assembling shipments that they had ordered in the Kerameikos before distribution to their customers. The long development of such an elaborate system reflects the complexity of the Etruscan market, with its proliferation of entrepôts. The clearest evidence for traders targeting particular sites (notably Cerveteri, Tarquinia and Vulci) comes during the sixth century (cf. p. 113 below), but even though a more general distribution of imports follows during the fifth, the continuing use of local distribution marks suggests that this was the result of improved Etruscan redistribution rather than a change of policy amongst traders. Clearly, this positive effort to secure imports raises a range of questions concerning attitudes to material innovation and the criteria by which elements of another society's material culture were selected and adapted.

Etruria and Attic production

In view of the suggestion that Athenians may have played a limited role in the distribution of their own finewares and that most activity seems to have been initiated by Etruscans, it is worth questioning whether the Etruscan market had any real impact on Athenian pottery production (a problem which has rarely been addressed: Scheffer 1988). There is limited archaeological evidence for Greek potters or painters from any region operating in Etruria. The appearance at Cerveteri in the mid-seventh century of a 'Greek' name (Aristonothos), of unknown ethnic origin, is exceptional as is the work of the Rondini and Bearded Sphinx Painters during the second half of the seventh century (in the East Greek and Etrusco-Corinthian traditions respectively; Camporeale 1985: 80); Pliny the Elder (*Natural History* 35, 151–2) also noted that three Corinthian artists, Eucheir, Diopos and Eugrammos, introduced clay modelling into Etruria (Arafat 1990b: 54). However, there is nothing to suggest that the vast majority of Attic vases found in Etruria were not made in Athens. Webster has sought to detach Athenian production from the Etruscan market altogether by proposing a second-hand trade in vessels ordered for Athenian symposia, used once and resold, yet there is no convincing evidence for the existence of such a trade or for how it might have operated (Boardman 1979: 34; Webster 1972: ch. 2), and there is no reason to suppose that the bulk of Attic pottery found in Etruria was not bought new for shipping directly or indirectly from Athens. The impact of Etruscan demand on Athenian production can only be assessed against the background of the organisation of the Athenian industry.

As noted, Attic pottery production can be characterised as a household-based system centred around extended families living in specific areas of the city centre and in certain scattered 'specialist' villages (Arafat and Morgan 1989). Along with other Athenian craftsmen, potters could lease, if not own, land (an essential mark of social status), and although there is a reasonable case for specialisation at oikos level, it is impossible to ignore the demands of the agricultural cycle. It will always be possible to find exceptional full-time workers or slaves (Canciani 1978), but it is generally less helpful to think of a division between full-time and part-time work than of a continuum of strategies relating pottery production to the agricultural base of the household economy. Potters could schedule their activities to ease out the burden of contracts through the year (especially those to be shipped during the short sailing season), but the overall organisation of the industry must have imposed limits on production (and perhaps also on the personal interests of potters), and it is easy to overestimate its scale. Even though Etruscan marketing was highly organised, the business of buying, or even commissioning, vessels in Athens was probably *ad hoc*, a matter of searching the Kerameikos for suitable vessels or someone prepared to make them (which in exceptional cases may have been the start of a regular commission from a particular workshop).

The two cases most often cited as showing the impact of the Etruscan market on Athenian potters do not contradict this view. Although the Etruscanising Tyrrhenian amphorae (fashionable *c.* 560–30; Carpenter 1983) have long been held to be Attic, doubts about their fabric, nonsense inscriptions, non-Attic elements in iconography and similarity to Pontic styles raise questions about their provenance (Carpenter 1984; Tiverios 1976). It has been suggested that they were Etruscan (Ginge 1988), yet the only example so far analysed has been shown to be Attic (Boardman and Schweitzer 1983: 270–1), and the question remains open. A non-Athenian Attic workshop, perhaps Attico-Boeotian, is another possibility. The second case is that of Nikosthenic amphorae, which were produced in the Nikosthenic workshop from *c.* 550, probably to fulfil a specific Etruscan commission (Eisman 1974). Their shape, derived directly from bucchero, belongs to an Etruscan tradition going back to ninth-century impasto (Gran Aymerich 1986; T. Rasmussen 1985: 34–5), and in addition to the majority decorated in black-figure, there is a group decorated predominantly in black-glaze with the occasional use of Six's technique on the neck which closely resembles bucchero. Along with most bucchero versions of the shape, Nikosthenic amphorae are mainly found at Cerveteri, and a specific local market may have lain behind the creation of a form new to Athenian potters. A further indication of the specific nature of this targeting is the fact that the small kyathoi produced by this same workshop are found overwhelmingly in two other cities, Orvieto and Vulci (Eisman 1974: 52; T. Rasmussen 1985: 35–6). The targeting apparently extends to the iconography of the vases, with, for example, three Nikosthenic amphorae showing boxers much as are seen on the contemporary wall painting from Tarquinia mentioned above (fig. 7.3; Beazley 1956: 217.8 (Rome, Torlonia), 225.9 (Rome, market). The products of the Nikosthenic workshop are by no means the earliest Attic imports in Etruria, but they reveal an exceptionally close link with a particular market, and a degree of 'product research' unparalleled during the second half of the sixth century (Scheffer 1988).

The Nikosthenic workshop was exceptionally large by Athenian standards; Eisman (1974: 48–9) suggests that it may have supported up to thirty men at any one time, and a great number of painters are known to have been associated with it. The small scale of most workshops (probably just single families and their dependents) facilitated the integration of pottery production with subsistence activities,

at least at oikos level, providing craftsmen with a valuable economic buffer. Since the size of the Nikosthenic workshop reflects a greater commitment to pottery production (perhaps at the expense of agriculture), and therefore greater economic vulnerability, extra income from commissions, however small, may have been useful. The fact that the Nikosthenic workshop is renowned for its innovations (pioneering Six's technique, for example, and being swift to employ red-figure painters) may reflect a particular need to keep abreast of the Athenian market (Eisman 1974: 49–52). Fragments of about one hundred Nikosthenic amphorae have been found in Etruria (perhaps all the work of Painter N, mostly in the 530s and 520s; Boardman 1974: 65), along with about 400 kyathoi from the same workshop over forty to fifty years (although their chronological distribution is uneven). Estimates of preservation vary greatly, yet whether one prefers a high rate (with a resulting

7.3 Neck detail of a Nikosthenic amphora (B64) signed by Nikosthenes as potter, from Cerveteri. From the collection of the Archaeological Society, Baltimore.

small number of vessels perhaps amounting to no more than a case or two or pottery each year) or a low (a figure of 1% for example, possibly resulting in as many as 1,700 amphorae exported per annum), production could be integrated into the annual output of the workshop, and a relatively small number of individuals could satisfy market demands via a long-standing trading relationship. The initial order may have resulted from a chance meeting between trader and potter in the Kerameikos, but it is easy to see how a long-term relationship and a regular commission could have developed. Since the trader who regularly marked pots 'SO' (Johnston 1979: 80–3) seems to have been responsible for moving many of the products of the Nikosthenic workshop (and also those of the Perizoma group), we see here a very personal system whereby one trader organised deals with one or two Athenian producers and supplied a defined local market around Cerveteri and Vulci.

The activities of the Nikosthenic workshop are by no means typical, however. The output of Athenian potters and painters does not appear to have been profoundly affected by Etruscan influences, and attempts to argue for market bias on the basis of the distribution of certain forms or scenes (e.g. Genière 1988) rarely take account of the total pattern. Ignorance of the provenance of most Attic vases (only 40%–60% of the output of most artists is securely traceable, Scheffer 1988: 536–7) and excavation biases make such statistics fallible. Although buyers exercised choice in selecting shapes and decoration suitable to their needs, this did not entail any significant addition to the repertoire produced for the home market (although cf. D. J. Williams 1988). That production for export was neither an essential part of the Athenian economy nor necessary for the survival of the pottery industry did not, of course, prevent skilled and inventive potters from adapting ideas from other regions to suit local tastes. Hence the introduction of eastern shapes like the rhyton or phiale, and also the possible impact of Etruscan metal or pottery shapes, especially kantharoi and kyathoi, on Attic black-glaze at least by the sixth century (Brijder 1988; T. Rasmussen 1985). Yet such experiments were first and foremost linked to the home market and did not result in the production of quantities of vessels unsaleable in Athens.

In assessing the strength of Athenian interest in trade with Etruria, it is important to consider the likely contents of cargoes. If Etruscan agents and non-Athenian shippers dealt with ordering and transport, they could presumably have stopped to pick up local produce almost anywhere en route: the Porticello wreck, for example, may have begun its journey as far east as Byzantium (Eiseman and Ridgway 1989: 107–13). A selection of wine, oil and fish from different regions, including Athens, could have formed a

major part of many cargoes, and Laurion silver and lead may also have been shipped (Eiseman and Ridgway 1989: 53–60; Gill 1988b). Yet the degree of direct Athenian input into the cargoes which reached Etruria is questionable, and what she gained in return is equally uncertain. Metals are possible (both finished vessels and ingots), since Etruria has a long history of metalworking, especially in iron and copper (d'Agostino 1985), and ceramic skeuomorphs of Etruscan metal forms are not uncommon (Brijder 1988; Gill 1987; T. Rasmussen 1985; cf. Vickers 1985b). Yet in view of the complex interests involved in assembling cargoes and marketing their contents, it would be simplistic to think purely in terms of input and return, and to devote too much attention to matching imports to exports, working out what Athenians wanted in return for their silver or pottery. Clearly selling produce to shipping agents brought returns, but we suggest that it is easy to overestimate the real value of Etruscan trade to Athenians.

Imports and Etruscan society

Returning to the question of Etruscan material behaviour, although it is easy to understand how Athenian pottery fitted into Etruscan elite display, its relationship to indigenous pottery production has been less well studied. Bronze vessels, beginning in the Late Bronze Age, outlasted and replaced Attic imports (van der Meer 1984 for depictions on wall paintings), and had a major impact on local pottery styles (especially bucchero). In Etruria, as in Athens, metal was perhaps a significant medium for the expression of wealth and status (cf. e.g. Gill 1988b). Equally, Attic pottery was not the only style to be imported; odd fragments of Cycladic and Euboean wares occur in graves as early as the eighth century (d'Agostino 1985: 46–7), but mass imports began with readily available Corinthian, followed by a brief period of Lakonian, and a major switch to Attic occurred only c. 560 (Martelli 1979: 44–5) (fig. 7.4). Earlier rich graves contained highly eclectic drinking sets, mixing bucchero with Lakonian, Attic and Ionian wares, or whatever was available (e.g. Cerveteri T170, second quarter of the sixth century; Martelli 1985: 195–9).

In considering why Attica came to be singled out, it is important to identify the ways in which it was suited to its specific role. One might point to its aesthetic affinity with indigenous products; Attic black-glaze resembles bucchero, and it is possible that the inlay effect of red-figure evoked metal styles (even if one does not accept Vickers' (1985b) argument that it was designed to do so). Equally, black- and red-figure techniques allow the depiction of complex narrative which is not easily rendered in bucchero (Gran Aymerich 1981; 1986; T. Rasmussen 1979: ch. 4; de Puma 1988 for an exceptional series of dance scenes on bucchero pesante oinochoai from Tarquinia dating from *c.* 550), and was not so popular in other Greek regional schools. The fact that mends are proportionally more common on Attic vessels found in Italy than in Attica (J. Boardman, pers. comm.) cannot solely be attributed to accidents en route, and suggests particular care of prized imports (especially as many mended imports in Etruria show signs of heavy wear; Boardman, pers. comm.). Occasionally, our evidence reveals the extent of Attic influence on Etruscan production, as in the case of a Nikosthenic amphora by the Etruscan Paris Painter which apparently imitates the decoration of the Attic Nikosthenic amphora (Dohrn 1937: 42–4; Jackson 1976: 38, 52 n. 1). However, it is neither adequate nor accurate to suggest that Etruscans sought to collect Attic vessels as possessions prized simply for their intrinsic worth (Beazley 1945: 158), nor was Etruria a passive recipient of Greek ideas, capable only of producing derivative art. Indeed, Etruscan art shows fundamental differences in the perception of the structure and role of iconography (Small 1987; Stoddart 1987: ch. 2). The argument that Attic vessels played an important and closely defined role in elite material behaviour should not be taken to imply that they were regarded as exceptionally valuable or copied as an ideal.

There is a strong case to be made for a more subtle role for Greek imports, as one element in a package of 'power art' by which the Etruscan elite reinforced their status as a group separate from the commons (Martelli 1985). In general, the means by which elites establish and express their status are vulnerable to change over time according to their contemporary social role, for example, or to perceived security of personal status. Non-staple imports imply wealth, but an equation between social stability and prosperity is more often assumed than demonstrated; indeed, such imports may be particularly important in times of social instability, when indigenous material systems may have required additional support. In Etruria, the fact that the growth of Attic imports coincides with a phase of generation of native art and iconography shows that they augmented rather than displaced local styles (e.g. Pontic vases, an urban style with an iconography reflecting elite interests, Lund and Rathje 1988). The importance of Attic vases rests upon the way in which elites expressed their status in relation to the populace. Ancestors and local genealogies played a central role in the maintenance of what was effectively a gerontocracy; this is reflected in funerary art, the use of inscriptions and the organisation of cemeteries such as those at Orvieto and Cerveteri (Colonna 1985b; Small 1986; Stoddart and Whitley 1988; Stoddart n.d.). The late sixth-century arrangement of family tombs, in 'streets' with regular frontages and similar internal structure, must be the result of a specific political decision, possibly emanating from the state

authority itself (the arrangement of the ninety tombs of the ring cemetery of Orvieto from *c.* 550–500 is a case in point; Cristofani 1979: 18–19). The perceived right of senior members of elite families to power permitted an emphasis on individualism rather than allegiance to the wider citizen body, and a preference in local art for scenes of aristocratic 'daily' life, and on imports for depictions of exotic heroes like Heracles, Achilles and Ajax, further reinforcing elite separation from the commons. Such Greek elements were readily comprehensible in view of the many points of comparison between Greek and Etruscan myth; Greek mythology was different from Etruscan, but it was meaningful and readily adaptable to Etruscan themes, and it is interesting that so many of the myth episodes derived from Etruscan (and early Roman) legend have come down to us in Greek guise (Spivey and Stoddart 1990: 98–106). Thus, for example, in later Etruscan art the Furies were used in infernal or funerary scenes to signify local female deities (Sarian 1986), and a long-lasting tradition developed in several media of the selective and 'uncanonical' use of Greek models to express Etruscan ideas (e.g. Bloch 1986; Scheffer 1984).

We suggest that much of the attraction of Attic vases lay in the value of their complex myth scenes for reinforcing the elite's exclusivity in their ability to read, comprehend and use such information (fig. 7.5). Control of myth information paralleled that of genealogy, and Attic iconography depicted

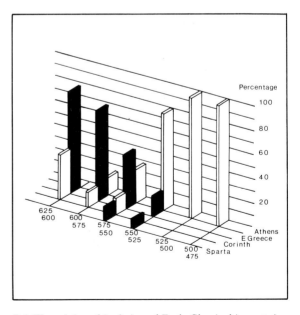

7.4 The origins of Archaic and Early Classical imports in Etruria (after Martelli 1985).

a much greater body of myth than anything on local vases; only the kind of people to whom such vases were available could have ready access to the information they conveyed. Shared knowledge of mythology was thus an elite social bond, and the connection was also expressed via continuing, if not numerous, dedications at a number of Greek sanctuaries, including Olympia and Delphi (Camporeale 1985; Colonna 1985c: 242–4, 256–7; Kilian 1977; Kilian-Dirlmeier 1985). The red-figure style also had great potential for development by Etruscan potters for Etruscan purposes (Gilotta 1986; 1988; Shefton 1967; early fourth-century Faliscan is a further case in point). This process began as the need for imports disappeared (effectively ending *c.* 450), and was not a matter of simple copying to augment imports, but rather the development of the red-figure technique for purely Etruscan purposes.

In investigating the context of Attic imports, and the relationship between material behaviour and the maintenance of the social system, it is important to consider the role of secondary or marginal centres. These centres appear to have varied in function, but since they were often too short-lived to develop complex urban structures they are not always easy to characterise (Stoddart 1987: ch. 7.3.2). Murlo (Poggio Civitate) is a particularly well-investigated case, located between polities and occupied between *c.* 650 and *c.* 530 with perhaps a short break at the end of the seventh century (Nielson 1984; Nielson and Phillips 1984; 1985; Talocchini and Phillips 1970). The presence of domestic debris and storage facilities, as well as the lack of any securely identifiable votive material, suggests some kind of residence, and the wealth of art of all kinds, terracottas, ivories and architectural ornament, reflects its high status. No Attic imports have been found (for Corinthian, Ionian and Lakonian vases: T. Rasmussen 1985/6: 119; Phillips 1984), but the range of indigenous artefacts is exceptionally rich (including terracottas, ivories and architectural ornament). There is also limited evidence of craft production (bronze and ironworking and the production of fine pottery).

The art of the secondary centres is eclectic but shows clear links with the status culture of the urban elites. Villanovan origins are often clear, but although a wide range of other stylistic influences can be traced, there are no signs of the thorough adoption of foreign (notably Greek) traits as found especially at entrepôts (e.g. Bianchi Bandinelli 1972; Edlund Gantz 1972; Torelli 1983: 478–82). The ritual character of much iconography at Murlo has led to the suggestion that Murlo's primary function was as a cult place, perhaps a meeting point for representatives of neighbouring polities (Edlund 1987: 87–92). Yet this is hard to equate with the site's residential function, and the suggestion that residence was confined to priests or sanctuary keepers does not take

into account the very personal character of scenes in many media, which seem rather to reinforce the status of the local ruler and his family. Terracotta akroteria (*c.* 575–550) probably show the ruler with the insignia of his office, and the banqueting frieze (*c.* 570) shows royal (or possibly divine) figures as onlookers at some ritual event (Small 1971). Ritual legitimised the local ruler's right to power and established his place in relation to the power structure of the urban elite. Yet the degree of investment evident in creating an iconography for the ruler of Murlo may reflect the instability and fragility of his position (Torelli 1983: 478–82). Innovations in iconography and other aspects of 'power art' were often developed, or quickly adopted, at secondary centres since these were least well established and in greatest need of legitimation. Styles are often closely linked to those found at primary centres (forms of terracotta decoration closely associated with a new version of the temple ground plan were first developed at Veii *c.* 600–570 (Piazza d'Armi), for example, but are subsequently found largely at marginal centres; cf. Colonna 1985a: ch. 3), yet the ways in which they are manipulated may be different. Rather than opting to emphasise imported status symbols, Murlo developed and copied experimental and very rich indigenous art forms, including those which harked back to its Villanovan ancestry. Partly this was a consequence of Murlo's geographical position, distant from other centres, inland and badly placed to receive direct imports, but the adoption and development of indigenous art styles must surely be a consequence of local political and social circumstances, especially as Murlo is not unique among secondary centres in its artistic development (Acquarossa is a similar case (Rystedt 1983) as is Bisenzio). In turn, challenges to the role of central places and to their mutually dependent relationship with the countryside are mirrored in the generation of art in urban centres, for example in the development, in Vulci or Cerveteri, of the so-called Pontic vase style, which these imports complement (e.g. Hannestad 1974; 1976).

The development of secondary sites (in two main phases, *c.* 750 and *c.* 550) may be taken as an index of change in the regional system. In view of the chronology of Attic ceramic imports, the second phase is especially interesting (although short lived). At the end of the sixth century, two major secondary centres, Acquarossa and Bisenzio, collapsed (perhaps because they had grown sufficiently large and powerful to disturb the primary centres and their relationship with rural producers), and a phase of renewed centralisation followed, heightening the imbalance in settlement organisation between very rich 'urbanised' principal sites, and country farms and remaining secondary centres. The peak of Attic pottery imports (*c.* 550–475) coincides with the second phase of secondary centre development, and its decline mirrors renewed centralisation. Since of all classes of artefact, Attic pots owed their place in Etruscan material culture to the way in which they can be used to reinforce and distinguish the qualities peculiar to the urban elite, it is possible that they were imported in greater quantities to reinforce the status of the elite at the time when it was most challenged.

Local versions of the black- and red-figured styles have their own distinctive stylistic traits and distribution, which do not accord with the notion that they simply served to augment Attic imports in urban contexts. The Micali Painter (*c.* 530–500) began to work in the black-figure style under Pontic influence and for much of his career made little attempt to imitate Attic, even though he served a local market around Vulci, a city which has produced some 52% of the Attic black-figure so far found in Etruria between *c.* 530 and 500, and where the final stages of Etrusco-Corinthian developed down to *c.* 540. His decorative style was eclectic (even at their height, Attic influences were relatively weak) and he consistently followed local preferences, for example in concentrating upon animal decoration (Spivey 1987). The distribution of the Micali Painter's vases is more like that of local finewares than Attic imports; they lie in a general scatter within an average radius of about 42 km around Vulci (70 km away at most), and their

7.5 *Cup by the Castelgiorgio Painter, from Vulci (London E67). Tondo: Zeus and Hebe(?) on Mt Olympus. Side A: Achilles and Memnon. Side B: Zeus and Hera with Ares on Mt Olympus (British Museum).*

distribution declines with distance. This suggests a geographically confined, provincial market, but no significant penetration of inner Etruria as one might expect if the material values of the urban elite served as a real role model for rural populations, with locally produced imitations supplying communities aspiring to imitate them. The technical standard of most vessels lies between that of Attic and local products (local clays could be refined, often to a high standard). Locally produced vases were not used by local elites as substitutes for Attic, but they filled a gap when Attic was scarce or expensive, serving as luxury items with fewer ideological connotations. Since some 40% of the Micali Painter's vases were neck amphorae, with the hydria as the next most popular form (about 18%), much of his output consisted of large 'best' pots, plus a wide range of smaller shapes, and it did not mirror the functional preferences revealed in the selection of Attic imports.

The decline of Attic imports

Attic imports in Etruria declined markedly in quantity around 450, in contrast with their prolonged popularity in the western Greek colonies and northwards, most notably in the mixed Greek and Etruscan settlement of Spina. The decline was sharpest at coastal centres, notably Cerveteri, Tarquinia and Vulci, and slightly more gradual at Chiusi and Orvieto. It is possible that Etruria's defeat at the battle of Cumae in 474 may have affected decisively the economic power of the southern urban centres, but it certainly did not bring an end to imports, as is clear from the quantity of material found at, for example, Orvieto (e.g. Beazley 1963: 598–608). The real role of red-figure in Etruscan urban centres was effectively ended by the mid-fifth century, even though Attic black-glazed wares are found at certain sites (especially entrepôts such as Pyrgi) into the fourth century.

The removal of imported wares is not paralleled by significant changes in Etruscan material culture or iconography: armed dance scenes appear on Etruscan vases mainly during the second half of the fifth century, but the theme is a much older one (Camporeale 1987; Jannot 1984: 332–8 [Chiusi reliefs]; Spivey 1988). A number of underlying factors may be significant. A change, or perhaps a return, to the use of metal vessels in symposia could have affected the selection of grave goods, and may be indicated on certain wall paintings (van der Meer 1984). Increased social stability, following the decline of secondary sites and renewed concentration on urban centres, may have reduced the need for imports to reinforce elite status, and may even have made them redundant, or socially passé, by encouraging a return to 'ancestral' values. In time, the development of local red-figured styles effectively filled whatever gap Attic imports left, creating a new element of indigenous elite

material culture from an import that had played a particular social role. Etruria's defeat at the battle of Cumae may have affected the economic power of the southern urban centres, and since the late fifth century saw the beginning of the rise of Rome and of a long-lived Celtic threat also, the need to respond to immediate challenges may have added to this problem, as well as encouraging a return to old native values. All of these factors probably contain an element of truth, but they carry no implications for the state of the Athenian industry and economic interests or for the state of the carrying trade.

Less convincing is the idea that the decline in imports resulted from a shift of Attic trade north to Spina (e.g. Collis 1984: 108–13; Cunliffe 1988: 23; Gill 1987; 1988d), even though the peak of imports at Spina and Bologna was later (*c.* 475–450). It is easy to point to a superficial coincidence of interests which may have diverted attention from southern Etruria (especially if Etruscan interests in the Mediterranean had been affected by her defeat in the battle of Alalia); an increasing number of Etruscan traits can be traced in Apennine material culture from *c.* 535, and the first Attic imports arrived at Spina *c.* 520 (Alfieri and Arias 1958; Boardman 1980: 228–9). It is also possible that the La Tène societies north of the Alps offered attractive markets (e.g. Bouloumié 1985). Yet trade was not a constant activity which could be moved around at will, and there is an important distinction in the nature of connections between Athens, Etruria and the head of the Adriatic. Etruscans purchased Attic pottery for their own purposes, and maintained only tenuous links with Athenian producers. By contrast, Spina and Bologna may have been Graeco-Etruscan emporia, and the import of marked batches of Attic pottery indicates the strength and directness of their connections with Athens (Gill 1988d: 3); indeed, a proportional rise in Attic exports to Spina through the fifth century (especially from *c.* 425), in comparison with what we can reconstruct of total Attic production, reinforces the strength of interest in this area. In short, there is no reason to assume that the patterns of Attic imports in two such different societies represent markets in any way interchangeable, or comparable in organisation, nor that the same Athenian workshops produced for the two areas (Eisman 1974). The notion that 'peripheral' interaction was a constant force which could shift in geographical intensity to serve only economic interests is highly questionable. One of the principal problems of any core–periphery model is defining the scale of the system, but although we accept that it is generally more accurate to think of Etruria and the Greek mainland as parallel interacting systems rather than as periphery and core (Stoddart 1989), the case of Etruria illustrates in microcosm many of the problems and points of principle which we will develop in considering the more controversial question of Greek contacts with western Europe.

Hallstatt Europe

Greek imports and western Europe

The Early Iron Age chiefdoms of western Europe are geographically, politically and ideologically far removed from the Greek world, with the sole visible link provided by a small and vulnerable network of Greek colonies along the southern French coast (Boardman 1980: 216–24) (fig. 7.6). These retained only tenuous links with the Greek world, and the Greek pottery found at these sites and in coastal areas was probably moved by Etruscan and Phoenician shippers (Bouloumié 1987; Clavel-Lévêque 1977: 9; Gill 1988d: 6–9; Johnston 1979: 117 for Iberian and Phoenician trademarks on Attic vessels; Kimmig 1983: 7–10; *pace* Bénoit 1965: 44). For most Greek states, Italy was the limit of contacts; there is a geographical, political and cultural division between the eastern and western Mediterranean, with comparatively low levels of pottery in southern France and Iberia (Gamito 1988: ch. 2.2.1–2). This is true even of Corinth, which maintained much closer material links with Italy, yet only sporadic contacts with North Africa and Spain, largely avoiding the colonial areas of southern France (Zimmerman-Munn 1983: e.g. 149–69, 186–211). The fascination which western exploration held for certain authors (notably Herodotus) may have rested on the fact that it was exceptional and provided a fund of good adventures, such as those of Kolaios of Samos who made the first voyage into the west Mediterranean in the 630s (Herodotus 4.152), told largely for their dramatic value (Alonso Nuñez 1987).

Yet the fact that links with the east Mediterranean were tenuous has not stopped European prehistorians from using colonial trade as the foundation of an elaborate economic network linking the 'Greek' world with central Europe. The most widely accepted reconstructions of the socio-economic organisation of Hallstatt west-central Europe are based on this (e.g. Brun 1987; Collis 1984: chs. 4 and 5; Cunliffe 1988: ch. 2; Wells 1980; 1984; Wells and Bonfante 1979; cf. T. Champion 1987: 100–3). According to this model, large centres (*Fürstensitze*), generally interpreted as centres of population and political power as well as focuses of trade and industry, emerged in eastern France, southwest Germany and northwest Switzerland between *c.* 600 and 450 (fig. 7.7). They are usually associated with rich burials (the upper levels of a four-tier mortuary hierarchy; Frankenstein and Rowlands 1978: 84–7). The means by which relations were maintained between peer rulers and within local hierarchies have been much debated (Bradley 1986; Gosden 1985; 1986; Rowlands 1986), yet the concept of a prestige goods economy (Frankenstein and Rowlands 1978: 75–81) has been consistently used to support the argument that Greek and Etruscan objects (mainly ceramics and Etruscan bronze jugs) found at *Fürstensitze* and in related wealthy graves served as essential symbols of power circulating within a prestige gift exchange network, and were obtained directly from the Phocaean colony of Massalia (fig. 7.8).[2] Thus long-distance trade with the Greek world played a vital role in maintaining sociopolitical relations in Hallstatt western Europe; according to Peter Wells, 'the emergence during the sixth century in west-central Europe of centers of

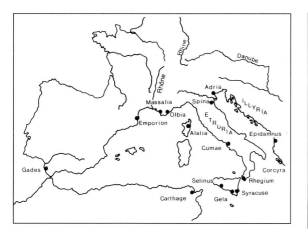

7.6 Principal sites in the Adriatic and west Mediterranean.

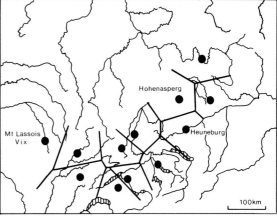

7.7 Fürstensitze with a hypothetical reconstruction of their territories (after Härke 1979).

trade, industry and population, as well as the appearance of an elite marked by sumptuous burials, came about as a result of the desire of central European chieftains to acquire the luxury trappings of Mediterranean civilisations' (Wells and Bonfante 1979: 21). Mediterranean goods have been interpreted not only as fulfilling a local demand for 'treasure' (F. Fischer 1973), but also as offering the elite access to one aspect of an exotic lifestyle (ritualised drinking), as a means of maintaining their status in a competitive system (Frankenstein and Rowlands 1978; cf. Rowlands 1984). In turn, dependence on long-distance trade to obtain luxury goods affected the organisation of local craft production and resource mobilisation, resulting in the creation of centralised workshops not only to supply the elite, but also to reward those who provided whatever commodities were in demand for trade. This model, in essence economic (a trade 'explosion' according to Collis 1984: ch. 2), has rarely been challenged; such debate as has taken place has concerned details rather than substance (the nature of exchange, for example, balancing market economics against social relations).

The end of intense activity at the *Fürstensitze* (just after 500) coincides with a change in settlement ordering, and the beginning of the Celtic migrations; the disappearance of archaeological evidence for local hierarchies from the end of La Tène is striking (Champion *et al.* 1984: 298–304; Collis 1984: 113–25). This coincides with a decline in imports of Attic pottery at Massalia (Gallet de Santerre 1977: 53; Vallet and Villard 1963: 18–35, a point to which we shall return), and so it has been argued that a cut-off in supply of Mediterranean trade goods (perhaps because of changing Greek requirements for raw materials) led to the collapse of a system dependent on them. Prosperity moved to the fringes of the Hallstatt chiefdoms (especially northeast towards the Alps), where a plentiful supply of Etruscan goods was available to maintain the system (Bouloumié 1985; Haffner 1976); here *Fürstengräber*, rich graves containing Mediterranean goods, continued into the fifth century. Underlying this view is the assumption that sudden change does not result from indigenous circumstances alone, and that dramatic endings need external causes, a common fallacy in many studies of culture change, as Tainter argues (1988: ch. 3). At best, some allowance is made for multivariate causality, considering factors such as breakdown in subsistence supply or population movement, but the resulting models have rarely been developed to the point where they have much explanatory power, and external causes continue to be given great weight (Cunliffe 1988: 32–7; Frankenstein and Rowlands 1978: 78–80; Härke 1982: 204). It is therefore considered legitimate to accord priority to Greek connections over and above consideration of

indigenous long-term development and change (a factor acknowledged by Frankenstein and Rowlands 1978: 109–10, but never fully discussed), and the resulting picture is of a Hallstatt system effectively controlled from outside, heavily dependent on the vagaries of Greek trade. Yet even if such theoretical objections were set aside, it would be wrong to place much emphasis upon chronological coincidence in relating Greek trading interests to the fate of Hallstatt Europe, since Mediterranean imports underpin Hallstatt chronology, and the danger of circular argument is clear (Dehn and Frey 1962; Gallet de Santerre 1977: 50). A coincidence of events is possible, but on chronological grounds, if no other, it is difficult to infer causality.

One aspect of this model of particular significance for the present discussion is the suggestion that long-distance trade with Hallstatt Europe was instigated and conducted by Greeks in need of raw materials of various kinds. The presence of Massaliote transport amphorae alongside other imports at Hallstatt sites confirms the principal route taken, and it is widely held that the prosperity of Massalia from the time of its foundation *c.* 600 rested on its success as an entrepôt (e.g. Cunliffe 1988: 19–23; Collis 1984: 65). Since few commodities of trade survive in the archaeological record, most reconstructions of Massaliote trade are based on later accounts of activity in this area (e.g. Strabo 4.1.3–5; 4.6.2–4), or in other regions bordering the Greek world (e.g. Polybius 4.38.4–5 on South Russia). On these grounds, slaves, timber and grain are favourite candidates, and metals, skins, furs, leather and wool have also been suggested (Cunliffe 1988: 9–10; Gill 1988d: 6). We will consider specific commodities presently, along with the problems inherent in this view of trade as a constant border phenomenon, but it is sufficient here to emphasise that even if one accepts that these commodities were imported by various Greek states during the Archaic and early Classical periods, it has become an article of faith that such imports *regularly* occurred via systematically organised, large-scale, long-distance trade in and around the Mediterranean.[3]

It is beyond the scope of the present article to examine possible alternative approaches to the reconstruction of Hallstatt society. However, it is important to stress the limitations of available evidence. Undoubtedly a greater body of settlement evidence would contribute greatly to the argument. Very few *Fürstensitze* (let alone subsidiary sites) have been excavated to *any* extent: about 40% of the Heuneburg (the site most frequently cited in regional reconstructions) has been investigated, and its stratigraphy is ill-understood, and the situation at supposed peer sites, such as the Goldberg or Wittnauer Horn, is even worse (Härke 1979: 7–11; 1982: 187–8). The accepted reconstruction of the Heuneburg may be correct and a reliable basis for generalisation, but at present we have no hope of testing it with any acceptable rigour. Most social reconstructions rest on grave material (despite problems of sample size and preservation), and the role of settlements is predicted on this basis rather than being investigated and tested independently (e.g. Frankenstein and Rowlands 1978: 84–93). It may be true that clustering of graves and lesser settlements around a central site is a characteristic of complex chiefdoms (cutting the cost of moving goods and tribute), but there is scant evidence with which to test this hypothesis in Hallstatt Europe. Equally, population levels are a matter of guesswork (extrapolating from the half-excavated Heuneburg; Wells 1984: 40–2, 108–10, 116–18 for an illustration of the tenuous nature of such reconstructions), and it is impossible to tell whether many lesser sites were ever permanently occupied. Despite the work of Heinrich Härke on settlement, many contentious assumptions about the organisation of Hallstatt society persist for want of large-scale excavations.

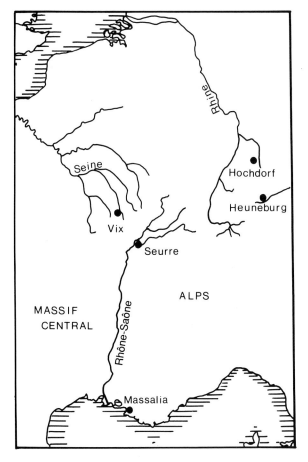

7.8 Massalia and the Fürstensitze.

Since, for example, the classification of sites is largely a matter of guesswork (Härke 1979: 165–78), the kind of factors which would contribute greatly to the dynamism of the settlement system (such as population movement, permanence of occupation, or the complexity of internal site organisation) are often those which are most difficult to investigate.

Even allowing for these limitations, the model as it stands depends on a considerable degree of selectivity, and a willingness to ignore material that does not fit (S. Champion n.d.). The notion of peer chiefdoms with uniform patterns of material culture is a case in point; it is possible to trace similarity via certain categories of site and artefact (Champion and Champion 1986), but it is easy to concentrate upon it at the expense of a much greater degree of variation in artefact styles and regional development. Equally, there is a qualitative difference in the degree of cultural homogeneity evident during the Hallstatt and La Tène phases, and it is possible to argue that homogeneity appears greatest at precisely the point when princely redistribution ceases. The notion of centralisation of production is equally disputable; it rests upon the assumption that the contents of rich graves were produced at the centres with which the graves are believed to be associated, yet there is at least as much evidence for metalworking outside *Fürstensitze* as on them (Champion and Champion 1986: 6; S. Champion n.d.; Härke 1979: 140), and almost no evidence for the location of pottery or wagon-making.

Greek imports and native values

Of particular relevance to our argument is the assumption in the models so far discussed of a high level of material interaction with the Mediterranean. Quantification (where possible) belies accounts of 'numerous' imported vases (e.g. Shefton 1989: 216–17; Wells and Bonfante 1979: 18–19; cf. Wells 1980: ch. 2). From the Heuneburg we have some forty sherds representing even fewer vessels (B. B. Shefton, pers. comm.) spanning ninety years from *c.* 540 (fig. 7.9). Since various versions of the Heuneburg stratigraphy exist and the site has yet to be definitively published, it is impossible to be precise about the chronological spread of imports, but they appear to be late, close to the transition to La Tène (Shefton 1989: 216–17, n. 45), and there is no obvious correlation between imports and the height of 'urbanisation' (Dammer 1978: 73–4; Gersbach 1976: 39–42; Härke 1982: 205 and n. 13; Kimmig 1971: 40–1; 1975: 200). Even if one were to assume that each sherd represents a single vessel (which is not the case) the rate of annual import would be just over forty-four vessels per annum (with a survival rate as low as 1%), and although no totals of native wares from the Heuneburg have been published, this hardly suggests a desperate rush to accumulate foreign luxuries (especially as many sherds show signs of conservation). This pattern is echoed at other sites: the twenty-four reconstructable Greek vases from Mt Lassois (from a sherd total of some 300) pale in comparison with the mass of local sherds (over a million from gisement 1 alone during the early phase of excavation; Joffroy 1960: 103–20 for local pottery, 120–1 for Greek imports), and although it would be interesting to know whether the context of imports represents ritual disposal or settlement use, evidence is as yet inadequate to answer such a question. Yet in certain modern accounts (e.g. Mildenberger 1963), it almost seems that a few Greek sherds are essential in the eyes of scholars to establish the 'status' of a site within its local system. Material evidence for elaborate trading schemes is therefore minimal in comparison with contemporary southern France, or later Roman patterns of activity (Dietler 1989: 129; Fulford 1987/8), and it is notable that intensification is most marked in locally produced high-status goods rather than imports. This in itself is significant; if, as we suggested in the case of Etruria, imported goods were used as status symbols mainly in time of instability, one would expect peaks of imports to coincide with periods of creativity in the generation of indigenous art styles, with imports supplementing rather than supplanting native goods. There is therefore no sound archaeological evidence for any constant or large-scale flow of Mediterranean goods into Hallstatt Europe.

How, then, do imports fit into existing patterns of social behaviour? By framing the question in this way, we echo Härke (1982) in challenging the view that the appearance of real wealth differentiation (warrior graves and rich burials with imports) during the sixth century is a turning point in the development of local chiefdoms, and that the appearance of Mediterranean imports acted as catalyst for the great social differentiation evident into the fifth century. Thus the Hallstatt C/D transition (*c.* 600) is perceived either as the time when local chiefdoms were created, or when there was so great an escalation in existing patterns of behaviour that the system was effectively transformed (Frankenstein and Rowlands 1978: 98). Indeed, Rowlands has suggested that the intensification and re-orientation of activity evident around the Hallstatt C/D transition not only reflected developing links with the Mediterranean world, but also localised patterns of resistance or acceptance of these links by either party (Rowlands 1984: 153). On either view, Mediterranean imports are accorded particular importance (e.g. Cunliffe 1988: ch. 2), and the idea that at the very least they introduced new stimuli into the existing system has rarely received critical examination (Dietler 1989: 129–30).

On the grounds of their scarcity if nothing else, we must surely think of imports as being accepted for their affinity to existing cultural practices, rather than as novelties with the power to change social action (Shennan 1989b; van der Leeuw and Torrence 1989: 1–15). Exchange relations governing the movement of salt, amber and copper had early origins and continued through the Hallstatt period (Champion *et al.* 1984: 284–90; Frankenstein and Rowlands 1978: 93–4), and produced a cross-cutting system of alliances extending over a wider area than that of the southern chiefdoms alone. One feature of the articulation of elite relations between and within chiefdoms was ritual drinking; this began during the Urnfield phase and from Hallstatt C onwards, an increasing variety of forms and styles of drinking vessel included cups, jugs and mixing bowls, with evidence of local variation in cup forms (e.g. Coles and Harding 1979: 370–6; Kimmig 1983: 47–50). It is therefore clear that the idea of social drinking was not exclusively Greek (as we have shown in the case of Etruria), and existed as an elite activity before the foundation of Massalia (Dietler 1990). At issue therefore is not the introduction of a new activity from the Mediterranean, but rather the impact of imports upon established patterns of behaviour; we should seek to investigate the indigenous role of feasting and drinking, and the way in which imports were incorporated in an existing system of elite consumption. It is, for example, notable that the Attic black-glazed and black-figured wares which were more commonly imported than red-figure show a stylistic affinity with earlier local graphite-burnished wares and also contemporary cup forms; this is reflected in the imitations of Attic wares (including Little Master cups) in local black-polished fabric found at the Heuneburg (Kimmig 1983: 69, fig. 61). As we emphasised in the case of Etruria, it is important to consider the ease and manner of incorporation of imported fine pottery into the material culture of the recipient society, and the idea that a society may structure its material behaviour around imports raises more questions than it answers.

Clearly, the emergence of Hallstatt chiefdoms did not depend on the acquisition of Mediterranean goods, nor was the emergence of the *Fürstensitze* simply a response to a new need for centres of trade and redistribution. In the case of Etruria, we examined the relationship between territorial organisation, social stability and innovation in material culture. In the case of Hallstatt Europe, it is clear that centralisation of wealth was a long process, yet the long-term development, stability and internal dynamics of separate chiefdoms have rarely been considered as problems in their own right. Although it is agreed that the apparent stability of Hallstatt D society is illusory (Rowlands 1984: 153), it is inadequate to externalise change by concentrating on the shifting balance of dominance between sites, or on developments on the fringes of the system (Cunliffe 1988: 33–7;

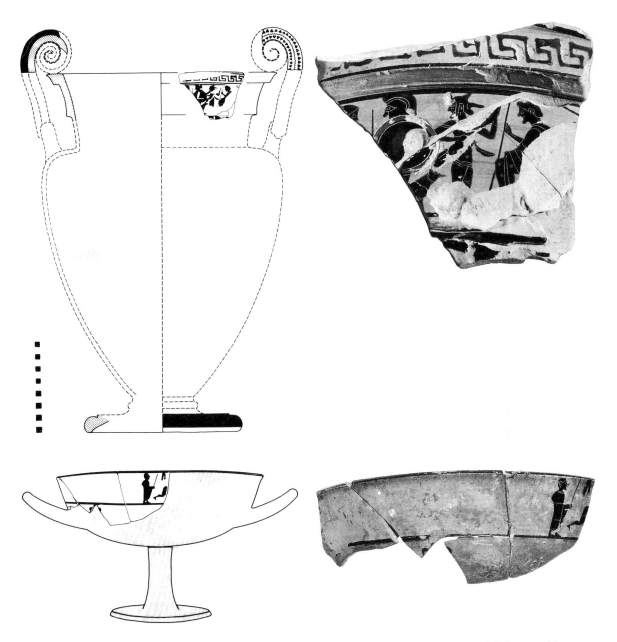

7.9 *Imported Attic pottery from Heuneburg. A and B: volute krater with a departing warrior. B and C: lip cup with scene of a contest.*

Frankenstein and Rowlands 1978), not least because the idea of changing patterns of dominant–subordinate site relations presupposes change within individual local systems. For example, the distribution of princely burials around *Fürstensitze* has been taken to indicate the extent of state territory (Härke 1979: 122–31), yet there is no reason to assume that constant borders mean a static social system; the major centres may have remained the same, but the emergence of marginal hillforts during Hallstatt D2 is reminiscent of the rise and fall of Etruscan secondary centres noted earlier, and may imply similar shifts in the distribution of power. Too little attention has been paid to long-term cycles of centralisation and decentralisation in western Europe which could help in the interpretation of archaeologically recoverable phenomena such as hillforts, or foreign imports and the generation of indigenous art works (Härke 1982). It is hard to take seriously the implication that early La Tène chiefs were prepared to sell their civilisations for a handful of Mediterranean imports, and explaining settlement discontinuity purely in terms of external factors cannot be satisfactory.

Massalia

The second area requiring re-examination, the role of the colony at Massalia, raises two related issues, the supposed activities of Mediterranean entrepreneurs and the nature of Massalia, which lie at the heart of the view of colonial–native relations central to the core–periphery model. As we noted, a failure to discover imports in the intervening area between the south French coast and Hallstatt Europe has been taken to indicate direct trade links and an absence of middlemen (e.g. Cunliffe 1988: 32). Yet the implications of such trade have only recently been considered. The dangers of travelling 500 km upstream along the notoriously fierce river Rhône are considerable, and a similar journey overland (without superiority in arms) would have required negotiation of safe passage through numerous small political groupings. If such journeys were actually made, they must have been in pursuit of some badly needed commodity, yet Hallstatt Europe offered little which could not have been obtained more easily closer to home (Dietler 1989: 131–2). There is no reason to suggest that Massaliote Greeks behaved differently from colonists in most other areas by initiating and conducting long-distance trade deep into native territory (Bénoit 1965; Villard 1960; Wells 1980 amongst many others), and as we shall show, there is no reason to suggest that additional incentives to trade existed in this case. The identification of a trade route does not imply the identification of the means by which it was exploited; it seems more likely that imports moved via long- and short-distance native exchange networks, and that the native

inhabitants of the areas surrounding Massalia played a significant role in articulating, or initiating, trading contacts with Hallstatt Europe (Dietler 1989: 129, 133–6). In recent years, archaeological investigation of the lower Rhône basin has produced Greek imports distributed more widely than hitherto thought, and also further evidence for the origins of the imported native vessels found with Greek imports on Hallstatt sites (Bellon *et al.* 1986). It is clear, therefore, that the nature of Massalia and its relations with local native communities stands in need of re-examination, and that this is a necessary prelude to any reconstruction of local trading relationships.

The common characterisation of Massalia as an entrepôt (e.g. Clavel-Lévêque 1977: 9–12, 16–27) rests on two assumptions. First, that its site, at the foot of the Rhône-Saône corridor, was chosen for its trading potential, a trait supposedly common to colonies all along the French and Iberian coasts; thus Kimmig (1983: 13–14) describes Emporion (Ampurias) as a free harbour, detached from the hinterland. Assessments of Massalia's agricultural potential range from a bleak picture of a rocky coastline (based on Strabo 4.1.5) to emphasis on local fertility and the density of nearby native settlement (e.g. Cunliffe 1988: 22, who also notes the ready availability of metal resources; cf. Wever 1966 for the most detailed assessment of the extent of the Massaliote *chora* and developments in Massaliote influence over it). The former view is almost certainly untrue, yet even those who stress the richness of Massalia's hinterland have not seen the question of Massaliote/native relations as central to studies of trade (and indeed, often base their assessment of those relations on the views of later Roman sources, notably Justin 43.4–5). Secondly, Massalia was founded by Phocaea, a city whose reputation for trading (Herodotus 1.163) has led to the attribution of commercial motives to most of its actions, even though there is scant evidence to support such assertions (Champion *et al.* 1984: 250–1; Cunliffe 1988: 19–23; Langlotz 1966; Morel 1975). Flawed as these arguments are, the identification of Massalia as a port of trade has rarely been questioned, and instead argument has centred around the role of trade in Greek colonial foundations. According to John Collis, for example, Massalia differed from Sicilian and south Italian colonies in being purely a trading foundation (1984: 65), whereas Barry Cunliffe has preferred to see it as part of a wider pattern of Greek colonial activity (1988: 13–23). A wider comparative study of economic, social and political aspects of colonialism in the Greek world would doubtless give a more secure basis on which to judge Massalia, but meanwhile, we suggest that there are two particular ways in which Massalia differs from Italian colonies which are significant for local economic organisation and thence exchange activity.

The first concerns the nature of links between colony and mother city. Massalia was founded (probably *c.* 600; Morel 1975: 866) against the background of a growing Lydian threat to the mother-city, Phocaea, which culminated in a siege and the city's destruction in 544/40. A move west, away from the threat, must have been inviting (especially as the Black Sea coast had been appropriated by Phocaea's rival, Miletos; Boardman 1980: 239–45), but it may have been difficult to find a suitable colonial site in Italy and Sicily, long divided between rival Corinthian and Euboean colonies and their daughter settlements. Although refugee groups from other similarly threatened Ionian communities did settle in the Greek cities of Italy and Sicily, the foundation of an independent city with its own territory must have presented greater difficulties. The western Mediterranean, of which the Phocaeans had prior knowledge through trade, may have appeared more accessible, and the site of Massalia has many features which would have been attractive anywhere (notably a fine harbour and fertile hinterland), as well as established contacts with Etruria and southern Italy. Yet the resulting colony was more isolated from its mother-city than earlier foundations elsewhere, not only because of the exceptional distances involved, but because the loss of Phocaean political independence divided colony from mother-city in an unprecedented fashion. The nature of relations between colonies and their mother-cities has long been a matter of debate (although it is clear that they were more usually a matter of ideology than economics; Graham 1983: pt II), but it seems likely that, unlike Italian and Sicilian foundations, Massalia would have had no connection on which to call. Furthermore, the foundation of Alalia *c.* 454 (Herodotus 1.166), and the subsequent battle in which local Greek communities defeated Etruscan and Phoenician opposition to the colony, began the process of consolidating 'Greek' interests in the western Mediterranean, ensuring a continuing role for Massalia within a localised network of 'Greek' settlements. It is no accident that the fall of Phocaea was followed by the beginning of Massalia's rise to prosperity (Euzennat 1980; Gallet de Santerre 1977: 41–3), exemplified by the construction of a treasury at Delphi in the late sixth century, a vital symbol of statehood in the Greek world (Lawrence and Tomlinson 1983: 168, 170; Morgan 1990: 18; Villard 1960: 90–1).

Second, whatever the limitations of links between Italy, the Greek mainland and Ionia, connections with the west Mediterranean were undoubtedly much more tenuous. As noted above, the extent to which Greeks from various areas of the mainland were regularly involved in the movement of goods in the west is debatable, and in view of the close similarity between the chronological pattern of imports of Attic pottery in Etruria and Massalia it could be argued that

there was a strong trading link between the two areas (Martelli 1979: 44–5) (fig. 7.10). If Massalia were somehow dependent upon Etruria for supplies of the kind of pottery which could have been used as material symbols of her 'Greek' identity (cf. Arafat and Morgan 1989: 335), then her lack of control over supply may help to explain the pattern of local pottery production, particularly the imitation of Attic wares and the ever wider spread of Phocaean gray ware (made near Massalia from *c.* 580; Arcelin-Pradelle *et al.* 1982: 54) and its wide distribution all along the Gulf of the Lion and up the Rhône-Saône corridor (Arcelin-Pradelle 1984; Kimmig 1983: fig. 25).

Such comparison provides useful information about the regional role of Massalia, but it is no substitute for a broader comparative analysis of colonial experience which would help us to trace the processes by which the kind of imports and local products which were central to the maintenance of colonial identity could spread into wider exchange systems without Greek intervention, and to understand how Massalia functioned as a colony in a heavily settled hinterland (for settlement in southern France: Gallet de Santerre 1977; Kimmig 1983; Py 1982). One possible approach would be to abandon models based on dominance or control (Bartel 1985) and instead to explore those stressing consensus and co-existence. In Whitehouse and Wilkins' (1985; 1989) study of Metapontum and Tarentum in southern Italy, the question of the nature of Greek/native relations was re-assessed via consideration of Greek pottery found at native sites beyond colonial boundaries. Whitehouse and Wilkins have sought to define the archaeological correlates of co-existence versus Greek domination of native settlement (considering factors such as the form, distribution and date of settlements in the hinterland in relation to the distribution of differential categories of Greek artefact), and

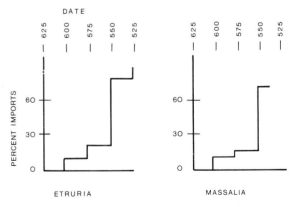

7.10 Proportions of Attic imports in Etruria and at Massalia (after Martelli 1985).

to test their hypotheses against the material record. As a result, they proposed a model based on mutual economic interests, notably the provision of subsistence supplies. With the exception of Pithekoussai, it is hard to think of any Greek colony that lacked access to sufficient prime agricultural land to feed its population via intensive cultivation, and even though colonial territories, where they can be defined, appear small by mainland standards (about 13,000 hectares in the case of Metapontum), no colony would have needed to import grain on a regular basis. Herding, by contrast, requires access to extensive areas of pasture, and would be more likely to provoke disputes with neighbouring native communities. It may therefore have been less disruptive to exchange wool, textiles and similar products, and in the case of Metapontum and Tarentum, the products traded in return included the votives found at native sanctuaries and Greek pottery (especially forms associated with wine drinking, also a native custom). Direct exchange between Greeks and natives was limited to a radius of 50–60 km (perhaps conducted at neutral locations such as marginal sanctuaries: Edlund 1987: 41, ch. 4), and beyond that, Greek goods moved within purely native systems; in the case of Massalia, such distances would extend to the Middle Rhine (as suggested by Dietler 1989). Clearly, therefore, there is no need to assume a massive imbalance in resources or the existence of formal markets to see how co-existence could be aided by exchange.

Not only would this model begin to explain how Greek and Massaliote goods came to enter native exchange systems, but it also enables us to assess the long-term impact of colonisation on native populations. New opportunities for control of trade could certainly be used to establish or reinforce dependent hierarchies, but it is also important to emphasise the divisive effects on native households competing for possession of status goods, and diverting produce from the reciprocal exchange structures which underpinned the traditional social order (Whitehouse and Wilkins 1989: 116–21).

Such processes may explain the long-term changes evident in the Massaliote hinterland and along the southern French coast during the sixth to fourth centuries (Py 1982). Pre-colonial maritime contacts (*c.* 625–580), although considerable (Shefton 1989: 208–13), never extended far inland: bucchero pottery, often associated with 'Phocaean' gray ware and Etruscan amphorae, occurs in small quantities all around the Gulf of the Lion and along the southern Mediterranean coast (*Actes*; Dietler 1989: 131; Jully 1982/3; Kimmig 1983: Fig. 6; Py 1985; T. Rasmussen 1979: 226, pl. 64). Following colonisation, there is a clear distinction between the early distribution of Attic black-figure, bucchero and Etruscan amphorae extending far inland, and

the later pattern of Attic red-figure, Massaliote amphorae and coins and pseudo-Ionian wares, resulting from the supposed 'Hellenisation' of the southern French coast (Kimmig 1983: figs. 27–9). The development of these 'long-distance' and 'middle-range' patterns may be explained via consideration of the long-term processes binding colony and hinterland which slowly altered the balance of exchange relationships between colonists and natives. A real change in Massalia's relations with the principal sites in the local native hierarchy is evident from the late sixth century onwards, with the expansion of a small number of native higher-order sites such as Enserune and Castelets (Py 1978; 1982; Wever 1966), where an increasing quantity and variety of Greek ceramics augmented the Etruscan wares imported from *c.* 625, and the fifth century saw an expansion of settlement area and the beginning of stone construction and regular planning also (Gallet de Santerre 1977; Jannoray 1955: 63–78, 169–224; Jully 1982/3; Py 1978: 49–64). These developments are paralleled by changes in the exploitation of the countryside (notably the spread of olive and vine cultivation), and the extension of production of Massaliote amphorae into the hinterland. Yet even at the small number of sites where imports or influences were common, the uses to which they were put showed that they were not part of any thorough-going 'Hellenisation'; native cult sites, symbols of community identity (and thus 'autonomy', desired if not real) were largely untouched, as evidence from sites such as Enserune or Roquepertuse shows (Bessac and Bouloumié 1985; Cunliffe 1988: 48–9; Jannoray 1955: 275–361). Instead, since native contacts with Massalia expanded just as Greek imports in central Europe declined (Jannoray 1955: 275–361), it seems likely that a coincidence of economic interests drew the native hierarchies of the hinterland away from networks extending further inland, and closer to Massalia (Clavel-Lévêque 1977: 18–20, 28–78, 169–209), establishing relationships cemented by the movement of material goods.

The commodities of long-distance trade

The third major area of difficulty with long-distance trade between Greeks and barbarians concerns the archaeologically invisible commodities exchanged for Greek goods. As we have suggested, it is hard to cast Massalia in the role of bulk consumer. Yet there is also a dangerous tendency to generalise about 'Greek' needs (usually on the basis of Athenian evidence), without considering which particular states were involved in any enterprise, the implications of variations in their social and economic organisation, and geographical biases in their respective patterns of contact (a danger stressed by Finley 1965: 34). Archaic and Classical Greece consisted of a collection of often warring states of greatly differing forms and degrees of organisational complexity, and it is impossible to generalise about their needs and interests. Equally, the same range of commodities, particularly slaves and grain, tend to be cited whenever it is necessary to invoke invisible imports; Blakeway (1933: 202) and T. J. Dunbabin (1948: 1–2, 7, 17–18) argued for the importance of slaves and grain in Italian and Sicilian colonial trade. Salmon (1984: 90) saw them as the incentive for the establishment of Corinthian links with Epirus at the beginning of the eighth century (cf. Morgan 1988, 220; Zimmermann-Munn 1983: ch. 1), and in the case of Hallstatt Europe, they are generally accepted to have been significant even by otherwise cautious prehistorians (e.g. Champion *et al.* 1984: 250–1; Dietler 1989: 133) or classicists who fail to evaluate the Greek markets supposedly supplied (e.g. Gill 1988c: 179–80; 1988d). Generalisations are easy, and it is vital to demonstrate the existence of supply and demand in each case considered.

To take the case of grain first. A full account of the structure and scope of the Greek grain trade is impossible here, but we would emphasise a few significant points. First, the only market on which we have any real information is Athens; references to trade controls by other states (e.g. Aegina: Herodotus 7.147.2; Teos: *SIG* 3.337–8) are rare before the fourth century (when changes in demography, warfare and the political and economic ordering of many states radically altered patterns of demand for grain; Garnsey 1988: chs. 9–10; Garnsey and Morris 1989; Osborne 1987a: 97–104, citing only much later evidence).[4] At issue therefore is the origin of the grain imported to Athens, one of the largest and most vulnerable *poleis* in Greece, and the date at which such trade began. The crucial distinction in assessing the level and frequency of imports is between normal shortage and dependence. Normal shortage results from the frequent, but haphazard, inter-annual climatic fluctuations which continually beset the Mediterranean (Garnsey 1988: 8–20; Halstead 1981; M. H. Jameson 1983). This was not a new problem during the Archaic period, and for centuries it had been solved via subsistence diversification, storage and occasional exchange between neighbours (Osborne 1987a: ch. 2). Normal shortage alone would not therefore have been sufficient reason to establish or exploit regular long-distance trading contacts. On the basis of the relationship between Athenian demography and the agricultural potential of Attica, Peter Garnsey has argued that the change from normal shortage to dependence occurred in Athens after the Persian Wars and no earlier, and that the first period of crisis occurred as late as the mid-fifth century, when the population of Athens was at its height (1988: chs. 6, 7). At this stage, Athens *may* have become attractive to traders; it is, however, worth noting Garnsey's conclusion

that fifth-century Athens experienced no standing food-supply problem (1988: 131, cf. 124), even though the role of the empire in guaranteeing food-supply should not be underestimated. If Garnsey's chronology is correct, the beginning of Athenian bulk imports occurred too late to account for developments in Hallstatt Europe, and is instead better traced in revived Athenian interest in the Black Sea area (Noonan 1973). Certainly, the shift to the kind of markets described in most long-distance trade models was essentially a fourth-century phenomenon.

In any case, there is no reason to suppose that Athens would have looked west for supplies (even Rome never looked to this part of western Europe). The import of grain from any western source is not attested in Athens until the fourth century, there is no evidence that colonisation had anything to do with the provision of a regular grain supply, and it is clear that, even into the fifth century, Athens was less dependent on distant sources than is often supposed (Garnsey 1988: 105, 128–31). By contrast with the modern commodities market, Athens relied to a great extent upon the maintenance of good diplomatic relations with states in a few specific, highly productive, areas to ensure supplies; Athenian colonies and states around the Black Sea were particularly important (although there is no evidence to show that colonies were founded for this purpose, and it is dangerous to make *post hoc* judgements in interpreting pottery scatters found in regions later known to be important in the grain trade; Bravo 1983; Hahn 1983; cf. Garnsey 1988: ch. 7). A trading system exploiting friendly relations established over many years is unlikely to be abandoned lightly, and the need to keep an open passage through the Hellespont demanded constant diplomatic and practical investment (notably during the Peloponnesian War; Garnsey 1988: 120–3; Kagan 1987: 211–46). It is clear that Athenian needs were exceptional among Mediterranean states, but she had invested so much in the east that it is hard to see why she would import grain via Massalia. Equally, it is hard to find other Greek states needing grain and likely to break the *ad hoc* habits of centuries and to search for it in the western Mediterranean during the Archaic and early Classical period (at least in the quantities which would support a trading scheme of the magnitude assumed for Hallstatt Europe).

The export of slaves presents similar problems. From a European point of view, slaves would be a plausible export, since ranked, centralised political structures are generally well placed to exploit their populations thus (B. Arnold 1988), but the problem again lies in finding a market at the right time. Advocates of a Massaliote slave trade usually argue from the analogy of Roman evidence to suggest that a regular supply was needed to maintain the 'Greek' labour force (Nash 1985: 53), but even if this were true, it is a significant further step to suggest that the western Mediterranean was a major source of slaves shipped via Massalia. Here also, Athens is our main source of evidence, the only state in which we can even begin to consider large-scale slavery, but there is no reason to assume that Athens was typical. A number of states (including Thessaly and Sparta) used indigenous or conquered unfree labour, and evidence for slavery on any scale in Greek colonies is slight (although cf. Herodotus 7.155 on Syracuse), not least because the suppression of native populations in such marginal vulnerable colonial communities would surely have entailed great risk. In the absence of evidence from Etruria, it is therefore likely that such trade as existed was designed to benefit just a few mainland Greek states.

The principal difficulty in reconstructing the Athenian slave market is the lack of literary or epigraphical evidence to provide reliable statistics for slave numbers or ethnic origins.[5] However, this is not the only problem. First, the term 'slave' is used in ancient sources in a very vague and inconsistent fashion, and it is often difficult to define the exact meaning of a particular reference (Wiedemann 1987). Modes of categorisation (notably Marxist) which equate slavery with an abstract concept of servile labour are therefore attractive for economic analysis, but are useless for present purposes. Secondly, even though difficulties of definition mean that estimated numbers of slaves in Athens vary greatly, it is impossible to relate these estimates to annual slave imports as we have no idea of the rate of manumission; since the link between social status, citizenship and state identity in Athens had become institutionalised by the end of the Archaic period, we might expect increasingly low social mobility to limit the ongoing demand for slaves, but this is impossible to quantify. Equally, attempts to reconstruct the role of slaves in the economy, and thus assess the likelihood that a large slave population existed, face the difficulty that there were no reserved slave occupations in Athens (mining is a possible exception; Lauffer 1979: 8–13); slaves worked alongside freemen and metics in the countryside and in workshops, operating within what remained essentially a household system (Arafat and Morgan 1989: 325–6; Wiedemann 1987: ch. 4; E. M. Wood 1988: ch. 2, although, *pace* Cunliffe 1988: 29, the army is one of the few places where slaves played a more restricted role during the Archaic and early Classical period, since military service was one of the principal criteria of *polis* membership; cf. Welwei 1974: 8–107). Whatever their contribution to the Athenian economy, their function was fundamentally different from the Roman model, and it is impossible to be precise about their use, origins, numbers, or any of the 'details' essential to

identifying the kind of market necessary for regular long-distance trade. And if the case cannot be demonstrated at Athens, it is even less plausible elsewhere. As with grain, it is possible to speculate (but no more) that Athens would have obtained most slaves (with the exception of prisoners of war) via long-standing relationships with states on the fringes of the Greek world, which would surely lead us to consider regions such as Thrace or the Black Sea before Massalia (Finley 1962).

It therefore seems most unlikely that trade with the Greek world in any of the commodities proposed existed in the west Mediterranean on a scale which could sustain a dependent relationship between Hallstatt Europe and the east Mediterranean (Etruria being a separate problem worthy of investigation in its own right). We are not debating the level of long-distance trade between the east Mediterranean, Massalia and Hallstatt Europe, but questioning whether it took place at all. It is, of course, impossible to prove or disprove the existence of trade in any archaeologically invisible commodity, and we do not dispute that many of the commodities commonly listed were imported into the Greek world during the period in question; our reservations centre on the mechanisms and markets supposedly involved, and the scale of operations. Arguments for long-distance trade in commodities such as slaves and grain reveal a lack of caution in failing to use the considerable bodies of evidence available from Archaic and Classical Greece to assess what is likely and what is not.

The transition to La Tène

The final stage in the argument, that a shift in trade between peripheral centres contributed to their rise and decline, is equally difficult to demonstrate. The foundation of Spina by Greeks and Etruscans at the end of the sixth century has been regarded as contributing to the decline of Massaliote trade and thence the early La Tène chiefdoms, and the development of Athenian interests in Olbia (Boardman 1980: 238–55; Wasowicz 1975) and the Black Sea has also been invoked. Since, it is argued, long-distance trade with Massalia was costly, new and closer sites, especially around the head of the Adriatic, offered more profitable opportunities; as a result European trade shifted, and trade in the western Mediterranean bypassed Massalia to focus first (from *c.* 500) on the Punic and Iberian markets, and later on Emporio (Ampurias). It would certainly be convenient if trade in a constant set of basic commodities could be transferred from Massalia to Spina at will (Cunliffe 1988: 32; Gill 1987), but this would be a facile assumption to make. We have already touched upon the difficulty of considering border trade as a constant and movable phenomenon in the case of Etruria, and the problems are greater in this case. Quite apart from the question of whether Greeks were ever directly involved in Massaliote trade, and that of the importance accorded to trading via sustained relationships between producers, shippers and consumers (maintaining vested interests), it is very difficult to reconcile the different structure of activity suggested by imports at Massalia and Spina. It also seems that different carriers were involved in shipping to both sites (and in so far as we have evidence, the products of different Athenian ceramic workshops were represented also; Eisman 1974: 53–4). The nature of contacts therefore appears very different, and it is hard to see these sites as alternatives within some wider trading scheme. Equally, the notion of simple commercial advantage governing shifts in border trade belongs within a tradition of debate on the structure of the Greek economy, in that it directly contradicts an accepted and well-documented picture of Archaic and Classical Greek trade as an unsystematic amalgam of *ad hoc* arrangements, with no concept of maximising profit or organisational efficiency (Finley 1985a: 17–34, 150–76; cf. Cartledge 1983; Snodgrass 1980a: ch. 4; 1983). One may side with those who disagree with this view but one cannot ignore it.

This debate is especially important when considering the application of core–periphery models to Greece, since it is the economic aspect of Wallerstein's work (the world economy) which has most frequently been applied to ancient data (despite Wallerstein's own very different conception of the pre-capitalist world; Woolf 1990). It has long been recognised that ancient trade was not a purely economic activity, yet this approach leaves no room to evaluate its social aspects in any particular situation. This in itself is a backward step; it is unlikely that anyone would approach the question of interaction within their own personal study region in so simplistic a fashion, and by pursuing the issue of the western Mediterranean alongside a discussion of links between Athens and Etruria, we have sought to highlight this point. From the point of view of classical archaeology and ancient history, therefore, much of what has been written about 'Greek' trading interests outside the Greek world should be treated with a far greater degree of scepticism than it is at present.

Conclusion

In this article, we have sought to show that the investigation of the material culture of any region (Greek, Italian or Western European) from a starting point of trade or exchange inevitably impedes understanding of local material behaviour and social development. It perpetuates untestable assumptions about the place of trade and exchange in the local economy, and effectively precludes detailed investigation of the role of imports and attitudes to innovation (van der Leeuw and Torrence 1989: 1–15). In seeking to test various aspects of the long-distance trade model against the Archaic and early Classical material record, we have been forced to simplify complex areas of discussion which could fill whole volumes in their own right. Models like those recently created from the world economy aspect of core–periphery can easily be applied in an unduly simplistic fashion and often need extensive discussion to unravel, so we have throughout endeavoured to achieve clarity without distortion of the evidence.

According to Barry Cunliffe, from as early as *c.* 600 BC the Classical and barbarian worlds were 'inextricably bound together in a network of economic interdependence' (1988: 193). From a Greek viewpoint, this does not make sense (cf. Finley 1985a: 177–80), especially as it requires a very narrow definition of 'economic'; for example, it ignores the social impact of the relatively tiny trickle of imported luxuries which acquired a symbolic importance far exceeding any 'economic' benefit they could bring to producer, trader or consumer. Social relations determined the supply and flow of goods of all kinds, and since Greek imports formed only a tiny part of the overall pattern in the West, their role must surely depend upon their affinity with existing local material cultures and the various ways in which they fitted into different patterns of material behaviour (as evident in the parallel case of Etruria). Underlying this discussion, therefore, is the question of attitudes to, and the impact of, material innovation in those areas where imports are found, and the acceptance of the fact that rejection of imports, however unpredictable, is also revealing of social values (M. L. Sørensen 1989). In applications of core–periphery models, material innovation appears exclusively in the form of universally desirable Mediterranean imports; not only is this theoretically implausible, but the simple question of why Hallstatt chiefs should find these imports desirable raises a whole set of questions about material values and aesthetics which are not, and cannot be, addressed via this approach.

A second difficulty arises with the way in which models based on border trade encourage simplistic identification of markets. Core–periphery modelling depends on drawing boundaries, a subjective process which is inevitably open to debate. In the case of the Archaic and Classical Mediterranean, the composition of the core is rarely made explicit; occasionally it seems to be just Greece with the rest of the Mediterranean consigned to the periphery, and sometimes the entire Mediterranean, with no dominant, privileged state and many regions sharing parallel processes of social and economic growth (T. Champion 1989: 16; cf. Nash 1985:

52–8). There are theoretical and practical difficulties with both versions, especially when one looks in detail at material evidence for interaction (the origins of artefacts, their function, etc.) and the practicality of moving particular commodities (considering sources and the existence of markets).

According to Wallerstein's world system model (1974: 347–57), when a core is deemed to be primarily an economic rather than a political or imperial entity, it usually consists of a group of states, rather than just one. In the Greek world, no single state could have acted alone in this way, and there is no evidence for the kind of coherence or coincidence of interest essential for the maintenance of a viable core. Mainland Greece alone incorporates a wide range of state forms, both *poleis* and *ethne* (Morgan 1991), and even within the most closely definable political category, the *polis*, it is widely accepted by historians of many shades of opinion that there is no such thing as a model state (e.g. Gawantka 1985; Gehrke 1986; Ruschenbusch 1978). Indeed, it is clear that similarities are more often expressed via symbols of statehood created for mutual recognition in a competitive world (Snodgrass 1986) than in the details of internal organisation which most closely determined patterns of trade and manufacturing. Real cultural boundaries existed between states, and material interchange, especially when it concerned 'personal' rather than 'state' categories of artefact, should never be taken for granted; we are only just beginning to understand how variant patterns of behaviour may be traced in the archaeological record (e.g. Arafat and Morgan 1989; Morgan 1991; Morgan and Whitelaw 1991). Particularly dangerous is the tendency, often implicit, to extrapolate from the case of Athens, a *polis* exceptional for the size of her territory and the complexity of her political structure; despite an unfortunate pro-Athenian bias in literary and archaeological evidence, there is no reason to assume that Athens was typical of mainland *poleis*, let alone of *ethne* or colonies. It is also important to remember that by *c.* 500, Cleisthenes' reforms were only just in place, and were almost immediately tested by a series of conflicts lasting over a century; the development of the Athenian *polis* was a long process, and certainly it would be wrong to regard the emerging state as stable and to accord it priority as more 'advanced' than others in the Mediterranean. Many of the papers in a recent volume on the archaeological applications of the core–periphery model (T. Champion 1989) were concerned with re-establishing the autonomy of a number of supposedly 'peripheral' areas (cf. Bernal 1987: 1–10). Just as Etruscologists, for example, are rightly eager to deny the peripheral status of Etruria (e.g. Stoddart 1989), so we would deny that the Greek world constitutes a core recognisable in Wallerstein's terms.

A second difficulty with treating the Greek world as a core is the tenet that expansion in the core is dependent on its ability to monopolise the periphery (Frankenstein and Rowlands 1978: 98; Wallerstein 1980: e.g. ch. 2), and that the subsequent development of competing points of accumulation in the core will create a crisis leading to a failure in the periphery. There is no evidence for expansion or crisis in the Greek world at this stage, the suggestion that the Peloponnesian war should be interpreted as such (Nash 1985: 58) rests upon a completely false notion of its real impact, and of the nature of the relationship between warfare, production and trade in the Classical Greek world (B. R. MacDonald 1979; Strauss 1986: 46–8). There is very little evidence for commercial market trade in any part of the Greek world before the late fifth century at the earliest; few states needed imported commodities in any quantity, and even fewer retained any interest in exported goods once they had been delivered to a trader (often a foreigner). As the case studies illustrated here show, as one moves further away from the centre of production of any particular type of artefact, it becomes increasingly difficult to trace real systemic links governing their movement. In short, if European prehistorians continue to regard the Greek world (or even the entire Mediterranean) as a 'core' without seeking to understand it more fully, and classical archaeologists either ignore the fringes of the classical world, or treat them as a useful market for luxuries, then a dialogue of the deaf is inevitable.

The dangers of investigating any archaeological question on the interface between a number of scholarly traditions and regional systems of research should be obvious (T. Champion 1987: 98–9). A study of trade in Archaic and Classical Attic fine pottery may seem an odd basis for evaluation of models of long-distance trade (and thence core–periphery theory). Yet fine decorated wares patently did move in quantity and are very difficult to fit into economic models; attempts to relate evidence for the organisation of production in Attica, patterns of transport and the nature of local markets, reveal that the very commodity used to construct vast trading schemes is that which most clearly reveals their weaknesses. A particular strength of Classical pottery analysis is that the weight of evidence for the organisation of production enables us to think directly in terms of human actions, limits and capabilities (Robertson 1985; 1987). It has been argued, notably by Vallet and Villard (1963: 209), that in cases where prolonged export activity occurs (Athens or Corinth, for example), detailed study of trading activity is a prerequisite for determining the internal economic development of the exporter state. We suggest that the reverse is true; the economic and social organisation of the state is a significant aspect of the background conditions which govern the production, appearance and use of fine decorated pottery, and thence its availability and potential desirability as an export commodity. Such an approach also avoids the extremes of studying pottery either from an art-historical viewpoint or from a position of market determinism. The movement of fine decorated pottery requires a producer capable of producing a surplus to export, a market willing to accept vessels made and decorated to suit the needs and tastes of another social group, and a trade route which allows carriage of pottery within a profitable cargo, and the existence of all three elements will undoubtedly vary through time and space. We would, however, emphasise that since every industry has its own technological requirements and social role, and the distribution of different raw materials varies, pottery should not be used as a basis for generalisation without detailed consideration of the circumstances surrounding other commodities.

In examining the movement and use of Attic finewares within and beyond the Mediterranean world, we have shown how common theoretical questions arise under very different circumstances. Once Attic finewares leave Attica, they cease to be 'Attic' in the sense that they were originally created; vessels selected by Etruria become part of Etruscan material culture, and Etruscan interests and values determine how and when they are used and traded on, and the same is true of Hallstatt Europe. The way in which different roles, meanings and values are ascribed to particular goods as they move through different societies may be obscured if one concentrates only on the two ends of a long exchange chain (Dietler 1989). Indeed, the vague (usually art-historical) concept of Hellenisation that is still current owes much to our predilection for drawing such boundaries (e.g. Olmos 1986). We do not suggest that pottery was necessarily an important component of any cargo, or that it everywhere served as an indicator of personal wealth. The significance of our arguments is rather the way in which we have been able to use detailed knowledge of the structure and local function of a particular industry to evaluate conclusions about the social and economic organisation of those societies which, directly or indirectly, imported its products. What at first may seem to be a very limited approach therefore has far-reaching implications.

Acknowledgements

We are grateful to John Boardman, Peter Callaghan, Sara and Tim Champion, Ian Morris and Brian Shefton for comments on earlier drafts of this paper, and to Sander van der Leeuw for discussion of many of the issues raised.

Notes

1 Specific objections should be brought to bear on the suggestion that clays were regularly transported (Boardman 1956: 56; 1980: 123; Casson 1938; Gill 1987: 82–3). Boardman speculates that clay was brought from Chios to Naukratis 'as ballast in the corn ships', but he offers no supporting evidence, putting the idea forward tentatively. There is nothing conclusive with which to support or refute this proposition; as Richard Jones notes (1984: 26), 'chemical analysis *per se* cannot clarify the issue of travelling clay in antiquity; that Chiot style chalices found at Naukratis have Chiot compositions cannot distinguish between Boardman's hypothesis that Chiot clay was imported as ballast in the wheat ships from the more conventional view that the pottery itself was imported from Chios'. Yet it is worth emphasising that although there may be a case for the movement of clay to the Nile Delta (which is almost unique in the Mediterranean for the absence of good potters' clay), there is no reason to extend this argument more widely, let alone to the West.

Gill's suggestion (1987: 82–3) is based partly on Boardman's, and partly on an Attic red-figured sherd found at Populonia which was marked in Etruscan before firing. This he takes as evidence of the movement of clay to Etruria, on the grounds that no Athenian potter or painter in Athens would put an Etruscan inscription on a vase; yet there are parallels for Etruscan dipinti and graffiti on vases (Johnston 1979: 238), and the very nature of trading in fine pottery makes such an occasional phenomenon readily explicable. It is quite possible that a trader, in Athens to collect vases for his return journey to Etruria, would be in the workshop of a particular painter, see that he was about to finish a vase and ask him to add a couple of words in Etruscan; the fact that the inscription is not readily comprehensible makes it at least as likely that it was added by a foreigner as by an Etruscan (cf. Williams 1988: 682). Equally, there is no evidence for Athenian workshops in Etruria (Spivey 1986: 284), and with the exception of the Suessula painter who worked in Athens and Corinth (Herbert 1977: 12; B. R. MacDonald 1979: 207–9; 1981: 162), there is scant evidence for itinerant Athenian potters (the migrants who probably helped to establish early south Italian workshops are a separate problem: Shefton 1967). To postulate an unnecessary movement of clay seems over-elaborate. Finally, the sherd is from a cup by the Penthesilea Painter Workshop, which was active *c.* 475–50 (Boardman 1989: 38–9), after the bulk of Attic imports to Etruria, and cannot therefore be taken as typical of Archaic trading patterns. Casson's work was based on modern ethnographic parallels; unfortunately his sources are of dubious reliability, and more recent investigations have reached the opposite conclusion (R. E. Jones 1986: 866, 872; cf. 1984: 26; 'most potters the writer has spoken to regard the transport of clay as an unnecessary and dubious exercise').

2 We accept the view of Dietler (1989: 134–5) that attempts to trace Greek influence in architecture (such as the use of mud brick, notably at the Heuneburg; Härke 1979: 92) or sculpture (local versions of *kouroi*; Wells 1980: 7) founder on our lack of detailed knowledge of native architectural and sculptural traditions, and we do not accept them as evidence for visiting Greek craftsmen. More seriously, for the purposes of this argument we shall set aside the outstandingly rich items which have been characterised as diplomatic gifts (listed by Wells 1980: 17; Champion and Champion 1986: 60–2), such as the Vix krater (Joffroy 1954) or the Grafenbühl couch (J. Fischer 1990). These clearly represent a non-commercial aspect of social relations, and although the question of the operation of gift exchange and elite symbolism within native social systems is of great importance (and probably accounts for a much wider range of imports than often allowed; Shefton 1990), a full study of this problem will only be possible once the ghost of long-distance Greek 'commerce' has been laid to rest, and our knowledge of the long-term development of Hallstatt society is increased to provide a proper context for the operation of such activities (as we argue in this article). There is also a pressing need for more detailed work on the role of Etruria and transalpine contact. At present, the study of imports and foreign contacts is clouded by the conflation of many issues, and this article should therefore be seen as an attempt to clear the way by dealing with the question of Greek commerce, whilst offering analogies from the eastern Mediterranean which may be helpful in considering the manipulation of imports by local communities.

3 It has been argued that trade in metals (especially tin from Spain, southern France or Cornwall) formed the basis for Massalia's prosperity (e.g. Clavel-Lévêque 1977: 22–4; cf. Villard 1960: 137–61). Yet, as Dietler has argued (1989: 132–3), the distribution of local resources and native traders makes the Rhône valley a most unlikely route for Massaliotes searching for metal supplies, and coastal trade would probably account for such movements as can be traced. We shall not therefore pursue the case here.

4 Aegina is the only Greek state which *may* have been in a worse position than Athens, although this judgement is largely impressionistic (Figueira 1981: 43–52 draws mainly on late fifth- and fourth-century evidence, and his figures are open to considerable revision). Yet there is no evidence for the scale and frequency of Archaic and early Classical imports, and limited evidence for Aeginetan trade points east rather than west (e.g. Herodotus 7.147), and especially to Egypt (e.g. Naucratis; Boardman 1980: 118–33; cf. Austin 1970). In the case of Athens, grain shipping remained in private hands throughout (M. H. Jameson 1983); state action was late and limited to such measures as fifth-century restrictions on the shipping of grain beyond the Piraeus or on the raising of maritime loans for other purposes, and the fourth-century establishment of magistracies to regulate the market (Osborne 1987a: 97–104). The earliest evidence for state intervention is the reference to *Hellespontophylakes* in Meiggs and Lewis 1969: 65 (relations between Athens and Methone in 426/5) who controlled shipping through the Hellespont and thus protected Athenian supplies. Equally, evidence for imports to any state from the western colonies is rare before the late fifth century; Thucydides 3.86 refers to the shipping of grain from Sicily to the Peloponnese, but it is hard to assess the extent to which this passing reference describes a regular practice (and one of long standing), or a response to new problems created or exacerbated by warfare.

5 The closest contemporary evidence comes from lists of property confiscated from those tried for the mutilation of the Herms in 415 (e.g. Meiggs and Lewis 1969: 79A). A total of forty-five slaves have so far been traced in these texts, and the ethnic origins of thirty-five are recorded (in all cases eastern or northern). Although there is a notable tendency for intermediate statuses to decrease as constitutions develop (Wiedemann 1987), ill-defined groups such as *oiketai* continue to appear in Athenian records, and it is difficult to know how to treat them. The argument that large-scale slavery was necessary to support popular participation in democracy (de Ste Croix 1981: 140–7, 284, 505–6, cf. 506–9; M. H. Jameson 1978) has been effectively refuted by Ober (1989: 24–7) amongst others.

PART IV

Artefacts in the landscape

8

Intensive survey, agricultural practice and the classical landscape of Greece

SUSAN E. ALCOCK, JOHN F. CHERRY and JACK L. DAVIS

The 'new wave' of survey in Greece

'A wave of activity in intensive survey has swept across the scene of Greek archaeology', claims Snodgrass (1990: 119). Survey in Greece, however, has a very long history indeed. A tradition of one-man topographic research extends back through antiquarians and painters such as Leake, Ross, Pashley or Lear (Tsigakou 1981; Constantine 1984; Eisner 1991) and aristocrats on the Grand Tour (Hibbert 1987), to Buondelmonti and Cyriac of Ancona in the late fourteenth and early fifteenth centuries (Simopoulos 1970–5). The opportunity of setting contemporary reconstructions of settlement history and land use in the context of earlier observations of this sort is one of the features which gives regional survey in Greece its characteristic flavour, and which distinguishes it sharply from that in other areas such as North America, whence some of its inspiration has certainly been derived.

The florescence of survey in Greece since 1970 is based partly on this local tradition of interest in the classical landscape and its political units (e.g. M. H. Jameson 1976), but also on the role of survey in the 'New Archaeology', with its assertion that field research must involve 'the detailed and systematic study of *regions* that can be expected to have supported cultural systems' (Binford 1964: 426; cf. C. A. Smith 1976; Johnson 1977). Consequently, most work in Greece has been of Anglo-Saxon inspiration (though in practice very international). Damage to sites from deep ploughing and bulldozing; the construction of buildings, roads, pipelines and reservoirs to serve Greece's growing population and tourist developments; rural depopulation; and the escalating costs of excavation have all fostered a sense of crisis in Greek archaeology (Bintliff and

Snodgrass 1985: 123–5), to which survey is one response.

Some of the current survey projects in Greece are in the forefront of methodological developments in Old World archaeology as a whole. Yet, oddly, the sort of *apologia* for survey (e.g. Ruppé 1966), which Schiffer *et al.* (1978: 1) some fifteen years ago thought anachronistic in North America, still seems necessary in Greek archaeology (e.g. Cherry 1982; 1983; Snodgrass 1982; 1987: 93–131; 1990: 113–19; cf. Popham 1990). In part, this may be due to the scarcity of publications in which survey data have been brought face-to-face with substantive issues of real interest to more traditionally minded classical archaeologists and ancient historians (e.g. M. H. Jameson 1976; Renfrew and Wagstaff 1982; Osborne 1985; 1987a; this volume; Snodgrass 1990; Cherry *et al.* 1991; Foxhall 1990). Large-scale, interdisciplinary, intensive surveys take time to complete in the field, and even longer for their results to be fully assimilated, so that the impact of the explosive growth in survey (fig. 8.1) is only now beginning to be felt. Equally characteristic of this 'new wave' (Cherry 1986) is a tendency to downplay many of the interpretative problems in handling survey data, choosing instead to promote survey by emphasising how this relatively simple, non-destructive and inexpensive technique can produce altogether new types of information, and in quantities previously unimagined. Debate has thus focused mainly on pragmatic and procedural issues (e.g. Keller and Rupp 1983; Hope Simpson 1984; Cherry 1984; Bintliff and Snodgrass 1985) – tiresome matters, no doubt, to those not themselves engaged in the field, but necessary for adapting a method first developed for generally sparser archaeological landscapes to the rich and complex evidence from Greece (Cherry and Davis 1988; Cherry *et al.* 1988).

These 'internal' debates have had a happy outcome, and some degree of consensus has been reached on two vital issues. First, although constraints of time and money and the unique circumstances of specific places mean that no single set of procedural guidelines can be generally applicable, only *intensive* survey techniques appear defensible – intensive here meaning quantified observations and controlled artefact collections, usually made in the course of line-walking by team members spaced at intervals of, at most, 15 to 20 metres. No one would claim that this constitutes 'total' coverage, but it is hard to deny the finding that such surveys have generated artefact collections that rival the size of those from excavations, and located up to one hundred times as many sites per square kilometre as earlier work at a less intensive level (Cherry 1983: 391 and fig. 1), even if at the expense of exploding traditional definitions of the 'site'. Second, coverage of every type of terrain within a clearly defined study region is now considered mandatory. This does not necessarily imply 'full coverage survey' (*sensu* Fish and Kowalewski 1990), since sampling – particularly when guided by sensible principles of sample stratification to account for landscape types and the known distribution of archaeological finds – can in some circumstances represent a compromise ensuring information of both regional scope and adequate quality. Even so, many recent surveys in Greece, because of their interest in the spatial configurations of past settlement, have concentrated on all available parts of a single *contiguous* block of landscape (or, at most, several such blocks); this is then broken up into a mosaic of small fields or artificial tracts for individual inspection (e.g. Cherry *et al.* 1988: fig. 4; 1991: figs. 2.2, 3.2–3.4; Snodgrass 1987: figs. 29–30; Snodgrass and Bintliff 1991: 92; Wright *et al.* 1990: figs. 5, 6, 10; Wells *et al.* 1990: figs. 7a–b). Fig. 8.2, illustrating over 5000 tracts covered by the survey undertaken by the Nemea Valley Archaeological Project, provides some notion of the complexity of survey data. For each tract, usually no larger than 1 or 2 hectares, we recorded not only data on visibility, environment and contemporary land-use, but also information about several categories of artefact for each 100 m section of the several traverses walked in each tract by each member of a team of half a dozen fieldwalkers. The consequences are obvious: managing and making sense of such a flood of data is a task that has only become feasible in the age of powerful, portable computers.

The application of such 'distributional archaeology' (Ebert 1986; Cherry and Davis 1988) in the classical lands has opened our eyes to a wealth of information not previously suspected, but also has raised a host of difficult problems that have yet to be tackled effectively. We concentrate on just one of these in the present paper.

Some earlier extensive-mode surveys seem not to have grasped the commonsense truth that 'the society did not exist that lived, worked, ate and died within a single site' (Gaffney and Tingle 1984: 135). However, subsequent experience has revealed the staggering range of features any survey may encounter – terraces, roads, bridges, quarries and mines, caves (used for cult, burial or settlement), pottery- and lime-kilns, cisterns, wells, individual graves, oil and wine presses, chipping floors, isolated towers, animal folds, agricultural storage sheds, farmhouses, rural sanctuaries and shrines, and so on (e.g. M. H. Jameson 1976: 86–7, writing of the Argolid Exploration Project, begun in 1972; cf. van Andel and Runnels 1987). These features have obvious modern counterparts in ethnoarchaeological studies of landscape utilisation and discard behaviour (e.g. Murray and Kardulias 1986; Gould and Schiffer 1981). At the other extreme, survey has been modified to study actual city sites (Bintliff

and Snodgrass 1988a; Snodgrass and Bintliff 1991; Whitelaw and Davis 1991; Alcock 1991). Yet still more significant is *the systematic recording of the density of artefacts over the whole landscape*, which emphasises the more-or-less continuous spatial distribution of cultural items across the landscape, some (but not all) of whose density peaks represent 'sites' in the traditional sense.

This need not involve rejection of the site concept itself (as suggested by D. H. Thomas 1975; Foley 1981; Shennan 1985), but it is clear that most consideration of site definition is either too vague, too formalised, or too dismissive (e.g. Gallant 1986: 408–9). The definition of a site is an act of interpretation. One major justification for the routine collection of data from *all* parts of the landscape is to provide quantitative criteria for fixing site boundaries which can only be established relative to the surrounding level of find-density. A real difficulty, however, is that almost all high-density clusters or 'sites' are multi-component. In one sense, all sites represent many components, since they are the outcome of multiple, repeated actions, even over a relatively short time-span; but we use the term 'multi-component' to refer to sites that produce finds of several distinct, often widely separated, periods. In Greece, characterised for so many millennia by sedentary arable communities, it is hardly surprising that people repeatedly occupied the same locations. Yet sometimes the amount of material of certain periods found 'on-site' is indistinguishable from that elsewhere in the landscape in those same periods, and its presence cannot be automatically assumed to be an index of settlement. Even if the site concept is retained, such problems are incapable of resolution without the availability of off-site information on a period-by-period basis (see Cherry *et al.* 1991: ch. 3).

Our chief point, however, is the very existence of an off-site landscape of artefact scatters. Why this should be so, and the processes that brought it into being, requires explanation. There is some consistency in the density thresholds used to define 'sites' in recent surveys (about thirty to fifty sherds per 100 sq. m; Cherry *et al.* 1991: ch. 3, table 3.4), but there is also great variation in density from one part of the landscape to another, with some areas producing virtually nothing and the densest urban areas sometimes exceeding 100 sherds per sq. m. Consequently, as Snodgrass and Bintliff (1991: 88) have remarked, 'artefacts are not distributed in neat, discrete packets corresponding to ancient sites. Instead the nearly millionfold variation in artefact density takes the form of a gradual distribution extending hundreds or even thousands of meters from "primary" sites.' But Bintliff and Snodgrass' 'almost unbroken carpet' of off-site pottery scatters (1988b: 506, fig. 1; Snodgrass 1987: fig. 30) is not precisely replicated everywhere. For instance,

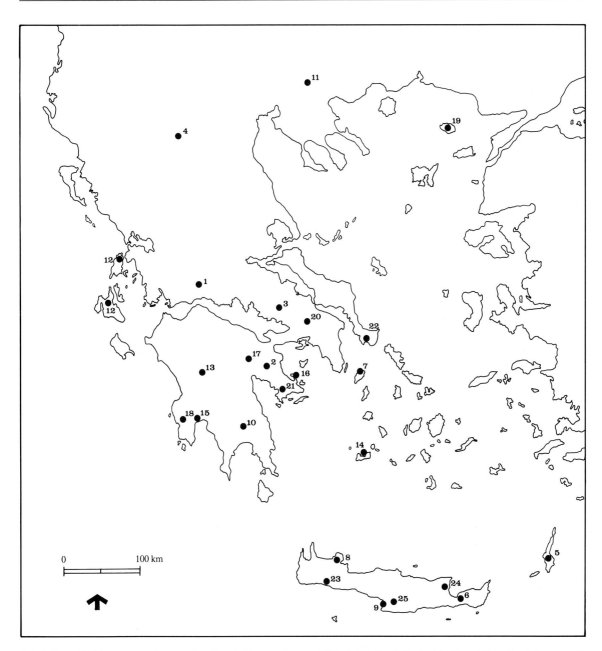

8.1 Selected field survey projects undertaken in Greece since c. 1975. 1 Aetolia, 2 Berbati Valley, 3 Boeotia, 4 Grevena, 5 Karpathos/Kasos, 6 Kavousi, 7 Keos, 8 Khania, 9 Kommos, 10 Lakonia, 11 Langadas Basin, 12 Leukas/Kephallenia, 13 Megalopolis Basin, 14 Melos, 15 Messenia (Five Rivers), 16 Methana, 17 Nemea Valley, 18 Pylos, 19 Samothrace, 20 Skourta Plain, 21 Southern Argolid, 22 Southern Euboea, 23 Sphakia, 24 Vrokastro, 25 Western Mesara

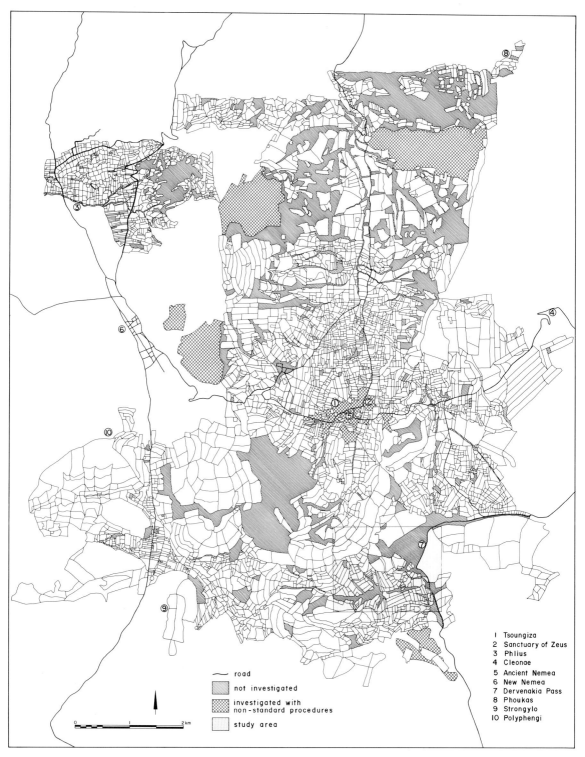

8.2 Nemea Valley Archaeological Project: the shape and distribution of about 5,500 individual survey tracts fieldwalked in 1984–9 (the box indicates the area of the case study discussed in this chapter, shown also in figs. 8.6–8.9).

the artefact distributions recorded on Keos (Cherry *et al.* 1991: figs. 3.3–3.4), in the Nemea region (Wright *et al.* 1990: figs. 5–6), in the Berbati-Limnes area (Wells *et al.* 1990: 238), and in other as yet unpublished projects, indicate a lower-density pattern, which is more variable and more discontinuous. In the southern Argolid, 'artefacts occurred for the most part in discrete clusters . . . Few were found in between; there was little background scatter' (van Andel and Runnels 1987: 33). For the Langadas Basin survey in Macedonia, Kotsakis (1989: 9) reports 'a surprisingly sparse occurrence of artefacts' suggesting that 'the phenomenon usually referred to as the "carpet" spread of artefacts does not seem to exist in the area we have covered so far' and noting that this is not 'the result of reduced artefactual visibility, as we repeatedly had the chance to verify this in freshly ploughed fields'.

Two other types of variation are also significant. The first is chronological. While the processes that produce distributions of artefacts on the surface are far from clear, it might be supposed either that they comprise a jumbled collection of finds from every period in which an area has been in use, or that the effects of alluviation, erosion and other destructive factors would cause a monotonic decrease in artefact counts as we move further back in time (e.g. Bintliff 1985: 214–15). In practice, neither seems generally to be the case. Virtually all recent surveys have found some periods to be very well represented, others much less so. Rutter (1983) has

argued that the distinctive artefacts of different periods cannot be recognised with equal ease, but clearly there is also some flux over the centuries in the rates at which artefacts are deposited in the landscape (Cherry *et al.* 1991: 328–33; Davis 1991). Moreover, there is a clear chronological correlation between the density of rural sites and the overall quantities of 'off-site' artefacts, while, despite differences from one survey to another, it is most often to the Classical to Early Hellenistic, Late Roman, and Middle Byzantine periods that the vast majority of the material belongs – both findings of some importance.

The second type of variation brings us to the central issue of this paper. Bintliff and Snodgrass (1985: 131; 1988b; 1990: 122–5; Bintliff 1985: 201–2; Snodgrass 1987: 113–17) have found that most sites, including urban centres, have what they term a 'halo' of finds around them, that is, an encircling zone substantially larger than the site, with artefact densities lower than those 'on-site', yet distinctly higher than those of the standard 'background' distribution (e.g. fig. 8.3). Absolute artefact densities defining such zones vary from one area to another (Snodgrass 1990: 233; cf. Bintliff and Snodgrass 1988b: fig. 2, with densities from about six to about forty-five sherds per 100 sq. m). Some locations lacking haloes may be tomb sites, while haloes without an accompanying site may indicate a location of activity without permanent settlement, or a failure to detect the site because of poor visibility conditions. Snodgrass

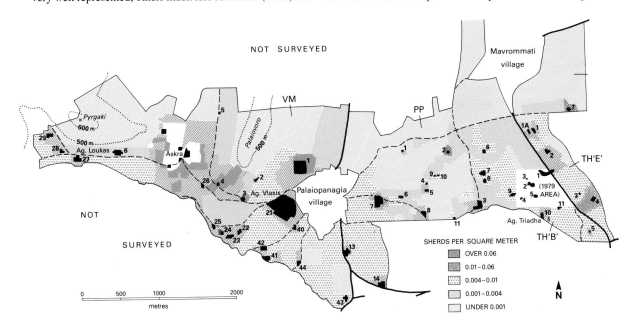

8.3 Boeotia Survey: total density of artefacts of all dates in the Valley of the Muses, Palaiopanagia and Thespiai areas, 1979–82 (after Snodgrass 1987: fig. 30).

(1987: 113) claims that haloes 'have often been encountered in survey work elsewhere', clearly referring to Wilkinson (1982) in the Middle East, or Williamson (1984) and Gaffney *et al.* (1985) in Britain. More recently (1990: 125), he has admitted that in Greece by no means all surveys have detected haloes. If we can satisfy ourselves that the procedures for recording artefact densities and defining sites allow comparability between projects (see Alcock 1989b; this volume), then this too would be a potentially important aspect of variability among different regions.

Snodgrass and Bintliff accept that rubbish disposal, natural processes of erosional smearing, and the dispersing action of modern ploughing over ancient sites may all have played some part in generating haloes. But they have repeatedly expressed their view that by far the most likely primary factor underlying off-site artefactual scatters is deliberate manuring of the cultivated landscape, using animal manure and household rubbish (incorporating pottery) collected at or near ancient sites and transported from them to be spread on the fields. The higher density of the halo around a site would be a consequence of locating the most intensive in-field cultivation or gardening closest to the site, just as von Thünen's *Der isolierte Staat* (P. Hall 1966) would lead us to expect. If this reasoning is correct, it has far-reaching implications:

> it means that the level of off-site density is an index of agricultural activity, and specifically of contemporary (that is, in this case, ancient) agricultural activity. The general areas of high density are areas of intensive ancient cultivation. Since in many cases these will coincide with areas of similar but later activity, we can see why it is that sites in the low-density areas are not only few, but also 'weak', in the sense that their interior density of finds is low: there has not been the same frequency of farming operations over subsequent centuries to bring their material to the surface. (Snodgrass 1990: 124)

As the philosopher Peter Kosso (1991: 623) has rightly comprehended, the extent of manuring in antiquity is not a matter of recondite curiosity, but one of real importance, related to intensity of land-use, methods of cultivation, and systems of land tenure. Indeed, the analysis of 'off-site' distributions could be the principal means to measure the amount of land under cultivation at particular times in the past. But is such a conclusion justified?

The idea has been widely (if somewhat uncritically) accepted by Mediterranean archaeologists, but it has yet to be demonstrated that this was the factor responsible for the bulk of the artefacts recorded in off-site contexts. If these artefacts were re-deposited during the occupation of the sites

from which they are thought to have derived, then such evidence would indeed offer significant insight into past agricultural practice, economic strategies, land-use and settlement. If it were *not* so, it does not necessarily follow, as Snodgrass (1990: 123) seems to imply, that the significance of off-site data is reduced 'almost to vanishing point', or that it becomes literally 'the junk you find on the surface – and nothing more' (Flannery 1976b: 51), since there exists a range of other human and non-human agencies which may have relevance and deserve exploration.

The 'manuring hypothesis' thus deserves closer examination. We try to provide this by drawing on several types of information and focusing on Greece in the Classical and Early Hellenistic periods (roughly the fifth to second centuries BC). This has several advantages. First, we have relevant documentary sources (although, as we shall see, they offer only a limited amount of *direct* evidence about problems of land tenure and animal husbandry), and ancient historians using this textual evidence have already studied agrarian conditions during these centuries (M. H. Jameson 1977/8; Finley 1973; Garnsey 1988; Gallant 1991). Next, intensive surveys have had success in dating material of this period, and throughout Greece and the Aegean islands they have detected broadly similar patterns: nucleated centres dominate rural landscapes characterised by numerous very small sites with assemblages comprised of finewares and domestic pottery, tile, and (occasionally) agricultural equipment such as querns or millstones. These have generally been considered as isolated farmsteads, occupied seasonally or year-round (cf. Osborne 1985), and most surveys have found that the number of rural sites in Classical and Early Hellenistic Greece attained levels unrivalled at virtually any other period. Such landscapes could be described as 'packed', perhaps even, in some areas, with dangerously high population densities (Bintliff 1985). Finally, this pattern has been interpreted as reflecting cultivation by numerous small-holders – a regime that, as we shall see, is one likely to encourage intensive, rational systems of land management and thus conditions in which manuring would be most likely.

We first consider the 'manuring hypothesis' itself, alongside alternative possible explanations for the same distributions, and note comparable case studies from outside Greece. Next follows an attempt to collate systematically the evidence for manuring in the ancient written sources, under variable circumstances of land management or ownership, intensity of production, choice of crop, environment, etc. Ethnographic information and recent theoretical models of alternative agricultural and residential strategies in antiquity also contribute to an informed perspective (e.g. about likely amounts of manure available and its use) from which to consider the archaeological record itself. Survey data from one small area examined as part of the Nemea Valley Archaeological Project provide a micro-level case study to illustrate some of the questions and techniques necessary to analyse low-density artefactual distributions more rigorously, to discriminate among possible causes for their presence, and to understand their significance.

The 'manuring hypothesis'

Bintliff and Snodgrass (1988b: 507–8) have summarised the interpretations that have been advanced to account for low-density scatters of artefacts over many square kilometres. They identify and evaluate four main types of explanation.

Model 1. They quite rightly refuse any significant role for purely accidental factors of loss and breakage – the amphora that fell off a donkey's back, or the wine-jug that broke in the fields during harvest – since these can scarcely account for the sheer quantity of material typically encountered.

Model 2. Off-site scatters reflect losses or discards in the course of behaviour at 'activity foci' or other less intensively used locations away from permanent occupation sites. While not denying the occurrence of such activities, they consider them more appropriate to low-density patterns with some spatial concentrations than to relatively uniform 'carpets' of artefacts from which sites emerge as peaks. At the same time, they admit that the boundaries of such activity foci would become fuzzy over time, and thus difficult to isolate clearly.

Model 3. Artefacts originating in sites have suffered post-depositional disturbance through erosion or activities like ploughing, so that landscape surfaces between sites and activity loci receive artefacts in secondary contexts, and initial patterns become blurred. The impact of factors such as these cannot be denied. In recent years there have been studies of downslope transport (e.g. Rick 1976; Pederson 1986), lateral displacement through ploughing (e.g. Ammerman 1985; Reynolds 1982; Yorston *et al.* 1990), site erosion (e.g. Kirkby and Kirkby 1976; Tasker 1980), and other sorts of disturbance (e.g. Wood and Johnson 1978; Schiffer 1983; Schofield 1991). Bintliff and Snodgrass, however, argue that 'the distribution of such off-site material ought to be highly preferential in landscape context', rather than 'reaching every sector of a settled landscape' (1988b: 508); they mean by this, for instance, that artefact spreads uphill from sites should be minimal, and that natural barriers such as trackways, stream-beds and field-walls would impede long-distance lateral transport, neither of which seems to be the case with their Boeotian data. Likewise, long-exposed and much-travelled artefacts would be more abraded and comminuted than those from the sites at which

they originated, but the fact that no such distinctions in quality could be made in Boeotia is regarded as an argument against ploughing and erosion as important mechanisms of transport.

Model 4. The most probable primary factor, therefore, is taken to be *manuring*. In other words, animal dung, night soil, organic wastes, ash, street sweepings, etc., in which cultural debris had been incorporated, were systematically collected, carted out, and spread on the cultivated parts of the landscape as fertiliser; once the organic component had decayed, the artefacts remained in the soil, to be brought to the surface by ploughing or by deflation of the soil matrix. They treat variations in aridity and lithology, rather than cultural factors, as the principal explanation for the consistent pattern of increase in absolute values of off-site densities from temperate northwestern Europe through the Mediterranean to the Middle East (Bintliff and Snodgrass 1988b: fig. 2).

While these authors allow some causal role to all the factors introduced in these models, their clear preference is for the manuring hypothesis. The recognition of the significance attached to manuring in our classical sources is nothing new, but it *is* new in classical archaeology to suggest that manuring has consequences which might give it some potential visibility in the archaeological record. Elsewhere, and most notably in Roman and medieval northwestern temperate Europe, such interpretations of field scatters have been current for much longer. Over forty years ago, P. P. Rhodes (1950: 13), writing about 'the thin but widespread scatter of Romano-British potsherds which can be picked up from the surface and lynchets of Celtic fields' on the Berkshire Downs of southern England, concluded that the pottery could only have got there by being 'conveyed to the fields casually amongst domestic rubbish used as manure'. This conclusion has been endorsed by many later writers (e.g. Bowen 1961: 6; Foard 1978: 363–4; P. Fowler 1981: 167; Rowley-Conwy 1981; Fenton 1981; Crowther 1983; Williamson 1984; Hayfield 1987: 192–6; Gaffney and Tingle 1985; 1989: 209–44; Astill 1988: 79), but usually without detailed consideration of the spatial and chronological characteristics of alleged 'manuring scatters', or of the social and economic contexts of the agricultural systems in which this sort of manuring might have occurred.

Support comes mainly from the agrarian history of Western Europe in the medieval and early modern periods, for which we have documentary evidence on settlement, landholding, field systems and agricultural practice. Irrespective of the specific patterns of landscape organisation, the overwhelming constraints were the ratio of arable and pasture, and the need to ensure adequate levels of soil fertility. As Slicher van Bath's (1963: 7–25) classic exposition demonstrated, these factors are tightly linked: the area cultivated depended on population and the possibilities for manuring, making livestock the key element where land shortage made long-fallow or turf-manuring impracticable. 'The extent of the stock was also determined by the surplus of agricultural produce on which it had to be fed during the winter. Under the fallow system one suffers from the evil of small harvest due to insufficient manuring, the lack of manure being in turn the result of small agricultural production making it impossible to keep more cattle' (1963: 10). One response was an infield/outfield system, with the transfer of plant nutrients to the arable infield, which was kept in permanent cultivation by receiving all the manure from stall-fed livestock and from the grazing of stubble after the harvest, and the input of many other fertilising agents (e.g. Olsson 1988; Dodgshon 1988: 144–5). As Astill (1988: 79) notes, the scarcity of rubbish pits or middens in medieval villages may imply that organic refuse was too important to be put in holes, being used instead as manure. In the crowded early modern landscapes – after the introduction of industrial crops needing very fertile soil, and the abandonment of fallowing, but before the advent of chemical fertilisers – massive quantities of manure were required. Slicher van Bath (1963: 254–63) describes the manure trade of eighteenth- and nineteenth-century England and Northern Europe; he cites manuring levels as high as 70–90,000 kg per hectare in the Netherlands, and refers to land in Norfolk being dressed with loam, gypsum, oyster shells, seaweed, burnt earth, mud, fish, rape-seed cakes, ash, buckwheat, compost, leaves, and night soil or garbage from towns.

Very substantial transfers of organic material thus took place between different parts of the agrarian system (Dodgshon 1988: figs. 1–2) and increasingly from outside it too. But it is only the manure from the byres or stockyards and the refuse from towns that have any relevance from the point of view of the cultural material spread by such transfers. Moreover, its distribution would be very selective, restricted not only to arable areas, but even to a core zone or to specific groups of fields. This, at least, is the conclusion of several studies in which 'manuring scatters' have *not* been found over all the arable belonging to known medieval settlements (see Astill 1988: 79–80); in Wharram Percy in East Yorkshire (Hayfield 1987: 195) the areas that seem to have received manure containing medieval cultural detritus are also those that have produced worn Roman pottery, thus raising the possibility that these were traditionally regarded as the more fertile lands and that there was some continuity in agricultural practice between the two periods. Even the most intensive manuring is not likely to generate an even-density spread of artefacts across the entire landscape.

Furthermore, there are dangers in interpreting changes in the amount and extent of pottery entering the surface off-site record solely in terms of changes in farming practice or in the intensity of production; apart from ignoring changes in pottery supply and circulation (Millett 1991), or in residential patterns affecting deposition (Davis 1991), this overlooks the fact that 'manuring scatters' – if that is what they really are – reflect only *settlement-derived* fertiliser, not the total area farmed, or even the total manured area. This is one weakness in what is otherwise the best study of manuring scatters in England, by Gaffney and Tingle (1989: 239–44; 1985; cf. Gaffney *et al.* 1985; Gaffney and Gaffney 1988) at the Romano-British estate of the Maddle Farm villa in Berkshire.

The scale and intensity of manuring are not simply a function of environment, but depend on a wide range of variables. These must include patterns of landholding; density and distribution of population; land forms and soil fertility; farming regimes, and the specific mixes of crops and animals involved; quantities of animal manure or other fertilising agents available, and the distances over which they must be transported; and the intensity of agricultural production, in response to wider economic and social constraints or opportunities. Broad generalisation seems inappropriate and possibly misleading. More chronologically and geographically specific consideration of manuring is necessary. One may therefore question the direct relevance for Classical and Early Hellenistic Greece of explanations drawn from other periods and other environmental zones (e.g. temperate Europe), whose climate, soils, plant and animal resources, and socioeconomic structure were all radically different. To cite but one significant difference, in hot and arid climates manures oxidise rapidly and easily lose their nutrients from excessive drying out or the leaching of the soluble constituents (Wilkinson 1982: 324). Their fertilising effect is limited, unless they are handled carefully (e.g. by composting; K. D. White 1970: 131–3), applied at the right time and in the right quantity, and immediately ploughed under rather than spread on the surface. Neither the assertion that 'it can be taken for granted that manure was part of the environment of early farming communities in Britain' (Fenton 1981: 217), nor the modern observation that 'manure is applied to tree crops, gardens and cereals throughout the Mediterranean and is evidently beneficial' (Halstead 1987: 82), nor even the evidence of the classical authors that the benefits of manuring were understood (see below), allow us to assume without question that manuring was ubiquitous in ancient Greece, and is the primary explanation for off-site artefact scatters. The case needs to be argued in detail *in its local context*. Yet such claims remain at the general level (e.g. Gallant 1986: 415;

Halstead 1987: 83; Osborne 1987a: 70; Hodkinson 1988: 40–1; Bintliff and Gaffney 1988: 152; Snodgrass 1990: 123–4).

Wilkinson's series of papers (1982; 1988; 1989; 1990; cf. Ball *et al.* 1989) on extensive, and sometimes very high-density, scatters in the vicinity of a number of ancient towns in Turkey, Syria, Iraq, Iran and Oman is probably the most sophisticated and sustained treatment of the 'manuring hypothesis'. By carefully counting artefacts within small quadrats located at regular intervals along transects running out from the major sites in each study area, Wilkinson has been able to build up quantified maps of sherd scatter and to compare these to the distributions of modern villages and of sites of various dates which might have been the points of origin for the scatters (e.g. fig. 8.4, from the north Jazira plain in Iraq). There is a general fall-off in density with increasing distance from the site, and the approximate radius of the scatter corresponds quite closely to the site's size, satellite villages being surrounded by zones of lower density and smaller radius (Wilkinson 1989: 44, table 1). In some cases (e.g. Siraf in Iran), the scatter corresponds closely to a clearly defined area of ancient fields, with traces of wells and water channels, so that it is reasonable to regard it as the most intensively cultivated land, which was irrigated and manured. Wilkinson concludes that such scatters result from the transport to the fields of settlement-derived refuse, and are episodic phenomena which correlate strongly with peak periods in total settlement area and city development (1989: fig. 8).

Wilkinson cites comparative archaeological, historical and ethnographic data on manuring from a wide range of times and places (1989: 38–41). He judiciously argues that field scatters 'should not be uncritically interpreted as result-ing from manuring in antiquity' (1989: 31). Thus, for instance, he carefully considers the possibility that scatters of prehistoric pottery are the result of the excavation of tells for fertiliser after their abandonment; the date of the material, its spatial distribution in relation to more recent centres of settlement, and its highly abraded condition are all advanced as counter-arguments (1989: 41; Ball *et al.* 1989: 13). Similarly, he acknowledges difficulties in discrimi-nating between high-density manuring scatters on intensively farmed land in the vicinity of cities, low-density scatters representing small-scale or short-term occupation sites, or even burials. Wilkinson has also examined the masking effects of sedimentation: he notes, for instance, that this may account for the lower sherd densities within a radius of some 0.5 km from a tell (1982: 329), although he also admits that the keeping of animal flocks adjacent to the settlement could have resulted in manuring on the hoof rather than from settlement-derived fertilisers (Ball *et al.*

1989: 13). Finally, he admits candidly that the area of sherd scatter, even if it does correspond to the manured zone, represents only a *minimum* estimate of the cultivated catchment of a site, so that it offers a shaky basis for estimating carrying capacity or modelling the agricultural regime as a whole (Wilkinson 1982: 332).

Such subtleties have yet to play a role in attempts to under-stand off-site artefact scatters in the classical lands. Our purpose in this paper is to encourage work of this kind, rather than to offer polished interpretations or complete solutions. In the following section, we discuss an important dimension of the problem, namely, what the classical sources reveal about the relationship between settlement-derived fertilisers and the organisation of farming practice under different environmental, economic and social constraints.

Agricultural practice and the formation of the classical landscape: the textual evidence

Recent work on animal husbandry in the classical world has addressed the role of animals in religious practice, in status rivalries, and in the economic strategies both of *poleis* and of individual households (e.g. Whittaker 1988). We focus on one by-product, manure (Greek *kopros*), and on the written evidence that could suggest a connection between the fertilisation of fields and the patterns of artefact distribution observed archaeologically. Our sources are not restricted to the classical period only, but our emphasis is on the types of landholding and agricultural regimes characteristic of that era.[1]

No one would deny that the use of *kopros* was well known and approved in antiquity. 'In agriculture there is nothing so good as manure', wrote Xenophon (*Oec.* 20.10), and manuring is rated second in importance only to ploughing and soil preparation (e.g. Theophrastus, *CP* 3.20.6; 3.2.1, 4.12.3; Cato 61; Varro 1.2.21; Columella 2.1.7; 2.13.3–4). Such fertilisation supplied necessary nutrients, improved the structure and aeration of the soil and – very important in the semi-arid Mediterranean – increased the amount of water the soil could retain (Follet *et al.* 1981: 479–81; Cooke 1975: 13; cf. Hadjichristodoulou 1983: 269; Gregory *et al.* 1984; Krentos and Orphanos 1979). From the superabundance of the Augean stables, to the dungheap where the dog Argos lay 'neglected, his master gone, in the deep dung of mules and cattle, which lay in heaps before the doors till the slaves of Odysseus should take it away to dung his wide lands' (Homer, *Odyssey* 17.296–9), *kopros* is a regular feature in the sources. It surfaces in Socratic dialogues, Old and New Comedy, even in personal and place names; demes in Attica and Keos were actually named *Kopros*, much to the satis-faction of Aristophanes, an author to whom we owe many of

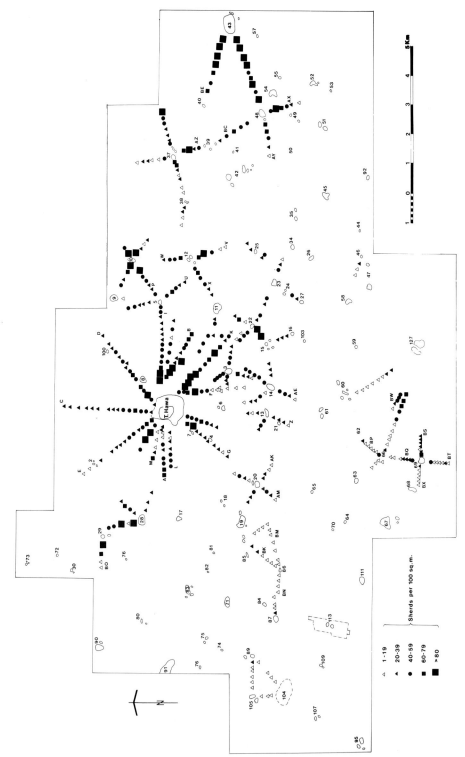

8.4 *North Jazira Project area, northern Iraq: archaeological sites (numbered) and off-site sherd densities around the Early Bronze Age centre of Tell Hawa (by courtesy of T. S. Wilkinson).*

our scatological data (Aristophanes, *Lysistrata* 1174; *Knights* 899; *Assemblywomen* 317; cf. Demosthenes 7.3.6; Isaeus 3.2.3). But despite the overwhelming impression that it was considered 'good to manure the land' (Xenophon, *Oec.* 20.4), it is still unclear how much manuring took place in classical Greece.

The extant literary data display a general bias against agriculture, and in particular against cultivators toward the lower end of the spectrum of landholding – the majority of farmers in most classical landscapes. The scarcity of useful references to specific methods of manuring, or to the scale on which it took place, displays that bias more than it reveals the realities of agricultural life. Agricultural leases go some way to fill the silence, although it is often unclear to what extent general farming practices are reflected in their prescriptions. For example, the rotation of cereals and pulses is sometimes forbidden (Attica, deme of Piraeus, *IG* II² 2498), yet elsewhere allowed (Attica, deme of Rhamnous, *IG* II² 2493; Attica, phratry, *IG* II² 1241 (M. H. Jameson 1982; Osborne 1987a: 42–3)). Two fourth-century sources deserve special mention: Xenophon's *Oeconomicus* (a description of a 'gentleman farmer's farm') and Theophrastus' *Historia Plantarum* and *De Causis Plantarum* (botanical treatises). Neither author wrote for small-scale cultivators, so their testimony is problematic, but they provide some guide to ancient attitudes to *kopros* and priorities for its use (Hodkinson 1988: 69–70 n. 3). Roman agronomists (Varro, Cato, Columella, Pliny), writing considerably later, also discuss manuring at some length, but the estates which concern them most were typically much larger than Classical and Hellenistic farms (Frayn 1979: 54–5; K. D. White 1970; Spurr 1986: x–xiii). Dio Chrysostom (*Oration* 7, the *Euboean Discourse*) describes a two-family household on Euboea around AD 100; unfortunately, despite its generally veristic description of the household, which is shown as existing quite happily at the subsistence level through a combination of hunting and agriculture, Dio's work is highly stylised (C. P. Jones 1978: 61). Ancient testimony thus gives a patchy picture, but it may be combined with ethnographic observations to provide some predictions against which to assess the archaeological data.

Several other methods of refreshing the land are also discussed in the sources. These included planting crops and ploughing them under as 'green manure'; stubble burning; application of mud, slime or other non-organic substances, such as marl, lime or nitrates; the use of 'tanner's manure' (i.e. by-products of the tanning process); and even the recognition that 'fields are fattened' by corpses or blood.[2] These techniques do not seem relevant to off-site artefact distributions; yet the very fact that alternative methods were known shows both the importance attached to fertilising the

fields and the feeling that *kopros* alone was not always sufficient.

Organic residues, however, were clearly the main ancient source of fertiliser. The word *kopros* had a wide semantic field: not only animal (and even human) dung, but any other organic substance that could be composted to provide soil nutrients. Xenophon's impatience with farmers careless about manuring demonstrates the point:

> So, too, everyone will say that in agriculture there is nothing so good as manure, and their eyes tell them that nature produces it. All know exactly how it is produced, and it is easy to get any amount of it; and yet, while some take care to have it collected, others care nothing about it. Yet the rain is sent from heaven, and all the hollows become pools of water, and the earth yields herbage of every kind which must be cleared off the ground by the sower before sowing; and the rubbish he removes has but to be thrown into water, and time of itself will make what the soil likes. For every kind of vegetation, every kind of soil in stagnant water turns into manure (*kopros*). (*Oec.* 20.10–11)

This terminological ambiguity raises problems, but since dung was the principal fertiliser, it is dung whose availability we need to consider, as well as the nature and goals of the households using it.

Our understanding of Classical and Early Hellenistic cultivation has been radically revised in recent years. Four basic features are usually thought to characterise ancient Greek agriculture: (1) highly nucleated residence at some distance from the fields; (2) regular fallowing, usually every other year; (3) fragmented landholdings; and (4) long-distance transhumant pastoral activity. Animals could not be kept on small, dispersed land parcels, especially since the adoption of fallow precluded the cultivation of fodder crops, and this (together with external climatic factors) tended to encourage regular seasonal transhumance. A fundamental divorce between stock husbandry and arable farming was thus taken for granted (Semple 1932: 300; Jardé 1925: 25–30; cf. Koster and Koster 1976). In this *extensive* system of agriculture, only limited manuring would be possible, because manure was so scarce. Agricultural yields are presumed to have been low, and this is blamed on the lack of fertilisation (Amouretti 1986: 62; Gamble 1982: 228).

Such a model of settlement and land use patterns, which Halstead (1987) has termed 'traditional', relies on extrapolation from early modern and present-day Greek agriculture. Recently, however, an alternative has been proposed, in part to take account of the traces of dispersed residence in the classical landscape detected by most intensive surface surveys. This model presupposes relatively intensive methods of cultivation and the practice of animal husbandry in close association with individual rural settlements; cereal/pulse rotation (rather than biennial fallow) would produce fodder crops, allowing animals to be kept on the arable and thus providing manure (Halstead 1987: 82–3; Garnsey 1988: 93–4; Hodkinson 1988: 38–41). It is also assumed that at least part of most individuals' total landholdings were concentrated in a relatively contiguous block, making an isolated rural base (rather than centralised urban or village residence) economically worthwhile (Cherry *et al.* 1991: ch. 17). Small-scale farming at subsistence or near-subsistence level is most closely associated with this regime, although agro-pastoral symbiosis would work at all levels of landholding (e.g. Spurr 1986: 117–19). Hints of such an association can certainly be found in the ancient sources: Xenophon (*Oec.* 5.3), for example, commented that 'the art of rearing animals is joined to agriculture, so that we may have the means to please the gods by sacrificing and may make use of them ourselves'. Many scholars now see long-distance transhumance as an anachronistic idea in the classical world and most earlier periods (Halstead 1987: 81; Cherry 1988; Hodkinson 1988; *contra* Skydsgaard 1988).

Extensive and intensive methods of farming could be employed simultaneously by different families from the same city, depending on their social and economic status, the size of their holdings and household, and other factors. Even individual families could vary their strategies through time, depending on changes in family composition or external political circumstances. The alternative model thus complements and modifies more traditional reconstructions; for instance fallowing, if not universally practised, was undoubtedly a feature of ancient agriculture (Hesiod, *Works and Days* 461–4; Xenophon, *Oec.* 16.10–15; Theophrastus, *CP* 3.20.8). The agricultural and residential choices made by individual cultivators, however, are very revealing of their economic and political situation. 'Traditional', centrally based, extensive cultivation is less labour intensive and buffers farmers more effectively against the potential risk of crop failure, yet tends to give low returns. Intensive agriculture, on the other hand, garners better yields for the amount of land cultivated, but requires more labour, demanding either much time away from an urban home or permanent residence in the countryside. The social implications of such decisions are obvious.

Tentatively, we suggest that the households most likely to adopt intensive cultivation are those with landholdings of moderate size – i.e. people under some pressure to work their fields intensively, yet still with the chance of meeting subsistence requirements from them. There was great variability in property sizes and systems of labour in the classical world, but a figure of 3.6–5.4 hectares nonetheless appears generally acceptable as the usual size of a 'family farm' (M. H. Jameson 1992; Burford Cooper 1977/8). It seems reasonable to equate the traces of dispersed rural settlement with property holding on this scale (always allowing generous margins of error on either side). Individuals with very much smaller landholdings would probably need additional economic resources, available only in the town, to supplement their agricultural holdings; so urban residence would be their obvious choice. Wealthy elite proprietors might install tenants on portions of their holdings, but would themselves prefer to live in town. Survey reports appear to have identified rural sites with small households in this range of landownership (e.g. Bintliff and Snodgrass 1985: 139–45).

The likelihood that the small Classical and Early Hellenistic sites observed in the countryside reflect intensive cultivation of moderate-sized landholdings is significant, since it has direct implications for the number and type of animals (both two- and four-legged) likely to be producing dung for the household unit. The mode of cultivation too is important: the traditional/intensive distinction affects the putative relationship between manuring and off-site artefact distributions, for strictly speaking the traditional model limits the links between manuring and the spread of cultural debris, whereas its alternative does the opposite. To see in dispersed settlement more labour-intensive land-use may not be controversial. But to go on to say that 'the background scatter of ancient pottery throughout the agricultural landscape frequently detected by archaeological survey . . . probably reflects the intensive spreading of manure' (Hodkinson 1988: 40–1) may be to miss a step in the argument. It is one thing to accept the importance of manuring for the ancient farmer, and to recognise that some cultural debris found its way out to the fields in the course of muck-spreading; quite another to quantify this process, or to equate it directly with the off-site scatters found by survey. In other words, we may have moved from under-estimating to over-estimating the use of *kopros*.

Urban wastes

Even at the height of Classical and Early Hellenistic dispersed settlements, many people in many *poleis* would have lived in their local urban centre, travelling out to cultivate their land in the 'traditional' way. Cities generate significant amounts of dung or other refuse that require removal and may be used as fertiliser on fields outside the town (e.g. Semple 1932: 408; Wilkinson 1982: 324; Day and Thompson 1988a; 1988b), as instances such as the Dung Gate at Jerusalem (Nehemiah 2.13) or the use of night soil in Chinese cities (Follet *et al.* 1981: 481–2; Fenton 1981: 210) illustrate. Greek cities as varied as Athens, Pergamon, Thasos and Thebes were concerned with urban sanitation (Vatin 1976; Martin 1974: 61–3; Owens 1983: 46; Plutarch, *Moralia* 811B). [Aristotle] (*Constitution of Athens* 50) numbered among the duties of the Athenian *astynomoi* that 'they keep watch to prevent scavengers [*koprologoi*] from depositing ordure within 10 stades [1,766 m] of the wall' (for *koprologoi*, see Aristophanes, *Peace* 9; Demosthenes 25.49). This may indicate the presence of a kind of sanitation department in Classical Athens, but Owens (1983: 48–50) suggests the *koprologoi* were private entrepreneurs profiting from their trade. The Athenian law was only concerned with removing ordure from the city, its further possible use not being a matter of public interest. At Hellenistic Pergamon, individuals were responsible, under the direction of city officials, for the cleanliness of streets and sewage removal. In Thasos too, keeping the streets in order was left to private citizens; one lease of about 300 BC, for the Garden of Heracles, required the lessor to clean up the rented area (which apparently was being treated as a thoroughfare and rubbish tip), and some consideration was given to the use of the *kopros* thus collected as fertiliser for the trees and vegetation in the garden (*IG* XII.8.265; Vatin 1976: 559–64; Salviat 1972: 370–3).

Sanitation thus seems largely to have been a private concern, and was not always well managed; in the first century BC Strabo reports the complaint that Athenian virgins could no longer 'draw pure liquid from the Eridanos, from which even cattle would hold aloof' (9.1.19). How much of the *kopros* removed from the city was sold to farmers as manure rather than simply dumped is uncertain. A trade certainly existed: provisions for the sale of dung are known from a late fifth-century BC inscription from Tegea, where herds grazed on the temple lands of Athena Alea (*IG* V.2.3; C. D. Buck 1955: 199–200, no. 18; cf. Trebatius, *Digest* 19.1.17.2; J. Thompson 1989: 83; and on such sales in other cultures, Wilkinson 1982: 324–5). This is an instance of trade in animal dung. *Human* excrement is a more pungent and powerful fertiliser, requiring dilution, composting or time to rot before it can be applied to most crops (Theophrastus, *HP* 2.7.4; Semple 1932: 410). In any case, few farmers could afford to buy dung, rather than relying on their own private supplies of it; its movement would be even more of a problem, since organic manures are heavy, bulky and unwieldy to handle (conditions of transport will be discussed again further below, p. 153). Nor is it yet very clear how much *cultural* detritus might have been transported in this way. The contents of *koprones* (privies) may have been dealt with separately from other rubbish, such as the sweepings from the streets, which would have contained animal dung (Aristophanes, *Thesmophoriazusai*

485; Plutarch, *Moralia* 1044D; Eupolis fr. 45–45A (= Edmonds 1957: 328–9); Athenaeus X.417D; for evidence from *horoi*, see Finley 1952: 186, no. 86A, 260 n. 116; Fine 1951: 8, no. 16). On the other hand, sewage and 'rubbish' in the modern sense scarcely seem to be distinguished in our sources. It is likely that the *koprologoi* or their equivalents carried out remains of food preparation or other kitchen debris, as well as the occasional broken pot tossed in the privy.

Just as von Thünen's *isolierte Staat* envisaged an 'inner zone' of intensive agriculture and manured land around market centres, so the immediate hinterland of the classical town must have been the chief recipient of urban refuse (p. 142, above; Chisholm 1968; P. Hall 1966: 122). Even at Athens there is evidence for the enrichment of gardens and olive groves about the city by urban *kopros*. The city's main sewer ran to a reservoir outside the Dipylon gate, from which canals ran to the cultivated plain of the Kephisos valley. One of the canals may have had a device to regulate the flow, possibly allowing the sale of sewage (Semple 1932: 414). Similar but less formal arrangements were in place for the fields and gardens we know existed not only immediately outside, but also within, many other Greek cities (Hanson 1983: 67, n. 3; Vatin 1974: 348–9; Phlius: Alcock 1991; Delos: Bruneau 1979: 89–99). Hardy city-dwellers may have loaded and carried out private supplies of *kopros*, but the amounts would probably have been relatively small, constrained especially by the number of animals that could be kept in the city. Even here, it was probably the family's holdings nearest the city, the ones on which the most labour-intensive crops would be grown, that would receive the household's limited offering.

In general, then, if manuring with urban wastes has any connection with the off-site artefact scatters detected by survey, its relevance is primarily to the areas immediately around the cities. Urban sites should certainly have an encircling 'halo' of ceramic debris from manuring with waste-products from the town; the Near Eastern examples discussed above had scatters extending out some 2 to 6 km (e.g. Wilkinson 1982). Intensive surveys in Greece that have included both the area of an ancient town *and* its immediate periphery (e.g. at Haliartos and Thespiai in Boeotia (Bintliff and Snodgrass 1988a; Snodgrass and Bintliff 1991) or at Phlius in the Corinthia (Wright *et al.* 1990: 611–16; Alcock 1991) are now providing data suitable for testing this hypothesis in more detail.

Manure in the countryside

The immediate periphery of a city, receiving relatively abundant refuse year-round, was substantially different from areas some distance away. The availability and uses of *kopros* generated in the countryside are more important for the present argument, particularly those processes which mixed artefacts with manure or other organic refuse available for spreading in the fields. This mixing would presumably have happened either in the dung heaps or elsewhere in the farmyard. The former are rarely mentioned in polite sources, but they were clearly a standard feature of a Greek farm. The Roman agronomists too advise about their location, construction and number (two: one for fresh and one for rotted manure; Varro 1.13.4; Columella 1.6.21–2; 2.14.6–8); 'keep the manure carefully', enjoined Cato (5.8; cf. 2.3). Late Roman legislation likewise provides testimony to their value (e.g. R. J. Buck 1983: 29–30).

Much of this dung would have been 'littered manure', straw and other plant material used as bedding in stables and animal pens. This made good *kopros*, since the straw absorbed nutritious urine and other liquids which would otherwise escape. Spurr (1986: 69, 126) quotes an old Italian proverb: 'He who has good litter has good manure' (cf. Theophrastus, *HP* 2.7.4; 7.5.1; K. D. White 1970: 125–6; Cooke 1975: 13, 22). Other organic material was added to the heap to compost it. Xenophon (*Oec.* 18.2) said stubble could be added to increase the pile's bulk; Cato (37.2) mentioned straw, lupins, chaff, bean stalks, husks, ilex and oak leaves (37.2); while Columella (2.14.6–8) cited ash, filth, sewage, straw and dirt (cf. K. D. White 1970: 132; Goffer *et al.* 1983). Theophrastus (*HP* 2.7.4), following an authority named Chartodras, listed types of manure in order of strength – human, swine, goat, sheep, ox and pack animals – and the Roman agronomists had similar rankings (Varro 1.38; Columella 2.15; K. D. White 1970: 126–9). Different types were recommended in different circumstances, or for different crops, although these may not have been separated on a small farm; such advice seems more appropriate to larger estates with more animals and a bigger labour force. As Foxhall (n.d.) notes, 'it is significant that Theophrastus . . . lumps manure with organic rubbish and "sweepings" (*surmatitis*). This provides another hint that all sorts of rubbish ended up in the same place.' The very ambiguity of the term *kopros* makes the same point.

Household rubbish and kitchen refuse, including broken pots, must have formed part of this general heap. Three references from ancient authors, two fifth-century BC comedians and a first-century AD philosopher, provide explicit references to the depositional processes involved:

(1) 'Nor a treasure thrown away on a dunghill neither' (Strattis fr. 43 = Edmonds 1957: 826–7).
(2) 'You will see the shaft of the kottabos rolling neglected in the chaff, and Manes pays no attention to wine-drops tossed at him; as for the unhappy pan, you may see that resting beside the socket of the back door in a pile of sweepings' [*or* 'you could see the wretched kottabos disc with its pivot in the rubbish out the back door' (trans. Foxhall)] (Hermippus fr. 47 = Edmonds 1957: 300–1).
(3) 'What confidence am I to place in you? If you were a vessel so cracked that it was impossible to use you for anything, you would be cast forth upon the dunghills and even from there no one would pick you up; but if, although a man, you cannot fill a man's place, what are we going to do with you?' (Epictetus 2.4.4).

Cato (5.8) advised cleaning the manure of foreign matter before applying it in the fields, but peasant farmers would probably not be bothered. The dung heap would thus accumulate some artefacts which would accompany the *kopros* to its destination.

Farmyards normally had an open central court (Pečírka 1973: 126–7; Jones *et al.* 1962), and in some cases also a boundary wall (Young 1956: 138). The fourth-century BC Vari house in Attica had a large and apparently subdivided enclosure, which yielded a significant amount of pottery (J. E. Jones *et al.* 1973: 370–2, 442; cf. J. H. Young 1956; Lohmann 1983; 1985). Such enclosures probably contained either gardens or animal shelters, perhaps used interchangeably, since the use of former pens as gardens is certainly attested in other settings (Chang and Koster 1986: 114; cf. Dio Chrysostom 7.16). Ordure, straw and rubbish gathered in these areas were periodically swept together for use as *kopros*. Thus Simiche, slave to Menander's Dyskolos, was put in a panic for losing the farm's only mattock: 'master wants to shift some dung / That's lying in the yard, as luck would have it' (*Dyskolos* 584–5); while in Longus' *Daphnis and Chloe* (4.1), a servant preparing for his master's arrival 'mucked the yard, lest the dung should offend him with the smell'. Varro (1.13.4) remarked that the yard 'becomes the handmaid of the farm because of what is cleared off it'. In the dung heap and farmyard, *kopros* was mixed with cultural refuse potentially including artefacts from earlier periods which re-entered the discard cycle.

In considering the contribution of various animals, we should not underestimate humans as significant contributors to a farm's *kopros*. Columella (2.14.8; cf. Spurr 1986: 128) estimated humans as equivalent to a 'large animal' (e.g. ox, mule) in terms of manure production, 'for they can gather and heap together not only the waste matter from their own bodies, but also the dirt which the yard and the buildings produce every day'. On the Classical farmstead most human waste would have gone the way of all others and been added to the general dung heap. Hesiod (*WD* 731) advises 'going to the wall of a well-fenced yard', where straw and other litter would soak up the valuable urine, while Varro (1.13.4) noticed that some people constructed slave privies over their dung heaps.

Traction animals were equally associated with the rural settlement itself: as Hesiod (*WD* 405) put it, 'First house and wife and an ox for the plough, for the ox is the poor man's slave.' However, recent estimates suggest that only holdings of at least 5 hectares could spare sufficient area for fodder cropping to make use of plough oxen feasible. Estates of that size fall in the range for a citizen-hoplite allotment, presumably leaving many cultivators below that level (e.g. for an Athenian *thes* about 2–4 hectares; Burford Cooper 1977/8: 168–72; K. D. White 1970: 336; Clark and Haswell 1970: 64–8; M. H. Jameson 1977/8: 125 n. 13, 131; Halstead 1987: 84 and n. 49; Garnsey 1988: 46 and n. 6; cf. Barker 1985: 52–3). Foxhall (n.d.) lowers the figure, arguing that farmsteads offered more fodder than is usually assumed; she mentions agricultural waste products such as chaff, straw and stubble, legume haulms and husks, weeds, leaves, and vine and tree prunings. Even so, oxen, horses, mules or donkeys would have been beyond the means of many small landowners.[3] However, Halstead (1987: 84) points out that it is in the 'traditional' agricultural model, with its emphasis on plough cultivation and travel to distant and fragmented plots, that draught animals are most significant; on the smaller and more concentrated holdings associated with dispersed settlement, hoeing, spading and family or slave labour would suffice, and indeed would result in the higher yields typical of hand, rather than plough, cultivation. Likewise, individual animals may have been shared with, or borrowed from, a neighbour or landlord (Hesiod, *WD* 451; Aschenbrenner 1972: 57; A. H. M. Jones 1952: 53; Foxhall 1990: 107). The fields would then get ploughed, but without any regular contribution of manure to the farm. The scarcity or absence of large animals is significant, for they are not only most productive of manure, but also the most likely to be kept in stalls regularly mucked out to provide much of the *kopros* liable to become mixed with cultural refuse.

Horses too were expensive to keep. Some regions were unable to provide the necessary resources for such animals, and even in the more favoured areas many landholdings were too small to accommodate horses or to grow the fodder crops they needed. Horses, 'the useless animal *par excellence* in an era before the invention of the harness' (Hodkinson 1988: 64; cf. Semple 1932: 305–7, 318–23), functioned almost exclusively as status markers and military mounts; they were animals for the elite. If kept at all, horses would have been stall-fed, but then probably turned out to pasture by day, thus removing part of their manure from the household context (Xenophon, *Art of Horsemanship* 4.4; Plutarch, *Lysander* 20.6). For our purposes, their presence can largely be disregarded.

Pigs and poultry would usually have been kept close to home. In some forested areas, pigs ran free to feed themselves, being rounded up only when necessary (Homer, *Iliad* 11.670–84; *Odyssey* 14.96–104; Semple 1932: 301; Xenophon, *Memorabilia* 2.7.6). Their digging and rooting could do some good on fallow land, but there was a risk of crop damage too (Halstead 1981a: 323). Other households kept pigs in sties, feeding them whatever was available and collecting what was given in return (Dio Chrysostom 7.73–4; Pritchett 1953: 265, V.39–40). Jameson (1988: 99) suspects that in view of dense population and the shortage of feed, swine would not have been intensively raised on the classical farm. Poultry must have been more common: 'a domestic fowl will often, though its own food lies near at hand, slip into a corner and scratch where one sole barley grain perhaps appears in the dung heap' (Plutarch, *Moralia* 516D; cf. Aristophanes, *Clouds* 1430). Poultry dung contains several nutrients in a more concentrated form than general farmyard manure (Wilkinson 1982: 324; K. D. White 1970: 126–7). Roman agronomists made much of bird droppings (e.g. Varro 1.38; 3.7; Columella 2.15.2; Cato 36; cf. Semple 1932: 409–10), but the Greeks showed little interest. This may be because poultry-raising on a large scale was almost unknown, the general pattern being the possession of just a few birds for household needs.

Sheep and goats dominated Greek animal husbandry, both ancient and modern, but two distinct stock-raising patterns can be distinguished (cf. Gamble 1982: 162). In the first, quite common in antiquity, 'house goats' or 'house sheep', kept close to the settlement for milk and other by-products, are fed with household refuse and agricultural residues (Forbes 1976b: 239). Thus Dio Chrysostom (7.47) records that two families kept eight such goats. According to Aischylides of Keos,

> Each of the farmers owns but few sheep, the reason being that the soil of Keos is exceedingly poor and has no pasture land. So they throw *kytisos* and fig leaves and the fallen leaves of the olive to the flocks, and also husks of various kinds of pulse, and they even sow thistles among the crops, all of which afford excellent feeding for the sheep. And from them they obtain milk which when curdled provides the finest cheese; and the same writer says that it is called Kythnian and that it is sold at the rate of 90 drachmas a talent. And lambs are also produced which are of remarkable beauty and are sold not at the price of ordinary lambs but at a far more impressive figure. (Aelian, *On the characteristics of animals* 16.32; cf. Hodkinson 1988: 46; Cherry *et al.* 1991: 462)

Wealthy men too sometimes kept small numbers of sheep close to home; these tended to be more valuable animals, sometimes 'jacketed' to protect their fleeces. Their owners expected to profit from their sale (e.g. Polybius 9.17.6; Hodkinson 1988: 46). Locating these animals near the settlement allowed closer supervision and maximum convenience, but only at the cost of higher labour input and the need to provide fodder (Wagstaff 1976: 24–7; Wagstaff and Augustson 1982: 120–3). Above a certain flock size, fodder crops needed to be raised specifically for animal feed, a difficult thing to achieve on small landholdings. The number of 'house' animals would thus inevitably be limited. Intensive sheep- and goat-raising, with manure deposited near the farmstead, may have been very common; but it would have been on a small scale.

The second pattern, often complementary to the first, was to take sheep and goats away from the farm to graze on pastures which may have been private property, rented space, or communal land. In crowded classical landscapes, lowland pastures would chiefly have been such non-arable land as marsh or water meadows, where available, most of it publicly owned and restricted to citizen usage (Theophrastus, *HP* 4.8.13; Hodkinson 1988: 47–8; Semple 1922: 23). Goats, with their browsing habits, tolerance for a wide range of foods and lower water requirements, could be taken to maquis-covered hillslopes. Some classical urban centres had large enceintes to provide both safe pasturage and cultivation zones (Hanson 1983: 67 n. 3; Winter 1971: 111–14). Short-distance movement of sheep and goats is quite clear; when he mentions a theft of fifty sheep, Demosthenes (47.52–3) notes that they were not at their home farm during the day.

Apart from pasturing on non-arable land, flocks could be taken to cultivated fields and orchards. Grazing in stubble, the animals could eat weeds and any grain missed by the reapers, while grazing them on fallow kept down weeds and improved soil tilth, and among tree crops helped with pruning (Theophrastus, *HP* 8.9; K. D. White 1970: 134; Spurr 1986: 125; J. Thompson 1989). Even cereals could be grazed while young, the nibbling of early shoots ensuring a better secondary growth (Theophrastus, *HP* 3.6.3; 8.7.4; *CP* 3.23.3). A fragment from Eupolis' comedy *The Goats* describes foraging in the wild and in cultivated zones run amok:

> On arbutus, oak and fir we feed,
>   all sorts and conditions of trees,
> Nibbling off the soft young green
>   of these, and of these, and of these;
> Olives tame and olives wild
>   are theirs and thine and mine . . .
>   (Eupolis fr. 14 = Edmonds 1957: 320–1)

More controlled forms of agro-pastoral symbiosis are still practised today (Chang and Koster 1986: 112; Gavrielides 1976: 155; Koster and Koster 1976: 282; Delano Smith 1979: 213; Hodkinson 1988: 45–50; for Italy, Spurr 1986: 131; Varro 2.2.12). Indeed, it was often actively sought by farmers with insufficient flocks of their own, as one metaphorical passage suggests:

> And this contributes not a little to prosperity; for wherever the greatest throng of people comes together, there necessarily we find money in greatest abundance, and it stands to reason that the place should thrive. For example, it is said, I believe, that the district in which the most flocks are quartered proves to be the best for the farmer because of the dung, and indeed many farmers entreat the shepherds to quarter their sheep on their land. (Dio Chrysostom 35.16–17)

These are instances of *direct* manuring, what Theophrastus evidently intended us to understand when, in his discussion of tree crops (*HP* 2.7.4), he distinguished dung from litter manure. Any manure deposited in this way is beneficial, although many nutrients are lost if dung is merely deposited on a field's surface. Careful timing and supervision of the animals are also needed (Theophrastus, *CP* 5.17.6; Halstead 1990: 148; Amouretti 1986: 62). But the point is that the more time animals spend out to pasture, the less likely it is that their dung will redeposit cultural materials. There are references to dung collection and dung baskets, presumably to reclaim manure from non-arable fields,[4] but we may ask how much labour could be spared for this task and how much dung collected; in any case, it is less likely that *kopros* would be carted back to the farmyard than simply being piled up *in situ* or put to immediate use on other fields.

Goats and sheep would usually be penned for the night, when most animals void the majority of their dung, and perhaps also for delicate stages in their life-cycle (Barker 1985: 52; Chang and Koster 1986: 113). Winter may have necessitated keeping animals in shelter, and fodder-fed as well. Literary references to byres are common enough, although their structure probably varied considerably (J. H. Kent 1948: 295; Aristophanes, *Clouds* 45; *Greek Anthology* 6.263, 7.174). In many cases, the pens must have been close to home, and their mucking out may well have brought dung in contact with household debris. Sometimes, however, animals would be kept in temporary holdings which could be moved from field to field, directly manuring each and saving labour (for Italy, Pliny 18.194; Cato 30; Spurr 1986: 131; Aschenbrenner 1972: 58; Barker 1985: 52; Chang and Koster 1986: 114; Dodgshon 1988: fig. 1). And we should not forget that activity areas like these folds, or accidental artefact loss by shepherds, represent additional mechanisms for the deposition of cultural material in the countryside, albeit in modest quantities. In short, the total manure output of sheep and goats was not wasted by the ancient farmer, but clearly it is only some portion of that total which has any potential relevance to the genesis of off-site artefact distributions, nor is manuring the only explanation possible.

Estimates of manure production and application

We may now attempt to calculate how much dung would be produced in a 'typical' Classical farm. For most Classical or Early Hellenistic small-holders, flock sizes were clearly quite modest. Aelian's Keian farmers, for example, had 'few' sheep, while Dio Chrysostom allots his rustics only eight goats, and even rich landowners seem to have run small flocks: a raid by Theophemus snatched fifty sheep (Demosthenes 47.52–3), Isaios (11.41) mentions an estate of sixty sheep and a hundred goats, one of the Hermokopidai possessed eighty-four sheep and sixty-seven goats (Pritchett 1953: 272, VI 68–73; 1956: 255–60), while Hellenistic grants of *epinomia* offered grazing rights to flocks ranging in size from fifty to two hundred head.[5]

Several forces kept numbers low. Most farmers, even the wealthy, simply had insufficient land to graze many animals or to produce sufficient fodder; Burford Cooper (1977/8: 170) has argued that the maximum in Attica was only 27 hectares. Fees for using public pasture were also a deterrent, and, as already discussed, significant amounts of lowland grazing – whether on private or communal land – were sometimes unavailable (Andreyev 1974: 44–5; cf. Grigg 1980: 27, 65; M. H. Jameson 1988: 94, with reference to cattle). There were also political problems, since shepherds following the transhumant routes necessary to provide grazing for large flocks had to violate territorial boundaries; this became a source of inter-*polis* contention, as border disputes from the Hellenistic Argolid testify (Osborne 1987a: 47–51; Hodkinson 1988: 51–8). Above all, we must remember the limited and inflexible market for animal products, so that even though windfall profits were possible and livestock could be a way to 'bank' surplus production, pastoralism was mainly a supplementary, not an independent, source of subsistence and cash income (Hodkinson 1988: 63–6). While some degree of regional variability must certainly be allowed – on the margins of smaller states, for instance, or in the mountainous interiors of larger ones (M. H. Jameson 1992: 135 n. 1) – specialised pastoral activity, in this period at least, was not a dominant element of the agrarian regime.

In table 8.1 we estimate the numbers of animals and their likely manure production on a rural classical farm. The procedure followed is akin to that in Spurr's work (1986: 128–31; cf. Applebaum 1986: 262; Slicher von Bath 1963:

254–62; Olsson 1988). Rates of manure production and use are modelled for three rather different household units. Two of these are purely hypothetical cases, designed to give a range of possible values; the third is based on Dio Chrysostom's description of the (real?) extended family grouping in his *Euboean Discourse*.

All these values are, of course, very approximate. The rates of manure production, taken from modern Western sources, are undoubtedly too generous considering the impact of diet and health on such figures (e.g. Loehr 1974: 112; 1977: 81; Cooke 1975: 23; cf. Barker 1985: 52). Baticle (1974: 131), for example, uses ethnographic evidence to suggest a manure production rate for a sheep of 500 kg per year, rather than the 840 kg used here; but, on the other hand, we must allow for the litter and other items already mentioned (filth, sweepings, leaves, etc.) used to bulk out the supply of *kopros*. As for rates of manure application, we have practically no data from the Greek world. One obligation in a fourth-century lease from an estate of Zeus Temenites on Amorgos was the annual deposition of 10.5 cu m of *kopros*, a not insignificant amount; but, since the area it was to dress remains unknown, this cannot help us, although it may be worth noting that such leases were generally held by wealthy men (*SIG*[3] 963; Osborne 1987a: 37; Jardé 1925: 26). Consequently, we rely on the application rates suggested by Spurr (1986: 129), taken from modern Italian sources. Each element in these calculations is approximate: but cumulatively, and in terms of orders of magnitude, they present a clear picture.

(1) *Hypothetical household A:* With fresh manure, two hectares could receive a light dressing, or 1.3 ha a heavy one; with rotted manure, a light dressing would cover 0.9 ha, a heavy one 0.6 ha. Assuming a holding of 5 ha (to accommodate the ox), less than half of the estate, even under the best of circumstances, would be manured in any year, and at worst it would be as little as about 12%.

(2) *Hypothetical household B:* With fresh manure, this would allow a heavy dressing of 0.4 ha, or a light one of 0.6 ha. With rotted manure, 0.25 ha could be heavily dressed, 0.17 ha lightly. Even with an extremely small estate (about 2 ha), only about a quarter of it could have been manured over the course of a year, at the most optimistic estimate; at worst, no more than 9%.

(3) *The household described in the 'Euboean Discourse':* With fresh manure, 3 ha could be covered with a light dressing, or 2 ha with a heavy one; with rotted manure, 1.4 ha light and 1 ha heavy. On a 5 ha holding, the area that could be manured over the course of a year would be at best about 60%, at worst about 20%. (It should be noted that this was a two-family household.)

However tentative, these figures show the restricted scale

Table 8.1. *Estimates of manure production on Classical farmsteads*

	Hypothetical Household A		Hypothetical Household B		Extended household in *Euboean Discourse*	
	No. of animals	Manure (kg/year)	No. of animals	Manure (kg/year)	No. of animals	Manure (kg/year)
Oxen	1	16,000	—	—	2	32,000
'House' sheep/goats	4	4,800	4	4,800	8	9,600
Sheep/goats grazed elsewhere part-time	8	4,800	6	3,600	—	—
Pigs	2	5,000	—	—	1	2,500
Chickens	10	365	5	183	10	365
Humans	5	365	5	365	10	730
Household total:	30	31,330	20	8,948	31	45,195
Fresh manure (m³)		78		22		113
Rotted manure (m³)		36		10		52

Note: Rates of manure production and application used in this analysis. (*Sources:* Loehr 1974: Table A37; 1977: Table 4.2; Spurr 1986: 129; Gaffney and Tingle 1989: 235)

Cattle	40 kg/day (plus 4 kg litter)	= 16,000 kg/year
Pigs	6 kg/day (plus 1 kg litter)	= 2,500 kg/year
Sheep/goats	2.3 kg/day (plus 1kg litter)	= 1,200 kg/year
Humans	0.2 kg/day	= 73 kg/year
Chickens	0.1 kg/day	= 36.5 kg/year

1 cu m of fresh manure with straw	= 400 kg
1 cu m of rotted manure	= 875 kg
Rate of manure dressing	40–60 cu m per hectare

of the manuring that was feasible for households of this size. They also include the *total* amount of available dung: *kopros* which had passed through the farmyard or dung heap, becoming mixed with cultural refuse, would be even scarcer.

This shortage of manure should come as no surprise. Roman agronomists were aware that supplementary or alternative fertilisers were needed (Cato 37.2; Columella 2.14.6, 8; 2.15.5; K. D. White 1970: 144). Spurr's calculations on the manure available on Columella's model farm reveal that 'even on the well-managed arable estate which produced for the market, there is no superabundance of manure' (1986: 131); small farms, particularly, 'had nothing like sufficient quantities of manure for the best yields' (1986: 126, 109). Legislation preserved in the late imperial digests indicates that damage or theft of a manure pile was an offence; anyone who 'sets fire to it or scatters it about so that it cannot be used in agriculture' was liable for punishment (R. J. Buck 1983: 30). There was chronic medieval shortage too (Barker 1985: 53–4); eighteenth-century wills on Keos, which allocate different parts of individual dung heaps to named heirs, imply the same problem (Cherry *et al.* 1991: 238; Davis 1991).

Classical sources also reveal this anxiety. There are strictures against the removal of manure, topsoil, or even straw, stubble, mud, brush or litter from a rented property in several leases; conserving the strength of the soil was important to the lessor (Amouretti 1982: 62–3; Salviat 1972: 369).[6] The sale of mud, the range of alternative fertilisers already mentioned, or the very act of laboriously collecting dung by hand – well-documented practices in the historical sources – reveal vividly the persistent problem of inadequate supplies of manure. It was precisely those who needed it most who often had the least: for *kopros*, as for much else in Greek agriculture, there was intense pressure upon limited resources.

Priorities in the application of manure

Given such scarcity, it is vital to understand the priorities that governed its application. First, we must briefly consider problems of transport and labour demands.

To use a Roman measure, one load of manure (720 litres) would weigh over 250 kg, or over 600 kg if rotted (Spurr 1986: 129); at the minimum manuring rate suggested here of 40 cu m per ha, between 16,000 and 34,000 kg would need to be carried out to fertilise a single hectare of land. Not surprisingly, therefore, manure has been transported by water in many societies (Grigg 1980: 154; Wilkinson 1982: 324). One recent set of calculations takes 5 km as the furthest that manure can be moved for its use still to make economic sense, even with modern transport technology (Follett *et al.* 1981: 474; Cox and Atkins 1964: 642). For *kopros* to be moved in bulk, animal labour would be required. Roman sources mention manure baskets carried by pack asses, with the manure possibly spread by harrows (Cato 10.3; Spurr 1986: 55 n. 59; K. D. White 1975: 66, fig. 22, 67). In Messenia before the introduction of chemical fertilisers earlier this century, stable manure was hauled out to the fields in huge baskets carried by a horse, mule or donkey (Aschenbrenner 1972: 56). The limits on such animal power in the classical world have already been discussed; fertilisers would often have been shifted by human effort, perhaps in dung baskets – a task made no easier by Greek topography. Moreover, once the manure reached its destination, it had to be worked into the soil as quickly as possible, or many valuable nutrients would be leached out and lost (Cooke 1975: 182; Cox and Atkins 1964). It is difficult to estimate the labour in this operation; following Spurr, we might guess at two days to manure 1 ha of vines, or four days to manure 1 ha of cereals. Many crops, especially trees, would probably have been treated on an individual plant-by-plant basis, a very labour-intensive practice (Theophrastus, *CP* 3.6.1–2; Semple 1932: 407).

Neither Theophrastus nor the Roman agronomists rank which crops are to be manured at the expense of others

(though cf. Cato 29), but we can make some predictions about preferential usage. Distance from the farm and the crop being grown would directly affect a particular plot's chance of being manured, and off-site scatters related to manuring should be densest around the rural centre. Modern-day patterns of land-use around preferred sites vary in detail, but show a clear tendency for vegetables and fruit to receive the most intensive care, followed by olives, vines and cereals (fig. 8.5; Wagstaff and Augustson 1982: 119, fig. 10.6; Wagstaff 1976: fig. 8).

The garden, being closest to the house, would be an economical place to manure carefully (Spurr 1986: 127; M. H. Jameson 1977/8: 129). We read, for instance, of the garden of Simulus, 'tiny in extent but fertile and richly stocked', or of that of the rustics in the *Euboean Discourse*, 'very pretty indeed with all its vegetables and trees' (Kenney 1984: 60–2; Dio Chrysostom 7.64; cf. Vatin 1974: 348–50). House animals would have been close by, and the possible alternation of garden areas and animal pens has already been mentioned. Gardens too were more frequently watered than other holdings; water is noted as desirable, even essential, for the application of *kopros* (Theophrastus, *CP* 2.6.3; 3.9.5; *HP* 2.6.3; 7.1.8; 7.5.2; Semple 1932: 414; K. D. White 1970: 130). Theophrastus states that many herbs 'are lovers of water and of dung' (*HP* 6.7.6; 7.1.8; *CP* 3.19.1); liquid manure, including fresh human dung, could be used on vegetables, thus 'manuring and watering them at once' (*CP* 3.9.2; *HP* 7.5.1); herbs and other plants are 'started' or 'forced' with manure (*HP* 2.2.1; 7.3.5; Athenaeus 2.60F; 15.684A). Vegetable gardens which were manured had the

(A) GREECE, 1955

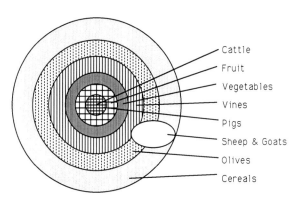

- Cattle
- Fruit
- Vegetables
- Vines
- Pigs
- Sheep & Goats
- Olives
- Cereals

(B) MELOS, 1974

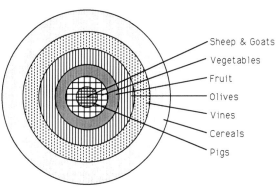

- Sheep & Goats
- Vegetables
- Fruit
- Olives
- Vines
- Cereals
- Pigs

8.5 Schematic zonation of land use with increasing distance from farm centres, using labour intensity values: (a) for Greece as a whole in 1955 (after Wagstaff 1976: fig. 8, data from Pepelasis and Yotopoulos 1962); and (b) for Melos in 1974 (after Wagstaff and Augustson 1982: fig. 10.6).

advantage of increasing the amount of refuse available for the livestock to eat.

It is revealing that Theophrastus places his detailed discussion of the varieties of dung in his section on tree crops (*HP* 2.7.4; cf. *CP* 3.9.5). Manuring trees was desirable: 'as to cultivation and tendance some requirements apply equally to all trees, some are peculiar to one. Those which apply equally to all are spadework, watering and manuring' (*HP* 2.7.1). He often refers to types of trees unlikely to concern the average farmer: the date palm, the myrtle, or the pomegranate (*HP* 2.2.11; 2.6.3; *CP* 3.17.5; but cf. Menander, *Georgos* 34-41). However, the olive is included among trees requiring the most pungent manures and the heaviest watering (*HP* 2.7.3; *CP* 3.9.3; cf. Columella 11.2.87), though usually the strongest manures are not considered suitable for trees (*CP* 3.8.2, though cf. 3.17.5). Manuring after pruning is recommended (*CP* 3.7.8). Application by hand was probably done tree by tree, but simply allowing animals to graze in the orchards is also beneficial. But despite all the benefits of manuring, Theophrastus urges caution: 'Even things that favour the tree and lend it aid will destroy it if accumulated in too great quantity or strength or at the wrong time, as manure applied either uninterruptedly or in too great quantity or possessing too great power' (*CP* 5.15.2–3; 3.9.1). Some practices deliberately introduced pottery into the countryside: when planting slips, he says, 'to let the roots profit from the rains in winter and be cooled in summer . . . others bury a pot of water alongside, and others a stick . . . all so that the slips may be ensured a constant supply of food' (*CP* 3.4.3); sherds could also be applied to cover the cuttings on a tree slip (*CP* 3.5.5); or branches bearing fruit could be bent to the ground, and the fruit buried in a pot to encourage its growth (*CP* 5.6.1; Varro 1.59.3–4). However rare such practices may have been, they remind us that many aspects of agriculture could spread cultural material through the countryside.

Over-manuring could be dangerous for the vine as well. According to Theophrastus, vines were manured once in 'every three years or at even greater intervals, since the vine cannot stand more frequent manuring, and watering is here no remedy, as it is with trees, but the vine is burnt and dries out' (3.9.5). Whether manure was even appropriate was questioned; Columella's uncle believed that dung spoiled the wine's flavour (2.15.5), and lupins or dust were sometimes recommended instead (Columella 2.15.3; Spurr 1986: 113 n. 26; Theophrastus, *HP* 2.7.5; *CP* 3.16.3). Cato believed that old manure applied to a vine's roots gave its wine a laxative property (Cato 114).

Following the logic of the model, cereals, and perhaps pulses, would have been grown furthest from the settlement, and manure would have been spread on them in a thin blanket, maximising the distribution of associated artefacts. Columella says that cereal cultivation was profitable 'where herds of four-footed animals are kept' (Columella 2.14.7; Spurr 1986: 126–7). Theophrastus was aware that such crops could be manured: he claimed that the process is beneficial (*HP* 8.7.7), cowdung produces vigorous lentils (*CP* 5.6.11; *HP* 2.4.2), and wheat does better than barley in fields that have not been so fertilised (*HP* 8.6.4; *CP* 3.21.2, 4). The speed of cereal growth was related to soil treatment; planting times might also vary depending on the presence of 'warming' dung (*HP* 8.1.7; on manure's warmth, *HP* 8.7.7; *CP* 3.21.4; 3.6.1–2; 3.9.1; 5.13.1; cf. Gregory *et al.* 1984, where fertilisers increased early growth in barley). Indeed, Theophrastus seems as conscious of what occurs when cereals are not manured, as when they are.

It was once believed that manuring could harm cereals, especially on light and dry soils, accelerating water loss and 'burning' the crops (Amouretti 1986: 62–3; Semple 1932: 411; K. D. White 1970: 129). This has been refuted (Halstead 1987: 81–2). Nevertheless, an excess of manure, or application at the wrong time, could harm the plants. Theophrastus knew that manures and soils had to be matched: 'one should (they say) manure poor country more but good country less, both because the soil is excellent in good country and because the grain by taking too much food on account of the manure gets heavy-headed and lodges' (*CP* 3.20.2). Only 'moderate manuring' was advised in 'dry country with thin soil', lest cereals wither (*CP* 3.9.2; cf. 3.9.5). Heavy and repeated applications of manure would not be wise, even if possible.

Theophrastus has much to say on the use of *kopros*. Much of this was irrelevant for most farmers (e.g. lucerne: *HP* 8.7.7; date palms: *HP* 8.6.3; 2.6.3; *CP* 3.17.3–4; cypress: *HP* 2.7.1), but other warnings – for example about inappropriate or excessive manuring – directly affect our argument (*CP* 3.9.4–5; 5.15.2–3; *HP* 8.7.7; Salviat 1972: 370–3). Even if this knowledge was not universally shared, or if Theophrastus' strictures were not always obeyed, the general scarcity of manure imposed constraints on farmers: manuring was not, and could not be, an indiscriminate process.

Discussion

We have assumed so far that farmers followed an economically optimising strategy, using *kopros* to improve agricultural yields wherever possible. This is clearly unrealistic. Some farmers annoyed Xenophon with their laziness in the matter. But he himself, by ploughing fallow rather than allowing it to be grazed, divorced arable agriculture and animal husbandry; hence his need for 'artificial' manure (*Oec.* 20.10–11; Hodkinson 1988:

41–2). Inscriptions forbid the 'dumping' of *kopros* in certain places, especially sacred ground: 'If anyone is caught dumping dung he shall pay five staters before he is right with the god.'[7] This reflects the temple officials' need to keep things tidy, but the idea that people abandoned valuable manure or that they had to be asked to take it away is intriguing (*IG* I[3] 4 = Sokolowski 1969: no. 3; Owens 1983: 46). *Kopros* served other functions as well, such as fuel (Halstead 1987: 82 n. 38; Miller and Smart 1984; Bryer 1986: 46–7). And finally there were some estates, even large ones, which apparently lacked animals completely (e.g. the Hermokopidai, Pritchett 1953: 265, V 39–40, 27, VI 68–73; Hodkinson 1988: 37).

In the traditional model of Greek agriculture, manuring was down-played, but the danger now lies in the opposite direction. We take a more minimalist line here: the classical farmstead was never 'chock-full of droppings' (Eupolis, *Goats*, fr. 16 = Edmonds 1957: 320–2). The archaeological implications are clear. We do not dispute that spreading *kopros* also spread cultural refuse, but the zone involved would have been more restricted than many recent writers have envisaged. Whether the practice accounts for the background density detected by surface survey requires investigation as well. We conclude that the 'manuring hypothesis' is inadequate as the *only* explanation for off-site pottery distributions; whether it was nonetheless the *chief* factor, as Bintliff and Snodgrass (1988b: 508) claim, is still *sub judice*, and in any case probably varied substantially with time and place, in ways that would repay exploration.

Our conclusion, based largely on texts, clearly requires testing against data that only archaeology can provide. There are several prerequisites and constraints. First, a detailed and well-controlled archaeological database is necessary, with quantitative information about artefact densities and types recorded throughout the whole countryside, not just as high-density concentrations (i.e. 'sites'); there are still few Mediterranean surveys that can provide such data. Second, the area examined must be sufficiently far from a city to avoid the zone spread with urban refuse (p. 147). Third, rural settlement must be predominantly of one era (here Late Archaic, Classical and Early Hellenistic), in an attempt to relate the causes of off-site scatters to the rural activities of a single period. And last, the distribution of settlement should approximate as far as possible to the pattern of dispersed farmsteads already identified as probably indicating small-scale intensive farmers – those with the best opportunity to fertilise their fields and with the most at stake in maximising their output. Most of these conditions are met in the following brief case study, which focuses on data from a small block of landscape within the larger region studied

during the 1980s by the Nemea Valley Archaeological Project (NVAP).

An archaeological case study from Nemea

In antiquity, as Pausanias (2.15.2, 1–7) noted, the most suitable vehicular passage between Corinthia and the Argolid led through the valley of Ayios Vasilios, via the Tretos Pass (modern Dervenakia), to the head of the Argive Plain near Mycenae (Wiseman 1978: 113–26). Before NVAP began its work, only two significant archaeological sites were known here: a Roman villa (Kritzas 1972: 212–15) and an ancient tower high in the hills to the east (Wiseman 1978: 113–17). Investigations by NVAP between 1984 and 1989, however, revealed a surprisingly dense distribution of ancient finds, and many more sites were recorded here than in an area of comparable size within the Nemea valley itself, immediately to the north (fig. 8.6). Prehistoric, later Roman and Byzantine ceramics were particularly common. Several settlements in the area of the pass have already been published, including an important Middle Neolithic site (no. 702; Cherry *et al.* 1988); an Early Bronze Age settlement, apparently on the same spot as a small Classical-Hellenistic rural sanctuary (no. 204; Wright *et al.* 1990: 611–12); a Byzantine community in the area of the known Roman villa (no. 704; Athanassopoulos 1992); and the now virtually abandoned early modern settlement of Papoutsaïka (Wright *et al.* 1985: fig. 8). However, prior to the Byzantine period, the area was occupied by relatively short-lived small settlements. Changes through time in their number, nature and location allow us to examine how different systems of settlement and land-use have affected the scatter of artefacts across the contemporary landscape. And since intervening hills separate the area from the nearest ancient cities – the *poleis* of Phlius and Cleonae, 7–10 km away – we can effectively ignore their influence, at least in artefactual terms.

Figs. 8.7, 8.8 and 8.9 show one part of the pass where small-scale settlement existed only between later Archaic and Early Hellenistic times (A–HL, *c.* sixth to third centuries BC).[8] We found at least half a dozen probable farmsteads of A–HL date, with contemporary artefacts in the scatters between them, but few of earlier or later date. More than two-thirds of the 120 or so tracts which we surveyed in detail in this area produced pre-modern finds, and in all some 3,500 artefacts were tallied; allowing for the 15 m spacing of walkers, who could scan the ground carefully only for a metre or two to either side of their path, the total of artefacts on the surface of this landscape must be far higher, perhaps 15,000 to 25,000. The number of potsherds, pieces of tile and other artefacts seen by a walker in a typical 100 m transect

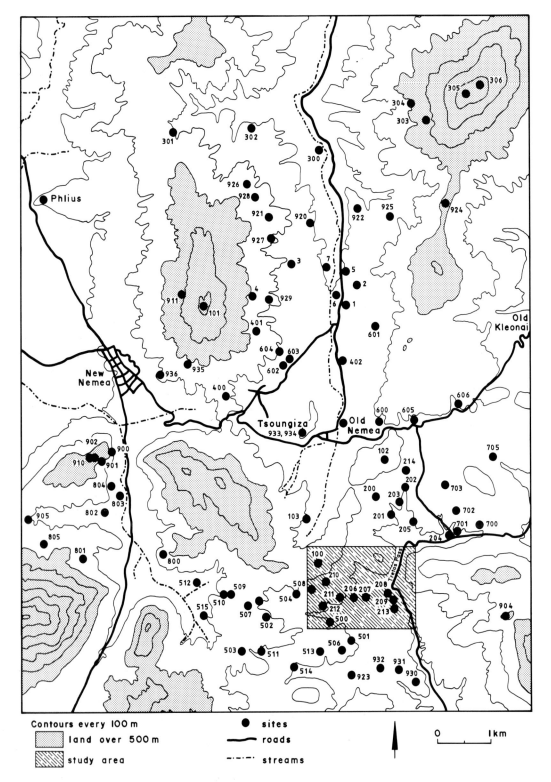

8.6 The distribution of sites recorded by the Nemea Valley Archaeological Project, 1984–9 (the box indicates the area of the case study in this chapter, shown also in figs. 8.2 and 8.7–8.9).

Table 8.2. *Archaic to Hellenistic sites in the study area*

Site	Periods	Size (ha)	Max. site density [X][a] (artefacts ha)	Max. tract density [Y][b] (artefacts ha)	X/Y	Tile %	Sherd %
206	A–HL	0.2	106,000	680–1700	62–156	88	12
207	A–HL	1.3	112,000	1340–3350	33–84	82	18
208	A–HL (Roman?)	1.0	18,000	640–4100	4–11	86	14
210	A–HL (Early Roman)	0.5	184,000	520–1300	141–354	78	22
211	A–HL	0.2	110,000	1664–4150	27–66	62	38
212	C–HL (Medieval?)	0.4	766,000	3040–7600	100–252	90	10

[a]Based on systematic samples collected at sites subsequent to initial tract-walking.
[b]Range, assuming that a walker scans a linear transect between 2 and 5 m in width (Cherry *et al.* 1991; Bintliff and Snodgrass 1988a: 506).

segment is generally quite low (less than five, and often zero); but higher counts tend to cluster, and it is these clusters that we treat as 'sites' – by which we mean discrete, well-bounded, artefactual concentrations of above-average density. The term 'site' implies nothing about the activities conducted at a location, nor about the presence beneath the surface of a reservoir of artefacts, but is merely a label for places where repetitive activity deposited relatively large numbers of artefacts. Establishing whether such artefacts are even approximately in their primary discard locations, or have been transported by non-human postdepositional agencies, is crucial to considering a site's function and place in the overall settlement system. In other words, we need to consider site definition in the context of geomorphic processes before it is possible to consider the relationship of material found on and off site.

8.7 The Tretos Pass and the valley to the west, within which lies the study area shown in figs. 8.8 and 8.9.

The definition of sites in the study area

We defined nine locations as 'sites'. After investigation by standard tract-walking methods, further finds were collected from potential sites using 'transect and grab' procedures (see Wright *et al.* 1990: 604–8; Cherry *et al.* 1991: 54 n. 10), to provide a larger and more representative sample, and to define more accurately the limits of each site's surface distributions. Naturally, locations initially treated as 'sites' were the ones in which the highest find-densities were encountered during tract walking. Table 8.2 lists the densities at the six defined A–HL sites, leaving aside Site 209 (see below) and Sites 213 and 508 (both of whose assemblages are multi-period). The maximum densities in the tracts associated with these locations fall below the thresholds used elsewhere to define sites (e.g. in Boeotia, >4500 artefacts/ha: Bintliff and Snodgrass 1988b: fig. 2; 1985: 130; for other examples, cf. Cherry *et al.* 1991: table 3.4); this demonstrates the need for relative, locally applicable criteria, rather than the rigid application of absolute thresholds (Gallant 1986).

The size of these nine 'sites' has no doubt been influenced by the dispersal of artefacts through geomorphic processes. Site 209 is a good example. Plotting the ceramic finds along each transect showed that the areas of greatest density were concentrated near the foot of the steep scarp at its southern end. We examined the micro-topography of the area more closely, and discovered that a slight depression in the surface acts as a natural path for the run-off of water from the ridge to the south. Erosion had carried virtually all the artefacts which we found from the cultural deposits at Site 213 on the ridge top itself to the foot of the scarp. This appears to be a location which has little, if any, cultural relevance, in spite of meeting the criteria of above-average artefact density and discreteness. None of the six A–HL sites has been so modified as this, but erosion requires careful attention.[9]

Site 206, for example, is located on level ground. Transects did not extend much beyond 40 m from the site centre in any direction, and finds were strongly concentrated within the central 20 × 20 m area. Ploughing alone, rather than manuring or erosion, might move sherds such small distances. Equally, manuring of gardens within a farmyard could account for the pattern, and this must be balanced with the possibility of natural processes 'smearing' the surface assemblages. The two are by no means mutually exclusive. The original surface distribution at the site (recorded here as 0.2 ha), at any rate, may have been no larger than the 0.04 ha implied by the 20 × 20 m central concentration.

The area defined by transects at Site 207 is larger. Apart from the modern farmer's stone pile (which includes tile and potsherds), the highest artefact counts fall within a small area of 200–400 sq. m, near the middle of the site, and on the crest of a hill. From here the ground slopes down in the direction of all four transects, so the occurrence of small numbers of artefacts on every side may well be caused by erosion from central 'core' deposits. The apparent size difference between Sites 206 and 207 may be the result simply of differences in topography. Site 210 offers a yet clearer illustration. What must have been the original concentration of material forms a core just 40 × 60 m; upslope from it, density counts fall off rapidly, while the downslope counts were appreciably higher all the way to a gully on the southwest, marking a clear limit. Terrain thus played an important role in shaping these surface distributions. The actual 'core' concentrations of artefacts, both here and at Sites 211 and 212, appear to be as small or smaller than at 206 and 207 – perhaps about 0.1–0.25 ha or even less.[10]

Similar but more detailed discussion of this and other areas at Nemea may be found in the study by Pederson (1986), with comparable work by Tasker (1980) on Melos, or Peter James (unpublished) for the Methana survey. Our point is simple. In Schiffer's (1983) terms, the 'manuring hypothesis' concerns a C-transform, whereby artefacts end up in secondary discard contexts as a result of human agency; but a logically prior consideration is the impact of N-transforms, in which artefacts are moved from their primary discard contexts through natural processes. In surveys in classical lands, we must deal properly with the latter before giving credence to the former.

Site function and patterns in settlement

The identification of these artefact concentrations as farmsteads is supported by several types of evidence (Snodgrass 1987: 117–19). First, although there is later material at several of the sites, the finds are in general fairly

Table 8.3. *Classes of pottery and other finds from sites in the study area*

	Site numbers						
	206	207	208	210	211	212	508
Fine glazed pottery							
Cups			X				
Jugs					X		
Other	X	X	X	X	X	X	X
Plain pottery							
Basins/bowls	X	X			X	X	
Amphorae					X	X	
Pithoi	X	X					X
Cookware		X	X	X	X		
Other			X	X	X	X	X
Other finds							
Lamps					X	X	
Loomweights		X			X	X	
Whorls			X				
Glazed tiles	X	X		X	X	X	
Querns					X		

homogeneous and seem to be associated with a single phase of use. Second, the very modest extent of the surface distributions is in keeping with the sizes of Classical farms elsewhere (no more than 0.5 ha, and generally very much less; it is hard to imagine that anything more than a single household of half a dozen individuals could have occupied such places. Third, the finds (table 8.3) include fine black-glaze tablewares and coarser vessels for food preparation and/or storage, as well as loomweights, lamps and querns, which imply an established residence. Lastly, A–HL roof-tiles, mostly glazed, are plentiful and suggest roofed structures (though not, of course, necessarily for human occupancy).

Although these surface scatters are small, they must still be bigger than the presumed farmhouses themselves. The Dema House in Attica covers only 0.04 ha (J. E. Jones *et al.* 1962: 79–80) and the Vari House 0.02 ha (with court, 0.19 ha: J. E. Jones *et al.* 1973: 360, 370). J. H. Young (1956) gives further examples, with floor areas much smaller than those scatters which surveys have called Classical farms. The smearing of refuse during occupation and erosion since abandonment may account for this. But it also reflects the inclusion of the farmyard, courtyard and outbuildings, where dungheaps with cultural refuse would have been, as well as the intensively cultivated vegetable gardens, fruit trees, etc. This is the equivalent of a 'halo' around the actual

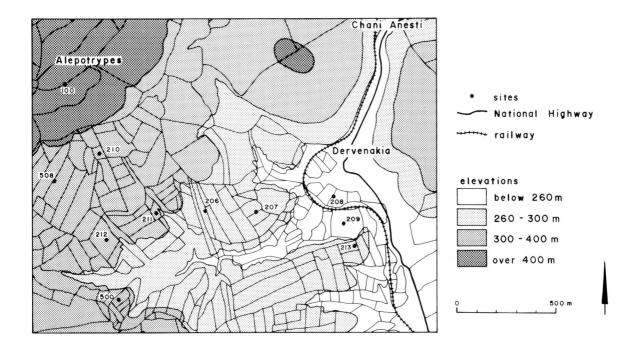

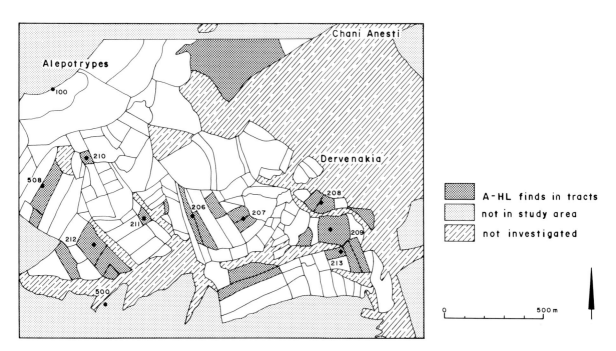

8.8 *Intensively surveyed block of land to the west of the Tretos Pass (see fig. 8.6 for location): (a) contours, toponyms and other modern features; (b) ancient sites and individual tracts with A–HL finds.*

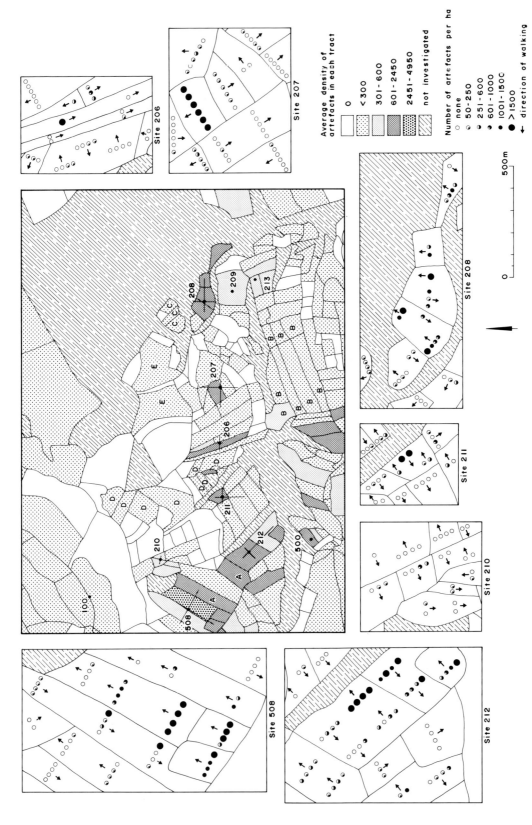

8.9 Intensively surveyed block of land to the west of the Tretos Pass (see fig. 8.6 for location). Central map: ancient sites with average densities of all artefacts discovered in tracts (for those labelled A–E, see nn. 11–13 on p. 167 below). Other diagrams: detailed plots of artefact densities recorded by individual fieldwalkers in the vicinity of A, C, and HL sites (arrows indicate the direction in which transects were walked).

building(s) on the site; but it is perhaps not what Bintliff and Snodgrass (1985) and others mean in writing of 'manuring haloes' around the high-density scatters they interpret as independent farmsteads. There is a danger of confusing observed data and its functional interpretation here.

There has been much debate over the character of such sites, and in particular whether they were continuously occupied, or merely served as seasonal bases for peasants, tenants or farm-workers (Snodgrass 1987: 117–19; 1990: 125–8; Osborne 1985). Attributes such as the presence of household pottery imply that they were more than sheds or barns, but to argue that the haloes around some of them show that they were bases from which cultivation was carried out begs the question we are trying to explore. Lloyd (1991: 236–7), discussing the same problem in early Roman times, claims that excavation, and the recovery of palaeoenvironmental data in particular, offers the only hope of resolving the issue; but we share Snodgrass' (1990: 128) pessimism over the likelihood of ever obtaining unambiguous information about the status of the occupants, or whether it was their only residence. In any case, this would be too simplistic an approach. The uses of these structures may have changed over quite short periods of time, depending on their owners' current needs, as Whitelaw (1991) concludes from an ethnoarchaeological study of nineteenth- and early twentieth-century rural structures in Keos.

These difficulties complicate attempts to estimate population levels or to ascertain the demographic balance between nucleated communities and scattered farms (e.g. Alcock 1989b; Cherry *et al.* 1991; Davis 1991; Lloyd 1991: 238). Yet for the more specific issue of manuring they may not be so damaging. Even if they were only 'animal shelters temporarily shared by human occupants at times of peak agricultural activity (thus explaining the household pottery), round which would be concentrated vegetable plots or other intensive cultivation' (Snodgrass 1987: 119), animal dung and other organic matter would still come into contact with cultural refuse, if on an irregular basis. New techniques may shed light on this. At the late Hellenistic and early Roman site PP17 of the Boeotian Survey (fig. 8.10), it has been possible to compare the shape and extent of surface scatters of pottery and tile with features detected by resistivity survey (Gaffney and Gaffney 1986), seemingly indicating a small structure with attached yard, as well as with the pattern of trace metal residues which have accumulated as a result of occupation (Davies *et al.* 1988). Likewise, the Laconia Survey has built up a picture of small rural sites by relating topography, sherd and tile counts and geophysical data to analysis of soil phosphate levels; among other things, they found that 'on-site' soil phosphate levels often extend well beyond the minimum area of the site as defined by its surface scatter alone (Buck *et al.* 1988; Cavanagh *et al.* 1988). We

do not yet have such data from our sites, but it seems safe to argue that these places were the principal agricultural *foci* in this part of the Tretos Pass, and the evidence is consistent with their interpretation as homestead farms. As often with survey data, the vagueness of the dating framework cannot demonstrate, but certainly allows, the possibility of a coherent system of agriculture and settlement.

This last point seems to be reinforced by the regularity of site spacing, generally some 250–400 m apart, implying catchments of 5–15 ha – similar to what the ancient sources indicate for farms of this sort (Burford Cooper 1977/8; M. H. Jameson 1992), and with a Classical farmstead whose complete boundary wall is extant (Keller and Wallace 1988: fig. 4, site C-54, enclosing about 9 ha). We cannot know how much land belonged to or was used by people at each of these sites; Foxhall (1990) points out that owner-occupancy cannot be taken for granted, while Snodgrass (1990: 126–7) notes the inexorable trend towards fragmentation of a family's landholdings under the inheritance laws in parts of ancient Greece, which would make 'the construction of a farmstead on any one plot . . . a questionable step in the first place'. Yet the evidence suggests that these sites were foci for agricultural production, and perhaps also residence, for a small group such as a family, which implies the establishment of sufficient landholdings in the

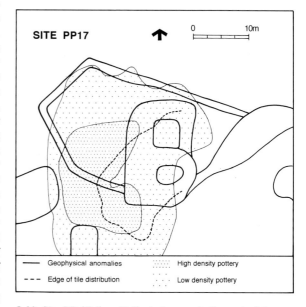

8.10 Site PP 17 (late Hellenistic to early Roman) of the Boeotia Survey: comparison of the shape and extent of surface scatters of pottery and roof-tile with features detected by resistivity survey (after Gaffney and Gaffney 1986: figs. 32–3; Davies et al. *1988: fig. 3).*

vicinity to make the investment worthwhile. Even today, with the use of irrigation and chemical fertilisers, fewer than 70 ha within this area are under cultivation; but that would have supported the households we envisage as dependent, or resident, on these sites in C–HL times with hypothetical livestock numbers in keeping with those set out in table 8.1.

Mechanisms of artefact dispersal

Much of the preceding discussion is speculative. But it follows from it that signs of agricultural intensification, including manuring, should be most plentiful for the A–HL periods. Residence on the land increases the opportunities for integrating arable cultivation and animal husbandry by locating dung-producers near cultural refuse and close to fields requiring fertilisation. If manuring *was* an important mechanism of artefact dispersal in classical times, then low-density distributions of that date should be more common than for other periods in the past.

Off-site finds are not chronologically mixed, but are virtually entirely limited to the A–HL periods. There are no prehistoric artefacts, even though there is a substantial Early Bronze Age and Mycenaean site (213) nearby. Neither problems of survey technique nor peculiar characteristics of prehistoric pottery can account for this, since low-density distributions of Mycenaean date have been recorded in several areas over the hills 2 or 3 km to the north (Cherry and Davis 1988; Wright *et al.*, in press). Similarly, Roman, Byzantine and modern pottery is usually scarce both on and off site in this area, except at Sites 213 and 508. We conclude that since only Site 508 remained in use after Hellenistic times, *later* manuring activities cannot account for the spread of A–HL artefacts. The question, then, is whether A–HL manuring produced these low-density scatters. We must look first at overall patterns of artefact density relative to our sites, and then at specific locations where datable artefacts were collected 'off-site' (fig. 8.8).

We cannot speak of a continuous and homogeneous 'carpet' of low-density material, as do Bintliff and Snodgrass (1988b) for Boeotia, since no artefacts whatsoever were seen in over one-third of all tracts. More than thirty of these forty 'empty' tracts are today cultivated, and may have been so in antiquity. Moreover, while artefact densities were generally higher in tracts near sites, the only contiguous blocks of empty tracts also lie next to sites (206, 210 and 211). In the case of Site 210, for instance, scatters were recorded on the southwest side of the ridge, downslope from the site, but *not* on its northeast slope, which could also have been farmed. If manuring was indeed the principal mechanism responsible for artefact transport, it seemingly did not result in the consistent spread of artefacts across all arable land close to their presumed source.

In the case of certain localised patterns of artefact distribution, erosion, rather than manuring, seems the most natural explanation (Wright *et al.* 1990: 607–8; Pederson 1986). It cannot be coincidence that two high-density tracts[11] producing late Roman and Byzantine-Modern finds (which are not otherwise very common) lie downslope of their probable source at Site 508, yet the entire ridge east and northeast of this site has produced nothing later than Hellenistic; the manuring hypothesis could be retained here only by invoking some highly preferential pattern of farming after Hellenistic times. But other cases are not so easily explained by natural processes, such as the diffuse but quite high-density finds in the tracts along the top and slopes of the ridge southwest of Site 213[12] – spots to which artefacts could not travel except by human intervention. Several other areas with low-density distributions,[13] for which no up-slope source of artefacts can be identified, are indicated in fig. 8.9. Manuring may well be the primary mechanism of transport in these cases.

Such a conclusion rests heavily on the composition of the finds themselves. Fertilising fields with settlement-derived manure should result in material of similar date and character both off and on site, and testing whether this is so requires data *collected under identical conditions* from both contexts (table 8.4). One obvious difference here is the ratio of tile to pottery: on average, tracts on or adjacent to sites have three times as many tile fragments as potsherds, whereas off-site tracts have more potsherds than tiles. *Purgatio* (i.e. picking out larger chunks of refuse from the midden before carting manure out to the fields) may explain this imbalance; or perhaps broken pots were more likely to end up in the dungheap than building debris. But we cannot actually rule out the possibility that the sherd-to-tile ratio reflects some other activity altogether, actually carried out in the fields. The functional character of the artefacts themselves could provide more clues, but here the data from this limited study area fail us: only a handful of the sherds noted in off-site tracts were diagnostic (mostly A–HL black-glaze lekane and skyphos fragments), and we cannot make any valid comparison between sites and the areas outside them.

Our conclusions are open-ended, but we have dealt in detail here only with 2 or 3% of NVAP's several thousand tracts, and we expect that the mapping and quantitative analysis of that much larger sample will shed more light on the problem. Other surveys in Greece have begun to compile large datasets of a similar kind. The chief problem is not shortage of data, but the failure to analyse them in detail or to recognise that no single model – such as the manuring hypothesis – can embrace the huge variety of patterns created by different types of activity in different landscape settings at different periods in the past.

Table 8.4. *Pottery and tile counts from tracts in the study area*

(A) Tracts associated with sites				(B) Tracts not clearly associated with sites		
Tract number	Associated site number	Sherd count[a]	Tile count[b]	Tract number	Sherd count[a]	Tile count[b]
90-1	206	1(1)	18	80-9	4(1)	0
90-2	206	1	0	80-11	7(1)	5
90-3	206	28(3)	6	81-7	8(3)	0
90-32	210	3(4)	16	90-8	1(1)	0
90-33	211	2	1	90-10	1(1)	1
90-35	211	6	10	90–11	5	5
90-36	211	32(1)	183(2)	90-18	1	1
90-44	211	11	5	90-19	6	4(1)
90-47	211	6	9	90-21	1	0
90-48	212	30(10)	217(4)	90-22	3(1)	2
90-49	212	19(3)	156(3)	90–23	3(2)	3
90-50	212	16(3)	51	90-24	1	0
91-8	208	1	2	91-1	5	2
91-9	208	19(2)	87(2)	91-2	3	1
91-10	208	12(3)	68(1)	91-4	0	2
91-11	208	3	21	91-6	2	2
91-12	208	8(2)	37	91-44	1	0
91-47	207	4	15	91-66	0	3
91-48	207	10(2)	5	Totals:	52(10) (63%)	31(1) (37%)
91-49	207	53(9)	88			
91-50	207	14(1)	4			
91-51	207	0	1			
91-52	207	1(1)	0			
Totals:		283(45) (22%)	1000(12) (78%)			

[a]Figures in parentheses indicate the number of diagnostic sherds collected
[b]Figures in parentheses indicate the number of tile fragments collected

We should not generalise widely from this limited example, but it does suggest five points. First, the bulk of all the finds from this block of landscape are associated with high-density A–HL concentrations, which were probably bases for agricultural activity in surrounding fields and may in some cases have been occupied residentially. Second, although there are sites of other periods within the study area and nearby, they produced hardly any off-site finds; from this we infer either that fertilising with settlement-derived manure was unusual during those other periods, or that manuring did not extend far from the sites themselves. Third, some scatters, at both low and high densities, result from erosion of high-density concentrations, and they tell us nothing about human activity. Fourth, where no such artefactual sources are obvious, it is possible that objects reached their find-locations by manuring, but *in situ* discard from other types of rural activity cannot easily be excluded,

except through detailed comparisons of on- and off-site finds. Lastly, even when settlement was densest in the A–HL period, off-site scatters are spatially discontinuous, very low density, and rarely extend far outside sites; thus, even if manuring was the cause, it was very restricted, as argued above (p. 151).

Conclusion

We have tried to show that detailed analysis can narrow the range of explanatory possibilities in understanding off-site scatters. Our study of textual sources for classical manuring shows the importance of the specific historical context. Our failure to reach definitive conclusions may hearten those who stress the supposedly inherent limitations of surface information (e.g. Hope Simpson 1983; 1984; Popham 1990; less dogmatically, Lloyd 1991), but only survey can provide a regional perspective on the ancient world, about which the written sources are reticent and for which excavation alone is too restricted. The fact that surface data are often 'noisy' and hard to interpret is no excuse for neglecting thoughtful and detailed analysis of them. But the gains of recent years, achieved by the development of efficient and sophisticated field procedures, will not be capitalised upon unless similar sophistication is brought to bear on the interpretation of results.

The past two decades have seen a growing awareness everywhere of the complexities of site formation and taphonomy, leading, in some cases, to radical reappraisal or even reversal of standard interpretative frameworks (e.g. Schiffer 1987; Binford 1983). The off-site record is now coming under similar scrutiny, with 'distributional archaeology' in North America (Ebert 1986), and 'the archaeology of the ploughzone' (Haselgrove *et al.* 1985) or 'the interpretation of artefact scatters' (Schofield 1991) in northern Europe. These studies reveal the need for high-quality data and the difficulty of unscrambling all the relevant generative mechanisms and post-depositional transformations. In Greece, however, insufficient attention has yet been paid to such detailed analysis and the building of logical arguments. More specifically, in this chapter we have criticised attempts to account for off-site scatters in Greek surveys in terms of a single mechanism, what we have referred to as the 'manuring hypothesis'.

We do not deny the importance of manuring in antiquity, nor that this practice could be a significant mechanism for the transport of artefacts. But we do see a need to specify the links between (a) the likely manuring patterns under varying kinds of residence and land-use, and (b) archaeologically observed artefact scatters, taking into account (c) the full range of cultural deposition and possible artefact discard behaviours, and (d) the probable scale of postdepositional distortion. For the classical world, better understanding of (a) will come from the exhaustive, rather than anecdotal, use of textual evidence, and from simple model-building of the kind attempted here and elsewhere (e.g. Hayes 1991). High-intensity survey provides the information needed for (b), although it is still rare to find a set of survey data in which on- and off-site data have been collected under truly comparable conditions, and in which there is tight quantitative and spatial control over the material in terms of its functional type, date, preservation, distance from nearest site, etc. We comment further on (c) and (d) below.

Even where all, or most, of these conditions are met, inferences about the relationship of residence, land-use and the agrarian regime at different periods should be made with caution. The area which received artefacts via manuring is likely to be only a sub-set of the total manured area, and the latter in turn only a sub-set of the exploited arable area; so the evidence of manuring scatters cannot stand as a direct measurement of the areas cultivated at different times. Some care, therefore, is required in accepting for any given region that 'the level of off-site density is an index of agricultural activity' (Snodgrass 1990: 124). We cannot adopt static models, for instance by making inferences about the past on the basis of idealised notions about the untouched and time-less character of rural Greek life (cf. Sutton, in Wright *et al.* 1990: 594–6): we must pay close attention to temporal and spatial variability.

We seek to replace interpretations of sweeping generality with detailed micro-level studies which can tease out the relative importance of the various factors. We single out five points which demand special attention.

(1) *Landscape and geomorphology.* Manuring is simply one facet of agricultural exploitation of the landscape which, in some parts of Greece, has been under way for eight millennia. Cycles of intensification have taken place in the context of tectonic and climatic changes, on soils which are fragile, unstable and easily degraded. This has led to complex local patterns of erosion and deposition. The presence of geomorphologists on most surveys has certainly led to a subtler understanding of artefact distributions, and an appreciation that both high- and low-density scatters can arise from postdepositional processes. But understanding artefact distributions at the regional scale in terms of colluvial and alluvial activity, in a manner that reliably distinguishes natural from cultural deposition, is very challenging. For example, in the Berbati-Limnes survey, Wells *et al.* note erosional and depositional phases in which soils were stripped from hillsides, presumably carrying away artefacts from the steeper slopes: such instability, they suggest, 'is likely to destroy the remains of fossil cultural landscapes' (1990: 238). How then to interpret the existence of low-density scatters in such settings? Are they the 'remnants of once more extensive cultural landscapes'? We need to ascertain just how destructive geological processes have been in those settings that probably saw the most intensive arable agriculture in antiquity.

(2) *The condition of artefactual material.* In our case study we stress the need to establish whether off-site scatters parallel the full range of finds at the sites from which they may have been carried. But useful information can also be gleaned from their state of preservation. For instance, it is often asserted that the smaller size and more abraded condition of sherds found off-site is evidence for their interpretation as a manuring scatter (e.g. Gaffney and Tingle 1989: 210); but we could also argue that pottery which reached its final findspot through erosion would be more severely comminuted, and that 'manuring pottery' transported there

directly would be fresher. And even if some soils had been manured and enriched with artefacts in antiquity, subsequent ploughing could have reduced once-fresh pottery to a heavily abraded condition. The degree of abrasion need not be an index of manuring itself. What, then, can the state of off-site material tell us about the processes which generated it?

(3) *Differential discard of different artefact types*. In many discussions of off-site archaeology and manuring scatters 'artefact' and 'sherd' are used as synonyms, but fieldwalkers encounter many non-ceramic finds. There are often scatters of lithics in the topsoil (e.g. Cherry *et al.* 1991: fig. 3.4). In Greece and elsewhere (e.g. Schofield 1987; Gaffney and Tingle 1989: 31–69) it is widely assumed that this represents *in situ* discard of portable, expediently used stone resources, mainly in prehistory. This may be largely true, but there is plentiful evidence from Greece for the use of chipped stone in historical times, and its discard must have occurred on- as well as off-site. Lithics may have been included in manuring scatters at any period. The processes behind different materials entering the archaeological record may themselves be entirely different (Crowther, in Haselgrove *et al.* 1985: 65). To understand the contents of artefact scatters we need to know more about the discard behaviours associated with specific categories of material. How, for example, should the differences between on- and off-site ratios of potsherds to tile noted in our case study be understood? If the larger pieces of tile were deliberately 'weeded' from the midden before transport to the fields, this would lower its representation in off-site scatters. Under natural conditions of downslope erosion, on the other hand, potsherds and tiles probably move different distances and at different rates. Such differences are important and require close attention.

(4) *Problems of contemporaneity*. Snodgrass (1990: 124) proposes that the level of off-site artefact density is an index 'specifically of contemporary (that is, in this case, ancient) agricultural activity'. This may be true of short-lived settlements whose occupants dealt systematically with domestic refuse. But what of messier sites which had long histories of occupation by the time manuring took place? Can we not imagine old sherds, building debris, and whatever other materials were on the surface being scraped up as the dung-heap was shovelled into the manure-wagon? The dates of the material in the manuring scatter would then tell us little about the intensity of land-use in the period the sherds were made, and at most could provide a *terminus ante quem* (Cherry *et al.* 1991: 328–31). The same is true on a bigger scale for the inhabitants of Near Eastern tells digging into earlier levels for phosphate-rich deposits to use as fertilisers (Wilkinson 1982: 330; 1989: 41). Some ingenuity will be required to distinguish between these possibilities.

The artefactual inventory of a modest Classical farmstead and its rates of pottery acquisition, breakage and discard raise similar problems. Little is known even from sites such as the Dema and Vari houses, but some vessel classes (e.g. cooking pots, or cups/plates/bowls in everyday use) probably cycled through the system rapidly, others (e.g. a fine dinner service) might last longer because used less often, and yet others (e.g. large storage vessels incorporated into the fabric of the building) would be well-nigh indestructible under normal conditions. Numerous ethnographic studies have demonstrated how important differential breakage rates are for reconstructing assemblages actually in use (e.g., DeBoer 1974; DeBoer and Lathrap 1979; van der Leeuw and Pritchard 1984). Our understanding of manuring scatters is affected in two ways. First, breakage and discard rates materially affect the supply of sherds which might reach the fields: would a farm in use over several decades or several centuries break enough pots to generate the densities recorded by survey? There is scope here for simulation modelling. Second, some classes of artefact have substantial time-lags between use, breakage and discard, and transport to the field: Archaic pithoi, for instance, turn up in Hellenistic contexts (Marangou 1980: 181). This too bears on the problem of contemporaneity.

(5) *The full range of discard behaviour*. We should also ask what activities besides (or in addition to) manuring would generate finds in the countryside. Ethnoarchaeologists in Greece (e.g. Murray and Kardulias 1986; Whitelaw 1991) have documented a surprising variety of rural contexts for discard. The seemingly wider range of findspots in these modern site surveys may be a function of modern cultural attitudes to dirt and refuse disposal, or of a limited imagination where ancient practices are concerned. To the obvious categories of simple artefact loss and accidental breakage, we can add artefacts associated with special structures such as temporary field-houses, animal pens and toolsheds; all aspects of pastoral activity, whether divorced from the arable sector or not; deliberate dumps (perhaps most likely in the vicinity of villages and towns with their greater need for regulated rubbish disposal on a large scale); various agricultural tasks that might involve *in situ* tool manufacture, storage, breakage, or loss; ritual activities such as the deposition of votives at rural shrines; the artefactual accompaniments of resource procurement (e.g. quarrying, mining), or of land clearance (e.g. broken axes); and many other possibilities besides. Excessive recourse to manuring as the mechanism causing artefact scatters may lead us to underrate other uses of the landscape, not always agricultural or even economically rational. But it is still unclear how far the material outcomes of such activities can be distinguished when they

only survive as a degraded palimpsest (Gaffney *et al.* 1991: 76).

Does it matter, finally, whether we can solve these difficult puzzles? We think it does. Distributional archaeology is concerned with the products of human behaviour across entire landscapes. Ultimately, this involves considering individual decision-making: what are the costs and benefits of different residential locations and agricultural strategies, and how are these constrained by socioeconomic relations? In the Classical world the concept of the landed citizen-farmer was a crucial part of the ideology of the *polis*, at least in its progressive form. This sometimes made viable a dispersed pattern of tenancy and residence on the land, and removed some of the constraints on adopting an 'intensive' agricultural regime. One consequence was a higher rate of artefact deposition in the landscape, giving sites of this period greater archaeological visibility than those of earlier and later date (Cherry *et al.* 1991: 50–2; Davis 1991; Alcock 1993). Put another way, rural artefact densities are correlated not with overall levels of production within the polity, but with the intensification of individual landholdings; so the formation of artefact distributions is strongly conditioned by the specific relations of production obtaining at that time.

If even a portion of these arguments is adopted, artefact scatters are very much more than 'surface junk', and relegating them to limbo as 'background noise' ignores a crucial aspect of our evidence for agriculture, settlement and production in the Classical landscape. Distributional archaeology has been most successful in developing models for the low-density, non-site 'signatures' of mobile hunter-foragers, but these models are in many respects inappropriate for the off-site archaeology of areas dominated for millennia by sedentary, arable agriculture. It is gratifying, therefore, to see that classical archaeologists – not noted for their methodological innovations or interest in model-building – are now beginning to develop sophisticated field techniques and thoughtful analyses of survey data. With hindsight, this will surely be regarded as one of the more significant new directions pursued by the classical archaeologists of the late twentieth century.

Acknowledgements

We are grateful to Peter Garnsey, Paul Halstead, Michael Jameson, Curtis Runnels and Tony Wilkinson for their comments on earlier drafts of parts of this paper, and to Julie Pfaff for the preparation of figs. 8.2, 8.6, 8.8 and 8.9. Some of the data we discuss here comes from the Nemea Valley Archaeological Project (NVAP), which was sponsored by Bryn Mawr College and conducted under the auspices of the American School of Classical Studies at Athens with permissions from the Greek Ministry of Culture and Sciences. The project has been funded by grants from the National Endowment for the Humanities (RO-20731, RO-21715), the Institute for Aegean Prehistory (1984–7, 1989), the National Geographic Society (2971-84 and 3265-86), and numerous institutional and private donors. James C. Wright directed the project as a whole; the archaeological survey was directed jointly by John F. Cherry, Jack L. Davis and Eleni Mantzourani.

Abbreviations

CP	Theophrastus, *De Causis Plantarum*
HP	Theophrastus, *Historia Plantarum*
IG	*Inscriptiones Graecae*
Oec.	Xenophon, *Oeconomicus*
WD	Hesiod, *Works and Days*

Notes

1 Many of the sources cited in this section were located by conducting searches, using an IBYCUS-SC computer, of the 55 million words of ancient Greek literary texts (about 90% of all extant texts for the period down to AD 600) held on the compact disc version of the *Thesaurus Linguae Graecae*.

2 *Green manure:* Follett *et al.* 1981: 497–500; Xenophon, *Oec.* 16.12, 17.10; Spurr 1986: 113 and n. 26, 119; Theophrastus, *HP* 8.9.1; Varro 1.23.2. *Stubble burning:* Delano Smith 1979: 197; Xenophon, *Oec.* 18.2; Theophrastus, *CP* 3.21.4. *Tanner's manure:* Amouretti 1986: 63. *Mixing soil types and minerals:* Theophrastus, *CP* 3.20.3; Amouretti 1986: 63; Semple 1932: 414–16; K. D. White 1970: 138–41. *Mud and slime:* Salviat 1972: 369. *Blood and corpses:* Plutarch, *Marius* 21; *Moralia* 669A; Strabo 16.4.26; Goffer *et al.* 1983: 235.

3 Wealthier, larger landowners would undoubtedly own such animals, but even they may only have kept modest numbers; one of the Hermokopidai, for example, owned only two work oxen and six cattle with calves (Pritchett 1953: 272, VI 68–73; 1956: 255–60).

4 Literary references to dung collection include the following: 'Some take care to have it [dung] collected' (Xenophon, *Oec.* 20.10). 'Just take a basket and go dung gathering' (Aristophanes fr. 662 = Edmonds 1957: 752–3). 'In a dung basket' (Crates fr. 13 = Edmonds 1957: 156–7). 'Is a dung basket beautiful then? Of

course, and a golden shield is ugly, if the one is well made for its special work and the other badly' (Xenophon, *Memorabilia* 3.8.6–7).

5 Euboulos, who was granted pasturage for 220 large and 1,000 small animals by Orchomenos, is an exception to this pattern; but he was a man of some importance, and patterns of animal husbandry may also have begun to shift by the time of this award in the third century BC (*IG* VII.3171; Hodkinson 1988: 62; Hennig 1977; Alcock 1989b).

6 For leases forbidding removal of manure, topsoil and dung: Attica, Rhamnous, *IG* II² 2493; Rhodian Peraea, Fraser and Bean 1954: 6–20, nos. 8–10; Attica, Aixone, *IG* II² 2492; maybe *IG* XII Suppl. 353 (Thasos); Attica, Piraeus, *IG* II² 2498; Delphi, *IG* II² 1126 = Sokolowski 1969: no. 78.

7 Fourth-century Tegea: *IG* V.2.3; Osborne 1987a: 49; Chios: *SIG*³ 986; Argos: *IG* IV 557 = Sokolowski 1969: no. 57; Delos: Sokolowski 1962: no. 51, ll. 7–8; Epidauros: Sokolowski 1962: no. 24, ll. 8–9.

8 The area in question is a block of about 1 sq. km, lying immediately west of the National Highway, south of the houses of Chani Anesti and the conical hill of Agrilovouno (at Stena Dervenakion), and north of a high ridge that rises to about 275 m at its eastern end; several side-valleys run down from Alepotrypes – the horse-shoe shaped ring of hills that divides the Tretos Pass from the head of the Nemea valley – to converge on the tiny modern village of Dervenakia, where they join the main stream that flows south through the pass to the Argive Plain.

9 None of these sites was very large (table 8.2). Size estimates are based on artefact density counts made during site collection, and subsequently evaluated by comparison with results from initial tract-walking. A first rough approximation of a site's area is provided by the product of the lengths of two orthogonal transects laid out across it; all finds were collected from circles 5 sq. m in area at 5 or 10 m intervals along each line, and sampling ceased when two consecutive sampling stations produced no finds. Inevitably, this level of search intensity results in densities much higher than tract-walking, and a site's area thus probably includes parts of the landscape in which very few finds would have been recognised by standard fieldwalking procedures; conversely, as table 8.2 suggests, on-site artefact densities calculated from transect collection may be an order of magnitude greater than tract-walking might have indicated.

10 Site 208, which seems relatively large, is more problematic. Artefacts were plentiful in four tracts (91-9 to

91-12), with highest density near the border of 91-9 and 91-10, but without any obvious 'core' to the concentration. However, the ground in all these tracts slopes very steeply, and the ground uphill from the site has been badly disturbed by the excavation of a passage for the railway to Argos; the main focus of the artefactual concentration may have been removed by the railway builders, leaving only its eroded remnants on the slope below. The two remaining sites in the study area (213 and 508) also produced A–HL material, but mixed with abundant finds of earlier and later dates, making it difficult to estimate the size of these sites in the A–HL periods alone; at no period, however, can they have been appreciably greater than those sites listed in table 8.2.

11 Tracts 90-55 and 57 (marked 'A' in fig. 8.9).

12 Tracts 91-16, 24–28, 54, 55 (marked 'B' in fig. 8.9).

13 Tracts 91-1, 2 and 3; Tracts 80-9, 90-8, 10, 11, 17–25; Tracts 91-6, 66. (These are marked as 'C', 'D' and 'E' in fig. 8.9).

Reply to Anthony Snodgrass, by Susan E. Alcock, John F. Cherry and Jack L. Davis

In his Response (below, pp. 197–200), Snodgrass has paid us the compliment of commenting in detail on our arguments about the relationship between ancient fertilising operations and the artefact scatters encountered by intensive surveys. He uses quantitative data from an unpublished study by Bradley Ault, not available to us at the time our paper was written, of the artefactual contents of stone-lined pits in the courtyards of houses at Classical Halieis. These yielded cultural debris in sufficient quantity, he maintains, to suggest that most off-site finds might have reached the countryside in the form of 'manuring scatters' – indeed (to use his own words) that 'the "manuring hypothesis" is, after all, powerful enough to explain the phenomena virtually unaided'. Such a monocausal explanation runs counter to the entire thrust of our paper, and we are therefore grateful to the editor for the chance to offer a brief response.

We note first that, in the absence of soil analyses, the pits in question are not identifiable with certainty as *koprones* and could equally well have served other functions during at least part of their use-life (e.g., as rainwater soak-aways); at any rate, as built features within the courtyards of *urban* structures they cannot be taken as directly comparable to the manure-pits recommended for Roman *rural* estates by Columella (I.6.21; II.14.6) and Varro (I.13.4). Our calculations were intended to apply to the small farming establishments of the Classical countryside, and because so little is known about rates of ceramic consumption and discard in either town or country contexts it seems premature to assume that 'the order of magnitude of the result' would be the same in either case. In any case, if manure containing sherds was indeed carted out from city *koprones*, it would most likely either be spread nearby (resulting in a 'halo' around the town itself) or be taken to the *scattered* land-holdings of city-resident farmers (and would thus not contribute significantly to the very pattern Snodgrass hopes to explain in this way, namely the creation of haloes around rural sites).

As for the specifics of Snodgrass' calculations, it should be remembered that (like our own) they involve a number of variables for which only the vaguest of 'guesstimates' can be offered – for instance, the number of times the *kopron* was cleaned out, the proportion of the cultural debris in the *kopron* actually removed at each cleaning, the size and use-life of a rural site, the rate of manure-spreading, the percent-age of the sherds in the plough-soil present on the surface, and so on. Ingenious as these computations may be, they are inevitably subject to the dangers of cumulative error. The fact is that, on the basis of the available information (which

does not, for instance, say anything about the sizes or condition of the sherds, or the organic content of the soil matrix), the circumstances leading to the deposition of the cultural material excavated from the Halieis pits remain very obscure. Even so, is it really plausible to take the 900 tile-fragments as a product of house-roof collapse, while also interpreting the 1200 sherds from the same context as the cumulative product of decades of on-going domestic discard activity?

Clearly, what is needed is a better understanding of formation processes – not only of this deposit at Halieis, but also of the low-density distributions encountered by many intensive surveys. Our paper was intended as a contribution towards a more subtle understanding of the latter, but we fear that Snodgrass' insistence on a single explanation will discourage not only serious analysis, but even collection in the field. Our argument is not that manuring did *not* serve as a dispersal mechanism, but rather that it is one of a number of potential factors whose relative importance in any given situation needs to be thought through carefully, not assumed *a priori*.

9
Breaking up the Hellenistic world: survey and society

SUSAN E. ALCOCK

In one way or another, this paper revolves around breakages: geographical, temporal, disciplinary. Its original purpose was to apply a particular investigatory technique, archaeological surface survey, to an under-appreciated, certainly under-studied, epoch of the ancient world. Results of this application have proved surprisingly helpful: both constructively, in contributing a novel and unique perspective to the period, and destructively, by underscoring the necessity of a sharp break with many past treatments of the Hellenistic age.

Conventionally (and negatively), the Hellenistic era is defined as the time-span stretching between the meteoric career of Alexander the Great (died 323 BC) and the formal imposition of Roman power in the east – in other words, very approximately the last three centuries BC. In another conventional definition, the Hellenistic world comprises all the lands conquered or under the informal control of Alexander and the royal dynasties that succeeded his rule: most significantly the Antigonids of Macedonia, the Ptolemies of Egypt and the Seleucids of Asia. A use of Greek (the *koine*) as a common tongue is also taken as one indicator of this world's boundaries (for fundamental studies see Préaux 1978; Will 1979a; 1982; Walbank 1981; Green 1990). West to east, this *oikoumene* (a Hellenistic term for the inhabited world) extended from mainland Greece to modern-day Afghanistan and northwest India, north to south it reached from Macedonia and Thrace to Egypt and the Gulf of Arabia (fig. 9.1).

Hellenistic historiography: devise and rule

... if you examine the results of Alexander's instruction, you will see that he educated the Hyrcanians to respect the marriage bond, and taught the Arachosians to till the soil, and persuaded the Sogdians to support their parents, not to kill them, and the Persians to revere their mothers and not to take them in wedlock. O wondrous power of Philosophic Instruction, that brought the Indians to worship Greek gods, and the Scythians to bury their dead, not to devour them! (Plutarch, *Moralia* 328C, *c.* AD 65?)

From a late twentieth-century, postmodernist perspective, much of the past historical treatment of this period is highly problematic. In the mid-nineteenth century, the German historian J. G. Droysen inaugurated its formal academic study, defining the Hellenistic epoch in scholarly terms and coining the term 'Hellenismus' – not a title the ancients themselves would have recognised. Droysen perceived the chief significance of the era to lie in its transitional nature, in providing the necessary cultural fusion of Greek (pagan) and Oriental (Jewish) elements that proved the 'avenue to Christianity' (Droysen 1952 [first published 1833–43]; Bravo 1968). The ordained 'mixture' of West and East, instigated and fostered by the providential conquests of Alexander, was unquestioned – and thus unexplored – by Droysen and many of his successors. Other early and influential interpretations of the epoch were coloured by contemporary imperialist beliefs and behaviour (Wilamowitz-Moellendorf 1924; Tarn 1948; 1951; Momigliano 1977: 307–23). Enlightenment for the backward masses, the gift of superior government, adoption of a common language (the Greek *koine*), economic stimulation: the European 'white man's burden' was transferred neatly to the sturdy shoulders of those precursors of the British Raj – the Greeks and Macedonians. The triumph of Greek culture, overlying and civilising the undifferentiated 'Oriental' populations effortlessly defeated by Alexander, has continued to dominate numerous discussions of the 'harvest of Hellenism' (e.g. Peters 1970). Consequently, apart from Jewish thought and culture, a general scholarly disregard has greeted the innumerable native societies and traditions which became enmeshed within the Graeco-Macedonian kingdoms. Even major pre-existent imperial regimes – for example, the Achaemenid (or Persian) empire, which itself had held much of the Hellenistic world in its grasp – were little considered. The Near and Middle East was viewed by and large as a *tabula rasa*, awaiting the imprint of civilisation.

One result both of an over-ready assumption of 'cultural fusion' and of a lopsided, 'Hellenocentric' focus has been the perception of the Hellenistic world as a relatively unitary phenomenon: sharing a common tongue, imbibing Greek culture, trading and exchanging at an unprecedented rate, displaying 'the unity and homogeneity of the Hellenistic

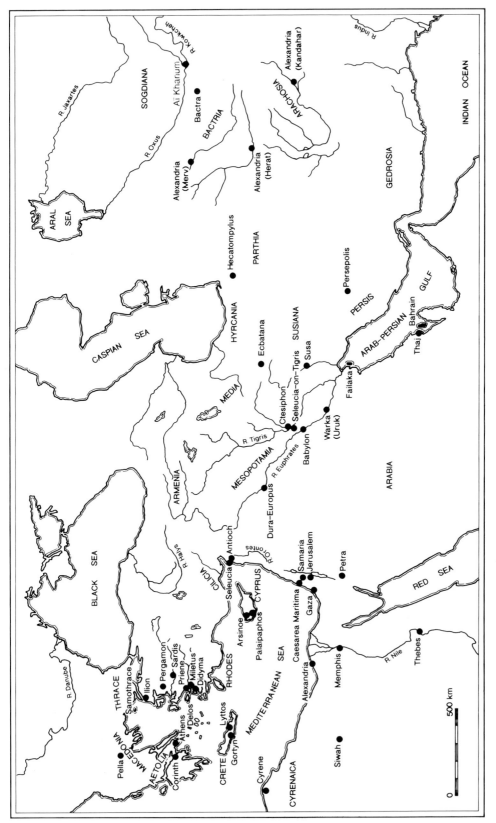

9.1 Sites mentioned in the text.

world from the point of view of civilisation and mode of life' (Rostovtzeff 1941: 1040; Tarn and Griffith 1952: 3). Such an approach to the study of the Hellenistic period can be traced to the scholarly stress laid on the dominant, persuasive power of Greek influence in these foreign lands. Yet it is also due in part to the nature of the sources most frequently consulted. Attention has chiefly been paid to the Greek documentary evidence, centring as always on the world of the elite, on the life of the courts, the urban wealthy, intellectuals and artists. The accessibility and familiarity of these doubly biased sources (biased in favour of the victor, and in favour of the wealthy) came to dictate the accepted historical reality (Sancisi-Weerdenburg and Kuhrt 1987; Briant 1982: 491–506). The study of alternative documentary traditions from literate, highly sophisticated Near Eastern cultures (for example, demotic texts from Egypt) has lagged behind or, more commonly, their analysis has not yet been integrated into the dominant histories of the Hellenistic era: those written from the conqueror's perspective.

In short, much Hellenistic history is fundamentally colonialist history, as recent scholarship has soberly observed (Kuhrt and Sherwin-White 1987a: ix–x; Préaux 1978: 5–9; Samuel 1989; Briant 1982: 7–12; Davies 1984: 263). To a great extent, of course, a much larger issue is engaged here, namely the nature of Western discourse about the East. Scholarly ignorance of those indigenous cultures conquered by Alexander was replaced by readily available preconceptions of the 'Oriental'; such inventions have obvious parallels in numerous other 'Third World' studies. Both in past and present, the history of these peoples has been defined chiefly through the fact of their conquest and domination by external authorities (Said 1978; Prakash 1990; Inden 1986; Kabbani 1986). Nowhere does 'Hellenism' meet 'Orientalism' more forcefully than in Hellenistic scholarship – though this has been only recently acknowledged (Morris, this volume).

Eurocentric attitudes of this sort have tended to colour other general perceptions of the period. One alternative view is to consider the era as unstable and ultimately unsuccessful: Hellenistic political structures, somehow 'weakened' by their contact with the East, were deprived of the purity and integrity of the Classical *polis*. Yet they also lacked the single-minded military prowess of Rome which proved capable of cowing into submission the once mighty kingdoms of Alexander's successors. This perception of Hellenistic 'decadence' constitutes one important aspect of much influential criticism (reaching back to no less an authority than Winckelmann himself) of the period's highly idiosyncratic artistic production (B. S. Ridgway 1990: 3–12). Also lurking in many analyses is the ready assumption that decline and decay (the Hellenistic era) must

naturally and inevitably follow youth, vigour and greatness (classical Greece).

Perhaps not surprisingly, therefore, the Hellenistic age has been perceived as playing little part in the construction of Western civilisation, aside from forming one stage in certain Marxist formulations (e.g. P. Anderson 1974; Ranowitsch 1958). In the academic study of the ancient world, one common didactic ploy has been to leap-frog through time from the 'Greeks' to the 'Romans' – the next important founders of the Western cultural tradition. As a result, more often than not the Hellenistic period gets remarkably short shrift in academic curricula (Austin 1981: vii). The lack of a single major narrative source for much of its duration also does nothing to endear the period to primarily text-bound classicists. Even when given every possible benefit of the doubt, for most scholars and teachers the Hellenistic era remains an untidy, unwieldy and confusing inter-regnum between 'Greek' and 'Roman' history. Such deep-rooted ambivalence is all the more striking given the number and variety of scholars who have drawn close and often unflattering parallels between the Hellenistic world and the modern age, expressed for instance by Edouard Will in articles entitled 'Le monde hellénistique et nous' and 'Pour une "anthropologie coloniale" du monde hellénistique' (Will 1979b; 1985; cf. Green 1990: xxi). For Will, the two periods share common problems of foreign domination, of intervention and interference with native cultures, of local resistance or acquiescence, of tension between conqueror and conquered.

The implications of such self-recognition have been sinking in for some time now, and it would be unjust to suggest that scholarly attitudes have remained unchanged since Droysen. The legacy of colonialism is increasingly acknowledged and resisted. In opposition, various scholars are now stressing the validity of pre-existing cultures and the precise nature of their interaction with the ruling powers (e.g. Kuhrt and Sherwin-White 1987b; Préaux 1978). Preoccupation with 'Hellenism' is being countered with more hardheaded assessments: for example, that power and wealth lured the Greeks east and that the impact of their conquest was 'first and foremost economic and demographic rather than cultural' (e.g. Green 1990: 316). Appreciation of the immensely complex cultural mosaic encompassed within the Hellenistic world is generating new concern about the actual composition of 'Hellenistic society' and the inherent improbability of deep-seated cultural fusion (e.g. Davies 1984: 320). And yet, for all the awareness that traditional questions and traditional approaches are failing us, nonetheless historians still appear somewhat stymied in how to break from the constraints of their traditional evidence, where to turn for alternative sources of information.

Archaeology and the short sharp shock?

One fixture of the traditional view of Hellenistic history is the assumption, reaching back to Droysen himself, of a universal and major discontinuity following the Macedonian conquest. How not? With the coming of the Greeks, it was the end of one era and the birth of a new and better age. This position has now been rectified in the number of standard historical studies, drawn from both the classical and the Near Eastern world, which take the reign of Alexander either as a natural point of departure or – more frequently – as a final chapter (e.g. Bury and Meiggs 1975; Hornblower 1983; cf. Finegan 1979; J. M. Cook 1983). Different scholars then pick up the story, often following entirely different lines of questioning, studying different regions, attending different conferences, reading different journals. It is typical, for example, that there is no overlap in the contributors to the *Cambridge ancient history* vol. VII.1 (*The Hellenistic world*) and the *Cambridge history of Iran* vol. III (*The Seleucid, Parthian and Sasanian periods*) (Walbank *et al.* 1984; Yarshater 1983). A sharp break in academic discourse goes a long way towards ensuring that the Hellenistic world always appears as something new under the sun.

This ready assumption of a historical caesura has recently come under vigorous attack, chiefly from scholars of the Achaemenid empire, and most notably by Pierre Briant. In an article entitled 'Des Achéménides aux rois hellénistiques: continuités et ruptures' (reprinted in *Rois, tributs et paysans*) Briant assailed the accepted wisdom, isolating the basic problem in this way:

> how are we to appreciate, in all its manifestations, implications and consequences, the Graeco-Macedonian conquest and assumption of power in the Near and Middle East without knowing anything about the interior of the Achaemenid empire? How are we seriously to discuss continuity and discontinuity between two historical phases (A and B), if A is *a priori* only the foil of B, and if we base all our reasoning on the assumption of a decisive break between A and B? Is it not quite clear that, in its turn, such an assumption justifies the lack of interest in A? (1982: 8)

The solution, of course, is to study the preceding regimes in their own right: 'Observations banales et de bon sens? Certes! Mais, on doit bien constater, pour le déplorer, qu'elles ne sont guère mises en pratique par les historiens' (Briant 1982: 304). Briant himself based his arguments for relative continuity between Achaemenid and Hellenistic rule upon his perceptions of similar organisational structures, of a basically unchanged rural infrastructure, and of continuities in imperial administration and policy (pp. 154–60,

291–330). Wishing to reinstate the period of conquest within the *longue durée* of eastern history, Briant concluded by re-anointing Alexander, not only as the first of the Hellenistic rulers, but as 'le dernier des Achéménides' (p. 330). Briant has been supported in other recent work, largely emerging from Near Eastern scholarship, which is equally critical of the tendency to isolate the period, leaving it a backwater in both Mediterranean and Near Eastern history (Davies 1984: 320; Kuhrt and Sherwin-White 1987b; Sancisi-Weerdenburg 1987; Sancisi-Weerdenburg and Kuhrt 1987; Kuhrt and Sancisi-Weerdenburg 1988). Among other research imperatives, two specific immediate goals have been identified: a longer-term perspective on the effects of Alexander's conquest and a need to penetrate to the lower echelons of society, outside the narrow elite circle.

What role has archaeological research so far played in all this? If the limited testimony of Greek documentary sources has led to some of this mischief, could not archaeological evidence have served to balance the picture? Much useful research focusing on the Hellenistic period has been undertaken: art-historical studies (e.g. Litvinskiy and Pichikyan 1984; Pollitt 1986; B. S. Ridgway 1990; Schlumberger 1970; A. Stewart 1979); architecture (e.g. Lauter 1986), jewellery (e.g. Hoffmann and Davidson 1965), mosaics (e.g. K. Dunbabin 1979), numismatics (e.g. Davis and Kraay 1975), as well as the excavation of Hellenistic levels at a number of large and important sites from the Aegean to Afghanistan (e.g. Aï Khanum, Delos, Didyma, Dura-Europus, Miletus, Pella, Pergamon, Priene, Samothrace, Sardis). Most of these studies, however, merely reinforce our evidential bias towards the wealthy ranks of Hellenistic society, where luxury items or other aspects of elite material culture are most likely to reflect – indeed, actively to emulate – dominant intrusive styles. Such evidence cannot be expected to provide much insight on behavioural responses to conquest at all levels within society (for an Achaemenid parallel: Haerinck 1987).

More problematic still, the archaeology of the period (like its historical treatment) could be judged as largely 'colonialist', following Trigger's categorisation (Trigger 1984: 360–3; Morris, this volume). Since the modern Western heirs of Greece acknowledge no close historical tie to the peoples of the Middle East, archaeological interest has chiefly lain in tracing Greek objects or studying the seemingly inevitable influence of Greek culture upon native traditions. There are, to be sure, some honourable exceptions. Examples include, for instance, studies of evidence for the lack of physical segregation between Greek and non-Greek in some settings (Roueché and Sherwin-White 1985: 37–8); of housing (Hoepfner and Schwandner 1986: 205–46; Moormann 1988) and of pottery and trade (papers in Empereur and Garlan 1986; Lévêque and Morel 1980; 1987). Yet even this close attention to material culture change has rarely made any sophisticated contribution to the issues of cultural fusion or resistance which have become increasingly insistent in recent years, both in Hellenistic scholarship and in archaeological studies elsewhere (Miller *et al.* 1989).

Fresh approaches are just as necessary, therefore, to the archaeology of the Hellenistic period as to its historical study. To my knowledge, the evidence of archaeological surface survey has not been brought to bear in any systematic fashion on the study of the epoch. Yet in some ways survey is an ideal antidote to many of the problems so far reviewed. Certainly it escapes the Hellenocentric, colonialist and elite bias of the documentary sources and of the majority of archaeological excavations and art-historical studies. Surface survey data yield up long-term patterns of settlement and land-use which, when interpreted, inform about demographic trends, residential preferences and economic decision-making across the full spectrum of a society: both rich and poor, native and colonist. Survey's inability to distinguish particular individuals, let alone their race or colour, social or juridical status, place of origin or religion, has often been regarded as a fatal shortcoming; but in this context, it can actually be taken as a positively useful blindness. Since survey cannot contribute directly to any debate about the progress of 'Hellenisation' (as it is most frequently defined, the diffusion of Greek language and culture), alternative questions must be asked. Immediate, relatively ephemeral disruption will not usually be revealed here, nor the particular reaction of individuals to foreign domination. Instead, survey forces into new prominence such issues as change in the agrarian economic base, or in regional population structures. The long-term impact of the Graeco-Macedonian conquest and period of control is observable in terms of certain basic parameters of human existence: where people lived, how intensively they worked their land, how large was the population. Naturally, a trade-off is involved in any such approach. Few sets of survey data offer chronological control better than a century or two, so that temporal trends cannot be traced in close detail. Yet in return for that loss of precision comes an enormous widening of scope. One might almost say that it becomes possible, for the first time, to receive a majority, rather than minority, report on those societies subsumed within the Hellenistic kingdoms. This development brings the study of the Hellenistic age more in line with other schools of historical research, where an obligation to recover something of the 'people without history' is increasingly felt (e.g. Marxist studies or the *Annales* school; Wolf 1982).

The advantages of survey in this context go still further.

The technique's inherently diachronic approach allows a direct re-examination of the theme of 'continuités et ruptures'. Survey results work against harsh and arbitrary chronological disjunctions, comparing like data with like data over long stretches of time, demanding that each period be considered naturally as part of a long-term trajectory. Individual survey projects are also by definition regionally focused, concentrating on a particular area and its *individual* history of development. Any traditional view of the Hellenistic world as a unitary phenomenon will quickly stand or fall under this kind of examination. Through survey evidence we can begin to re-explore the Hellenistic *oikoumene* piece by piece: watching for discontinuities from region to region, watching for breaks in patterns of human behaviour.

A survey of the Hellenistic world

Assembled here is a preliminary review of much of the evidence available, using data from archaeological surveys conducted in as many parts of the Hellenistic world as possible (table 9.1 and fig. 9.2). The review remains preliminary for several reasons. First, coverage is not uniform; some regions (modern-day Greece, Jordan) have witnessed a florescence of archaeological survey, while others remain relatively unexplored. Notable by its absence, for example, is Egypt, home of the Ptolemies, nor do other central zones, such as modern-day Turkey or Syria, yet boast much relevant work. The review is also restricted, somewhat arbitrarily, to surveys of a relatively intensive standard, thus excluding some forms of extensive reconnaissance (e.g. Bean 1979), but nonetheless including work that falls well short of the sophisticated methodologies now routinely adopted in some parts of the Mediterranean (Keller and Rupp 1983; Macready and Thompson 1985). The basic criteria for the inclusion of a survey have been that it gives some systematic view of activity *below* the level of the city or large village, and that it is primarily archaeological in character, rather than an epigraphically or historically based topographic study (e.g. S. Mitchell 1982). The result, obviously, is a heterogeneous collection of surveys, often operating with quite different field methodologies and research goals, but for present purposes some measure of comparability between projects has been taken largely for granted. Any further, more detailed comparisons between areas would naturally require more rigorous treatment.

A problem of a different sort is the admittedly imperfect chronological precision of many of these projects, owing to an imperfect understanding of both Greek and local ceramic traditions. The problem may be exacerbated if the period's diagnostic artefacts are chiefly foreign imports or externally

Table 9.1. *Major survey projects mentioned in this chapter*

Region		Survey	Principal publications
Greece	(1)	Aetolian Studies Project	Bommeljé and Doorn 1987
	(2)	Argolid Exploration Project	van Andel and Runnels 1987
	(3)	Southwest Boeotia	Bintliff and Snodgrass 1985
	(4)	Southern Euboea	Keller 1985
	(5)	Northern Keos	Cherry *et al.* 1991
	(6)	Lakonia	Cavanagh and Crouwel 1988
	(7)	Megalopolis	Roy *et al.* 1988
	(8)	Melos	Renfrew and Wagstaff 1982
	(9)	Messenia	McDonald and Hope Simpson 1972
	(10)	Nemea Valley	Wright *et al.* 1990
	(11)	Panakton	Munn and Zimmerman Munn 1989
Macedonia	(12)	Grevena	Wilkie 1988; Wilkie *et al.* 1990
	(13)	Langadas	Kotsakis 1989
Crete	(14)	Mesara Plain	Sanders 1976; 1982
	(15)	Ayiofarango Valley	Blackman and Branigan 1975; 1977
	(16)	Sphakia Survey	Nixon *et al.* 1988; 1989; 1990
	(17)	Lasithi Plain	Watrous 1982b
Cyprus	(18)	Polis region	Raber 1987
	(19)	Canadian Palaipaphos	Rupp *et al.* 1984; Rupp 1986
Asia Minor/Turkey	(20)	Troad	J. M. Cook 1973
	(21)	Lower Maeander Plain	Marchese 1986
	(22)	Northern Caria	Marchese 1989
	(23)	Cilician Survey	Seton-Williams 1954
	(24)	Chicago Euphrates Project	Marfoe *et al.* 1986
Syria	(25)	Tell Rifa'at Survey	Matthers *et al.* 1978; Matthers 1981
Palestine/Israel	(26)	Golan	Arav 1989
	(27)	Galilee	Meyers *et al.* 1978
	(28)	Plain of Sharon	Roller 1982a
	(29)	Western Samaria	Dar 1986
Jordan	(30)	Southern Ghors/'Arabah	MacDonald *et al.* 1987; Macdonald *et al.* 1988
	(31)	Wadi el-Yabis	Mobry and Palumbo 1988
	(32)	East Jordan Valley Survey	Ibrahim *et al.* 1976
	(33)	Limes Arabicus Desert	V. A. Clark 1987
	(34)	Limes Zone Survey	Koucky 1987
	(35)	Central Moab	Miller 1979a
	(36)	Northern Jordan	Kerestes *et al.* 1977/8
	(37)	Wadi Mujib	Miller 1979b
	(38)	'Ain Ghazal	Simmons and Kafafi 1988
	(39)	Wadi Ziqlab	Banning and Fawcett 1983
	(40)	Wadi Arab	Hanbury-Tenison 1984
	(41)	Wadi el-Hasa	B. Macdonald 1982; 1984; 1988; MacDonald *et al.* 1982; 1983; MacDonald and d'Annibale 1983
	(42)	Edom	Hart and Falkner 1985

Table 9.1 (*cont.*)

Region		Survey	Principal publications
Arab-Persian Gulf	(43)	Bahrain	Boucharlat and Salles 1981; C. E. Larsen 1983
	(44)	Arabian peninsula	Adams *et al.* 1977
Mesopotamia/Iraq	(45)	Tell-al Hawa Project	Ball *et al.* 1989
	(46)	Diyala Plain	Adams 1965
	(47)	Warka Survey	Adams and Nissen 1972
	(48)	Central Euphrates Floodplain	Adams 1981
Susiana/Iran	(49)	Susa Plain	Wenke 1975/6; 1987
Bactria	(50)	Aï Khanum	Gardin and Gentelle 1976; 1979; Gardin and Lyonnet 1978/9

influenced finewares – material of a sort which does not necessarily reach all contexts, particularly the more mundane ceramic assemblages typical of survey results. (This difficulty, of course, is not confined to the Hellenistic era or to survey assemblages alone; in some areas of the Achaemenid empire, for example, little trace of 'alien' Persian cultural influence can be identified (van der Kooij 1987; Haerinck 1987)). Survey projects have also tended to employ idiosyncratic chronologies, in which the Hellenistic period is not always defined in precisely comparable ways. Unless specifically stated otherwise, it is to the last three centuries BC that the term refers, and for purposes of the present discussion such coarse chronology is acceptable. Survey technique's relative youth, the geographical range of this review, and a general lack of interest in the Hellenistic epoch all help to account for this chronological variability.

Such limitations apart, these various projects allow roughly contemporaneous, roughly equivalent glimpses to be taken into twelve different regions of the Hellenistic world. The regional divisions adopted here are largely for convenience, and by 'region', it must be emphasised that only the surveyed area proper is intended. Generalising from these results across any significantly wider expanse is unwise, as well as undercutting our desire to monitor local variability in as much detail as possible. With the information available, we shall move roughly from west (beginning in Greece) to east (ending in Afghanistan). My goal in this review, it should be emphasised, is not to perform an in-depth analysis and explanation for the particular developmental trajectory of each and every region. Lengthy historical introduction and complex exposition are eschewed in favour of a brief general overview of the major trends observed (urban foundations, demographic fluctuations, agricultural intensification) and in looking for signs of continuity or discontinuity – for breaks.

Greece and the Aegean islands

This region, though small when located within the Hellenistic sphere at large, boasts several of the most intensive survey projects available for this study. A remarkably uniform and relatively detailed sequence of settlement and land-use patterns emerges from these results. I have discussed this phenomenon in some detail elsewhere (Alcock 1989a; 1989b); the surveys utilised are listed in table 9.1.

In the traditional chronology for this area, the Hellenistic period extends from 323 BC, the year of Alexander's death, to 31 BC, the victory of Octavian at Actium. The period's earlier stage (very approximately late fourth century to mid-third century) is characterised by a highly dispersed settlement pattern, with a great number of rural sites, especially of very small sites often believed to represent farmsteads or seasonal agricultural shelters. This Early Hellenistic pattern, largely a continuation of that generally observed in the Classical period, has been interpreted to suggest intensive cultivation of an unprecedented amount of territory at this time. Demographic pressures are believed to play a part in this trend, though no automatic correlation can, of course, be made between numbers of sites (admittedly higher in this period than almost any other) and absolute population levels. For the most part, small-scale landed holdings, of the type associated with 'peasant' agriculture, are believed to have been the norm in this densely populated landscape, though some larger estates must also have existed.

At some point during the Hellenistic period, however, a radical alteration in the distribution of settlement and in land-use practices took place; this shift is visible to a greater or lesser extent in all the areas consulted. In some of the survey projects, the change can be dated very approximately to the mid-third century BC. A sharp drop in rural site numbers, pointing to a slackening in agricultural production

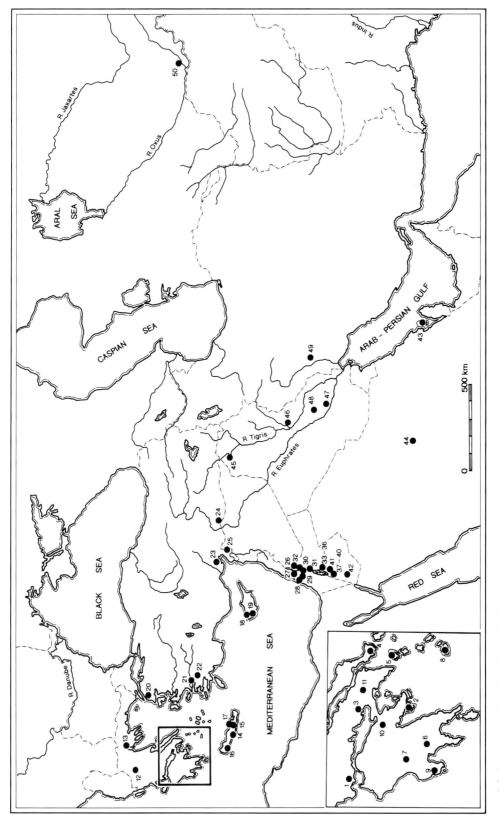

9.2 *Locations of sites listed in table 9.1.*

and therefore some measure of population decline, marks this later Hellenistic development. An increasing preference for nucleated residence, in cities or large villages, may also partly explain this trend. Of those sites remaining in the rural landscape, peasant cottages in many cases now gave way to more substantial properties, suggesting the growth of significant agricultural estates. Major reorganisation in demographic behaviour, residential priorities and land-holding patterns are thus clearly signalled during the course of this era; it should be noted that the new pattern continued relatively unchanged through the Early Roman period in Greece (approximately first to third centuries AD).

This basic reconstruction of settlement and land-use trends is replicated more or less faithfully in all the survey projects consulted here. One major possible exception is the Aetolia Studies Project, which records a net *gain* of sites in the Hellenistic period (Bommeljé and Doorn 1987). Given the florescence of the Aetolian League at this time, coupled with the region's previous obscurity, it is entirely possible that a variant settlement history evolved in that relatively northern and more mountainous region. Unfortunately, the pottery chronologies utilised by that project are still very coarse, and no sure distinctions can be based upon these data.

From this evidence, it is clear that the 'Hellenistic' period in central and southern Greece and the Aegean islands, when defined in terms of socioeconomic conditions rather than of political events, is very far from being a coherent whole. Instead, the Classical and Early Hellenistic periods (roughly fifth to third centuries BC) stand as one unit, the Late Hellenistic and Early Roman epoch (roughly third century BC to third century AD) as another. As a general point, dissatisfaction with purely political chronologies has long been expressed but infrequently challenged in any concrete sense; survey data, with their account of settlement organisation, demography and land-use, present one valid alternative structure. Certainly it is now impossible to consider the Hellenistic period in Greece as a uniform, essentially static, epoch.

Macedonia

Moving further north into Macedonia, the home base for Alexander's conquests and later the seat of the Antigonid dynasty, there is sadly little survey evidence to consider. What can be said is that the Hellenistic period witnessed a trend towards greater urbanisation; unlike Greece to the south, Macedon had not previously been a land of cities (Papazoglou 1988: 37–51). One predictable, if still unrecorded, result would be a significant reorganisation of rural activity. For settlement history *below* the urban level,

only two very preliminary hints exist, again suggesting a situation markedly different from that to the south. In the nome of Grevena, an American survey team reports that Hellenistic and Early Roman sites are 'quite common' (Catling 1988: 50; 1989: 75; Wilkie 1988; Wilkie *et al.* 1990); results of a survey by the University of Thessaloniki in the Langadas basin of central Macedonia are still very preliminary, but a similar phenomenon may yet emerge there (Kotsakis 1989; 1990).

Crete

Crete also differs from the Greek model, for the data available do not suggest any overriding uniformity in settlement and land-use patterns. The results of four survey projects can be examined. The first of these lay in the Mesara plain, the island's largest fertile area. During the Hellenistic period settlement there appears to have been chiefly fixed in cities and towns, with very little sign of isolated rural living. No evidence from earlier periods is present, so we cannot compare this pattern to its Classical predecessor and monitor the transition. It is known, however, that formerly independent cities of the area were incorporated within the territory of Gortyn, a neighbouring city, in Hellenistic times (Bennet 1990: 200–3, fig. 2). No associated alterations in rural population distribution were noted, however, nor in this particular study could any variation within the Hellenistic period as a whole be identified (Sanders 1976: 131). The pattern thus detected in the Mesara plain by Sanders, admittedly the result of only relatively extensive investigation, is fundamentally one of urban sites dominating the landscape. By contrast, the period following the Roman conquest saw an increase in site numbers and an associated intensification of agricultural activity (Sanders 1976: 137; 1982: 20–4, 30).

A much more intensive investigation of a far more limited zone was undertaken in the Ayiofarango valley, on the south coast of Crete. Significant reoccupation in this area, after a centuries-long hiatus, began in Early Hellenistic times; the Later Hellenistic period saw 'increasing settlement', both at a small nucleated settlement (Agia Kyriaki) and in isolated farmsteads (Blackman and Branigan 1977: 74). Further development of this pattern of dispersed settlement is seen in the valley during the Early Roman era. The survey zone apparently lay in the *chora* of the city Lasaia, where settlement had commenced in the late Classical period before spreading to the Ayiofarango valley proper. In its turn, Lasaia was probably dependent on Gortyn at this time (Blackman and Branigan 1975: 28–32). The Ayiofarango evidence contraverts the results of the Mesara work by arguing the presence of small rural farmsteads and a measure of settlement expansion in the Hellenistic landscape of

Crete. A genuinely different pattern of human activity may have been in operation here, though the relative intensities of the two surveys might play some part as well. The Ayiofarango pattern is reinforced by results from the Sphakia survey, a project in progress still further to the west of the island. There, in the territory of the city of Anopolis, small hamlets and isolated farms were found dating to the Classical-Hellenistic and the Hellenistic-Roman periods, 'the most common of all periods'. The ceramics of these periods cannot yet be properly differentiated (Nixon *et al.* 1988; 1989: 208; 1990).

If the Ayiofarango and Sphakia surveys testify to dispersed rural settlement, more intensive land-use and a possible increase in population levels beginning in Hellenistic times, the evidence of the upland plain of Lasithi in eastern Crete argues against accepting this as a general Cretan pattern. Settlement in that very fertile area is barely represented for both the Classical and Hellenistic periods, possibly reflecting pressures exerted by the local central power, the city of Lyttos, in determining residential priorities (Watrous 1982b: 23; Sanders 1982: 18–19). Only in Roman times, most clearly the Late Roman period, does significant utilisation of the plain reappear (Watrous 1982b: 23–4). Variability in settlement and land-use patterns is apparent across Hellenistic Crete, with an expansion of settlement and possible demographic growth ushered in within some, if not all, areas during this time. The dominance of the major settlements, the cities, and their impact upon rural hinterlands are, however, factors common to each of these survey analyses (Sanders 1982: 16–31).

Cyprus

Cyprus passed under Ptolemaic suzerainty early in the Hellenistic period, remaining in that kingdom's possession until the island's annexation by Rome in 58 BC (Vessberg and Westholm 1956: 220–37; Bagnall 1976: 57–79; Mitford 1980). Of the several surveys conducted in the island (e.g. Adovasio *et al.* 1975; 1978; Baird 1984; 1985; Sheen 1981; P. W. Wallace 1984), two are suitable for use in this analysis.

Part of the Khrysokou river drainage in the Paphos district was examined by a survey targeting the organisation and distribution of copper production in that region, the area around modern Polis. Settlement and metallurgical sites were recorded, allowing shifts through time in the region's economic structure to emerge. In the Iron Age (1050–325 BC), settlement had chiefly centred on the *polis* of Marion; copper production, though locally controlled, was mobilised to respond to both local and external demands, for example by exporting to fifth-century Athens (Raber 1987: 305, 309). However, the Hellenistic-Early Roman era (325 BC–AD 300) witnessed both a 'drastic decline' in this local

industry and a reorganisation of settlement, with the Hellenistic foundation of Arsinoe (285 BC) replacing Marion (which was destroyed by the Ptolemies). Raber explains this sharp decline in production as 'correlated with the incorporation of Cyprus into the Hellenistic (Ptolemaic) economic and political system and the appearance of larger copper-smelting centres elsewhere on the island. The overall pattern suggests that, with the ability to efficiently exploit the resources of the entire island, the Hellenistic and Roman rulers of Cyprus chose to locate their smelting installations with regard to convenience of supply and access.' The relative isolation of the Polis area 'made it a poor choice for the location of a state-directed industry' (Raber 1987: 305). Copper production did continue – but only as a local enterprise by and for the local population. Some variation in the distribution of both settlement and metallurgical sites marked the Late Roman-Byzantine period (AD 300–1200), but the basic pattern of small-scale, locally based industry endured (pp. 305–6, 309). This specialist survey reveals the highly localised, but nevertheless decisive, impact of Hellenistic incorporation upon the economy of one relatively remote region.

This development can be compared with the data of the Canadian Palaipaphos Survey project in southwestern Cyprus (Rupp *et al.* 1984; Rupp 1982; 1984; 1987; L. W. Sørensen 1983; cf. Hadjisavvas 1977). Instead of unbroken continuity in settlement throughout the Iron Age, a severe drop in site numbers in the Cypro-Classical period (*c.* 500–300 BC) has been observed, attributed to the Persian destruction of Palaipaphos, the central settlement of the survey region. A problem with ceramic identifications for the period may play some part in this hiatus as well (L. W. Sørensen *et al.* 1987: 274; Rupp 1986: 35). As in the Polis survey, the Hellenistic period is not a quiet continuation of its Classical predecessor. A 'dramatic growth' in site numbers (approximately five times the Classical total) occurred, suggesting – in the most recent opinion of the investigators – a period of prosperity, rising population and a booming economy; this favourable state endured into the Early Roman period (L. W. Sørensen *et al.* 1987: 277, tables 1 and 2; Rupp 1986: 28). Peaceful conditions, ensured by Ptolemaic and Roman rule, are believed to underlie this impressive development. Another undoubtedly important factor was the late fourth-century BC foundation of Nea Paphos some 17 km to the west of the survey area; in the second century BC this city was transformed into the island's capital, first for the Ptolemies, later for the Romans (Mitford 1980: 1309). Instead of being drained of population or resources by this foundation, the neighbouring survey region appears to have benefited; the maintenance of the international sanctuary of Aphrodite at Palaipaphos itself also undoubtedly contributed to the area's well being (Rupp

1982: 325). Although sites of Hellenistic and Early Roman date were discovered throughout the survey region, an especially high concentration of settlement on the coastal plain and in the lower portions of river drainages has been interpreted as reflecting the proximity of these centres, one political and one religious (Rupp 1986: 35; cf. Bagnall 1976: 61–2). Attention has already been drawn to the role played by Nea Paphos, and Ptolemaic influence in general, in the expanded settlement of the Paphos district (Winter and Bankoff 1989). The changed political and economic status of the island appears to have had significant repercussions upon local patterns of life, both by marginalising areas (Polis region) or by bringing them to greater prominence (Palaipaphos).

Asia Minor/Turkey

Originally part of the Seleucid empire before becoming the home of later 'splinter' dynasties such as the Attalids of Pergamon, Asia Minor at present can offer little to this investigation. While a great deal of excavation has been done at many major centres (Miletus, Pergamon, Priene), the majority of surveys have been restricted to city-oriented architectural studies, rather than regional explorations (e.g. A. Hall 1976; Mitchell and Waelkens 1987; 1988; Coulton, Milner and Reyes 1988). One highly intensive and methodical survey, at the Keban reservoir in east-central Turkey, admitted little knowledge or interest in the Hellenistic and Roman periods (Whallon 1979: 274). Only the results of more extensive work are available, therefore, for this study.

In the Hellenistic Troad, the chief alterations in settlement density and distribution came about through civic synoecisms – reorganisations that cut the number of cities in the area by more than half (J. M. Cook 1973: 360–3). Despite the growth of individual civic territories (with, for example, half of the Troad now divided between only two cities, Ilion and Alexandria Troas), little evidence for secondary settlement at the village level was found; the Hellenistic period was thus judged to be an 'age of city dwellers' (J. M. Cook 1973: 368). This can be accepted as a preliminary statement, but verification through regular and systematic survey is still desirable. A similar concentration on the upper level of the settlement hierarchy dominates work in the lower Maeander floodplain, where the Hellenistic period was described as witnessing 'a consolidation of populations through the extension of municipal territory or newly incorporated territory'. While occurrences of site relocation and abandonment are observed, for much of this area the investigator still found it doubtful that 'the change in municipal status greatly affected local population patterns' (Marchese 1986: 322). Investigative work along similar lines suggests that the region of northern Caria was somewhat more

profoundly affected, with certain native villages transformed into Greek *poleis* and a number of new urban foundations demanding the reorganisation of local populations (Marchese 1989).

A broader settlement spectrum did emerge from a non-systematic but relatively thorough investigation of the Cilician plain, which lay under Seleucid control for much of Hellenistic history. Although pottery chronologies for the pre-Classical periods were not of the best, a distinct rise in the number of Hellenistic sites (compared to the preceding Persian period) was reported, indicating 'how thickly the area was populated, especially towards the sea where the sites were mostly the size of small farmsteads' (Seton-Williams 1954: 139; but cf. Davesne *et al.* 1987 for Achaemenid activity). Parts of the plain were also said to have been put under cultivation for the first time (Seton-Williams 1954: 145). Also under Seleucid control was an area further to the east, along the lower Euphrates and near the modern-day border between Turkey and Syria. There too a steady increase in settlement was observed in the later first millennium, though the region's population peak was not reached until Late Roman and Byzantine times (Marfoe *et al.* 1986).

Syria

Although numerous surveys have been undertaken in this region (cf. Maxwell Hyslop *et al.* 1942; Tchalenko 1953; Matthers 1981: 2–3; Grainger 1990: 204–10; Sanlaville 1985), these rarely meet the necessary criteria for this study. One exception is from northern Syria, in the vicinity of Tell Rifa'at. While no identifiable sites of Persian date were found, the Hellenistic period witnessed a significant repopulation of the landscape, particularly marked in the Late Hellenistic period (Matthers 1978: 123, 147). After this, another break in occupation is recorded for the early centuries of this era; for all these data, however, it should be noted that only the survey's finewares have so far been consulted (Kenrick 1981). Assembling all available hints from Syrian surveys, however, it can tentatively be stated that an increase in settlement numbers and population, with more territory placed under cultivation than before, did indeed occur. This development has been directly linked with the foundation of the Dekapolis, the implantation of ten new cities by Seleucid rulers (Grainger 1990: 110–19). The resultant impact on rural populations and settlement patterns must have been great, but no finer resolution on this process is possible from the extant survey evidence (cf. Millar 1987).

Palestine/Israel

An uncommon amount of archaeological activity, including surface survey, is carried out in the modern state of Israel.

Most attention is devoted to periods dominated by biblical scholarship and to the early history of the Israelites; the Hellenistic period, here as elsewhere, has tended to suffer in consequence (Roller 1982a: 44–5; Arav 1989: 7–8). Nonetheless, through culling pieces of evidence from both survey and excavation, an archaeological framework for Hellenistic Palestine is beginning to emerge (Arav 1989). During this epoch, Palestine had fallen under the suzerainty first of the Ptolemies and then of the Seleucids, before the mid-second-century BC Maccabean revolt and the subsequent formation of the independent Hasmonean kingdom.

No detailed recapitulation of survey results from areas such as Idumaea, Judaea, Philoteria or Transjordan will be given (Arav 1989 and Stern 1982: 1–46 for reviews; for Judaea cf. Applebaum 1977). In many of these regions, fairly unbroken continuity from the preceding Persian period was noted, with only minor fluctuations in site numbers. Exceptions, however, were noted; a few are detailed here. In the Golan, for example, an efflorescence of definite or possible Hellenistic foundations was observed, findings very much at odds with results elsewhere (Arav 1989: 117). Inland Galilee possessed scant Persian and no trace of Early Hellenistic occupation, before emerging with several new sites in the later Hellenistic era; settlement density, and presumably population, continued to grow through Roman times, peaking in the Late Roman and Early Byzantine periods (Meyers *et al.* 1978). Finally, in the northern Plain of Sharon, the agricultural potential of the area seems to have been reached after approximately 200 BC (Roller 1982a: 50). A 'dense network' of rural settlement, including wealthy 'manor farms', then developed within this coastal zone, which later became the territory of Caesarea Maritima (Roller 1980; 1982a; 1982b; 1983).

More detailed rural developments can be examined in the northern region of Palestine known as Samaria, lying between Galilee and Judaea (Josephus, *Jewish War* 3.4). This region had revolted against the governor installed by Alexander; as punishment a Macedonian colony was placed at Shomron (Roman Sebaste) disrupting the existing settlement and landholding patterns of the area. It is also believed that a considerable part of Samaria may have passed into royal hands (Applebaum 1976: 257; Bickerman 1988: 8–12).

Fieldwork by Dar in the western part of this region has revealed two major settlement developments during the Hellenistic era. The first of these was the appearance of 'military farmsteads', sites resembling small defensive posts in the landscape, with impressive central buildings and advantageous sitings. Since these are also associated with holdings of 4–7 ha, significantly larger than the apparent norm in the area, it has been concluded that 'the dwellers of the military farmsteads were not simple peasants', but that these sites belonged to 'military settlers of the Hellenistic period and, in view of their size, as belonging to officers and commanders' (Dar 1986: 12, 15, 224, 249). If Dar's inferences are correct, we see here the direct transformation of the landscape by the physical imposition of new residential landowners.

The second rural phenomenon observed in Hellenistic Samaria was the proliferation of field towers, massive stone structures associated with agricultural equipment and lying in the territory surrounding nucleated settlements. Over twelve hundred of these towers were located and examined. While some slight traces of material of earlier, Persian date were found in towers, the chief period of occupation clearly fell in the third to second centuries BC, with activity continuing until the first and second centuries AD, the time of the anti-Roman revolts (Dar 1986: 109). From the towers' great number, wide distribution and uniform nature, as well as the degree of investment they required, a single, central agency has been assumed to be responsible for their planning and construction. The investigators believe the tower pattern is evidence for colonisation in Samaria after its turbulent Early Hellenistic history; it may 'have been one of the results of the confiscation of Samaritan estates and village lands for the benefit of military settlers and other elements' (Applebaum 1986: 260). This rural development may be related to the 'King's Mountain Country' referred to in Jewish sources, but the date and precise meaning of that term remain very problematic (Dar 1986: 119–21, 248; Applebaum 1986: 258–60; Applebaum *et al.* 1978).

The towers have been interpreted as individual centres for an intensive viticulture industry aimed at an external market, but it remains uncertain if they were indeed such specialised production centres or more mixed farms (Dar 1986: 110, 163–4). Who precisely the residents of these towers were is likewise undetermined. What does seem to emerge with the pattern of towers is a major change in the social organisation of rural life. In the Iron Age, the extended family or clan (*beth av*) had been the basic unit of residence. With the towers, and the implied military or civilian colonisation, nuclear family units now began to dominate (Dar 1986: 20; Applebaum 1986: 257–8). Organisation along the line of the clan's communal interests was given up in favour of the individual family; it is hypothesised that 'the Hellenistic conquest initiated – at least in Samaria – the breakup of the extended family as it existed in the rural areas (was this governmental coercion?)' (Applebaum 1986: 262).

In western Samaria, confiscation, colonisation and a major reorganisation of the agrarian landscape is associated with the Hellenistic era. Established landholding and residential practices were overthrown, and the presence of newly introduced settlers detected – in the military farmsteads if not in the tower pattern at large. The dramatic changes observed here, however, were not universal. In Judaea, for example, field towers are rare, possibly reflecting a smaller amount of land taken from local residents (Applebaum 1986: 260). Even within Samaria itself, different patterns of rural settlement and abandonment can be observed (Finkelstein 1981; Stern 1982: 31; Arav 1989: 131–3, 138). Considering the survey evidence from Israel *in toto* reiterates the need to be prepared for great regional and local variability.

Jordan

Archaeological surface survey also flourishes in the modern state of Jordan, and, as in Greece, numerous projects combine to provide a strikingly similar picture of human activity (table 9.1). In the Hellenistic period, the region would for the most part have lain under Seleucid control, though parts of central and southern Jordan may have retained their independence under Nabataean leadership, until that kingdom's annexation by Rome (Negev 1977: 534–5; Hammond 1973). In all results from Jordanian surveys, only a slight Hellenistic presence (typically dated from the end of the fourth century to the mid-first century BC) is ever attested, a pattern very similar to the preceding, equally lightly populated Persian period (*c*. 539–332 BC). In central and southern areas, where most of these surveys are located, the post-Hellenistic period is termed Nabataean, dating from roughly the first century BC until the Roman conquest of AD 106 (although this period's precise chronological range – especially in terms of surface survey material – remains very flexible, possibly beginning somewhat earlier). What is clear is that the Nabataean period saw a remarkable upsurge in settlement numbers, intensification of land-use, and – by extension – some population growth. As just one example, the Wadi el-Hasa survey in west-central Jordan discovered a more than ten-fold increase in Nabataean site numbers over Hellenistic levels (B. MacDonald 1988: 11). This development may in part reflect increased sedentism by the residents of the area. Further to the north, a somewhat stronger Hellenistic presence was detected in a survey of the East Jordan valley, along the border of modern Jordan and Israel. Even there, however, site numbers more than doubled in the Early Roman period (Ibrahim *et al.* 1976). It seems clear that the region remained largely unsettled during the Hellenistic period, continuing in the tradition of the preceding Persian epoch. It was not until the era of Nabataean or Roman domination that a stimulus to more vigorous exploitation and permanent settlement was felt in this area.

Arab-Persian Gulf

The chief interest of the Seleucid monarchy in this zone lay in its undoubted communications and commercial potential, notably in long-distance trade with Mesopotamia and the Eastern Mediterranean. To secure the route, a military presence, in the form of a fleet and fortified garrisons, has been proposed as one Seleucid tactic of domination (Salles 1982; 1987: 108–9; cf. Larsen 1983: 57–8). One such fortress was discovered on Failaka (ancient Icarus), an island off the coast of Kuwait. Of early third-century BC date, the site boasted a Greek-style sanctuary with associated finds, including inscriptions in Greek. This *asylon* gives the strongest attestation of a Seleucid presence in the Gulf region (Hannestad 1984; Salles 1987: 85–6; Boucharlat and Salles 1981: 73–4). 'Hellenising' features are likewise seen at other sites in Eastern Arabia, for example Thaj – sometimes linked to the powerful trading city of Gerrha mentioned in many Graeco-Roman sources (Boucharlat and Salles 1981: 76–80; D. Potts 1983, 1989; generally, Boucharlat and Salles 1981; Salles 1984; al-Wohaibi 1980).

At these and other sites both in the Gulf itself and the Arabian peninsula, an increasing amount of archaeological evidence is now becoming available for the Hellenistic period (D. Potts 1990). Or rather for what most archaeologists, following classical authorities, would term the 'Hellenistic' period; that particular label is rejected in several of the local chronological schemas, where the epoch can be recognised as the 'Seleucid complex' (D. Potts 1983: 94) or the Middle Hasaean period (D. Potts 1984: 119–20; cf. Boucharlat 1984: 190–1; De Cardi 1984: 206; Hannestad 1984: 67). Some general impressions can be registered, for example that activity is relatively better attested in Arabia's Eastern Province than in the rest of the Arabian peninsula at this time (D. Potts 1983: 94; 1984: 85; Adams *et al.* 1977; Salles 1987: 78; Boucharlat 1984: 191). Again, the intensification of Hellenistic trade along routes to the Indian Ocean is connected with this development (Adams *et al.* 1977: 26; al-Wohaibi 1980: 97).

Despite this growing database, only occasionally are more detailed observations available of diachronic regional activity. One such case is the island of Bahrain, most famous in its late third- and early second-millennium BC incarnation as part of the land of Dilmun (Bibby 1970). Foodcrops, dates and pearls were the chief products of this intensively cultivated island, known as Tylus in classical antiquity (Bowersock 1986). Archaeological and geomorphological studies have estimated that approximately 65 sq. km were cultivated in the Achaemenid (Persian) and Seleucid periods, supporting a total population somewhere between 8,000 and 19,000 people (Larsen 1983: 55–8, 196). The distribution of archaeological sites on the island is interesting; apart from one large urban settlement proper (Qala'at al-Bahrain), all known sites are either necropoleis or single tombs (Salles 1987: 80; Boucharlat 1986).

Qala'at al-Bahrain (or Tylus City Va, dated to *c.* 300–100 BC) displays a distinct foreign influence in its urban material culture: in coins, Attic black-glaze sherds, terracotta figurines and Greek graffiti. These signs of contact with a 'Hellenised world' relate the site to Failaka, a contemporary foundation. Salles has recently suggested that Qala'at al-Bahrain likewise served as a Seleucid base in the Arab-Persian Gulf (cf. Boucharlat 1986: 439–42). He proceeded to relate this assumption to the associated archaeological patterns in that centre's hinterland by claiming that an urban-based tribal aristocracy organised the trading and marketing of the produce (agricultural and otherwise) of the population at large, a population whose status remains uncertain. Qala'at al-Bahrain then became a 'gateway community' not only because of its external military presence but also because of its status as the island's central, indeed only, market. Primary producers lived in dispersed, and today archaeologically invisible, settlements (e.g. palm-leaf *barastis*) with only the scattered cemeteries revealing their former residential distribution (Salles 1987: 102–5; Larsen 1983: 83).

Yet was this pattern, shaped as it was by the particular role played by the island within the specific socioeconomic structure of the Gulf, a direct product of the Seleucid presence? Salles for one argues not. The 'commercial axis' of the Gulf and the interest of external authorities in the area was long established, for example by the Achaemenid rulers; it was not novel in Hellenistic times. Only the urban centre with its elite community would experience and reflect the direct impact of a new political or military power; 'the rest of the island remained entirely untouched by any process of colonization'. However strong the Seleucid presence in Qala'at al-Bahrain/Tylus, it would remain 'isolated from the world and the inhabitants of the island' (Salles 1987: 104). In other words, a plural response, varying between city and country, rich and poor, can be observed through these archaeological data (Boucharlat and Salles 1981: 74–6; cf. Kervran 1986).

Mesopotamia/Iraq

Located in northern Mesopotamia is the North Jazira project, which centres around the major settlement of Tell al-Hawa. Because of difficulties with ceramic classifications, no comparison with the preceding Median/Achaemenid epoch is possible, but a Hellenistic pattern was established of settlement dispersed in villages and hamlets across the North Jazira plain. The investigators noted that while this dispersion ensured that almost all of the plain could have

been farmed, an absence of off-site pottery of Hellenistic date might indicate relatively less intensive cultivation (i.e. manuring) practices (Ball *et al.* 1989: 18; see Alcock, Cherry and Davis, this volume). Tell al-Hawa itself, in former times the central place of the plain, yielded no trace of Hellenistic settlement. One explanation advanced for this break in urban occupation is that the region's rural settlement may have become dependent upon and peripheral to a more remote urban centre at this time: an observation which emphasises the need to keep surveyed 'micro-regions' within a wider geographical context (Ball *et al.* 1989: 43).

Central and southern Mesopotamia are represented here by the monumental surveys, combining aerial photography and surface reconnaissance, which have been directed by Robert Adams since the 1960s. Three major volumes have been published, detailing settlement history in the land behind Baghdad, the Diyala plain (Adams 1965), in the area further to the south around Warka – ancient Uruk, classical Orchoi (Adams and Nissen 1972) – and in the central flood-plain of the Euphrates (Adams 1981). In none of these studies is the chronological resolution for our period very refined; a paucity of clear ceramic indicators requires that the Seleucid period proper always be lumped within a longer chronological span (e.g. Seleucid-Parthian: 300 BC–AD 226): 'the uncertainty obviously affects any developmental as well as historical explanations that may be offered on the basis of survey data, basically requiring that very little be said about the Seleucid period' (Adams 1981: 229, 176, 228–30; 1965: 61, 130–1; Adams and Nissen 1972: 57, 103; for more general problems, Brinkman 1984). Despite this extreme judgement, general conclusions from Adams' work can be summarised to some purpose, as long as it is remembered that the trends described cannot be linked firmly to the period of Seleucid suzerainty alone.

The most striking development of the Seleucid-Parthian era was the sudden cultural emergence of the Diyala plain in the northern part of the surveyed territory, now over-shadowing the formerly pre-eminent regions to the south. The Diyala region experienced 'explosive developments' in settlement numbers, population levels and irrigation works, only one expression of which was a fifteen-fold increase over the Achaemenid period in the recorded amount of occupied settlement area. Several contributory factors have been put forward to explain this phenomenon, with the effects of urbanisation taking pride of place. For the first time in its history, the Diyala plain lay in the immediate hinterland of major imperial centres: Seleucia-on-Tigris, founded by Seleucus I, and later the Parthian capital of Ctesiphon, 'the crowning ornament of Persia' (Gullini 1964; Invernizzi 1976). These foundations undoubtedly attracted population from surrounding areas, notably from the south; it is often argued that numerous inhabitants of Babylon were transferred forcibly to Seleucia-on-Tigris. In addition to these two well-known cities, which actually lay just outside the survey area to the west, a whole new class of unidentified urban settlements, as well as significant numbers of large towns, sprang up in the surveyed territory proper, indicating a decisive move away from residence in villages or other small communities. Also contributing to the Diyalan expansion was the region's position on a 'central artery of imperial administration and trade', a royal road from Seleucia to Bactria. A shift from interaction and communication along the Euphrates to a new emphasis on the Tigris river, visible in the Seleucid-Parthian period, similarly boosted the Diyala in relation to other areas (Adams 1981: 192, 251). A general interest in improving communications and commerce is held to be a shared feature of both the imperial regimes, and relative stability under their rule – in this area at least – allowed for peaceful and prosperous development.

Impressive population growth is believed to be reflected in the multiplication of Seleucid-Parthian settlements in the Diyala region. Support for this assumption is also derived from activity in the agricultural sphere, with evidence for a substantial expansion in cultivated territory based on a new system of lateral canals. The irrigation system as a whole moved in the direction of 'a more intensive, large scale, artificially maintained and regionally interdependent enterprise' (Adams 1965: 68). There is evidence to suggest that these new irrigation programmes in the north disrupted – in the very long run – regular water supplies downstream, a debilitating factor in the south's subsequent development (Adams 1981: 196–7). But however marked the intensification of settlement and agriculture in the Diyala region, it did remain notably uneven in distribution, with areas of dense occupation juxtaposed with more empty zones (generally, Adams 1965: 59–68; 1981: 192–4).

If the hinterland of Seleucia-on-Tigris and Ctesiphon was booming, how does this compare to the territories further south? The Warka region of southern Mesopotamia experienced relative continuity from Neo-Babylonian to Seleucid times (800–120 BC), with settlement and irrigation patterns implying an element of centralised planning and labour management; no comments peculiar to the Seleucid era can however be made. A subsequent decline and disruption in settlement and prosperity in the Early Parthian period (c. 120 BC to early first century AD) has been attributed to unstable political conditions and the importance of Seleucia-on-Tigris and Ctesiphon. Nonetheless, the region recovered to record its densest population and most intensive agricultural activity in the first and second centuries AD (Adams and Nissen 1972: 55–9). A similar overall pattern emerges in the central Euphrates floodplain, lying between the Warka and Diyala regions. Site numbers and total areas of occupation rose steadily from the Neo-Babylonian through the Seleucid-Parthian period, the net result appearing as an ongoing intensification of a system established early within that time span (Adams 1981: 196–200). In neither area, however, was the expansion of settlement density, population and agricultural intensity as rapid and discontinuous as it was in the Diyala plain.

Any 'decline' in the importance of central and southern Babylonia, for the Seleucid-Parthian period at any rate, must not be exaggerated; both remained settled and cultivated zones, but the more dramatic growth to the north, coupled with the new imperial foundations, signalled the rise of a new 'core area' in Babylonia at large: 'after the intense development of the lands along the lower Diyala the preeminence of southern Babylonia was irretrievably lost' (Adams 1981: 196, 194). How closely this wide-ranging reorganisation can be assigned to the Seleucid period proper remains, of course, unclear. In the earliest publication of these results, there was no hesitancy about proclaiming many of these changes to be 'aspects of the broader Hellenistic milieu that swept the Orient', the product of the 'intensive Hellenistic influence that followed in the wake of Alexander's conquest' (Adams 1965: 61, 115). Less is made of that 'Hellenistic influence' in later publications. Yet surely the foundation of Seleucia-on-Tigris, and the accompanying imposition of the Seleucid imperial regime, must have played some part in the trends observed, and in the regional transformation of central and peripheral areas in ancient Mesopotamia.

Susiana/Iran

For Iran, adequate settlement data from survey evidence come only from northern Khuzistan, centring on the Susiana plain (Wenke 1975/6; 1987; Johnson 1987: 290–1). Susa was refounded by Seleucus I and the area began the period under Seleucid control, before passing to the Parthians in the mid-second century and then to the Elymaeans in the mid-first BC. Our period of interest is here defined as the 'Seleuco-Parthian' epoch (c. 324–25 BC). Ceramic chronologies, as in Mesopotamia, are not sufficiently detailed to allow any further refinement, nor has research interest in the period run high. Yet some patterns within this time span still emerge, especially when compared to the previous Achaemenid regime.

If Susa, under the Achaemenids, had been a 'capital of the world', textual and numismatic evidence suggests it remained a wealthy and important city under the Seleucids and Parthians, continuing to mediate trade between the Persian Gulf and markets to the north and west. In the settlement patterns of the city's hinterland too, certain features remained constant: zones uninhabited in the Achaemenid period remained uninhabited, the areas of densest occupation remained roughly the same, approximately one third of all Achaemenid sites continued in use in the Seleuco-Parthian period (Wenke 1987: 254; 1975/6: 112).

New features in the settlement and land-use patterns of the region are, however, equally clear for the Seleuco-Parthian period. One striking development is an increasing density of sites in the vicinity of Susa itself, within a radius of approximately 20 km (Wenke 1975/6: 110, figs. 16–17; 1987: figs. 74–5). The construction of major irrigation canal systems in the Susiana plain, another innovation of the time, has been connected with this phenomenon, as well as signalling a move away from dry farming and towards more labour-intensive crops such as rice and orchard products (Wenke 1975/6: 106–9). In comparing the Seleuco-Parthian to the Achaemenid period, a significant decrease in average site size has also been observed. This may in part reflect a lessening concern with problems of security, but it can also be related profitably to new agricultural strategies and priorities. With this site size decline, Susa takes on something of the appearance of a primate settlement in the region (Wenke 1987: 261, fig. 80). Increased economic activity during this period, focusing on Susa, may have bound the region into a more tightly integrated unit; certainly there appears to have been some economic 'rationality' to the distribution of its larger villages (Wenke 1975/6: 111). Overall, the population density of the Seleuco-Parthian period records an increase over that of the Achaemenid domination, but the rate of increase here, as far as can be determined, does not appear to have been remarkable.

Despite the demographic growth and agricultural intensification of the Seleuco-Parthian period, it was in the subsequent Elymaean or Middle Parthian era (c. 26 BC– c. AD 125) that Susa reached its economic zenith and rural Susiana experienced 'a considerable increase in population densities, vastly greater investments in irrigation systems, and the emergence of a ring of substantial settlements around Susa itself' (Wenke 1987: 254). As far as can be determined, the Seleuco-Parthian period laid the foundations for this development, witnessing innovations (e.g. irrigation, rice cultivation) that eventually allowed a more significant transformation of the region's agricultural regime and settlement structure. This reconstruction is somewhat paralleled, though much more crudely, in the evidence from the Deh Luran plain, some 125 km northwest of Susa (Wenke 1987: 256; Neely 1970).

Bactria/Afghanistan

Originally a satrapy of the Seleucid empire and later on independent kingdom, Bactria has often been referred to as a 'lost chapter' of Hellenistic history, for we possess little documentary evidence beyond occasional eye-opening claims: 'The Greeks who made Bactria independent became so powerful because of the wealth of the country that they established control over Ariane and India . . . and they subdued more peoples than Alexander did . . . ' (Strabo 11.11.1; Austin 1981: 313–15; Tarn 1951; Briant 1984). As for archaeological evidence, art historians have long been entranced by a series of remarkable coin and sculptural portraits of the local Euthydemid dynasty (cf. Holt 1984a: 3; Pollitt 1986: 70–2, 284–9). Excavations were also carried out at a few major centres, most importantly at the site of Aï Khanum (Lady Moon in Uzbek), lying at the confluence of the Oxus and Kowkcheh rivers in northern Afghanistan. The settlement may well have been a foundation of Alexander himself (possibly Alexandria-Oxiana), Hephaistion or Seleucus I Nicator (Musti 1984: 182; Holt 1988: 62–3). Many aspects of the city's material culture display undoubted signs of Greek influence, including the famous Delphic maxims inscribed in a Greek heroon. Aï Khanum has been triumphantly described as 'first and foremost a Greek polis', becoming a favourite example of Greek culture penetrating and dominating the east (Bernard 1967; 1982; Colledge 1984; Green 1990: 332–3; Walbank 1981: 60–2).

The plain of Aï Khanum, and much surrounding territory, has been the subject of a French archaeological project combining aerial photography and surface reconnaissance (Gardin and Gentelle 1976; 1979; Gardin and Lyonnet 1978/9; Gentelle 1978). A complex system of irrigation canals, allowing for the more intensive exploitation of the land, has been traced, and contemporary settlement patterns located in association, revealing a programme of overall regional land management. In the investigators' first opinion, these developments were linked specifically to the Graeco-Bactrian period in the area, and the sophisticated engineering feats hailed as the outcome of the expertise of Greek military engineers and the 'génie grec' (Gardin and Gentelle 1979: 15). Further research, however, has significantly altered that reconstruction. Irrigation systems can now be traced well back before the Greek arrival in Bactria, possibly even to the Bronze Age. Certainly in the 'préhellénistique' period (first millennium BC), the territory was already densely populated and intensively utilised: the Greek colonists were not pioneers on virgin land (Gardin and Lyonnet 1978/9: 132–7).

The Graeco-Bactrian period did indeed witness a further intensification of this pre-existing pattern: 'c'est en effet à l'époque hellénistique, semble-t-il, que la plaine d'Aï

Table 9.2. *Changes in certain key areas in the study regions*

Region	Level of urbanisation?	Signs of colonisation?	Population	Agricultural intensification
Greece	Unchanged, some synoecism	—	Down in LHL	Down in LHL
Macedonia	Up	—	Up?	Up?
Crete	Unchanged, some synoecism	—	Variable	Variable
Cyprus	Unchanged, destructions/foundations	Yes?	Variable	Variable
Asia Minor/Turkey	Up, synoecisms	—	Up?	Up?
Syria	Up	—	Up?	Up?
Palestine/Israel	Up	—	Variable	Variable
Jordan	—	—	Unchanged	Unchanged
Arab-Persian Gulf	Unchanged	Yes?	Unchanged?	Up?
Mesopotamia/Iraq	Up	Yes?	Up	Up
Susiana/Iran	Unchanged	Yes?	Up	Up
Bactria/Afghanistan	Up	Yes?	Up	Up

Kanoum connut son développement le plus grand . . . le temps le plus prospère de son histoire' (Gardin and Gentelle 1979: 9, 18–19). The foundation of Aï Khanum itself, providing a populous central place within the region, must be responsible for stimulating much of this increasing activity. One pattern, tentatively established by the French archaeologists, is an increasing concentration of settlement density around the urban centre, suggesting some centripetal movement (willing or forced) on the part of the local population. That the territory in the vicinity of the city was the most intensively exploited is also suggested by developments in irrigation works. This concentration obviously required ever greater efforts in construction and more spectacular engineering designs, yet the object of such investment was frequently not the most productive land: more effort was now apparently being made for less return (Gardin and Lyonnet 1978/9: 137–8). At the same time, zones at a greater distance from the city, even those of greater agricultural promise, were often either abandoned or left relatively under-developed; the intensification of land-use in the Graeco-Bactrian period was by no means a uniform or economically 'rational' phenomenon (Gardin and Gentelle 1979: 14; Gardin and Lyonnet 1978/9: 137–9, 145–6). The nomadic invasions of the first century BC, and the inception of the Kushan period, put an end to this first millennium development, at least in Eastern Bactria.

Pierre Briant gleefully hailed the results of this work, as well as the belated recognition of clearly non-Hellenic features in Aï Khanum's material culture, as a demonstration of continuity between periods, of trends in Hellenistic economy and society perpetuating an already existing structure. He opposed this reconstruction to the more usual (indeed here the investigators' first) interpretation of the Hellenistic epoch as the beginning of a new age: *ex occidente lux* (Briant 1982: 314–17; Holt 1988: 43–4; Bernard 1976). Yet a balanced assessment is surely necessary: although the basic settlement and agricultural framework pre-dated the Graeco-Bactrian period, it still must be acknowledged that this portion of Eastern Bactria witnessed an intensification of agricultural cultivation, an increasing population concentration and a distinct new concentration upon an urban foundation. This picture of an overall Hellenistic *acceleration* of settlement and exploitation has been tentatively extended, on the basis of very limited archaeological evidence, to other areas of Bactria and other parts of the far eastern reaches of the Hellenistic world (Gardin and Gentelle 1979: 23; cf. Holt 1984a; 1984b).

Discussion

Can a 'break' then be detected in the diachronic record of human occupation and activity with the inception of the Hellenistic period? To that question, each region provides its own particular response. Table 9.2 summarises the situation in each region as measured by four key parameters: level of urbanisation, signs of colonisation, demographic variability, and agricultural intensification or disintensification. When viewed in this fashion, from the 'bottom up' as it were, regional variability is everywhere apparent: in the distinct contraction of settlement and population half-way during the Hellenistic period in Greece, the apparently static situation in Jordan, the variable picture emerging from Crete and Israel, the clear signs of demographic growth and economic intensification in several areas, including Bactria and Central

Mesopotamia. All previous scholarly concern about the perils of generalisation across a world of such geographical and cultural complexity have been amply confirmed.

Returning then to Pierre Briant's arguments about 'continuités et ruptures', has the survey evidence decided the case one way or another? On the one hand, the evidence rarely presents a static picture; hardly ever are Hellenistic conditions identical to those of the preceding era. 'Continuité' then, if defined strictly as the absence of change, does not agree with the survey data. Yet 'rupture', if defined as a sudden break and an abandonment of previous modes of operation, is clearly not applicable either. While this might be claimed in one or two cases (the significant alteration in mainland Greece for example), for the most part no catastrophic restructuring of these Hellenistic landscapes is to be observed. The legacy of the preceding regimes in each region remains clearly reflected to a very great extent. Increasing social complexity, urbanisation, population growth and improved agricultural technology were not confined solely to the Hellenistic period, especially in those areas formerly under Achaemenid control. Nonetheless, forces were at work to alter basic settlement and land-use patterns across much of the Hellenistic world – and with them the lives of multitudes within these far-flung kingdoms.

To identify at least some of these forces, we can turn again to table 9.2. Urbanisation and colonisation are scarcely neglected factors to cite in Hellenistic studies; city foundations and population implantations have long been considered prime hallmarks of the period (e.g. Bikerman 1939; A. H. M. Jones 1940; Kreissig 1974; G. M. Cohen 1978). In earlier studies, however, the dominant line of research focused on the status, administration and population structure of these enclaves (percentage of Graeco-Macedonians, origin of other settlers), as well as showing a healthy interest in their role as a 'motor of acculturation', energetically civilising local indigenous populations. The presumed ubiquity of these foundations and their 'Hellenising' capacity is now under serious attack (e.g. Briant 1982: 156–7, 294; Millar 1987: 129; van der Spek 1987; Grainger 1990). Survey evidence allows us to take a somewhat different approach to the problem. Where urban foundations or re-foundations, with or without a formal colonial component, did take place (and the areas surveyed are biased towards such areas), impressive knock-on effects are visible: characteristically, a reorganisation of residential patterns, a rise in associated rural settlement and population numbers, and a concomitant increase in levels of agricultural productivity. Urbanisation and colonisation may not appear novel factors to consider – until it is realised that, with the help of regional survey evidence, the interaction of such

foundations with their rural hinterlands can now be traced. Exploring the impact of these creations upon local indigenous communities (in ways apart from the important but not all-encompassing issue of their adoption of Greek culture) suddenly becomes a viable option for the archaeologist. That this impact was often far from negligible is obvious even in a brief and preliminary review such as this.

Other changes within these various landscapes also stemmed from large- and small-scale shifts in the geopolitics of the Hellenistic world. Juggling of local civic hierarchies, through synoecism, co-optation or destruction, was not infrequent (particularly so in Greece, Crete, Cyprus and Anatolia). Such restructuring was motivated in part by the enlarged scale of the political system within which the cities were operating (Alcock 1989a: 116–17; Walbank 1981: 141–52; Tarn and Griffith 1952: 91–2). In addition, new imperial preferences and priorities could be expressed by a redistribution of cities and populations. The proximity of an important route of communications or trade could, for example, dictate regional development. This factor has been argued as significant for the Arab-Persian Gulf, for the Diyala region in Mesopotamia and for Susiana, although reactions to this proximity were not uniform. On Bahrain, Seleucid imperial demands were mediated and controlled through the urban centre, leading to an interesting 'dual' response to the external presence. Elsewhere in the Gulf, a greater density of settlement and population in key areas was attributed by investigators to the stimulus of trade and external contact. Similar increases were explained, at least in part, by similar stimuli in the Diyala and Susa plains. Conversely, areas could be bypassed through changes in wider patterns of commerce and communication. The 'marginalisation' of the Polis region of Cyprus, as the island was introduced within the broad Ptolemaic sphere of control, offers one localised example of this phenomenon. On a higher level too, new 'core' and 'peripheral' zones emerged, as has been noted for Mesopotamia. From this perspective, developmental differences between those areas under indirect royal control (e.g. Greece, Crete) versus direct sovereignty (Israel, Bactria) also become intriguing.

Despite the variety of regional trajectories, the dominant trend to emerge from table 9.2 is towards higher levels of urbanisation, increasing population numbers and more intensive land-use. In some cases, sudden and (comparatively) rapid change was apparently initiated as a result of socioeconomic developments taking place during the Hellenistic period proper. This appears to be the case in Macedonia, western Cyprus, Syria, Diyala in Mesopotamia and, to some extent, Susiana. Elsewhere (for example, in Bahrain, southern Mesopotamia, Bactria and possibly Anatolia), demographic and economic growth appears rather as part of a long-term process of regional development. Yet even in the latter cases, as I emphasised for Bactria, Hellenistic acceleration in settlement, population and agricultural production must be appreciated and understood in its own terms, and not dismissed as simply part of an ongoing gradualist development.

Does this general, if far from universal, pattern support the belief that Greek conquest and colonisation brought positive economic stimulation to the Oriental lands? While much work remains to be done on other aspects of the Hellenistic economy (e.g. trade and monetarisation studies), the ideological underpinnings of that assumption, born of nineteenth-century imperial theory, have already been challenged, nor can the survey data be employed to endorse them. More intensive exploitation of the land can be triggered by numerous factors, not least of which is escalating external pressure, through tribute or taxation, upon a local population. General prosperity need not necessarily be reflected in this survey evidence, and it seems more likely that Briant's observation (1982: 119) about the rural population of Asia Minor ('pour lesquelles la conquête macédonienne s'est certainement soldée par une dégradation de leur situation sociale et économique') often must have held true. In a somewhat different context, an important point was made by Susan Sherwin-White, rebuking a general 'failure to recognise policies that seem simply characteristic of an imperial power . . . instead these are seen as somehow peculiarly characteristic of Greek colonial rule in the east' (1987: 4, 30–1). The major developments observed in these survey data will never be satisfactorily explained by the fact that 'Greeks' conquered and controlled these lands, but by the fact that these territories were incorporated, re-incorporated or influenced by powerful political entities: here imperialism was more significant than 'Hellenisation'. Further comparison of Hellenistic imperial strategies with both their predecessors (Achaemenids) and their successors (Romans, Parthians) would place these kingdoms within a longer-term perspective, while at the same time evading the Hellenocentric snare (M. T. Larsen 1979; Wenke 1987).

Conclusion

Particular stress has been laid in this collection of papers upon the need to 're-people' classical antiquity, to remove material artefacts from pride of place and restore issues of social action, conflict and power to the agenda of the classical archaeologist. At first glance, archaeological surface survey may not appear the most obvious place to begin this repopulation. The lives and decisions of any one individual, family or even small community can rarely be discerned (though see Alcock *et al.*, this volume). Survey evidence works most successfully at the aggregate level, reflecting the activity and choices of innumerable nameless people over relatively long stretches of time. The role of individual human agency is lost in general trends.

Despite this fact, I would argue that survey nevertheless returns human behaviour to the forefront of our investigations. Survey, manifestly, is not about the beautiful *objet d'art*; the material finds generally are fit only to serve as a means to an end. That end is an insight into conditions of human life: residential priorities, responses to social, economic and demographic pressures. If archaeology provides the *only* way to retrieve information about the majority of people in the past, then survey evidence offers the most broadly based reconstruction of their existence. Moreover, survey data can serve as a springboard to further, more specific questions, for instance about relationships of land and labour (Kreissig 1980; Welwei 1979; Briant 1982: 95–135) or the interactions of town and countryside (e.g. Préaux 1978: 9). Regional survey, then, forms an essential component in the redevelopment of the discipline.

Fortunately enough, archaeological survey no longer really requires apology or lengthy explanation among practitioners of classical archaeology; the technique now claims its fair share of prestige, student interest, conference proceedings and funding. Most encouragingly, ancient historians interested in social and economic processes are increasingly willing to accept and utilise the vital range of evidence that the technique provides (e.g. Brinkman 1984; Osborne 1987a). The convergence of classical archaeology and ancient history is demonstrated in this volume, and survey yet again is proving an important component in this healthy rapprochement.

What is noteworthy, however, is that survey results have so far been treated primarily in terms of the diachronic history of each discrete project. Sufficient data are now available to try a new tactic. In this analysis I have approached the evidence in a different fashion, adopting a relatively tight chronological focus and juxtaposing the results from several diverse areas. Comparative survey analyses hold out great promise for the exploration of long-term change across a wide territorial spectrum, a perspective denied to almost every other form of historical or archaeological investigation. If a defence of surface survey is no longer required in a volume such as this, advocacy is still demanded for broad synthesis of its results, across a range of geographical regions and with a view to answering more general historical questions.

I said at the beginning that this article would be about breakages: my final destructive concern involves the disciplinary nature of the period's study. As has been made clear, any valid understanding of the Hellenistic *oikoumene* is greatly hampered by sharp scholarly divides: Greek versus Near Eastern history, Classical versus Hellenistic versus Roman history, Achaemenid versus Seleucid history, and so on. This lack of communication is damaging, not least because it perpetuates the old colonialist, Hellenocentric treatment of the period, and it has quite rightly been increasingly stigmatised (Kuhrt and Sherwin-White 1987a: ix–xi; Briant 1982: 159–60; Adams 1981: 242–3). Surface survey reinforces the need to avoid any such arbitrary divisions, paradoxically demonstrating that, while the Hellenistic world must be studied on a region-by-region basis, its dissection cannot follow the geographical and cultural lines traditionally laid down. Established boundaries are slipping as more and more multi-disciplinary and inter-disciplinary projects are being undertaken – or at very least desired. Symptomatic of this recent change is the fact that one major bastion of classical archaeology, the *American Journal of Archaeology*, has now added 'Archaeology in Iran' to its long-running feature on 'Archaeology in Anatolia', as well as including papers on eastern subjects (e.g. Sumner 1986; Mellink 1988; Nashef 1990).

Many of the difficulties underlying the archaeological study of the Hellenistic period are not peculiar to it. The ongoing controversy over Martin Bernal's *Black Athena* (1987), in which the author addressed head on problems of Western prejudice and disciplinary inflexibility, has been revealing (Peradotto and Levine 1989; Muhly 1990). Classical archaeologists are becoming increasingly sensitive to changing attitudes towards the Western cultural heritage and its relation to the 'Oriental'. If one of the major challenges facing the discipline of classical archaeology today is the legacy – and the loss – of Hellenism, then breaking up the Hellenistic world, to reveal its complexities and scholarly inadequacies, as well as its untapped research potential, has been a timely exercise.

Acknowledgements

I would like to thank Paul Cartledge, John Cherry and Amélie Kuhrt for their comments on an earlier draft of this paper.

PART V

Responses

10
Response

MICHAEL JAMESON

Ian Morris (in Ch. 1) has given a chilling account of the history of Greek archaeology (not 'classical' – Rome has not part in his tale) and an assessment of its future that strikes me as bleak, though he tries to put a good face on it. In his view, Greek archaeology grew up in the shadow of 'Hellenism', the appropriation by the elites of Western Europe of the language, literature and art of classical Greece for the purpose of maintaining superiority within their own societies and of asserting the superiority of the West in general over the non-Western world. In many respects Morris apparently agrees with the thesis of Martin Bernal (1987). Morris sees this Hellenism as resistant to the notion of change in the world of classical Greece and unwilling to consider the existence of orders of society other than those presented in, or conjured out of, the nineteenth-century canon of Greek literature. Archaeology by revealing a harsher, unromantic reality, posed a threat to Hellenism and was swiftly neutralised by confinement to the description of excavation, the analysing and cataloguing of artefacts, and attempts to annotate major historical events or personalities, when not serving simply as the art history branch of Hellenism. With the increasing theoretical and methodological sophistication of other archaeologies, Greek archaeology has become increasingly isolated by being subservient to a master that has lost its *raison d'être* as classical education withers, postmodernism shatters the intellectual consensus and the West after colonialism claims other bases for its superiority. Under such circumstances Morris' call to rethink the role of Greek archaeology may seem not timely but fatally late.

Before considering the solutions Morris proposes I have to return to the history of the disciplines which I find considerably more complex and contradictory. First, 'Hellenism' – there is no question that the languages and symbols of arcane cultures, as they seemed to the majority of the population, were among the instruments of social domination in Western Europe and America, though I suspect much more superficially and less effectively, especially in America, than their proponents and their critics have supposed. All aspects of high culture can be seen as tools of social and political domination, but does this exhaust their role while they prevail, does it mean that when their exploitation is exposed or becomes obsolete they have only antiquarian interest? Greek literature and philosophy, art and architecture, history and political thought, also served as vehicles of intellectual dissent. The rationalism of Greek discourse, however idealised and exaggerated, could be used to break from the bonds of church, state and social convention, as well as to reinforce them. The modes of thought the West used to colonise intellectually were, more remotely, imbued with the derivatives of Hellenism, and, for better or worse, it is through these modes that the world now carries on intellectual communication. Greece may not have been 'the origin of the West' but it has been seen as, and to some degree truly is, an inextricable component.

When the dead hand of traditional classics teaching was lifted in the West, even fewer undertook the laborious regime of learning the classical languages and their scholarly disciplines. While such efforts might gain amused admiration they were no longer (if they ever had been) necessary accomplishments for political power and social prestige. And yet the study of the Greek and Roman world survives with the philological component reduced but stubbornly resistant. Teachers at elite institutions proclaim its marginality and irrelevance while at the same time at *all* types of institution students of all backgrounds, given the opportunity and exposure to good teachers, continue to find the subject stimulating and rewarding. This is not because there is a single, powerful lure for them, or because a single effective doctrine inspires the teachers, or because the claims for classics made in the past are all still valid. All of us engaged with classical antiquity have our explanations which, when compared, are often contradictory. (I shall give my own views in a moment.) My point here is that neither now nor in the past does Morris' analysis account for all of the appeal of classics in the West and beyond, and that if archaeology has been the handmaiden of classics her service too is not adequately explained.

Morris' characterisation of most Greek archaeology of the past century I find persuasive, but not his explanation of it. According to Morris, Greek archaeology had to be 'de-peopled', made to seem scientific and neutral, so as to shield conventional classics from the reality of the ancient world and the notion of change. But of course there was plenty in the textual tradition that showed brutality

(Homer), irrationality (Euripides), sexuality and scatology (Aristophanes), and evidence of change and decline was not avoided (cf. the common view of the Hellenistic period and sometimes of the fourth century BC). Nonetheless the life of the majority of the ancient population (women, the unfree and those below the level of the elite) was given little attention and while that life was not well represented in the texts, the texts selected for study were restricted and sometimes bowdlerised. But except for the fact that no ancient Greeks, not even the apex of the elite, dwelt in marble mansions, it is not clear to me that field archaeology threatened shocking revelations or that a more prestigious (?) philology consciously or unconsciously shackled the young discipline of archaeology. Rather it seems to me that classics as a whole, with ancient history and archaeology in tow, maintained its focus on 'the finest' products of the civilisation, and the same tended to be the case when other periods and cultures were the object of scholarship and sometimes education. For antiquity this was perhaps inevitable since it was accepted that the texts available were already a selection of the best that had survived by virtue of their quality (which by some criteria is, of course, true). Only with the opening up of ancient history, and history in general, to social and economic issues did a broader role for field archaeology become possible. It could be argued that meanwhile the 'scientific' procedures of detailed observation and analysis of objects, buildings, landscapes and inscriptions provided a haven for those who had a curiosity about an alien reality and were not predisposed to romanticise. Aegean prehistory, even before the widespread adoption of the techniques of other archaeologies, had begun to present a more comprehensive view of the societies it excavated. Morris regrets the banishing of narrative from Greek archaeology but I wonder how much benefit would have come from it so long as the historical framework was limited. Morris, following Snodgrass (1987), is sharply critical of 'the wrong kind of archaeology' that tries to link the material record to major historical events. That kind of narrative was attempted and showed its limitations (and is seen by Morris as still 'desperately seeking contacts with a postmodern [?] narrative'), though, in my view, it would be irresponsible *not* to keep testing the possibilities, in part to demonstrate what does not show in the archaeological record. Shrines, houses, farmsteads and graves need not reflect historical events but I do not see how fortifications and walls, prominent features of many Greek landscapes, can be studied effectively without attention to political and military history.

The call for a genuinely historical archaeology, 'returning human beings to the centre of an intellectual landscape that has been systematically dehumanised', is welcome and should now be widely accepted, despite the melodramatic language. It is well illustrated by a number of the papers in this volume. The material remains should indeed be means, not ends in themselves. But a caution – not all good scholars and archaeologists have a bent for asking historical and theoretical questions, and not all who do are good archaeologists in the sense that they know the evidence and how to use it. Accurate chronologies and attributions, no doubt often prepared by incurious experts, are indispensable for the surveys examined by Alcock, Cherry and Davis, and again by Alcock in this volume, and for Whitley's Protoattic pots and the movement of ceramics examined by Gill and by Arafat and Morgan. If such information is significantly off the mark much of the argumentation in these articles collapses. Incurious experts, for whatever motives, are committed to months and years of often tedious work. I am not sure their liberation in the past to create narratives would have done much more than obscure and even skew their analyses. But Morris' new archaeologists need intellectual commitment, and here we have to ask with Morris not only 'Why Greek archaeology?' but 'Why Greek classical studies?', especially if the chief motive for their study hitherto has been the promotion of Western and elite superiority. Morris and before him Snodgrass and Chippindale (1988) give a disappointing answer: because we have so many data, produced for so long (by the wrongheaded or incurious). The case becomes a bit stronger when it is added that we have *both* textual and archaeological evidence, an argument I am sure I am not alone in having used in writing grant applications. But are not other high cultures – China, South Asia, the Near East and most recently the Maya – equally, and in some ways more, deserving of attention by this standard? Purely in terms of the complexity and challenging character of the material record they may have a stronger case. We may get our grant but will we be able to maintain our place in the educational system? Here, it seems to me, we need to come up with our justification for the study of ancient Greece as a whole, which makes up a large part of classics in the present day, if we are to make any successful claims for classical archaeology.

When I spoke earlier of the various reasons that have led inquiring minds to the study of Greek culture in the past, I suggested that the reasons given are likely to be personal and inconsistent, though they will have much in common. A 'response' is not a review so I need not hide behind a mask of impersonal objectivity. My own answer is surely the product of my origins and experiences and I do not expect others to agree with it. Barely returned to the university after the interruption of World War II, I was interviewed for a prized overseas fellowship and was asked why one should study Greek civilisation rather than, for instance, that of

Classical China (I had had a Peking childhood and became involved again in the Orient during the war). I would like to think that my willingness to accept the point lost me the fellowship, though I know there were much more substantial reasons. And yet why had I, at one time bilingual and with an abiding interest in non-Western cultures, on the road as I thought to a career in archaeology, become captured by Greece – its language, literature and history, in that order, not its archaeology until later? The sheer power of Archaic and Classical literature and art and the intellectual inventiveness of cultural life can be challenged by other remarkable periods (in the West by Renaissance Florence and Elizabethan England, for instance). What is more difficult to match (and this is where my fascination becomes more personal) is the small scale and variety of the societies of Greece, the possibility of following the interplay of force and principle, of the public and the personal, social ideology and economic reality, in these 'cities of reason' (Murray 1990). Finally, and most personally, on coming to the land of Greece after studying with Robert Braidwood and Robert Redfield as well as in classical philology, there was the realisation that the economic, ecological and, to some degree, social underpinnings of the culture could be uncovered through archaeology. (Six years earlier Karl Lehmann had assured me that I neither could nor should contemplate the excavation of a Greek village!) That this was likely to provide contradictions and problems when compared with the literary record (problems compounded by the study of inscriptions, a subject which this volume largely eschews) only encouraged a young man's sceptical and left-leaning bent.

I have indulged in autobiography in order to underline that whereas my own predilections when it comes to actual research are not far from those of Morris and his contemporaries, I am not satisfied with his account of Greek studies in either the past or the present. Perhaps, rootless and socially marginal as I was, I was hoping, unconsciously, to be co-opted by the establishment and therefore began my initiation into the classics. Today when few who come to classics are any more affiliated with the elite than I was fifty years ago, I suggest that the continuing attraction and justification for Greek studies, including Greek archaeology, is that it offers us much of the Western tradition, both establishmentarian and anti-establishmentarian, Christian or anti-Christian or neutral as we wish, while at the same time providing us with the opportunity through archaeology and anthropology (for Morris it would be rather through literary theory though his acquaintance with the anthropological literature is formidable) of questioning and undermining, of appreciating Greece's deep differences from our contemporary world for all its apparent familiarity.

I tend to take for granted the necessity of constant comparison with other cultures, especially with the ancient Near East, and with other phases of Greek history, without making any assumption of superiority (by what standard?) for Classical Greece. In essence, I think the response that Greek studies still elicit from amateurs and professionals alike, when cleaned of the labels of class snobbery and racism, comes from the imaginative power of texts and art and the interconnections that history (through texts and archaeology) enables us to trace. This extends, in my experience, to a world that is becoming increasingly engaged with the West when not already part of it, and yet wants nothing of its religious and political hegemony. Ancient Greece offers common ground, within a diverse society such as contemporary America and between societies.

The papers that follow Morris' critical history all deal with substantial problems and touch for the most part only incidentally on theoretical issues. Generally they might be called 'contextual', while two essays (Hoffmann's and Osborne's) make use of 'currents of study in the psychology of art', both these quotations, as it happens, taken from what our most outspoken champion of traditional classical archaeology sees as desirable new directions (Boardman 1988c: 177). The fragmentation and variety of outlook in all current archaeology, as in postmodern thought in general, stressed by Morris, may mean that there can be convergence and unexpected alliances as well as conflict.

Alongside the opportunities that are being opened up, the larger ambitions reveal some of the constant difficulties in recovering the context and entering into the experience of the individual in antiquity. How, without circular reasoning, can Whitley argue that the Attic elite of the seventh century (unlike other contemporary elites?) 'rationed' the use of Orientalising art and confined it to 'liminal' uses, when non-archaeological history is lacking, when the zealously protected symbolic system is inferred from the art of the previous century, and when the Orientalising art itself comes from domestic as well as funerary contexts? How can Hoffmann link the use of the Sphinx and the family of Kekrops seen on a single vessel by their allusions to initiation, when the characteristic features of initiation appear to be absent from the induction of Athenian ephebes into the citizen body? (For one exploration of the consequences of their absence, see Winkler 1990.) Arafat and Morgan commendably look at Attic exports from the point of view of the receiving cultures of Etruria and northwestern Europe, something that is long overdue in view of the dismissive and incurious attitude to Etruscan culture by archaeologists of Greece (cf. Boardman 1980: 199–200). But while common assumptions are demolished effectively, the reader will come away with agnosticism about the actual social context of transalpine societies and doubt about that of Etruria if the decline of Attic imports can be assigned with equal likelihood, it seems, to (a) a change in sympotic practice, (b) economic decline, (c) the greater security of the elite. While the jolt the authors give to modernist application of the 'core/periphery' model is healthy, I find their conception of the 'core' old-fashioned and simplistic and regret that here I can only be negative and not specific. Osborne's ventures into artistic analysis are stimulating (though I wish he had developed his thoughts on Lucian's pederastic view of the Knidian Aphrodite as seen from the rear) and he places the contrasts between *kouros* and *kore* convincingly in Archaic society. But when marriage is used as the specimen of the changes between Archaic and Classical Athens we are in the end left with the disappearance of aristocratic, international marriages, which could only have affected a tiny fraction of the society. Surely it is the general effacement of aristocratic display from public view in favour of the forms of *polis* art (well suggested by Osborne although the striking ritual of the Nike parapet is overlooked) rather than any change in marriage that occurs. The two papers making use of evidence from archaeological surveys, being more focused and crossing fewer boundaries, bring with them fewer problems along with their positive contributions.

My role as respondent rather than reviewer, I take it, has been neither to applaud blandly nor to try to subvert a worthy enterprise. Appreciation of the methods and issues of anthropological archaeology are necessary for any archaeologist but, as Morris says, that is not enough. One must also become engaged in the particulars of the civilisation on which one is working. In the last analysis I am impressed by the scope and ambition of the archaeologies proposed, and also by the need to change our modes of research and publication. Morris speaks of the trade-offs: more attention to anthropological and historical comparisons and to theory means less to languages, texts, traditional history and the painstaking assembling of minutiae characteristic of traditional classical archaeology. The first, language, has already largely been lost to classical archaeology in America. The difficulties I have with the treatment of history and religion in these papers and the frustrations the writers on survey work have with the nature of their evidence suggest that dialogue and collaboration between different specialists will be needed if these new archaeologies are to produce more than a series of lively position papers.

11
Response: the archaeological aspect

ANTHONY SNODGRASS

To start with the obvious, indeed the hackneyed: who could have imagined, say fifteen years ago, the creation of such a book as this in such a field as classical archaeology? The decade of the 1970s saw most of the authors of these papers completing, or in some cases only just embarking on, their first degrees. Were they already burning to bring about a change in their chosen subject? Perhaps, but I doubt it. That leaves Herbert Hoffmann, Michael Jameson and myself: what are *we* doing here, and what were we doing then? Were our writings and our teaching already pointing our pupils along this new trail? In my own case, I can say that nothing of this kind began to happen until that same decade was well under way, though I would risk doing an injustice to my two friends and colleagues if I associated them with me in this admission. I believe, however, that the same wave of change, at the same juncture, affected all of us, whether we were then in our teens or our forties.

The impetus for that change is commonly said to have come from other disciplines; certainly there was enough ferment in both history and non-classical archaeology at the time. But again I must speak for myself: of the forces operating within academe, it was the feeling of professional isolation from the main intellectual discourse that was the strongest factor – the inherited, hermetic sealing-off of the subject and its content. In this respect, non-classical archaeology, for all its ferment, was of no immediate inspiration: there were few disciplines whose practitioners fitted so uncomfortably into the intellectual milieu of a university. Classical archaeology could at least claim affiliation to a once dominant and still 'respectable' subject.

But in any case I believe that the strongest pressure, as Ian Morris hints at several points in his chapter, came from the external, non-academic world. The feeling of being 'cut off from a recognisable function' is, I suspect, one that first comes home to someone already embarked on a career. In my own case, it has been an increasingly strong feeling, and with it has grown a dissatisfaction with the *status quo* in classical archaeology. The subject had become one for which the contemporary world no longer had obvious uses – or if it had, they were uses in which I wanted no part.

An image comes to mind for all archaeology: in the past generation, its position has come to resemble that of the beautiful actress who wants to undertake serious roles, whereas her public only wishes her to take off her clothes. As often as archaeologists protest that the past of mankind is a serious business, so often does the cry go up, 'Show us your assets! Give us another exhibition called "Treasures of . . ."! Give us the chance to indulge our material appetites, as safely as voyeurs do, by directing them into the distant past!' (The cry is as often raised by the media, on the presumed behalf of the public, as by the public itself.) But so often, too, there are archaeologists more than happy to answer the call. The most traditional branches of the subject, those concerned with the Mediterranean and Egypt, are the readiest to comply, just as they have been the least voluble in the claims to seriousness. Instead, their traditional priorities are ones that in no way conflict with such materialism, and are readily shared by the public: the artefact as fetish, excavation as the means of generating it.

'Yesterday the classic lecture / on the origin of Mankind. But today the struggle.' How firm and how deceptively simple were the old certainties: the object, when it stayed put, was predestined for monographs, corpora and museum shelves; when it travelled, it was 'trade'. Excavation was a rite of passage for the young, a field of *aristeia* for those in mid-career, and a monument for the elderly. And how attractive and stimulating it was to assail these certainties, to call for a new vision of the past. Somehow we have progressed to the point where a book like this can not only emerge, but also (I predict) arouse interest beyond, as well as within, the subject. If it does so, the main reason will surely be because it is on a higher intellectual level than its innumerable predecessors in the established tradition.

I have already admitted, by palpable implication, that Ian Morris is right: analysis of recent intellectual history is vital to the understanding of contemporary practices. By this means we can not only understand the current quest for 'deep meaning and wide relevance', but even take the first small steps towards achieving it. Let me now turn to the specific issues which are raised in the individual papers, and thence to some of the actual arguments used.

The central issue of the first main section of the book – Chs. 2, 3 and 4 – is a kind of analogue for the investigation of our whole subject initiated by Ian Morris in Ch. 1. The question which he asks about classical archaeology as a whole, they apply to painted pottery and sculpture: 'Yes, but what was it *for*? Who was it *for*?' It would take a real die-hard to object to the asking of such questions, though there will be plenty of die-hards who will consider their work unaffected by them. For me, the great advance achieved by James Whitley's paper is to bring Protoattic pottery into the total material culture of its epoch, to bring it into real archaeology. A reviewer of his recent *Style and society in Dark Age Greece* has made the same point about the treatment of the earlier painted pottery covered by that book: Whitley has rescued the material from the art historians. For, make no mistake, the real opponents of the new approach in this chapter are not the pure classicists, looking down their noses at those who use non-literary evidence – in my experience, few classicists can any longer afford such attitudes; nor is it the prehistorians, who will be puzzled but gratified to find tactics similar to their own being employed in 'enemy territory'; no, it is the new art historians who regard the concept of 'total material culture' as a tedious impediment to their own mystic communication with the viewers and users of the pottery.

But Herbert Hoffmann is not like that. His approach here, as often, is to start from a single artefact or a tiny, often aberrant group, but to set them against an intimidatingly grand panorama. Within a bare twenty lines, we have grave-goods evaluated along the lines established by Gordon Childe, and vases dismissed as 'mere symbols'. What differentiates the treatment from most recent art history is precisely, once again, that Hoffmann shows that he knows and cares about the 'total material culture' of Classical Athens (as well as many other aspects of it). One thing that worries me is the apparent friction between two of the assumptions that underlie the paper: the view of painted vases as relatively cheap surrogates for vessels in precious metals, and the view of their decoration as being expressive of ideas sometimes subtle, sometimes grandiose ('the creation of immortality'). Are these two views in fact compatible? Can there be intimations of immortality not only in the 'recollections of early childhood', but in the iconography of the souvenir earthenware ashtray? This last is, I admit, a stupid way in which to re-phrase the question. The answer is that in another culture, *mutatis mutandis*, there could be. Only we must find out a great deal more about the cultural role of the painted pottery in that culture; and this knowledge can only come from more and better archaeology.

Sculpture is, of course, a different matter entirely. The hard economic facts about the carving of life-sized stone statues have not changed much. The documentary evidence for the contexts in which statues were set up in ancient

Athens is not so bad either. It is only the evidence for the contemporary *viewer's* reaction that is in desperately short supply, though some progress has been made with specific categories (portraits, colossal cult-statues). The strength of Robin Osborne's paper is that he is therefore free to hypothesise about the messages that a statue would convey to different groups of viewers, but can at the same time firmly assume that there *was* a message, conscious or unconscious on the part of sculptor and client, but neither trivial nor haphazard: the cost and labour of setting up the statue would ensure that. One of the many reasons for welcoming this paper is that it throws new light on the attraction of Archaic sculpture for our own age. The 'challenge to the viewer' has, I suggest, been getting through to us, without our often realising it.

The papers in the next section return us firmly to the domain of archaeology, *sensu stricto*. As Ian Morris has already said, they are handling the same issues as have been recently preoccupying European prehistorians, especially those working on the Iron Age. I hope that this will start a genuine dialogue between the two groups, surmounting the barriers of terminology and language that have so long prevented this happening. The most important common feature between David Gill's approach and that of Catherine Morgan and Karim Arafat is their shared suspicion of the 'modernising' view of Greek overseas exchange. In traditional classical archaeology, as I admitted on the previous page, 'trade' was a central, uncritical, unanalysed concept; one of the distinctive recent trends in the subject has been the growing dissatisfaction with, often the outright rejection of, that concept. The laws of supply and demand do not cover all cases; 'the market' shrinks to little more than a metaphor; profit is often beside the point. For this enlightenment, as everyone will acknowledge, we are indebted to the Finley school of ancient historians. But it has now acquired another, less desirable significance, as a further feature which divides classical from other archaeology. No such trend of dissatisfaction has taken place there: trade is now taken for granted, now exalted to a yet more dominant role. Even if our emphasis has swung too far in one direction, their contrary one could do with a bit more examination. If this were to be the only lesson which non-classical archaeologists learned from this book, it would still be a flying start.

So to the final section, the papers centred on and inspired by the advance of surface survey in the Greek world. Here, it is hardly necessary to say, it is a lesson that *we* have learned from non-classical archaeology, and put into practice with increasing enthusiasm. Not since stratigraphic excavation began to be adopted in early twentieth-century work in Greece has anything so far-reaching taken place. Greek surveys are becoming, yearly, more intensive, more comprehensive in terms of period coverage, more versatile in employment of ancillary techniques. These developments are still regarded with a mixture of bewilderment and hostility in some quarters, but the undeniable fact is that survey has now progressed, from the prehistoric or geographically peripheral borders of Greek archaeology, to arrive in its most central, strictly 'Classical' core. The papers by Sue Alcock, John Cherry and Jack Davis reflect this fact in an admirable way. They pose a most vigorous challenge, not just to the critics of survey but to the hitherto unconcerned 'neutrals'.

For the informed 'neutral' in Hellenistic studies – let us say a military historian or a student of pastoral poetry – archaeology has been something that could, with impunity, be largely ignored. Sculpture and urban architecture required at least a nodding acquaintance, but not much more. By investigating the changes in the Hellenistic rural landscape, therefore, Sue Alcock is introducing far more of an innovation than the rest of us who have pioneered survey in prehistoric, classical and Roman studies. That may be how survey fits in best to a sequence of investigation: not as a corrective for entrenched views, but as an exploratory start, in the light of which archaeological orthodoxy can grow up for the first time. It will be interesting to see whether the archaeologists accept the life-line that is being thrown to them.

I turn to Chapter 7, whose central theme is a feature which has come to be recognised as a central justification for modern intensive survey. If there were no artefact scatters across the landscape, around and between the known and inferred settlement sites, then intensive survey would become an unreasonably laborious and expensive alternative to mere site location (which is more or less what some of its critics think it is). But why are these artefact scatters there in the first place? Is it *really* possible, the authors ask, that ancient fertilising operations were the prime factor in generating them? No one doubts that manuring took place: the real difficulty is a quantitative one, that of accepting that sherds, tile and occasionally other material could be discarded and embedded in the rubbish heaps at such a rate as to create the density of these materials that we find across the landscape.

It is here that the ethnographic evidence, used to such good effect by the authors as a supplement to the textual information, lets us down. As has often been observed, few if any modern societies match the ancient Greek world in the range and intensity of its uses for ceramics. It is thus easier to calculate the likely rates of production and distribution of manure (though I am awestruck at the ingenuity and thoroughness with which it has been done here) than it is to

offer even a vague estimate of the rate of discard of pottery and tile.

When textual and ethnographic evidence both fall silent, it is not obvious where to turn. How about giving good old archaeology a try? A recent, as yet unpublished study by Bradley Ault of the stone-lined pits, undoubtedly *koprones*, in the yards of Classical houses at Halieis in the southern Argolid, gives us a chance of filling this gap in the calculations. In one of the *koprones*, whose capacity was 5 cu m, Ault counted some 1200 sherds and 900 tile fragments. The tiles may perhaps be explained as having fallen into the pit when the house-roof collapsed, but this will hardly do for the sherds. Let us assume minimum figures throughout. If the pit was full of manure at the time of abandonment (thus giving the lowest density of sherds), we obtain the figure of 240 sherds per cu m. It would be unreasonable to use this as a representative figure, since each time the *kopron* was cleaned out, the manure would be assiduously collected, but not the sherds. The *kopron* did not have a long life and, on the rates of production given in Ch. 7, it may only have been cleared about 100 times. Let us assume that 10% of the sherds fell out on each occasion: that will give *24* rather than 240 per cu m. as the original density. What we are looking for is a quantification of the *rate of inclusion of sherds in manure*; so the special factors operating at Halieis – that other waste from oil-presses was also fed into the *koprones*, or that built *koprones* are most unlikely to have existed in rural locations – are beside the point for our purposes.

We should pay the authors the compliment of adopting wholesale their calculations (table 7.1) of manure production and rate of dressing in the form of fertiliser; and take the example of the relatively impoverished 'Hypothetical household B', along with their 'worst of circumstances', a light dressing of rotted manure at 40 cu m per hectare. The 10 cu m available for this small estate will then cover 0.25 ha, one-eighth of the cultivated land belonging to it. Ten cu m., at 24 sherds per cu m. will give a prediction of 240 spread in one year; over eight years, this density (960 per ha) can be extended over the whole estate. Our evidence relates to the Classical period in southern Greece: a time and place where the picture of the spread of isolated rural sites is at its fullest. On the estimates of some surveys, the typical duration of occupation of these sites might be 150 years, but let us be minimalist again and say eighty years. On an eight-year cycle, the cultivated land of the household will have been covered ten times: this will generate 19,200 sherds over the whole area, or 9600 Classical sherds per ha. For the proportion of these that would be found on the surface, we can refer to the calculations of Dr Peter Reynolds, based on experimentation at the Butser Farm project in Britain and strikingly confirmed when he carried out sampling in

Boeotia in 1991. Assuming a plough-soil depth of 20 cm, he found that each modern ploughing operation was bringing to the surface the remarkably high proportion of 15.9% of the sherds in the plough-soil. The calculation is thus completed: the prediction will be that 1526 sherds per ha, or 15.26 per 100 cu m, or 0.153 per sq m, will be visible on the surface wherever both fertilisation in the Classical period and ploughing in the current year have taken place.

This figure is high for a 'site-halo' or any other off-site location; even if a further proportion of the sherds were discarded or recycled within the site itself, the residue would still form a respectable 'halo' level. There could be challenges to these calculations – for instance, on the grounds that rural buildings might be less well endowed with pottery than urban houses – but I do not think that they could change the order of magnitude of the result. What it suggests is that the 'manuring hypothesis' is, after all, powerful enough to explain the phenomena virtually unaided. On a broader front, it reminds us that the employment and consumption of ceramics in Classical Greece may have taken place at a level of intensity that we cannot readily imagine – a conclusion that might not come as a surprise to the exponents of traditional classical archaeology.

I hope, however, that surprise will be the main reaction among the varied groups of readers into whose hands this book falls: surprise that writing in this subject can interest a new audience without boring the old; surprise at the outward-looking attitudes shown in much of that writing; surprise, if nothing else, at the length and scope of the bibliography that follows.

I would like to thank Bradley Ault for generously agreeing to my use of his still unpublished data (p. 199). For a summary of his paper, see *American Journal of Archaeology* 97 (1993) 324–5.

Bibliography

Abbott, A. 1988. *The system of professions*. Chicago: University of Chicago Press.

Abramson, H. 1979. 'A hero shrine for Phrontis at Sounion', *California Studies in Classical Antiquity* 12: 1–19.

Ackerman, R. 1971. 'Some letters of the Cambridge Ritualists', *Greek, Roman and Byzantine Studies* 12: 113–36.

　1972. 'Jane Ellen Harrison: the early work', *Greek, Roman and Byzantine Studies* 13: 209–30.

　1991. 'The Cambridge Group: origins and composition', in Calder 1991: 1–19.

Actes. 1979. Actes de la table ronde d'Aix-en-Provence. *Le bucchero nero étrusque et sa diffusion en Gaule méridionale*. Brussels: Collection Latomus 160.

Adams, R. McC. 1965. *Land behind Baghdad: a history of settlement on the Diyala plain*. Chicago: University of Chicago Press.

　1981. *Heartland of cities*. Chicago: University of Chicago Press.

Adams, R. McC. and Nissen, H. J. 1972. *The Uruk countryside*. Chicago: University of Chicago Press.

Adams, R. McC., Parr H., Ibrahim, M. and Al-Mughannum, A. 1977. 'Saudi Arabian archaeological reconnaissance 1976', *Atlal* 1: 21–40.

Adcock, F. E. 1927. 'The breakdown of the Thirty Years Peace, 445–431 BC', in J. D. Bury, S. A. Cook and F. E. Adcock, eds., *Cambridge ancient history* V: *Athens 478–401 BC*: 165–92. Cambridge: Cambridge University Press.

Adovasio, J. M., Fry, G. F., Gunn J. D. and Maslowski, R. F. 1975. 'Prehistoric and historic settlement patterns in Western Cyprus', *World Archaeology* 6: 339–64.

　1978. 'Prehistoric and historic settlement patterns in Western Cyprus: an overview', *Report of the Department of Antiquities, Cyprus*: 39–57.

Africa, T. 1991. 'Aunt Glegg among the dons or Jane Harrison at her word', in Calder 1991: 21–35.

Ahlberg, G. 1971a. *Fighting on land and sea in Greek Geometric art*. Stockholm: Skrifter utgivna i svenska institutet i Athen.

　1971b. *Prothesis and ekphora in Greek Geometric art*. Göteborg: Studies in Mediterranean Archaeology 32.

al-Khalifa, Shaika Haya Ali and Rice, M., eds. 1986. *Bahrain through the ages: the archaeology*. London: Kegan Paul International.

al-Wohaibi, F. 1980. *Studio storico-archeologico dello costa occidentale del Golfo Arabico in età ellenistica*. Rome: L'Erma di Bretschneider.

Alcock, S. E. 1989a. 'Archaeology and imperialism: Roman expansion and the Greek city', *Journal of Mediterranean Archaeology* 2: 87–135.

　1989b. 'Roman imperialism in the Greek landscape', *Journal of Roman Archaeology* 2: 5–34.

　1991. 'Urban survey and the polis of Phlius', *Hesperia* 60: 421–63.

　1993. *Graecia capta: an archaeological and historical study of Roman Greece*. Cambridge: Cambridge University Press.

Alexander, G. 1982. *The prelude to the Truman Doctrine: British policy in Greece, 1944–1947*. Oxford: Oxford University Press.

Alexandri, O. 1968. 'Nyterini anaskaphi skammatos kata mikos tis Odou Kriezi', *Athens Annals of Archaeology* 1: 20–30.

Alfieri, N. and Arias, P. 1958. *Spina*. Munich: Hirmer Verlag.

Alimentazione. 1987. *L'alimentazione del mondo antico*. Rome: Instituto poligrafico e zecca dello stato.

Alonso-Nuñez, J.-M. 1987. 'Herodotos on the far West', *L'Antiquité Classique* 56: 241–9.

Amin, S. 1989. *Eurocentrism*. New York: Monthly Review.

Ammerman, A. J. 1985. 'Plow-zone experiments in Calabria, Italy', *Journal of Field Archaeology* 12: 33–40.

Amouretti, M.-C. 1986. *Le pain et l'huile dans la Grèce antique*. Paris: Les Belles Lettres.

Anderson, B. 1991. *Imagined communities*. 2nd edn. London: Verso.

Anderson, P. 1974. *Passages from antiquity to feudalism*. London: Verso.

　1983. *In the tracks of historical materialism*. Chicago: University of Chicago Press.

Andreae, B. 1988. *Laokoon und die Gründung Roms*. Mainz: Zabern.

Andreyev, V. N. 1974. 'Some aspects of agrarian conditions in Attica in the 5th to 3rd centuries BC', *Eirene* 12: 5–46.

Angelomatis-Tsougarakis, H. 1991. *The eve of the Greek revival*. London: Routledge.

Ankersmit, F. 1989. 'Historiography and postmodernism', *History and Theory* 28: 137–53.

Appadurai, A. 1986a. 'Introduction: commodities and the politics of value', in Appadurai 1986b: 3–63.

Appadurai, A., ed. 1986b. *The social life of things*. Cambridge: Cambridge University Press.

Applebaum, S. 1977. 'Judaea as a Roman province', *Aufstieg und Niedergang der römischen Welt* II.8: 355–96.

1986. 'The settlement pattern of Western Samaria from Hellenistic to Byzantine times: a historical commentary', in Dar 1986: 257–313.

Applebaum, S., Dar, S. and Safrai, Z. 1978. 'The towers of Samaria', *Palestine Exploration Quarterly*: 91–100.

Arafat, K. 1990a. *Classical Zeus*. Oxford: Clarendon Press.

1990b. 'Fact and artefact: texts and archaeology', *Hermathena*: 45–67.

Arafat, K. and Morgan, C. 1989. 'Pots and potters in classical Athens and Corinth: a review', *Oxford Journal of Archaeology* 8: 311–46.

Arav, R. 1989. *Hellenistic Palestine*. Oxford: British Archaeological Reports International Series 485.

Arcelin-Pradelle, C. 1984. *La céramique grise monochrome en Provence*. Paris: *Revue Archéologique de Narbonnaise* supp. 10.

Arcelin-Pradelle, C., Dedet B. and Py, M. 1982. 'La céramique grise monochrome en Languedoc centrale', *Revue Archéologique de Narbonnaise* 15: 19–67.

Arnheim, R. 1969. *Visual thinking*. Berkeley: University of California Press.

Arnold, B. 1988. 'Slavery in late prehistoric Europe', in Gibson and Geselowitz 1988: 179–92.

1990. 'The past as propaganda: totalitarian archaeology in Nazi Germany', *Antiquity* 64: 464–78.

Arnold, D. 1985. *Ceramic theory and cultural process*. Cambridge: Cambridge University Press.

Aschenbrenner, S. 1972. 'A contemporary community', in McDonald and Rapp 1972: 47–63.

1976. 'Karpofora: reluctant farmers on a fertile land', in Dimen and Fridel 1976: 207–21.

Astill, G. 1988. 'Fields', in G. Astill and A. Grant, eds., *The countryside of medieval England*: 62–85. Oxford: Blackwell.

Athanassopoulos, E. 1992. 'Intensive survey and medieval settlement: the case of Nemea', *American Journal of Archaeology* 96: 366.

'Athenian'. 1972. *Inside the Colonels' Greece*. London: Chatto and Windus.

Austin, M. M. 1970. *Greece and Egypt in the Archaic age*. Cambridge: Cambridge Philological Society supp. vol. 2.

1981. *The Hellenistic world*. Cambridge: Cambridge University Press.

Baeumer, M. L. 1986. 'Klassizität und republikanische Freiheit in der ausserdeutschen Winckelmann-Rezeption des späten 18. Jahrhunderts', in Gaehtgens 1986: 195–219.

Baglione, M. P. 1988. 'Quelques données sur les plus récentes fouilles de Pyrgi', in Christiansen and Melander 1988: 17–24.

Bagnall, R. 1976. *The administration of Ptolemaic possessions outside Egypt*. Leiden: Brill.

Baird, D. 1984. 'Survey in the Dhrousha area of W. Cyprus', *Levant* 14: 55–65.

1985. 'Survey in Peyia village territory, Paphos, 1983', *Report of the Department of Antiquities, Cyprus*: 340–9.

Baker, K., ed. 1987. *University of Chicago readings in western civilization* 7: *The Old Regime and the French Revolution*. Chicago: University of Chicago Press.

Ball, W., Tucker D. and Wilkinson, T. J. 1989. 'The Tell al-Hawa project: archaeological investigations in the North Jazira 1986–87', *Iraq* 51: 1–66.

Bammer, A. 1989. 'Zur Archäologie von griechischen Mythen und Ritualen', in H. C. Ehalt, ed., *Volksfrömmigkeit*: 29–65. Vienna: Böhlau Verlag.

Banning, E. and Fawcett, C. 1983. 'Man–land relationships in the ancient Wadi Ziqlab: report of the 1981 survey', *Annual of the Department of Antiquities of Jordan* 27: 291–309.

Bapty, I. and Yates, T., eds. 1990. *Archaeology after structuralism: post-structuralism and the practice of archaeology*. London: Routledge.

Barker, G. 1985. *Prehistoric farming in Europe*. Cambridge: Cambridge University Press.

1988. 'Archaeology and the Etruscan countryside', *Antiquity* 62: 772–85.

Barnes, B. 1977. *T. S. Kuhn and social science*. London: Methuen.

Bartel, B. 1985. 'Comparative historical archaeology and archaeological theory', in S. Dyson, ed., *Comparative studies in the archaeology of colonialism*: 8–37. Oxford: British Archaeological Reports International Series 233.

Barthes, R. 1975. *S/Z*. New York: Hill and Wang.

Baticle, Y. 1974. *L'élevage ovin days les pays européens de la Méditerranée occidentale*. Paris: Les Belles Lettres.

Bayly, C. A. 1986. 'The origins of swadeshi (home industry): cloth and Indian society 1700–1930', in Appadurai 1986b: 283-321.

Bazant, J. 1991. 'Otto Jahn's "Griechische Kunstgeschichte" today', in W. M. Calder III, H. Cancik and B. Kytzler, eds., *Otto Jahn (1813–1868)*: 11–28. Stuttgart: Steiner.

Bean, G. 1979. *Aegean Turkey*. London: Murray.

Beard, M. 1991. 'Adopting an approach', in Rasmussen and Spivey 1991: 12–35.

Beaton, R. 1988. 'Romanticism in Greece', in R. Porter and M. Teich, eds., *Romanticism in national context*: 92–108. Cambridge: Cambridge University Press.

Beazley, J. D. 1918. *Attic red-figured vases in American museums*. Cambridge, MA: Harvard University Press.

1926. 'Early Greek art', in J. D. Bury, S. A. Cook and F. E. Adcock, eds., *Cambridge ancient history* IV: *The Persian empire and the west*: 579–600.

1945.'The Brygos tomb at Capua', *American Journal of Archaeology* 49: 153–8.

1951. *The development of Attic black-figure*. Oxford: Clarendon Press. Reissued Berkeley: University of California Press, 1986. Ed. D. von Bothmer and M. B. Moore.

1956. *Attic black-figure vase painters*. Oxford: Clarendon Press

1963. *Attic red-figure vast painters*. 2nd edn. 2 vols. Oxford: Clarendon Press.

1971. *Paralipomena*. Oxford: Clarendon Press.

1989. *Greek vases: lectures by J. D. Beazley*. Ed. D. C. Kurtz. Oxford: Oxford University Press.

Becker, E. 1973. *The denial of death*. New York: Free Press.

Bellon, C., Burnouf, J. and Martin, J.-M. 1986. 'Premiers résultats des fouilles sur le site protohistorique de Gorge-de-Loup (Vaise, Lyon, Rhône)', *Revue Archéologique de l'Est et du Centre Est* 37: 247–51.

Benario, H. W. 1989. 'The APA as a North American organization', in Culham *et al.* 1989: 285–93.

Bennet, J. 1990. 'Knossos in context: comparative perspectives on the Linear B administration of LM II–III Crete', *American Journal of Archaeology* 94: 291–309.

Bénoit, F. 1965. *Recherches sur l'hellénisation du midi de la Gaule*. Aix-en-Provence: Annales de la Faculté des Lettres 43.

Benson, J. L. 1970. *Horse, bird and man*. Amherst: University of Massachusetts Press.

Bérard, C. 1989a. 'The order of women', in Bérard 1989b: 89–107.

Bérard, C., ed. 1989b. *The city of images*. Princeton: Princeton University Press.

Bérard, C. and Bron, C. 1986. 'Bacchos au cœur de la cité', *Collection de l'Ecole Française de Rome* 89: 13–30.

1989. 'Satyric revels', in Bérard 1989b: 131–49.

Berger, J. 1972. *Ways of seeing*. Harmondsworth: Penguin.

Berkhofer, R. F. 1988. 'The challenge of poetics to (normal) historical practice', *Poetics Today* 9: 435–52.

Berlin, I. 1979. *Against the current*. Oxford: Oxford University Press.

Bernal, M. 1987. *Black Athena* I: *The fabrication of ancient Greece, 1785–1985*. New Brunswick, NJ: Rutgers University Press.

1989a. '*Black Athena* and the APA', in Peradotto and Levine 1989: 17–38.

1989b. 'Classics in crisis: an outsider's view in', in Culham *et al.* 1989: 67–74.

1990. 'Responses to critical reviews of *Black Athena*', *Journal of Mediterranean Archaeology* 3: 111–37.

1991. *Black Athena* II: *The archaeological and documentary evidence*. New Brunswick, NJ: Rutgers University Press.

Bernard, P. 1967. 'Aï Khanum on the Oxus: a Hellenistic city in central Asia', *Proceedings of the British Academy* 53: 71–95.

1976. 'Les traditions orientales dans l'architecture gréco-bactrienne', *Journal Asiatique* 264: 245–75.

1982. 'An ancient Greek city in central Asia', *Scientific American* 246: 148–59.

Bernstein, R. 1983. *Beyond objectivity and relativism: science, hermeneutics and praxis*. Philadelphia: University of Pennsylvania Press.

Bernstein, R., ed. 1985. *Habermas and modernity*. Cambridge, MA: MIT Press.

Bessac, J.-C. and Bouloumié, B. 1985. 'Les stèles de Glanum et de Sainte-Blaise et les sanctuaires pré-romaines du midi de la Gaule', *Revue Archéologique de Narbonnaise* 18: 127–87.

Betancourt, P. 1985. *The history of Minoan pottery*. Princeton: Princeton University Press.

Betterton, R. 1987. *Looking on: images of femininity in visual arts and media*. London: Pandora.

Bianchi Bandinelli, R. 1972. 'Osservazione sulle statue acroteriali di Poggio Civitate (Murlo)', *Dialoghi di Archeologia* 6: 236–47.

Bibby, G. 1970. *Looking for Dilmun*. Harmondsworth: Penguin.

Bickerman, E. 1988. *The Jews in the Greek age*. Cambridge, MA: Harvard University Press.

Biers, W. 1992. *Art, artefacts and chronology: classical archaeology*. London: Routledge.

Biersack, A. 1989. 'Local knowledge, local history: Geertz and beyond', in Hunt 1989b: 72–96.

Bikerman, E. 1939. 'La cité grecque dans les monarchies hellénistiques', *Revue de Philologie* 65: 335–49.

Binford, L. R. 1962. 'Archaeology as anthropology', *American Antiquity* 28: 217–25, reprinted in Binford 1972: 20-32.

1964. 'A consideration of archaeological research design', *American Antiquity* 29: 425–41.

1972. *An archaeological perspective.* New York: Academic Press.

1982. 'Objectivity-explanation-archeology 1981', in A. C. Renfrew, M. J. Rowlands and B. Segraves, eds., *Theory and explanation in archaeology*: 125–38. New York: Academic Press.

1983. *In pursuit of the past.* London: Thames and Hudson.

1987. 'Data, relativism and archaeological science', *Man* 22: 391-404.

1989. 'The "New Archaeology", then and now', in Lamberg-Karlovsky 1989b: 50–62.

Binford, L. R. and Sabloff, J. 1982. 'Paradigms, systematics and archeology', *Journal of Anthropological Research* 3: 137–53.

Binford, S. R. and Binford, L. R., eds. 1968. *New perspectives in archaeology.* New York: Academic Press.

Bingen, J. *et al.* 1965a. 'Thorikos: rapport préliminaire sur la première campagne de fouille', *L'Antiquité Classique* 34: 1–46.

1965b. *Thorikos I, 1963.* Brussels: Comité des fouilles belges en Grèce.

1967a. *Thorikos II, 1964.* Brussels: Comité des fouilles belges en Grèce.

1967b. *Thorikos III, 1965.* Brussels: Comité des fouilles belges en Grèce.

1969. *Thorikos IV, 1966/7.* Brussels: Comité des fouilles belges en Grèce.

1978. *Thorikos VII, 1970/1.* Brussels: Comité des fouilles belges en Grèce.

1984. *Thorikos VIII, 1972/6.* Brussels: Comité des fouilles belges en Grèce.

Bintliff, J. L. 1985. 'The Boeotia survey', in Macready and Thompson 1985: 196–216.

1986. 'Archaeology at the interface: an historical perspective', in Bintliff and Gaffney 1986: 4–31.

Bintliff, J. L., ed. 1991. *The Annales School and archaeology.* Leicester: Leicester University Press.

Bintliff, J. and Gaffney, C. F., eds. 1986. *Archaeology at the interface.* Oxford: British Archaeological Reports International Series 300.

1988. 'The Ager Pharensis/Hvar Project 1987', in J. C. Chapman, J. Bintliff, V. Gaffney and B. Slapsak, eds., *Recent developments in Yugoslav archaeology*:

151–75. Oxford: British Archaeological Reports International Series 431.

Bintliff, J. L. and Snodgrass, A. M. 1985. 'The Cambridge/Bradford Boeotia Expedition: the first four years', *Journal of Field Archaeology* 12: 123–61.

1988a. 'Mediterranean survey and the city', *Antiquity* 62: 57–71.

1988b. 'Off-site pottery distributions: a regional and interregional perspective', *Current Anthropology* 29: 506–13.

Bittel, K. 1980. 'The German perspective and the German Archaeological Institute', *American Journal of Archaeology* 84: 271–7.

Blackman, D. J. and Branigan, K. 1975. 'An archaeological survey on the south coast of Crete between Ayiofarango and Chrisostomou', *Annual of the British School at Athens* 70: 17–36.

1977. 'An archaeological survey of the lower catchment of the Ayiofarango valley', *Annual of the British School at Athens* 72: 13–84.

Blakeway, A. 1933. 'Prolegomena to the study of Greek commerce with Italy, Sicily and France in the eighth and seventh centuries BC', *Annual of the British School at Athens* 33: 170–208.

Bloch, R. 1986. 'Réflexions sur le destin et la divination haruspicionale en Grèce et en Etrurie', in *Iconographie classique et identités régionales*: 77–85. Paris: *Bulletin de Correspondance Hellénique* supp. 14.

Blondé, F. 1978. 'Two fenestrated stands', in Bingen *et al.* 1978: 111–21.

Bloom, A. 1987. *The closing of the American mind.* New York: Simon and Schuster.

Boardman, J. 1956. 'Chian and Naucratite', *Annual of the British School at Athens* 51: 55–62.

1959. 'Greek potters at Al Mina?', *Anatolian Studies* 9: 163–9.

1974. *Athenian black figure vases: a handbook.* London: Thames and Hudson.

1975. *Attic red figure vases: the Archaic period: a handbook.* London: Thames and Hudson.

1979. 'The Athenian pottery trade. The classical period', *Expedition* 21: 33–9.

1980. *The Greeks overseas.* 3rd edn. London: Thames and Hudson.

1982. 'Heracles, Theseus and Amazons', in D. Kurtz and B. Sparkes, eds., *The eye of Greece*: 1–28. Cambridge: Cambridge University Press.

1984. 'Image and politics in sixth-century Athens', in Brijder 1984: 239–47.

1987. 'Silver is white', *Revue Archéologique*: 279–95.

1988a. 'Trade in Greek decorated pottery', *Oxford Journal of Archaeology* 7: 27–33.

1988b. 'The trade figures', *Oxford Journal of Archaeology* 7: 371–3.

1988c. 'Classical archaeology: whence and whither?', *Antiquity* 62: 795–7.

1989. *Attic red figure vases: the Classical period: a handbook*. London: Thames and Hudson.

1990. 'Al Mina and history', *Oxford Journal of Archaeology* 9: 169–90.

Boardman, J. and Hayes, J. W. 1966. *Excavations at Tocra 1963–1965: the Archaic deposits* I. London: British School at Athens supp. vol. 4.

Boardman, J. and Schweitzer, F. 1973. 'Clay analyses of Greek pottery', *Annual of the British School at Athens* 68: 267–83.

Boegehold, A. 1987. 'The time of the Amasis Painter', in von Bothmer 1987b: 15–32.

Bogue, A. 1986. 'Systematic revisionism and a generation of ferment in American history', *Journal of Contemporary History* 21: 1–17.

Böhlau, J. 1887. 'Frühattischen Vasen', *Jahrbuch des deutschen archäologischen Instituts* 2: 33–66.

Böhner, K. 1981. 'Ludwig Lindenschmit and the three-age system', in Daniel 1981b: 120–6.

Boitani, F. 1985. 'Cenni sulla distribuzione delle anfore da trasporto archaiche nelle necropoli dell'Etruria meridionale', in Cristofani and Pelagatti 1985: 23–6.

Bolgar, R. R. 1979a. 'Classical influences in the social, political and educational thought of Thomas and Matthew Arnold', in Bolgar 1979b: 327–88.

Bolgar, R. R., ed. 1979b. *Classical influences on western thought AD 1650–1870*. Cambridge: Cambridge University Press.

Bommelaer, J. F. 1972. 'Nouveaux documents de céramique protoargienne', *Bulletin de Correspondance Hellénique* 96: 229–51.

Bommeljé, S. and Doorn, P., eds. 1987. *Aetolia and the Aetolians*. Utrecht: Parnassus Press.

Borbein, A. H. 1986. 'Winckelmann und die klassische Archäologie', in Gaehtgens 1986: 289–99.

Boucharlat, R. 1984. 'Les périodes pré-islamiques récentes aux Emirates Arabes Unis', in Boucharlat and Salles 1984: 189–99.

1986. 'Some notes about Qal'at al-Bahrain during the Hellenistic period', in al-Khalifa and Rice 1986: 435–44.

Boucharlat, R. and Salles, J.-F. 1981. 'The history and archaeology of the Gulf from the fifth century BC to the secenth century AD: a review of the evidence', *Proceedings of the Seminar for Arabian Studies* 11: 65–94.

Boucharlat, R. and Salles, J.-F., eds. 1984. *Arabie orientale. Mésopotamie et Iran méridionale: de l'âge du fer au début de la période islamique*. Paris: Editions Recherche sur les civilisations.

Bouloumié, B. 1982. 'Le bucchero nero d'Etrurie', *Latomus* 41: 773–84.

1985. 'Les vases de bronzes étrusques et leur diffusion hors d'Italie', in Cristofani and Pelagatti 1985: 167–78.

1987. 'Le rôle des étrusques dans la diffusion des produits étrusques et grecs en milieu préceltique et celtique', in F. Fischer, B. Bouloumié and C. Lagrand, eds., *Hallstatt-Studien/Etudes halstattiennes*: 20–1, 34–41. Weinheim: VCH.

Bound, M. 1985. 'Una nave mercantile di età arcaica all'isola del Giglio', in Cristofani and Pelagatti 1985: 65–70.

Bourdieu, P. 1977. *Outline of a theory of practice*. Cambridge: Cambridge University Press.

1988. *Homo academicus*. Stanford: Stanford University Press.

Bowden, H. 1991. 'The chronology of Greek painted pottery', *Hephaistos* 10: 49–59.

Bowen, H. C. 1961. *Ancient fields*. London: British Association for the Advancement of Science.

Bowen, J. 1975. *A history of western education* II. New York: St Martin's Press.

1989. 'Education, ideology and the ruling class', in G. W. Clarke 1989: 161–86.

Bowersock, G. 1986. 'Tylos and Tyre', in al-Khalifa and Rice 1986: 399–406.

Bowler, P. J. 1989. *The invention of progress*. Oxford: Basil Blackwell.

Bracken, C. P. 1975. *Antiquities acquired*. North Pomfret, VT: David and Charles.

Bradley, R. 1986. 'Modernist fantasies in prehistory', *Man* 21: 747–8.

1987. 'Against objectivity', in C. Gaffney and V. Gaffney, eds., *Pragmatic archaeology: theory in crisis?*: 115–19. Oxford: British Archaeological Reports 167.

Brandt, R. 1986. '" . . . ist endlich eine edle Einfalt, une eine stille Grösse . . . "', in Gaehtgens 1986: 41–53.

Brann, E. 1961. 'Protoattic well groups from the Agora', *Hesperia* 30: 305–79.

1962. *The Athenian Agora* VIII: *Late Geometric and Protoattic pottery*. Princeton: American School of Classical Studies.

Braudel, F. 1972. *The Mediterranean and the Mediterranean world at the time of Philip II*. Glasgow: Fontana.

Bravo, B. 1968. *Philosophie, histoire, philosophie de l'histoire: étude sur J. G. Droysen, historien de l'antiquité.* Warsaw: Polskij Ajkademii Nauk.

    1983. 'Le commerce des céréales chez les grecs de l'époque archaïque', in Garnsey and Whittaker 1983: 17–29.

Brekis, S. L. 1984. *To 1848 stin Ellada.* Athens: Hermes.

Bremmer, J. 1984. 'Greek maenadism reconsidered', *Zeitschrift für Papyrologie und Epigraphik* 55: 267–86.

Briant, P. 1982. *Rois, tribus et paysans.* Paris: Les Belles Lettres.

    1984. *L'Asie centrale et les royaumes proche-orientaux du premier millénaire (c. VIIIe–IVe siècles avant notre ère).* Paris: Editions Recherche sur les civilisations.

Brijder, H. A. G., ed. 1984. *Ancient Greek and related pottery.* Amsterdam: Allard Pierson Series 5.

    1988. 'The shapes of Etruscan bronze kantharoi from the seventh century BC and the earliest Athenian black figure kantharoi', *Babesch* 63: 103–14.

Brinkman, J. A. 1984. 'Settlement surveys and documentary evidence: regional variation and secular trends in Mesopotamian demography', *Journal of Near Eastern Studies* 43: 169–80.

Brokaw, C. 1963. 'Concurrent styles in Late Geometric and Early Protoattic vase painting', *Mitteilungen des Deutschen Archäologischen Instituts, Athenische Abteilung* 78: 68–73.

Brouskari, M. 1979. *Apo to Athinaiko kerameiko tou 8ou. p. Chr. aiona.* Athens: I en Athinais Arkhaiologiki Etaireia.

Brown, B. and Cousins, M. 1986. 'The linguistic fault: the case of Foucault's archaeology', in M. Gane, ed., *Towards a critique of Foucault*: 33–60. London: Routledge.

Browning, R. 1983. 'The continuity of Hellenism in the Byzantine world: appearance or reality?', in T. Winfrith and P. Murray, eds., *Greece old and new*: 111–28. New York: St Martin's Press.

Bruford, W. H. 1962. *Culture and society in classical Weimar, 1775–1806.* Cambridge: Cambridge University Press.

    1975. *The German tradition of self-cultivation: 'Bildung' from Humboldt to Thomas Mann.* Cambridge: Cambridge University Press.

Brulé, P. 1987. *La fille d'Athènes.* Paris: Annales littéraires de l'université de Besançon 363.

Brun, P. 1987. *Princes et princesses de la celtique: le premier âge du fer (850–450 av. J.C.).* Paris: Errance.

Bruneau, Ph. 1979. 'Deliaca (III)', *Bulletin de Correspondance Hellénique* 103: 83–107.

Bryer, A. 1986. 'Byzantine agricultural implements', *Annual of the British School at Athens* 81: 45–80.

Bryson, N. 1984. *Tradition and desire: from David to Delacroix.* Cambridge: Cambridge University Press.

Buck, C. D. 1955. *The Greek dialects.* Chicago: University of Chicago Press.

Buck, C. E., Cavanagh, W. G. and Litton, C. D. 1988. 'The spatial analysis of site phosphate data', in S. P. Q. Rahtz, ed., *Computer and quantitative methods in archaeology, 1988*: 151–60. Oxford: British Archaeological Reports International Series 446.

Buck, R. J. 1983. *Agriculture and agricultural practice in Roman law.* (*Historia* Einzelschrift 45). Wiesbaden: Franz Steiner.

Bullock, A. W. 1985. *Callimachus: the fifth hymn.* Cambridge: Cambridge University Press.

Burford Cooper, A. 1977/8. 'The family farm in Greece', *Classical Journal* 73: 162–75.

Burkert, W. 1966. 'Kekropidensage und Arrhephorie', *Hermes* 94: 1–25.

    1985. *Greek religion.* Berkeley: University of California Press.

    1987. *Ancient mystery cults.* Cambridge, MA: Harvard University Press.

Burr, D. 1933. 'A Geometric house and a Proto-attic votive deposit', *Hesperia* 2: 542–640.

Bury, J. B. and Meiggs, R. 1975. *A history of Greece to the death of Alexander.* 4th edn. London: Macmillan.

Butler, E. M. 1935. *The tyranny of Greece over Germany.* Cambridge: Cambridge University Press.

Calder, W. M. III. 1984. *Studies in the modern history of classical scholarship.* Naples: Jovene Editore.

Calder, W. M. III, ed. 1991. *The Cambridge Ritualists reconsidered.* Atlanta: *Illinois Classical Studies* supp. vol. 2.

Calder, W. M. III and Traill, D. A. 1986. *Myth, scandal and history.* Detroit: Wayne State University Press.

Callinicos, A. 1990. 'Reactionary postmodernism?', in R. Boyne and A. Rattansi, eds., *Postmodernism and society*: 97–118. New York: St Martin's Press.

Callipolitis-Feytmans, D. 1965. *Les 'louteria' attiques.* Athens: I en Athinais Arkhaiologiki Etaireia.

Camp, J. McK. 1979. 'A drought in the late eighth century BC', *Hesperia* 48: 397–411.

Camporeale, G. 1985. 'La cultura dei "principi"', in Cristofani 1985: 79–84.

    1987. 'La danza armata in Etruria', *Mélanges de l'Ecole Française de Rome: Antiquités* 99: 11–42.

Canciani, G. 1978. 'Lydos der Sklave?', *Antike Kunst* 21: 17–22.

Cannon, A. 1989. 'The historical dimension in mortuary

expressions of status and sentiment', *Current Anthropology* 30: 437–58.

Capps, E. 1932. 'Foreword', *Hesperia* 2: 89–95.

Carpenter, R. 1960. *Greek sculpture*. Chicago: University of Chicago Press.

Carpenter, T. H. 1983. 'On the dating of the Tyrrhenian group', *Oxford Journal of Archaeology* 2: 279–93.

1984. 'The Tyrrhenian group: problems of provenance', *Oxford Journal of Archaeology* 3: 45–56.

1989. *Beazley addenda*. 2nd edn. Oxford: Oxford University Press.

Cartledge, P. A. 1983. '"Trade and politics" revisited', in Garnsey *et al.* 1983: 1–15.

1986. 'A new classical archaeology?', *Times Literary Supplement*, 12 September: 1011–12.

1990. 'Herodotus and "the other": a meditation on empire', *Echos du Monde Classique/Classical Views* 34: 27–40.

Casson, S. 1938. 'The modern pottery trade in the Aegean', *Antiquity* 12: 463–73.

Catling, H. W. 1988. 'Archaeology in Greece, 1987–88', *Archaeological Reports* 34: 1–85.

1989. 'Archaeology in Greece, 1988–89', *Archaeological Reports* 35: 3–116.

Cavanagh, W. G. and Crouwel, J. H. 1988. 'The Lakonia survey', *Lakonikai Spoudai* 9: 77–88.

Cavanagh, W. G., Hirst, S. and Litton, C. 1988. 'Soil phosphate, site boundaries, and change-point analysis', *Journal of Field Archaeology* 15: 67–83.

Champion, S. n.d. 'A multiplicity of models, or how the Iron Age came to mean all things to all people'. Unpublished paper.

Champion, T. 1986. Review of P. S. Wells 1984, *Man* 21: 554.

1987. 'The European Iron Age: assessing the state of the art', *Scottish Archaeological Review* 4: 98–108.

Champion, T., ed. 1989. *Centre and periphery: comparative studies in archaeology*. London: Unwin Hyman.

Champion, T. and Champion S. 1986. 'Peer polity interaction and the European Iron Age', in Renfrew and Cherry 1986: 59–68.

Champion, T., Gamble, C., Shennan, S. and Whittle, A. 1984. *Prehistoric Europe*. New York: Academic Press.

Chang, C. and Koster, H. A. 1986. 'Beyond bones: toward an archaeology of pastoralism', in M. Schiffer, ed., *Advances in Archaeological Method and Theory* 9: 97–148. New York: Academic Press.

Charbonneaux, J., Martin R. and Villard, F. 1972. *Classical Greek art*. New York: Braziller.

Cherry, J. F. 1981. 'Pattern and process in the earliest colonization of the Mediterranean islands', *Proceedings of the Prehistoric Society* 47: 41–68.

1982. 'A preliminary definition of site distribution in Melos', in Renfrew and Wagstaff 1982: 10–23.

1983. 'Frogs round the pond: perspectives on current archaeological survey projects in the Mediterranean region', in Keller and Rupp 1983: 375–416.

1984. 'Commonsense in Mediterranean survey?', *Journal of Field Archaeology* 11: 117–20.

1986. 'The "New Wave" of Greek surveys: problems and prospects'. Unpublished paper.

1988. 'Pastoralism and the role of animals in the pre- and protohistorical economies of the Aegean', in Whittaker 1988: 6–34.

Cherry, J. F. and Davis, J. L. 1988. 'High-density distributional archaeology: a Mediterranean perspective'. Unpublished paper.

Cherry, J. F., Davis, J. L. and Mantzourani, E. 1991. *Landscape archaeology as long-term history: northern Keos in the Cycladic islands from earliest settlement to modern times*. Los Angeles: UCLA Institute of Archaeology (Monumenta Archaeologica 16).

Cherry, J. F., Davis, J. L., Demitrack, A., Mantzourani, E., Strasser, T. F. and Talalay, L. E. 1988. 'Archaeological survey in an artifact-rich landscape: a Middle Neolithic example from Nemea, Greece', *American Journal of Archaeology* 92: 159–76.

Childe, V. G. 1945. 'Directional changes in funerary practices during 50,000 years', *Man* 45: 13–19.

Chisholm, M. 1968. *Rural settlement and land use*. London: Hutchinson.

Christenson, A. L., ed. 1989. *Tracing archaeology's past*. Carbondale: Southern Illinois University Press.

Christiansen, J. and Melander, T., eds. 1988. *Ancient Greek and related pottery*. Copenhagen: Ny Carlsberg Glypotek and Thorvaldsens Museum.

Christiansen, R. 1988. *Romantic affinities: portraits from an age, 1780–1830*. London: Methuen.

Clark, C. and Haswell, M. 1970. *The economics of subsistence agriculture*. 4th edn. London: Macmillan.

Clark, K. 1956. *The nude*. New York: Pantheon.

Clark, V. A. 1987. 'The desert survey', in S. T. Parker 1987: 107–63.

Clarke, D. L. 1962. 'Matrix analysis of British Beaker pottery', *Proceedings of the Prehistoric Society* 28: 371–83, reprinted in Clarke 1979: 489–502.

1968. *Analytical archaeology*. 1st edn. London: Methuen.

1973. 'Archaeology: the loss of innocence', *Antiquity* 47: 6–18, reprinted in Clarke 1979: 83–103.

1979. *Analytical archaeologist*. Ed. R. W. Chapman. London: Methuen.

Clarke, G. W., ed. 1989. *Rediscovering Hellenism: the Hellenic inheritance and the English imagination*. Cambridge: Cambridge University Press.

Clarke, M. L. 1962. *George Grote: a biography*. London: Athlone.

Clavel-Lévêque, M. 1977. *Marseille grecque: la dynamique d'un impérialisme marchand*. Marseilles: Jeanne Lafitte.

Clifford, J. 1988. *The predicament of culture*. Cambridge, MA: Harvard University Press.

Clogg, R., ed. 1983. *Greece in the 1980s*. New York: St Martin's Press.

1986a. *A short history of modern Greece*. 2nd edn. Cambridge: Cambridge University Press.

1986b. *Politics and the academy: Arnold Toynbee and the Koraes Chair*. London: Cass.

Clogg, R. and Yannopoulos, G., eds. 1972. *Greece under military rule*. New York: Basic Books.

Close, P. 1990. 'Conservatism, authoritarianism and fascism in Greece, 1915–45', in M. Blinkhorn, ed., *Fascists and conservatives*: 200–17. London: Unwin Hyman.

Cohen, E. 1990. 'Commercial lending by Athenian banks', *Classical Philology* 85: 117–90.

Cohen, G. M. 1978. *The Seleucid colonies*. Wiesbaden: Steiner.

Coldstream, J. N. 1968. *Greek Geometric pottery*. London: Methuen.

1977. *Geometric Greece*. London: Methuen.

1984. 'A Protogeometric nature goddess from Knossos', *Bulletin of the Institute of Classical Studies* 31: 93–104.

Coles, J. and Harding, A. 1979. *The Bronze Age in Europe*. London: Methuen.

Colledge, M. A. R. 1984. 'The Greek kingdoms in Bactria and India', in Walbank *et al.* 1984: 25–32.

Collis, J. 1984. *The European Iron Age*. London: Batsford.

Colonna, G. 1985b. 'Il culto dei morti', in Cristofani 1985: 290.

1985c. 'Le forme ideologiche della città', in Cristofani 1985: 242–4.

1985d. 'Anfore da trasporto a Gravisca', in Cristofani and Pelagatti 1985: 5–18.

Colonna, G., ed. 1985a. *Santuari d'Etruria*. Milan: Electa.

Connor, P. 1989. 'Cast-collecting in the ninteeenth century: scholarship, aesthetics, connoisseurship', in G. W. Clarke 1989: 187–235.

Connor, W. R. 1989. 'The new classical humanities and the old', in Culham *et al.* 1989: 25–38.

Constantine, D. 1984. *Early Greek travellers and the Hellenic ideal*. Cambridge: Cambridge University Press.

1989. 'The question of authenticity in some early accounts of Greece', in G. W. Clarke 1989: 1–22.

Constantinides, C. N. 1982. *Higher education in Byzantium in the thirteenth and early fourteenth centuries (1204–ca. 1310)*. Nicosia: Cyprus Research Center, Texts and Studies in the History of Cyprus 11.

Conway, R. S. 1926. 'Sir William Ridgeway 1853–1926', *Proceedings of the British Academy* 12: 327–36.

Conze, A., Hauser, A. and Benndorf, O. 1880. *Neue archäologische Untersuchungen auf Samothrake*. Vienna: C. Gerolds.

Conze, A., Hauser, A. and Niemann, G. 1875. *Archäologische Untersuchungen auf Samothrake*. Vienna: C. Gerolds.

Cook, J. M. 1935. 'Protoattic pottery', *Annual of the British School at Athens* 35: 165–219.

1947. 'Athenian workshops around 700', *Annual of the British School at Athens* 42: 139–55.

1973. *The Troad*. Oxford: Clarendon Press.

1983. *The Persian empire*. London: Dent.

Cook, R. M. 1972a. *Greek painted pottery*. 2nd edn. London: Methuen.

1972b. *Greek art*. Harmondsworth: Penguin.

1987. 'Pots and Pisistratan propaganda', *Journal of Hellenic Studies* 107: 167–9.

1989. 'The Francis-Vickers chronology', *Journal of Hellenic Studies* 109: 164–70.

Cooke, G. W. 1975. *Fertilizing for maximum yield*. 2nd edn. London: Crosby Lockwood Staples.

Coufoudakis, V. 1987. 'Greek foreign policy, 1945–1985', in Featherstone and Katsondas 1987: 230–52.

Couloumbis, T. A. 1991. 'Greek–American relations since 1974', in Vryonis 1991: 81–95.

Coulton, J. J., Milner, N. P. and Reyes, A. 1988. 'Balboura survey: Onesimos and Meleager, part 1', *Anatolian Studies* 38: 121–45.

Courbin, P. 1955. 'Un fragment de cratère protoargien', *Bulletin de Correspondance Hellénique* 79: 1–49.

1988. *What is archaeology?* Chicago: University of Chicago Press.

Couve, L. 1893. 'Un vase proto-attique du Musée de la Société Archéologique d'Athènes', *Bulletin de Correspondance Hellénique* 17: 25–30.

Cowan, M. 1963. *An anthology of the writings of Wilhelm von Humboldt*. Detroit: Wayne State University Press.

Coward, R. 1987. 'Underneath we're angry', in Parker and Pollock 1987: 144–6.

Cox, G. W. and Atkins, M. D. 1964. *Agricultural ecology*. San Francisco: Freeman.

Crane, G. 1989. 'Computers and research in the classics', in Culham *et al.* 1989: 117–31.

—— 1991. 'Composing culture: the authority of an electronic text', *Current Anthropology* 32: 293–311.

Cristofani, M. 1979. *The Etruscans*. London: Orbis.

—— 1987. 'Il banchetto in Etruria', in *Alimentazione*: 123–32.

Cristofani, M., ed. 1985. *Civiltà degli Etruschi*. Milan: Electa.

Cristofani, M. and Pelagatti, P., eds. 1985. *Il commercio etrusco arcaico*. Rome: Consiglio nazionale delle ricerche.

Cristofani, M. and Zevi, F. 1985. 'L'espansione politica', in Cristofani 1985: 121–8.

Crowther, D. 1983. 'Old land surfaces and modern plough-soil: implications of recent work at Maxey, Cambs.', *Scottish Archaeological Review* 2: 31–44.

Cuddon, J. A. 1979. *A dictionary of literary terms*. Revised edn. Harmondsworth: Penguin.

Culham, P., Edmunds, L. and Smith, A., eds. 1989. *Classics: a discipline and profession in crisis?* Lanham, MD: University Press of America.

Cunliffe, B. 1988. *Greeks, Romans and barbarians: spheres of interaction*. London: Batsford.

Dacos, N. 1979. 'Arte italiana e arte antica', in G. Previtali, ed., *Storia dell'arte italiana* 3: 5–68. Turin: G. Einaudi.

d'Agostino, B. 1985. 'La formazione dei centri urbani', in Cristofani 1985: 43–6.

—— 1989. 'Image and society in Archaic Etruria', *Journal of Roman Studies* 79: 1–10.

—— 1990a. 'Military organization and social structure in Archaic Etruria', in Murray and Price 1990: 59–82.

—— 1990b. 'Relations between Campania, Southern Etruria and the Aegean in the eighth century BC', in Descouedres 1990: 73–85.

Dammer, H.-W. 1978. *Die bemalte Keramik der Heuneburg*. Mainz: Zabern.

Daniel, G. 1950. *A hundred years of archaeology*. London: Duckworth.

—— 1981a. 'Introduction: the necessity for an historical approach in archaeology', in Daniel 1981b: 9–13.

Daniel, G., ed. 1981b. *Towards a history of archaeology*. London: Thames and Hudson.

Dar, S., ed. 1986. *Landscape and pattern: an archaeological survey of Samaria: 800 BCE–636 CE*. Oxford: British Archaeological Reports International Series 308.

Davesne, A., Lemaire, M. A. and Lozachmeur, H. 1987. 'Le site archéologique de Meydancikkale (Turquie)', *Comptes Rendus de l'Académie des Inscriptions et Belles-Lettres*: 359–82.

Davies, B. E., Bintliff, J. L., Gaffney, C. F. and Waters, A. T. 1988. 'Trace metal residues in soil as markers of ancient site occupance in Greece', in D. D. Hemphill, ed., *Trace substances in environmental health, XXII: a symposium*: 391–8. Columbia: University of Missouri.

Davies, J. K. 1971. *Athenian propertied families 600–300 BC*. Oxford: Clarendon Press.

—— 1984. 'Cultural, social and economic features of the Hellenistic world', in Walbank *et al.* 1984: 257–320.

Davis, J. L. 1991. 'Contributions to a Mediterranean rural archaeology: historical case studies from the Ottoman Cyclades', *Journal of Mediterranean Archaeology* 4: 131–216.

Davis, N. and Kraay, C. 1973. *The Hellenistic kingdoms: portrait coins and history*. London: Thames and Hudson.

Day, A. D. and Thompson, R. K. 1988a. 'Effects of dried sewage sludge on wheat cultivars in the southwestern US', *Journal of Arid Environments* 14: 93–9.

—— 1988b. 'Sewage sludge as fertilizer for wheat forage in an arid environment', *Journal of Arid Environments* 15: 209–14.

DeBoer, W. R. 1974. 'Ceramic longevity and archaeological interpretation: an example from the Upper Ucayali, Peru', *American Antiquity* 39: 335–43.

DeBoer, W. R. and Lathrap, D. W. 1979. 'The making and breaking of Shipibo-Conibo ceramics', in C. Kramer, ed., *Ethnoarchaeology: implications of ethnography for archaeology*: 102–38. New York: Columbia University Press.

De Cardi, B. 1984. 'Survey in Ras al-Khaimah', in Boucharlat and Salles 1984: 201–15.

de la Genière, J. 1988. 'Les acheteurs des cratères Corinthiens', *Bulletin de Correspondance Hellénique* 112: 83–90.

de Polignac, F. 1984. *La naissance de la cité grecque*. Paris: Editions de la découverte.

de Puma, R. D. 1988. 'Nude dancers: a group of bucchero pesante oinochoai from Tarquinia', in Christiansen and Melander 1988: 130–43.

de Ridder, A. 1896. *Catalogue des bronzes trouvés sur l'acropole d'Athènes*. Paris: Bibliothèque des écoles françaises d'Athènes et de Rome 74.

de Ste Croix, G. E. M. 1981. *The class struggle in the ancient Greek world*. London: Duckworth.

de Vries, K. 1977. 'Attic pottery in the Achaemenid empire', *American Journal of Archaeology* 81: 544–8.

de Wever, J. 1966. 'La chora massaliote d'après les fouilles récentes', *L'Antiquité Classique* 35: 71–117.

Deetz, J. 1988. 'History and archaeological theory: Walter Taylor revisited', *American Antiquity* 53: 13–22.

—— 1989. 'Archaeography, archaeology, archeology?', *American Journal of Archaeology* 93: 429–35.

Dehn, W. and Frey, O.-H. 1962. 'Die absolute Chronologie der Hallstatt- und Frühlatènezeit Mitteleuropas auf Grund des Südimports', in *Congresso internazionale delle scienze preistoriche e protostoriche* VI, vol. 3: 197–208. Florence.

Delano Smith, C. 1979. *Western Mediterranean Europe: a historical geography of Italy, Spain and Southern France since the Neolithic*. London: Academic Press.

Derber, C., Schwartz, W. A. and Magrass, Y. 1990. *Power in the highest degree*. Oxford: Oxford University Press.

Desborough, V. R. 1952. *Protogeometric pottery*. Oxford: Clarendon Press.

1972. *The Greek Dark Ages*. London: Methuen.

Descouedres, J.-P., ed. 1990. *Greek colonists and native populations*. Oxford: Clarendon Press.

Di Gennaro, F. 1982. 'Organizzazione di territorio nell'Etruria meridionale protostorica: applicazione di un modello grafico', *Dialoghi di Archeologia* 4: 102–12.

Diamandouros, N. P., Anton, J. P., Petropulos, J. A. and Topping, P., eds. 1976. *Hellenism and the first Greek War of Liberation (1821–1830)*. Thessaloniki: Institute for Balkan Studies 156.

Diehl, C. 1977. *Americans and German scholarship 1770–1870*. New Haven: Yale University Press.

Dietler, M. 1989. 'Greeks, Etruscans and thirsty barbarians', in T. Champion 1989: 127–41.

1990. 'Driven by drink: the role of drinking in the political economy and the case of Early Iron Age France', *Journal of Anthropological Archaeology* 9: 352–406.

Dimaras, A. 1980. *Neoellinikos diaphostismos*. Athens: Hermes.

1982. *Ellinikos Romandismos*. Athens: Hermes.

1983. 'Europe and the 1980s: a double challenge for Greek education', in Clogg 1983: 231–44.

Dimen, M. and Friedl, E., eds. 1976. *Regional variation in modern Greece and Cyprus: toward a perspective on the ethnography of Greece*. New York: The New York Academy of Sciences.

Dittenberger, W., ed. 1960 [1915–24]. *Sylloge Inscriptionum Graecarum*. 3 vols. 3rd edn. Hildesheim: Georg Olms.

Dodgshon, R. A. 1988. 'The ecological basis of Highland peasant farming, 1500–1800 AD', in H. H. Birks *et al.*, eds., *The cultural landscape: past, present and future*: 139–51. Cambridge: Cambridge University Press.

Dohrn, T. 1937. *Die schwarzfiguren etruskischen Vasen aus der zweiten Hälfte des sechsten Jhs*. Berlin: Triltsch and Huther.

Donahue, A. A. 1985. 'One hundred years of the *American Journal of Archaeology*: an archival history', *American Journal of Archaeology* 89: 3–30.

D'Onofrio, A. M. 1982. 'Korai e kouroi funerari attici', *Annali Istituto Orientale di Napoli. Archeologia e Storia Antica* 4: 135–70.

1988. 'Aspetti e problemi del monumento funerario Attico arcaico', *Annali Istituto Orientale di Napoli. Archeologia e Storia Antica* 10: 82–96.

Dontas, D. N. 1966. *Greece and the Great Powers, 1863–1875*. Thessaloniki: Institute for Balkan Studies.

Dort, A. V. 1954. 'The Archaeological Institute of America – early days', *Archaeology* 7: 195–201.

Dover, K. J. 1988. 'Byron on the ancient Greeks', in K. J. Dover, *The Greeks and their legacy: collected papers* II: 292–303. Oxford: Basil Blackwell.

Dowden, K. 1988. *Death and the maiden: girls' initiation rites in Greek mythology*. London: Routledge.

Dronke, P., ed. 1988. *A history of twelfth-century western philosophy*. Cambridge: Cambridge University Press.

Droysen, J. G. 1952. *Geschichte des Hellenismus*. 3 vols. Basel: Schwabe.

Ducat, J. 1971. *Les kouroi du Ptoion*. Paris: Boccard.

Dunbabin, K. 1979. 'Techniques and materials of Hellenistic mosaics', *American Journal of Archaeology* 83: 265–77.

Dunbabin, T. J. 1937. '"Echthre palaie"', *Annual of the British School at Athens* 37: 83–91.

1948. *The Western Greeks*. Oxford: Clarendon Press.

1962. *Perachora* II. Oxford: Clarendon Press.

Dyson, S. 1981. 'A classical archaeologist's response to the "New Archaeology"', *Bulletin of the American Schools of Oriental Research* 242: 15–29.

1985. 'Two paths to the past: a comparative study of the last fifty years of *American Antiquity* and *American Journal of Archaeology*', *American Antiquity* 50: 452–63.

1989a. 'The role of ideology and institutions in shaping classical archaeology in the nineteenth and twentieth centuries', in Christenson 1989: 127–35.

1989b. 'Complacency and crisis in late twentieth century classical archaeology', in Culham *et al.* 1989: 211–20.

Eagleton, T. 1983. *Literary theory: an introduction*. Minneapolis: University of Minnesota Press.

Earle, T. K. and Preucel, R. W. 1987. 'Processual archaeology and the radical critique', *Current Anthropology* 28: 501–38.

Ebert, J. I. 1986. 'Distributional archaeology: nonsite discovery, recording and analytical methods for application to the surface archaeological record'. PhD dissertation, University of New Mexico.

Echallier, J.-C. 1982. 'La provenance des amphores massaliètes', *DAM* 5: 139–44.

Edlund, I. 1987. *The gods and the place*. Göteborg: Paul Åström.

Edlund Gantz, I. 1972. 'The seated statue akroteria from Poggio Civitate (Murlo)', *Dialoghi di Archeologia* 6: 167–219.

Edmonds, J. M. 1957. *The fragments of Attic comedy* I. Leiden: Brill.

Edmunds, L. 1983. 'The sphinx in the Oedipus legend', in Edmunds and Dundes 1983: 147–53.

Edmunds, L. and Dundes, A., eds. 1983. *Oedipus: a folklore casebook*. Königsten: Beiträge zur klassische Philologie 127.

Eilmann, R. and Gebauer, K. 1938. *Corpus Vasorum Antiquorum: Deutschland, Berlin Antiquarium* I. Munich: Beck.

Eiseman, C. and Ridgway, B. S. 1989. *The Porticello shipwreck: a Mediterranean merchant vessel of 415–385 BC*. College Station: Texas A & M University Press.

Eisman, M. M. 1974. 'Nikosthenic amphorae: the J. Paul Getty Museum amphora', *J. Paul Getty Museum Journal* 1: 43–54.

1975. 'Attic kyathos production', *Archaeology* 28: 76–83.

Eisner, R. 1991. *Travelers to an antique land: the history and literature of travel to Greece*. Ann Arbor: University of Michigan Press.

Eizennat, M. 1980. 'Ancient Marseille in the light of recent excavations', *American Journal of Archaeology* 84: 133–40.

Embree, L. 1989a. 'The structure of American theoretical archaeology: a preliminary report', in Pinsky and Wylie 1989: 28–37.

1989b. 'Contacting the theoretical archaeologists', in Christenson 1989: 62–74.

Empereur, J.-Y. and Garlan, Y., eds. 1986. *Recherches sur les amphores grecques*. Paris: *Bulletin de Correspondance Helléniques* supp. 13.

Engel, A. 1983. *From clergyman to don: the rise of the academic profession in nineteenth-century Oxford*. Oxford: Clarendon Press.

Fagan, B. M. 1989. 'The backward-looking curiosity: a glance at archaeology in the year of our lord 1989', *American Journal of Archaeology* 93: 445–9.

Fahnestock, P. 1984. 'History and theoretical development: the importance of a critical historiography of archaeology', *Archaeological Review from Cambridge* 3: 7–18.

Fallmereyer, J. P. 1830. *Geschichte der Halbinsel Morea während des Mittelalters* I. Stuttgart: J. G. Cotta.

Farnsworth, M., Perlman, I. and Asaro, F. 1977. 'Corinth

and Corfu: a neutron activation study of their pottery', *American Journal of Archaeology* 81: 455–68.

Farrar, C. 1988. *The origins of democratic thinking*. Cambridge: Cambridge University Press.

Featherstone, K. and Katsondas, D. K., eds. 1987. *Political change in Greece*. London: Croom Helm.

Fellmann, B. 1972. 'Die Geschichte der deutschen Ausgrabung', in B. Fellmann, ed., *100 Jahre deutsche Ausgrabungen in Olympia*: 37–48.

Felperin, H. 1985. *Beyond deconstruction*. Oxford: Oxford University Press.

Femia, J. V. 1971. *Gramsci's political thought*. Oxford: Clarendon Press.

Fenton, A. J. 1981. 'Early manuring techniques', in R. Mercer, ed., *Farming practice in British prehistory*: 210–27. Edinburgh: Edinburgh University Press.

Figueira, T. 1981. *Aegina*. New York: Arno Press.

Fine, J. V. A. 1951. *Horoi: studies in mortgage, real security and land tenure in ancient Athens*. Athens: American School of Classical Studies (*Hesperia* supp. vol. 9).

Finegan, J. 1979. *An archaeological history of the ancient Middle East*. Boulder, CO: Westview.

Finkelstein, I. 1981. 'Israelite and Hellenistic farms in the foothills and in the Yarkon Basin', *Eretz Israel* 15: 86, 331–48 (in Hebrew, English abstract).

Finley, M. I. 1952. *Studies in land and credit in ancient Athens, 500–200 BC: The horos inscriptions* (reprinted 1985). New Brunswick: Rutgers University Press. Reprinted New York, Arno, 1979; Cambridge, Cambridge University Press, 1985.

1962. 'The slave trade in antiquity: the Black Sea and Danubian regions', *Klio* 40: 51–9.

1965. 'Classical Greece', in *Deuxième conférence internationale d'histoire économique*: 11–35. Paris: Mouton. Reprinted New York, Arno, 1979.

1975. *The use and abuse of history*. London: Chatto and Windus. Reissued by the Hogarth Press, London, 1986.

1985a. *The ancient economy*. 2nd edn. London: Hogarth Press.

1985b. *Ancient history: evidence and models*. London: Chatto and Windus.

1985c. *Democracy ancient and modern*. 2nd edn. London: Hogarth Press.

Finley, M. I., ed. 1973. *Problèmes de la terre en Grèce ancienne*. Paris: Mouton.

Fischer, F. 1973. 'KEIMILIA: Bemerkungen zur kultur-geschichtlichen Interpretation des sogenannten Südimports in der späten Hallstatt- und frühen Latènekultur des westlichen Mitteleuropas', *Germania* 51: 436–59.

Fischer, J. 1990. 'Zu einer griechischen Kline und weiteren Südimportan aus dem Fürstengrab Grafenbühl, Asperg, Kr. Ludwigsburg', *Germania* 68: 115–27.

Fish, S. 1980. *Is there a text in this class? The authority of interpretive communities.* Cambridge, MA: Harvard University Press.

1990. 'Commentary: the young and the restless', in Veeser 1990: 303–16.

Fish, S. K. and Kowalewski, S. A., eds. 1990. *The archaeology of regions: a case for full-coverage survey.* Washington, DC: Smithsonian Institution.

Fittschen, K. 1969. *Untersuchungen zum Beginn der Sagendarstellungen bei den Griechen.* Berlin: Bruno Hessling.

Flannery, K. 1976a. 'A plea for an endangered species', in Flannery 1976b: 369–73.

Flannery, K., ed. 1976b. *The early Mesoamerican village.* New York: Academic Press.

Foard, G. 1978. 'Systematic fieldwalking and the investigation of Saxon settlement in Northamptonshire', *World Archaeology* 9: 357–74.

Foley, A. 1988. *The Argolid 800–600 BC: an archaeological survey.* Göteborg: *Studies in Mediterranean Archaeology* 80.

Foley, R. 1981. 'Off-site archaeology: an alternative approach for the short-sited', in Hodder *et al.* 1981: 157–83.

Follett, R. H., Murphy, L. S. and Donahue, R. L. 1981. *Fertilizers and soil amendments.* Englewood Cliffs, NJ: Prentice-Hall.

Forbes, H. A. 1976a. 'The "thrice-ploughed-field": cultivation techniques in ancient and modern Greece', *Expedition* 19: 5–11.

1976b. '"We have a little of everything": the ecological basis of some agricultural practices in Methana, Trizinia', in Dimen and Friedl 1976: 236–50.

Forrest, W. G. 1966. *The emergence of Greek democracy.* London: Weidenfeld and Nicolson.

Foucault, M. 1970. *The order of things.* London: Tavistock.

1972. *The archaeology of knowledge.* New York: Pantheon.

1977a. *Discipline and punish: the birth of the prison.* New York: Vintage.

1977b. *Language/counter-memory/practice.* Ithaca, NY: Cornell University Press.

Fowler, D. D. 1987. 'Uses of the past: archaeology in the service of the state', *American Antiquity* 52: 229–48.

Fowler, P. 1981. 'Later prehistory', in S. Piggott, ed., *The agrarian history of England and Wales*: 61–298. Cambridge: Cambridge University Press.

Foxhall, L. 1990. 'The dependent tenant: land leasing and labour in Italy and Greece', *Journal of Roman Studies* 80: 97–114.

n.d. 'Snapping up the unconsidered trifles: the use of agricultural residues in ancient farming'. Unpublished paper.

Francis, E. D. 1990. *Image and idea in fifth-century Greece: art and literature after the Persian wars.* London: Routledge.

Francis, E. D. and Vickers, M. 1985. 'Greek .Geometric pottery at Hama and its implications for Near Eastern chronology', *Levant* 17: 131–8.

1988. 'The Agora revisited: Athenian chronology c. 500–458 BC', *Annual of the British School at Athens* 83: 143–67.

Frankenstein, S. and Rowlands, M. 1978. 'The internal structure and regional context of Iron Age society in south-western Germany', *Bulletin of the Institute of Archaeology* 15: 73–112.

Fraser, P. M. and Bean, G. E. 1954. *The Rhodian Peraea and islands.* Oxford: Oxford University Press.

Frayn, J. M. 1979. *Subsistence farming in Roman Italy.* Fontwell: Centaur Press.

Freeman, E. A. 1880. *Historical essays: second series.* 2nd edn. London: Macilllan.

French, E. B. and Wardle, K. A., eds. 1988. *Problems in Greek prehistory.* Bristol: Bristol Classical Press.

Freud, S. 1977. *On sexuality.* Harmondsworth: Pelican.

Freytag, B. von gen. Löringhoff. 1974. 'Ein spätgeometrisches Frauengrab vom Kerameikos', *Mitteilungen des Deutschen Archäologischen Instituts, Athenische Abteilung* 89: 1–25.

1975. 'Neue frühattische Funde aus dem Kerameikos', *Mitteilungen des Deutschen Archäologischen Instituts, Athenische Abteilung* 90: 49–81.

Friedl, E. 1962. *Vasilika: a village in modern Greece.* New York: Holt, Rinehart and Winston.

Friis Johansen, K. 1951. *The Attic grave reliefs of the classical period.* Copenhagen: Munksgaard.

Fulford, M. 1978. 'The interpretation of British late Roman trade: the scope of medieval historical and archaeological analogy', in H. Cleere and J. du Plat Taylor, eds., *Roman shipping and trade: Britain and the Rhine provinces*: 59–69. London: Council for British Archaeology.

1987/8. 'Economic interdependence among urban communities in the Roman Mediterranean', *World Archaeology* 19: 58–75.

Fürst, L. 1969. *Romanticism.* London: Methuen.

Furtwängler, A. 1885. *Königliche Museen der Berlin: Beschreibung der Vasensammlung im Antiquarium.* 2 vols. Berlin: Asher.

1886. *Mykenische Vasen: Vorhellenische Tongefässe aus dem Gebiet des Mittelmeers*. Berlin: Asher.

Furtwängler, A. and Löschke, G. 1879. *Mykenische Tongefässe*. Berlin: Asher.

Furumark, A. 1941. *The Mycenaean pottery*. 2 vols. Stockholm: Kungl. Vitterhets Historie och Antikivitets Akademien. Reprinted 1972, Stockholm, Skrifter Utgivna i Svenska Institutet i Athen.

Gaehtgens, T. W., ed. 1986. *Johann Joachim Winckelmann 1717–1768*. Hamburg: Felix Meiner Verlag.

Gaffney, C. F. and Gaffney, V. L. 1986. 'From Boeotia to Berkshire: an integrated approach to geophysics and rural field survey', *Prospezione Archeologiche* 10: 65–71.

1988. 'Some quantitative approaches to site territory and land use from the surface record', in J. L. Bintliff, D. A. Davidson and E. G. Grant, eds., *Conceptual issues in environmental archaeology*: 82–90. Edinburgh: Edinburgh University Press.

Gaffney, C., Gaffney, V. and Tingle, M. 1985. 'Settlement, economy or behaviour? Micro-regional land use models and the interpretation of surface artifact patterns', in C. Haselgrove, M. Millett and I. Smith, eds., *Archaeology from the ploughsoil: studies in the collection and interpretation of field survey data*: 95–107. Sheffield: Department of Archaeology and Prehistory.

Gaffney, V. L., Bintliff, J. and Slapsak, B. 1991. 'Site formation processes and the Hvar Survey Project, Yugoslavia', in A. J. Schofield, ed., *Interpreting artifact scatters: contributions to ploughzone archaeology*: 59–77. Oxford: Oxbow Books (Oxbow Monograph 4).

Gaffney, V. and Tingle, M. 1984. 'The tyranny of the site: method and theory in field survey', *Scottish Archaeological Review* 3: 134–40.

1985. 'The Maddle Farm (Berks.) Project and micro-regional analysis', in Macready and Thompson 1985: 67–73.

1989. *The Maddle Farm project: an integrated survey of prehistoric and Roman landscapes on the Berkshire Downs*. Oxford: British Archaeological Reports 200.

Gallagher, C. 1990. 'Marxism and the new historicism', in Veeser 1990: 37–48.

Gallant, T. 1986. Background noise and site definition: a contribution to survey methodology', *Journal of Field Archaeology* 13: 403–18.

1991. *Risk and survival in ancient Greece*. Stanford: Stanford University Press.

Gallay, A. 1986. *L'archéologie demain*. Paris: Belfond.

1989. 'Logicism: a French view of archaeological theory founded in computational perspective', *Antiquity* 63: 27–39.

Gallet de Santerre, H. 1977. 'La diffusion de la céramique attique aux Ve et IVe siècles av. J.-C. sur les rivages français de la Méditerannée', *Revue Archéologique de Narbonnaise* 10: 33–57.

Gamble, C. 1982. 'Animal husbandry, population and urbanisation', in Renfrew and Wagstaff 1982: 161–71.

Gamito, T. J. 1988. *Social complexity in South-West Iberia 800–300 BC*. Oxford: British Archaeological Reports International Series 439.

Gardin, J.-C. 1987. *Systèmes experts et publications savantes*. London: British Library Board.

Gardin, J.-C and Gentelle, P. 1976. 'Irrigation et peuplement dans la plaine d'Aï Khanoum de l'époque achéménide à l'époque musulmane', *Bulletin de l'Ecole Française de l'Extrême Orient* 63: 59–99.

1979. 'L'exploitation du sol en Bactriane antique', *Bulletin de l'Ecole Française de l'Extrême Orient* 66: 1–29.

Gardin, J.-C. and Lyonnet, B. 1978/9. 'La prospection archéologique de la Bactriane orientale (1974–78)', *Mesopotamia* 13/14: 99–154.

Gardner, E. 1894/5. 'Sir Charles Newton, KCB', *Annual of the British School at Athens* 1: 67–77.

Garin, E. 1990, 'Polibio e Machiavelli', *Quaderni di Storia* 31: 5–22.

Garland, R. 1985. *The Greek way of death*. London: Duckworth.

Garnsey, P. 1988. *Famine and food supply in the Greco-Roman world*. Cambridge: Cambridge University Press.

Garnsey, P., Hopkins K. and Whittaker, C. R., eds. 1983. *Trade in the ancient economy*. Cambridge: Cambridge University Press.

Garnsey, P. and Morris, I. 1989. 'Risk and polis', in P. Halstead and J. O'Shea, eds., *Bad year economics*: 98–105. Cambridge: Cambridge University Press.

Garnsey, P. and Whittaker, C. R., eds. 1983. *Trade and famine in classical antiquity*. Cambridge: Cambridge University Press.

Gathercole, P. and Lowenthal, D., eds. 1990. *The politics of the past*. London: Unwin Hyman.

Gauer, W. 1988. 'Parthenonische Amazonomachie und Perserkrieg', in H. Schmidt, ed., *Kanon. Festschrift Ernst Berger*: 26–41. Basel: *Antike Kunst* suppl. vol.

Gavrielides, N. 1976. 'Olive growing in the Fourni Valley', in Dimen and Friedl 1976: 143–57.

Gawantka, W. 1985. *Die sogennante Polis*. Stuttgart: Franz Steiner.

Geanakopoulos, D. J. 1976. 'The diaspora Greeks', in Diamandouros *et al.* 1976: 59–77.

Geertz, C. 1973. *The interpretation of cultures.* New York: Basic Books.

1988. *Works and lives: the anthropologist as author.* Stanford: Stanford University Press.

Gehrke, H.-J. 1986. *Jenseits von Athen und Sparta: das dritte Griechenland und seine Staatenwelt.* Munich: Beck.

Gellner, E. 1985. *The psychoanalytic movement.* London: Paladin.

Gentelle, P. 1978. *Etude géographique de la plaine d'Aï Khanoum et de son irrigation depuis les temps anciens.* Paris: Editions du CNRS.

Gernet, L. 1981. *The anthropology of ancient Greece.* Baltimore: Johns Hopkins University Press.

Gero, J., Lacy D. and Blakey, M., eds. 1983. *The sociopolitics of archaeology.* Amherst: University of Massachusetts Department of Anthropology Research Report 23.

Gersbach, E. 1976. 'Das Osttor (Donautor) der Beuneburg bei Hundersingen (Donau)', *Germania* 54: 17–42.

Gerstenberg, J. 1949. *Die Wiedergewinnung Olympias als Stätte und Idee: ein Beitrag zur Geistesgeschichte.* Baden Baden.

Gibbins, D. 1990. 'Analytical approaches in maritime archaeology: a Mediterranean perspective', *Antiquity* 64: 376–89.

Gibbon, G. 1985. 'Classical and anthropological archaeology: a coming rapprochement?', in N. C. Wilkie and W. D. E. Coulson, eds., *Contributions to Aegean archaeology*: 283–94. Minneapolis: University of Minnesota Press.

1989. *Explanation in archaeology.* Oxford: Basil Blackwell.

Gibson, D. B. and Geselowitz, M. N., eds. 1988. *Tribe and polity in late prehistoric Europe.* London / New York: Plenum.

Giddens, A. 1990. *The consequences of modernity.* Stanford: Stanford University Press.

Giddens, A. and Turner, J., eds. 1987. *Social theory today.* Stanford: Stanford University Press.

Gilbert, N. W. 1977. 'A letter of Giovanni Dondi dall'Orologio to Fra Guglielmo Centueri: a fourteenth-century episode in the quarrel of the ancients and moderns', *Viator* 8: 339–46.

Gill, D. 1986. 'Attic black-glazed pottery', in F. M. Kenrick, ed., *Excavations at Sabratha 1948–1951*: 275–96. London: Society for the Promotion of Roman Studies (*Journal of Roman Studies* supp. vol. 2).

1987. 'METRU. MENECE: an Etruscan painted inscrip-

tion on a mid-5th-century BC red-figure cup from Populonia', *Antiquity* 61: 82–7.

1988a. '"Trade in Greek decorated pottery": some corrections', *Oxford Journal of Archaeology* 7: 369–70.

1988b. 'Expressions of wealth: Greek art and society', *Antiquity* 62: 735–42.

1988c. 'The distribution of Greek vases and long distance trade', in Christiansen and Melander 1988: 175–85.

1988d. 'Silver anchors and cargoes of oil', *Papers of the British School at Rome* 56: 1–12.

1988e. 'The temple of Aphaia on Aegina: the date of the reconstruction', *Annual of the British School at Athens* 83: 169–77.

1990. '"Ancient fictile vases" from the Disney collection', *Journal of the History of Collections* 2: 227–31.

1991a. 'Pots and trade: spacefillers or *objets d'art?*', *Journal of Hellenic Studies* 111: 29–47.

1991b. 'An archaeological note on two ostraca from the Fitzwilliam collection', *Zeitschrift für Papyrologie und Epigraphik* 86: 277.

Gill, D. and Vickers, M. J. 1989. 'Pots and kettles', *Revue Archéologique*: 297–303.

1990. 'Reflected glory: pottery and precious metal in classical Greece', *Jahrbuch des Deutschen Archäologischen Instituts* 105: 1–30.

Gilotta, F. 1986. 'Appunti sulla più antica ceramica etrusca a figure rosse', *Prospettiva* 45: 2–18.

1988. 'Notes on some early Etruscan red-figure workshops', in Christiansen and Melander 1988: 195–200.

Ginge, B. 1988. 'A new evaluation of the origins of Tyrrhenian pottery', in Christiansen and Melander 1988: 201–10.

Goffer, Z., Molcho, M. and Beit-Arieh, I. 1983. 'The disposal of wastes in ancient Beer-Sheba', *Journal of Field Archaeology* 107: 77–87.

Goldberg, S. 1990. 'Goldberg appointed new editor of *TAPA*', *American Philological Association Newsletter* 13.3: 1–2.

Gosden, C. 1985. 'Gifts and kin in early Iron Age Europe', *Man* 20: 475–93.

1986. 'Modernist fantasies in prehistory', *Man* 21: 746–7.

Gould, R. and Schiffer, M. B., eds. 1981. *Modern material culture: the archaeology of us.* New York: Academic Press.

Graef, B. and Langlotz, E. 1925. *Die antiken Vasen von der Akropolis zu Athen.* 9 vols. Berlin: de Gruyter.

Grafton, A. 1991. *Defenders of the text: the traditions of scholarship in an age of science, 1450–1800.* Cambridge, MA: Harvard University Press.

Graham, A. J. 1983. *Colony and mother city in ancient Greece*. 2nd edn. Chicago: Ares Press.

Grainger, J. D. 1990. *The cities of Seleukid Syria*. Oxford: Clarendon Press.

Gramsci, A. 1971 [1926–35]. *Selections from the 'Prison notebooks'*. Ed. Q. Hoare and G. N. Smith. New York: International Publishers.

Gran Aymerich, J. M. J. 1981. 'Compositions figurées et compositions narratives d'époque archaïque en Etrurie', in L. Kahil and C. Augé, eds., *Mythologie gréco-romaine, mythologies périphériques: études d'iconographie*: 19–26. Paris: Editions CNRS.

1986. 'Les données décoratives dans les céramiques antiques: bilan de deux expériences', in *Iconographie classique et identités régionales*: 93–104. Paris: *Bulletin de Correspondance Hellénique* supp. vol. 14.

Gräslund, B. 1987. *The birth of prehistoric chronology*. Cambridge: Cambridge University Press.

Green, P. 1990. *Alexander to Actium: the Hellenistic age*. London: Thames and Hudson.

Greenblatt, S. 1990. 'Towards a poetics of culture', in Veeser 1990: 1–14.

Greenfield, J. 1989. *The return of cultural treasures*. Cambridge: Cambridge University Press.

Greenhalgh, M. 1989. *The survival of Roman antiquities in the Middle Ages*. London: Duckworth.

Gregory, P. J., Shepherd, K. D. and Cooper, P. J. 1984. 'Effects of fertilizer on root growth and water use of barley in north Syria', *Journal of Agricultural Science* 103: 429–38.

Grigg, D. 1980. *Population growth and agrarian change: an historical perspective*. Cambridge: Cambridge University Press.

Grote, G. 1826. 'Fasti hellenici', *Westminster Review* 5: 269–331.

1847. *A history of Greece* IV. London: Murray.

Guidi, A. 1985. 'An application of the rank-size rule to protohistoric settlements in the middle Tyrrhenian area', in Malone and Stoddart 1985: 217–42.

Gullini, G. 1964. 'First report on the results of the first excavation campaign at Seleucia and Ctesiphon (1st October–17th December 1964)', *Sumer* 20: 63–5.

Gunn, B. 1943. 'Notes on the Naucratis stela', *Journal of Egyptian Archaeology* 29: 55–9.

Gutting, G. 1989. *Michel Foucault's archaeology of scientific reason*. Cambridge: Cambridge University Press.

Haas, J., Pozorski, S. and Pozorski, T., eds. 1989. *The origins and development of the Andean state*. Cambridge: Cambridge University Press.

Habermas, J. 1984. *Theory of communicative action* I: *Reason and the rationalization of society*. Cambridge, MA: MIT Press.

1985. 'Neoconservative culture criticism in the United States and West Germany: an intellectual movement in two political cultures', in Bernstein 1985: 78–94.

Hadjichristodoulou, A. 1982. 'The effects of annual precipitation and its distribution on grain yield of dryland cereals', *Journal of Agricultural Science* 99: 261–80.

Hadjisavvas, S. 1977. 'The archaeological survey of Paphos: a preliminary report', *Report of the Department of Antiquities, Cyprus*: 222–31.

Haerinck, E. 1987. 'La neuvième satrapie: archéologie confronte histoire?', in Sancisi-Weerdenburg 1987: 139–45.

Haffner, A. 1976. *Die westliche Hunsrück-Eifel Kultur*. Berlin: de Gruyter.

Hägg, R. 1987. 'Gifts to the heroes in Geometric and Archaic Greece', in T. Linders and G. Nordqvist, eds., *Gifts to the gods*: 93–9. Uppsala: *Boreas* 15.

Hahn, I. 1983. 'Foreign trade and foreign policy in Archaic Greece', in Garnsey *et al*. 1983: 30–6.

Hall, A. 1976. 'The Oenoanda survey: 1974–76', *Anatolian Studies* 26: 191–7.

Hall, E. 1990. *Inventing the barbarian*. Oxford: Oxford University Press.

Hall, P., ed. 1966. *Von Thünen's isolated state*. Oxford: Pergamon Press.

Hallett, J. 1989. 'The women's classical caucus', in Culham *et al*. 1989: 339–50.

Halporn, J. W. 1989. 'Foreign scholars and American classical education', in Culham *et al*. 1989: 305–15.

Halstead, P. 1981a. 'Counting sheep in Neolithic and Bronze Age Greece', in Hodder *et al*. 1981: 307–39.

1981b. 'From determinism to uncertainty: social storage and the rise of the Minoan palace', in A. Sheridan and G. Bailey, eds., *Economic archaeology*: 187–213. Oxford: British Archaeological Reports International Series 96.

1987. 'Traditional and ancient rural economies in Mediterranean Europe: plus ça change?', *Journal of Hellenic Studies* 107: 77–87.

1990. 'Waste not, want not: traditional responses to crop failure in Greece', *Rural History* 1: 147–64.

Halstead, P. and Jones, G. 1989. 'Agrarian ecology in the Greek islands: time stress, scale and risk', *Journal of Hellenic Studies* 109: 41–55.

Hammond, P. C. 1973. *The Nabataeans*. Göteborg: Paul Åströms Verlag.

Hanbury-Tenison, J. W. 1984. 'Wadi Adab survey, 1983',

Annual of the Department of Antiquities of Jordan 28: 385–424.

Hannestad, L. 1974. *The Paris Painter*. Copenhagen: Munksgaard.

1976. *Followers of the Paris Painter*. Copenhagen: Munksgaard.

1984. 'The pottery from the Hellenistic settlements on Fikala', in Boucharlat and Salles 1984: 67–83.

Hansen, M. H. 1984. 'Athenian maritime trade in the fourth century BC, operation and finance', *Classica et Medievalia* 35: 71–92.

1989. *Was Athens a democracy?* Copenhagen: Royal Danish Academy.

Hansen, P. A. 1983. *Carmina epigraphica Graeca, saeculorum VII–V a. Chr.* Berlin: de Gruyter.

Hanson, V. D. 1983. *Warfare and agriculture in classical Greece*. Pisa: Giardini Editori e Stampatori.

1989. *The western way of war*. Oxford: Oxford University Press.

Härke, H. 1979. *Settlement types and settlement patterns in the West Hallstatt province*. Oxford: British Archaeological Reports International Series 57.

1982. 'Early Iron Age hill settlement in west central Europe: patterns and developments', *Oxford Journal of Archaeology* 1: 187–211.

Harrison, J. E. 1903. *Prolegomena to the study of Greek religion*. Cambridge: Cambridge University Press. Reprinted 1962, London: Merlin Press.

1912. *Themis: a study of the social origins of Greek religion*. Cambridge: Cambridge University Press. Reprinted 1963, London: Merlin Press.

1965 [1921]. 'Reminiscences of a student's life', *Arion* 4: 312–46. First published as a book by the Hogarth Press, London.

Hart, S. and Falkner, R. 1985. 'Preliminary report on a survey in Edom, 1984', *Annual of the Department of Antiquities of Jordan* 29: 255–77.

Hartog, F. 1988. *The mirror of Herodotus*. Berkeley: University of California Press.

Hartwig, P. 1893. *Die griechischen Meisterschalen*. Stuttgart: Spemann.

Harvie, C. 1976. *The limits of liberalism: university liberals and the challenge of democracy, 1860–1886*. London: Allen Lane.

Hasebroek, J. 1933. *Trade and politics in ancient Greece*. London: Bell.

Haselgrove, C., Millett, M. and Smith, I., eds. 1985. *Archaeology from the ploughsoil: studies in the collection and interpretation of field survey data*. Sheffield: Dept of Archaeology and Prehistory.

Haskell, F. 1987. 'The baron d'Hancarville: an adventurer and art historian in eighteenth-century Europe', in F. Haskell, ed., *Past and present in art and taste*: 30–45. New Haven: Yale University Press.

Haskell, F. and Penny, N. 1981. *Taste and the antique: the lure of classical sculpture, 1500–1900*. New Haven: Yale University Press.

Haskell, T. L. 1977. *The emergence of professional social science*. Urbana: University of Illinois Press.

Häsler, B. 1973a. 'Winckelmanns Verhältnis zur griechischen Literatur', in Häsler 1973b: 39–42.

Häsler, B., ed. 1973b. *Beiträge zu einem neuen Winckelmannbild*. Berlin: Akademie-Verlag. Schriften der Winckelmann-Gesellschaft 1.

Hayes, P. P. 1991. 'Models for the distribution of pottery around former agricultural settlements', in A. J. Schofield, ed., *Interpreting artifact scatters: contributions to ploughzone archaeology*: 81–92. Oxford: Oxbow Books (Oxbow Monograph 4).

Hayfield, C. 1987. *An archaeological survey of the parish of Wharram Percy, east Yorkshire* I: *The evolution of the Roman landscape*. Oxford: British Archaeological Reports 172.

Haynes, H. W. 1900. 'Progress of American archaeology during the past ten years', *American Journal of Archaeology* n.s. 4: 17–39.

Hennig, D. 1977. 'Die Berichte des Polybios über Boiotien und die Lage von Orchomenos in der 2. hälfte des 3. Jahrhunderts v. Chr.', *Chiron* 7: 119–48.

Herbert, S. 1977. *Corinth* VII.4. *The red-figure pottery*. Princeton: American School of Classical Studies.

Herman, G. 1987. *Ritualised friendship in the Greek city*. Cambridge: Cambridge University Press.

Herrmann, H.-V. 1972. *Olympia: Heiligtum und Wettkampfstätte*. Munich: Hirmer.

Herrmann, J. 1992. 'Heinrich Schliemann – forschungsgeschichtliche Leistung, wissenschaftsmethodischer Neuansatz und zentenare Wirkung', in J. Herrmann, ed., *Heinrich Schliemann*: 93–102. Berlin: Akademie Verlag.

Hertzberg, H. 1989. 'History and progressivism: a century of reform proposals', in P. Gagnon, ed., *Historical literacy*: 69–99. Boston: Houghton Mifflin.

Herzfeld, M. 1982. *Ours once more: folklore, ideology and the making of modern Greece*. Cambridge: Cambridge University Press.

1987. *Anthropology through the looking glass: critical ethnography in the margins of Europe*. Cambridge: Cambridge University Press.

Herzog, R. 1983. 'On the relation of disciplinary development and historical self-preservation – the case of classical philology since the end of the eighteenth century', *Functions and Uses of Disciplinary Histories* 7: 281–90.

Heyck, T. W. 1982. *The transformation of intellectual life in Victorian England*. New York: St Martin's Press. Reprinted Chicago: Pantheon, 1989.

Hibbert, C. 1987. *The grand tour*. London: Methuen.

Hignett, C. 1952. *A history of the Athenian constitution*. Oxford: Clarendon Press.

Hill, J. 1972. 'The methodological debate in contemporary archaeology: a model', in D. Clarke, ed., *Models in archaeology*: 61–107. London: Methuen.

Hinsley, C. M. 1985. 'From shell-heaps to stelae: early anthropology at the Peabody Museum', in G. Stocking, ed., *Objects and others*: 49–74. Madison: University of Wisconsin Press (*History of Anthropology* 3).

1986. 'Edgar Lee Hewitt and the School of American Research in Santa Fe 1906–1912', in Meltzer *et al.* 1986: 217–33.

Hirschon, R. 1989. *Heirs of the Greek catastrophe*. Oxford: Clarendon Press.

Hitchens, C. 1987. *The Elgin marbles: should they be returned to Greece?* London: Chatto and Windus.

Hobhouse, H. 1985. *Seeds of change: five plants that transformed mankind*. London: Sidgwick and Jackson.

Hobsbawm, E. J. 1962. *The age of revolution, 1789–1848*. New York: Mentor.

1987. *The age of empire, 1875–1914*. New York: Mentor.

1990. *Nations and nationalism since 1780*. Cambridge: Cambridge University Press.

Hodder, I. 1982a. *Symbols in action*. Cambridge: Cambridge University Press.

1982b. *The present past*. London: Batsford.

1982c. 'Theoretical archaeology: a reactionary view', in Hodder 1982d: 1–12.

1985. 'Postprocessual archaeology', in M. Schiffer, ed., *Advances in archaeological method and theory* 8: 1–26. New York: Academic Press.

1989a. 'Writing archaeology: site reports in context', *Antiquity* 63: 268–74.

1989b. 'Post-modernism, post-structuralism, and post-processual archaeology', in Hodder 1989c: 64–78.

1990. *The domestication of Europe*. Oxford: Basil Blackwell.

1991. *Reading the past*. 2nd edn. Cambridge: Cambridge University Press.

Hodder, I., ed. 1982d. *Symbolic and structural archaeology*. Cambridge: Cambridge University Press.

1987a. *Archaeology as long-term history*. Cambridge: Cambridge University Press.

1987b. *The archaeology of contextual meanings*. Cambridge: Cambridge University Press.

1989c. *The meanings of things*. London: Unwin Hyman.

Hodder, I., Isaac, G. and Hammond N., eds. 1981. *Patterns of the past: studies in honour of David Clarke*. Cambridge: Cambridge University Press.

Hodgkin, T. 1905/6. 'Ernst Curtius', *Proceedings of the British Academy* 2: 31–54.

Hodkinson, S. 1988. 'Animal husbandry in the Greek polis', in Whittaker 1988: 35–74.

Hoepfner, W. and Schwandner, E.-L. 1986. *Haus und Stadt im klassischen Griechenland*. Munich: Deutsche Kunstverlag.

Hoesterey, I., ed. 1991. *Zeitgeist in Babel*. Bloomington: Indiana University Press.

Hoffmann, H. 1979. 'In the wake of Beazley', *Hephaistos* 1: 61–70.

1983. '*Ybrin Orthian Knodalon*', in D. Metzler, ed., *Antidoron: Festschrift für Jürgen Thimme*: 61–73. Karlsruhe: C. F. Müller.

1986. 'From Charos to Charon: some notes on the human encounter with death in Attic red-figured vase-painting', *Visible Religion* 4/5: 173–204.

1988. 'Why did the Greeks need imagery?', *Hephaistos* 9: 143–62.

1989. '*Aletheia*: the iconography of death/rebirth in three cups by the Sotades painter', *Res* 17/18: 69–88.

Forthcoming. 'Dulce et decorum est pro patria mori: heroic immortality imagery on Greek painted vases', in R. Osborne and S. Goldhill, eds., *Art and text*. Cambridge: Cambridge University Press.

Hoffmann, H. and Davidson, P. F. 1965. *Greek gold jewellery from the age of Alexander*. Mainz: Zabern.

Hoffmann, H. and Metzler, D. 1990. 'Audiatur et altera pars: zur Doppeldeutigkeit einer griechischen Amazone aus dem Sudan', *Visible Religion* 7: 172–98.

Hofstadter, R. 1961. *Anti-intellectualism in American life*. New York: Knopf.

Hohendahl, P. U. 1989. *Building a national literature: the case of Germany, 1830–1870*. Ithaca, NY: Cornell University Press.

Hole, F., ed. 1987. *The archaeology of Western Iran*. Washington, DC: Smithsonian Institution Press.

Holland, P. 1987. 'The page three girl speaks to women too', in Betterton 1987: 105–19.

Hollein, H.-G. 1988. 'Bürgerbild und Bildwelt der athenischen Demokratie auf den rotfiguren vasen des 6.–4. Jhs. v. Chr'. PhD thesis, Hamburg University.

Hollinger, D. A. 1991. 'Postmodernist theory and *wissenschaftliche* practice', *American Historical Review* 96: 688–92.

Holt, F. L. 1984a. 'Discovering the lost history of ancient Afghanistan', *The Ancient World* 9: 3–11.

1984b. 'Select bibliography of recent research and studies on Hellenistic Bactria', *The Ancient World* 9: 13–28.

1988. *Alexander the Great and Bactria*. Leiden: Brill.

Hondros, J. 1983. *Occupation and resistance: the Greek agony, 1941–1944*. New York: Pella.

Hood, M. S. F. 1987. 'An early British interest in Knossos', *Annual of the British School at Athens* 82: 85–94.

Hope Simpson, R. 1983. 'The limitations of surface surveys', in Keller and Rupp 1983: 45–7.

1984. 'The analysis of data from surface surveys', *Journal of Field Archaeology* 11: 115–17.

Hornblower, S. 1983. *The Greek world, 479–323 BC*. London: Methuen.

Horstmann, A. 1979. 'Die Forschung in der klassischen Philologie des 19. Jahrhunderts', *Studien zur Wissenschaftstheorie* 12: 27–57.

Hugo, H. E. 1957. *The portable Romantic reader*. New York: Viking.

Humphreys, S. C. 1978. *Anthropology and the Greeks*. London: Routledge.

1980. 'Family tombs and tomb cult in ancient Athens: tradition or traditionalism?', *Journal of Hellenic Studies* 100: 96–126.

1983. *The family, women and death*. London: Routledge.

Hunt, L. 1989a. 'Introduction: history, culture and text', in Hunt 1989b: 1–22.

Hunt, L., ed. 1989b. *The new cultural history*. Berkeley: University of California Press.

Hussey, J. 1978. 'Jakob Philipp Fallmerayer and George Finlay', *Byzantine and Modern Greek Studies* 4: 78–87.

Hutcheon, L. 1988. *A poetics of postmodernism: history, theory, fiction*. London: Routledge.

1989. *The politics of postmodernism*. London: Routledge.

Iatrides, J. 1972. *Revolt in Athens: the Greek communist 'second round', 1944–1945*. Princeton: Princeton University Press.

1983. 'Greece and the United States: the strained partnership', in Clogg 1983: 150–72.

Ibrahim, M., Sauer, J. and Yassine, K. 1976. 'The East Jordan valley survey, 1975', *Bulletin of the American Schools of Oriental Research* 221: 41–66.

Iggers, C. 1983. *The German conception of history*. 2nd edn. Middletown, CT: Wesleyan University Press.

Immerwahr, H. 1990. *Attic script: a survey*. Oxford: Clarendon Press.

Inden, R. 1986. 'Orientalist constructions of India', *Modern Asian Studies* 20: 401–46.

1990. *Imagining India*. Oxford: Basil Blackwell.

Inglehart, R. 1990. *Culture shift in advanced industrial societies*. Princeton: Princeton University Press.

Invernizzi, A. 1976. 'Ten years of research in the Al-Mada'in area: Seleucia and Ctesiphon', *Sumer* 32: 167–75.

Irmscher, J. 1986. 'Johann Joachim Winckelmann in der Sicht seiner altmärkischen Zeitgenossen', in Gaehtgens 1986: 31–40.

Isler-Kerenyi, C. 1979. 'Beazley und die Vasenforschung', in C. Isler-Kerenyi, ed., *Vasenforschung nach Beazley*: 1–14. Mainz: Schriften des deutschen archäologen-Verbandes 4.

Jackson, D. A. 1976. *East Greek influence on Attic vases*. London: Society for the Promotion of Hellenic Studies.

Jacoby, F., ed. 1923–58. *Die Fragmente der griechische Historiker*. Berlin: de Gruyter.

Jameson, F. 1989. 'Marxism and postmodernism', *New Left Review* 176: 31–45, reprinted in Kellner 1989b: 369–87.

1991. *Postmodernism, or the cultural logic of late capitalism*. Durham, NC: Duke University Press.

Jameson, M. H. 1976. 'The Southern Argolid: the setting for historical and cultural studies', in Dimen and Friedl 1976: 74–91.

1977/8. 'Agriculture and slavery in Classical Athens', *Classical Journal* 73: 122–45.

1982. 'The leasing of land in Rhamnous', in *Studies in Attic epigraphy, history and topography presented to Eugene Vanderpool*: 66–74. Princeton: *Hesperia* supp. vol. 19.

1983. 'Famine in the Greek world', in Garnsey and Whittaker 1983: 6–16.

1988. 'Sacrifice and animal husbandry in Classical Greece', in Whittaker 1988: 87–119.

1992. 'Agricultural labor in classical Greece', in B. Wells, ed., *Agriculture in classical Greece*, 135–46. Stockholm: Paul Åströms Förlag.

Janko, R. 1989. 'Dissolution and diaspora: Ptolemy Physcon and the future of classical scholarship', in Culham *et al.* 1989: 321–31.

Jannoray, J. 1955. *Enserune: contribution à l'étude des civilisations préromaines de la Gaule méridionale*. Paris: Boccard.

Jannot, J.-R. 1984. *Les reliefs archaïques de Chiusi*. Rome: Ecole française de Rome supp. 71.

1985. 'De l'agôn du geste rituel. L'example de la boxe étrusque', *L'Antiquité Classique* 54: 66–75.

Jantzen, U. 1986. *Einhundert Jahre Athener Institut 1874–1974*. Mainz: Deutsches archäologisches Institut, Geschichte und Dokumente 10.

Jardé, A. 1925. *Les céréales dans l'antiquité grecque*. Paris: Boccard. Reprinted 1979.

Jay, M. 1985. 'Habermas and modernism', in Bernstein 1985: 125–39.

1991. 'Habermas and postmodernism', in Hoesterey 1991: 98–110.

Jeanmaire, J. 1939. *Couroi et courètes*. Lille: Bibliothèque universitaire.

1978. *Dionysos*. Paris: Payot.

Jeffery, L. H. 1962. 'The inscribed gravestones of Archaic Attica', *Annual of the British School at Athens* 57: 115–53.

Jencks, C. 1991. 'Postmodern vs. late-modern', in Hoesterey 1991: 4–21.

Jenkyns, R. 1980. *The Victorians and ancient Greece*. Oxford: Blackwell.

1992. *Dignity and decadence: Victorian art and the classical inheritance*. Cambridge, MA: Harvard University Press.

Joffroy, R. 1954. *Le trésor de Vix*. Paris: Presses universitaires de France.

1960. *L'oppidum de Vix et la civilisation halstattienne finale dans l'Est de la France*. Paris: Publications de l'Université de Dijon 20.

Johnson, G. A. 1977. 'Aspects of regional analysis in archaeology', *Annual Review of Anthropology* 6: 479–508.

1987. 'Nine thousand years of social change in Western Iran', in Hole 1987: 283–91.

Johnston, A. W. 1972. 'The rehabilitation of Sostratos', *Parola del Passato* 27: 416–23.

1978a. 'Lists of contents: Attic vases', *American Journal of Archaeology* 82: 222–6.

1978b. 'Some non-Greek ghosts', *Bulletin of the Institute of Classical Studies* 25: 79–84.

1979. *Trademarks on Greek vases*. Warminster: Aris and Philips.

1985. 'Etruscans in the Greek vase trade', in Cristofani and Pelagatti 1985: 249–55.

1987. 'Amasis and the Greek vase trade', in von Bothmer 1987b: 125–40.

1990, 'Supplement', in L. H. Jeffery, *The local scripts of Archaic Greece*. 2nd edn. Oxford: Clarendon Press.

Jones, A. H. M. 1940. *The Greek city from Alexander to Justinian*. Oxford: Oxford University Press.

1952. 'Census records of the Later Roman Empire', *Journal of Roman Studies* 42: 49–64.

Jones, C. P. 1978. *The Roman world of Dio Chrysostom*. Cambridge, MA: Harvard University Press.

Jones, G. D. and Kautz, R. R., eds. 1981. *The transition to statehood in the New World*. Cambridge: Cambridge University Press.

Jones, H. 1991. *'A new kind of war' – America's global strategy and the Truman doctrine in Greece*. Oxford: Oxford University Press.

Jones, J. E., Graham, A. J. and Sackett, L. H. 1973. 'An Attic country house below the cave of Pan at Vari', *Annual of the British School at Athens* 68: 355–452.

Jones, J. E., Sackett, L. H. and Graham, A. J. 1962. 'The Dema house in Attica', *Annual of the British School at Athens* 57: 75–114.

Jones, N. 1974. *Men of influence in Nuristan*. London: Seminar Press.

Jones, R. E. 1984. 'Greek potters' clays: questions of selection, availability and adaption', in Brijder 1984: 21–30.

1986. *Greek and Cypriot pottery: a review of scientific studies*. Athens and London: Fitch Laboratory Occasional Papers.

Jones, R. E. and Johnston, A. W. 1978. 'The "SOS" amphora', *Annual of the British School at Athens* 73: 101–41.

Jully, J.-J. 1982/3. *Céramiques grecques ou de type grec et autres céramiques en Languedoc méditerranéen, Roussillon et Catalogne*. Paris: Société des Belles Lettres.

Just, R. 1989. 'Triumph of the ethnos', in E. Tonkin, M. McDonald and M. Chapman, eds., *History and ethnicity*: 71–88. London: Routledge. ASA monograph 27.

Justi, C. 1898. *Winckelmann und sein Zeitgenossen*. 2 vols. Leipzig: C. F. W. Vogel. Reissued 1943, Leipzig: Koehler and Ameland; 1956, Köln: Phaidon.

Kabbani, R. 1986. *Europe's myths of Orient*. London: Macmillan.

Kaempf-Dimitriadou, S. 1979. *Die Liebe der Götter in der attischen Kunst des 5. Jhs. v. Chr*. Bern: Antike Kunst Beiheft 11.

Käfer, M. 1986. *Winckelmanns hermeneutische Prinzipien*. Heidelberg: C. Winter.

Kagan, D. 1987. *The fall of the Athenian empire*. Ithaca, NY: Cornell University Press.

Kampen, N. 1975. 'Hellenistic artists: female', *Archeologia Classica* 27: 9–17.

Karady, V. 1980. 'Educational qualifications and university careers in France', in R. Fox and G. Weisz, eds., *The organisation of science and technology in France, 1808–1914*: 95–125. Cambridge: Cambridge University Press.

Kardulias, P. N. Forthcoming. 'Archaeology in modern Greece: politics, bureaucracy, and science'.

Kedurie, E. 1970. *Nationalism*. London: Hutchinson.

Keller, D. R. 1985. 'Archaeological survey in Southern Euboea, Greece'. PhD thesis, Indiana University.

Keller, D. R. and Rupp, D. W., eds. 1983. *Archaeological*

survey in the Mediterranean area. Oxford: British Archaeological Reports International Series 155.

Keller, D. R. and Wallace, M. B. 1988. 'The Canadian Karystia Project: two Classical farmsteads', *Echos du Monde Classique/Classical Views* 7: 151–8.

Kelley, J. H. and Hanen, M. P. 1988. *Archaeology and the methodology of science*. Albuquerque: University of New Mexico Press.

Kellner, D. 1989a. *Jean Baudrillard*. Stanford: Stanford University Press.

Kellner, D., ed. 1989b. *Postmodernism/Jameson/critique*. Washington, DC: Maisonneuve Press.

Kelman, M. 1987. *A guide to critical legal studies*. Cambridge, MA: Harvard University Press.

Kenner, H. 1935. 'Das Luterion im Kult', *Jahrshefte des österreichischen archäologischen Instituts in Wien* 29: 109–54.

Kenney, E. J., ed. 1984. *The ploughman's lunch (Moretum)*. Bristol: Bristol Classical Press.

Kenrick, P. M. 1981. 'Fine wares of the Hellenistic and Roman periods', in Matthers 1981: 439–58.

Kent, J. H. 1948. 'The temple estates of Delos, Rheneia and Mykonos', *Hesperia* 17: 243–338.

Kent, S., ed. 1990. *Domestic architecture and the use of space*. Cambridge: Cambridge University Press.

Kerestes, J. M., Lundquist, J. M., Wood, B. G. and Yassine, K. 1977/8. 'An archaeological survey of three reservoir areas in Northern Jordan, 1978', *Annual of the Department of Antiquities of Jordan* 22: 108–35.

Kervran, M. 1986. 'Qal'at al-Bahrain', in al-Khalifa and Rice 1986: 462–9.

Keuls, E. 1985. *The reign of the phallus*. New York: St Martin's Press.

Keylor, W. R. 1975. *Academy and community*. Cambridge, MA: Harvard University Press.

Kilian, K. 1977. 'Zwei italische Kannhelme aus Griechenland', in *Etudes Delphiques*: 429–42. Paris: *Bulletin de Correspondance Hellénique* supp. 4.

Kilian-Dirlmeier, I. 1985. 'Fremde Weihungen in griechischen Heiligtümern vom 8. bis zum Beginn des 7. Jhs. v. Chr.', *Jahrbuch des Römisch-Germanischen Zentralmuseums Mainz* 32: 215–54.

Kimball, R. 1990. *Tenured radicals: how politics has corrupted our higher education*. New York: Harper.

Kimmig, W. 1971. 'Grabungsverlauf und Funde', in W. Kimmig and E. Gersbach, 'Die Grabungen auf der Heuneburg 1966–1969', *Germania* 49: 21–60.

1975. 'Die Heuneburg auf der oberen Donau', in *Ausgrabungen in Deutschland 1950–1975*: 192–211. Mainz: *Jahrbuch des Römisch-Germanischen Zentralmuseums Mainz* supp, vol.

1983. 'Die griechische Kolonisation im westlichen Mittelmeergebiet und ihre Wirkung auf die Landschaften des westlichen Mitteleuropa', *Jahrbuch des Römisch-Germanischen Zentralmuseums Mainz* 30: 3–78.

Kirkby, A. and Kirkby, M. J. 1976. 'Geomorphic processes and the surface area of archaeological sites in semi-arid areas', in D. A. Davidson and M. L. Shackley, eds., *Geoarchaeology: earth science and the past*: 229–53. London: Duckworth.

Kloppenberg, J. T. 1989. 'Objectivity and historicism: a century of American historical writing', *American Historical Review* 94: 1011–30.

Koliopoulos, J. 1987. *Brigands with a cause*. Oxford: Clarendon Press.

Konstans, D. C. 1991. 'Greek foreign policy objectives: 1974–1986', in Vryonis 1991: 37–69.

Kopytoff, I. 1986. 'The cultural biography of things: commoditization as process', in Appadurai 1986b: 64–91.

Koselleck, R. 1985. *Futures past: on the semantics of historical time*. Cambridge, MA: MIT Press.

Kosso, P. 1991. 'Method in archaeology: middle-range theory as hermeneutics', *American Antiquity* 56: 621–7.

Koster, H. A. and Koster, J. B. 1976. 'Competition or symbiosis: pastoral adaptive strategies in the Southern Argolid, Greece', in Dimen and Friedl 1976: 275–85.

Kotsakis, K. 1989. 'The Langadas Basin intensive survey: first preliminary report, the 1986 season', *Egnatia* 1: 3–14.

1990. 'The Langadas survey and the organisation of space in central Macedonia'. Unpublished paper.

1991. 'The powerful past: theoretical trends in Greek archaeology', in I. Hodder, ed., *Archaeological theory in Europe: the last three decades*: 65–90. London: Routledge.

Koucky, F. L. 1987. 'Survey of the Limes zone', in S. T. Parker 1987: 41–105.

Kousser, M. 1984. 'The revivalism of narrative', *Social Science History* 8: 133–49.

Kreissig, H. 1974. 'Die Polis in Griechenland und im orient in der hellenistischen Epoche', in E. C. Welskopf, ed., *Hellenische Poleis* II: 1074–84. Berlin: Akademie Verlag.

1980. 'Free labour in the Hellenistic age', in P. Garnsey, ed., *Non-slave labour in the Greco-Roman world*: 30–3. Cambridge: Cambridge Philological Society supp. vol. 6.

Krentos, V. D. and Orphanos, P. I. 1979. 'Nitrogen and phosphorus fertilizers for wheat and barley in a semi-arid region', *Journal of Agricultural Science* 93: 711–17.

Kristiansen, K. 1981. 'A social history of Danish archaeology (1805–1975)', in Daniel 1981b: 20–44.

Kritzas, Ch. 1972. 'Arkhaiotites kai mnimeia Argolidokorinthias', *Archaiologikon Deltion* 27.2: 192–219.

Kron, U. 1976. *Die zehn attischen Phylenheroen*. Berlin: Gebr. Mann.

Kübler, K. 1954. *Kerameikos*. V.1. *Die Nekropole des 10. bis 8. Jhs.* 2 vols. Berlin: de Gruyter.

1959. *Kerameikos* VI.1. *Die Nekropole des späten 8. bis frühen 6. Jhs.* 2 vols. Berlin: de Gruyter.

1970. *Kerameikos* VI.2. *Die Nekropole des späten 8. bis frühen 6. Jhs.* 2 vols. Berlin: de Gruyter.

Kuhn, A. 1985. *The power of the image: essays on representation and sexuality*. London: Pandora.

Kuhn, T. S. 1970. *The structure of scientific revolutions*. 2nd edn. Chicago: University of Chicago Press.

1977. *The essential tension*. Chicago: University of Chicago Press.

Kuhrt, A. and Sancisi-Weerdenburg, H., eds. 1988. *Achaemenid history* III. *Method and theory*. Leiden: Proceedings of the Leiden 1985 Achaemenid History Workshop.

1987a. 'Preface', in Kuhrt and Sherwin-White 1987b: ix–xii.

Kuhrt, A. and Sherwin-White, S., eds. 1987b. *Hellenism in the East*. London: Duckworth.

Kurtz, D. C. 1983. 'Gorgos' cup', *Journal of Hellenic Studies* 103: 68–86.

Kurtz, D. C. and Boardman, J. 1971. *Greek burial customs*. London: Thames and Hudson.

Kushner, G. 1973. 'Archeology as anthropology', *Science* 183: 616–18.

La Fontaine, J. 1985. *Initiation*. Harmondsworth: Penguin.

Laclau, E. and Mouffe, C. 1985. *Hegemony and socialist strategy*. London: Verso.

Lamberg-Karlovsky, C. C. 1989a. 'Introduction', in Lamberg-Karlovsky 1988b: 1–16.

Lamberg-Karlovsky, C. C., ed. 1989b. *Archaeological thought in America*. Cambridge: Cambridge University Press.

Lambert, S. 1986. 'Herodotus, the Cylonian conspiracy and the "prytaneis ton naukraron"', *Historia* 35: 105–12.

Lane, E. W. 1836. *Manners and customs of the modern Egyptians*. London: J. M. Dent. Reissued London, 1978: East-West Publishers.

Lang, B. 1986. 'Postmodernism in philosophy: nostalgia for the future, waiting for the past', *New Literary History* 18: 209–23.

Langdon, M. K. 1976. *A sanctuary of Zeus on Mt Hymettos*. Princeton: *Hesperia* supp. vol. 16.

Langlotz, E. 1966. *Die kulturelle und künstlerische Hellenisierung der Küsten des Mittelmeers durch die Stadt Phokaia*. Cologne: Westdeutscher Verlag.

Larsen, C. E. 1983. *Life and land use on the Bahrain islands*. Chicago: University of Chicago Press.

Larsen, M. T. 1989. 'Orientalism and Near Eastern archaeology', in Miller *et al.* 1989: 229–39.

Larsen, M. T., ed. 1979. *Power and propaganda: a symposium on ancient empires*. Copenhagen: Akademisk Forlag.

Larson, M. S. 1977. *The rise of professionalism: a sociological analysis*. Berkeley: University of California Press.

Lauffer, S. 1979. *Die Bergwerkssklaven von Laureion*. 2nd edn. Wiesbaden: Steiner.

Lauter, H. 1985a. *Lathuresa: Beiträge zur Architektur und Sidelungsgeschichte in spätgeometrischer Zeit*. Mainz: von Zabern.

1985b. *Der Kultplatz auf dem Turkovuni*. Berlin: Gebrüder Mann.

1986. *Die Architektur des Hellenismus*. Darmstadt: Wissenschaftliche Buchgesellschaft.

Lawrence, A. W. and Tomlinson, R. A. 1983. *Greek architecture*. 4th edn. Harmondsworth: Penguin.

Layton, R., ed. 1989a. *Conflict in the archaeology of living traditions*. London: Unwin Hyman.

1989b. *Who needs the past? Indigenous values and archaeology*. London: Unwin Hyman.

Lazzarini, M. 1976. *Le formule delle dediche votive nella Grecia arcaica*. Rome: Atti della Accademia nazionale dei Lincei, classe di scienze morali, storiche e filologiche: ser. 8, vol. 19, fasc. 2.

Leach, E. R. 1970. *Claude Lévi-Strauss*. London: Fontana.

1976. *Culture and communication*. Cambridge: Cambridge University Press.

Leclant, J. 1982. 'Champollion et le Collège de France', *Bulletin de la Société Française d'Egyptologie* 95: 32–46.

Leone, M. 1972. 'Issues in anthropological archaeology', in M. Leone, ed., *Contemporary archaeology*: 14–27. Carbondale: Southern Illinois University Press.

Lévêque, P. and Morel, J.-P., eds. 1980. *Céramiques hellénistiques et romaines* I. Paris: Editions des Belles Lettres.

1987. *Céramiques hellénistiques et romaines II*. Paris: Editions des Belles Lettres.

Lévi-Strauss, C. 1963. *Structural anthropology*. Harmondsworth: Pelican.

Levine, J. M. 1987. *Humanism and history: origins of modern English historiography*. Ithaca, NY: Cornell University Press.

Levine, M. 1992. 'The use and abuse of *Black Athena*', *American Historical Review* 97: 440–60.

Levine, P. 1986. *The amateur and the professional: antiquarians, historians and archaeologists in Victorian England, 1838–1886*. Cambridge: Cambridge University Press.

Lewis, B. 1990. 'Other people's history', *American Scholar* 59: 397–405.

Lewis, D. M. 1987. 'Bowie on elegy: a footnote', *Journal of Hellenic Studies* 107: 188.

Lewis, D. M. and Stroud, R. 1979. 'Athens honors king Evagoras of Salamis', *Hesperia* 48: 180–93.

Lewthwaite, J. 1986. 'Archaeologists in academe: an institutional confinement?', in Bintliff and Gaffney 1986: 52–87.

Lippold, G. 1952. 'Der plaste Sotades', *Münchner Jahrbuch des Bildenden Kunst* (ser. 3) 3: 85–95.

Lissarrague, F. 1990. *The aesthetics of the Greek banquet*. Princeton: Princeton University Press.

Litvinskiy, B. A. and Pichikyan, I. R. 1984. 'Monuments of art from the sanctuary of Oxus (North Bactria)', in J. Harmatta, ed., *From Hecataeus to al-Huwarizmi*: 25–83. Budapest: Akadémiai Kiadó.

Livadie, C. A. 1985. 'La situazione in Campania', in Cristofani and Pelagatti 1985: 127–54.

Lloyd, J. 1991. 'Forms of rural settlement in the early Roman landscape', in G. Barker and J. Lloyd, eds., *Roman landscapes*, 233–40. London: British School at Rome.

Loehr, R. C. 1974. *Agricultural waste management: problems, processes and approaches*. New York: Academic Press.

1977. *Pollution control for agriculture*. New York: Academic Press.

Lohmann, H. 1983. 'Atene: eine attische Landgemeinde klassischer Zeit', *Hellenika Jahrbuch*: 98–117.

1985. 'Landleben in klassischen Attika', *Ruhr-Universität Bochum Jahrbuch*: 71–96.

Loraux, N. Forthcoming. 'Kreusa the autochthon: a study of Euripides' *Ion*'.

Lord, L. E. 1947. *A history of the American School of Classical Studies at Athens, 1882–1942: an intercollegiate project*. Cambridge, MA: Harvard University Press.

Lowenthal, D. 1988. 'Classical antiquities as national and global heritage', *Antiquity* 62: 726–35.

1990. 'Conclusion: archaeologists and others', in Gathercole and Lowenthal 1990: 302–14.

Lowenthal, D. and Bowden, M. J., eds. 1976. *Geographies of the mind*. New York: Oxford University Press.

Lund, J. and Rathje, A. 1988. 'Italic gods and deities on Pontic vases', in Christiansen and Melander 1988: 352–68.

Luscombe, D. E. and Evans, G. R. 1988. 'The twelfth-century renaissance', in J. H. Burns, ed., *The Cambridge history of medieval political thought*: 306–38. Cambridge: Cambridge University Press.

Lyotard, J.-F. 1984. *The postmodern condition: a report on knowledge*. Minneapolis: University of Minnesota Press.

McCredie, J., ed. 1990. *Anamneseis*. Princeton: Institute for Advanced Study.

MacDonald, B. 1982. 'The Wadi el-Hasa survey 1979 and previous archaeological work in Southern Jordan', *Bulletin of the American Schools of Oriental Research* 245: 35–52.

1984. 'The Wadi el Hasa archaeological survey', in H. O. Thompson, ed., *The answers lie below*: 113–27. Lanham, MD: University Press of America.

1988. *The Wadi el Hasa archaeological survey 1979–82, west central Jordan*. Waterloo, Ontario: Wilfred Laurier University Press.

MacDonald, B. and d'Annibale, C. 1983. 'The classical period (322 BC–AD 640) sites of the Wadi el Hasa archaeological survey, Southern Jordan: a preliminary report', *Echos du Monde Classique/Classical Views* 2: 149–58.

MacDonald, B., Clark, G. A. and Neeley, M. 1988. 'Southern Ghors and Northeast 'Arabah archaeological survey 1985 and 1986, Jordan', *Bulletin of the American Schools of Oriental Research* 272: 23–45.

MacDonald, B., Clark, G. A., Neeley, M., Adams, R. and Gregory M. 1987. 'Southern Ghors and Northeast 'Arabah archaeological survey 1986, Jordan', *Annual of the Department of Antiquities of Jordan* 31: 391–418.

MacDonald, B., Rollefson, G. O., Banning, E. B., Byrd, B. F. and d'Annibale, C. 1983. 'The Wadi el Hasa archaeological survey 1982: a preliminary report', *Annual of the Department of Antiquities of Jordan* 27: 311–23.

MacDonald, B., Rollefson, G. O. and Roller, D. W. 1982. 'The Wadi el Hasa survey 1981: a preliminary report', *Annual of the Department of Antiquities of Jordan* 26: 117–31.

MacDonald, B. R. 1979. 'The distribution of Attic pottery from 450 to 375 BC. The effects of politics on trade'. PhD thesis, University of Pennsylvania.

1981. 'The emigration of potters from Athens in the late

fifth century BC and its effects on the Attic pottery industry', *American Journal of Archaeology* 85: 159–68.

1982. 'The import of Attic pottery to Corinth and the question of trade during the Peloponnesian war', *Journal of Hellenic Studies* 102: 113–23.

McDonald, W. A. and Hope Simpson, R. 1972. 'Archaeological exploration', in McDonald and Rapp 1972: 117–47.

McDonald, W. A. and Rapp, G., eds. 1972. *The Minnesota Messenia expedition: reconstructing a Bronze Age regional environment.* Minneapolis: University of Minnesota Press.

McDonald, W. A. and Thomas, C. G. 1990. *Progress into the past.* 2nd edn. Bloomington: Indiana University Press.

McGann, J. J. 1983. *The Romantic ideology.* Chicago: University of Chicago Press.

McGlew, J. 1984. 'J. G. Droysen and the Aechylean hero', *Classical Philology* 79: 1–14.

McGuire, R. H. and Paynter, R., eds. 1991. *The archaeology of inequality.* Oxford: Blackwell.

Macintosh, H. 1974. 'Etruscan bucchero imports from Corinth', *Hesperia* 43: 34–45.

McNeill, W. 1976. *The metamorphosis of Greece since World War II.* Chicago: University of Chicago Press.

1989. *Arnold J. Toynbee: a life.* Oxford: Oxford University Press.

Macready, S. and Thompson, F. H., eds. 1985. *Archaeological field survey in Britain and abroad.* London: Society of Antiquaries.

Malina, J. and Vasícek, Z. 1990. *Archaeology yesterday and today.* Cambridge: Cambridge University Press.

Malone, C. and Stoddart, S., eds. 1985. *Papers in Italian archaeology* IV. Oxford: British Archaeological Reports International Series 245.

Manganaro, M., ed. 1990. *Modernist anthropology: from fieldwork to text.* Princeton: Princeton University Press.

Mansuelli, G. A. 1985. 'L'organizzazione del territorio e la città', in Cristofani 1985: 111–20.

Mara, D. 1976. *Sewage treatment in hot climates.* Chichester: Wiley.

Marangou, L. 1980. 'Ekthesi yia tin anaskaphi tou Panepistimiou Ioanninon stin Amorgo 1979 (Lefkes-Ayia Eirini)', *Dodoni* 9: 175–94.

Marchese, R. 1986. *The lower Maeander floodplain: a regional settlement study.* Oxford: British Archaeological Reports International Series 292.

1989. *The historical archaeology of Northern Caria.* Oxford: British Archaeological Reports International Series 536.

Marcus, G. and Fischer, M. 1986. *Anthropology as cultural critique.* Chicago: University of Chicago Press.

Marfoe, L. *et al.* 1986. 'The Chicago Euphrates archaeological project 1980–1984', *Anatolica* 13: 37–148.

Marichal, R. 1982. 'Champollion et l'Académie', *Bulletin de la Société Française d'Egyptologie* 95: 12–31.

Martelli, M. 1979. 'Prima considerazioni sulla statistica della importazione greche in Etruria nel periodo arcaico', *Studi Etruschi* 47: 37–52.

1985. 'I luoghi e i prodotti dello scambio', in Cristofani 1985: 175–81.

Martin, R. 1974. *L'urbanisme dans la Grèce antique.* 2nd edn. Paris: Picard.

Martino, F. de 1976. *La terra del remorso: contributo a una storia religiosa del Sud.* Milan: Il Saggiatore.

Matthers, J., ed. 1981. *The River Qoueiq, Northern Syria and its catchment.* Oxford: British Archaeological Reports International Series 98.

Matthers, J. *et al.* 1978. 'Tell Rifa'at 1977', *Iraq* 40: 119–62.

Maxwell Hyslop, R., Du Plat Taylor, J., Seton Williams, M. V. and D. A. and Waechter, J. 1942. 'An archaeological survey of the plain of Jabbul, 1939', *Palestine Exploration Quarterly*: 8–40.

Mayo, M. E. 1982. *The art of South Italy: vases from Magna Grecia.* Richmond: Virginia Museum of Fine Arts.

Mazower, M. 1991. *Greece and the inter-war economic crisis.* Oxford: Oxford University Press.

Megill, A. 1985. *Prophets of extremity.* Berkeley: University of California Press.

1987. 'The reception of Foucault by historians', *Journal of the History of Ideas* 48: 117–41.

1991. 'Fragmentation and the future of historiography', *American Historical Review* 96: 693–8.

Meiggs, R. and Lewis, D. M. 1969. *A selection of Greek historical inscriptions.* Oxford: Oxford University Press.

Mellink, M. 1988. 'Archaeology in Anatolia', *American Journal of Archaeology* 92: 101–31.

Mellor, A. K., ed. 1988. *Romanticism and feminism.* Bloomington: Indiana University Press.

Meltzer, D. J. 1979. 'Paradigms and the nature of change in American archaeology', *American Antiquity* 44: 644–57.

1983. 'Prehistory, power and politics in the Bureau of American Ethnology, 1879–1906', in Gero *et al.* 1983: 67–77.

1985. 'North American archaeology and archaeologists, 1879–1934', *American Antiquity* 50: 249–60.

1989. 'A question of relevance', in Christenson 1989: 5–20.

Meltzer, D., Fowler, D. and Sabloff, J., eds. 1986. *American archaeology past and future*. Washington, DC: Smithsonian Institution Press.

Meritt, L. S. 1984. *History of the American School of Classical Studies at Athens, 1939–1980*. Princeton: American School of Classical Studies at Athens.

Merkouri, M. 1982. 'Anaskaphes Xenon Arkhaiologikon Idrymaton pou leitourgoun stin Ellada', circular no. 4883 of the Ministry of Culture and Science, 21 July 1982. Athens.

Meyer, J. C. 1980. 'Roman history in the light of the import of Attic vases to Rome and Etruria in the sixth and fifth centuries BC', *Analecta Romana Instituti Danici* 9: 47–68.

Meyers, E. M., Strange, J. F. and Groh, D. E. 1978. 'The Meiron excavation project: archaeological survey in Galilee and the Golan', *Bulletin of the American Schools of Oriental Research* 230: 1–24.

Michell, H. 1957. *The economics of ancient Greece*. Cambridge: Cambridge University Press.

Mildenberger, G. 1963. 'Griechische Scherben vom Marlenberg in Würzburg', *Germania* 41: 103–4.

Millar, F. 1987. 'The problem of Hellenistic Syria', in Kuhrt and Sherwin-White 1987b: 110–33.

Miller, D. 1984. 'Modernism and suburbia as material ideology', in Miller and Tilley 1984: 37–49.

1987. *Material culture and mass consumption*. Oxford: Basil Blackwell.

Miller, D., Rowlands, M. and Tilley, C., eds. 1989. *Domination and resistance*. London: Unwin Hyman.

Miller, D. and Tilley, C., eds. 1984. *Ideology, power and prehistory*. Cambridge: Cambridge University Press.

Miller, J. M. 1979a. 'Archaeological survey of central Moab', *Bulletin of the American Schools of Oriental Research* 234: 43–52.

1979b. 'Archaeological survey south of Wadi Mujib: Glueck's sites revisited', *Annual of the Department of Antiquities of Jordan* 23: 79–92.

Miller, N. and Smart, T. 1984. 'Intentional burning of dung as fuel: a mechanism for the incorporation of charred seeds into the archaeological record', *Journal of Ethnobiology* 4: 15–28.

Millett, M. 1991. 'Pottery: population or supply patterns? The *Ager Tarraconensis* approach', in G. Barker and J. Lloyd, eds., *Roman landscapes*: 18–26. London: British School at Rome.

Millett, P. 1983. 'Maritime loans and the structure of credit in fourth-century Athens', in Garnsey *et al.* 1983: 36–52.

Mitchell, S. 1982. *Regional epigraphic catalogues of Asia Minor* II. *The Ankara district, the inscriptions of North*

Galatia. Oxford: British Archaeological Reports International Series 135.

Mitchell, S. and Waelkens, M. 1987. 'Sagalassus and Cremna 1986', *Anatolian Studies* 37: 37–47.

1988. 'Sagalassus and Cremna 1987', *Anatolian Studies* 38: 53–65.

Mitchell, T. 1991. *Colonising Egypt*. Berkeley: University of California Press.

Mitford, T. B. 1980. 'Roman Cyprus', *Aufstieg und Niedergang der römischen Welt* II.7.2: 1285–384.

Mobry, J. and Palumbo, G. 1988. 'The 1987 Wadi el-Yabis survey', *Annual of the Department of Antiquities of Jordan* 32: 275–305.

Momigliano, A. 1966. *Studies in historiography*. Oxford: Blackwell.

1977. *Essays in ancient and modern historiography*. Oxford: Basil Blackwell.

Moon, W. 1979. *Greek vase-painting in midwestern collections*. Chicago: Art Institute of Chicago.

Moore, F. G. 1919. 'A history of the American Philological Association', *Transactions of the American Philological Association* 50: 5–32.

Moormann, E. M. 1988. 'Het woonhuis in de hellenistische Stad', *Lampas* 21: 137–55 (English summary).

Morel, J.-P. 1975. 'L'expansion phocéenne en occident: dix années de recherches (1966–1975)', *Bulletin de Correspondance Hellénique* 99: 853–96.

1983. 'La céramique comme indice du commerce antique (réalités et interprétations)', in Garnsey and Whittaker 1983: 66–74.

Moret, J.-M. 1984. *Oidipe, la sphinx et les Thébains: essai de mythologie iconographique*. Rome: Institut suisse de Rome.

Morgan, C. 1988. 'Corinth, the Corinthian Gulf and western Greece during the eighth century BC', *Annual of the British School at Athens* 83: 313–38.

1990. *Athletes and oracles*. Cambridge: Cambridge University Press.

1991. 'Ethnicity and early Greek states: historical and material perspectives', *Proceedings of the Cambridge Philological Society* 217: 131–63.

Morgan, C. and Whitelaw, T. 1991. 'Pots and politics: ceramic evidence for the rise of the Argive state', *American Journal of Archaeology* 95: 79–108.

Morris, I. 1987. *Burial and ancient society*. Cambridge: Cambridge University Press.

1991. 'The early polis as city and state', in J. Rich and A. Wallace-Hadrill, eds., *City and country in the ancient world*: 24–57. London: Routledge.

1992. *Death-ritual and social structure in classical antiquity*. Cambridge: Cambridge University Press.

Morris, S. P. 1981. 'A Middle Protoattic workshop from Aigina and its historical background'. PhD thesis, Harvard University.

1984. *The Black and White style*. New Haven: Yale University Press.

Mountjoy, P. 1986. *Mycenaean decorated pottery: a guide to identification*, Göteborg: *Studies in Mediterranean Archaeology* 73.

Muhly, J. D. 1980. Review of G. Rapp and S. Aschenbrenner, eds., *Excavations at Nichoria in southwest Greece* I (1978) in *American Journal of Archaeology* 84: 101–2.

1990. '*Black Athena* versus traditional scholarship', *Journal of Mediterranean Archaeology* 3: 83-110.

Müller, D. K. 1987. 'The process of systematisation: the case of German secondary education', in D. K. Müller, F. Ringer and B. Simon, eds., *The rise of the modern educational system: structural change and social reproduction 1870–1920*: 16–52. Cambridge: Cambridge University Press.

Mulvey, L. 1987. 'You don't know what is happening, do you Mr Jones?', in Parker and Pollock 1987: 127–31.

Munn, M. H. and Zimmerman Munn, M. L. 1989. 'Studies on the Attic-Boiotian frontier: the Stanford Skourta project, 1985', in J. M. Fossey, ed., *Boiotia Antiqua* I: 73–127. Amsterdam: Gieben.

Murray, O. 1980. *Early Greece*. Glasgow: Fontana.

1983. 'The symposion as social organisation', in R. Hägg, ed., *The Greek renaissance of the eighth century BC*: 195–9. Stockholm: Skrifter utgvina i svenska institutet i Athen.

1990. 'Cities of reason', in Murray and Price 1990: 1–25.

Murray, O. and Price, S., eds. 1990. *The Greek city from Homer to Alexander*. Oxford: Oxford University Press.

Murray, P. and Kardulias, N. 1986. 'A modern-site survey in the Southern Argolid, Greece', *Journal of Field Archaeology* 13: 21–41.

Musti, D. 1984. 'Syria and the East', in Walbank *et al.* 1984: 175–220.

Mylonas, G. 1957. *O protoattikos amphorefs tis Elefsinos*. Athens: I en Athinais Arkhaiologiki Vivliothiki.

1961. *Eleusis and the Eleusinian mysteries*. Princeton: Princeton University Press.

1975. *To dytikon nekrotapheion tis Elefsinos*. 3 vols. Athens: I en Athinais Arkhaiologiki Vivliothiki.

N.N. 1972. 'Traditionalism and reaction in Greek education', in Clogg and Yannopoulos 1972: 128–45.

Napier, A. D. 1986. *Masks, transformations, and paradox*. Berkeley: University of California Press.

Nash, D. 1985. 'Celtic territorial expansion and the Mediterranean world', in T. Champion and J. Megaw, eds., *Settlement and society: aspects of West European prehistory in the first millennium BC*: 45–67. Leicester: Leicester University Press.

Nashef, K. 1990. 'Archaeology in Iraq', *American Journal of Archaeology* 94: 259–89.

Neely, J. A. 1970. 'The Deh Luran region', *Iraq* 8: 202–3.

Negev, A. 1977. 'The Nabataeans and the Provincia Arabia', *Aufstieg und Niedergang der römischen Welt* II.8: 520–686.

Newbould, I. 1990. *Whiggery and reform 1830–41*. Stanford: Stanford University Press.

Nielson, E. O. 1984. 'Recent excavations at Poggio Civitate', *Studi e Materiali* 6.

Nielson E. O. and Philips, K. M. 1983. 'Poggio Civitae (Siena). The excavations at Murlo in 1976–1978', *Notizie degli Scavi*: 5-24.

1985. 'Poggio Civitate (Murlo)', in S. Stoppone, ed., *Case e palazzi d'Etruria*: 64–154. Milan: Electa.

Nilsson, M. P. 1948. *Greek piety*. Oxford: Clarendon Press.

Nimis, S. 1984. 'Fussnoten: das Fundament der Wissenschaft', *Arethusa* 17: 105–34.

Nixon, L., Moody, J., Niniou-Kindeli, V., Price, S. and Rackham, O. 1990. 'Archaeological survey in Sphakia, Crete', *Echos du Monde Classique/Classical Views* 9: 213–20.

Nixon, L., Moody, J., Price, S. and Rackham, O. 1989. 'Archaeological survey in Sphakia, Crete', *Echos du Monde Classique/Classical Views* 8: 201–15.

Nixon, L., Moody, J. and Rackham, O. 1988. 'Archaeological survey in Sphakia, Crete', *Echos du Monde Classique/Classical Views* 7: 159–73.

Nock, A. D. 1944. 'The cult of heroes', *Harvard Theological Review* 37: 141–74.

Noonan, T. S. 1973. 'The grain trade of the Northern Black Sea in antiquity', *American Journal of Philology* 94: 231–42.

Norton, C. E. 1900. 'The progress of the Archaeological Institute of America: an address', *American Journal of Archaeology* n.s. 4: 1–16.

Novick, P. 1988. *That noble dream: the 'objectivity question' and the American historical profession*. Cambridge: Cambridge University Press.

1991. 'My correct views on everything', *American Historical Review* 96: 699–703.

Nussbaum, M. 1987. 'Undemocratic vistas', *New York Review of Books*, 5 November: 20–6.

Nylander, C. 1962. 'Die sog. mykenischen Säulenbasen auf der Akropolis in Athen', *Opuscula Atheniensia* 4: 31–77.

Ober, J. 1989. *Mass and elite in democratic Athens*. Princeton: Princeton University Press.

O'Boyle, L. 1969. 'Klassische Bildung und soziale Struktur in Deutschland zwischen 1800 und 1848', *Historische Zeitschrift* 207: 584–608.

O'Brien, P. 1989. 'Michel Foucault's history of culture', in Hunt 1989b: 25–46.

Oleson, A. and Voss, J., eds. 1979. *The organization of knowledge in modern America, 1860–1920*. Baltimore: Johns Hopkins University Press.

Olmos, R. 1986. 'Quelques observations sur l'assimilation de l'iconographie grecque dans le monde ibérique (II)', in *Iconographie classique et identités régionales*: 157–66. Paris: *Bulletin de Correspondance Hellénique* supp. vol. 14.

Olsson, G. 1988. 'Nutrient use and productivity for different cropping systems in South Sweden during the 18th century', in H. H. Birks *et al.*, eds., *The cultural landscape: past, present and future*: 123–37. Cambridge: Cambridge University Press.

Orme, B. 1981. *Anthropology for archaeologists*. London: Duckworth.

Osborne, R. 1985. 'Buildings and residence on the land in Classical and Hellenistic Greece: the contribution of epigraphy', *Annual of the British School at Athens* 80: 119-28.

1987a. *Classical landscape with figures: the ancient Greek city and its countryside*. London: George Philip.

1987b. 'The viewing and obscuring of the Parthenon frieze', *Journal of Hellenic Studies* 107: 98–105.

1988a. 'Death revisited, death revised: the death of the artist in Archaic and Classical Greece', *Art History* 11: 1–16.

1988b. 'Social and economic implications of the leasing of land and property in Classical and Hellenistic Greece', *Chiron* 18: 279–323.

1989. 'A crisis in archaeological history? The seventh century BC in Attica', *Annual of the British School at Athens* 84: 297–322.

1991. 'Whose image and superscription is this?', *Arion* n.s. 1: 255–75.

Owens, E. J. 1983. 'The *koprologoi* at Athens in the fifth and fourth centuries BC', *Classical Quarterly* 33: 44–50.

Page, D. L. 1976. *Epigrammata Graeca*. Oxford: Clarendon Press.

Panofsky, E. 1955. *Meaning in the visual arts*. New York: Doubleday.

Papaspyridi-Karouzou, S. 1963. *Ta angeia tou Anayiroundos*. Athens: I en Athinais Arkhaiologiki Vivliothiki.

Papazoglou, F. 1988. *Les villes de Macédoine à l'époque romaine*. Paris: *Bulletin de Correspondance Hellénique* supp. 16.

Pappas, P. C. 1985. *The United States and the Greek War for Independence, 1821–1828*. Boulder, CO: East European Monographs 173.

Pappé, H. O. 1979. 'The English utilitarians and Athenian democracy', in Bolgar 1979b: 295–308.

Paraskevopoulou, P. 1987. *I dokimasia tis dimokratias, 1974–1986: 12 krisima khronia*. Athens: Phytrakis.

Parker, A. 1990. 'The maritime in classical antiquity', *Antiquity* 64: 335–46.

Parker, R. 1986. 'Myths of early Athens', in J. Bremmer, ed., *The interpretation of Greek mythology*: 187–214. London: Routledge.

Parker, R. and Pollock, G. 1987. *Framing feminism: art and the women's movement 1970–1985*. London: Pandora.

Parker, S. T., ed. 1987. *The Roman frontier in central Jordan: interim report on the Limes Arabicus project, 1980–1985* I. Oxford: British Archaeological Reports International Series 340.

Parker Pearson, M. 1982. 'Mortuary practices, society and ideology: an ethnoarchaeological case study', in I. Hodder, ed., *Symbolic and structural archaeology*: 99–113. Cambridge: Cambridge University Press.

Patterson, T. C. 1986. 'The last sixty years: toward a social history of Americanist archaeology in the United States', *American Anthropologist* 88: 7–26.

1989a. 'History and the post-processual archaeologies', *Man* 24: 555–66.

1989b. 'Post-structuralism, post-modernism: the implications for historians', *Social History* 14: 83–8.

1990. 'Some theoretical tensions within and between the processual and postprocessual archaeologies', *Journal of Anthropological Archaeology* 9: 189–200.

Payne, H. 1931. *Necrocorinthia*. Oxford: Clarendon Press.

Peacock, D. and Williams, D. 1986. *Amphorae and the Roman economy, an introductory guide*. London: Longman.

Peacock, S. J. 1988. *Jane Ellen Harrison*. New Haven: Yale University Press.

Pecircka, J. 1973. 'Homestead farms in Classical and Hellenistic Hellas', in M. I. Finley, ed., *Problèmes de la terre en Grèce ancienne*: 113–47. Paris: Mouton.

Pederson, J. E. 1986. '"Background Noise" in pedestrian archaeological survey: a geomorphological evaluation in the Nemea valley, Greece'. Unpublished MA thesis, University of Illinois at Chicago.

Pelekides, S. 1916. 'Anaskaphi Phalirou', *Arkhaiologikon Deltion* 2: 13–64.

Pemble, J. 1987. *The Mediterranean passion: Victorians*

and Edwardians in the South. Oxford: Oxford University Press.

Pepelasis, A. A. and Yotopoloulos, P. A. 1962. *Surplus labor in Greek agriculture, 1953–1960*. Athens: Centre of Economic Research (Research Monograph Series 2).

Peradotto, J. 1983. 'Oedipus and Erichthonius', in Edmunds and Dundes 1983: 179–96.

1989. 'Texts and unrefracted facts: philology, hermeneutics and semiotics', in Culham *et al.* 1989: 179–98.

Peradotto, J. and Levine, M. M., eds. 1989. *The challenge of 'Black Athena'*. Buffalo, NY: *Arethusa* special issue, Fall 1989.

Perkin, H. 1989. *The rise of professional society: England since 1880*. London: Routledge.

Peters, F. 1970. *The harvest of Hellenism: a history of the Near East from Alexander the Great to the triumph of Christianity*. London: Allen.

Petrakos, V. 1987. *I en Athinais Arkhaiologiki Etaireia: i istoria ton 150 khronon tis 1837–1987*. Athens: I en Athinais Arkhaiologikis Etaireias.

Petropulos, J. A. 1968. *Politics and statecraft in the kingdom of Greece, 1833–1843*. Princeton: Princeton University Press.

Pfeiffer, R. 1976. *History of classical scholarship from 1300 to 1850* II. Oxford: Clarendon Press.

Philips, K. M. 1984. 'Greek objects at Poggio Civitate, Murlo', *Studi e Materiali* 6.

Phillips, J. A. 1984. *Eve: the history of an idea*. San Francisco: Harper and Row.

Pilbeam, P. M. 1990. *The middle classes in Europe 1789–1914*. Chicago: Lyceum.

Pinsky, A. 1989. 'Introduction: historical foundations', in Pinsky and Wylie 1989: 51–4.

Pinsky, V. and Wylie, A., eds. 1989. *Critical traditions in contemporary archaeology*. Cambridge: Cambridge University Press.

Polignac, F. de. 1984. *La naissance de la cité grecque*. Paris: Editions de la Découverte.

Pollitt, J. J. 1972. *Art and experience in Classical Greece*. Cambridge: Cambridge University Press.

1986. *Art in the Hellenistic age*. Cambridge: Cambridge University Press.

Pollock, G. 1987a. 'What's wrong with "Images of women"', in Parker and Pollock 1987: 132–8.

1987b. 'Feministry', in Parker and Pollock 1987: 238–43.

Pomeroy, S. 1977. '*Technikai kai mousikai*: the education of women in the fourth century and in the Hellenistic period', *American Journal of Ancient History* 2: 51–68.

Pomeroy, S., ed. 1991. *Women's history and ancient history*. Chapel Hill: University of North Carolina Press.

Popham, M. R. 1990. 'Reflections on "An Archaeology of Greece": surveys and excavations', *Oxford Journal of Archaeology* 9: 29–35.

Popham, M. R., Sackett, L. H. and Themelis, P. G. 1980. *Lefkandi* I: *The Iron Age*. 2 vols. London: British School at Athens supp. vol. 11.

Poster, M. 1982. 'The future according to Foucault: the *Archaeology of knowledge* and intellectual history', in D. LaCapra and S. Kaplan, eds., *Modern European intellectual history*: 137–52. Ithaca, NY: Cornell University Press.

Potter, T. W. 1979. *The changing landscape of South Etruria*. London: Elek.

Potts, A. 1982. 'Winckelmann's construction of history', *Art History* 5: 377–407.

Potts, D. 1983. 'Thaj in the light of recent research", *Atlal* 7: 86–101.

1984. 'Northeastern Arabia in the later pre-Islamic era', in Boucharlat and Salles 1984: 85–144.

1989. *Miscellanea Hasaitica*. Copenhagen: Museum Tusculanum Press.

1990. *The Arabian Gulf in antiquity*. 2 vols. Oxford: Oxford University Press.

Powell, B. B. 1991. *Homer and the origin of the Greek alphabet*. Cambridge: Cambridge University Press.

Prakash, G. 1990. 'Writing post-Orientalist histories of the third world: perspectives from Indian historiography', *Comparative Studies in Society and History* 32: 383–408.

Préaux, C. 1978. *Le monde hellénistique*. 2 vols. Paris: Presses Universitaires de France.

Preziosi, D. 1989. *Rethinking art history: meditations on a coy science*. New Haven: Yale University Press.

Pritchett, W. K. 1953. 'The Attic stelai, Part I', *Hesperia* 22: 225–99.

1956. 'The Attic stelai, Part II', *Hesperia* 25: 178–328.

1965–82. *Studies in Ancient Greek Topography* I–IV. Berkeley: University of California Press.

Psomiades, H. J. 1976. 'The character of the new Greek state', in Diamandouros *et al.* 1976: 147–55.

Py, M. 1978. *L'oppidum de Castelets à Nages (Gard). Fouilles 1958–1974*. Paris: *Gallia* supp. 35.

1982. 'Civilisation indigène et urbanisation durant la protohistoire en Langudeoc-Roussillon', *Ktema* 7: 101–19.

1985. 'Les amphores étrusques de Gaule méridionale', in Cristofani and Pelagatti 1985: 73–94.

Raber, P. 1987. 'Early copper production in the Polis region, Western Cyprus', *Journal of Field Archaeology* 14: 297–312.

Radet, G. 1901. *L'histoire et l'œuvre de l'Ecole française d'Athènes*. Paris: Fontemoing.

Ramage, N. H. 1990. 'Sir William Hamilton as collector, exporter, and dealer: the acquisition and dispersal of his collections'. *American Journal of Archaeology* 94: 469–80.

Rankavis, A. R. 1837. 'Synoptiki ekthesis tis tykhis ton arkhaion mnimeion eis tin Ellada kata ta teleftaia eti', *Ephemeris Arkhaiologiki* 1: 5–13,

Ranowitsch, A. 1958. *Der Hellenismus und seine geschichtliche Rolle*. Berlin: Akademie Verlag.

Rasmussen, D. 1990. *Reading Habermas*. Oxford: Basil Blackwell.

Rasmussen, T. 1979. *Bucchero pottery from Southern Etruria*. Cambridge: Cambridge University Press.

1985. 'Etruscan shapes in Attic pottery', *Antike Kunst* 28: 33–9.

1985/6. 'Archaeology in Etruria, 1980–1985', *Archaeological Reports for 1985/6*: 102–22.

Rasmussen, T. and Spivey, N., eds. 1991. *Looking at Greek vases*. Cambridge: Cambridge University Press.

Raubitschek, A. 1949. *Dedications from the Athenian Akropolis*. Cambridge, MA: Archaeological Institute of America.

Redfield, J. M. 1991. 'Classics and anthropology', *Arion* 3rd ser. 1: 5–23.

Renfrew, A. C. 1972. *The emergence of civilisation*. London: Methuen.

1973. *Before civilisation*. London: Jonathan Cape.

1978. *Problems in European prehistory*. Edinburgh: Edinburgh University Press.

1980. 'The great tradition versus the great divide: archaeology as anthropology?', *American Journal of Archaeology* 84: 287–98.

Renfrew, A. C. and Cherry, J., eds. 1986 *Peer polity interaction and the development of sociocultural complexity*. Cambridge: Cambridge University Press.

Renfrew, A. C. and Shennan, S. J., eds. 1982. *Ranking, resource and exchange*. Cambridge: Cambridge University Press.

Renfrew, A. C. and Wagstaff, J. M., eds. 1982. *An island polity: the archaeology of exploitation in Melos*. Cambridge: Cambridge University Press.

Reynolds, P. J. 1982. 'The ploughzone', in *Festschrift zum 100 jährigen Jubiläum der Abteilung Vorgeschichte der Naturhistorischen Gesellschaft Nürnberg*: 315–400. Nuremberg.

Rhodes, P. J. 1981. *A commentary on the Aristotelian Athenaion Politeia*. Oxford: Clarendon Press.

Rhodes, P. P. 1950. 'The Celtic field systems of the Berkshire Downs', *Oxoniensia* 13: 1–28.

Ricciardi, L., Constantini, L., Giorgio, J. A. and Scale, S. 1985. 'Biera: l'insediamento agricolo di Le Pozze', in *Alimentazione*: 83–7.

Rice, P. M. 1981. 'Evolution of specialized pottery production: a model', *Current Anthropology* 22: 219–27.

1987. *Pottery analysis: a sourcebook*. Chicago: University of Chicago Press.

Rice, P. M., ed. 1984. *Pots and potters*. Los Angeles: UCLA Institute of Archaeology monograph 24.

Richlin, A. 1989. '"Is classics dead?" The 1988 women's classical caucus report', in Culham *et al.* 1989: 51–65.

Richter, G. M. A. 1904/5. 'The distribution of Attic vases', *Annual of the British School at Athens* 11: 224–42.

1961. *The archaic gravestones of Attica*. New York: Phaidon.

1968. *Korai: Archaic Greek maidens*. New York: Phaidon.

Rick, J. W. 1976. 'Downslope movement and archaeological intra-site spatial analysis', *American Antiquity* 41: 133–44.

Ricoeur, P. 1981. *Hermeneutics and the human sciences*. Ed. J. Thompson. Cambridge: Cambridge University Press.

Ridgeway, W. 1908. 'The relationship of anthropology to classical studies', *Journal of the Royal Anthropological Institute* 39: 10–25.

Ridgway, B. S. 1990. *Hellenistic sculpture*. Bristol: Bristol Classical Press.

Ridgway, F. 1990. 'Etruscans, Greeks, Carthaginians: the sanctuary at Pyrgi', in Descouedres 1990: 511–30.

Ridley, R., 1992. *The eagle and the spade*. Cambridge: Cambridge University Press.

Ringer, F. K. 1979a. 'The German academic community', in Oleson and Voss 1979: 409–29.

1979b. *Education and society in modern Europe*. Bloomington: Indiana University Press.

Robbin, K. 1989. *Nineteenth-century Britain*. Oxford: Oxford University Press.

Robert, C. 1915. *Oidipus*. Stuttgart.

Roberts, J. T. 1989. 'Athenians on the sceptred isle', *Classical Journal* 84: 193–205.

Robertshaw, P. T., ed. 1988. *History of African archaeology*. London: Currey.

Robertson, M. 1957. 'Europa', *Journal of the Warburg and Courtauld Institute* 20: 1–3.

1975. *A history of Greek art*. 2 vols. Oxford: Clarendon Press.

1985. 'Beazley and Attic vase painting', in D. Kurtz, ed., *Beazley and Oxford*: 19–30. Oxford: Oxford University Press.

1987. 'The state of Attic vase painting in the mid-sixth century' in von Bothmer 1987b: 13–28.

1989. 'Beazley's use of terms', in T. H. Carpenter, *Beazley addenda*: xii–xx. Oxford: Oxford University Press, for the British Academy.

1991. 'Adopting an approach', in Rasmussen and Spivey 1991: 1–12.

Roe, N. 1988. *Wordsworth and Coleridge: the radical years*. Oxford: Oxford University Press.

Roller, D. W. 1980. 'Hellenistic pottery from Caesarea Maritima', *Bulletin of the American Schools of Oriental Research* 238: 35–42.

1982a. 'The Northern Plain of Sharon in the Hellenistic period', *Bulletin of the American Schools of Oriental Research* 246: 43–52.

1982b. 'The Wilfred Laurier University survey of North-eastern Caesarea Maritima', *Levant* 14: 90–103.

1983. 'The problem of the location of Straton's tower', *Bulletin of the American Schools of Oriental Research* 252: 61–8.

Rombos, T. 1988. *The iconography of Attic Late Geometric II pottery*. Jonsered: *Studies in Mediterranean Archaeology* Pocketbook 68.

Rorty, R. 1985. 'Habermas and Lyotard on postmodernism', in Bernstein 1985: 161–75.

Rosen, F. 1992. *Bentham, Byron, and Greece*. Oxford: Oxford University Press.

Rostovtzeff, M. I. 1941. *The social and economic history of the Hellenistic world*. 1st edn. Oxford: Oxford University Press.

Roueché, C. and Sherwin-White, S. 1985. 'Some aspects of the Seleucid empire: the Greek inscriptions from Falaika, in the Arabian Gulf', *Chiron* 15: 1–39.

Rowlands, M. J. 1984. 'Conceptualizing the European Bronze and Early Iron Ages', in J. Bintliff, ed., *European social evolution*: 147–56. Bradford: Bradford University Press.

1986. 'Modernist fantasies in prehistory?', *Man* 21: 745–6.

1987a. 'The concept of Europe in prehistory', *Man* 22: 558–9.

1987b. '"Europe in prehistory": a unique form of primitive capitalism?', *Culture and History* 1: 63–78.

1987c. 'Centre and periphery: a review of a concept', in Rowlands *et al.* 1987: 1–12.

1989. 'The archaeology of colonialism and constituting the African peasantry', in Miller *et al.* 1989: 261–83.

Rowlands, M. J., Larsen M. and Kristiansen, K., eds. 1987. *Centre and periphery in the Ancient world*. Cambridge: Cambridge University Press.

Rowley-Conwy, P. 1981. 'Slash and burn in the temperate European Neolithic', in R. Mercer, ed., *Farming practice in British prehistory*: 85–96. Edinburgh: Edinburgh University Press.

Roy, J., Owens, E. J. and Lloyd, J. A. 1988. 'Tribe and polis in the chora at Megalopolis', *Praktika*: 179–82.

Runnels, C. N. 1989. Review of Snodgrass 1987, in *American Journal of Archaeology* 93: 145–6.

Rupp, D. W. 1982. 'The Canadian Palaipaphos survey project: an overview of the 1979 and 1980 seasons', *Echos du Monde Classique/Classical Views* 1: 179–85.

1984. 'The Canadian Palaipaphos survey project: an overview of the 1982 and 1983 seasons', *Echos du Monde Classique/ Classical Views* 3: 147–56.

1986. 'The Canadian Palaipaphos (Cyprus) survey project: third preliminary report', *Acta Archaeologica* 57: 27–45.

1987. 'The Canadian Palaipaphos survey project: an overview of the 1986 season', *Echos du Monde Classique/Classical Views* 6: 217–24.

Rupp, D. W., Sørensen, L. W., King, R. H. and Fox, W. A. 1984. 'Canadian Palaipaphos (Cyprus) survey project: second preliminary report, 1980–1982', *Journal of Field Archaeology* 11: 133–54.

Ruppé, R. J. 1966. 'The archaeological survey: a defence', *American Antiquity* 31: 313–33.

Ruschenbusch, E. 1978. *Untersuchungen zu Staat und Politik in Griechenland vom 7–4. Jhs. v. Chr.* Bamberg: Fotodruck.

Rutter, J. B. 1983. 'Some thoughts on the analysis of ceramic data generated by site surveys', in Killer and Rupp 1983: 137–42.

Rystedt, E. 1983. *Acquarossa IV. Early Etruscan akroteria from Acquarossa and Poggio Civitate (Murlo)*. Göteborg: Paul Åström.

Sabloff, J. A. 1989. 'Analyzing recent trends in American archaeology from a historical perspective', in Christenson 1989: 34–40.

Said, E. W. 1978. *Orientalism*. New York: Vintage.

St Clair, W. 1972. *That Greece might still be free: the Philhellenes in the Greek War of Independence*. Oxford: Oxford University Press.

1983. *Lord Elgin and the marbles*. 2nd edn. Oxford: Oxford University Press.

Salles, J.-F. 1982. 'The Gulf area during the first millennium', *Dilmun* 10: 4–8.

1984. 'Bahrain "hellénistique": données et problèmes', in Boucharlat and Salles 1984: 151–63.

1987. 'The Arab-Persian Gulf under the Seleucids', in Kuhrt and Sherwin-White 1987b: 75–109.

Salmon, J. 1984. *Wealthy Corinth*. Oxford: Clarendon Press.

Salviat, F. 1972. 'Bail Thasien pour un terrain planté', *Bulletin de Correspondance Hellénique* 96: 363–73.

Samuel, A. E. 1989. *The shifting sands of history: interpretations of Ptolemaic Egypt*. Lanham, MD: University Press of America.

Sancisi-Weerdenburg, H., ed. 1987. *Achaemenid history* I. *Sources, structures and synthesis*. Leiden: Proceedings of the Groningen 1983 Achaemenid History Workshop.

Sancisi-Weerdenburg, H. and Kuhrt, A., eds. 1987. *Achaemenid history* II. *The Greek sources*. Leiden: Proceedings of the Groningen 1984 Achaemenid History Workshop.

Sanders, I. 1976. 'Settlement in the Hellenistic and Roman periods on the plain of Mesara, Crete', *Annual of the British School at Athens* 71: 131–7.

1982. *Roman Crete*. Warminster: Aris and Philips.

Sanlaville, P., ed. 1985. *Holocene settlement in N. Syria*. Oxford: British Archaeological Reports International Series 239.

Sarafis, S. 1980. *ELAS: the Greek resistance army*. London: Humanities Press.

Sarian, H. 1986. 'Réflexions sur l'iconographie des érinyes dans le milieu grec, italiote et étrusque', in *Iconographie classique et identités régionales*: 25–35. Paris: *Bulletin de Correspondance Hellénique* supp. 14.

Scheffer, C. 1984. 'The selective use of Greek motifs in Etruscan black-figured case painting', in Brijder 1984: 229–33.

1988. 'Workshop and trade patterns in Athenian black figure', in Christiansen and Melander 1988: 536–46.

Schiffer, M. 1983. 'Toward the identification of formation processes', *American Antiquity* 48: 675–706.

1987. *Formation processes of the archaeological record*. Albuquerque: University of New Mexico Press.

1988. 'The structure of archaeological theory', *American Antiquity* 53: 461–85.

Schiffer, M. B., Sullivan, A. P. and Klinger, T. C. 1978. 'The design of archaeological surveys', *World Archaeology* 6: 107–16.

Schilardi, D. U. 1975. 'Anaskaphi para tin Makra Teikhi kai i oinokhoi tou Tavrou', *Arkhaiologiki Ephemeris*: 66–149.

Schlesier, R. 1990. 'Jane Ellen Harrison', in W. Briggs and W. Calder III, eds., *Classical Scholarship: a biographical encyclopedia*: 127–41. New York: Garland.

Schlörb-Vierneisel, B. 1966. 'Eridanos-Nekropole I: Gräber und Opferstellen hS 1–204', *Mitteilungen des Deutschen Archäologischen Instituts, Athenische Abteilung* 81: 4–111.

Schlumberger, D., 1970. *L'Orient hellénisé: l'art grec et ses hériteurs dans l'Asie non Méditerranéenne*. Paris: Albin Michel.

Schnapp, A. 1982. 'Archéologie et tradition académique en Europe aux XVIIIe et XIXe siècles', *Annales, Economies, Sociétés, Civilisations* 37: 760–77.

Schofield, A. J. 1987. 'Putting lithics to the test: non-site analysis and the Neolithic settlement of southern England', *Oxford Journal of Archaeology* 6: 269–86.

1989. 'Understanding early medieval pottery distributions: cautionary tales and the implications for further research', *Antiquity* 63: 460–70.

Schofield, A. J., ed. 1991. *Interpreting artifact scatters: contributions to ploughzone archaeology*. Oxford: Oxbow Books (Oxbow Monograph 4).

Segal, C. 1961. 'The character and cults of Dionysos and the unity of *The Frogs*', *Harvard Studies in Classical Philology* 65: 209–42.

Seidman, D. 1983. *Liberalism and the origins of European political thought*. Berkeley: University of California Press.

Semple, E. C. 1922. 'The influence of geographic conditions upon ancient Mediterranean stock-raising', *Annals of the Association of American Geographers* 12: 3–38.

1932. *The geography of the Mediterranean region: its relation to ancient history*. London: Constable.

Senjak, R., ed. 1990. *Fieldnotes: the making of anthropology*. Ithaca, NY: Cornell University Press.

Seton-Williams, M. V. 1954. 'Cilician survey', *Anatolian Studies* 4: 121–74.

Shanks, M. and Tilley, C. 1987. *Social theory and archaeology*. Oxford: Polity Press.

Shapiro, H. A. 1989. *Art and cult under the tyrants*. Mainz: von Zabern.

Shapiro, W. 1988. 'Ritual kinship, ritual incorporation and the denial of death', *Man* 23: 275–97.

Shear, T. L. Sr. 1932. 'The program of the first campaign of excavation in 1931', *Hesperia* 2: 96–109.

1938. 'The campaign of 1937', *Hesperia* 7: 311–62.

Sheen, A. 1981. 'Stavros tis Psokas survey, 1979', *Levant* 13: 39–42.

Sheftel, P. S. 1979. 'The Archaeological Institute of America, 1879–1979. A centennial review', *American Journal of Archaeology* 83: 3–17.

Shefton, B. B. 1967. 'Attisches Meisterwerk und etruskische Kopie', in G. von Lucken and K. Zimmermann, eds., *Die griechische Vase*: 529–37. Rostock.

1970. 'The Greek Museum, University of Newcastle upon Tyne', *Archaeological Reports for 1969–70*: 52–62.

1982. 'Greeks and Greek imports in the South of the Iberian peninsula', in H. G. Niemeyer, ed., *Phönizier im*

Westen: 337–70. Mainz: Philip von Zabern (*Madrider Mitteilungen* 8).

1989. 'Zum Import und Einflusse Mediterraner Güter in Alteuropa', *Kölner Jahrbuch für Vor- und Frühgeschichte* 22: 207–20.

Shelton, J. C. 1991. 'More ostraca from the Fitzwilliam Museum', *Zeitschrift für Papyrologie und Epigraphik* 86: 267–76.

Shennan, S. J. 1985. *Experiments in the collection and analysis of archaeological survey data: the East Hampshire survey*. Sheffield: Department of Prehistory and Archaeology.

1989a. 'Archaeology as archaeology or as anthropology?', *Antiquity* 63: 831–5.

1989b. 'Cultural transmission and cultural change', in van der Leeuw and Torrence 1989: 330–46.

Shero, L. R. 1964. *The American Philological Association: an historical sketch*. Philadelphia: University of Pennsylvania Press.

Sherratt, A. 1989. 'Gordon Childe: archaeology and intellectual history', *Past and Present* 125: 151–70.

Sherwin-White, S., 1987. 'Seleucid Babylonia: a case-study for the installation and development of Greek rule', in Kuhrt and Sherwin-White 1987b: 1–31.

Shorey, P. 1919. 'Fifty years of classical scholarship', *Transactions of the American Philological Association* 50: 33–61.

Sifakis, G. M. 1991. 'The impasse of Greek higher education', in Vryonis 1991: 285–304.

Silberman, N. 1989. *Between past and present: archaeology, ideology and nationalism in the modern Middle East*. New York: Holt.

1990. 'The politics of the past: archaeology and nationalism in the Eastern Mediterranean', *Mediterranean Quarterly* 1: 99–110.

Simmons, A. and Kafafi, Z. 1988. 'Preliminary report on the 'Ain Ghazal archaeological survey, 1987', *Annual of the Department of Antiquities of Jordan* 32: 27–39.

Simon, E. 1981. *Das Satyrspiel Sphinx des Aischylos*. Heidelberg: Winter.

1982. 'Satyr plays in the time of Aeschylus', in D. Kurtz and B. Sparkes, eds., *The eye of Greece*: 123–48. Cambridge: Cambridge University Press.

Simopoulos, K. 1970–5. *Xenoi taxidiotes stin Ellada*. 4 vols. Athens: Eptalophos.

Singer, B. 1982. 'The ascendancy of the Sorbonne: the relations between centre and periphery in the academic order of the Third French Republic', *Minerva* 20: 269–300.

Skias, A. N. 1912. 'Neoterai anaskaphai en to panarkhaia Elefsiniaki nekropolei', *Arkhaiologiki Ephemeris*: 1–39.

Skinner, M. 1989. 'Expecting the barbarians: feminism, nostalgia and the "epistemic shift" in classical studies', in Culham *et al.* 1989: 199–210.

Sklenár, K. 1983. *Archaeology in Central Europe: the first 500 years*. Leicester: Leicester University Press.

Skydsgaard, J. E. 1988. 'Trahshumance in ancient Greece', in Whittaker 1988: 75–86.

Slaska, M. 1985. 'Le anfore da trasporto a Gravisca', in Cristofani and Pelagatti 1985: 19–21.

Slicher van Bath, B. H. 1963. *The agrarian history of western Europe, AD 500–1850*. London: Edward Arnold.

Small, J. 1971. 'The banquet frieze from Poggio Civitate', *Studi Etruschi* 39: 25–61.

1986. 'Choice of subject on late Etruscan funerary urns', in *Iconographie classique et identités régionales*: 87–92. Paris: *Bulletin de Correspondance Hellénique* supp. 14.

1987. 'Left, right and centre: direction in Etruscan art', *Opuscula Romana* 16: 123–35.

Smart, B. 1986. 'The politics of truth and the problem of hegemony', in D. C. Hoy, ed., *Foucault: a critical reader*: 157–73. Oxford: Basil Blackwell.

Smelser, N. and Content, R. 1977. *The changing academic marketplace*. Berkeley: University of California Press.

Smith, C. A. 1976. 'Regional economic systems: linking geographical models and socioeconomic problems', in C. A. Smith, ed., *Regional analysis* I: *Economic systems*: 3–63. New York: Academic Press.

Smith, W. D. 1991. *Politics and the sciences of culture in Germany, 1840–1920*. Oxford: Oxford University Press.

Smithson, E. L. 1968. 'The tomb of a rich Athenian lady, c. 850 BC', *Hesperia* 37: 77–116.

Snodgrass, A. M. 1964. *Early Greek armour and weapons*. Edinburgh: Edinburgh University Press.

1965a. 'The hoplite reform and history', *Journal of Hellenic Studies* 85: 110–22.

1965b. 'Barbarian Europe and Early Iron Age Greece', *Proceedings of the Prehistoric Society* 31: 229–40.

1971. *The Dark Age of Greece*. Edinburgh: Edinburgh University Press.

1977. *Archaeology and the rise of the Greek state*. Cambridge: Cambridge University Press.

1980a. 'Iron and early metallurgy in the Mediterranean', in T. Wertime and J. D. Muhly, eds., *The coming of the age of iron*: 335–74. New Haven: Yale University Press.

1980b. *Archaic Greece: the age of experiment*. London: Dent.

1982. 'La prospection archéologique en Grèce et dans le monde méditerranéen', *Annales, Economies, Sociétés, Civilisations* 37: 800–12.

1983. 'Heavy freight in Archaic Greece', in Garnsey *et al.* 1983: 16–26.

1985a. 'Greek archaeology and Greek history', *Classical Antiquity* 4: 193–207.

1985b. 'The new archaeology and the classical archaeologist', *American Journal of Archaeology* 89: 31–7.

1986. 'Interaction by design: the Greek city state', in Renfrew and Cherry 1986: 47–58.

1987. *An archaeology of Greece: the present state and future scope of a discipline*. Berkeley: University of California Press.

1989a. 'The coming of the Iron Age in Greece: Europe's earliest bronze/iron transition', in M. L. Sørensen and R. Thomas, eds., *The Bronze Age–Iron Age transition in Europe* I: 22–35. 2 vols. Oxford: British Archaeological Reports International Series 483.

1989b. 'The rural landscape and its political significance', *Opus* 6–8: 53–65.

1990. 'Survey archaeology and the rural landscape of the Greek city', in Murray and Price 1990: 113–36.

1991a. 'Archaeology and the study of the Greek city', in J. Rich and A. Wallace-Hadrill, eds., *City and country in the ancient world*: 1–24. London: Routledge.

1991b. 'Structural history and classical archaeology', in Bintliff 1991: 57–72.

Snodgrass, A. M. and Bintliff, J. L. 1991. 'Surveying ancient cities', *Scientific American* 264: 88–93.

Snodgrass, A. M. and Chippindale, C. 1988. 'Classical matters', *Antiquity* 62: 724–5.

Sokolowski, F. 1962. *Lois sacrées des cités grecques (Supplément)*. Paris: Boccard.

1969. *Lois sacrées des cités grecques*. Paris: Boccard.

Sørenson, L. W. 1983. 'Canadian Palaepaphos survey project: preliminary report of 1980 ceramic finds', *Report of the Department of Antiquities, Cyprus*: 283–99.

Sørenson, L. W., Guldager, P., Korsholm, M., Lund, J. and Gregory T. 1987. 'Canadian Palaepaphos survey project: second preliminary report of the ceramic finds 1982–83', *Report of the Department of Antiquities, Cyprus*: 259–78.

Sørenson, M. L. 1989. 'Ignoring innovation – denying change. The role of iron and the impact of external influences on the transformation of Scandinavian societies 800–400 BC', in van der Leeuw and Torrence 1989: 182–202.

Sotiropoulos, D. 1977. 'Diglossia and the national language question in modern Greece', *Linguistics* 17: 5–31.

Sourvinou-Inwood, C. 1986. *Studies in girls' transitions*. Athens: Kardamitsa.

1989. 'The fourth stasimon of Sophocles' *Antigone*', *Bulletin of the Institute of Classical Studies* 36: 141–65.

1991. *'Reading' Greek culture*. Oxford: Clarendon Press.

Spawforth, A. 1989. 'Breaking the potter's mould', *Daily Telegraph*, 6 February: 12.

Spencer, P., ed. 1990. *Anthropology and the riddle of the sphinx*. London: ASA monograph 28.

Spivey, N. 1986. Review article, *Journal of Roman Studies* 76: 281–6.

1987. *The Micali Painter and his followers*. Oxford: Clarendon Press.

1988. 'The armed dance on Etruscan vases', in Christiansen and Melander 1988: 592–603.

1991. 'Greek vases in Etruria', in Rasmussen and Spivey 1991: 131–50.

Spivey, N. and Stoddart, S. 1990. *Etruscan Italy*. London: Batsford.

Spurr, M. S. 1986. *Arable cultivation in Roman Italy, ca. 200 BC–ca. AD 100*. London, The Society for the Promotion of Roman Studies (*Journal of Roman Studies* Monograph 3).

Staïs, V. 1890a. 'O tymvos en Vourva', *Mitteilungen des Deutschen Archäologischen Instituts, Athenische Abteilung* 15: 318–29.

1890b. 'Tymvos en Vourva', *Arkhaiologikon Deltion*: 105–12.

1917. 'Sounio anaskaphi', *Arkhaiologiki Ephemeris*: 168–213.

Starr, C. G. 1961. *The origins of Greek civilization*. New York: Knopf.

1986. *Community and individual: the rise of the polis 800–500 BC*. Oxford: Oxford University Press.

Stavrakis, P. J. 1990. *Moscow and Greek communism, 1944–1949*. Ithaca, NY: Cornell University Press.

Stern, E. 1982. *Material culture of the land of the Bible in the Persian period, 538–322 BC*. Warminster: Aris and Philips.

Sterud, E. L. 1973. 'A paradigmatic view of prehistory', in C. Renfrew, ed., *The explanation of culture change*: 3–17. London: Duckworth.

Stewart, A. 1979. *Attika: studies in Athenian sculpture of the Hellenistic age*. London: Society for the Promotion of Hellenic Studies.

Stewart, J. 1959. *Jane Ellen Harrison: a portrait from letters*. London: Merlin Press.

Stocking, G. 1987. *Victorian anthropology*. New York: The Free Press.

Stoddart, S. 1987. 'Complex polity formation in Northern Etruria and Umbria 1200–500 BC'. PhD thesis, Cambridge University.

　1989. 'Divergent trajectories in central Italy', in T. Champion 1989: 88–101.

　n.d. 'The appropriation of the past and the formation of the Etruscan and Italic states'. Unpublished paper.

Stoddart, S. and Whitley, J. 1988. 'The social context of literacy in Archaic Greece and Etruria', *Antiquity* 62: 761–72.

Stone, P. 1989. 'Interpretations and uses of the past in modern Britain and Europe', in Layton 1989b: 195–206.

Stone, P. and MacKenzie, R., eds. 1989. *The excluded past*. London: Unwin Hyman.

Strauss, B. 1986. *Athens after the Peloponnesian war*. Ithaca, NY: Cornell University Press.

Stroud, R. 1968. *Drakon's law on homicide*. Berkeley: University of California Press.

　1979. *The axones and kyrbeis of Drakon and Solon*. Berkeley: University of California Press.

Struever, S., 1985. *Koster: Americans in search of their prehistoric past*. 2nd edn, revised with F. A. Holton. New York: Mentor.

Sumner, W. 1986. 'Achaemenid settlement in the Persepolis plain', *American Journal of Archaeology* 90: 3–31.

Sykes, C. J. 1988. *Profscam: professors and the demise of higher education*. New York: St Martin's Press.

Szegedy-Maszak, A. 1987. 'True illusions: early photographs of Athens', *J. Paul Getty Museum Journal* 15: 125–38.

　1988. 'Sun and stone: images of ancient, heroic times', *Archaeology* 41: 20–31.

Szilágyi, J. G. 1975. *Etruszko-Korinthosi vásafestézct*. Budapest: Akadémias Kiadó.

Tainter, J. 1988. *The collapse of complex societies*. Cambridge: Cambridge University Press.

Talocchini, A. and Phillips, K. M. 1970. *Il santuario arcaico: catalogo della mostra Firenze-Siena 1970*. Florence.

Tarn, W. W. 1948. *Alexander the Great*. 2 vols. Cambridge: Cambridge University Press.

　1951. *The Greeks in Bactria and India*. 2nd edn. Cambridge: Cambridge University Press.

Tarn, W. W. and Griffith, G. T. 1952. *Hellenistic civilisation*. 3rd edn. London: Edward Arnold.

Tasker, C. M. K. 1980. 'Archaeological site erosion: studies in Britain and the Aegean'. PhD dissertation, University of Strathclyde.

Tatsios, T. G. 1984. *The 'megáli ídea' and the Greek–Turkish war of 1897*. Boulder, CO: East European Monographs 156.

Tchalenko, G. 1953. *Villages antiques de la Syrie du nord*. 3 vols. Paris: Librairie Orientaliste Paul Geuthner.

Thomas, B. 1990. 'The new historicism and other old-fashioned topics', in Veeser 1990: 182–203.

Thomas, D. H. 1975. 'Non-site sampling in archaeology: up the creek without a site?', in J. W. Mueller, ed., *Sampling in Archaeology*: 61–81. Tucson: University of Arizona Press.

Thompson, H. A. 1940. *The tholos of Athens and its predecessors*. Princeton: *Hesperia* supp. vol. 4.

　1947. 'The excavation of the Athenian Agora, 1940–1946', *Hesperia* 16: 193-213.

　1968. 'Activity in the Athenian Agora 1966–67', *Hesperia* 37: 36–76.

　1980. 'In pursuit of the past: the American role, 1879–1979', *American Journal of Archaeology* 84: 263–70.

Thompson, J. 1989. 'Transhumant sheep-raising and the rural economy of Roman Italy, 200 BC–AD 200'. Unpublished PhD thesis, University of Cambridge.

Tickner, L. 1987. 'The body politic: female sexuality and women artists since 1970', in Parker and Pollock 1987: 273–76 and Betterton 1987: 235–53.

Tilley, C. 1989a. 'Excavation as theatre', *Antiquity* 63: 275–80.

　1989b. 'Discourse and power: the genre of the Cambridge inaugural lecture', in Miller *et al.* 1989: 41–62.

　1989c. 'Interpreting material culture', in Hodder 1989c: 185–94.

　1989d. 'Archaeology as socio-political activity in the present', in Pinsky and Wylie 1989: 104–16.

　1990. 'Michel Foucault: towards an archaeology of archaeology', in C. Tilley, ed., *Reading material culture*: 281–347. Oxford: Basil Blackwell.

　1991. *Material culture and text: the art of ambiguity*. London: Routledge.

Tiverios, A. E. 1976. 'I "Tyrriniki" (Attiki) amphoreis. I skhesi tous me tous "Pondiakous" (Etrouskiakous) kai ton Nikostheni', *Arkhaiologiki Ephemeris*: 44–57.

Tomlinson, R. A. 1991. *The Athens of Alma Tadema*. Stroud: Alan Sutton.

Torelli, M. 1983. 'Polis e "palazzo". Architettura, ideologia e artigianato greco in Etruria tra VII e VI sec. a.C.', in *Architecture et société*: 471–99. Paris: Editions du CNRS.

Touloupa, E. 1972. 'Bronzebleche von der Akropolis in Athen. Gehämmerte geometrische Dreifüsse',

Mitteilungen des deutschen archäologischen Instituts, Athenische Abteilung 87: 57–76.

Toynbee, A. J. 1916. *The treatment of the Armenians in the Ottoman Empire, 1915-1916*. London: His Majesty's Government.

1919. *The place of medieval and modern Greece in history*. London: University of London Press.

1920. *The tragedy of Greece*. Oxford: Oxford University Press.

1934. *A study of history* I–III. Oxford: Oxford University Press.

Travlos, J. 1981. 'Athens after the liberation: planning the new city and exploring the old', *Hesperia* 50: 391–407.

Treholt, A. 1972. 'Europe and the Greek dictatorship', in Clogg and Yannopoulos 1972: 210–27.

Trendall, A. D. 1989. *Red figure vases of South Italy and Sicily: a handbook*. London: Thames and Hudson.

1990. 'On the divergence of South Italian from Attic red-figure vase-painting', in Descoudres 1990: 217–30.

Trigger, B. 1984. 'Alternative archaeologies: nationalist, colonialist, imperialist', *Man* 19: 355–70.

1985. 'Writing the history of archaeology: a survey of trends', in G. Stocking, ed., *Observers observed*: 218–55. Madison: University of Wisconsin Press.

1989. *A history of archaeological thought*. Cambridge: Cambridge University Press.

1990. 'The 1990s: North American archaeology with a human face?', *Antiquity* 64: 778–87.

Trigger, B. and Glover, I., eds., 1981/2. 'Regional traditions of archaeological research', *World Archaeology* 13: 133–371.

Tsaousis, D. G., ed. 1983. *Ellinismos kai ellinikotita*. Athens: Hermes.

Tsigakou, F.-M. 1981. *The rediscovery of Greece: travellers and painters of the Romantic era*. London: Thames and Hudson.

Tsoucalas, C. 1981. 'The ideological impact of the civil war', in J. Iatrides, ed., *Greece in the 1940s: a nation in crisis*: 318–41. Hanover, NH: University Press of New England.

Turner, D. 1990. 'Heinrich Schliemann: the man behind the masks', *Archaeology* 43: 36–42.

Turner, F. M. 1981. *The Greek heritage in Victorian Britain*. New Haven: Yale University Press.

1986. 'British politics and the demise of the Roman Republic', *Historical Journal* 29: 577–99.

1989a. 'Why the Greeks and not the Romans in Victorian Britain?', in G. W. Clarke 1989: 61–81.

1989b. 'Martin Bernal's *Black Athena*: a dissent', in Peradotto and Levine 1989: 97–109.

Turner, R. S. 1980. 'The Prussian universities and the concept of research', *International Archiv für Sozialgeschichte der deutschen Literatur* 5: 68–93.

Usener, H. 1903. *Dreiheit: ein Versuch mythologischer Zahlenlehre*. Berlin. Reprinted Darmstadt, 1962.

Vallet, G. 1968. 'La cité et son territoire dans les colonies grecques de l'occident', in *La città e il suo territorio*: 67–142. Naples: Centre Jean Bérard.

Vallet, G. and Villard, F. 1963. 'Céramique grecque et histoire économique', in P. Courbin, ed., *Etudes archéologiques*: 205–17. Paris: SEVPEN.

van Andel, T. H. and Runnels, C. N. 1987. *Beyond the acropolis: a rural Greek past*. Stanford: Stanford University Press.

van der Kooij, G. 1987. 'Tell Deir 'Alla (East Jordan valley) during the Achaemenid period', in Sancisi-Weerdenburg 1987: 97–102.

van der Leeuw, S. E. and Pritchard, A. C., eds. 1984. *The many dimensions of pottery: ceramics in archaeology and anthropology*. Amsterdam: Albert Egges Van Giffen Instituut vor Prae- en Protohistorie.

van der Leeuw, S. E. and Torrence, R., eds. 1989. *What's new? A closer look at the process of innovation*. London: Unwin Hyman.

van der Meer, L. B. 1984. 'Kylikeia in Etruscan tomb paintings', in Brijder 1984: 298–304.

van der Spek, R. J. 1987. 'The Babylonian city', in Kuhrt and Sherwin-White 1987b: 57–74.

van Gelder, K. 1978. 'A Protoattic oinochoe with dolphins', in Bingen *et al.* 1978: 122–9.

Vatin, C. 1974. 'Jardins et vergers grecs', in *Mélanges helléniques offerts à Georges Daux*: 345–67. Paris: Editions de Boccard.

1976. 'Jardins et services de voirie', *Bulletin de Correspondance Hellénique* 100: 555–64.

Veeser, H. A., ed. 1990. *The new historicism*. London: Routledge.

Veremis, T. 1991. 'Greece and NATO', in Vryonis 1991: 71–80.

Vermeule, E. 1979. *Aspects of death in early Greek art and poetry*. Berkeley: University of California Press.

Vernant, J.-P. 1980. *Myth and society in ancient Greece*. Brighton: Harvester.

1983. *Myth and thought among the Greeks*. London: Routledge.

1989. *L'individu, la mort, l'amour*. Paris: Maspero.

Vernant, J.-P. and Detienne, M. 1978. *Cunning intelligence in Greek culture and society*. Brighton: Harvester.

Vernant, J.-P. and Vidal-Naquet, P. 1988. *Œdipe et ses mythes*. Paris: Maspero.

Verney, S. 1987. 'Greece and the European Community', in Featherstone and Katsondas 1987: 253–70.

Vessberg, O. and Westholm, A. 1956. *The Swedish Cyprus Expedition* IV.3: *The Hellenistic and Roman periods in Cyprus*. Stockholm: Swedish Cyprus Expedition.

Vickers, M. J. 1984. 'The influence of exotic materials on Attic white-ground lekythoi', in Brijder 1984: 88–97.

1985a. 'Greek and Roman antiquities in the seventeenth century', in O. Impey and A. MacGregor, eds., *The origins of museums: the cabinet of curiosities in sixteenth- and seventeenth-century Europe*: 223–31. Oxford: Oxford University Press.

1985b. 'Artful crafts: the influence of metalwork on Athenian painted pottery', *Journal of Hellenic Studies* 105: 108–28.

1986. 'Imaginary Etruscans: changing perceptions of Etruria since the fifteenth century', *Hephaistos* 7/8: 153–68.

1987. 'Value and simplicity: eighteenth-century taste and the study of Greek vases', *Past and Present* 116: 98–137.

1990a. 'Impoverishment of the past: the case of ancient Greece', *Antiquity* 64: 455–63.

1990b. 'Attic *symposia* after the Persian Wars', in O. Murray, ed., *Sympotika*: 105–21. Oxford: Oxford University Press.

1990c. 'Golden Greece: relative values, minae, and temple inventories', *American Journal of Archaeology* 94: 613–25.

Vidal-Naquet, P. 1986. *The black hunter: forms of thought and forms of society in the Greek world*. Baltimore: Johns Hopkins University Press.

1990. *La démocratie grecque vue d'ailleurs*. Paris: Flammarion.

Villard, F. 1960, *La céramique grecque de Marseille*. Paris: Boccard.

Vlavianos, H. 1992. *Greece, 1941–1949: from resistance to civil war*. London: Macmillan.

von Bothmer, D. 1987a. 'Greek vase painting: 200 years of connoisseurship', in von Bothmer 1987b: 184–204.

von Bothmer, D., ed. 1987b. *Papers on the Amasis Painter and his world*. Malibu: J. Paul Getty Museum.

Vryonis, S., ed. 1991. *Greece on the road to democracy: from the junta to PASOK 1974–1986*. New Rochelle, NY: Caratzas.

Wagstaff, M. 1976. *Aspects of land use in Melos*. Southampton: Department of Geography.

Wagstaff, M. and Augustson, S. 1982. 'Traditional land use', in Renfrew and Wagstaff 1982: 106–33.

Walbank, F. W. 1981. *The Hellenistic world*. Glasgow: Fontana.

Walbank, F. W., Astin, A. E., Frederiksen, M. W. and Ogilvie, R. M., eds. 1984. *Cambridge ancient history* VII part 1: *The Hellenistic world*. 2nd edn. Cambridge: Cambridge University Press.

Walberg, G. 1986. *Tradition and innovation: essays in Minoan art*. Mainz: von Zabern.

Waldstein, C. 1905. *The Argive Heraeum* II. Boston: Houghton Mifflin.

Wallace, E. R. 1985. *Historiography and causation in psychoanalysis*. Hillsdale, NJ: Analytic Press.

Wallace, P. W. 1984. 'The Akamas promontory of Cyprus', *Report of the Department of Antiquities, Cyprus*: 341–7.

Wallace, R. W. 1989. *The Areopagus council*. Baltimore: Johns Hopkins University Press.

Wallerstein, I. 1974. *The modern world system* I. New York: Academic Press.

Walter, O. 1940. 'Archäologische Funde in Griechenland vom Frühjahr 1939 bis Frühjahr 1940', *Archäologischer Anzeiger*: 121–308.

Ward-Perkins, J. B. 1962. 'Etruscan engineering: road building, water supply and drainage', in M. Renard, ed., *Hommages à Albert Grenier*: 1636–43. Brussels: Collection *Latomus* 58.3

Wasowicz, A. 1975. *Olbia Pontique et son territoire*. Paris: Annales Littéraires de l'Université de Besançon.

Waterhouse, H. 1986. *The British School at Athens: the first hundred years*. London: Thames and Hudson. British School at Athens supp. vol. 19.

Watrous, L. V. 1982a. 'An Attic farm near Laurion', *Studies in Attic epigraphy, history and topography presented to Eugene Vanderpool*: 193–7. Princeton: *Hesperia* supp. vol. 19.

1982b. *Lasithi: a history of settlement on a highland plain in Crete*. Princeton: *Hesperia* supp. vol. 18.

Watson, R. 1991a. 'Ozymandias, king of kings: post-processual radical archaeology as critique', *American Antiquity* 55: 673–89.

1991b. 'What the New Archaeology has accomplished', *Current Anthropology* 32: 275–91.

Weber, M. 1947. *The theory of social and economic organization*. Ed. T. Parsons. New York: The Free Press.

Webster, T. B. L. 1972. *Potter and patron in classical Athens*. London: Methuen.

Wehrli, H.-U. 1970. 'Bismarck's imperialism 1862–1890', *Past and Present* 48: 119–55.

Weil, R. 1897. 'Geschichte der Ausgrabung von Olympia', in E. Curtius and F. Adler, eds., *Olympia* I: *Die*

Ergebnisse der von dem deutschen Reich veranstalteten Ausgrabung: 101–45. Berlin: Asher.

Weintraub, K. J. 1988. 'Jacob Burckhardt: the historian among the philologists', *American Scholar* 57: 273–82.

Weiss, R. 1988. *The Renaissance discovery of classical antiquity*. 2nd edn. Cambridge: Cambridge University Press.

Weisz, G. 1983. *The emergence of modern universities in France 1863–1914*. Princeton: Princeton University Press.

Wells, B., Runnels, C. and Zangger, E. 1990. 'The Berbati-Limnes archaeological survey, the 1988 season', *Opuscula Atheniensia* 18: 207–38.

Wells, P. S. 1980. *Culture contact and culture change: Early Iron Age central Europe and the Mediterranean World*. Cambridge: Cambridge University Press.

1984. *Farms, villages and cities: commerce and urban origins in late prehistoric Europe*. Ithaca, NY: Cornell University Press.

Wells, P. S. and Bonfante, L. 1979. 'West-central Europe and the Mediterranean. The decline of trade in the fifth century BC', *Expedition* 21: 18–24.

Welwei, K.-W. 1974. *Unfreie im Antike Kriegdienst* I. Wiesbaden: Steiner.

1979. 'Abhängige Landbevölkerungen auf "Tempel-territorien" in hellenistischen Kleinasien und Syrien', *Ancient Society* 10: 97–118.

Wendy, E. and Kaplan, C. 1991. *The arts-and-crafts movement*. London: Thames and Hudson.

Wenke, R. J. 1975/6. 'Imperial investments and agricultural developments in Parthian and Sasanian Khuzestan: 150 BC to AD 640', *Mesopotamia* 10/11: 31–157.

1987. 'Western Iran in the Partho-Sasanian period', in Hole 1987: 251–81.

Weston, C. C. 1960. 'The theory of mixed monarchies under Charles I and after', *English Historical Review* 75: 426–43.

1984. 'Co-ordination: a radicalising principle in Stuart politics', in M. and J. Jacob, eds., *The origins of Anglo-American radicalism*: 85–104. London: Routledge.

Wever, J. de. 1966. 'La *chora* massaliote d'après les fouilles récentes', *L'Antiquité Classique* 35: 71–117.

Whallon, R. 1979. *An archaeological survey of the Keban reservoir area of east-central Turkey*. Ann Arbor: Memoirs of the Museum of Anthropology, University of Michigan 11.

White, H. 1973. *Metahistory: the historical imagination in nineteenth-century Europe*. Baltimore: Johns Hopkins University Press.

1987. *The content of the form: narrative discourse and historical representation*. Baltimore: Johns Hopkins University Press.

White, K. D. 1970. *Roman farming*. London: Thames and Hudson.

1975. *Farm equipment of the Roman world*. Cambridge: Cambridge University Press.

Whitehouse, R. B. and Wilkins, J. B. 1985. 'Magna Graecia before the Greeks: towards a reconciliation of the evidence', in Malone and Stoddart 1985: 89–109.

1989. 'Greeks and natives in south-east Italy', in T. Champion 1989: 102–26.

Whitelaw, T. M. 1991. 'The ethnoarchaeology of recent rural settlement and landuse in northwest Keos', in Cherry *et al.* 1991: 403–54.

Whitelaw, T. M. and Davis, J. L. 1991. 'The *polis* center of Koressos', in Cherry *et al.* 1991: 265–81.

Whitley, J. 1986. 'Style, burial and society in Dark Age Greece'. PhD thesis, Cambridge University.

1988. 'Early states and hero cults: a reappraisal', *Journal of Hellenic Studies* 108: 173–82.

1991. *Style and society in Dark Age Greece*. Cambridge: Cambridge University Press.

Whitman, J. 1984. 'From philology to anthropology in mid-nineteenth-century Germany', in G. Stocking, ed., *Functionalism historicized*: 214–29. Madison: University of Wisconsin Press.

Whittaker, C. R., ed. 1988. *Pastoral economies in classical antiquity*. Cambridge: Cambridge Philological Society supp. vol. 14.

Wiedemann, T. 1987. *Slavery*. Oxford: *Greece and Rome* New Surveys in the Classics.

Wilamowitz-Moellendorf, U. von. 1924. *Hellenistische Dichtung in der Zeit des Kallimachos* I. Berlin: Wiedmannsche Buchhandlung.

Wilkie, N. C. 1988. 'The Grevena project, 1987'. *American Journal of Archaeology* 92: 241.

Wilkie, N. C., Rosserm, J., Savina, M. and Doyle, R. 1990. 'The Grevena project, 1988–89', *American Journal of Archaeology* 94: 309.

Wilkinson, T. J. 1982. 'The definition of ancient manuring zones by means of extensive sherd sampling techniques', *Journal of Field Archaeology* 9: 323–33.

1988. 'The archaeological component of agricultural soils in the Middle East: the effects of manuring in antiquity', in W. Groenman van Waateringe and M. Robinson, eds., *Man-made soils: symposia of the association for environmental archaeology* 6: 93–114. Oxford: British Archaeological Reports International Series 410.

1989. 'Extensive sherd scatters and land-use intensity:

some recent results', *Journal of Field Archaeology* 16: 31–46.

1990. 'Soil development and early land use in the Jazira region, Upper Mesopotamia', *World Archaeology* 22: 87–103.

Will, E. 1979a. *Histoire politique du monde hellénistique (323–30 av. J-C)* I. 2nd edn. Nancy: Annales de l'Est.

1979b. 'Le monde hellénistique et nous', *Ancient Society* 10: 79–95.

1982. *Histoire politique du monde hellénistique (323–30 av. J-C)* II. 2nd edn. Nancy: Annales de l'Est.

1985. 'Pour une "anthropologie coloniale" du monde hellénistique', in J. Eadie and J. Ober, eds., *The craft of the ancient historian*: 273–301. Lanham, MD: University Press of America.

Willey, G. and Sabloff, J. 1980. *A history of American archaeology*. 2nd edn. New York: Freeman.

Williams, D. J. 1988. 'The Late Archaic class of eye cups', in Christiansen and Melander 1988: 674–83.

1992. 'The Brygos tomb reassembled', *American Journal of Archaeology* 96: 617ff.

Williams, R. 1958. *Culture and society: 1780–1950*. London: Chatto and Windus.

Williamson, T. M. 1984. 'The Roman countryside: settlement and agriculture in NW Essex', *Britannia* 15: 225–30.

Wilshire, B. 1990. *The moral collapse of the university: professionalism, purity and alienation*. Albany: State University of New York Press.

Wilson, R. 1988. 'Archaeology in Sicily, 1982–87', *Archaeological Reports for 1987–88*: 105–50.

Winckelmann, J. J. 1968 [1764]. *History of ancient art*. 2 vols. New York: Ungar.

Winkler, J. J. 1990. 'The ephebes' song: *tragoidia* and the *polis*', in J. J. Winkler and F. Zeitlin, eds., *Nothing to do with Dionysos? The social meaning of Athenian drama*: 20–62. Princeton: Princeton University Press.

Winter, F. E. 1971. *Greek fortifications*. London: Routledge and Kegan Paul.

Winter, F. E. and Bankoff, H. A. 1989. 'Ptolemaic conquest and influence outside Egypt: the Hellenic response', *American Journal of Archaeology* 93: 247.

Wiseman, J. 1978. *The land of the ancient Corinthians*. Göteborg: *Studies in Mediterranean Archaeology* 50.

1980a. 'Archaeology in the future: an evolving discipline', *American Journal of Archaeology* 84: 279–85.

1980b. 'Archaeology as archaeology', *Journal of Field Archaeology* 7: 149–51.

1989. 'Archaeology today: from the classroom to the field and elsewhere', *American Journal of Archaeology* 93: 437–44.

Wobst, M. 1989. 'Commentary: a socio-politics of socio-politics in archaeology', in Pinsky and Wylie 1989: 136–40.

Wolf, E. F. 1982. *Europe and the people without history*. Berkeley: University of California Press.

Wolters, P. 1899. 'Vasen auf Menidi II', *Jahrbuch des deutschen archäologischen Instituts* 14: 103–35.

Wood, E. M. 1988. *Peasant-citizen and slave: the foundations of Athenian democracy*. London: Verso.

Wood, R. W. and Johnson. D. L. 1978. 'A survey of disturbance processes in archaeological site formation', in M. B. Schiffer, ed., *Advances in archaeological method and theory* I: 315–81. New York: Academic Press.

Woodford, S. 1986. *An introduction to Greek art*. Ithaca, NY: Cornell University Press.

Woodhouse, C. M. 1976. *The struggle for Greece, 1941–1949*. London: Granada.

1982. *Karamanlis: the restorer of Greek democracy*. Oxford: Oxford University Press.

1985. *Greece under the Colonels*. London: Granada.

Woolf, G. 1990. 'World-systems analysis and the Roman empire', *Journal of Roman Archaeology* 3: 44–58.

Woolley, C. L. 1938. 'Excavations at Al Mina, Suedia I. The archaeological report', *Journal of Hellenic Studies* 58: 1–30.

Wright, J. C., Cherry, J. F., Davis, J. L. and Mantzourani, E. 1985. 'To erevnitiko archaiologiko programma stin Koilada tis Nemeas kata ta eti 1984–1985', *Athens Annals of Archaeology* 18: 86–104.

Wright, J. C., Cherry, J. F., Davis, J. L., Mantzourani, E., Sutton, S. B. and Sutton, R. F. 1990. 'The Nemea Valley Archaeological Project: a preliminary report', *Hesperia* 59: 579–659.

Wright, J. C., Davis, J. L. and Mantzourani, E. In press. 'Early Mycenaean settlement in the Nemea region', in G. Korres, ed., *Proceedings of the sixth international colloquium on Aegean prehistory*. Athens.

Wright, J. H. 1897. 'Editorial announcement', *American Journal of Archaeology* n.s. 1: 1–4.

Xydis, A. G. 1972. 'The military regime's foreign policy', in Clogg and Yannopoulos 1972: 191–209.

Yarshater, E., ed. 1982. *Cambridge history of Iran* III (1 and 2). *The Seleucid, Parthian and Sasanian periods*. Cambridge: Cambridge University Press.

Yorston, R. M., Gaffney, V. L. and Reynolds, P. J. 1990. 'Simulation of artifact movement due to cultivation', *Journal of Archaeological Science* 17: 67–83.

Young, J. H. 1956. 'Studies in South Attica: country estates at Sounion', *Hesperia* 25: 122–46.

Young, R. 1991. *White mythologies*. London: Routledge.

Young, R. S. 1938. 'Pottery from a seventh-century well', *Hesperia* 7: 412–28.

   1939. *Late Geometric graves and a seventh-century well in the Agora*. Princeton: *Hesperia* supp. vol. 2.

   1952. 'Graves from the Phaleron cemetery', *American Journal of Archaeology* 46: 23–57.

Zaimis, A. and Petridis, P. 1928. 'Peri tropou ekteleseos arkhaiologikon anaskaphon', Presidential Decree (ΦΕΚ 6/1929/tA'). Athens. ·

   1932. 'Peri arkhaiotiton', People's Law 5351. Athens.

Zeitlin, F. 1982. 'Cultic models of the female', *Arethusa* 15: 129–57.

Zimmerman-Munn, M. L. 1983. 'Corinthian trade with the West in the classical period'. PhD thesis, Bryn Mawr College.

Zinn, H. 1990. *The politics of history*. 2nd edn. Urbana: University of Illinois Press.

Zinserling, G. 1973. 'Winckelmann und die Kunst der Gegenwart', in Häsler 1973b: 93–112.

Index

Achaemenids, *see* Persia
Achilles Painter, 103
Ackerman, R., 29
Acquarossa, 118
Adams, R., 184–6
Aegina, 25, 26, 51, 53, 57, 62, 65, 66 n. 3,
      67 n. 11, 99, 106, 109, 129, 134 n. 4
Aelian, 149, 153
Aetolia, 179
Afghanistan, 186–7
Africa, 11
agalma, 90, 94
Agia Kyriaki, 179
agriculture, 147–8, 153, 157, *see also*
      manuring
Aï Khanum, 186–7
AIA, *see* Archaeological Institute of
      America
ainigma, 77
Aiskhylides, 151
Aixone, 169 n. 6
AJA, see American Journal of Archaeology
akroteria, 118
Al Mina, 105–7
Alalia, battle of, 120, 127
Alcock, S., 6–7, 45, 194, 199–200
aletheia, 77
Alexander, 171, 173
Altertumswissenschaft, 18–19, 20, 25–6, 27
Amasis, 107
Amasis Painter, 101–2
Amelung's goddess, 88
American Anthropological Association,
      42
American Historical Association, 32
American Journal of Archaeology, 31–2,
      35, 190
American Journal of Philology, 44
American Philological Association, 19, 33
American revolution, 30

American School of Classical Studies at
      Athens, 32–5
Amorgos, 153
amphorae
      Etruscan, 128
      Massaliote, 128
      Nikosthenic, 101–2, 115–16, 117
      SOS, 105
      Tyrrhenian, 102, 115
Ampurias, 126, 130
Animal husbandry, 145–8
Annales school, 175
Anopolis, 180
Antigonids, 179
Antoninus Liberalis, 84
APA, *see* American Philological
      Association
Aphrodite of Knidos, 81–6, 196
Apollodorus, 74, 74, 77
Appadurai, A., 59, 60
Applebaum, S., 182
Arabia, 183–4
Arabs, 23
Arafat, K., 6, 99, 104, 194, 195, 198
Archaeological Institute of America, 31–2
Archaeological Service, 34
Archaeological Society of Athens, 34, 35
archaeology
      American, 14, 31–54, 38, 137
      anthropological, 8, 9, 28, 40, 43, 35,
            47 n. 2
      colonialist, 174
      contextual, 4, 43, 52
      distributional, 138, 166
      logicist, 42
      prehistoric, 21, 26, 27, 38, 39, 51, 194,
            198
Argive Heraeum, 33, 54, 67 n. 14
Argos, 67 n. 14, 159 n. 7
Aristocracy, 60

Aristophanes, 79, 135–7, 149, 151,
      168 n. 4, 194
Aristotle, 16, 51, 58, 66 n. 1, 94, 149
Armenia, 33
Arnheim, R., 80
Arsinoe, 180
art collecting, 15, 24
art market, 4, 24
Arts-and-Crafts movement, 37
Aryans, 21
Ashmolean Museum, 28
Astill, G., 144
Athena, 79, 85–7
Athenaeus, 149, 155
Athens, 30, 32, 34, 38
      Agora, 34–5, 54, 55–6 66 n. 5
      Acropolis, 24, 25, 34, 54, 58, 67 n. 8, 94
      Dipylon, 65, 149
      Erechtheiou St, 66 n. 5
      Kerameikos, 54, 56–7, 60, 62, 65,
            66 n. 5, 67 n. 9, 67 n. 10, 94
      Kriezi St, 67 n. 9
      Kynosarges, 65
      Piraeus Gate, 92
      Piraios St, 65
Augustan Age, 16
Augustine, 16
Ault, B., 167–8, 199–200
Ayiofarango valley, 179

Babylon, 184–5
Bactria, 184, 186–7, 188–9
Baghdad, 184
Bahrain, 183–4, 188
Bammer, A., 73
bandits, 22–3
Bapty, I., 43
Barthes, R., 84
Baudrillard, J., 41
Bayly, C., 61

Beazley, J., 28, 36–8, 52, 103, 104–5
Becker, C., 21
Bennett, W., 44
Bérard, C., 37
Berbati-Limnes survey, 141, 166
Berger, J., 84
Berkeley, University of California at, 39
Berkshire Downs, 143
Berlin Painter, 37
Bernal, M., 18, 22, 26, 34, 190, 193
beth av, 182
Bible, 16
big-dig approach, 33, 35, 38
Bildung, 18, 19, 32, 44
Binford, L., 10–11, 42, 43
Bintliff, J., 6, 138, 141–3, 163, 164
Bisenzio, 118
Bismarck, 25
Black Sea, 129, 130
Blakeway, A., 105–6, 129
Bloom, A., 44
Boardman, J., 8, 39, 99, 101–6, 109, 117,
    195
Boegehold, A., 102
Boeotia, 6, 143, 163, 164
Böhlau, J., 52
Bologna, 120
Botticelli, 37
Bourdieu, P., 9, 42, 92, 94, 96 n. 5
Bowen, J., 26
Bradley, R., 45
Braidwood, R., 195
Brann, E., 55
Brauron, 54
breakage patterns, 167
Breasted, J., 21
Bremmer, J., 78
Briant, P., 174, 188, 189
Brinkman, A., 184, 189
Britain, 17, 30–1
British Museum, 24, 28, 71
British School at Athens, 28
bronze vessels, 116
Bronzino, 84
Brown University, 33
Bruford, W. H., 18
Bryson, N., 86
Bull Painter, 103
Buondelmonti, 137
Bureau of Ethnology, 32
Burford-Cooper, A., 153
burials, 51, 54, 55, 56–7, 60, 62, 63–5, 71,
    83, 88, 94, 114, 121
Burrows, R., 33
Butser Farm, 199–200
Byzantium, 116

Caere, 105
Callinicos, A., 41
Cambridge ancient history, 174
Cambridge University, 19, 29, 43
Camirus, 105

Capps, E., 33, 35
Capua, 71, 103
Caria, 181
Carpenter, R., 82
Cartledge, P., 103
Castelets, 128
Cato, 145, 147, 150–2, 154, 156, 169
causation, 9, 10
Celts, 120, 122
Centre Union, 38
Cerveteri, 101, 112, 114, 116–18, 120
Champion, T., 43
Champollion, J. F., 21
Cherry, J. F., 66, 66–7 n. 7, 194, 199–200
Chicago, University of, 21, 42
Childe, V. G., 71, 198
China, 16, 17, 194–5
Chios, 169 n. 7
Chiusi, 105, 112, 120
Choiseul-Gouffier, Comte de, 24
chronology, regional, 175–7, 181, 185
Cicero, 94
Cilicia, 181
citizenship, 95
Civil Service, 19
Clark, K., 82, 84
Clarke, D., 42
classical scholarship, 18–20
Classics, 11
clay, 109, 133–4 n. 1
Cleisthenes, 5, 30, 57, 93–5, 132
Cleonae, 157
cognitivism, 9
Collis, J., 122, 126
Colonels, junta of, 38
colonialism, 20–3, 25, 173, 182
colonisation, 126–8, 188
Columella, 145, 147, 150–2, 154, 156,
    169
communism, 36, 37, 52
Connor, W. R., 41
conservatism, 44
Constant, B., 17
Constantine, D., 15
Conway, R., 29
Conze, A., 26
Cook, A. B., 29
Cook, J. M., 52, 181
Cook, R. M., 82, 85
Corcyca, 113
core culture, 42
core-periphery models, 108, 131–2, 188
Corinth, 61, 111, 119
Cornford, F., 29
Corpus vasorum antiquorum, 28
counter-Enlightenment, 17
Courbin, P., 8, 47 n. 2
Crates, 168 n. 4
Crete, 179–80
Critias, 102
Ctesiphon, 185
Cumae, battle of, 120

Cunliffe, B., 1; 26, 131
Curtius, E., 25–6, 32
Cylon, 51, 57, 66 n. 1
Cyriac of Ancona, 15, 137
Cyprus, 103, 180–1, 188

Dalboki, 103
Daniel, G., 9
Dartmouth College, 33
Dattilo shipwreck, 105
Davis, J., 6, 194, 199–200
de la Gernière, J., 113
de Sacy, S., 20
death, 63–5, 75–80, 198
Deetz, J., 27
Deh Luran, 186
Dekapolis, 181
Delos, 169 n. 7
Delphi, 33, 58, 118, 127, 169 n. 6
Dema house, 167
democracy, 30
demography, 177–89
Demosthenes, 149, 152, 153
Denmark, 26
depositional practices, 52, 57
Desborough, V. R., 39
d'Hancarville, Baron, 24
Dietler, M., 134 n. 3
Digest, 149
diglossia, 23
Dilmun, 183–4
Dio Chrysostom, 147, 150–3, 155
Dionysos, 79
Dipylon oinochoe, 62
discard behaviour, 167–8
Diyala plain, 184–5, 188
Donahue, A., 34
Draco, 51, 66 n. 1
drought, 57, 66–7 n. 7
Droysen, J. G., 171, 173, 174
Ducat, J., 90
Dunbabin, T., 66 n. 2, 129
Duvanli, 103
Dyson, S., 35, 38

EAM/ELAS, 36
Earle, T., 42
eastern establishment, 42
economic rationality, 186, 187
Edmunds, L., 79
education, 18–20
Education Reform Bill, 44
Egypt, 17, 20–1, 24, 44, 107, 173
Egyptology, 21, 28, 42, 44
Eisman, M., 101–2, 115
Eleusis, 24, 54, 56, 64, 77, 79
Elgin, Lord, 24
Elgin marbles, 25, 38
Eliot, T. S., 44
elite ideologies, 57–62, 112, 117, 118,
    122
Elymaeans, 185

Embree, L., 46 n. 2
engineering, 19
Enserune, 128
ephebes, 75–6, 195
Epictetus, 150
epinomia, 153
Epirus, 129
epistemes, 10
ethnoarchaeology, 138, 167
ethnos, 132
Etruria, 99–105, 110–20, 132, 195–6
Euboea, 60, 61, 106, 147
Euboulos, 169 n. 5
Eupatridae, 58
Euphrates, 184
Eupolis, 149, 152, 157
Euripides, 72, 74, 78, 90, 95 n. 3, 194
Europeanness, 3, 8, 11, 43
Evans, A., 28
Everett, W., 31–2
evolution, 28, 29
Exekias, 37
externalism, 9
extremist scholarship, 14

Failaka, 183, 184
Fallmereyer, J., 23, 38
fallow, 147–8
family farms, 148
farmsteads, 112, 142, 148, 150, 157,
    163–4, 179–80, 181, 182
  military, 182
Farrar, C., 94, 95
Fauvel, P., 24
feasting, 112
femininity, 85
feminism, 37, 44
Finley, M. I., 45, 99, 104, 128
Fiorelli, G., 26
Fish, S., 45
Fittschen, K., 67 n. 11
Flannery, K., 10, 142
Foce della Marangane, 112
Foucault, M., 10, 22, 27, 35, 40, 41
Foxhall, L., 150, 151, 173
France, early modern, 15, 16
Francis, E. D., 106
Frankenstein, S., 122
Frazer, J., 29
Freeman, E., 29, 30
French revolution, 17, 30, 46
French School of Archaeology at Athens,
    25, 33
Freud, S., 73, 84, 87
Fulford, M., 99
Fürstengräber, 122
Fürstensitze, 121–6
Furtwängler, A., 21, 28, 36
Furumark, A., 36, 37

Gaffney, V., 142, 144
Galilee, 182

Gandhi, M., 61
Garnsey, P., 99, 102, 104, 129
Geertz, C., 80
Gennadius, J., 34
German
  Institute in Athens, 25, 29, 31
  language, 17, 19
  occupation of Greece, 35
Germany, early modern, 16, 25–6
Gerrha, 183
Gestalt, 80
GI Bill, 42
Giglio Islands, 104, 105, 107, 109
Gill, D., 5–6, 194
Gladstone, W., 31
goats, 151–2
goddesses, 81, 83
Golan Heights, 182
Goldberg, 122
golden age, 77–8
good death, 78
Gosden, C., 43
Göttingen, University of, 18, 26
Grafenbühl, 134 n. 2
graffiti, 99–101, 103–4
Grafton, A., 16, 28
grain, 102, 129
Gramsci, A., 13–14
graves, *see* burials
Gravisca, 99, 101, 113
great divides, 14–15, 45
great tradition, 14, 32
Greece
  modern, 11, 22–3, 31–6, 38–9
  prehistoric, 11, 15
Greek
  civil war, 36
  Dark Age, 15, 39, 45, 59
  language, 15–16, 34, 44, 195, 196, *see
    also katharevousa*
  war of independence, 22–3, 25, 31
Greek Anthology, 152
Green, P., 173
Grevena survey, 179
Grote, G., 30–1
Gymnasien, 18

Habermas, J., 40
Hale, W. G., 33
Haliartos, 149
Halieis, 168–9, 199–200
haloes of artefacts, 141–2, 163
Halstatt society, 121–31
Halstead, P., 147–8, 151
Hama, 107
Hamilton, W., 24, 99
Härke, H., 123, 124
Harrison, J., 29
Hartwig, P., 75
Harvard University, 31, 33
Hasebroek, J., 103, 105
Hasmonean kingdom, 182

Hegel, G. W. F., 71
hegemony, 13–14
Hellenisation, 113, 128, 171–5, 183, 186,
    188–90
Hellenism, 8, 9, 11, 20–3, 26, 27, 47 n. 4,
    190, 193
Hellenismus, 171
Hellespontophylakes, 134 n. 4
Hempel, C., 42
Heraclitus, 77
Herbert, S., 106
Herculaneum, 17
Hermippus, 150
Hermokopidai, 134 n. 4, 153, 157, 168 n. 3
Hermonax, 77
Herodotus, 6, 20, 51, 94, 99, 101, 107, 121,
    126, 127, 129, 130, 134 n. 4
heroic passage, 72
Herzfeld, M., 3, 11, 23
Hesiod, 78, 87, 148, 150, 151
Hesperia, 35
Heuneberg, 122–4, 134 n. 2
Heyne, C. G., 18
hieroglyphs, 21
Hinsley, F., 32
historiography, 39–31, 39, 40, 45
Hobsbawm, E., 17
Hodder, I., 5, 42, 43, 52
Hodkinson, S., 148
Hoffmann, H., 4–5, 63, 195, 197, 198
Holland, P., 92
Holy Alliance, 22
Homer, 30, 60, 77, 145, 151, 194
homosexuality, 78
hoplites, 39, 62, 75–7, 151
horses, 151
household production, 109, 114–15, 130,
    147–8
Humanismus–Realismus, 19
Hunnekens, L., 68
Hyginus, 78

idealisation, 17–18
ideology, 13–14
Idumenaea, 182
Ilion, 181
imperialism, 171
India, 61
Indian Ocean, 183
initiation, 74–7, 195
inscriptions, 89–92, 102–3, 106, 116, 130,
    149, 157
Instituto di corrispondenza archeologica, 25
internalists, 9
Ionian Islands, 22
Iran, 143, 185–6
Iraq, 143, 184–5
iron, 39, 102
irrigation, 185, 186
Isaios, 153
Israel, 181–3
Italy, modern, 24

Jahn, O., 25
Jameson, F., 35, 40
Jameson, M. H., 39, 197
Jazira plain, 145, 184–5
Jebb, R. C., 31
Jerusalem, 148
Johnston, A., 99–101, 114
Jordan, 183
Josephus, 182
Journal of Hellenic Studies, 29
Judaea, 182, 183
Justin, 126

Kallimakhos, 84
Kalyvia Kouvara, 92
Karamanlis, K., 38
katharevousa, 23
Kedourie, E., 23
Kekrops, 77–9
Kenner, H., 52
Keos, 141, 154, 163
Khrysokou River, 180
Kimmig, W., 126
Knidos, 81–2
Knossos, 28, 53, 60
koine, 171
Kolokotronis, Th., 22
koprologoi, 149
koprones, 149, 169–70, 199–200
kopros, 145–53
Koraes, A., 23
Koraes chair, 33–4
korai, 88–93, 196
Kossinna, G., 21
Kosso, P., 142
Kotsakis, K., 141
kouroi, 88–93, 196
Kristiansen, K., 26
Kron, U., 78
Kuhn, A., 84
Kuhn, T., 12–13
Kul Oba, 103
Kunstwollen, 28
Kurtz, D., 37
Kuwait, 183
kyathoi, 102

Laconia, 163
Lamberg-Karlovsky, C., 43
Lane, E., 21
Langadas basin survey, 141, 179
language, 13, 15, *see also* German, Greek, Latin
Laocoon, 18
Lapps, 23
Larsen, M. T., 21
Lasithi plain, 180
Lathouresa, 55
Latin, 15–16, 19
Lazzarini, M., 90
Leach, E. R., 73–4
leases, 147, 153, 169 n. 6

Leeds Grammar School, 19
Lefkandi, 60
Lehmann, K., 195
Leone, M., 42
Lévi-Strauss, C., 79
Lewis, D. M., 92
Lion, Gulf of the, 128
liberalism, 30
Lippold, G., 71
Little Master cups, 124
Livy, 16
Lloyd, J., 163
London, University of, 33, 36
Longus, 150
[Lucian], 82, 84
luxury goods, 103, 131
Lyotard, J.-F., 40–1
Lyttos, 180

Maccabees, 182
MacDonald, B. R., 104
Macedonia, 30, 179
Machiavelli, N., 16
Maddle Farm, 144
Maeander floodplain, 181
manuring, 142–57, 199–200, *see also kopros*
Marchese, T., 181
Marion, 105, 180
markets, 101–2, 109, 114, 116, 128, 129–30, 131, 132, 149, 153, 198
marriage, 78, 90–1, 92–5, 196
Marseilles, *see* Massalia
Marshall, F. H., 34
Marshall Plan, 36
Marxism, 41, 130, 173, 175
Massalia, 105, 121, 122, 124, 126–8, 130–1
Maya, 194
meaning, 4–5, 65, 80, 81
megáli idea, 22
Melos, 6, 26
men of letters, 31
Menander, 150, 156
Menidhi, 54, 55
Merkouri, M., 38
Mesara plain, 179
Mesopotamia, 183, 184–5, 188
Messenia, 6, 155
metal trade, 134 n. 3
metalwork, 61–2
Methone, 134 n. 4
Metropolitan Museum, 33, 76
Micali Painter, 119–20
Michell, H., 99
micro-regions, 184
middle classes, 26, 43
Miletus, 181
Miller, D., 43
mining, 130
Mitford, W., 29–30
mixed constitution, 16

Modern Languages Association, 32
modernity, 40
Mohammed Ali, 22
Montelius, O., 21
Moon, W., 103
Morel, J.-P., 99
Moret, J.-F., 76
Morgan, C., 6, 99, 103, 104, 194, 195, 198
Morris, I., 54, 56, 57, 193–4, 198
Morris, S., 66 n. 3
Mt Hymettus, 54, 62, 64
Mt Lassois, 124
Muhly, J., 14, 29, 38
multiculturalism, 12
Murlo, 118
Murray, G., 29
Murray, O., 60, 195
museums, 4, 24, 25, 28, 33
Mycenae, 24, 25, 34
mystery cults, 77
mythology, 62

Nabataeans, 183
Nafplion, 34
Napoleon, 18–22
narrative, 15, 27–8, 37, 41, 84, 87, 88, 92, 93, 194
Nash, D., 105
nationalism, 11, 22–3, 25
NATO, 38
Naucratis, 107, 134 n. 4
Navarino, battle of, 22
Nea Paphos, 180, 181
Nektanebos II, 107
Nemea valley, 138, 141, 157–65
Nessos Painter, 62
New Archaeology, 4, 11, 42–3, 47 n. 2, 137
New directions in archaeology, 3, 4
'New Rome', 15, 16
Newton, C., 28
Nichoria, 38
Niebuhr, B., 26
Nike, 78, 85–7
Nilsson, M., 77
Nodier, C., 17
non-cognitivism, 9
Norton, C. E., 31–2, 37
Novick, P., 14, 40
Nuristan, 59, 60

Oedipus, 72–3, 74–5, 77, 79
Oedipus Painter, 75
off-site activity, 143
oiketai, 134 n. 5
oikumene, 171, 175
Olbia, 130
Olympia, 17, 24, 25–6, 27, 33, 35, 54, 58, 118
Olympic games, 19
Orchoi, 184

Oriental Institute, University of Chicago, 21
orientalism, 7, 10, 20–3, 44, 47 n. 3, 173, 190
Orthodox Church, 22
Orvieto, 105, 117, 120
Osborne, R., 4, 5, 37, 45, 63–5, 189, 195, 196, 198
Otho I, 23, 26
Owens, E., 149
oxen, 151, 168 n. 3
Oxford University, 19, 39

Page 3 girl, 85, 92
Painter N, 115
Palaeolithic, 26
Palaipaphos, 180–1
Palestine, 181–3
Pandora, 77–8, 86, 87
Panofsky, E., 80
panoptic gaze, 27, 37
Papandreou, A., 38
Papandreou, G., 38
Papoutsaïka, 157
paradigms, 12–13
Paris Painter, 117
Paris School, 5
Parkman, F., 31
Parthenon, 86–7
Parthians, 184, 185
PASOK, 38
Patterson, T. C., 4, 38, 42–3
patronage, 14
Pausanias, 78
peak sanctuaries, 54–5
Pedersen, J., 160
Peisistratos, 93
Peloponnesian War, 105, 106, 129, 132
Perachora, 54
Peradotto, J., 79
Pergamon, 149, 181
Pericles, 93, 94
Perry, B., 19
Persia, 94, 95, 109, 171, 174, 181, 183–4, 185–6
Persian Gulf, 183–4, 188
Phaleron, 56, 64
Ph.D. programmes, 13
Pheidias, 16, 86–7
Phigaleia marbles, 25
philhellenes, 25
philiki etaireia, 22
philology, 11, 25–6, 193
Philosophic Radicals, 30
Philoteria, 182
Phlius, 149, 157
Phocaea, 126, 127
Phoenicians, 105, 109, 121, 127
photography, 24
Photius, 83
Phrasikleia, 92
Pindar, 71, 103

Pinsky, V., 42
Piraeus, 134 n. 4, 147, 169 n. 6
Pithekoussai, 128
Plato, 81
Pliny the Elder, 81–2, 87, 152
Pliny the Younger, 147
Plutarch, 51, 94, 149, 151, 171
Poggio Civitate, *see* Murlo
Polis, 180
politeia, 57–8
Pollitt, J., 85–6
Polybius, 16, 122, 152
Polyphemus vase, 63–4
Pompeii, 17, 26
Populonia, 102
Porticello shipwreck, 109, 116
positivism, 99, 106
postmodernism, 40–2, 43, 171
poststructuralism, 4, 65
pottery
    black-figure, 36–8, 99–102, 108, 113–14, 115, 119, 124
    bucchero, 116, 128
    Chinese, 99
    Corinthian, 107, 113
    Geometric, 51, 53, 59–60, 61
    Mycenaean, 36, 37, 47 n. 10
    mythological scenes, 62–5, 71–80, 115–16
    Orientalising, 53, 55, 57, 61, 63, 67 n. 13, 195
    prices, 102–4, 109
    Protoattic, 51–69
    Protocorinthian, 51, 56, 62, 105
    Protogeometric, 60
    Protogeometric B, 53
    red-figure, 36–8, 71–80, 108, 113–14, 124
    Roman, 99, 144
    south Italian, 113–14
    Subgeometric, 51, 53, 55, 56, 64
poultry, 151–2
Praxiteles, 16, 81–6
Preucel, R., 42
Preziosi, D., 9, 27, 45
Priene, 181
professionalism, 13, 18
Protestantism, 16
Prussia, 18, 19, 25, 26
pseudo-Scylax, 105
Ptolemies, 180, 182
public schools, 19
public space, 83
Punta della Vipera, 112
purgatio, 164
Pyrgi, 113

Qala'at al-Bahrain, 184

Raber, P., 180
rainfall, annual variability in, 129
rape, 88

rationing, 60, 62
Realschulen, 19
rebirth, 75–8
Redfield, J. M., 44–5
Redfield, R. M., 195
refiguring, 4, 9
Renaissance, 81
Renfrew, A. C., 14–15, 43
republicanism, 17, 30
resistivity survey, 163
revolution, 17
Reynolds, J., 24
Reynolds, P., 199–200
Rhamnous, 147, 169 n. 6
Rhine, 128
Rhodes, 169 n. 6
Rhodes, P. J., 66 n. 1
Rhodes, P. P., 143
Rhône, 126
rhyta, 71–2, 77, 116
Ricoeur, P., 11
Ridgeway, W., 29
rites of passage, 74
Robertson, M., 37, 38, 81, 86, 88
Rockefeller, J. D., 35
Romanticism, 17, 23, 24, 31, 47 n. 7
Rombos, Th., 53
Rome, 4, 16, 17, 120, 129, 193
Roquepertuse, 128
Rowlands, M., 11, 43, 122, 124
Rutter, J. J., 141

Sabloff, J., 9
Sabratha, 105, 106
Sachphilologen/Sprachphilologen, 19, 28
Said, E., 20–1, 47 n. 3
Salles, J.-F., 184
Salmon, J., 101, 129
Samaria, 182–3
Samothrace, 26
sanctuaries, 51, 54–5, 58, 71, 81, 85–7, 88, 112, 113, 118
Sanders, I., 179
Santa Fe, 32
Scaliger, J., 16
Schiffer, M., 150
Schliemann, H., 25, 34
schools of archaeology, 14, 34, *see also* American, British, French, German
Schuchhardt, E., 21
science, 26, 28, 194
Scotland, 26
scripture, 16
sculpture, 16–18, 81–96, 198
secondary centres, 118–19
Seleucia-on-Tigris, 184–5
Seleucids, 181, 182, 183, 186–7
Seminar, 18
Seton-Williams, M., 181
settlement patterns, 111–13, 118–19, 122, 177–89

sexuality, 81, 82, 85, 87
Shanks, M., 27, 43
Sharon, plain of, 182
Shear, L., Sr., 35
sheep, 151–2
Shelley, P. B., 22–3
Sherwin-White, S., 189
shipwrecks, 104, 105–6, 109
Shomron, 182
Shorey, P., 20
silver, 102–3
Siraf, 145
site definition, 138, 159
site function, 160
Six's technique, 115
slaves, 129–30, 134 n. 5
Slavs, 23
Snodgrass, A. M., 4, 6, 7, 15, 27, 39–40,
    45, 47 n. 2, 99, 103, 106, 137, 138,
    141–3, 163, 164, 166, 167, 194
Society for American Archaeology, 32
Society of Dilettanti, 24
Solon, 51, 94
Sophocles, 72, 74
Sostratos, 99–101
Sotades Painter, 71–9
Sounion, 54
Southern Argolid Project, 141
Spain, 99, 121
Sparta, 30, 130
Sphakia survey, 180
sphinxes, 62, 63, 71–80, 195
Spina, 105, 120, 130–1
Spurr, M., 150, 153, 154
Starr, C., 39
Strabo, 122, 124, 149, 186
Strattis, 150
structuralism, 4, 27, 52
Struever, S., 8, 47 n. 2
Stuarts, 16
Studniczka-Langlotz chronology, 106
survey, 6–7, 38, 39, 137–43, 165–6,
    198–200
Susa, 185–6
Susiana, 185–6, 188
symbolic capital, 90–1, 92
symposia, 112, 122, 124
Syracuse, 130
Syria, 181
Switzerland, 26

Tainter, J., 122
Tarquinia, 105, 114, 117, 119
Tasker, C., 160
Tavros, 57
Tegea, 149
Tell al-Hawa, 184
Tell Rifa'at, 181

temples, *see* sanctuaries
Teos, 129
Thaj, 183
Thasos, 149
Thebes, 72–3, 74, 149
Theophrastus, 145, 147, 148, 150, 152,
    155–6
Theseus, 79, 109
Thesmophoria, 91
Thespiai, 149
Thessaly, 130
thetes, 151
Thomas, B., 5
Thomsen, C., 26
Thorikos, 54, 55, 56
three, 75
Thucydides, 51, 78, 134 n. 4
Tilley, C., 10, 27, 43
Tingle, M., 144
Tocra, 106
Tompkins, J., 5
towers, 182
Toynbee, A., 33–4
trademarks, 99–101, 103–4, 109–10,
    116
*Transactions of the American Philological
    Association*, 44
transhumance, 148, 153
Transjordan, 182
trasformismo, 13, 15
travellers to Greece, 17, 18
Tretos Pass, 157–9, 163
Trigger, B., 11, 26, 34, 42–3, 174
Trikoupis, Ch., 23, 33, 34, 47 n. 9
Troad, 181
Troy, 25
Truman Doctrine, 36
Tsoucalas, C., 36
Tsountas, Ch., 34
Turkey, 22–3, 33, 34, 181
Turkovuni, 54
Turner, F. M., 15, 24, 29, 31
Tylus, 183

unconscious, positive and negative, 10
universities, 17, 18
urban waste, 148–9
urbanisation, 188–9
Urnfields, 124
Uruk, 184

Vallet, G., 132
van Bath, S., 143–4
Vanderpool, E., 6
Vari, 54, 57
Vari house, 150, 167
Varro, 145, 147, 151, 156, 169
vase painting, 36–8, 51–69

Veii, 112
Venizelos, E., 33
Venus de Milo, 25
Vernant, J.-P., 79, 90, 93–4
Vickers, M. J., 5, 24, 37, 102, 103, 106
Vietnam, 43
viewer response, 95 n. 1, 198
Villard, F., 132
Vix, 134 n. 2
Volk, 18
von Bothmer, D., 28, 36–7
von Humboldt, A., 18, 26, 44
von Riedesel, J., 17
von Thünen, J., 142, 149
Vourva, 54, 57
Vulci, 99, 105, 114, 116, 118, 119

Wadi el-Hasa, 183
Waldstein, C., 33
wall paintings, 112
Wallace, R., 66 n. 1
Wallerstein, I., 131–2
Warka, 184, 185
Webster, T. B. L., 114
Wedgewood, J., 24
well deposits, 55
Wells, B., 166
Wells, P., 43, 121–2
Wenke, R. J., 186
Wesleyan College, 33
Westmacott, R., 24
Wharram Percy, 144
White, H., 9, 15, 28, 45
White, L., 42
Whitehouse, R., 127–8
Whitelaw, T., 163
Whitley, J., 4, 45, 194, 195, 198
Wilkinson, T., 142, 145
Will, E., 173
Willey, G., 9
Williamson, T., 142
Winckelmann, J. J., 16–18, 24, 28, 173
Wiseman, J., 45
Wittnauer Horn, 122
Wolf, F., 18
women, 81–96, 194, *see also* feminism
Woolley, L., 106
Wright, J. H., 32
writing, 21, 62

Xenophon, 145, 147, 148, 151, 156,
    168 n. 4

Yale University, 33
Yates, T., 43

Zeitgeist, 18, 20, 23, 28, 33
Zeus, 109